APPLICATIONS OF
DISCRETE MATHEMATICS

APPLICATIONS OF DISCRETE MATHEMATICS

Edited by

John G. Michaels

State University of New York
College at Brockport

Kenneth H. Rosen
AT&T Bell Laboratories

McGRAW-HILL, INC.

New York St. Louis San Francisco Auckland Bogotá Caracas
Hamburg Lisbon London Madrid Mexico Milan
Montreal New Delhi Paris San Juan São Paulo
Singapore Sydney Tokyo Toronto

APPLICATIONS OF DISCRETE MATHEMATICS

ISBN 0-07-041823-3

The editor was Richard Wallis;
the production supervisor was Friederich W. Schulte.
The cover was designed by Joan Greenfield.
R. R. Donnelley & Sons Company was printer and binder.

Cover painting: "Between the Clock and the Bed."
© Jasper Johns /VAGA New York 1990. Virginia Museum of Fine Arts, Richmond. Gift of the Sydney and Frances Lewis Foundation.

This book was typeset on a Macintosh IICX using TEXTURES Version 1.2. The illustrations were done using SuperPaint 1.0.

Macintosh is a registered trademark of Apple Computer, Inc.
SuperPaint is a trademark of Silicon Beach Software, Inc.
TEXTURES is a trademark of Blue Sky Research.

Library of Congress Catalog Card Number: 91-61089

Preface

Goals

The goal of this book is to present a wide variety of interesting applications of discrete mathematics in a flexible and accessible format. The intended audience includes students who are currently studying or have previously studied discrete mathematics from any of the texts now available.

The book can be used as a supplement since it provides material on many interesting and important applications not usually covered in an introductory course. This volume can also be used as a text for a second course in discrete mathematics — a short course, a semester-long course, or an independent study course. The range of applications covered makes it appealing for summer courses, including those for in-service secondary teachers who want to develop new skills.

Each chapter can be studied independently since there are no dependencies between chapters. Although the chapters have been written by different authors, a great deal of effort has been devoted to ensure consistency of format, writing styles, accessibility, completeness, and terminology. Devoting an entire chapter to each application permits a thorough treatment not usually possible in an introductory text.

We have covered a broad range of applications in different areas of discrete mathematics, arranged in three sections: discrete structures and computing, combinatorics, and graph theory. Although some applications could fit in two or even three of these sections, each application is placed into the section in which it most strongly fits. The applications come from a wide range of subjects including computer science, the social sciences, the natural sciences, the physical sciences, and mathematics.

The field of discrete mathematics has a tremendous variety of applications. We feel that those discussed here are interesting and important, but that many other applications would fit nicely in this work. In future editions we hope to broaden the scope by including other applications, especially in areas not currently represented.

Features

Some prominent features of this book are:

Accessibility   Each chapter of the book has been written so that it is easily accessible. The basic ideas of each application are carefully and clearly explained, with more sophisticated ideas given in later parts of the chapters.

Prerequisites   Prerequisite topics are listed at the beginning of each chapter, and a basic understanding of those topics will suffice for the study of that chapter. (For students and faculty who have used or are using *Discrete Mathematics and Its Applications* by Kenneth H. Rosen, the appropriate sections in the Second Edition of that text are listed.)

Exercise Sets   Each chapter includes a comprehensive exercise set containing routine, intermediate, and challenging exercises. Difficult exercises are marked with a star and very difficult exercises are marked with two stars. Solutions to all exercises are given in a separate section at the end of the book.

Suggested Readings   A bibliography of suggested readings appears in each chapter and suggests publications that are useful for surveying related topics as well as proving particular results mentioned in the text.

Algorithms   Many of the chapters include a description of algorithms, both in English and in an easily-understood form of Pascal-like pseudocode.

Biographical and Historical Information   The historical background of each application is described, and biographical information about mathematicians and computer scientists is also given.

Computer Projects   Each chapter concludes with a set of computer projects related to the topics covered in that chapter.

Future Editions

We plan to issue future editions of this volume that will include additional applications. Instructors using this book, or *Discrete Mathematics and Its Applications* by Kenneth H. Rosen, are invited to submit chapters on additional applications for possible inclusion. Users of this book are also invited to suggest additional applications for subsequent editions. Submissions and/or suggestions can be sent to either editor of this volume.

Acknowledgements

We would like to thank Richard Wallis, our editor at McGraw-Hill, for his support and enthusiasm for this project. The first editor appreciates the encouragement of his family, Lois and Margaret, during all phases of the development of this text. We also thank Fred Roberts of Rutgers University for his helpful advice and his many contributions to the area of discrete mathematics. We would also like to thank the contributors to this volume for their diligence, flexibility, patience, creativity, and, especially, their excellent work. Finally, we shall be very grateful to all instructors and students who send us their helpful suggestions. This feedback will make future editions of this volume more useful.

Contents

PART III — Graph Theory

PART I

DISCRETE STRUCTURES
AND COMPUTING

1

The Apportionment Problem

Author: Russell B. Campbell, Department of Mathematics and Computer Science, The University of Northern Iowa.

Prerequisites: The prerequisites for this chapter are big-O notation, mathematical induction, counting, and sorting. See, for example, Sections 1.8, 3.2, 4.6, and 8.4 of *Discrete Mathematics and Its Applications*, Second Edition, by Kenneth H. Rosen.

Introduction

How should I divide a bag of jelly beans among my six nephews? How should Uncle Sam divide his military bases among his fifty "nephews"? How should the House of Representatives assign its 435 seats to the fifty states which make up this union? These are different *apportionment problems*, which are made difficult by the assumption that the apportionment should be "fair".

The apportionment problem is a problem which has no one correct answer. Instead of being given an answer to a problem, the reader will learn how to ask questions which can be answered, and make use of the answers. This process includes deciding upon objectives, building algorithms to obtain those objectives, determining whether the algorithms will work within reasonable time constraints, and determining when two algorithms achieve the same final output. Apportionment is an especially timely topic following the decennial census (1990, 2000, etc.) when the U. S. House of Representatives is reapportioned.

Historical Background

The Constitution of the United States reads

> "Representatives ... shall be apportioned among the several States ...,
> according to their respective Numbers, which shall be determined ...".

It is not specified how this apportionment is to be achieved. The only requirements for the apportionment are that each state shall have at least one representative, but not more than one per 30,000 residents. The total number of seats in the House of Representatives, which is determined by Congress, is at present 435. Prior to the reapportionment based on the 1990 census, several states had only one representative, while California had the largest delegation with 45 representatives. (The United States Constitution specifies that each state have two senators, hence there is no problem determining how many senators to assign to each state.)

The Problem

The basic apportionment problem is how to "fairly" divide discrete objects among competing demands. There are many examples other than those given in the introduction including the number of teachers each school in a district is assigned, or the number of senators each college in a university has on the university senate. We shall focus on dividing the seats in the U. S. House of Representatives among the states. The crux of the problem is that although "one man, one vote" (proportional representation) will usually require that states have a fractional number of representatives, an integral number of representatives must be assigned to each state. The third Congress (formed in 1793) was the first time a census (the first census of the United States, taken in 1790) was used to apportion seats in the House; we shall consider the composition of the first Congress, which is specified in the Constitution, contrasted to various "fair" apportionments based on the 1790 census, in the sequel.

Example 1   Let n be the number of states entitled to representatives. For example, $n = 13$ when the United States was formed, $n = 50$ today. We denote the population of the ith state by p_i and let

$$P = \sum p_i$$

the total population of the United States. In 1790 the population of Connecticut was 236,840.4 (this is not an integer because slaves were counted as 0.6 each), and the total population was 3,596,687. Therefore, Connecticut should have received

$$\frac{236,840.4}{3,596,687} = 6.58\%$$

of the representatives. The total size of the House of Representatives, which will be denoted by H, was 65 in 1789. Therefore Connecticut should have received

$$0.0658 \cdot 65 = 4.28$$

representatives. The **quota** for the ith state will be denoted by

$$q_i = \frac{p_i}{P} \cdot H,$$

so that $\sum q_i = H$. We will denote the actual number of representatives allotted to the ith state (which must be an integer) by a_i, subject to the constraint $\sum a_i = H$. The Constitution specifies the number of representatives each state was entitled to before the first (1790) census; the Constitution assigned Connecticut five representatives prior to the first census. (The complete apportionment specified by the Constitution for use prior to the first census is given in Table 1 in the column labeled "C".)   □

If an apportionment is not externally mandated (e.g., specified in the Constitution), we must construct one in a "fair" manner. In order to illustrate the construction of apportionments, it is useful to assume fewer than 13 states with population sizes which do not distract from the concepts being presented.

Example 2   Consider a mythical country with four states A, B, C, and D, with populations 1000, 2000, 3000, and 4000 respectively. The total number of seats for this country is 13 ($H = 13$). Find the quota for each state and choose integers $\{a_i\}$ which provide a "fair" apportionment.

Solution: A "fair" apportionment should have the a_i as close to the q_i as possible; i.e., the integer number of seats assigned to each state should be as close as possible to its quota, which in general will not be an integer. This is easily obtained by rounding off the quota for each state. For our fictitious country the quotas are

$$\frac{1000}{10000} \cdot 13 = 1.3,$$

$$\frac{2000}{10000} \cdot 13 = 2.6,$$

$$\frac{3000}{10000} \cdot 13 = 3.9,$$

$$\frac{4000}{10000} \cdot 13 = 5.2.$$

These round off to the integers 1, 3, 4, and 5 for the actual number assigned, a_i. However this procedure is naïve in that it may not yield the specified house size. In particular, Table 1 shows that this method would have provided 66 representatives for the 1790 census.   □

Therefore, another criterion of closeness must be employed. One method is to construct a global index of closeness and then find the apportionment which optimizes it. The term **global index** means that all the deviations of the a_i from the q_i are combined in some manner to form a single number which serves as a measure of fairness; this contrasts the pairwise criteria of fairness discussed below. Examples of global indices include

$$\sum |a_i - q_i|$$

and

$$\sum |a_i - q_i|^2.$$

Minimizing either of these two indices provides a sense of fair apportionment.
     In Example 2, where $H = 13$ and $\mathbf{p} = (1000, 2000, 3000, 4000)$, these indices are equal to
$$0.3 + 0.4 + 0.1 + 0.2 = 1$$

and
$$0.09 + 0.16 + 0.01 + 0.04 = 0.3,$$

respectively, for our fictitious country with the apportionment 1, 3, 4, 5. It can easily be shown that for this case these values provide the minima for the respective indices. However, especially for more complicated indices, we may need to evaluate the index for every possible apportionment of the seats to the states to find the apportionment which will minimize the index, and hence provide the fairest apportionment. Even if we could decide which index best embodies "fairness", it is not feasible to check all possible apportionments because there are too many apportionments to check.

Example 3   Find the number of possible apportionments that must be checked for the country of Example 2.

Solution: The formula for combinations with repetition (Section 4.6 in *Discrete Mathematics and Its Applications*, Second Edition, by Rosen) can be modified to find the number of possible apportionments which must be checked. We first assign one representative to each state (as mandated by the Constitution) and then divide the remaining seats among the states (sample with replacement from among the states until the House is filled). An alternative motivation for the formula lines up the H seats in the House so that there are $H - 1$ spaces between them and then chooses $n-1$ of the spaces to demarcate the number of seats each state receives. For our fictitious country with four states and thirteen seats there are $12!/(3!9!) = 220$ possible apportionments. $\qquad\square$

Example 4   For 13 states and a House with 65 seats, the same reasoning yields

$$\frac{64!}{12!\,52!} \approx 3.3 \times 10^{12}$$

apportionments to check, which is about 10^5 cases for every man, woman, and child in the United States in 1790. Although we now have computers to do calculations, the current size of the House and current number of states leaves checking all possible apportionments unfeasible because the number of cases far exceeds the power of our computers. (Estimating the current number of possible apportionments is left as Exercise 12.) $\qquad\square$

Algorithms for Apportionment

Construction of indices of fairness is easy, but they are not useful unless there is a means to find the apportionment which optimizes them. To apportion the House fairly, we need to have an algorithm to obtain that end. Several algorithms for apportioning the House are presented below. Reconciliation of these algorithms with the fairness of the resultant apportionments is addressed later.

Largest fractions

The problem with rounding off the quota to determine the number of assigned seats, i.e., setting

$$a_i = \lfloor q_i + .5 \rfloor,$$

is that too few or too many seats may be assigned, as was noted for the quota column in Table 1. An easy way to correct this problem is to assign each state the integer part of its quota, $\lfloor q_i \rfloor$, and then assign the remaining seats to the states with the largest fractional parts until the House is full. If rounding off produces a House of the proper size, this method provides the same apportionment. This method is known as the method of **largest fractions**, and also known as the **Hare quota** method. Alexander Hamilton was a proponent of this method, but its use was vetoed by George Washington. (It was subsequently used from 1850–1910, at which time it was referred to as the **Vinton**

method, named after Congressman S. F. Vinton*.) This method is easy to implement, we merely need to calculate the quota for each state and then rank order the fractional parts. The complexity of this algorithm is governed by the sort which rank orders the fractional parts, since calculating all the quotas entails only $O(n)$ operations, but the complexity of a sort of n objects is $O(n \log n)$. (See Section 8.4 of *Discrete Mathematics and Its Applications*, Second Edition, by Rosen.) Although this algorithm is concise, it is not useful until the resultant apportionment has been shown to be "fair".

Example 5   Find the largest fractions apportionment for the fictitious country from Example 2.

Solution: The quotas are

$$1.3, \ 2.6, \ 3.9, \ 5.2.$$

Rounding down guarantees the states 1, 2, 3, and 5 representatives, respectively, which leaves 2 more to be assigned. The largest fractional part is 0.9 which belongs to state C and the second largest fractional part is 0.6 which belongs to state B. Hence the largest fractions apportionment is 1, 3, 4, 5.   □

The apportionment for a House of 65 seats based on the 1790 census using the method of largest fractions is given in Table 1 in the column labeled "LF".

λ–method

The λ–method is a generalization of rounding off the quota which provides that the requisite number of seats will be assigned. There are several alternative versions (which often produce different apportionments). All of the versions entail finding a λ to modify the quotas so that the proper number of seats will be assigned. One version, known as the method of **major fractions**, or the method of the **arithmetic mean**, was advocated by Daniel Webster; it was used to apportion the House of representatives from 1911–1940 when it was advocated by Walter F. Willcox of Cornell University. To assign H seats, we need to find a λ such that

$$\sum \left\lfloor \frac{q_i}{\lambda} + .5 \right\rfloor = H$$

and set

$$a_i = \left\lfloor \frac{q_i}{\lambda} + .5 \right\rfloor.$$

---

* S. F. Vinton (1792–1862) was a congressman from Ohio who also served as president of a railroad.

State	Population	Quota	C	LF	GD	MF	EP	SD
NH	141,821.8	2.56	3	2	2	3	3	3
MA	475,327.0	8.59	8	9	9	8	9	8
RI	68,445.8	1.24	1	1	1	1	1	2
CT	236,840.4	4.28	5	4	4	4	4	4
NY	331,590.4	5.99	6	6	6	6	6	6
NJ	179,569.8	3.25	4	3	3	3	3	3
PA	432,878.2	7.82	8	8	8	8	8	8
DE	55,541.2	1.00	1	1	1	1	1	1
MD	278,513.6	5.03	6	5	5	5	5	5
VA	699,264.2	12.63	10	13	13	13	12	12
NC	387,846.4	7.01	5	7	7	7	7	7
SC	206,235.4	3.73	5	4	4	4	4	4
GA	102,812.8	1.86	3	2	2	2	2	2

Table 1.   Apportionment of the first House of Representatives, based on the 1790 census. Slaves were counted as 0.6. The apportionment specified in the Constitution (C) is followed by those given by the methods of largest fractions (LF), greatest divisors (GF), major fractions (MF), equal proportions (EP), and smallest divisors (SD).

Example 6   The value $\lambda=1$ works for our fictitious country of Example 2, since rounding off assigns the proper number of seats. However, rounding off provides 66 seats for the 1790 census with a House size of 65. By trial and error, we discover that any λ in the range 1.0107–1.0109 will provide a House with 65 seats as given in the column labeled "MF" in Table 1.   □

A variant known as the method of **greatest divisors**, or the method of **rejected fractions**, was advocated by Thomas Jefferson and used from 1791–1850. This method requires that we find a λ such that

$$\sum \left\lfloor \frac{q_i}{\lambda} \right\rfloor = H$$

and set

$$a_i = \left\lfloor \frac{q_i}{\lambda} \right\rfloor.$$

The apportionment based on the 1790 census using this method is given in the column labeled "GD" in Table 1. Another variant, for which John Quincy Adams was a proponent, is the method of **smallest divisors**. For this method we find a λ such that

$$\sum \left\lceil \frac{q_i}{\lambda} \right\rceil = H$$

and set

$$a_i = \left\lceil \frac{q_i}{\lambda} \right\rceil.$$

The apportionment based on the 1790 census using the method of smallest divisors is given in the column labeled "SD" in Table 1. The method of smallest divisors was never used to apportion the House of Representatives.

The time required to apportion the House by a λ–method depends on the particular algorithm used. A procedure analogous to bisecting an interval to find a root of an equation can be employed. Because there is an interval of λs which provide the proper House size (e.g., [1.0107, 1.0109] in Example 6), a value of λ for which the summation equals H (i.e., a $\lambda \in [1.0107, 1.0109]$) will be obtained after enough successive approximations. (The exact root of an equation is seldom found by the bisection method because there is often only an irrational root which is never reached by bisection.) For each λ which is tried, n summands must be calculated, which require a fixed number of operations each; then the summands must be added. Hence $O(n)$ calculations must be performed for each λ. The total complexity depends on how many λs it may be necessary to try. Values of λ which work may range from the number of states (n) to its reciprocal ($1/n$), but in general choosing 1 and then a number near 1 will serve as good initial choices for λ with the bisection method. (Of course, the second choice should be greater than 1 if $\lambda = 1$ assigned too many seats, and conversely.)

Huntington Sequential Method

An alternative approach for achieving the optimal apportionment is to start with no seats assigned (or with one seat allocated to each state), and then sequentially assign each seat to the "most deserving" state. E. V. Huntington[*] reformulated previously employed and proposed methods in this framework, and also proposed new methods of apportionment. These apportionment methods differ by the concept of "most deserving" they employ. Algorithm 1 incorporates the criterion of "most deserving" which Huntington favored. It is known as the method of **equal proportions** or the method of the **harmonic mean** and has been used since 1941 to apportion the U. S. House of Representatives.

---

[*] E. V. Huntington (1874–1952) was a Professor of Mechanics at Harvard University, and his many professional positions included presidency of the Mathematical Association of America in 1918. *Survey of Methods of Apportionment in Congress* (Senate document 304; 1940) is one of his lesser-known publications.

ALGORITHM 1   The method of equal proportions.

procedure *Huntington*(H: size of House; n: number of
states; p_i: population of state i)
for $i := 1$ **to** n
    $a_i := 1$
    $\{a_i$ is the number of seats assigned; start at 0 for some
    variations$\}$
$s := n$
$\{s$ is sum of assigned representatives; use 0 if 0 used for $a_i\}$
while $s < H$
begin
    $maxr := 0$
    $\{maxr$ is the largest value of any $r_i\}$
    $maxindex := 1$
    $\{maxindex$ is the subscript of an r_i that equals $maxr\}$
    for $i := 1$ **to** n
    begin
        $r_i := p_i/\sqrt{a_i(a_i + 1)}$
        $\{r_i$ measures how deserving state i is$\}$
        if $r_i > maxr$ **then**
        begin
            $maxr := r_i$
            $maxindex := i$
        end
    end
    $a_{maxindex} := a_{maxindex} + 1$
    $\{$next seat is assigned to most deserving state$\}$
    $s := s + 1$
end $\{a_i$ is the number of representatives assigned to state $i\}$

The largest value of r_i indicates that the smallest number of representatives relative to its population has been assigned to that state, hence that state merits the next seat. It is not obvious whether the next seat should be given to the state which is most underrepresented now, or would be most underrepresented if given another seat; taking the geometric mean of a_i and $a_i + 1$ as illustrated in Algorithm 1 is a compromise of these two philosophies in that it provides an average of the merit under each philosophy.

Changing the definition of r_i provides different methods of apportionment. Employing the **arithmetic mean** of a_i and $a_i + 1$ in the denominator instead of the geometric mean produces the **major fractions** apportionment; employing the **harmonic mean** produces an apportionment which has been advocated, but has not been used, for apportioning the House of Representatives. If a_i alone is in the denominator, the **smallest divisors** apportionment results, and if $a_i + 1$ alone is in the denominator, the **greatest divisors** apportionment results.

The number of operations required to calculate all the r_i is $O(n)$, since each requires only a few algebraic operations. (Specifically, perhaps adding 1 to the a_i of record, perhaps averaging that sum with a_i in some manner, and then dividing p_i by the resultant.) To find the maximum of the r_i, $O(n)$ comparisons are required. (See Section 2.1 of *Discrete Mathematics and Its Applications*, Second Edition, by Rosen for finding a maximum and Section 8.4 for a bubble sort which will find the maximum with a single pass.) Since this must be done for each of the H seats in the House of Representatives, a total of $O(nH)$ operations are required for this algorithm. We cannot compare the efficiency of the λ and sequential algorithms because we do not have a bound on how many λs we will need to try. In the case of equal proportions there is no λ analog. (See Table 2.)

Reconciliation

We first presented fairness criteria which we could not achieve, and then algorithms for which we had no way to assess the fairness of the resultant apportionments. It is indeed possible to reconcile the algorithms which have been discussed to indices of fairness.

Largest fractions

The method of largest fractions minimizes $\sum |a_i - q_i|$. This is readily verified by first noting that if $\sum |a_i - q_i|$ is minimized, each a_i equals either $\lfloor q_i \rfloor$ or $\lceil q_i \rceil$. To see this, suppose some a_i is greater than $\lceil q_i \rceil$. Then the sum can be reduced by subtracting 1 from a_i and adding 1 to an a_j where $a_j < q_j$. (Such a state must exist since $\sum a_i = \sum q_i = H$.) If some a_i is less than $\lfloor q_i \rfloor$, the sum can be reduced by adding 1 to a_i and taking 1 from a state with $a_j > q_j$. (Such a state must exist since $\sum a_i = \sum q_i = H$.) If all the assigned numbers a_i, $i = 1, 2, \ldots, n$, result from either rounding up or rounding down the quota, then the summation is clearly minimized by rounding up those with the largest fractional parts. It also follows that the resultant apportionment minimizes the maximum value of $|a_i - q_i|$ taken over all states i. This follows since the maximum with respect to i of $|a_i - q_i|$ is the maximum of the $|a_i - q_i|$ where $a_i > q_i$ (where the quotas were rounded up) or the maximum of the $|a_i - q_i|$ where $a_i < q_i$ (where the quotas were rounded down). Any reassignment

Method	When used	Proponent	Global minimization	Pairwise minimization	λ-method $H =$	r_i
LF	1850–1910	Hamilton	$\sum \|a_i - q_i\|$			
GD	1791–1850	Jefferson	$\max_i \frac{a_i}{p_i}$		$\sum \lfloor \frac{q_i}{\lambda} \rfloor$	$\frac{p_i}{a_i+1}$
MF	1911–1940	Webster	$\sum \frac{(a_i-q_i)^2}{q_i}$	$\left\| \frac{a_i}{p_i} - \frac{a_j}{p_j} \right\|$	$\sum \lfloor \frac{q_i}{\lambda} + .5 \rfloor$	$\frac{p_i}{.5(a_i+(a_i+1))}$
EP	1941–present	Huntington	$\sum \frac{(a_i-q_i)^2}{a_i}$	$\left\| \log \frac{a_i/p_i}{a_j/p_j} \right\|$		$\frac{p_i}{\sqrt{a_i(a_i+1)}}$
SD	never	J.Q.Adams	$\max_i \frac{p_i}{a_i}$		$\sum \lceil \frac{q_i}{\lambda} \rceil$	$\frac{p_i}{a_i}$

Table 2.   The apportionment methods employed are given with the sense in which they are fair and alternative algorithms to achieve them.

of states to the categories "round up" and "round down" will result both in rounding up a smaller fractional part and in rounding down a larger fractional part than when the largest fractional parts are rounded up and the smallest fractional parts are rounded down. (Because the House size H is fixed, so is the number of fractional parts which are rounded up.) This correspondence between the algorithms and optimality criteria for largest fractions is given in Table 2.

Greatest Divisors

For the method of greatest divisors (or rejected fractions), we will first show that the λ–method with rounding down and the Huntington sequential method with $a_i + 1$ in the denominator produce the same apportionment. Then we will show that this apportionment maximizes the minimum size of congressional districts, i.e., maximizes the minimum over i of p_i/a_i. (This can be interpreted alternatively as minimizing the maximum power of a voter, i.e., minimizing the maximum over i of a_i/p_i.) For demonstrating the equivalence of the λ and sequential algorithms, we shall reformulate the λ–method as finding μ such that

$$\sum \left\lfloor \frac{p_i}{\mu} \right\rfloor = H \qquad (\mu = \lambda \cdot P/H).$$

This converts the λ–method into a sequential method as μ is decreased.

Theorem 1   The lambda and sequential algorithms for greatest divisors provide the same apportionment.

Proof: We will prove this theorem using induction on H, the number of seats in the House. The proposition to be proved for all H is $P(H)$, the lambda and sequential algorithms for greatest divisors provide the same apportionment for a House of size H. If $H = 0$, no state has any representative, and the two assignment methods give the same result. Assume that they give the same result for House size H. Then for House size $H + 1$, μ will have to be further reduced until rounding down gives a state another representative. At that value of μ, $p_i/\mu = a_i + 1$ for the state i which will get another seat and $p_j/\mu < a_j + 1$ for all other states j. Therefore $p_i/(a_i + 1) = \mu$ for the state which gets the next seat and $p_j/(a_j + 1) < \mu$ for all other states. Hence the Huntington sequential algorithm assigns the same state the next seat as the lambda method. This proves $P(H)$ implies $P(H+1)$, which, with the verity of $P(0)$ mentioned above, completes the proof by induction on H.   ∎

Theorem 2   The greatest divisors apportionment maximizes the minimum district size. (This can be interpreted as assuring that no persons are overrepresented.)

Proof: We will prove this by induction on k, the number of seats which have been assigned. The proposition to be proven for all k is $P(k)$, the greatest divisors apportionment maximizes the minimum district size when k seats are assigned.

Before any seats are assigned, all the ratios p_i/a_i (i.e., district sizes) are infinite because the denominators are zero. This shows that $P(0)$ is true. The first seat is assigned to the state for which $p_i/(0+1)$ is greatest, which ratio becomes the minimum district size and is the largest possible value for the minimum district size. This proves $P(1)$. If after k of the seats have been assigned the minimum district size is as large as possible, the next state to receive a seat will have the new minimum district size. (If a state which did not receive the $(k+1)$st seat retained the minimum district size, then giving one of its seats to the state which received the $(k+1)$st seat while only k seats were assigned would would have increased the minimum district size when k seats were assigned. This contradicts the induction hypothesis that the minimum district size was maximized for k seats assigned.) The new minimum district size will be $p_j/(a_j + 1)$ for that state, where j was chosen as the state which gave the maximum value for that ratio. This completes the proof by induction on the number of seats.   ∎

The method of greatest divisors sequentially assigns seats to the states which would be least represented with an additional seat, which anticipation maximizes the minimum district size.

Equal proportions

Huntington employed pairwise concepts of fairness rather than global indices of fairness for his apportionment method. Rather than measuring the total disparity in representation among all states, he posited that an apportionment was fair if no disparity between two states could be lessened by reassigning a representative from one of them to the other. For the method of equal proportions, which he favored, the criterion is to pairwise minimize

$$\left| \log \frac{a_i/p_i}{a_j/p_j} \right|.$$

This quantity employs the ratio rather than the difference between states of representatives per person (or, alternatively, congressional district sizes) to measure disparity in representation. If the representation were equal, this ratio would equal 1, and hence its logarithm would equal 0. There is also a global index,

$$\sum \frac{(a_i - q_i)^2}{a_i},$$

which equal proportions minimizes, but no intuitive interpretation of this global index is readily available.

Optimization criteria corresponding to the other apportionment methods discussed earlier are given in Table 2. The method of major fractions minimizes

$$\left| \frac{a_i}{p_i} - \frac{a_j}{p_j} \right|$$

(the absolute disparity in representatives per person) pairwise, and minimizes the global index $\sum (a_i - q_i)^2/q_i$ (subject to the constraint $\sum a_i = H$). There are also pairwise criteria for the methods of smallest divisors and greatest divisors, but they are difficult to interpret and are omitted from Table 2.

Problems with Apportionment

The most obvious obstacle to providing the best apportionment is that different methods provide different apportionments. A survey of Table 1 reveals that there is a bias which changes from favoring the large states under greatest divisors to favoring the small states under smallest divisors. This bias can be demonstrated rigorously, but the mathematics is beyond of the scope of this chapter. Is it a mere coincidence that Thomas Jefferson (who favored greatest divisors) was from the Commonwealth of Virginia, and John Quincy Adams (who favored smallest divisors) was from the Commonwealth of Massachusetts, whose neighbors included the states of New Hampshire and Rhode Island and Providence Plantations? Since no incontrovertible argument favoring one method exists, states will always argue for a method which gives them more seats.

What has come to be called the *Alabama Paradox* was discovered in 1881 when tables prepared to show the composition of the House for various sizes showed that Alabama would have 8 representatives if the House had 299 members, but only 7 representatives if the House had 300 members. Several other states were affected in a similar manner, which caused extensive rhetoric on the Senate floor and the ultimate replacement of the method of largest fractions by major fractions in 1911. It is obvious that sequential assignment methods will not produce an Alabama paradox, but there are also problems associated with those methods.

It is certainly intuitive that a_i should equal $\lfloor q_i \rfloor$ or $\lceil q_i \rceil$. If a_i is less than the former or more than the latter, the apportionment is said to *violate lower quota* or *violate upper quota*, respectively. For example, following the census of 1930, when the method of major fractions was being used, New York received more than its upper quota. The method of greatest divisors cannot violate lower quota since the choice $\lambda = H$ gives each state its lower quota, and decreasing λ to achieve a full House cannot reduce any assignments. However, the method of greatest divisors can violate upper quota.

Example 7   Suppose $H = 20$ with quotas 2.4, 3.4, 3.4, and 10.8 for four states. The value $\lambda = 0.9$ provides the apportionment 2, 3, 3, 12 for the method of greatest divisors. This apportionment violates upper quota. $\square$

The method of largest fractions never violates quota, but violation of quota is possible under all the sequential assignment methods in Table 2 including the method of equal proportions which is currently used.

There are other properties which an apportionment method could satisfy. For example, when the House size is fixed a state should not lose a seat when its quota, q_i, increases. However, it is quite unreasonable to expect this to hold: if it held, a given quota would always assign the same number of seats independent of the quotas of the other states. The less restrictive condition that a state whose quota increases should not lose a seat to a state whose quota decreases is more reasonable. Unfortunately, it has been shown that there is no apportionment method which never violates quota, never decreases a state's delegation when the house size increases, and never gives a seat to a state whose quota decreased from one whose quota increased. Hence, we must prioritize what properties we want our apportionment method to have. The method of equal proportions which is currently used can violate quota, but satisfies the other two properties.

Suggested Readings

1. M. Eisner, "Methods of Congressional apportionment", UMAP Module 620, Educational Development Center, Newton, Massachusetts, 1982.

2. E. Huntington, "A New Method of Apportionment of Representatives", *Quarterly Publication of the American Statistical Association*, 1921, pp. 859–870.

3. E. Huntington, "The Apportionment of Representatives in Congress", *Transactions of the American Mathematical Society 30*, 1928, pp. 85–110.

4. W. Lucas, "Fair Division and Apportionment", Chapter 12 in L. Steen, ed. *For All Practical Purposes*, W. H. Freeman, New York, 1988, pp. 230–249.

5. W. Lucas, "The Apportionment Problem" in S. Brams, W. Lucas, and P. Straffin, ed. *Political and Related Models*, Springer-Verlag, New York, 1983, pp. 358–396.

Exercises

1. Suppose a fictitious country with four states with populations 2000, 3000, 5000, and 8000 has a house with eight seats. Use each of the apportionment methods listed in Tables 1 and 2 to apportion the house seats to the states.

2. Consider the same country as in Exercise 1, but with nine seats in the house.

3. The Third Congress had 105 seats in the House. For apportioning the Third Congress, the population figures in Table 1 must be modified by reducing North Carolina to 353,522.2 to reflect the formation of the Southwest Territory (which eventually became Tennessee), reducing Virginia to 630,559.2 to reflect the formation of Kentucky, adding Kentucky at 68,705, and adding Vermont at 85,532.6 (there were no slaves in Vermont, but 16 reported as "free colored" were recorded as slave). Find the apportionment for the Third Congress according to each of the five methods listed in Tables

1 and 2. (This can be done with a hand calculator, but computer programs would save time.)

4. Suppose that $n \geq H$. Which of the five apportionment methods assure at least one seat for each state?

5.   a) Modify both the λ and Huntington sequential methods for the greatest divisors apportionment to assure at least 3 representatives per state.
   b) Show that they produce the same result.

6. Use the algorithms constructed in Exercise 5 to apportion a 15-seat house for the fictitious country of Example 2.

7. Show that the λ and sequential algorithms for the smallest divisors apportionment produce the same result.

8. Show that the λ and sequential algorithms for the smallest divisors apportionment minimize $\max_i (p_i / a_i)$.

9.   a) Show that smallest divisors can violate lower quota.
   b) Can it violate upper quota?

10.   a) Construct an example illustrating the Alabama paradox. (Recall that this can only happen under the largest fractions apportionment.)
   b) Can this happen if there are only two states?

11. How many apportionments are possible with 15 states and 105 seats if each state has at least one seat?

12. How many apportionments are possible with 50 states and 435 seats if each state has at least one seat?

13. Solve Exercise 3, but for the 1990 census with a House size of 435. (Ask your friendly librarian for the 1990 census. *Computer programs are strongly recommended for this problem.*) Which of the five methods would benefit your state the most?

14. (Calculus required) The denominators in the Huntington sequential method (labeled r_i in Table 2) involve averages of the form

$$(.5(a_i^t + (a_i + 1)^t))^{1/t}.$$

(The choices $t = 1$, 0, and -1 provide the arithmetic, geometric, and harmonic means, respectively.)
   a) Show $\lim_{t \to 0}(.5(a_i^t + (a_i+1)^t))^{1/t} = \sqrt{a_i(a_i + 1)}$ (the geometric mean).
   b) Show that $\lim_{t \to \infty}(.5(a_i^t + (a_i + 1)^t))^{1/t} = a_i + 1$ (the maximum).
   c) Show that $\lim_{t \to -\infty}(.5(a_i^t + (a_i + 1)^t))^{1/t} = a_i$ (the minimum).

Computer Projects

1. Write a computer program to apportion the House by the method of major fractions using the lambda method.

2. Write a computer program to apportion the House by the method of major fractions using the sequential (r_i) method.

3. Write a program which will check all apportionments consistent with rank order of size (no state which is smaller than another state will receive more seats, but equality of seats is allowed).

2

Finite Markov Chains

Author: Eric Rieders, Department of the Mathematical Sciences, DePaul University.

Prerequisites: The prerequisites for this chapter are finite probability, matrix algebra, mathematical induction, and sequences. See, for example, Sections 1.7, 2.5, 3.2, and 4.4 of *Discrete Mathematics and Its Applications*, Second Edition, by Kenneth H. Rosen.

Introduction

Probability theory is the mathematical basis of the study of phenomena that involve an element of chance. There are many situations in which it is not possible to predict exactly what is going to happen. A gambler at the roulette table cannot say with certainty how much money he or she will win (if any!) after one round of play. The exact number of users logged on to a time-share computer at 2 p.m. tomorrow can only be guessed. The eye or hair color of a child is a subject of speculation prior to its birth. Yet, in all three of these cases, we feel that it is reasonable to give the probability of observing a particular outcome.

These probabilities may be based on past experience, such as the number of users "typically" logged on around 2 p.m. They might also derive from a *mathematical model* of the phenomenon of interest. Combinatorial arguments lead one to the computation of probabilities associated with betting at roulette, and models of heredity may be used to predict the likelihood of a child inheriting certain genetic characteristics (such as eye color) from its parents.

The preceding examples may be extended to *sequences* of consecutive observations, where the sequence of outcomes cannot be predicted in advance. The rising and falling fortunes of the gambler; the number of users requiring cpu time at, say, one minute intervals; or the eye color of succeeding generations of children are all examples of random processes. A **random process** is any phenomenon which evolves in time and whose evolution is governed by some random (i.e. chance) mechanism. Questions relating to the likelihood that the gambler reaches a preset goal (before going broke), the response time of the computer, or the chance that one of your grandchildren will have green eyes all may be addressed by analyzing the underlying random process.

In this chapter, we will examine an important kind of random process known as a *Markov chain*. All of the foregoing examples of random processes may in fact be modeled as Markov chains. The basic property of a Markov chain is that in making the best possible predictions about the future behavior of the random process, given the information yielded by a sequence of observations up to the present, only the most recently observed outcome need be considered. Prior observations yield no additional information useful for the purposes of prediction.

Markov chains were first studied systematically by the Russian mathematician Andrei Markov*. In the course of his investigations in probability theory, Markov wished to extend the investigation of the properties of sequences of *independent* experiments (i.e. those for which the outcome of one experiment does not influence, nor is influenced by, any of the other experiments) to an investigation of sequences of experiments for which the present outcome does in fact affect future outcomes. That is, the outcomes of the experiments are "chained" together by the influence each outcome exerts on the probability of observing a particular outcome as the result of the next experiment.

The widespread applicability of the Markov chain model to such diverse fields as population genetics, decision sciences, physics and other fields has gone hand in hand with the large amount of mathematical research concerning the properties of this kind of random process. Markov chain models are simple enough to be analyzed, yet realistic enough to be of genuine use in understanding real random processes. We will touch only on the more basic definitions and properties of Markov chains. For further study, see the references at the end of this chapter.

---

* Andrei Andreevich Markov, born in 1856 in Ryazan, Russia, showed an early mathematical talent. He studied at St. Petersburg University, where he was heavily influenced by the father of the Russian school of probability, P. Chebyshev. Markov remained as a professor at St. Petersburg, where he distinguished himself in a number of mathematical disciplines. Markov died in 1922, his health having suffered from a winter spent teaching high school mathematics in the interior of Russia.

The State Space

We now develop a precise definition of a Markov chain. Suppose that a sequence of "experiments" is to be performed and that each experiment will result in the observation of exactly one outcome from a finite set S of possible outcomes. The set S is called the **state space** associated with the experiments, and the elements of S are called **states**. Typically these experiments are carried out to investigate how some phenomenon changes as time passes by classifying the possible types of behavior into states.

We denote the sequence of observed outcomes by $X_1, X_2, \ldots$ (which presumably we do not know in advance). We denote by X_k the outcome of experiment k. Note that $X_k \in S$. In our description of a random process, we will usually include a state X_0, which is the state in which we initially find the phenomenon. We can think of the sequence $X_0, X_1, X_2, \ldots$ as being the observations of some phenomenon (such as the gambler's net winnings) as it evolves from state to state as time goes by. For our purposes, the random process is simply the sequence of observed states $X_0, X_1, X_2, \ldots$.

Example 1   Set up a Markov chain to model the following gambling situation. A gambler starts with \$2. A coin is flipped; if it comes up heads, the gambler wins \$1, and if it comes up tails the gambler loses \$1. The gambler will play until having gone broke or having reached a goal of \$4. After each play, the observation to be made is how much money the gambler has.

Solution: The possible amounts are $0, 1, 2, 3$ and 4 dollars. Thus, the state space is $S = \{0, 1, 2, 3, 4\}$; the five elements of S describe the status of the gambler's fortune as the game progresses.

Initially (before the first "experiment" begins), the gambler has \$2, and we write $X_0 = 2$ to describe this "initial state". X_1 is the amount of money the gambler has after the first coin toss. Note that the only information required to give predictions about the quantity X_2 (the amount of money the gambler has after the second toss) is in fact the value of X_1. If the coin is fair, we easily see that the probability of winning \$1 on the second toss is 0.5, that is,

$$p(X_2 = X_1 + 1) = 0.5.$$

Similarly,

$$p(X_2 = X_1 - 1) = 0.5.$$

If the gambler wins the first round and then loses the next 3 rounds, we will observe $X_0 = 2$, $X_1 = 3$, $X_2 = 2$, $X_3 = 1$, $X_4 = 0$. For $k \geq 5$, we will have $X_k = 0$, since once the gambler is broke, nothing more happens. In general, X_k is the amount that the gambler has after k coin tosses, where the state space S was described above. We can make probabilistic predictions about the value of X_{k+1} as soon as the value of X_k is known, *without* knowing anything about $X_0, X_1, \ldots X_{k-1}$. In fact, we can state explicitly

$$p(X_k = j | X_{k-1} = i) = \begin{cases} 1 & \text{if } i = j = 0 \text{ or } i = j = 4 \\ \frac{1}{2} & \text{if } 0 \leq j = i - 1 \leq 3 \text{ or } 1 \leq j = i + 1 \leq 4 \\ 0 & \text{otherwise} \end{cases} \quad (1)$$

where $p(X_{k+1} = j | X_k = i)$ is a conditional probability (see Section 4.5 of *Discrete Mathematics and Its Applications*, Second Edition, by Rosen), namely, the probability that the gambler will have $\$j$ after the $(k+1)$st coin toss, given that the gambler had $\$i$ after k tosses. $\square$

The probabilities expressed in (1) are called **transition probabilities**. A transition probability is associated with each pair of states in the state space; such a quantity represents the probability of the phenomenon moving from the first state of the pair to the second state.

Example 2   Suppose that the gambler of Example 1 is given a choice of five envelopes containing $0, 1, \ldots, 4$ dollars, respectively. Find the probability distribution of X_0.

Solution: Assuming the gambler is equally likely to choose any of the proffered envelopes, we have that $p(X_0 = i) = 0.2$, $0 \leq i \leq 4$. $\square$

More generally, we might have

$$p(X_0 = i - 1) = q_i \quad 1 \leq i \leq 5$$

where q_i is the probability that the gambler has $i - 1$ dollars to start with, and $\sum_{i=1}^{5} q_i = 1$. The 1×5 matrix

$$\mathbf{Q} = (q_1 \ q_2 \ q_3 \ q_4 \ q_5)$$

is called the **initial probability distribution**. The entries of $\mathbf{Q}$ are the probabilities of the various possible initial states of the gambler's wallet. For ease of notation, it is often useful to list the elements of the state space sequentially. In this gambling example, we would write $S = \{s_1, s_2, s_3, s_4, s_5\}$, where s_1 is the state where the gambler is broke (i.e., has 0 dollars), s_2 is the state where the gambler has 1 dollar, and so on. Thus, with probability q_i the gambler is initially in state s_i, for $1 \leq i \leq 5$.

Example 3   Suppose that we have a package of 1000 seeds of a plant that has the following life cycle. The plant lives exactly one year, bearing a single flower that is either red, yellow or orange. Before dying, the plant produces a single seed which, when it blooms, produces a flower the color of which depends (randomly) on the color of the flower of its "parent". Use Table 1 to model the color of the flower during succeeding years as a Markov chain.

| | | | Offspring | |
		Red	Yellow	Orange
		s_1	s_2	s_3
	Red s_1	0.3	0.5	0.2
Parent	Yellow s_2	0.4	0.4	0.2
	Orange s_3	0.5	0.5	0

Table 1.   Transition Probabilities

Solution: Here, the state space S is the set of colors red (denoted s_1), yellow (s_2) and orange (s_3), and the random process $X_0, X_1, X_2 \ldots$ is the yearly succession of flower colors produced by succeeding generations of plants beginning with the one that grows from the first seed you have chosen. The rule which describes how the color of the flower of the offspring depends on that of its parent is summarized in Table 1.

This table gives the probability that the offspring will bear a flower of a particular color (corresponding to a column of the table), given the color of its parent's flower (corresponding to a row of the table). For example, the probability that a plant having a red flower produces a plant with a yellow flower is 0.5. This is the probability of the random process moving from state s_1 to state s_2; we denote this as p_{12}. (Note that we are assuming the probability of observing a particular flower color in any given year depends only on the color of the flower observed during the *preceding* year.) The quantity p_{12} is the probability of a transition from state s_1 to state s_2.   □

We can use basic facts about conditional probability together with the Markov chain model to make predictions about the behavior of the Markov chain.

Example 4   In the preceding example, suppose you choose a seed at random from the package which has 300 seeds that produce red flowers, 400 producing yellow flowers and the remaining 300 produce orange flowers. Find the probability that the colors observed in the first two years are red and then orange.

Solution: Denote by X_0 the color of the flower produced (the "initial state"); the initial probability distribution is

$$Q = (0.3 \quad 0.4 \quad 0.3).$$

To make predictions about the sequence of flower colors observed we need the information in Table 1 as well as knowledge of the initial probability distribution. With probability 0.3, we have $X_0 = s_1$, i.e., the first flower is red. Given that $X_0 = s_1$, we have $X_1 = s_3$ (the next plant has an orange flower) with probability 0.2. That is, $p(X_1 = s_3|X_0 = s_1) = 0.2$; this comes from Table 1. Recall that

$$p(X_1 = s_3|X_0 = s_1) = \frac{p(X_0 = s_1, X_1 = s_3)}{p(X_0 = s_1)}$$

where $p(X_0 = s_1, X_1 = s_3)$ is the probability that the sequence of colors red, orange is observed in the first two years. It is the probability of the *intersection* of the two events $X_0 = s_1$ and $X_1 = s_3$. Rewriting this expression, we then have

$$p(X_0 = s_1, X_1 = s_3) = p(X_0 = s_1) \cdot p(X_1 = s_3|X_0 = s_1)$$
$$= 0.3 \cdot 0.2$$
$$= 0.06 \qquad \square$$

Can we deduce the probability of observing a particular sequence of flower colors during, say, the first 4 years using an argument similar to the one just carried out? We in fact can, using Theorem 1 (later in this chapter), and the fact that the random process in Example 4 is a Markov chain.

Now suppose that $X_0, X_1, X_2, \ldots$ are observations made of a random process (including the initial state) with state space $S = \{s_1, s_2, \ldots, s_N\}$. We denote the probability of observing a particular sequence of states $s_{i_0}, s_{i_1}, \ldots, s_{i_k}$, beginning with the initial one, by

$$p(X_0 = s_{i_0}, X_1 = s_{i_1}, \ldots, X_k = s_{i_k}).$$

The (conditional) probability of observing the state $s_{i_{k+1}}$ as the $(k+1)$st outcome, given that the first k outcomes observed are $s_{i_0}, s_{i_1}, \ldots, s_{i_k}$, is given by

$$p(X_{k+1} = s_{i_{k+1}}|X_0 = s_{i_0}, X_1 = s_{i_1}, \ldots, X_k = s_{i_k}) =$$
$$\frac{p(X_0 = s_{i_0}, X_1 = s_{i_1}, \ldots, X_k = s_{i_k}, X_{k+1} = s_{i_{k+1}})}{p(X_0 = s_{i_0}, X_1 = s_{i_1}, \ldots, X_k = s_{i_k})}.$$

Example 5   With reference to Example 1, find an expression which gives the probability that the gambler has \$1 after 2 rounds, given that the gambler started with \$1 and then won the first round.

Solution: We have $s_{i_0} = 1$, $s_{i_1} = 2$, and $s_{i_2} = 1$. The desired probability is then given by

$$p(X_2 = s_{i_2}|X_0 = s_{i_0}, X_1 = s_{i_1}). \qquad \square$$

Markov Chains

The foregoing examples provide motivation for the formal definition of the Markov chain.

Definition 1   A random process with state space $S = \{s_1, s_2, \ldots s_N\}$ and observed outcomes $X_0, X_1, X_2, \ldots$ is called a *Markov chain* with initial probability distribution $\mathbf{Q} = (q_1 \ q_2 \ \cdots \ q_N)$ if

(i) $p(X_{k+1} = s_{i_{k+1}} | X_0 = s_{i_0}, X_1 = s_{i_1}, \ldots, X_k = s_{i_k})$

$$= p(X_{k+1} = s_{i_{k+1}} | X_k = s_{i_k}) \quad \text{for } k = 1, 2, \ldots$$

(ii) $p(X_{k+1} = s_j | X_k = s_i) = p_{ij} \quad \text{for } k = 0, 1, 2, \ldots$

(iii) $p(X_0 = i) = q_i \quad \text{for } i = 1, 2, \ldots, N.$ $\square$

The numbers p_{ij} are the transition probabilities of the Markov chain. The **Markov property**, (i), says that we need only use the most recent information, namely, $X_k = s_{i_k}$, to determine the probability of observing the state $s_{i_{k+1}}$ as the outcome of the experiment number $k + 1$, given that the sequence of states $s_{i_1}, \ldots, s_{i_k}$ were the outcomes of the first k experiments (and the initial state is s_{i_0}).

Property (ii) requires that the underlying random mechanism governing the chance behavior of the random process does not change; the probability of moving from one particular state to another is always the same regardless of when this happens. (Sometimes Markov chains are defined to be random processes satisfying condition (i). Those that also satisfy (ii) are said to have **stationary transition probabilities**.)

It might happen that the initial state of the random process is itself determined by chance, such as in Examples 2 and 3. To compute probabilities associated with a Markov chain whose initial state is unknown, one needs to know the probability of observing a particular state as the initial state. These are the probabilities given in (iii). Note that if the initial state is known, as in Example 1, we still can express this in terms of an initial distribution. For example, if the Markov chain is known to be initially in state s_k, then we have $q_k = 1$ and $q_i = 0$ for $i \neq k$. This says that with probability 1, the Markov chain is initially in state s_k.

It is very useful to arrange the transition probabilities p_{ij} in an $N \times N$ matrix $\mathbf{T}$ (N is the number of elements in the state space), so that the (i, j)th entry will be p_{ij}.

Example 6   Find the matrix of transition probabilities for the Markov chain of Example 3.

Solution: Using Table 1, this matrix is

$$\mathbf{T} = \begin{bmatrix} 0.3 & 0.5 & 0.2 \\ 0.4 & 0.4 & 0.2 \\ 0.5 & 0.5 & 0 \end{bmatrix}.$$

For instance, the entry in the first row and second column, 0.5, is p_{12}, the probability that a red flower will produce an offspring that bears a yellow flower. Since it is impossible for an orange flower to produce an offspring that bears an orange flower, we have $p_{33} = 0$. $\square$

We will show that knowing the transition probabilities p_{ij} and the initial probability distribution $\mathbf{Q}$ of a Markov chain suffices for determining all probabilities of interest in connection with the Markov chain. Indeed, all such probabilities can be computed if we know the probability of observing any specific sequence of outcomes; any other events of interest are made up of such sequences.

Example 7   In Example 2, find the probability of starting out with 3 dollars, and losing the first two rounds, i.e., having 1 dollar left after flipping the coin twice.

Solution: We must compute $p(X_0 = 3, X_1 = 2, X_2 = 1)$. Using the definition of conditional probability, we have

$$
\begin{aligned}
& p(X_0 = 3, X_1 = 2, X_2 = 1) \\
& = p(X_0 = 3, X_1 = 2)p(X_2 = 1 | X_0 = 3, X_1 = 2) \\
& = p(X_0 = 3)p(X_1 = 2 | X_0 = 3)p(X_2 = 1 | X_0 = 3, X_1 = 2) \\
& = p(X_0 = 3)p(X_1 = 2 | X_0 = 3)p(X_2 = 1 | X_1 = 2) \quad \text{(Property (i) of} \\
& \hspace{9cm} \text{Markov chains)} \\
& = q_4 p_{43} p_{32} \\
& = 0.05.
\end{aligned}
$$

Note that, for example, p_{43} is the probability of going from state s_4, where the gambler has 3 dollars, to state s_3, where the gambler has 2 dollars. $\square$

More generally, we have the following basic result.

Theorem 1   If $X_0, X_1, \ldots, X_k$ denote the first k observed outcomes of the Markov chain with initial probability distribution $\mathbf{Q} = (q_1 \; q_2 \; \cdots \; q_N)$ then

$$p(X_0 = s_{i_0}, X_1 = s_{i_1}, \ldots, X_k = s_{i_k})$$
$$= p(X_0 = s_{i_0})p(X_1 = s_{i_1}|X_0 = s_{i_0}) \times \cdots \times p(X_k = s_{i_k}|X_{k-1} = s_{i_{k-1}})$$
$$= q_{i_0}p_{i_0 i_1}p_{i_1 i_2} \cdots p_{i_{k-1} i_k}.$$

Proof: We will demonstrate this using mathematical induction.

Basis step: The case $k = 1$ is an immediate consequence of the definition of conditional probability.

Induction step: Assuming the truth of the result for some particular k, we must then deduce its truth for $k + 1$. We have

$$p(X_0 = s_{i_0}, X_1 = s_{i_1}, \ldots, X_k = s_{i_k}, X_{k+1} = s_{i_{k+1}})$$
$$= p(X_{k+1} = s_{i_{k+1}}|X_0 = s_{i_0}, X_1 = s_{i_1}, \ldots, X_k = s_{i_k})$$
$$\times p(X_0 = s_{i_0}, X_1 = s_{i_1}, \ldots, X_k = s_{i_k})$$
$$= p(X_{k+1} = s_{i_{k+1}}|X_0 = s_{i_0}, X_1 = s_{i_1}, \ldots, X_k = s_{i_k})$$
$$p(X_0 = i_0)p(X_1 = s_{i_1}|X_0 = s_{i_0}) \times \cdots \times p(X_k = s_{i_k}|X_{k-1} = s_{i_{k-1}})$$
$$= p(X_{k+1} = s_{i_{k+1}}|X_k = s_{i_k})p(X_0 = i_0)p(X_1 = s_{i_1}|X_0 = s_{i_0}) \times \cdots$$
$$\times p(X_k = s_{i_k}|X_{k-1} = s_{i_{k-1}}),$$

which is the result. (The definition of conditional probability was used at the first step, the induction assumption at the second step, and property (i) at the third step.)   ■

Example 8   Compute the probability of the sequence of outcomes described in Example 1 ($X_0 = 2$, $X_1 = 3$, $X_2 = 2$, $X_3 = 1$, $X_4 = 0$) using Theorem 1.

Solution: Note that $q_3 = 1$ (state s_3 occurs when the gambler has \$2), since we are certain that we begin with \$2. We have

$$p(X_0 = 2, X_1 = 3, X_2 = 2, X_3 = 1, X_4 = 0) = q_3 p_{34} p_{43} p_{32} p_{21}$$
$$= 1 \cdot 0.5 \cdot 0.5 \cdot 0.5 \cdot 0.5$$
$$= 0.0625. \qquad \square$$

Example 9   With reference to Example 4, what is the probability that, having planted one of the seeds in the package (chosen at random), we observe the sequence of flower colors "red, red, yellow, red" over the first four years?

Solution: Using the notation for the state space and Theorem 1, we compute

$$p(X_0 = s_1, \; X_1 = s_1, \; X_2 = s_2, \; X_3 = s_1)$$
$$= q_1 p_{11} p_{12} p_{21}$$
$$= 0.3 \cdot 0.3 \cdot 0.5 \cdot 0.4$$
$$= 0.018. \qquad \square$$

Example 10   Referring again to Example 4, compute the probability that after having planted a randomly chosen seed, we must wait 3 years for the first *red* flower.

Solution: This means that one of the following sequences of outcomes must have occurred:

$$s_2 s_2 s_1 \quad s_2 s_3 s_1 \quad s_3 s_2 s_1 \quad s_3 s_3 s_1.$$

As in Example 9, we can use Theorem 1 to compute the probabilities of observing these sequences of outcomes; they are (respectively)

$$0.064, 0.04, 0.06, 0.$$

Thus, the "event" that the first red flower is observed during the third year is the sum of these, 0.164. Notice that knowledge of the initial distribution is essential for computing the desired probability. In this computation, we wish to suggest how knowledge of the probability that a particular sequence is observed allows one to compute the probability of a particular event related to the random process, by simply adding up the probabilities of all the sequences of outcomes which give rise to the event.   ☐

Long-term Behavior

A very important aspect of the analysis of random processes involves discerning some regularity in the long-term behavior of the process. For example, can we be assured that in Example 1 the game will necessarily end after a finite number of coin tosses, or is it conceivable that the game could be indefinitely prolonged with the gambler never going broke and never reaching his $4 goal? In Example 4, we might wish to predict the proportion of plants with a particular flower color among the succeeding generations of the 1000 plants, after planting all 1000 seeds. In fact, it turns out that these proportions tend to certain equilibrium values (that after a period of time will remain virtually unchanged from one year to the next), and that these proportions are not affected by the initial distribution.

We will see that the Markov chains of Examples 1 and 3 exhibit dramatic differences in their long-term behavior. The gambler's ultimate chances of reaching a particular state (like winning four dollars) depend very much on the initial distribution; this is in contrast to the situation in Example 3. For Markov chains, the kinds of questions we have just suggested can in fact be answered once the initial probability distribution and the transition probabilities are known.

We first determine the conditional probability that the random process is in state s_j after k experiments, given that it was initially in state s_i, i.e., we compute $p(X_k = s_j | X_0 = s_i)$. Theorem 2 shows that these probabilities may be found by computing the appropriate power of the matrix of transition probabilities.

Theorem 2   Let $\mathbf{T} = [p_{ij}]$ be the $N \times N$ matrix whose (i, j)th entry is the probability of moving from state s_i to state s_j. Then

$$\mathbf{T}^k = [p_{ij}^{(k)}], \tag{5}$$

where $p_{ij}^{(k)} = p(X_k = s_j | X_0 = s_i)$.

Remark: Note that $p_{ij}^{(k)}$ is *not* the kth power of the quantity p_{ij}. It is rather the (i, j)th entry of the matrix $\mathbf{T}^k$.

Proof: We will prove the Theorem for the case $n = 2$. (The case $n = 1$ is immediate from the definition of $\mathbf{T}$.) The general proof may be obtained using mathematical induction (see Exercise 5). First, note that

$$p(X_2 = s_j, X_0 = s_i) = \sum_{n=1}^{N} p(X_2 = s_j, X_1 = s_n, X_0 = s_i)$$

since X_1 must equal exactly one of the elements of the state space. That is, the N events $\{X_2 = s_j, X_1 = s_n, X_0 = s_i\}$, $(1 \le n \le N)$, are disjoint events whose union is $\{X_2 = s_j, X_0 = s_i\}$. Using this fact, we compute

$$
\begin{aligned}
p_{ij}^{(2)} &= p(X_2 = s_j | X_0 = s_i) \\
&= \frac{p(X_2 = s_j, X_0 = s_i)}{p(X_0 = s_i)} \\
&= \sum_{n=1}^{N} \frac{p(X_2 = s_j, X_1 = s_n, X_0 = s_i)}{p(X_0 = s_i)} \quad \text{(by addition rule for probabilities)} \\
&= \sum_{n=1}^{N} p(X_2 = s_j | X_1 = s_n) \frac{p(X_1 = s_n, X_0 = s_i)}{p(X_0 = s_i)} \quad \text{(by property (i))} \\
&= \sum_{n=1}^{N} p(X_2 = s_j | X_1 = s_n) p(X_1 = s_n | X_0 = s_i) \\
&= \sum_{n=1}^{N} p_{in} p_{nj}. \quad \text{(by property (ii))}
\end{aligned}
$$

This last expression is the (i, j)th entry of the matrix $\mathbf{T}^2$.   ∎

Example 11   What happens in the long run to the gambler in Example 1? In particular, give the long term probabilities of the gambler either reaching the $4 goal or going broke.

Solution: From (1), the matrix of transition probabilities is

$$\mathbf{T} = \begin{bmatrix} 1 & 0 & 0 & 0 & 0 \\ 0.5 & 0 & 0.5 & 0 & 0 \\ 0 & 0.5 & 0 & 0.5 & 0 \\ 0 & 0 & 0.5 & 0 & 0.5 \\ 0 & 0 & 0 & 0 & 1 \end{bmatrix}.$$

According to Theorem 2, computing the powers of T will provide the probabilities of finding the gambler in specific states, given the gambler's initial state.

$$\mathbf{T}^2 = \begin{bmatrix} 1 & 0 & 0 & 0 & 0 \\ 0.5 & 0.25 & 0 & 0.5 & 0 \\ 0.25 & 0 & 0.5 & 0 & 0.25 \\ 0 & 0.25 & 0 & 0.25 & 0.5 \\ 0 & 0 & 0 & 0 & 1 \end{bmatrix},$$

$$\mathbf{T}^3 = \begin{bmatrix} 1 & 0 & 0 & 0 & 0 \\ 0.625 & 0 & 0.25 & 0 & 0.125 \\ 0.25 & 0.25 & 0 & 0.25 & 0.25 \\ 0.125 & 0 & 0.25 & 0 & 0.625 \\ 0 & 0 & 0 & 0 & 1 \end{bmatrix},$$

$$\mathbf{T}^{20} = \begin{bmatrix} 1 & 0 & 0 & 0 & 0 \\ 0.749 & 0 & 0.001 & 0 & 0.250 \\ 0.499 & 0.001 & 0 & 0.001 & 0.499 \\ 0.250 & 0 & 0.001 & 0 & 0.749 \\ 0 & 0 & 0 & 0 & 1 \end{bmatrix},$$

$$\mathbf{T}^{50} = \begin{bmatrix} 1 & 0 & 0 & 0 & 0 \\ 0.750 & 0 & 0 & 0 & 0.250 \\ 0.500 & 0 & 0 & 0 & 0.500 \\ 0.250 & 0 & 0 & 0 & 0.750 \\ 0 & 0 & 0 & 0 & 1 \end{bmatrix}.$$

(We have rounded the entries to three decimal places.) The matrices $\mathbf{T}^k$ for $k > 50$ will be the same as $\mathbf{T}^{50}$ (at least up to 3 decimal place accuracy). According to Theorem 2, the probability of the gambler going broke after three rounds, given that he starts with $1 is the entry of $\mathbf{T}^3$ in the second row and first column, 0.625. If we want to know the probability that, starting with $2, we will have $3 after 20 rounds (i.e. we want to compute $p_{34}^{(20)}$), we need only look at the entry in the third row and fourth column of the matrix $\mathbf{T}^{20}$, which is 0.001. Notice that the probability of reaching the goal of $4 (after many rounds) depends upon the state in which the gambler is initially observed. Thus, it is with probability 0.75 that the goal is reached if the gambler starts with \$3, 0.5 if he starts with \$2 and 0.25 if he starts with \$1. These are the probabilities that comprise the fifth column of the matrix $\mathbf{T}^k$, for large k ($k = 50$, say). Similar statements concerning the chances of the gambler eventually going broke can easily be made. $\qquad\qquad\qquad\qquad\qquad\qquad\qquad\qquad\qquad\qquad\qquad$ □

The following result may be deduced as a corollary of Theorem 2. It describes how to compute the probability that the Markov chain will be in any particular state after k experiments, thus allowing one to make predictions about the future behavior of the Markov chain.

Corollary 1   Suppose that a Markov chain has initial probability distribution $\mathbf{Q}$ and $N \times N$ matrix $\mathbf{T}$ of transition probabilities. Then the $1 \times N$ matrix $\mathbf{QT}^k$, denoted $\mathbf{Q}_k$, has as ith entry the probability of observing the Markov chain in state s_i after k experiments. $\qquad\qquad\qquad\qquad$ ■

Example 12   Suppose now that the gambler initially gets to pick one of ten envelopes, 6 of them containing \$1, and the other four, \$2. Find the probabilities of the gambler being each possible state after one round of gambling, and estimate the long-term chances of the gambler reaching the \$4 goal.

Solution: The initial probability distribution is

$$(0 \quad 0.6 \quad 0.4 \quad 0 \quad 0),$$

i.e., the gambler has a probability of 0.6 of starting with \$1 and 0.4 of starting with \$2. By Corollary 1,

$$\mathbf{Q}_1 = \mathbf{QT} = (0.2 \quad 0.3 \quad 0.2 \quad 0.3 \quad 0).$$

This means that after the first round of gambling, the probabilities that the gambler has 0,1,2,3, or \$4 are, respectively, 0.2, 0.3, 0.2, 0.3, 0. The probability is 0 that the goal of \$4 has been reached.

We have observed that for large k, $\mathbf{T}^{(k)}$ will be almost exactly equal to $\mathbf{T}^{(50)}$. This means that the long-term chances of the gambler reaching the \$4 goal (or going broke) are approximately equal to the probabilities of being in these states after 50 coin tosses. These probabilities will depend on the initial distribution. Using Corollary 1, if

$$\mathbf{Q} = (0 \quad 0.6 \quad 0.4 \quad 0 \quad 0),$$

we obtain

$$\mathbf{Q}_{50} = (0.6 \quad 0 \quad 0 \quad 0 \quad 0.4).$$

This means that with this initial distribution, the gambler's long-term chances of going broke are 0.6 and are 0.4 of reaching the $4 goal.   □

In the previous example, if the initial distribution is changed to

$$Q = (0 \ \ 0 \ \ 0.4 \ \ 0.6 \ \ 0),$$

then we find that

$$Q_{50} = (0.35 \ \ 0 \ \ 0 \ \ 0 \ \ 0.65);$$

and if the initial distribution were

$$Q = (0 \ \ 0.4 \ \ 0 \ \ 0.6 \ \ 0),$$

then

$$Q_{50} = (0.45 \ \ 0 \ \ 0 \ \ 0 \ \ 0.55).$$

Thus, we see that the probability distribution of this Markov chain after many rounds of play depends very much on its initial distribution. This should be contrasted to the behavior of the Markov chain of Example 3 (see Example 13).

The entries in the matrices T^{20} and T^{50} suggest that in the long run the probability is (essentially) 0 that the gambler will not have either gone broke or reached his goal, *irrespective* of his initial state. The only reasonably large entries in these matrices are in columns 1 and 5, corresponding to the probabilities of entering states s_1 and s_5 respectively. In fact, what our computations indicate is indeed the case. As the number of rounds gets very large, the probability of being in states $s_2, s_3,$ or s_4 (corresponding to a fortune of $1, $2 or $3, respectively) tends to 0. In this setting, this means that the game cannot last indefinitely; eventually, the gambler will reach $4 or go broke trying. The states s_1 and s_5 thus have a different character than the other 3 states; eventually the gambler enters one of these two states and can never leave it (since we have assumed the game will stop when one of these states is reached).

Example 13   Analyze the long-term behavior of the Markov chain of Example 3.

Solution: We have already used Table 1 to write down the matrix of transition probabilities of the Markov chain of Example 2:

$$T = \begin{bmatrix} 0.3 & 0.5 & 0.2 \\ 0.4 & 0.4 & 0.2 \\ 0.5 & 0.5 & 0 \end{bmatrix}.$$

We then compute

$$T^2 = \begin{bmatrix} 0.39 & 0.45 & 0.16 \\ 0.38 & 0.46 & 0.16 \\ 0.35 & 0.45 & 0.2 \end{bmatrix} \quad T^3 = \begin{bmatrix} 0.377 & 0.455 & 0.168 \\ 0.378 & 0.454 & 0.168 \\ 0.385 & 0.455 & 0.160 \end{bmatrix}$$

$$T^4 = \begin{bmatrix} 0.379 & 0.455 & 0.166 \\ 0.379 & 0.455 & 0.166 \\ 0.378 & 0.455 & 0.168 \end{bmatrix} \quad T^{19} = \begin{bmatrix} 0.379 & 0.454 & 0.167 \\ 0.379 & 0.454 & 0.167 \\ 0.379 & 0.454 & 0.167 \end{bmatrix}$$

$$T^{20} = \begin{bmatrix} 0.379 & 0.454 & 0.167 \\ 0.379 & 0.454 & 0.167 \\ 0.379 & 0.454 & 0.167 \end{bmatrix}.$$

We also observe that all larger powers of **T** are the same (to within three decimal place accuracy), as was true in Example 11. Thus, in the long run, the behavior of the Markov chain "settles down" in the sense that the probability of observing a particular state remains essentially constant after an initial period of time.

The states of a Markov chain are typically classified according to a criterion suggested by the last two examples.

Definition 2   A state s_i of a Markov chain is called *recurrent* if, given that the chain is in this state at some time, it will return to this state infinitely often with probability 1, i.e.

$$p(X_n = s_i \text{ for infinitely many } n > k | X_k = s_i) = 1.$$

States that are not recurrent are called **transient**; these are the states which will not be observed after enough experiments have been performed.   □

None of the states in Example 3 are transient, whereas in Example 1, states s_2, s_3, and s_4 are transient. We have not proved this, but the truth of this fact is certainly suggested by the computations, since the probability of being in any of these states after only 20 rounds is essentially zero. Criteria for determining if a state is transient are developed, for example, in [2].

To summarize, in Example 1 there are two states (s_1 and s_5) which are recurrent, and the remaining three are transient. Consequently, the long term behavior of this random process may be succinctly described by saying that eventually the Markov chain will reach one of the two recurrent states and stay there. Furthermore, the probability of reaching a particular recurrent state depends upon the initial state of the random process.

In Example 2, all states are recurrent. The fact that the numbers in the columns of the higher powers of the matrix of transition probabilities are the same means that the probability of observing the particular state corresponding to the given column after enough experiments have been performed is the same, regardless of the initial state. For example, the probability of observing a red flower (i.e. state s_1) after 19 (or 20 or more) years is 0.379, irrespective of the color of the flower produced by the seed that is originally planted! If all 1000 seeds are planted, then after 20 years we expect to see approximately 379 red flowers, 454 yellow and 167 orange flowers. The same is true of all succeeding years, although we don't expect to find the same colors in the same places; it is the overall proportion of these colors that remains constant.

The random process of Example 3 belongs to a special class of Markov chain which we now define.

Definition 3   A Markov chain with matrix of transition probabilities $\mathbf{T}$ is called *regular* if for some k, $\mathbf{T}^k$ contains all positive entries.   □

Regular Markov chains exhibit a long-term behavior quite different from that of Markov chains that have transient states (such as that of Example 1). In particular, it turns out that irrespective of the initial distribution $\mathbf{Q}$, the entries of $\mathbf{Q}_k$ tend toward specific values as k gets large. That is, the probabilities of observing the various states in the long term can be accurately predicted, without even knowing the initial probability distribution. To see why this is so, note that in Example 13 we showed that the Markov chain in Example 3 is regular. In contrast to the Markov chain discussed in Example 12, the probability of observing a particular state after a long period of time does *not* depend on the state in which the random process is initially observed. If $\mathbf{Q} = (q_1 \ q_2 \ q_3)$ is an arbitrary initial probability distribution for this Markov chain, we have $q_1 + q_2 + q_3 = 1$. Now for large k,

$$\mathbf{T}^k = \begin{bmatrix} 0.379 & 0.454 & 0.167 \\ 0.379 & 0.454 & 0.167 \\ 0.379 & 0.454 & 0.167 \end{bmatrix},$$

so that

$$\mathbf{Q}_k = \mathbf{Q}\mathbf{T}^k$$
$$= (\ (q_1 + q_2 + q_3)0.379 \quad (q_1 + q_2 + q_3)0.454 \quad (q_1 + q_2 + q_3)0.167)$$
$$= (0.379 \ 0.454 \ 0.167).$$

Thus, we see that it does not matter what the proportions of colors in the original package of seeds were. In the long run, the proportion of colors tends to 0.379 red, 0.454 yellow and 0.166 orange. This distribution of flower colors is called the *equilibrium distribution* for the Markov chain.

Definition 4   A Markov chain with matrix $\mathbf{T}$ of transition probabilities is said to have an *equilibrium distribution* $\mathbf{Q}_e$ if $\mathbf{Q}_e\mathbf{T} = \mathbf{Q}_e$.   □

Note that if $\mathbf{Q}_e\mathbf{T} = \mathbf{Q}_e$, then

$$\mathbf{Q}_e\mathbf{T}^2 = (\mathbf{Q}_e\mathbf{T})\mathbf{T} = \mathbf{Q}_e\mathbf{T} = \mathbf{Q}_e$$

and in general (by the principle of mathematical induction),

$$\mathbf{Q}_e\mathbf{T}^k = \mathbf{Q}_e$$

for all positive integers k. According to the Corollary to Theorem 2, this means that if the initial distribution of the Markov chain is an equilibrium distribution, then the probability of observing the various possible states of the random process does not change with the passage of time.

For the Markov chain of Example 3, we deduced that the equilibrium distribution is

$$(0.379 \quad 0.454 \quad 0.167);$$

furthermore, there is no other equilibrium distribution. To summarize the observations made concerning this Markov chain, we find that all three possible flower colors can be expected to be repeatedly observed, regardless of the seed chosen the first year for planting. If many seeds are planted, the proportion of the flowers bearing red, yellow, and orange flowers in the long run will be, respectively, 0.379, 0.454, and 0.167.

If a random process is known to be a regular Markov chain, then it is of great interest to determine its equilibrium distribution, since this gives a good idea of the long-term behavior of the process. Notice that the entries of the rows of the higher powers of $\mathbf{T}$ are in fact the entries of the equilibrium distribution. This is what in general happens with regular Markov chains: the equilibrium distribution will appear to within any desired accuracy as the entries of the rows of high enough powers of the matrix of transition probabilities. See Exercise 13 for more on this point.

It is no coincidence that the regular Markov chain of Example 3 possesses an equilibrium distribution. We conclude our discussion with the statement of a very important result, the proof of which may be found in any reference on Markov chains, such as [2].

Theorem 3   Every regular Markov chain has a unique equilibrium distribution.   ■

Thus, the analysis of the long-term behavior of regular Markov chains can always be carried out by computing the equilibrium distribution.

Suggested Readings

1. W. Feller, *An Introduction to Probability Theory and its Applications*, Vol.1, Third Edition, Wiley, New York, 1963. (Chapter 15 deals with Markov chains. This text contains a wealth of ideas and interesting examples in probability theory and is considered a classic.)

2. J. Kemeny and J. Snell *Finite Markov Chains*, Springer-Verlag, New York, 1976. (This text provides a rigorous and thorough development of the subject, and is directed to the serious undergraduate. Some applications are given.)

3. J. Kemeny, J. Snell and G. Thompson *Introduction to Finite Mathematics*, Prentice-Hall, Englewood Cliffs, N.J., 1956. (This was probably the first finite mathematics text specifically written to introduce non-science majors to this subject. The basic ideas of a Markov chain are laid out, and many applications can be found throughout the text.)

4. K. Trivedi, *Probability and Statistics with Reliability, Queueing and Computer Science Applications*, Prentice-Hall, Englewood Cliffs, N.J., 1982. (This intermediate-level text provides many applications relevant to computer science.)

Exercises

---

1. In Example 4, suppose one seed is selected at random from the package.

   a) Find the probability of observing an orange flower two years after observing a red flower.

   b) Find the probability that in the first four years the flower colors are: yellow, orange, red, red.

   c) Find the probability of having to wait exactly three years to observe the first yellow flower.

2. In Example 1, suppose the coin being flipped is not necessarily fair, i.e., the probability of heads is p and the probability of tails is $1 - p$, where $0 < p < 1$. Find the matrix of transition probabilities in this case.

3. Two jars contain 10 marbles each. Every day, there is a simultaneous interchange of two marbles between the two jars, i.e., two marbles are chosen, one from each jar, and placed in the other jar. Suppose that initially, the first jar contained two red marbles and eight white, and that the second jar

initially contained all white marbles. Let X_k be the number of red marbles in the first jar after k days (so $X_0 = 2$).

a) Explain why this random process, with observed outcomes X_0, X_1, X_2, ..., is a Markov chain. Find the state space of the process.

⋆b) Find the matrix of transition probabilities of this Markov chain.

c) What is the probability that after three days, there is one red marble in each jar, i.e., $X_3 = 1$?

4. If $\mathbf{T} = [p_{ij}]$ is the matrix of transition probabilities of some Markov chain, explain why the sum of the entries in any of the rows of $\mathbf{T}$ is 1 (i.e. $\sum_{j=1}^{N} p_{ij} = 1$ for $1 \leq i \leq N$).

5. Give the complete proof of Theorem 2.

6.   a) Are either of the following matrices the matrix of transition probabilities of a regular Markov chain?

$$ A = \begin{bmatrix} 1 & 0 & 0 \\ 0.5 & 0.3 & 0.2 \\ 0.1 & 0.9 & 0 \end{bmatrix} \qquad B = \begin{bmatrix} 0 & 0.5 & 0.5 \\ 1 & 0 & 0 \\ 0.3 & 0 & 0.7 \end{bmatrix}. $$

b) If $\mathbf{T}$ is the matrix of transition probabilities of a regular Markov chain, prove that there is an integer k such that the entries of the matrix $\mathbf{T}^m$ are all positive for any $m \geq k$.

7. In a certain country, it has been observed that a girl whose mother is an active voter will with probability 0.5 also vote . A girl whose mother *doesn't* vote is found to become a nonvoter with probability 0.9.

a) Model this phenomenon as a Markov chain with two states. Describe the state space and find the matrix $\mathbf{T}$ of transition probablities.

b) Find the equilibrium distribution $\mathbf{Q}_e = (p \; q)$ of this Markov chain by solving the system of equations $\mathbf{Q}_e \mathbf{T} = \mathbf{Q}_e$, $p + q = 1$. Give an interpretation of the equilibrium distribution in this setting.

8. A state s_k of a Markov chain is called *absorbing* if once the random process enters the state, it remains there, i.e.

$$ p_{kj} = \begin{cases} 1, & \text{if } k = j; \\ 0, & \text{otherwise} \end{cases} $$

a) Are there any absorbing states for the random process described in Example 1?

b) Are there any absorbing states for the random process described in Example 3?

c) Is it possible for a *regular* Markov chain to have absorbing states? *Hint:* Look at Exercise 6 b).

⋆9.   a) Suppose that A and B are events such that exactly one of A or B occurs, i.e., $P(A \cup B) = 1$ and $P(A \cap B) = 0$. If E is any event, prove that

$P(E) = P(A)P(E|A) + P(B)P(E|B).$

b) Referring to Example 1, let r_k be the probability that the gambler reaches his \$4 goal before going broke, given that he starts out with \$$k$ ($0 \leq k \leq 4$). Note that $r_0 = 0$ and $r_4 = 1$. For $0 < k < 4$, use part a) to determine a recurrence relation satisfied by the r_k. Hint: Let E be the event that, starting with \$$k$, the gambler reaches his goal before going broke, A the event that he wins the first round, and B the event that he loses the first round.

c) Extend the result of part b) to the situation where the gambler's goal is to reach \$$N$ before going broke.

d) Verify that $r_k = k/N$, $0 \leq k \leq N$, satisfies the recurrence relation found in part c).

10. A drunkard decides to take a walk around the perimeter of the Pentagon. As he reaches each corner of the building (there are 5 corners!), he flips a coin to determine whether to go back to the last corner or to go to the next one.

a) Find the appropriate state space for this random process. Model the position of the drunkard as a Markov chain with 5 states. In particular, find the appropriate transition probability matrix.

b) Show that the equilibrium distribution of this Markov chain is given by (0.2 0.2 0.2 0.2 0.2). Give a description of the long-term behavior of the Markov chain.

c) Suppose that the drunkard has found his way to a square building, and uses the same method of walking around it. Find the matrix of transition probabilities in this case, and determine the equilibrium distribution, if it exists.

⋆11. A dice game has the following rules: Two dice are rolled, and the sum is noted. If doubles are rolled at any time (including the first), the player loses. If he hasn't rolled doubles initially, he continues to roll the dice until he either rolls the same sum he started out with (in which case he wins) or rolls doubles and loses. The game ends when the player either wins or loses.

a) Find the appropriate state space for the random process described above, and discuss why it is a Markov chain. Hint: You will need to include a state corresponding to winning and one corresponding to losing.

b) Find the initial distribution of the Markov chain.

c) Find the matrix of transition probabilities.

12. Let S be the state space of a Markov chain with transition probabilities p_{ij}. A state s_j is said to be *accessible* from state s_i if $p_{ij}^n > 0$ for some $n \geq 0$, i.e., s_j can be reached (eventually) if the random process starts out from state s_i. (We will agree that every state is accessible from itself). States s_i and s_j are said to *communicate* if s_i is accessible from s_j and s_j

is accessible from s_i. When the states communicate, we write $s_i \leftrightarrow s_j$.

★ a) Show that the relation "$\leftrightarrow$" is an equivalence relation on S.

b) If s_k is an absorbing state, show that the equivalence class $[s_k]$ contains only s_k itself.

c) If s_i is a transient state and s_j is a recurrent state, is it possible that $s_i \in [s_j]$?

d) Find the equivalence classes under $\leftrightarrow$ in Examples 1 and 3.

★ e) If the Markov chain is *regular*, what can you say about the equivalence classes?

★★**13.** Show that there are many (in fact, infinitely many) equilibrium distributions for the Markov chain of Example 1.

★★**14.** Let $\mathbf{T}$ be the $N \times N$ matrix of transition probabilities of a regular Markov chain. It is a fact (mentioned in this chapter) that for large k, each row of $\mathbf{T}^k$ will be very close to the equilibrium distribution $\mathbf{Q}_e = (r_1 \; r_2 \; \ldots \; r_N)$. More precisely, if a number e (e stands for "error") is specified, then there is a number k_0 such that $k > k_0$ implies that for each $1 \leq j \leq N$, $|p_{ij}^{(k)} - r_j| \leq e, \quad 1 \leq i \leq N$.

a) Show that if $\mathbf{Q}$ is *any* initial probability distribution, then $\mathbf{Q}_k$ will be close to the equilibrium distribution for large k.

b) Refer to Corollary 1. There, $\mathbf{Q}_k$ is obtained from the equation $\mathbf{Q}_k = \mathbf{Q}\mathbf{T}^k$. If we want to compute $\mathbf{Q}_k$ by first computing $\mathbf{T}^k$ with k matrix multiplications and then computing $\mathbf{Q}_k = \mathbf{Q}\mathbf{T}^k$, how many arithmetic operations (i.e. multiplications and additions) would be required?

c) Prove that $\mathbf{Q}_k$ can be computed from $\mathbf{Q}_{k-1}$ recursively: $\mathbf{Q}_k = \mathbf{Q}_{k-1}\mathbf{T}$. Use this to find a quicker way to compute $\mathbf{Q}_k$ than that suggested in part b). Determine the number of arithmetic operations required with this method.

d) Refer to Exercise 7. Find $\mathbf{Q}_e$ using the method you developed in part c).

Computer Projects

1. Write a computer program to find the equilibrium distribution of any regular Markov chain using the method suggested in Exercise 14c. This is known as the *power method*.

2. Write a computer program that simulates a Markov chain. It should take as input the matrix of transition probabilities and the initial distribution, and give as output the sequence $X_0, X_1, \ldots$. Such a sequence is known as a **sample path** of the Markov chain.

3

Rational Election Procedures

Author: Russell B. Campbell, Department of Mathematics and Computer
Science, The University of Northern Iowa.

Prerequisites: The prerequisites for this chapter are sets and relations. See,
for example, Sections 1.4, 6.1, 6.5, and 6.6 of *Discrete Mathematics and Its
Applications*, Second Edition, by Kenneth H. Rosen.

Introduction

The word democracy, derived from the Greek *dēmos* (the people) and *kratia*
(power), means rule or authority of the people. If a democracy is to be successful, it must manifest the will of the people. A collective will reflecting the diverse
wills of the individuals must be followed. Over the centuries several means to
achieve this end have been proposed. In 1951 Kenneth Arrow* showed that
no such collective will exists. Hence there is inherent inequity which cannot be

---

* Kenneth J. Arrow (1921–) published *Social Choice and Individual Values* [1] in
1951, which demonstrated that no such collective will exists. That monograph was
essentially his Ph.D. dissertation, and is the primary reason that he received the Nobel
prize in Economics in 1972. Arrow has been on the faculty of Stanford University for
forty years during which time he has received numerous fellowships and honorary
degrees.

avoided.

Individuals are often unhappy if their candidate does not win an election. But sometimes the outcome indeed does not reflect what the majority of the people want. One example is that if 60% of the voters are liberal, but divide their votes evenly between two candidates, the single conservative candidate wins with only 40% of the vote. Another example occurs in an election with a runoff, where a candidate who would have won any two-way race may be eliminated from the runoff. Elections should not result in outcomes the voters did not want.

A *rational election procedure* is one under which each individual's vote will positively affect his candidate's standing in the outcome. (This notion is made precise below.) There is no rational election procedure if there are more than two candidates. This chapter illustrates some of the reasons why. But more importantly, it illustrates how the concept of relations and various properties of relations can be used to concretely formulate the vague notion of fairness in election procedures. The election procedures in the latter half of this chapter employ some of the notation introduced in the first half, but do not require understanding the theorems.

The Problem

The problem was originally posed as choosing a *social welfare function* (i.e., a function which converts the preferences of individuals for alternative social states into a single collective preference schedule for alternative social states). We shall specialize to the problem of conducting an election and refer to the social welfare function which Arrow discussed as a rational election procedure (REP). Although elections are usually discussed in the context of electing government officials, ranking college football teams by a vote of sportswriters also requires an election procedure (EP) to convert the individual rankings into a collective ranking. In order to define an election procedure, and add properties which will make it a rational election procedure, it is necessary to introduce some notation.

Let n denote the number of alternative choices (for example, candidates $A, B, C, \ldots$). The fundamental assumption is that each voter has preferences among the candidates:

> For every voter i, there is a relation R_i which represents his preferences for the candidates. The statement $A R_i B$ means that voter i likes candidate A at least as well as candidate B. Each relation R_i must satisfy two axioms: (i) transitivity and (ii) connectivity.

Transitivity provides order to the preferences: if a voter prefers A to D and also prefers D to B, it is reasonable to expect that the voter prefer A to B. *Connectivity* requires that the voter will have a preference (or indifference) between every pair of candidates; it means that if presented with two alternative candidates, a voter will either prefer one to the other or be indifferent between them (i.e., consider them a tie), thus every pair of candidates is comparable. A formal definition of connected for a relation R_i follows.

Definition 1   A relation R_i is *connected* if, given any two alternatives X and Y, either $X R_i Y$ or $Y R_i X$ (both may hold).   □

Together transitivity and connectivity require that every individual must be able to rank the candidates preferentially, but allows for indifference among some of the candidates.

Definition 2   A relation which is connected and transitive is called a *weak order*.   □

Example 1   A weak order may be represented in the following manner:

$$\{C \succ B, A \succ E \succ D, F\},$$

where the candidates to the left of $\succ$ are preferred to those to the right, and the voter is indifferent between candidates separated by commas. Thus, in this example, the voter prefers candidate C to all alternatives; is indifferent between B and A which are preferred to D, E, and F; and is also indifferent between D and F. Every possible preference of a voter may be represented in the above manner.   □

Definition 3   Let W be the set of all weak orders on n candidates and assume there are N voters. An *election procedure (EP)* is a function $W^N \to W$, i.e., a mapping from sets of individual preferences to collective preferences.   □

Transitivity is a property which was used to define both an equivalence relation and a partial order relation. Connectivity forces reflexivity (see Exercise 3), which was also part of the definition of both an equivalence relation and a partial order relation. Therefore, if a weak order is symmetric, it is also an equivalence relation. The characterization of relations which are both weak orders and equivalence relations is determined by connectivity and symmetry.

Theorem 1   If a relation R is connected and symmetric, it is the universal relation (everything is related to everything, i.e., ARB for all A and B).

Proof: We prove that $A \not{R} B$ cannot happen. Suppose $A \not{R} B$. By connectivity BRA, and symmetry forces ARB, which is a contradiction. Therefore ARB. ∎

The universal relation is transitive. Hence the only equivalence relation (which by definition is symmetric) which is a weak order (which by definition is connected) is the universal relation, which has a single equivalence class. The only weak order on a the set of six candidates which is an equivalence relation can be represented as

$$\{A, B, C, D, E, F\},$$

i.e., indifference among all candidates.

A weak order is by definition transitive, and connected implies reflexive. Hence if a weak order is antisymmetric, it is also a partial order. Indifference between distinct alternatives A and B entails that ARB and BRA, hence antisymmetry precludes indifference among distinct alternatives.

Definition 4   A relation which is antisymmetric, transitive, and connected is called a *total order* or *linear order* (see Section 6.6 in *Discrete Mathematics and Its Applications*, Second Edition, by Rosen).   □

A weak order which is a partial order (hence a total order) on a set of six candidates can be represented as a single "chain", such as

$$\{A \succ B \succ E \succ C \succ D \succ F\}.$$

A weak order on a set with more than one element cannot be both an equivalence relation and a partial order relation (see Exercise 7). The weak order displayed in Example 1 is neither an equivalence relation nor a partial order.

An important feature of weak orders is that they only express preferences qualitatively. No numerical values are assigned to the preference rankings. We are not allowing voting procedures which assign 5 points to a first choice, 3 to a second, and 1 to a third choice, and then add up the total points to determine the winner. Such procedures are used for scoring athletic contests such as track and field, and ranking sports teams based on the votes of sportswriters; but Arrow did not allow such assignments because he felt it is not possible to quantify preferences, especially on a scale which is consistent between voters.

Desired Properties of the REP

Arrow summarized the heuristic notions of fair and rational with two properties which the collective relation R resulting from the EP must have in order to justify characterizing an EP as rational:

(i)   It must positively reflect the wills of individuals (PR).

(ii) It must be independent of irrelevant alternatives (IA).

To formulate these conditions precisely, we introduce a relation derived from a weak order.

Definition 5   A *strict preference* is a relation P defined by

$$XPY \Leftrightarrow XRY \wedge Y\not\!RX,$$

where R is a weak order.   □

This provides that X is related to Y in P if and only if X is strictly preferred to Y in R. P is irreflexive, and hence not connected. We use accents (such as $\hat{\ }, ', \tilde{\ }$) to indicate the correspondence of various relations (relations which are derived from each other share the same accent): $\tilde{R}$ is the collective preference which comes from the individual preferences $\{\tilde{R}_i\}$; $\hat{P} = \hat{R} - \hat{R}^{-1}$ (the strict preference derived from the weak order $\hat{R}$). Relations without any accent also correspond to each other.

Positively reflecting individual preferences is the heuristic notion that if a voter changes his vote in favor of a candidate, that candidate should not fare worse in the outcome of the election. Property PR is defined by contrasting two sets of individual preferences $\{R_i\}$ and $\{\tilde{R}_i\}$ which are identical with respect to all candidates except Z, but some of the $\tilde{R}_i$ may manifest a greater preference for Z than the corresponding R_i. Property PR then requires that $\tilde{R}$ ranks Z at least as high as R does. A more concise statement of the definition follows:

Definition 6   An election procedure (EP) *positively reflects the wills of individuals* (satisfies property PR) if the following holds:

If, whenever two sets of individual preferences $\{R_i\}$ and $\{\tilde{R}_i\}$ satisfy for all X and Y different from a specified Z and for all i:

1. $XR_iY \Leftrightarrow X\tilde{R}_iY$,
2. $ZR_iX \Rightarrow Z\tilde{R}_iX$, and
3. $ZP_iX \Rightarrow Z\tilde{P}_iX$,

then $ZPX \Rightarrow Z\tilde{P}X$.   □

In other words, if, all other preferences being the same, there is a stronger preference for Z in the individual rankings, Z will not manifest a lower preference in the collective function (it could be the same).

Independence of irrelevant alternatives says that if a candidate withdraws from a race, it will not affect the relative rankings of the other candidates. This is expressed by considering relations on a set T restricted to a set $S \subset T$ (i.e., if R is a relation on T, R restricted to $S \subset T$ is $R \cap (S \times S)$).

Definition 7 *Independence of irrelevant alternatives* is satisfied if, whenever $R_i = \tilde{R}_i$ for all i when the relations are restricted to S, then $R = \tilde{R}$ when restricted to S. □

The preceding two definitions allow us to define when an election procedure is rational

Definition 8 A *rational election procedure* (REP) is an election procedure (EP) which satisfies properties PR and IA. □

Plurality voting is not a REP as illustrated in the Introduction with the example of two liberal versus one conservative candidate. If either liberal were to withdraw, the other would win; hence the victory of the conservative over either liberal is not independent of irrelevant alternatives. Sequential runoffs also violates IA as the example in the Introduction shows.

The General Possibility Theorem

The *general possibility theorem* of Arrow is really an *impossibility* theorem. It states that if there are at least two voters and three candidates, there is no rational election procedure which reflects the preferences of the voters. More specifically, it states that the only functions from the individual preferences $\{R_i\}$ (which are weak orders) to a collective preference R (which is a weak order) which satisfy positively reflecting individual preferences (PR) and independence of irrelevant alternatives (IA) either select one of the individual preferences (i.e., $R = R_i$ for some i) or impose a weak order between at least two of the candidates independent of the individual preferences (i.e., XRY for some X and Y independent of the R_i). The former provides a dictatorship by the ith voter, while the latter, which is referred to as **externally imposed**, does not reflect anyone's preferences. Neither of these election procedure alternatives is consistent with our notion of democracy.

To simplify the proof of the general possibility theorem, we restrict our attention to the case of only two voters and three candidates.

Theorem 2 Arrow's General Possibility Theorem The only functions $F : W^2 \to W$ which satisfy PR and IA are
  1. $F(R_1, R_2) = R_1$ or $F(R_1, R_2) = R_2$ (i.e., dictatorships), or
  2. $F(R_1, R_2) = R$ with XRY for some X and Y independent of R_1 and R_2 (i.e., externally imposed).
(R_1 and R_2 are weak orders on the three candidates; the subscripts identify voters 1 and 2 respectively.) ∎

For notational convenience, we denote the three candidates with A, B, and C; and use X and Y generically for the candidates A, B, and C. The proof is based on a series of lemmas under the assumption that the REP is not externally imposed, which successively characterize the REP until it is shown to be a dictatorship. A contradiction is then obtained by applying the lemmas.

Lemma 1   If XP_1Y and XP_2Y, then XPY.

Recall that P is the strict preference defined from the weak order R which results from weak orders R_1 and R_2 which define the strict preferences P_1 and P_2; the mapping which produces R is assumed to satisfy properties IA and PR in accordance with the hypothesis of the theorem. (This is certainly a desirable property. If both individuals prefer X to Y, the collective preference should, but it must be shown.)

Proof: If YRX for all choices of P_1 and P_2, R is an externally imposed weak order, which is one of the forms of the function in the conclusion of the theorem, so assume $X\widehat{P}Y$ for $\widehat{P}_1$ and $\widehat{P}_2$ (i.e., such $\widehat{P}_i$ exist). We may alter the preference orderings $\widehat{P}_1$ and $\widehat{P}_2$ by making X strictly preferred to the other alternatives (if that is not already the case) while leaving the relationships between the other two alternatives unchanged; denote these preferences as P_1' and P_2'. Because the REP positively reflects individual preferences (PR), $XP'Y$. Hence, by property IA this will hold for all preferences satisfying the hypothesis of Lemma 1. ∎

The next lemma treats a circumstance when the preferences of the two voters differ, which the following lemma will show cannot occur.

Lemma 2   If whenever XP_1Y and YP_2X, XPY; then whenever XP_1Y, XPY. ∎

This is also intuitive, it says that if individual 1's preferences win out when opposed, they will also win when not opposed. The proof (see Exercise 8) follows from property PR.

Before proceeding, we need to define a class of relations which will be denoted with I. I stands for **indifferent**, i.e., $XIY \Leftrightarrow XRY \wedge YRX$. We leave it as an exercise to show that indifference is an equivalence relation (see Exercise 4). This notation allows us to characterize collective preference functions when voter preferences are opposite.

Lemma 3   If XP_1Y and YP_2X, then XIY.

This says that if the two voters' preferences for two candidates are opposite, the REP must show indifference between the two candidates ("their votes cancel").

Proof: The alternative is that the REP provides P satisfying XPY (or YPX which would be handled analogously). Property IA extends "XP_1Y and YP_2X and XPY" to "whenever XP_1Y and YP_2X, XPY", which is the hypothesis of Lemma 2. The conclusion of Lemma 2 will be used to draw a contradiction.

Assume that AP_1B, BP_2A, and APB. By property IA this holds for all sets of voter preferences $\{\dot{P_i}\}$ with voter 1 preferring A to B and voter 2 preferring B to A. Consider $\dot{P_1}$ prescribing the preference $A \succ B \succ C$ and $\dot{P_2}$ prescribing the preference $B \succ C \succ A$. (We use $X \succ Y$ to denote XPY, commas separate alternatives between which the voter is indifferent.) It follows by Lemma 1 that $B\dot{P}C$, hence $A\dot{P}C$ by transitivity for these preferences. As noted above, a single case ($\{\dot{P_i}\}$) satisfies the hypotheses of Lemma 2 by property IA, hence $AP_1C \Rightarrow APC$. We now have $AP_1B \Rightarrow APB$ and $AP_1C \Rightarrow APC$.

Next consider $\widehat{P_1}$ prescribing the preference $B \succ A \succ C$ and $\widehat{P_2}$ prescribing the preference $C \succ B \succ A$. It follows by Lemma 1 that $B\widehat{P}A$. $A\widehat{P}C$ since it is true for $\widehat{P_1}$. Hence $B\widehat{P}C$ by transitivity. $B\widehat{P_1}C$, $C\widehat{P_2}B$ and $B\widehat{P}C$ is equivalent to the hypothesis of Lemma 2. We now have $AP_1B \Rightarrow APB$, $AP_1C \Rightarrow APC$, and $BP_1C \Rightarrow BPC$.

Consideration of the individual preferences $B \succ C \succ A$ and $C \succ A \succ B$ adds $BP_1A \Rightarrow BPA$ to our list. Continuing in this fashion we can show that the preference of the first individual governs, i.e., the REP is given by $R = F(R_1, R_2) = R_1$ (a dictatorship). This proves Lemma 3 since the assumption XIY implied that the REP is a dictatorship, which is one of the forms of the REP specified in Theorem 2. Our initial choice AP_1B, BP_2A, and APB was made without loss of generality, hence provides the result for arbitrary X and Y (the reader may repeat the proof with BPA and all the other 2–permutations of A, B, and C). ∎

These lemmas allow us to proceed with the proof of the general possibility theorem.

Proof of Theorem 2:   Consider the preferences P_1 prescribing $A \succ B \succ C$ and P_2 prescribing $C \succ A \succ B$. It follows from Lemma 1 that APB and from Lemma 3 that AIC and BIC. The latter two relationships imply AIB by transitivity, which contradicts APB. Hence there is no REP with the desired properties. ∎

Extension to more than three candidates is immediate since IA allows us to restrict any REP to three candidates, but extension to more than two voters is more recondite and will not be proven here. There is, however, an additional assumption (which is included in many definitions of "fair") that simplifies the proof. This assumption is symmetry, both with respect to voters and with respect to candidates.

Symmetric Election Procedures

The hypotheses of Theorem 2 put no restriction on the REP (rational election procedure) other than that it provide a weak order and satisfy properties PR and IA. It is reasonable to further require that the election procedure be symmetric with respect to both candidates and voters. *Symmetry* with respect to candidates means that no candidate has an inherent advantage built into the election procedure, i.e., all candidates are entering the race as equals. A formal characterization is that if XRY (or XPY or XIY) and everyone interchanged their votes for X and Y, then YRX (or YPX or YIX). *Symmetry* with respect to voters means that all voters are equal, it only matters what votes are cast, not who cast them. This is formally stated as: permuting the indices of the voters associated with the preference schedules, without changing the preference schedules, will leave the resultant R unchanged.

There are circumstances where these assumptions are not reasonable for constructing a REP, such as declaring the incumbent the winner if there is a tie or weighting the votes of women as half the votes of men, but these are rather anomalous.

Assuming symmetry greatly simplifies the proof of Lemma 3, which reduces to the conclusion that indifference is the only symmetric weak order (see Exercise 9). The following lemmas are preparation for the proof that in the symmetric case, if there are at least three candidates, there is no REP satisfying PR and IA other than total indifference for any number of voters.

Lemma 4   If XP_iY for all i, then XPY.

Proof: The proof of Lemma 4 is is analogous to the proof of Lemma 1. If there is not total indifference, there is a set of preference schedules under which some candidate is preferred to another. By symmetry there must be a set of preference schedules for each pair of candidates and, in particular, a set of preferences yielding XPY. By PR, we still have XPY if X is raised above Y on each schedule in that set, and Lemma 4 follows by IA.   ∎

The following lemma provides an easy way to determine the collective preference if none of the individual preference schedules contain indifference.

Lemma 5   If there is no indifference in the individual preference schedules and $|\{i|XP_iY\}| > |\{i|YP_iX\}|$, then XPY.

(Note that $|\ |$ denotes cardinality. This says that if more people strictly prefer X to Y than Y to X, then the collective will will strictly prefer X to Y.)

Proof: Construct individual preference schedules for three candidates of the form $X \succ Z \succ Y$ and $Z \succ Y \succ X$ where there are more of the former than the latter. By symmetry (and PR), XRY and XRZ. By Lemma 4, ZPY. If XIY, ZPX by transitivity which contradicts XRZ. Because IA extends this special case to the hypothesis of Lemma 5, Lemma 5 is proven.   ∎

These lemmas provide the proof of the general possibility theorem in the case of symmetric election procedures.

Theorem 3   If there are at least three candidates, then there is no REP which is symmetric with respect to both voters and candidates except complete indifference.

Proof: With Lemma 5, the preference schedules

$$A \succ B \succ C \qquad B \succ C \succ A \qquad C \succ A \succ B$$

provide APB, BPC, and CPA; thereby violating transitivity of the REP. Since there is no REP which works if individual preferences are restricted to strict preferences, there cannot be one for general individual preferences. This example is easily extended to show there cannot be a REP with any number of voters.   ∎

In the case of only two candidates, majority rule provides a REP for any number of voters. The proof is left as Exercises 5 and 6.

Election Procedures

Approval voting

The fact that there is no rational election procedure if there are more than two candidates may have contributed to the pervasiveness of the two party system. But there is a rational election procedure which will produce a collective weak order of any number of candidates based on individual preferences consistent with PR and IA. However, although any number of candidates is allowed, all individual preference functions must be dichotomous: individuals either approve or disapprove of each candidate, but do not distinguish preferentially among the candidates in each category. The REP is simple — it is the rank order based on the number of approval votes each candidate receives.

Example 2   The operation of approval voting can be illustrated by a five candidate race (A, B, C, D, E). Each voter votes for whichever candidates he approves. For illustrative purposes assume that the ten ballots cast are

$$ABE, B, BCE, BD, AE, BCD, CE, BCDE, ABE, ABDE$$

(i.e., each voter lists the candidates of whom he approves; voter 1 approves Alfred, Barthowlamew, and Ethelred). Then A received 4 votes, B received 8 votes, C received 4 votes, D received 4 votes, and E received 7 votes. This provides the preferential order $B \succ E \succ A, C, D$. Ties (indifferences) are possible; it is not necessary that anyone receive approval from 50% of the voters, nor does receiving such approval assure election.   □

The utility of approval voting is given in the following theorem.

Theorem 4   Approval voting provides a REP on the restricted domain where each voter has dichotomous preferences.

Proof: A dichotomous preference (i.e., a partition of the candidates into two sets: the "approved" set, whose members are related to every candidate, and the "nonapproved" set, whose members are only related to members of that set,) is a weak order. It must be shown that the resultant preference schedule is a weak order, and further that it satisfies properties PR and AI.

The vote tally identifies each candidate with an integer (the number of votes received). XRY if the number of votes X received is greater than or equal to the number of votes received by Y. The trichotomy for two integers a and b ($a > b$, $a = b$, or $b > a$) is equivalent to connectivity, and the transitive property of inequality is equivalent to transitivity; hence R is a weak order. Property PR is satisfied since giving an additional vote to a candidate will increase his vote count without affecting other vote counts, hence cannot result in his vote count becoming less than another candidate's. Property IA is satisfied since the relative ranking of two candidates depends solely on the number of votes they receive, i.e., is independent of the number of votes other candidates receive. Hence approval voting provides a REP if all individual preferences are dichotomous.   ∎

Example 3   Unfortunately, allowing individuals only the option of indicating approval or disapproval for each candidate significantly restricts their ability to express their preference. Consider the dilemma of an individual who, in a three candidate race, prefers A to B and prefers B to C (hence prefers A to C). It is clear that he should not vote for all three candidates or withhold his vote from all, because then his ballot would not affect the relative totals. He should vote for A because whatever the vote count is without his ballot, adding a vote to A can only serve his interest. Similarly he should not vote for C. But it is not clear whether he should vote for B. If without his ballot there is a tie between

B and C, then voting AB will serve his interest; but if there is a tie between A and B voting AB will retain the tie which he could have broken in his favor had he voted only A. If he does not know how others will vote, he does not know how to vote to favor his interests.   □

Majority election procedures

Although approval voting produces a REP, it puts an unreasonable constraint on the individual preference functions. Since in the case of only two candidates majority rule provides a rational election procedure, it is natural to try to modify election procedures so that they entail only two candidates and majority rule will provide a rational election procedure. Are there satisfactory ways to dichotomize all elections, i.e., to make all elections a choice between two alternatives? The answer is no, but it is worth surveying some methods which have been employed in order to illustrate the problems which have manifested.

Sequential elections

Example 4   One possibility, perhaps more commonly used for passing legislation than for electing candidates, is to put two alternative choices to a vote at a time. For example, if there are three candidates A, B, and C; a vote could first be taken between A and B, and then between the winner of that contest and C. However, as the individual preferences of three voters $(A \succ B \succ C)$, $(B \succ C \succ A)$, and $(C \succ A \succ B)$ illustrate, the ultimate winner could be different if the first vote were between B and C, followed by the winner of that contest versus A.   □

Condorcet criterion

The paradox in Example 4 was noted by Marie-Jean-Antoine-Nicolas de Caritat, marquis de Condorcet*. Although election procedures are fraught with paradoxes, he concluded, based on two candidate results, that if any candidate would win all two way races, that person should be the winner. Such a person is called the **Condorcet** winner. If such a winner exists, the above paradox will not occur. It is easy to show that a Condorcet winner is unique, but such a winner need not exist. A. H. Copeland suggested generalizing the Condorcet

---

* Marie-Jean-Antoine-Nicolas de Caritat, marquis de Condorcet (1743–1794) was a protégé of Jean Le Rond d'Alembert. His *Essai sur l'application de l'analyse à la probabilité de décisions rendues à la pluralité des voix* (1785) assured him permanent place in the history of probability. He is also known as one of the first people to declare for a republic in the French revolution, but died an outlaw because he was too moderate when Robespierre came to power.

criterion by selecting as the winner the person who wins the most two way contests in the event that there is no Condorcet winner. Unfortunately, if there are fewer than five alternatives, there will never be a Copeland winner if there is not a Condorcet winner (see Exercise 22). Another method must be employed if one wishes to determine a winner.

Pluralities and runoffs

The essence of majority is maintained in plurality procedures, and runoff elections can be held in order to assure an actual majority. Runoffs may be held between the two recipients of the most votes (only first place votes count) or by sequentially eliminating the recipients of the fewest votes and transferring their votes to the next highest names on the respective ballots (these two methods are not equivalent).

Example 5   Although plurality decisions or runoff elections are widely used, they do not assure election of a Condorcet winner if one exists. In order to obtain a workable system, the most justifiable winner is often eliminated. The example with 9 voters, four with preference $(A \succ C \succ B)$, three with preference $(B \succ C \succ A)$, and two with preference $(C \succ B \succ A)$, illustrates that a Condorcet winner may lose either under plurality, a runoff between the top two vote-getters, or sequential runoffs eliminating the low vote-getter until somebody has a majority. (A voter whose top preference has been eliminated from a runoff votes for his most favored remaining candidate.) $\Box$

Applications to Sports

Most of the elections related to government are concerned only with determining a single winner rather than rank ordering the alternatives. But within the realm of our leisure activities there is a significant demand to for ranking alternatives. We conclude by considering some procedures employed to rank sports teams.

The Borda method

A vote count method to produce a collective ranking of alternative candidates based on individual rankings was proposed by Jean-Charles de Borda* in 1781. If there are n candidates, the Borda count assigns to the last name on each

---

* Jean-Charles de Borda (1733-1799) was a French mathematician best known for his work in fluid mechanics, navigation, and geodesy. While in the French navy he served on several scientific voyages, but also took part in the American Revolution and was captured by the British in 1782.

ballot 0 points, to the next-to-last name 1 point, ..., and to the first name $n-1$ points. The winner is then determined by summing for each candidate the number of points from each ballot. This is the method used to rank the top twenty college football teams by polling sportswriters. It has the advantage of converting the weak orders of individuals into a collective weak order. It reflects the entire preference schedules, not just the top candidates on each ballot.

However, the use of numerical rankings quantifies the degree of preference, which Arrow felt could not be justified. A major problem is that it encourages insincere voting. If you know that there are two candidates for the best team, it will be in your interest to rank the one you favor first and the other one (although you sincerely believe it to be the second best team) last. This gives voters the ability to essentially blackball a candidate. A Condorcet winner will not necessarily win by this procedure; in fact, a team which receives a majority of the first place votes may not win.

Example 6   Suppose three sportswriters decide to rank the football teams of Dartmouth, Harvard, Brown, and Yale. They might cast the following ballots: $(B \succ H \succ D \succ Y)$, $(H \succ D \succ Y \succ B)$, and $(B \succ H \succ Y \succ D)$. Even though Brown received a majority of the first place votes, the point total for Harvard is seven, while the total for Brown is only six. $\square$

Elimination tournaments

The national championship in collegiate basketball, unlike football, does not rely on a poll of sportswriters to determine the winner. Rather the "best" teams are paired off, with the winners subsequently paired against other winners. (These elimination trees can be found in newspapers during the NCAA playoffs.) Ultimately, one team wins the finals, and by transitivity is better than all the other teams in the tournament. But this method only picks a single winner; it is not clear whether the team defeated in the final game or the team defeated by the champion in the semi-final is the second best team; there are $n/2$ candidates remaining for the worst team. The amount of ambiguity can be diminished if there are consolation games, but too many games such as a round robin tournament could produce a violation of transitivity if teams did not perform consistently. (It is also possible that there is no transitive ranking; abilities to implement and defend against various styles of play may allow team A to consistently beat team B, team B to consistently beat team C, and team C to consistently beat team A.)

Example 7   It is desired to rank the teams RI, CT, NH, and VT. A tournament in which CT beats NH and RI beats VT in the first round followed by CT defeating RI in the final produces CT as the best team since it defeated NH and RI, and the RI victory over VT makes CT better than VT by transitivity.

Otherwise, all that has been demonstrated is that RI is better than VT; either VT or NH could be the worse team, either RI or or NH could be the second best team. A consolation game in which VT beat NH would establish the order $CT \succ RI \succ VT \succ NH$, but if NH beat VT it would not be determined which of RI and NH is better. ☐

Example 8   A round robin tournament of six games between four teams in which A beats B, B beats C, C beats D, D beats A, A ties C, and B ties D shows that transitivity need not hold. ☐

In summary, whether electing people who will determine the fate of the world or judging the entrants in a fiddle competition, there is no best procedure. All we can do is know the limitations of each of the various methods, and hope it does not matter.

Suggested Readings

1. K. Arrow, *Social Choice and Individual Values*, John Wiley, New York, 1963.

2. S. Brams, "Comparison voting" in S. Brams, W. Lucas, and P. Straffin, *Political and Related Models*, Springer-Verlag, New York, 1978, pp. 32–65.

3. S. Brams, and P. Fishburn, *Approval Voting*, Birkhäuser, Boston, 1983.

4. W. Lucas, "Social Choice: The Impossible Dream", *For All Practical Purposes*, ed. L. Steen, W. H. Freeman, New York, 1988, pp. 174–90.

5. R. Niemi and W. Riker, "The choice of voting system", *Scientific American*, Vol. 214, 1976, pp. 21–27.

6. P. Straffin, *Topics in the Theory of Voting*, Birkhäuser, Boston, 1980.

Exercises

1. Give an example, other than those discussed in the text, of a weak order which is not a total order.

2. Give an example, other than those discussed in the text, of a partial order which is not a weak order.

3. Show that connectivity implies reflexivity for all binary relations on a set A.

4. Show that indifference is an equivalence relation on a set A.

5. Show that the relation resulting from majority rule with just two candidates is connected and transitive, hence is a weak order.

6. Show that majority rule with just two candidates positively reflects individual preferences (PR) and is independent of irrelevant alternatives (IA), hence provides a REP.

7. Show that a total order cannot be an equivalence relation on a set with more than one element.

8. Prove Lemma 2: Given that properties PR and IA hold, if whenever $X P_1 Y$ and $Y P_2 X$, $X P Y$; then whenever $X P_1 Y$, $X P Y$.

9. Prove Lemma 3 in the case that the REP is symmetric with respect to voters and candidates.

In Exercises 10–15, consider an election with three candidates in which the preferences of the nine voters are: $(A \succ B \succ C), (A \succ C \succ B), (A \succ C \succ B),$ $(A \succ C \succ B), (B \succ C \succ A), (B \succ C \succ A), (B \succ C \succ A), (C \succ B \succ A),$ and $(C \succ B \succ A)$.

10. Does any candidate have a majority of the first place votes? Which candidate wins by the plurality criterion?

11. Which candidate wins if there is a runoff between the top two candidates?

12. If every voter found only his favorite candidate acceptable, which candidate would win under approval voting? If every voter found his first two choices acceptable, which candidate would win under approval voting?

13. If there are sequential elections with the first election between A and B and then the winner of that contest versus C, which candidate will win?

14. Is there a Condorcet winner?

15. Which candidate wins by the Borda count method?

16. Sometimes the Borda Count method is modified to favor candidates who receive first place votes by awarding n points for a first place vote, $n - 2$ points for a second place vote, and in general $n - m$ points for an mth place vote ($2 \leq m \leq n$). What would be the ranking of the teams in Example 6 if this method were used?

17. In a round robin tournament (everyone plays every other team) with four teams A beats B and D, C beats A and B. What outcomes for B vs. D and C vs. D will provide a transitive ranking of the teams?

18. In a round robin tournament with n teams, what is the least number of games that can be played and violate transitivity?

19. Extend the example in the proof of Theorem 3 to show that there is no REP with any number of voters greater than two.

20. Continue the proof of Lemma 3 to show $BP_1A \Rightarrow BPA$ and $CP_1A \Rightarrow CPA$.

21. Show that $|\{i|XP_iY\}| > |\{i|YP_iX\}| \Rightarrow |XRY|$ using symmetry and PR.

22. Show that for three or four alternatives there cannot be a Copeland winner unless there is a Condorcet winner.

23. If there is a single elimination tournament with no consolation games for eight teams, how many total orderings of the teams will be consistent with the final outcome (i.e., how many total orderings are consistent with $A \succ B$, $C \succ D$, $E \succ F$, $G \succ H$, $A \succ C$, $E \succ G$, and $A \succ E$)?

24. If A can beat B and C, B can beat C and D, C can beat D, and D can beat A; how should a single elimination tournament be organized so that A will win? How should a single elimination tournament be organized so that A will not win?

Computer Projects

1. Write a computer program to determine the winner of an election if there is a runoff between the top two vote-getters (assuming no candidate had a majority of votes on the first ballot). The input will be the preference schedules of each voter (i.e., ordered n-tuples), with the first votes cast for the names on the top of the lists, and the second votes cast for the highest ranking of the remaining two candidates.

2. Write a computer program to determine the winner of an election if there are sequential runoffs with the lowest vote recipient eliminated each round until one candidate has a majority. The input will be the preference schedules of each voter (i.e., ordered n-tuples), with the first votes cast for the names on the top of the lists, and the subsequent votes cast for the highest ranking of the remaining candidates.

3. Write a computer program to implement approval voting (what form should the input be in?). (*Solution*: Input the names of the approved candidates, adding 1 to their vote count each time the name is entered, or enter Boolean vectors indicating approval or disapproval and sum them componentwise.)

4

Gödel's Undecidability Theorem

Author: Stephen F. Andrilli, Mathematical Sciences Department, La Salle University

Prerequisites: The prerequisites for this chapter are logic, properties of integers, and techniques of proof. See, for example, Chapters 1 and 2 and Section 3.1 of *Discrete Mathematics and Its Applications*, Second Edition, by Kenneth H. Rosen.

Introduction

In high-school geometry and in your discrete mathematics course, you encountered many types of mathematical proof techniques. These included such methods as proof by contrapositive, proof by contradiction, and proof by induction. After becoming familiar with these methods, many students think mathematicians have so much "power" at their disposal that, surely, any given mathematical statement must either already have been proven or disproven.

But this is not the case! For instance, consider the following simple statement.

Goldbach Conjecture: Every even positive integer greater than 2 is the sum of two (not necessarily distinct) primes.

Note that $4 = 2 + 2$, $6 = 3 + 3$, $8 = 5 + 3$, $10 = 5 + 5$, $12 = 7 + 5$, and so on. Can we continue, expressing all larger even integers as the sum of two primes?

The answer is not yet known, despite extensive work by many mathematicians. Goldbach's Conjecture* is one of hundreds of mathematical "conjectures" whose truth value we have not been able to determine.

Now, of course, Goldbach's Conjecture is either true or false. Therefore, considering the huge battery of proof techniques available, it seems logical for us to predict with some confidence that eventually mathematicians will develop a proof that it is true or else find a counterexample to show that it is false. Until recently, the general attitude of most mathematicians was that every mathematical conjecture would, after enough effort, be resolved one way or the other. That is, it would either "become" a theorem or be identified as a false statement. However, as we will see later, the work of a brilliant 25-year-old German mathematician named Kurt Gödel** forever shattered this "belief", and led to a profound difference in the way we perceive mathematics as a whole.

Mathematical Systems: Examples from Geometry

To understand Gödel's work, we must first discuss the nature of general mathematical systems. Every statement in mathematics occurs in a *context*. This context might not always be stated directly, but is often implicit from previous statements. For example, a theorem in a high-school geometry can only be understood fully when we know what the terms in the theorem mean. These terms may have been *defined* previously in the text, or they may have been accepted as **undefined terms**. Undefined terms are terms that are so fundamental that we cannot fully describe them using other more basic terms. Terms such as "point", "line", "equal", and "between" are typical examples of undefined terms used in many texts.

Sometimes we cannot prove a theorem without the help of previous theorems. We may even need to use some *axioms* (sometimes called *postulates*). **Axioms** are statements that we accept as true, because they are so fundamental that we cannot prove them from other more basic results. In high-school

---

* The Goldbach Conjecture appeared in a letter from Christian Goldbach (1690–1764) to Leonhard Euler in 1742. Goldbach was a historian and professor of mathematics at the Imperial Academy of St. Petersburg (now Leningrad). He tutored Czar Peter II, and later worked in the Russian Ministry of Foreign Affairs. Among his research areas were number theory, infinite series, and differential equations.

** Kurt Gödel was born in Brno, Czechoslovakia in 1906. During the 1930s he taught at the University of Vienna and did research at the Institute for Advanced Study in Princeton, New Jersey. Gödel spent time in a sanatorium for treatment of depression in 1934 and again in 1936. In 1940, to escape Nazi fascism, he emigrated to the United States, and continued his work at the Institute for Advanced Study. He died in Princeton in 1978.

geometry, most axioms are based on common-sense notions. For example, a typical axiom in many geometry texts is: Every two distinct points lie on a unique straight line.

In any high-school geometry text, the undefined terms, definitions, axioms, and theorems, taken together, form a **mathematical system.** Most high-school geometry courses introduce students to the system of **Euclidean geometry,** so named because most of the results are essentially those handed down from classical times in *The Elements* of Euclid.* Within such a mathematical system, we can make new definitions and prove additional theorems.

Example 1   After accepting the axiom "Every two distinct points lie on a unique straight line", and the undefined terms listed above, we can introduce a new term: "midpoint". The *midpoint* between two given points is defined as the (unique) point on the line connecting the given points that divides the line segment between the points into two equal parts.

Additionally, once we have defined terms like "right triangle" and "hypotenuse", we can prove theorems such as the familiar Pythagorean Theorem: In any right triangle, the square of the hypotenuse is equal to the sum of the squares of the other two sides.   □

In this way, we can achieve the development of an entire mathematical system beginning with a few simple building blocks!

Non-Euclidean Geometries

One of the axioms that Euclid adopted in *The Elements* is equivalent to the following statement, commonly known as the **Parallel Postulate:**

> **Parallel Postulate:** If *l* is a line in a given plane, and P is a point of the plane not on *l*, then in this plane there is one and only one line going through P that is parallel to *l*.

This seems like a perfectly reasonable assumption — so reasonable, in fact, that even into the nineteenth century many mathematicians tried to prove that it was really a consequence of earlier axioms and definitions. Their efforts were ultimately unsuccessful. They next tried to deny this postulate to determine whether the resulting mathematical system contained a logical contradiction. But instead they obtained a set of new "strange" results!

We know now that it is possible to create several valid **non-Euclidean geometries** in which the Parallel Postulate is contradicted in different ways. For

---

* Euclid, who lived about 300 B.C., taught mathematics at Alexandria during the reign of the Egyptian Pharaoh Ptolemy Soter, and was most probably the founder of the Alexandrian School of mathematics. His classic work *The Elements* contains much of the basic geometrical knowledge accumulated up to that time.

example, we could decide to include the following axiom in our mathematical system instead of the Parallel Postulate:

Multi-Parallel Postulate: If *l* is a line in a given plane and *P* is a point in the plane not on *l*, then in the plane there is more than one line going through *P* parallel to *l*.

Adopting this axiom leads to a type of geometry known as **hyperbolic geometry**, which was discovered independently before 1830 by Nikolai Lobachevsky* and János Bolyai**. We can now prove theorems that are consequences of this new postulate. For instance, in hyperbolic geometry we can prove that, with *l* and *P* as in the statement of the Multi-Parallel Postulate, there are an *infinite* number of lines through *P* parallel to *l*. We can also show that the sum of the angles of any triangle is less than 180°.

Another type of non-Euclidean geometry is created when we replace the Parallel Postulate with:

No-Parallel Postulate: If *l* is a line in a given plane and *P* is a point in the plane not on *l*, then in the plane there is no line going through *P* parallel to *l*.

Such a geometry is called **elliptic geometry**, and was first created by Bernhard Riemann†. In this geometry, every pair of distinct lines meets in a point. Also, the angles of any triangle sum up to more than 180°.

---

* Nikolai Lobachevsky (1792–1856) taught at the University of Kazan, Russia, beginning in 1816. He later became Rector of the University. Lobachevsky published his first results on hyperbolic geometry in 1829. Another of his research interests was developing methods for approximating roots of algebraic equations.

** János Bolyai (1802–1860) studied at the Royal College of Engineering in Vienna and served in the army engineering corps. He was an expert swordsman and a superb violinist! Bolyai's father Farkas spent his lifetime to no avail trying to prove that the Parallel Postulate was a consequence of Euclid's earlier postulates. János continued this work, but realized that it might be impossible to prove. He began constructing a non-Euclidean geometry, a first draft of which was written in 1823. Bolyai's work went unnoticed at the time, and was largely overshadowed by Lobachevsky's publication. His contribution to non-Euclidean geometry was only recognized posthumously. Aside from his work in geometry, Bolyai also broke new ground in the theory of complex variables.

† Georg Friedrich Bernhard Riemann (1826–1866) was one of the most important mathematicians of the last century. He taught at Göttingen (University), and aside from his ground-breaking work in geometry, he developed many new concepts in complex and real analysis, and what is now topology and differential geometry. His discovery of elliptic geometry dates from about 1854 and was first published in 1867. Albert Einstein later based much of his theory of relativity on the geometrical ideas of Riemann.

Consistency of Mathematical Systems

As a result of these new observations in non-Euclidean geometry, mathematicians began to realize that abstract mathematical systems (with undefined and defined terms, axioms and theorems) could be created without any natural or obvious association with "reality" as we ordinarily perceive it. But this leads to a fundamental difficulty: once we choose an arbitrary set of axioms, how do we know that the system "makes sense"? That is, how can we be sure that none of the axioms are contradicted by the others?

It is important that any mathematical system we work in be **consistent**, that is, free from self-contradiction. It can be shown that Euclidean geometry is inwardly consistent, as are both of the non-Euclidean geometries discussed earlier. However, not all sets of axioms lead to consistent systems.

Example 2   Consider the following set of axioms with undefined terms "point" and "line":

(i) There are exactly three points in the system.
(ii) There are fewer than three lines in the system.
(iii) Every pair of points lies on exactly one line.
(iv) Not all points lie on the same line.

Notice that "line" as used here is a general term. A "line" does not necessarily have to agree with our "common-sense" notion of an object that consists of an infinite number of points, but may only contain a finite set of points. These axioms are not consistent, since the only way that axioms (i), (ii), and (iii) can be satisfied simultaneously is to have all three points lying on the same line. But this contradicts axiom (iv).   ☐

One way to be sure that none of the axioms in a given mathematical system contradict the others is to exhibit a **model** for the system that satisfies all of the axioms simultaneously.

Example 3   Consider the following collection of axioms, with undefined terms "point" and "line":

(i) At least two lines exist.
(ii) Every line contains at least two points.
(iii) Given any two distinct points, there is a line containing the first point but not the second point.

Notice also that the last axiom is "symmetric", because if we reverse the order of the points, axiom (iii) insists there is a line containing the original second point that does not contain the original first point.

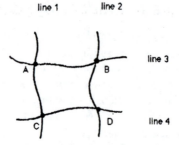

line 1   line 2

line 3

line 4

Figure 1.   A model of four points and four lines.

The model of four "points" and four "lines" in Figure 1 shows that these axioms are consistent.

For example, given points A and B, line 1 goes through A but not B, while line 2 goes through B but not A. Exercise 3 asks you to find another model for this system using fewer than four points. $\square$

Mathematicians are not interested in a system unless it is logically consistent. However, for a system that involves a large (possibly infinite) number of objects, a "model" of the system is often too difficult to construct. Such models would be extremely complicated, especially if we were trying to represent a system powerful enough to contain an entire branch of mathematics.

This can be seen even in a branch of mathematics as familiar as arithmetic. For instance, suppose we want to include an axiom that states that for every integer, there is a next largest integer. If we attempt to construct this system, then for every integer x that we list, we must list the integer y immediately following it as well. But then for this new integer y, we must list the integer z immediately following y, and so on. Thus, we would have to display an entire infinite sequence of integers, which is, of course, not physically possible. Mathematicians realized that a new approach was needed.

In 1910, two mathematicians, Alfred N. Whitehead* and Bertrand Russell** published a monumental treatise, *Principia Mathematica*. In this work,

---

* Alfred North Whitehead (1861–1947) was a philosopher and mathematician who held various academic positions in London from 1911 to 1924. From 1910–1913, he worked with Russell on *Principia Mathematica*. In 1924, he accepted a faculty post at Harvard University, and in the late 1920s he wrote a number of treatises on metaphysics.

** Bertrand Russell (1872–1970) was a philosopher and logician, who published numerous books on logic and the theory of knowledge. He was a student of Whitehead's before they collaborated on *Principia Mathematica*. Russell was active in many social causes, and was an advocate of pacifism (as early as World War I) and of nuclear disarmament.

they took a different approach to the consistency question. They attempted to derive all of arithmetic from principles of symbolic logic, which had been rigorously developed in the nineteenth century. (Symbolic logic includes such rules of inference as "modus ponens", "disjunctive syllogism", etc.) In this way, Whitehead and Russell could establish the consistency of arithmetic as a consequence of the basic laws of symbolic logic.

Resolving Logical Paradoxes

Whitehead and Russell's effort took on added importance because, at the turn of the century, mathematicians became more and more concerned about resolving **paradoxes** appearing in mathematical systems. Paradoxes are statements that are apparently self-contradictory. These paradoxes worried mathematicians because they seemed to imply that mathematics itself is ultimately inconsistent!

A typical paradox is **Russell's Paradox**. To understand this, let a **set** be described as a collection of objects (leaving "object" as an undefined mathematical term). Next, consider the set X of all sets having more than one element. Now X certainly contains more than one set. Thinking of these sets as elements of X, we see that X itself has more than one element. Hence, $X \in X$. Thus, it *is* possible to find sets that are elements of themselves. This leads us to the following.

> **Russell's Paradox:** Let S be the set of all sets that are not elements of themselves: i.e., $S = \{X \mid X \notin X\}$. Then either $S \in S$, or $S \notin S$. But either possibility leads to a contradiction. For, if $S \in S$, then by definition of S, $S \notin S$. On the other hand, if $S \notin S$, then by definition of S, $S \in S$.

In their *Principia Mathematica*, Whitehead and Russell devised methods to avoid Russell's Paradox and other similar paradoxes. They introduced the idea of "set types". They began with a fundamental collection of objects as above. These objects were considered to be of "type 0". Any set of objects of type 0 is considered to be a set of "type 1". Any set of objects of types 0 or 1 is considered to be a set of "type 2". In general, all objects in a set of "type n" must be of type less than n. Finally, only those collections of objects that have a "type" will be admitted into the system as sets. Such a scheme enabled Whitehead and Russell to avoid situations like Russell's Paradox where a set could be an element of itself.

In effect, what Whitehead and Russell did was to avoid mathematical paradoxes and "shift" the problem of the consistency of arithmetic to the consistency of a few basic logical principles. If these logical principles standing alone were consistent, then any mathematical system (in particular, arithmetic) derived solely from them would also be consistent. With this new method for checking consistency, many mathematicians felt it would only be a matter of time before other branches of mathematics would be proven consistent as well, and then, within those systems, eventually all statements could be proven or disproven.

Gödel's Undecidability Theorem

In 1931, Kurt Gödel published a paper "On Formally Undecidable Propositions of *Principia Mathematica* and Related Systems" in which he proved the following theorem.

Theorem 1   Gödel's Undecidability Theorem   Any mathematical system containing all the theorems of arithmetic is an incomplete system. (That is, there is a statement within this system that is true, but can never be proven true.)   ■

In other words, any system powerful enough to contain all of the rules of arithmetic, (e.g., the commutative and associative laws of addition and multiplication), must contain a mathematical statement that is true (has no counterexample), but for which *no proof can ever be found* using all of the results available in that system!

Another way of expressing Gödel's Undecidability Theorem is to say that, given a certain mathematical statement in this system, we may never learn whether it is true or false — and even if it is true, we may not ever have the resources to prove that it is true from within the system. Because of Gödel's Undecidability Theorem, we can no longer confidently predict that all open conjectures, such as Goldbach's Conjecture, will eventually be resolved one way or the other.

In his paper, Gödel produced a statement (let us call it G, for Gödel) that is true in any system similar to the system developed in *Principia Mathematica* but can never be proven true within that system. A natural question is: How do we know that G is true if we can't *prove* G is true? To explain this, we need to give some idea of Gödel's actual proof.

Gödel's actual paper is extremely complicated. The Undecidability Theorem is preceded by the establishment of several primitive objects called "signs", several variables of various "types" (as in *Principia Mathematica*), 45 definitions of functions (or relations), many other definitions, five axioms, one lemma, and seven theorems! Nevertheless, we can get the central thrust of Gödel's argument by studying the method he used for labeling items in *Principia Mathematica*. His technique is often referred to as *Gödel numbering*.

Gödel Numbering

Gödel assigned a distinct positive integer, a **Gödel number**, to each symbol, formula, and proof in the system. He assigned the first few odd integers to these seven basic symbols:

symbol	meaning	Gödel number
0	zero	1
f	successor	3
¬	not	5
∨	or	7
∀	for all	9
(	left parenthesis	11
)	right parenthesis	13

Other useful symbols such as ∧ (and), ∃ (there exists), and = (equals) can be "built" by using an appropriate combination of the seven basic symbols above. However, for the sake of simplicity, we will depart from Gödel's actual numbering, and assign Gödel numbers to these symbols as follows:

symbol	meaning	Gödel number
∧	and	15
∃	there exists	17
=	equals	19

Numerical variables (such as x, y, and z) that represent natural numbers are assigned larger odd values as their Gödel numbers — we assign 21 to x, and 23 to y.

Natural numbers after 0 can be represented in this system as follows:

$$\underbrace{f0}_{one}, \quad \underbrace{ff0}_{two}, \quad \underbrace{fff0}_{three}, \quad etc.$$

Formulas of this type that contain a sequence of symbols are assigned Gödel numbers by creating a product of powers of successive primes 2, 3, 5, 7, 11, ...

Example 4   Find the Gödel number for the sequence $fff0$.

Solution: The symbols in the sequence

$$fff0$$

have Gödel numbers 3, 3, 3, 1, respectively, and therefore we assign the Gödel number

$$2^3 3^3 5^3 7^1$$

to the entire sequence $fff0$.   □

Example 5   Find the Gödel number of the formula $\exists x(x = f0)$.

Solution: The symbols in the formula

$$\exists x(x = f0)$$

have Gödel numbers 17, 21, 11, 21, 19, 3, 1, 13, respectively. Hence we would assign the Gödel number

$$2^{17}3^{21}5^{11}7^{21}11^{19}13^{3}17^{1}19^{13}$$

to the formula $\exists x(x = f0)$.   □

By the way, the formula $\exists x(x = f0)$ in the last example asserts that there is some natural number that is the successor of zero. Since '1' is the successor of zero, we would consider this to be a true proposition. With the method of this example, we can assign to every logical proposition (and hence every theorem) an associated Gödel number.

We can generalize this even further by associating a Gödel number with a *sequence* of propositions. If there are k propositions in a sequence with Gödel numbers $n_1, n_2, \ldots, n_k$, then we assign the Gödel number $2^{n_1}3^{n_2}5^{n_3} \ldots p_k^{n_k}$ (where p_k is the kth prime in the list 2, 3, 5, 7, 11, $\ldots$) to this sequence.

Example 6   Find the Gödel number of the sequence

$$S = \left\{ \begin{array}{c} x = f0 \\ \neg(f0 = 0) \\ \neg(x = 0) \end{array} \right\}.$$

Solution: We first find the Gödel number of each individual proposition in the sequence. Now,

the Gödel number of $x = f0$ is $k_1 = 2^{21}3^{19}5^{3}7^{1}$,
the Gödel number of $\neg(f0 = 0)$ is $k_2 = 2^{5}3^{11}5^{3}7^{1}11^{19}13^{1}17^{13}$, and
the Gödel number of $\neg(x = 0)$ is $k_3 = 2^{5}3^{11}5^{21}7^{19}11^{1}13^{13}$.

Now, the Gödel numbers of these individual propositions are placed as exponents on the primes 2, 3, 5, respectively, to obtain the Gödel number

$$2^{k_1}3^{k_2}5^{k_3}$$

(an incredibly large number) for the entire sequence S.   □

Note that, in Example 6, if the first two statements in the sequence S have already been proven (or accepted as axioms), then the third statement follows logically from the first two. Hence, if $x = f0$, we can consider the sequence S to be a *proof* of the statement $\neg(x = 0)$. In this way, every proof in this mathematical system can be assigned a Gödel number.

In this manner, every basic symbol, variable, sequence of symbols and variables (e.g., proposition), and sequence of propositions (e.g., proof) that can be expressed in a system such as *Principia Mathematica* has its own *unique* Gödel number. Conversely, given any Gödel number, we can reconstruct the unique sequence of symbols corresponding to it. (This follows from the Fundamental Theorem of Arithmetic, which asserts that each positive integer has a *unique* expression as a product of primes, where the primes are listed in increasing order.) In other words, there is a one-to-one correspondence between valid sequences of symbols and valid Gödel numbers in our *Principia Mathematica*-like system.

A Few Additional Definitions

Suppose we consider all the possible formulas in our system having exactly one variable (say, x), and put them in increasing order according to Gödel number. Let $R(n)$ represent the nth such Gödel formula.

Gödel became interested in what would happen if the particular sequence of the form $fff \cdots f0$ representing the natural number n were substituted in place of the variable x in the nth Gödel formula $R(n)$. This produces a new formula, which we label as

$$\text{SUBST}[n, R(n)],$$

where "SUBST" stands for "substitution". (Gödel actually used $[R(n); n]$ in his paper to represent this new formula.) This new formula may or may not be *provable* within our mathematical system. That is, there may or may not be some sequence of previously established propositions that logically proves the new formula $\text{SUBST}[n, R(n)]$.

Suppose, for a particular n, the Gödel formula $\text{SUBST}[n, R(n)]$ is provable. We express this by writing

$$\text{PR}(\text{SUBST}[n, R(n)]),$$

where "PR" stands for "provable". (Gödel expressed this as $\text{Bew}[R(n); n]$.)

The Heart of Gödel's Argument

Consider the set Z of all integers n for which $\text{PR}(\text{SUBST}[n, R(n)])$ is true — that is, for which there exists a finite sequence of propositions to prove the statement obtained when the sequence $fff \cdots f0$ for n is substituted for the variable x in the nth Gödel formula. (In his paper, Gödel actually used the *complement* of this set as the set Z.) Now, a given integer n is either in Z or it is not. Consider the formula $\neg(x \in Z)$ (i.e., it is not true that $x \in Z$). It is not immediately obvious that this formula involving x has a Gödel number, but Gödel showed that there is a way of expressing the formula $x \in Z$ in terms of more basic symbols in the system. Therefore, let us suppose that $\neg(x \in Z)$ has a Gödel number, and that it is the qth Gödel formula (in the ordering of single-variable Gödel formulas discussed earlier). Then, $\neg(x \in Z)$ is $R(q)$.

Finally, let us consider $\text{SUBST}[q, R(q)]$ — the new formula obtained by putting the appropriate sequence of symbols of the form $fff \cdots f0$ for q into the formula $R(q)$. We will call this new formula G.

Now, either G is true or $\neg G$ is true. However,

Theorem 2   Neither G nor $\neg G$ is a provable statement.

Proof: We give a proof by contradiction. Suppose first that G is a provable statement. Then, $\text{PR}(\text{SUBST}[q, R(q)])$ is true — and so by definition of Z, we have $q \in Z$. But upon actually substituting q into $R(q)$, we obtain the statement $\neg(q \in Z)$, which is supposed to be provable. Since we cannot have both $q \in Z$ and $\neg(q \in Z)$ provable in our system, we have a contradiction.

On the other hand, suppose $\neg G$ is a provable statement. Then G is certainly not true, and therefore not provable. Hence, $\text{PR}(\text{SUBST}[q, R(q)])$ is not true, and so by definition of Z, it follows that $q \notin Z$. That is, $q \notin Z$ is a provable statement. But, since G is not provable, substituting q into $R(q)$ gives us the unprovable statement $\neg(q \in Z)$. Since we cannot have $q \notin Z$ both provable and unprovable, we have a contradiction.   ■

We have seen that either G or $\neg G$ is true but that neither of these two statements is provable. Thus, in our *Principia Mathematica*-like system, there is at least one statement that *is true, but is not provable!*

Applications of Gödel's Undecidability Theorem

Gödel's Undecidability Theorem has profound implications. It tells us that even such a fundamental branch of mathematics as arithmetic has its limitations. It is not always possible to find a proof for every true statement within that system. Thus, we may never be able to establish whether certain conjectures within the system are true. You might wonder whether we could enlarge our system to a more powerful one in the hopes of finding proofs for certain statements. But, we could then apply Gödel's Undecidability Theorem to this larger system to show that it also has limitations.

Rudy Rucker writes in [4] that "Gödel once told the philosopher of science Hao Wang that the original inspiration for his ... theorem was his realization that 'truth' has no finite description." That is, no mathematical system with a finite number of axioms such as we have described here can contain a full depiction of reality. No mathematical system like *Principia Mathematica* can be both consistent and complete.

In addition to the Undecidability Theorem, Gödel also demonstrated in his paper that a system like *Principia Mathematica* is not even powerful enough to establish its own consistency! That is, the consistency of the system cannot be proven using only the principles available within the system itself.

In recent years, the implications of Gödel's Undecidability Theorem in computer science have been studied widely, especially in the area of artificial intelligence. If we imagine giving to a computer an initial set of formulas (axioms) and a set of logical principles (operations) for calculating new formulas (theorems), then Gödel's Undecidability Theorem implies that, no matter how powerful the computer, there are always some true statements that the computer will never be able to derive. Although computers have been useful to mathematicians in proving computationally difficult results, Gödel's Undecidability Theorem destroys the myth many people have that any difficult mathematical problem will eventually be resolved by a powerful enough computer.

Computer scientists have drawn an even closer parallel between mathematical systems and computers. The initial state (register contents, data) of a computer is analogous to the initial set of formulas (axioms) in a mathematical system. Similarly, the logical operations (via hardware and software) that a computer is allowed to perform are analogous to the principles of logic permitted in the mathematical system. Extending this analogy, the mathematician (and pioneer computer scientist) Alan Turing* extended Gödel's results to prove that there is no general algorithm that can always correctly predict whether a randomly selected computer program will run or not.

In 1961, the British philosopher J. Anthony Lucas tried to use Gödel's Undecidability Theorem to show that a machine will never be able to "think"

---

* Alan Turing (1912–1954) was a British mathematician and logician, who received his Ph.D. from Princeton in 1938. In his landmark 1937 paper "On Computable Numbers", he proposed the notion of a general computer (later known as a *Turing machine*), that could execute finite mathematical algorithms, and proved there exist mathematical problems that can not be solved by such a machine. Turing also worked on the enormous problems of breaking secret codes during World War II with the Foreign Office of the British Department of Communications. He was the subject of a recent Broadway play (starring Derek Jacobi) by Hugh Whitemore entitled "Breaking the Code". After the war, Turing worked at the National Physical Lab at Teddington on the design of a large (automatic) computer, and became Deputy Director of the Computing Lab at the University of Manchester in 1949. Turing died from a dose of potassium cyanide poisoning, self-administered, but possibly accidental.

in quite the same manner as a human, and hence that the achievement of an artificial intelligence is impossible. However, Lucas' argument is refuted in Douglas Hofstadter's book [2]. In this book, Hofstadter also considers a number of other related artificial-intelligence questions, such as whether the human mind is essentially a computer system (i.e., a mathematical system). If so, are there some truths that the unaided human mind will never fathom?

Suggested Readings

1. M. Gardner, "Douglas R. Hofstadter's 'Gödel, Escher, Bach' ", *Scientific American*, 1979, pp. 16–24. (A quick tour through Hofstadter's book [2].)

2. D. Hofstadter, *Gödel, Escher, Bach: An Eternal Golden Braid*, Basic Books, New York, 1979. (Pulitzer Prize winning *tour de force* that relates the work of Gödel to the work of the artist M.C. Escher and the composer Johann Sebastian Bach.)

3. E. Nagel and J. Newman, *Gödel's Proof*, New York University Press, New York, 1958. (The classic reference on Gödel's Undecidability Theorem.)

4. R. Rucker, *Mind Tools: The Five Levels of Mathematical Reality*, Houghton-Mifflin, Boston, 1987. (See especially the section on Gödel's Undecidability Theorem, pp. 218–226.)

5. R. Smullyan, *Forever Undecided: A Puzzle Guide to Gödel*, Knopf, New York, 1987. (Understanding the concepts behind Gödel's Undecidability Theorem by solving successively more difficult puzzles.)

6. J. van Heijenoort, *From Frege to Gödel, A Source Book in Mathematical Logic, 1879–1931*, Harvard University Press, Cambridge, Mass., 1967. (Contains a complete English translation of Gödel's 1931 paper, as well as Gödel's abstract of the paper, and a related note that he wrote about the paper.)

Exercises

1. Verify that Goldbach's Conjecture is true for all the even integers from 14 to 50.

2. Another unproven conjecture in number theory is the following: Let f: $\mathcal{N} \longrightarrow \mathcal{N}$ be defined by

$$f(n) = \begin{cases} n/2 & n \text{ even} \\ 3n+1 & n \text{ odd}; \end{cases}$$

then, for every n, there is an integer i such that $f^i(n) = 1$. Verify that this conjecture is true for $n = 22$ and $n = 23$.

3. Exhibit a model for the axioms in Example 3 containing fewer than four points.

In Exercises 4–6, find a finite model for the system having the given set of axioms. Let "point" and "line" be undefined terms. (Remember, a "line" does not necessarily have to be straight or contain an infinite number of points.)

4. (i) There are exactly four points in the system.
   (ii) Not all points are on the same line.
   (iii) Through any three points there is exactly one line.

5. (i) There are at least two lines in the system.
   (ii) Each line contains at least two points.
   (iii) Every pair of points is on a line.
   (iv) No point is on more than two lines.

6. (i) There is at least one line and a point not on that line.
   (ii) Each line contains exactly three points.
   (iii) Each pair of points lies on exactly one line.
   Hint: Use seven points and seven lines.

7. In Exercise 5, can you find a model containing exactly 4 points?

In Exercises 8 and 9, show that the given set of axioms is inconsistent.

8. (i) There are exactly four points in the system.
   (ii) Each pair of points lies on exactly one line.
   (iii) Every line contains exactly three points.

9. (i) There is at least one line in the system.
   (ii) Every two points lie on exactly one line.
   (iii) Every point lies on exactly two distinct lines.
   (iv) Every line contains exactly three points.

10. Explain why the following statement is a paradox: "This sentence is false."

11. Suppose there are two types of people living on a certain island: truth-tellers (who never lie) and liars (who never tell the truth).
    a) An inhabitant of the island says, "I am lying." Explain the paradox.
    ★ b) An inhabitant of the island says, "You will never know that I am telling the truth." Is this a paradox?

12. Using the Gödel numbering scheme established earlier in this chapter, give the Gödel number for each of the following statements:

a) $x = ff0$.

b) $\neg((x = 0) \lor (y = 0))$.

c) $\forall x \exists y(\neg(fx = y))$.

d) $\forall x((x = f0) \lor \neg(x = f0))$.

13. Give the Gödel number for each of the following proofs (i.e., sequence of statements):

a) $S = \left\{ \begin{array}{l} x = f0 \\ y = fx \\ y = ff0 \end{array} \right\}$

b) $T = \left\{ \begin{array}{c} \exists y(x = fy) \\ \forall y(\neg(0 = fy)) \\ \neg(x = 0) \end{array} \right\}$

14. In each case, state the proposition that has the given Gödel number.

a) $2^5 3^{11} 5^{21} 7^{19} 11^{23} 13^{13}$.

b) $2^9 3^{21} 5^{17} 7^{23} 11^{11} 13^{21} 17^{19} 19^3 23^{23} 29^{13}$.

c) $2^{11} 3^{21} 5^{19} 7^1 11^{13} 13^7 17^5 19^{11} 23^{23} 29^{19} 31^1 37^{13}$.

15. In each case, state the sequence of propositions that has the given Gödel number.

a) $2^{k_1} 3^{k_2} 5^{k_3}$, where $k_1 = 2^{21} 3^{19} 5^3 7^3 11^1$, $k_2 = 2^5 3^{11} 5^{23} 7^{19} 11^{21} 13^{13}$, and $k_3 = 2^5 3^{11} 5^{23} 7^{19} 11^3 13^3 17^1 19^{13}$.

b) $2^{k_1} 3^{k_2} 5^{k_3}$, where $k_1 = 2^9 3^{23} 5^{17} 7^{21} 11^5 13^{11} 17^{21} 19^{19} 23^{23} 29^{13}$, $k_2 = 2^{23} 3^{19} 5^3 7^1$, and $k_3 = 2^{17} 3^{21} 5^5 7^{11} 11^{21} 13^{19} 17^3 19^1 23^{13}$.

⋆16. Suppose we enlarged our *Principia Mathematica*-like system to include Gödel's statement G as an axiom. If the new mathematical system is consistent (that is, if G is true), what does Gödel's Undecidability Theorem tell us about the new system?

Computer Projects

1. Write a program that takes as input an even positive integer greater than 2 and writes it as a sum of two primes (Goldbach's Conjecture).

2. Write a program that implements the function defined in Exercise 2.

3. Write a program that takes a list of primes and gives as output the string of symbols that constitutes the corresponding Gödel statement or recognizes that the list of primes is unacceptable.

5

Coding Theory

Author: Kenneth H. Rosen, AT&T Bell Laboratories.

Prerequisites: The prerequisites for this chapter are the basics of logic, set theory, number theory, matrices, and probability. See, for example, Sections 1.1, 1.4, 2.3, 2.5, and 4.4 of *Discrete Mathematics and Its Applications*, Second Edition, by Kenneth H. Rosen.

Introduction

The usual way to represent, manipulate, and transmit information is to use bit strings, that is, sequences of zeros and ones. It is extremely difficult, and often impossible, to prevent errors when data are stored, retrieved, operated on, or transmitted. Errors may occur from noisy communication channels, electrical interference, human error, or equipment error. Similarly, errors are introduced into data stored over a long period of time on magnetic tape as the tape deteriorates.

It is particularly important to ensure reliable transmission when large computer files are rapidly transmitted or when data are sent over long distances, such as data transmitted from space probes billions of miles away. Similarly, it is often important to recover data that have degraded while stored on a tape. To guarantee reliable transmission or to recover degraded data, techniques from *coding theory* are used. Messages, in the form of bit strings, are encoded by translating them into longer bit strings, called *codewords*. A set of codewords is called a *code*. As we will see, we can detect errors when we use certain codes. That is, as long as not too many errors have been made, we can determine whether one or more errors have been introduced when a bit string was transmitted. Furthermore, when codes with more redundancy are used, we can correct errors. That is, as long as not too many errors were introduced in transmission, we can recover the codeword from the bit string received when this codeword was sent.

   Coding theory, the study of codes, including error detecting and error correcting codes, has been studied extensively for the past forty years. It has become increasingly important with the development of new technologies for data communications and data storage. In this chapter we will study both error detecting and error correcting codes. We will introduce an important family of error correcting codes. To go beyond the coverage in this chapter and to learn about the latest applications of coding theory and the latest technical developments, the reader is referred to the references listed at the end of the chapter.

Error Detecting Codes

A simple way to detect errors when a bit string is transmitted is to add a **parity check bit** at the end of the string. If the bit string contains an even number of 1s we put a 0 at the end of the string. If the bit string contains an odd number of 1s we put a 1 at the end of the string. In other words, we encode the message $x_1 x_2 \ldots x_n$ as $x_1 x_2 \ldots x_n x_{n+1}$, where the parity check bit x_{n+1} is given by

$$x_{n+1} = (x_1 + x_2 + \ldots + x_n) \bmod 2.$$

Adding the parity check bit guarantees that the number of 1s in the extended string must be even. It is easy to see that the codewords in this code are bit strings with an even number of 1s.

   Note that when a parity check bit is added to a bit string, if a single error is made in the transmission of a codeword, the total number of 1s will be odd. Consequently, this error can be detected. However, if two errors are made, these errors cannot be detected, since the total number of 1s in the extended string with two errors will still be even. In general, any odd number of errors can be detected, while an even number of errors cannot be detected.

Example 1   Suppose that a parity check bit is added to a bit string before it is transmitted. What can you conclude if you receive the bit strings 1110011 and 10111101 as messages?

Solution: Since the string 1110011 contains an odd number of 1s, it cannot be a valid codeword (and must, therefore, contain an odd number of errors). On the other hand, the string 10111101 contains an even number of 1s. Hence it is either a valid codeword or contains an even number of errors.   □

Another simple way to detect errors is to repeat each bit in a message twice, as is done in the following example.

Example 2   Encode the bit string 011001 by repeating each bit twice.

Solution: Repeating each bit twice produces the codeword 001111000011. □

What errors can be detected when we repeat each bit of a codeword twice? Since the codewords are those bit strings that contain pairs of matching bits, that is, where the first two bits agree, the third and fourth bits agree, and so on, we can detect errors that change no more than one bit of each pair of these matching bits. For example, we can detect errors in the second bit, the third bit, and the eighth bit of when codewords have eight bits (such as detecting that 01101110, received when the codeword 00001111 was sent, has errors). On the other hand, we cannot detect an error when the third and fourth bit are both changed (such as detecting that 00111111, received when the codeword 00001111 was sent, has errors).

So far we have discussed codes that can be used to detect errors. When errors are detected, all we can do to obtain the correct codeword is to ask for retransmission and hope that no errors will occur when this is done. However, there are more powerful codes that can not only detect but can also correct errors. We now turn our attention to these codes, called error correcting codes.

Error Correcting Codes

We have seen that when redundancy is included in codewords, such as when a parity check bit is added to a bit string, we can detect transmission errors. We can do even better if we include more redundancy. We will not only be able to detect errors, but we will also be able to correct errors. More precisely, if sufficiently few errors have been made in the transmission of a codeword, we can determine which codeword was sent. This is illustrated by the following example.

Example 3   To encode a message we can use the *triple repetition code*. We repeat a message three times. That is, if the message is $x_1 x_2 x_3$, we encode it as $x_1 x_2 x_3 x_4 x_5 x_6 x_7 x_8 x_9$ where $x_1 = x_4 = x_7$, $x_2 = x_5 = x_8$, and $x_3 = x_6 =$

x_9. The valid codewords are 000000000, 001001001, 010010010, 011011011, 100100100, 101101101, 110110110, and 111111111.

We decode a bit string, which may contain errors, using the *simple majority rule*. For example, to determine x_1, we look at x_1, x_4, and x_7. If two or three of these bits are 1, we conclude that $x_1 = 1$. Otherwise, if two or three of these bits are 0, we conclude that $x_1 = 0$. In general, we look at the three bits corresponding to each bit in the original message. We decide that a bit in the message is 1 if a majority of bits in the string received in positions corresponding to this bit are 1s and we decide this bit is a 0 otherwise. Using this procedure, we correctly decode the message as long as at most one error has been made in the bits corresponding to each bit of the original message.

For example, when a triple repetition code is used, if we receive 011111010, we conclude that the message sent was 011. (For instance, we decided that the first bit of the message was 0 since the first bit is 0, the fourth bit is 1, and the seventh bit is 0, leading us to conclude that the fourth bit is wrong.) □

To make the ideas introduced by the triple repetition code more precise we need to introduce some ideas about the *distance* between codewords and the probability of errors. We will develop several important concepts before returning to error correcting codes.

Hamming Distance

There is a simple way to measure the distance between two bit strings. We look at the number of positions in which these bit strings differ. This approach was used by Richard Hamming* in his fundamental work in coding theory.

Definition 1   The *Hamming distance* $d(\mathbf{x}, \mathbf{y})$ between the bit strings $\mathbf{x} = x_1 x_2 \ldots x_n$ and $\mathbf{y} = y_1 y_2 \ldots y_n$ is the number of positions in which these strings differ, that is, the number of i $(i = 1, 2, \ldots, n)$ for which $x_i \neq y_i$. □

---

* Richard Hamming (1915–) is one of the founders of modern coding theory. He was born in Chicago and received his B.S. from the University of Chicago, his M.A. from the University of Nebraska, and his Ph.D. from the University of Illinois in 1942. He was employed by the University of Illinois from 1942 to 1944 and the University of Louisville from 1944 to 1945. From 1945 until 1946 he was on the staff of the Manhattan Project in Los Alamos. He joined Bell Telephone Laboratories in 1946, where he worked until 1976. His research has included work in the areas of coding theory, numerical methods, statistics, and digital filtering. Hamming joined the faculty of the Naval Postgraduate School in 1976, where he continues teaching. Among the awards he has won are the Turing Prize from the ACM and the IEEE Hamming Medal (named after him).

Note that the Hamming distance between two bit strings equals the number of changes in individual bits needed to change one of the strings into the other. We will find this observation useful later.

Example 4   Find the Hamming distance between the bit strings 01110 and 11011 and the Hamming distance between the bit strings 00000 and 11111.

Solution: Since 01110 and 11011 differ in their first, third, and fifth bits, $d(01110, 11011) = 3$. Since 00000 and 11111 differ in all five bits, we conclude that $d(00000, 11111) = 5$.   ☐

The Hamming distance satisfies all the properties of a *distance function* (or *metric*), as the following theorem demonstrates.

Theorem 1   Let $d(\mathbf{x}, \mathbf{y})$ represent the Hamming distance between the bit strings $\mathbf{x}$ and $\mathbf{y}$ of length n. Then

(i) $d(\mathbf{x}, \mathbf{y}) \geq 0$ for all $\mathbf{x}$, $\mathbf{y}$

(ii) $d(\mathbf{x}, \mathbf{y}) = 0$ if and only if $\mathbf{x} = \mathbf{y}$

(iii) $d(\mathbf{x}, \mathbf{y}) = d(\mathbf{y}, \mathbf{x})$ for all $\mathbf{x}$, $\mathbf{y}$

(iv) $d(\mathbf{x}, \mathbf{y}) \leq d(\mathbf{x}, \mathbf{z}) + d(\mathbf{z}, \mathbf{y})$ for all $\mathbf{x}$, $\mathbf{y}$, $\mathbf{z}$.

Proof: Properties (i), (ii), and (iii) follow immediately from the definition of the Hamming distance. To prove (iv), we use the fact that $d(\mathbf{x}, \mathbf{y})$ is the number of changes of bits required to change $\mathbf{x}$ into $\mathbf{y}$. Note that for every string $\mathbf{z}$ of length n the number of changes needed to change $\mathbf{x}$ into $\mathbf{y}$ does not exceed the number of changes required to change $\mathbf{x}$ into $\mathbf{z}$ and to then change $\mathbf{z}$ into $\mathbf{y}$. ∎

How can the Hamming distance be used in decoding? In particular, suppose that when a codeword $\mathbf{x}$ from a code C is sent, the bit string $\mathbf{y}$ is received. If the transmission was error-free, then $\mathbf{y}$ would be the same as $\mathbf{x}$. But if errors were introduced by the transmission, for instance by a noisy line, then $\mathbf{y}$ is not the same as $\mathbf{x}$. How can we correct errors, that is, how can we recover $\mathbf{x}$?

One approach would be to compute the Hamming distance between $\mathbf{y}$ and each of the codewords in C. Then to decode $\mathbf{y}$, we take the codeword of minimum Hamming distance from $\mathbf{y}$, if such a codeword is unique. If the distance between the closest codewords in C is large enough and if sufficiently few errors were made in transmission, this codeword should be $\mathbf{x}$, the codeword sent. This type of decoding is called *nearest neighbor decoding*.

Example 5   Use nearest neighbor decoding to determine which code word was sent from the code $C = \{0000, 1110, 1011\}$ if 0110 is received.

Solution: We first find the distance between 0110 and each of the codewords. We find that

$$d(0000, 0110) = 2,$$

$$d(1110, 0110) = 1,$$

$$d(1011, 0110) = 3.$$

Since the closest codeword to 0110 is 1110, we conclude that 1110 was the codeword sent.   □

Will nearest neighbor decoding produce the most likely codeword that was sent from a binary string that was received? It is not hard to see that it will if each bit sent has the same probability p of being received incorrectly and $p < 1/2$. We call a transmission channel with this property a *binary symmetric channel*. Such a channel is displayed in Figure 1.

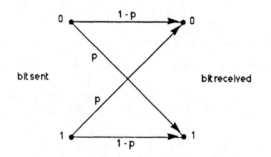

Figure 1.   A binary symmetric channel.

Example 6   Suppose that when a bit is sent over a binary symmetric channel the probability it is received incorrectly is 0.01. What is the probability that the bit string 100010 is received when the bit string 000000 is sent?

Solution: Since the probability a bit is received incorrectly is 0.01, the probability that a bit is received correctly is $1 - 0.01 = 0.99$. For 100010 to be received, when 000000 is sent, it is necessary for the first and fifth bits to be received incorrectly and the other four bits to be received correctly. The probability that this occurs is

$$(0.99)^4(0.01)^2 = 0.000096059601.$$ □

We will now show that nearest neighbor decoding gives us the most likely codeword sent, so that it is also *maximum likelihood decoding.*

Theorem 2   Suppose codewords of a binary code C are transmitted using a binary symmetric channel. Then, nearest neighbor decoding of a bit string received produces the most likely codeword sent.

Proof: To prove this theorem we first need to find the probability that when a codeword of length n is sent, a bit string with k errors in specified positions is received. Since the probability each bit is received correctly is $1 - p$ and the probability each bit is received in error is p, it follows that the probability of k errors in specified positions is $p^k(1-p)^{n-k}$. Since $p < 1/2$ and $1 - p > 1/2$, it follows that

$$p^i(1-p)^{n-i} > p^j(1-p)^{n-j}$$

whenever $i < j$. Hence, if $i < j$, the probability that a bit string with i specified errors is received is greater than the probability that a bit string with j specified errors is received. Since is more likely that errors were made in fewer specified positions when a codeword was transmitted, nearest neighbor decoding produces the most likely codeword. ∎

The Hamming distance between codewords in a binary code determines its ability to detect and/or correct errors. We need to make the following definition before introducing two key theorems relating to this ability.

Definition 2   The *minimum distance* of a binary code C is the smallest distance between two distinct codewords, that is,

$$d(C) = \min\{d(\mathbf{x}, \mathbf{y}) | \mathbf{x}, \mathbf{y} \in C, \mathbf{x} \neq \mathbf{y}\}. \qquad \square$$

Example 7   Find the minimum distance of the code

$$C = \{00000, 01110, 10011, 11111\}.$$

Solution: To compute the minimum distance of this code we will find the distance between each pair of codewords and then find the smallest such distance. We have $d(00000, 01110) = 3$, $d(00000, 10011) = 3$, $d(00000, 11111) = 5$, $d(01110, 10011) = 4$, $d(01110, 11111) = 2$, and $d(10011, 11111) = 2$. We see that the minimum distance of C is 2. $\square$

Example 8   Find the minimum distance of the code
$$C = \{000000, 111111\}.$$

Solution: Since there are only two codewords and $d(000000, 111111) = 6$, the minimum distance of this code is 6.   □

The minimum distance of a code tells us how many errors it can detect and how many errors it can correct, as the following two theorems show.

Theorem 3   A binary code C can detect up to k errors in any codeword if and only if $d(C) \geq k + 1$.

Proof: Suppose that C is a binary code with $d(C) \geq k + 1$. Suppose that a codeword $\mathbf{x}$ is transmitted and is received with k or fewer errors. Since the minimum distance between codewords is at least $k + 1$, the bit string received cannot be another codeword. Hence, the receiver can detect these errors.

Now suppose that C can detect up to k errors and that $d(C) \leq k$. Then there are two codewords in C that differ in no more than k bits. It is then possible for k errors to be introduced when one of these codewords is transmitted so that the other codeword is received, contradicting the fact that C can detect up to k errors.   ■

Theorem 4   A binary code C can correct up to k errors in any codeword if and only if $d(C) \geq 2k + 1$.

Proof: Suppose that C is a binary code with $d(C) \geq 2k + 1$. Suppose that a codeword $\mathbf{x}$ is transmitted and received with k or fewer errors as the bit string $\mathbf{z}$, so that $d(\mathbf{x}, \mathbf{z}) \leq k$. To see that C can correct these errors, note that if $\mathbf{y}$ is a codeword other than $\mathbf{x}$, then $d(\mathbf{z}, \mathbf{y}) \geq k + 1$. To see this note that if $d(\mathbf{z}, \mathbf{y}) \leq k$, then by the triangle inequality $d(\mathbf{x}, \mathbf{y}) \leq d(\mathbf{x}, \mathbf{z}) + d(\mathbf{z}, \mathbf{y}) \leq k + k = 2k$, contradicting the assumption that $d(C) \geq 2k + 1$.

Conversely, suppose that C can correct up to k errors. If $d(C) \leq 2k$, then there are two codewords that differ in $2k$ bits. Changing k of the bits in one of these codewords produces a bit string that differs from each of these two codewords in exactly k positions, thus making it impossible to correct these k errors.   ■

Example 9   Let C be the code $\{00000000, 11111000, 01010111, 10101111\}$. How many errors can C detect and how many can it correct?

Solution: Computing the distance between codewords shows that the minimum distance of C is 5. By Theorem 3, it follows that C can detect up to

$5 - 1 = 4$ errors. For example, when we use C to detect errors, we can detect the four errors made in transmission when we receive 11110000 when the codeword 00000000 was sent.

By Theorem 4, it follows that C can correct up to $\lfloor (5-1)/2 \rfloor = 2$ errors. For example, when we use C to correct errors, we can correct the two errors introduced in transmission when we receive 11100000 when the codeword 11111000 was sent.   □

Perfect Codes

To allow error correction we want to make the minimum distance between codewords large. But doing so limits how many codewords are available. Here we will develop a bound on the number of codewords in a binary code with a given minimum distance.

Lemma 1   Suppose $\mathbf{x}$ is a bit string of length n and that k is a nonnegative integer not exceeding n. Then there are

$$C(n,0) + C(n,1) + \cdots + C(n,k)$$

bit strings $\mathbf{y}$ of length n such that $d(\mathbf{x},\mathbf{y}) \leq k$ (where d is the Hamming distance).

Proof: Let i be a nonnegative integer. The number of bit strings $\mathbf{y}$ with $d(\mathbf{x},\mathbf{y}) = i$ equals the number of ways to select the i locations where $\mathbf{x}$ and $\mathbf{y}$ differ. This can be done in $C(n,i)$ ways. It follows that there are

$$C(n,0) + C(n,1) + \cdots + C(n,k)$$

bit strings such that $d(\mathbf{x},\mathbf{y}) \leq k$.   □

We can describe the statement in Lemma 1 in geometric terms. By the **sphere of radius** k centered at $\mathbf{x}$ we mean the set of all bit strings $\mathbf{y}$ such that $d(\mathbf{x},\mathbf{y}) \leq k$. Lemma 1 says that there are exactly $\sum_{i=0}^{k} C(n,i)$ bit strings in the sphere of radius k centered at $\mathbf{x}$.

Lemma 2   Let C be a binary code containing codewords of length n and let $d(C) = 2k + 1$. Then given a bit string $\mathbf{y}$ of length n, there is at most one codeword $\mathbf{x}$ such that $\mathbf{y}$ is in the sphere of radius k centered at $\mathbf{x}$.

Proof: Suppose that $\mathbf{y}$ is in the sphere of radius k centered at two different codewords $\mathbf{x}_1$ and $\mathbf{x}_2$. Then $d(\mathbf{x}_1,\mathbf{y}) \leq k$ and $d(\mathbf{x}_2,\mathbf{y}) \leq k$. By the triangle inequality for the Hamming distance this implies that

$$d(\mathbf{x}_1, \mathbf{x}_2) \le d(\mathbf{x}_1, \mathbf{y}) + d(\mathbf{x}_2, \mathbf{y}) \le k + k = 2k,$$

contradicting the fact that the minimum distance between codewords is $2k + 1$.

□

We can now give a useful bound on how many codewords can be in a code consisting of n-tuples that can correct a specified number of errors.

Theorem 5   The Sphere Packing or (Hamming) Bound   Suppose that C is a code of bit strings of length n with $d(C) = 2k + 1$. Then $|C|$, the number of codewords in C, cannot exceed

$$\frac{2^n}{C(n, 0) + C(n, 1) + \cdots + C(n, k)}.$$

Proof: There are 2^n bit strings of length n. By Lemma 1 the sphere of radius k centered at a codeword $\mathbf{x}$ contains

$$C(n, 0) + C(n, 1) + \cdots + C(n, k)$$

bit strings. Since no bit string can be in two such spheres (by Lemma 2), it follows that the number of bit strings of length n is at least as large as the number of codewords times the number of bit strings in each such sphere. Hence,

$$2^n \ge |C|[C(n, 0) + C(n, 1) + \cdots + C(n, k)].$$

We obtain the inequality we want by dividing by the second factor on the right-hand side of this inequality (and writing the inequality with the smaller term first).   ■

Example 10   Find an upper bound for the number of codewords in a code C where codewords are bit strings of length seven and the minimum distance between codewords is three.

Solution: The minimum distance between codewords is $3 = 2k + 1$, so that $k = 1$. Hence the sphere packing bound shows that there are no more than

$$2^7/[C(7, 0) + C(7, 1)] = 128/8 = 16$$

codewords in such a code.   □

The sphere packing bound gives us an upper bound for the number of codewords in a binary code with a given minimum distance where codewords are bit strings of length n. The codes that actually achieve this upper bound, that is, that have the most codewords possible, are of special interest because they are the most efficient error correcting codes. Such codes are known as *perfect codes*.

Example 11   Show that the code consisting of just two codewords 00000 and 11111 is a perfect binary code.

Solution: The minimum distance between codewords in this code is 5. The sphere packing bound states that there are at most

$$2^5/[C(5,0) + C(5,1) + C(5,2)] = 32/16 = 2$$

codewords in a code consisting of 5-tuples with minimum distance 5. Since there are 2 codewords in this code, it is a perfect binary code.   □

The code in Example 11 is called a *trivial perfect code* since it only consists of the two codewords, one containing only 0s and the other containing only 1s. As Exercise 8 demonstrates, when n is an odd positive integer there are trivial perfect codes consisting of the two codewords which are bit strings of length n consisting of all 0s and of all 1s. Finding perfect binary codes different from the trivial codes has been one of the most important problems in coding theory. In the next section we will introduce a class of perfect binary codes known as Hamming codes.

Generator Matrices

Before describing Hamming codes, we need to generalize the concept of a parity check bit. When we use a parity check bit, we encode a message $x_1 x_2 \ldots x_k$ as $x_1 x_2 \ldots x_k x_{k+1}$ where $x_{k+1} = (x_1 + x_2 + \cdots + x_k) \bmod 2$. To generalize this notion, we add more than one check bit. More precisely, we encode a message $x_1 x_2 \ldots x_k$ as $x_1 x_2 \ldots x_k x_{k+1} \ldots x_n$, where the last $n - k$ bits $x_{k+1}, \ldots, x_n$, are *parity check bits*, obtained from the k bits in the message. We will describe how these parity check bits are specified.

Consider a k-bit message $x_1 x_2 \cdots x_k$ as a $1 \times k$ matrix **x**. Let **G** be a $k \times n$ matrix that begins with the $k \times k$ identity matrix $\mathbf{I}_k$. That is, $\mathbf{G} = (\mathbf{I}_k | \mathbf{A})$, where **A** is a $k \times (n - k)$ matrix, known as a *generator matrix*. We encode **x** as $E(\mathbf{x}) = \mathbf{x}\mathbf{G}$, where we do arithmetic modulo 2. Coding using a parity check bit and using the triple repetition code are special cases of this technique, as illustrated in Examples 12 and 13.

Example 12   We can represent encoding by adding a parity check bit to a three-bit message as $E(\mathbf{x}) = \mathbf{xG}$, where

$$\mathbf{G} = \begin{pmatrix} 1 & 0 & 0 & 1 \\ 0 & 1 & 0 & 1 \\ 0 & 0 & 1 & 1 \end{pmatrix}.$$

Note that to obtain G we add a column of 1s to $\mathbf{I}_3$, the 3×3 identity matrix. That is, $G = (\mathbf{I}_3|\mathbf{A})$, where

$$\mathbf{A} = \begin{pmatrix} 1 \\ 1 \\ 1 \end{pmatrix}. \qquad \qquad \square$$

Example 13   We can represent encoding using the triple repetition code for three-bit messages as $E(\mathbf{x}) = \mathbf{xG}$, where

$$\mathbf{G} = \begin{pmatrix} 1 & 0 & 0 & 1 & 0 & 0 & 1 & 0 & 0 \\ 0 & 1 & 0 & 0 & 1 & 0 & 0 & 1 & 0 \\ 0 & 0 & 1 & 0 & 0 & 1 & 0 & 0 & 1 \end{pmatrix}.$$

Note that $\mathbf{G}$ is formed by repeating the identity matrix of order three, $\mathbf{I}_3$, three times, that is,

$$\mathbf{G} = (\mathbf{I}_3|\mathbf{I}_3|\mathbf{I}_3). \qquad \qquad \square$$

We now consider an example which we will use to develop some important ideas.

Example 14   Suppose that

$$\mathbf{G} = \begin{pmatrix} 1 & 0 & 0 & 1 & 1 & 1 \\ 0 & 1 & 0 & 1 & 1 & 0 \\ 0 & 0 & 1 & 1 & 0 & 1 \end{pmatrix},$$

that is, $\mathbf{G} = (\mathbf{I}_3|\mathbf{A})$, where

$$A = \begin{pmatrix} 1 & 1 & 1 \\ 1 & 1 & 0 \\ 1 & 0 & 1 \end{pmatrix}.$$

What are the codewords in the code generated by this generator matrix?

Solution: We encode each of the eight three-bit messages $\mathbf{x} = x_1 x_2 x_3$ as $E(\mathbf{x}) = \mathbf{x}\mathbf{G}$. This produces the codewords 000000, 001101, 010110, 011011, 100111, 101010, 110001, and 111100. For example, we get the third of these by computing

$$E(010) = (0\ 1\ 0)\mathbf{G} = (0\ 1\ 0) \begin{pmatrix} 1 & 0 & 0 & 1 & 1 & 1 \\ 0 & 1 & 0 & 1 & 1 & 0 \\ 0 & 0 & 1 & 1 & 0 & 1 \end{pmatrix} = (0\ 1\ 0\ 1\ 1\ 0). \quad \square$$

It is easy to see that we can find the codewords in a binary code generated by a generator matrix G by taking all possible linear combinations of the rows of G (since arithmetic is modulo 2, this means all sums of subsets of the set of rows of G). The reader should verify this for codewords in the code in Example 14.

It is easy to see that the binary codes formed using generator matrices have the property that the sum of any two codewords is again a codeword. That is, they are **linear codes**. To see this, suppose that $\mathbf{y}_1$ and $\mathbf{y}_2$ are codewords generated by the generator matrix $\mathbf{G}$. Then there are bit strings $\mathbf{x}_1$ and $\mathbf{x}_2$ such that $E(\mathbf{x}_1) = \mathbf{y}_1$ and $E(\mathbf{x}_2) = \mathbf{y}_2$, where $E(\mathbf{x}) = \mathbf{x}\mathbf{G}$. It follows that $\mathbf{y}_1 + \mathbf{y}_2$ is also a codeword since $E(\mathbf{x}_1 + \mathbf{x}_2) = \mathbf{y}_1 + \mathbf{y}_2$. (Here we add bit strings by adding their components in the same positions using arithmetic modulo 2.)

We will see that there is an easy way to find the minimum distance of a linear code. Before we see this, we need to make the following definition.

Definition 3   The *weight* of a codeword $\mathbf{x}$, denoted by $w(\mathbf{x})$, in a binary code is the number of 1s in this codeword. $\qquad \square$

Example 15   Find the weights of the codewords 00000, 10111, and 11111.

Solution: Counting the number of 1s in each of these codewords we find that $w(00000) = 0$, $w(10111) = 4$, and $w(11111) = 5$. $\qquad \square$

Lemma 3   Suppose that $\mathbf{x}$ and $\mathbf{y}$ are codewords in a linear code C. Then $d(\mathbf{x}, \mathbf{y}) = w(\mathbf{x} + \mathbf{y})$.

Proof: The positions with 1s in them in $\mathbf{x} + \mathbf{y}$ are the positions where $\mathbf{x}$ and $\mathbf{y}$ differ. Hence $d(\mathbf{x}, \mathbf{y}) = w(\mathbf{x} + \mathbf{y})$. $\qquad \blacksquare$

We also will need the fact that $\mathbf{0}$, the bit string with all 0s, belongs to a linear code.

Lemma 4   Suppose that C is a nonempty linear code. Then $\mathbf{0}$ is a codeword in C.

Proof: Let $\mathbf{x}$ be a codeword in C. Since C is linear $\mathbf{x} + \mathbf{x} = \mathbf{0}$ belongs to C. ∎

Theorem 6   The minimum distance of a linear code C equals the minimum weight of a nonzero codeword in C.

Proof: Suppose that the minimum distance of C is d. Then there are codewords $\mathbf{x}$ and $\mathbf{y}$ such that $d(\mathbf{x}, \mathbf{y}) = d$. By Lemma 3 it follows that $w(\mathbf{x} + \mathbf{y}) = d$. Hence w, the minimum weight of a codeword, is no larger than d.

Conversely, suppose that the codeword $\mathbf{x}$ is a nonzero codeword of minimum weight. Then using Lemma 4 we see that $w = w(\mathbf{x}) = w(\mathbf{x} + \mathbf{0}) = d(\mathbf{x}, \mathbf{0}) \geq d$. It follows that $w = d$, establishing the theorem. ∎

Parity Check Matrices

Note that in Example 14 the bit string $x_1 x_2 x_3$ is encoded as $x_1 x_2 x_3 x_4 x_5 x_6$ where $x_4 = x_1 + x_2 + x_3$, $x_5 = x_1 + x_2$, and $x_6 = x_1 + x_3$ (here, arithmetic is carried out modulo 2). Because we are doing arithmetic modulo 2, we see that

$$x_1 + x_2 + x_3 + x_4 = 0$$
$$x_1 + x_2 + x_5 = 0$$
$$x_1 + x_3 + x_6 = 0.$$

Furthermore, it is easy to see that $x_1 x_2 x_3 x_4 x_5 x_6$ is a codeword if and only if it satisfies this system of equations.

We can express this system of equations as

$$\begin{pmatrix} 1 & 1 & 1 & 1 & 0 & 0 \\ 1 & 1 & 0 & 0 & 1 & 0 \\ 1 & 0 & 1 & 0 & 0 & 1 \end{pmatrix} \begin{pmatrix} x_1 \\ x_2 \\ x_3 \\ x_4 \\ x_5 \\ x_6 \end{pmatrix} = \begin{pmatrix} 0 \\ 0 \\ 0 \end{pmatrix},$$

that is,

$$\mathbf{H}\mathbf{E}(\mathbf{x})^t = \mathbf{0},$$

where $\mathbf{E}(\mathbf{x})^t$ is the transpose of $\mathbf{E}(\mathbf{x})$ and $\mathbf{H}$, the parity check matrix, is given by

$$\mathbf{H} = \begin{pmatrix} 1 & 1 & 1 & 1 & 0 & 0 \\ 1 & 1 & 0 & 0 & 1 & 0 \\ 1 & 0 & 1 & 0 & 0 & 1 \end{pmatrix}.$$

Note that $\mathbf{H} = (\mathbf{A}^t | \mathbf{I}_{n-k})$. With this notation we see that $\mathbf{x} = x_1 x_2 x_3 x_4 x_5 x_6$ is a codeword if and only if $\mathbf{H}\mathbf{x}^t = \mathbf{0}$, since checking this equation is the same as checking whether the parity check equations hold.

In general, suppose that $\mathbf{G}$ is a $k \times n$ generator matrix with

$$\mathbf{G} = (\mathbf{I}_k | \mathbf{A}),$$

where $\mathbf{A}$ is a $k \times (n - k)$ matrix. To G we associate the *parity check matrix* $\mathbf{H}$, where

$$\mathbf{H} = (\mathbf{A}^t | \mathbf{I}_{n-k}).$$

Then $\mathbf{x}$ is a codeword if and only if $\mathbf{H}\mathbf{x}^t = \mathbf{0}$. Note that from a generator matrix $\mathbf{G}$ we can find the associated parity check matrix $\mathbf{H}$, and conversely, given a parity check matrix $\mathbf{H}$, we can find the associated generator matrix $\mathbf{G}$. More precisely, note that if $\mathbf{H} = (\mathbf{B} | \mathbf{I}_r)$, then $\mathbf{G} = (\mathbf{I}_{n-r} | \mathbf{B}^t)$.

We have seen that the parity check matrix can be used to detect errors. That is, to determine whether $\mathbf{x}$ is a codeword we check whether

$$\mathbf{H}\mathbf{x}^t = \mathbf{0}.$$

Not only can the parity check matrix be used to detect errors, but when the columns of this matrix are distinct and are all nonzero, it also can be used to correct errors. Under these assumptions, suppose that the codeword $\mathbf{x}$ is sent and that $\mathbf{y}$ is received, which may or may not be the same as $\mathbf{x}$. Write $\mathbf{y} = \mathbf{x} + \mathbf{e}$, where $\mathbf{e}$ is an *error string*. (We have $\mathbf{e} = \mathbf{0}$ if no errors arose in the transmission). In general, the error string $\mathbf{e}$ has 1s in the positions where $\mathbf{y}$ differs from $\mathbf{x}$ and 0s in all other positions. Now suppose that only one error has been introduced when $\mathbf{x}$ was transmitted. Then $\mathbf{e}$ is a bit string that has only one nonzero bit which is in the position where $\mathbf{x}$ and $\mathbf{y}$ differ, say position j. Since $\mathbf{H}\mathbf{x}^t = \mathbf{0}$, it follows that

$$\begin{aligned}
\mathbf{H}\mathbf{y}^t &= \mathbf{H}(\mathbf{x}^t + \mathbf{e}) \\
&= \mathbf{H}\mathbf{x}^t + \mathbf{e}^t \\
&= \mathbf{e}^t \\
&= \mathbf{c}_j
\end{aligned}$$

where $\mathbf{c}_j$ is the jth column of $\mathbf{H}$.

Hence, if we receive $\mathbf{y}$ and assume that no more than one error is present, we can find the codeword $\mathbf{x}$ that was sent by computing $\mathbf{H}\mathbf{y}^t$. If this is zero, we know that $\mathbf{y}$ is the codeword sent. Otherwise, it will equal the jth column of $\mathbf{H}$ for some integer j. This means that the jth bit of $\mathbf{y}$ should be changed to produce $\mathbf{x}$.

Example 16   Use the parity check matrix to determine which codeword from the code in Example 14 was sent if 001111 was received. Assume that at most one error was made.

Solution: We find that

$$
\mathbf{Hy}^t = \begin{pmatrix} 1 & 1 & 1 & 1 & 0 & 0 \\ 1 & 1 & 0 & 0 & 1 & 0 \\ 1 & 0 & 1 & 0 & 0 & 1 \end{pmatrix} \begin{pmatrix} 0 \\ 0 \\ 1 \\ 1 \\ 1 \\ 1 \end{pmatrix} = \begin{pmatrix} 0 \\ 1 \\ 0 \end{pmatrix}.
$$

This is the fifth column of **H**. If follows that the fifth bit of 001111 is incorrect. Hence the code word sent was 001101.   □

Hamming Codes

We can now define the Hamming codes. We define them using parity check matrices.

Definition 4   A *Hamming code of order r* where r is a positive integer, is a code generated when we take as parity check matrix **H** an $r \times (2^r - 1)$ matrix with columns that are all the $2^r - 1$ nonzero bit strings of length r in any order such that the last r columns form the identity matrix.   □

Interchanging the order of the columns leads to what is known as an *equivalent code*. For details on equivalence of codes the reader is referred to the references at the end of this chapter.

Example 17   Find the codewords in a Hamming code of order 2.

Solution: The parity check matrix of this code is

$$
\mathbf{H} = \begin{pmatrix} 1 & 1 & 0 \\ 1 & 0 & 1 \end{pmatrix}.
$$

We have $\mathbf{H} = (\mathbf{B}|\mathbf{I}_2)$ where $\mathbf{B} = \begin{pmatrix} 1 \\ 1 \end{pmatrix}$. Hence, the generator matrix **G** of this code equals $\mathbf{G} = (\mathbf{I}_{3-2}|\mathbf{B}^t) = (1\ 1\ 1)$. Since the codewords are linear combinations of the rows of G, we see that this code has two codewords, 000 and 111. This is the linear repetition code of order 3.   □

Example 18   Find the codewords in a Hamming code of order 3.

Solution: For the parity check matrix of this code we use

$$\mathbf{H} = \begin{pmatrix} 0 & 1 & 1 & 1 & 1 & 0 & 0 \\ 1 & 0 & 1 & 1 & 0 & 1 & 0 \\ 1 & 1 & 0 & 1 & 0 & 0 & 1 \end{pmatrix}.$$

We have $\mathbf{H} = (\mathbf{B}|\mathbf{I}_3)$ where

$$\mathbf{B} = \begin{pmatrix} 0 & 1 & 1 & 1 \\ 1 & 0 & 1 & 1 \\ 1 & 1 & 0 & 1 \end{pmatrix}.$$

Hence the generator matrix $\mathbf{G}$ of this code equals

$$\mathbf{G} = (\mathbf{I}_{7-3}|\mathbf{B}^t) = \begin{pmatrix} 1 & 0 & 0 & 0 & 0 & 1 & 1 \\ 0 & 1 & 0 & 0 & 1 & 0 & 1 \\ 0 & 0 & 1 & 0 & 1 & 1 & 0 \\ 0 & 0 & 0 & 1 & 1 & 1 & 1 \end{pmatrix}.$$

The 16 codewords in this code C can be found by taking all possible sums of the rows of $\mathbf{G}$. We leave this as an exercise at the end of the chapter. $\square$

To show that the Hamming codes are perfect codes we first need to establish two lemmas.

Lemma 5   A Hamming code of order r contains 2^{n-r} codewords where $n = 2^r - 1$.

Proof: The parity check matrix of the Hamming code is an $r \times n$ matrix. It follows that the generator matrix for this code is a $(n - r) \times n$ matrix. Recall that the codewords are the linear combinations of the rows. As the reader can show, no two linear combinations of the rows are the same. Since there are 2^{n-r} different linear combinations of row, there are 2^{n-r} different codewords in a Hamming code of order r.   ∎

Lemma 6   The minimum distance of a Hamming code of order r is 3 whenever r is a positive integer.

Proof: The parity check matrix $\mathbf{H}_r$ has columns which are all nonzero and no two of which are the same. Hence, from our earlier discussion, a Hamming code of order r can correct single errors. By Theorem 3 we conclude that the minimum distance of this code is at least 3. Among the columns of $\mathbf{H}_r$ are the following three columns:

$$
c_1 = \begin{pmatrix} 1 \\ 1 \\ 0 \\ \vdots \\ 0 \end{pmatrix}, \quad c_2 = \begin{pmatrix} 1 \\ 0 \\ 0 \\ \vdots \\ 0 \end{pmatrix}, \quad c_3 = \begin{pmatrix} 0 \\ 1 \\ 0 \\ \vdots \\ 0 \end{pmatrix}.
$$

Note that $c_1 + c_2 + c_3 = 0$. Let x be the bit string with 1 in the positions of these columns and zero elsewhere. Then $Hx^t = 0$, since it is $c_1 + c_2 + c_3$. It follows that x is a codeword. Since $w(x) = 3$, by Theorem 6 it follows that the minimum distance is no more than 3. We conclude that the minimum distance of a Hamming code of order r is 3.   ∎

Theorem 7   The Hamming code of order r is a perfect code.

Proof: Let $n = 2^r - 1$. By Lemma 5 a Hamming code of order r contains 2^{n-r} codewords, each of which is an n-tuple. By Lemma 6 the minimum distance of the Hamming code of order r is 3. We see that this code achieves the maximum number of codewords allowed by the sphere packing bound. To see this, note that

$$
2^{n-r}(1 + C(n,1)) = 2^{n-r}(1 + n) = 2^{n-r}(1 + 2^r - 1) = 2^n.
$$

This is the upper bound of the sphere-packing bound. hence a Hamming code of order r is perfect.   ∎

By Theorem 7 we see that the Hamming codes are examples of perfect codes. The study of perfect codes has been one of the most important areas of research in coding theory and has lead to the development of many important results. See the references at the end of the chapter to learn about what is known about perfect codes.

Summary

In this chapter we have studied how codes can be used for error detection and error correction. We have introduced an important class of codes known as the Hamming codes. However, we have only touched the surface of a fascinating and important subject that has become extremely important for modern computing and communications. The interested reader can consult the references listed at the end of this chapter to learn about many other classes of codes that have practical applications.

For example, pictures of the planets taken by space probes have been encoded using powerful codes, such as a code known as the *Reed-Muller* code (see [5] for details). This code has been used to encode the bit string of length 6 representing the brightness of each pixel of an image by a bit string of length 32. This Reed-Muller code consists of 64 codewords, each a bit string of length 32, with minimum distance 16. Another interesting example is the use of a family of codes known as *Reed-Solomon* codes used in digital audio recording (see [5] for details). Finally, many concepts and techniques from both linear algebra and abstract algebra are used in coding theory. Studying coding theory may convince the skeptical reader about the applicability of some of the more abstract areas of mathematics.

Suggested Readings

1. E. Berlekamp, editor, *Key Papers in the Development of Coding Theory*, IEEE Press, New York, 1974.

2. R. Hamming, *Coding and Information Theory*, Prentice-Hall, Englewood Cliffs, New Jersey, 1980.

3. R. Hill, *A First Course in Coding Theory*, Oxford University Press, Oxford, 1986.

4. V. Pless, *Introduction to the Theory of Error-Correcting Codes*, M.I.T. Press, 1972.

5. S. Vanstone and P. van Oorschot, *An Introduction to Error Correcting Codes with Applications*, Kluwer, Boston. 1989.

Exercises

1. Could the following bit strings have been received correctly if the last bit is a parity bit?
   a) 1000011
   b) 111111000
   c) 10101010101
   d) 110111011100

2. Find the Hamming distance between each of the following pairs of bit strings.

a) 00000,11111
b) 1010101,0011100
c) 000000001,111000000
d) 1111111111,0100100011

3. Suppose the bit string 01011 is sent using a binary symmetric channel where the probability a bit is received incorrectly is 0.01. What is the probability that
   a) 01011, the bit string sent, is received?
   b) 11011 is received?
   c) 01101 is received?
   d) 10111 is received?
   e) no more than one error is present in the bit string received?

4. How many errors can each of the following binary codes detect and how many can it correct?
   a) $\{0000000, 1111111\}$
   b) $\{00000, 00111, 10101, 11011\}$
   c) $\{00000000, 11111000, 01100111, 100101101\}$

5. Suppose that the probability of a bit error in transmission over a binary symmetric channel is 0.001. What is the probability that when a codeword with eight bits is sent from a code with minimum distance five, the bit string received is decoded as the codeword sent (when nearest neighbor decoding is used)?

★6. Show that if the minimum distance between codewords is four it is possible to correct an error in a single bit and to detect two bit errors without correction.

7. Use the sphere packing bound to give an upper bound on the number of codewords in a binary code where codewords are bit strings of length nine and the minimum distance between codewords is five.

8. Show that whenever n is an odd positive integer, the binary code consisting of the two bit strings of length n containing all 0s or all 1s is a perfect code.

9. Suppose that $\mathbf{x}$ and $\mathbf{y}$ are bit strings of length n and m is the number of positions where both $\mathbf{x}$ and $\mathbf{y}$ have 1s. Show that $w(\mathbf{x}+\mathbf{y}) = w(\mathbf{x})+w(\mathbf{y})-2m$.

10. Find the parity check matrix associated with the code formed by adding a parity check bit to a bit string of length 4.

11. Find the parity check matrix associated with the triple repetition code for bit strings of length 3.

12. Suppose that the generator matrix for a binary code is

$$\begin{pmatrix} 1 & 0 & 0 & 0 & 1 & 1 & 1 \\ 0 & 1 & 0 & 0 & 1 & 0 & 1 \\ 0 & 0 & 1 & 0 & 0 & 1 & 1 \\ 0 & 0 & 0 & 1 & 1 & 1 & 0 \end{pmatrix}.$$

What is the parity check matrix **H** for this code?

13. Suppose that the parity check matrix for a binary code is

$$\begin{pmatrix} 1 & 0 & 1 & 0 & 0 \\ 1 & 1 & 0 & 1 & 0 \\ 0 & 1 & 0 & 0 & 1 \end{pmatrix}.$$

What is the generator matrix **G** for this code?

14. Find the 16 codewords in the Hamming code of order 3 described in Example 18.

⋆15. Sometimes, instead of errors, bits are erased during the transmission of a message or from a tape or other storage medium. The position, but not the value, of an erased bit is known. We say that a code C can correct r erasures if a message received with no errors and with no more than r erasures can be corrected to a unique codeword that agrees with the message received in all the positions that were not erased.

a) Show that a binary code of minimum distance d can correct $d - 1$ erasures.

b) Show that a binary code of minimum distance d can correct t errors and r erasures if $d = 2t + r + 1$.

Computer Projects

1. Given a binary code, determine the number of errors that it can detect and the number of errors that it can correct.

2. Given a binary code with minimum distance k, where k is a positive integer, write a program that will detect errors in codewords in as many as $k - 1$ positions and correct errors in as many as $\lfloor (k - 1)/2 \rfloor$ positions.

PART II

COMBINATORICS

6

Stirling Numbers

Author: Thomas A. Dowling, Department of Mathematics, Ohio State University.

Prerequisites: The prerequisites for this chapter are basic counting techniques and equivalence relations. See, for example, Chapters 4, 5, and 6 of *Discrete Mathematics and Its Applications*, Second Edition, by Kenneth H. Rosen.

Introduction

A set of objects can be classified according to many different criteria, depending on the nature of the objects. For example, we might classify

— accidents according to the day of the week on which they occurred

— people according to their profession, age, sex, or nationality

— college students according to their class or major

— positions in a random sequence of digits according to the digit appearing there

— misprints according to the page on which they occur

— printing jobs according to the printer on which they were done.

In each of these examples, we would have a function from the set of objects to the set of possible levels of the criterion by which the objects are classified.

Suppose we want to know the number of different classifications that are possible, perhaps subject to additional restrictions. This would be necessary, for example, in estimating probabilities that a classification satisfied certain conditions. Determining the number of functions between finite sets, based on the sizes of the sets and certain restrictions on the functions, is an enumeration problem considered in Chapter 4 of *Discrete Mathematics and Its Applications*, Second Edition, by Rosen.

It may be the case, however, that the classification need not distinguish the various levels of the criterion, if such a distinction is even possible. There could be many levels, but the actual level on which an object falls is of no concern. Of interest might be how the set of objects is partitioned into disjoint subsets, with two objects being in the same subset whenever they fall at the same level of the criterion. A classification then represents a partition of the set of objects, where two objects belong to the same class of the partition whenever they fall at the same level of the criterion. In this case, rather than counting functions, partitions of the set of objects would be counted. It is then that the Stirling numbers* become appropriate.

Along with the binomial coefficients $C(n, k)$, the Stirling numbers are of fundamental importance in enumeration theory. While $C(n, k)$ is the number of k-element *subsets* of an n-element set N, the Stirling number $S(n, k)$ represents the number of *partitions* of N into k nonempty subsets. Partitions of N are associated with sets of functions defined on N, and they correspond to equivalence relations on N.

Because of their combinatorial interpretation, the numbers $S(n, k)$ will be met first, despite their name as the Stirling numbers of the *second* kind. After we establish their role in a classification of functions defined on N, we consider their part in relating two sequences of polynomials (as they were originally defined by Stirling). We will then be led to the Stirling numbers $s(n, k)$ of the first kind. We will see why they are referred to as being of the first kind, despite the fact that some of these integers are negative, and thus cannot represent the size of a set.

Occupancy Problems

Many enumeration problems can be formulated as counting the number of distributions of *balls* into *cells* or *urns*. The balls here correspond to the objects and the cells to the levels. These counting problems are generally referred to as **occupancy** problems. Suppose n balls are to be placed in k cells, and assume that any cell could hold all of the balls. The question "In how many ways can this be done?" asks for the number of distributions of n balls to k cells.

---

* They are named in honor of James Stirling (1692–1770), an eighteenth century associate of Sir Isaac Newton in England.

As posed, the question lacks sufficient information to determine what is meant by a distribution. It therefore cannot be correctly answered. The number of distributions depends on whether the n balls and/or the k cells are *distinguishable* or *identical*. And if the n balls are distinguishable, whether the order in which the balls are placed in each cell matters. Let us assume that the order of placement does not distinguish two distributions.

Suppose first that both the balls and the cells are distinguishable. Then the collection of balls can be interpreted as an n-element set N and the collection of cells as a k-element set K. A distribution then corresponds to a function $f : N \rightarrow K$. The number of distributions is then k^n.

If, however, the balls are identical, but the cells are distinguishable, then a distribution corresponds to an n-combination with repetition from the set K of k cells (see Section 4.5 of *Discrete Mathematics and Its Applications*, Second Edition, by Rosen). The number of balls placed in cell j represents the number of occurrences of element j in the n-combination. The number of distributions in this case is $C(k + n - 1, n)$.

Occupancy problems can have additional restrictions on the number of balls that can be placed in each cell. Suppose, for example, that at most one ball can be placed in each cell. If both the balls and the cells are distinguishable, we would then be seeking the number of *one-to-one* functions $f : N \rightarrow K$. Such a function corresponds to an n-permutation from a k-set, so the number is $P(k, n) = k(k - 1) \cdots (k - n + 1)$. If instead there must be at least one ball in each cell, we want the number of *onto* functions $f : N \rightarrow K$. Using inclusion-exclusion, that number is equal to

$$\sum_{i=0}^{k-1} (-1)^i C(k, i)(k - i)^n.$$

(See Section 5.5 of *Discrete Mathematics and Its Applications*, Second Edition.)

Partitions and Stirling Numbers of the Second Kind

An **ordered partition** of N with length k is a k-tuple $(A_1, A_2, \ldots, A_k)$ of disjoint subsets A_i of N with union N. By taking $K = \{1, 2, \cdots, k\}$, we can interpret any function $f : N \rightarrow K$ as an ordered partition of N with length k. We let A_i be the subset of N whose elements have image i. Then, since f assigns exactly one image in K to each element of N, the subsets A_i are disjoint and their union is N. Then A_i is nonempty if and only if i is the image of at least one element of N. Thus the function f is onto if and only if all k of the sets A_i are nonempty.

Recall that a **partition** of a set N is a set $P = \{A_i | i \in I\}$ of disjoint, *nonempty* subsets A_i of N that have union N. We shall call these subsets **classes**. An ordered partition of N of a given length may have empty subsets A_i, but the empty set is not allowed as a class in a partition. If it were, then even though the classes are disjoint, they would not necessarily be different sets, since the empty set might be repeated. Given an equivalence relation R on N, the distinct equivalence classes A_i are disjoint with union N. The reflexive property then implies that they are nonempty, so the equivalence classes form a partition of N. Conversely, given a partition $P = \{A_i | i \in I\}$, an equivalence relation R is defined by $a R b$ if and only if there is some class A_i of P containing a and b. Thus, there is a one-to-one correspondence between the set of partitions of N and the set of equivalence relations on N.

A *binary relation* on N is defined as a subset of the set $N \times N$. Since $N \times N$ has n^2 elements, the number of binary relations on N is 2^{n^2}. The number of these that are equivalence relations, which is equal to the number of partitions of N, is called a *Bell number**, and denoted by B_n. For example, the number of ways that ten people can be separated into nonempty groups is the Bell number B_{10}. Two of the people satisfy the corresponding equivalence relation R if and only if they belong to the same group.

Suppose we want instead the number of ways the ten people can be separated into exactly three nonempty groups. That is, how many equivalence relations are there on a ten-element set that have exactly three equivalence classes? More generally, of the B_n equivalence relations, we might ask how many have exactly k equivalence classes? Since this is the number of partitions of N into k classes, we are led to our definition of a Stirling number $S(n, k)$ of the second kind. (Note that the Bell number B_n is then the sum over k of these numbers, that is, $B_n = \sum_{k=1}^{n} S(n, k)$.)

Definition 1   The *Stirling number of the second kind*, $S(n, k)$, is the number of partitions of an n-element set into k classes.   □

Example 1   Find $S(4, 2)$ and $S(4, 3)$.

Solution: Suppose $N = \{a, b, c, d\}$. The 2-class partitions of the 4-element set N are

$$(\{a, b, c\}, \{d\}), \quad (\{a, b, d\}, \{c\}), \quad (\{a, c, d\}, \{b\}), \quad (\{b, c, d\}, \{a\})$$

$$(\{a, b\}, \{c, d\}), \quad (\{a, c\}, \{b, d\}), \quad (\{a, d\}, \{b, c\}).$$

It follows that $S(4, 2) = 7$.

The 3-class partitions of N are

$$(\{a, b\}, \{c\}, \{d\}), \quad (\{a, c\}, \{b\}, \{d\}), \quad (\{a, d\}, \{b\}, \{c\})$$

---

* We won't pursue the Bell numbers here, but see any of the references for more about them.

$$(\{b, c\}, \{a\}, \{d\}), \quad (\{b, d\}, \{a\}, \{c\}), \quad (\{c, d\}, \{a\}, \{b\})$$

We therefore have $S(4, 3) = 6$.   □

In occupancy problems, a partition corresponds to a distribution in which the balls are distinguishable, the cells are identical, and there is at least one ball in each cell. The number of distributions of n balls into k cells is therefore $S(n, k)$. If we remove the restriction that there must be at least one ball in each cell, then a distribution corresponds to a partition of the set N with at most k classes. By the sum rule the number of such distributions equals

$$S(n, 1) + S(n, 2) + \cdots + S(n, k).$$

Since the classes A_i of a partition $P = \{A_i | i \in I\}$ must be disjoint and nonempty, we have $S(n, k) = 0$ for $k > n$. Further, since $(\{S\})$ itself is the only partition of N with one class, $S(n, 1) = 1$ for $n \geq 1$. Given these initial conditions, together with $S(0, 0) = 1$, $S(n, 0) = 0$ for $n \geq 1$, the Stirling numbers $S(n, k)$ can be recursively computed using the following theorem.

Theorem 1   Let n and k be positive integers. Then

$$S(n + 1, k) = S(n, k - 1) + k S(n, k). \tag{1}$$

Proof: We give a combinatorial proof. Let S be an $(n + 1)$-element set. Fix $a \in S$, and let $S' = S - \{a\}$ be the n-element set obtained by removing a from S. The $S(n + 1, k)$ partitions of S into k classes can each be uniquely obtained from either

(i) a partition P' of S' with $k - 1$ classes by adding a singleton class $\{a\}$, or

(ii) a partition P' of S' with k classes by first selecting one of the k classes of P' and then adding a to that class.

Since the cases are exclusive, we obtain $S(n, k)$ by the sum rule by adding the number $S(n, k - 1)$ of partitions of (i) to the number $k S(n, k)$ of partitions in (ii).   ■

Example 2   Let P be one of the partitions of $N = \{a, b, c, d\}$ in Example 1. Then P is obtained from the $S(3, 1) = 1$ one-class partition $(\{a, b, c\})$ of $N' = N - \{d\} = \{a, b, c\}$ by adding $\{d\}$ as a second class, or from one of the $S(3, 2) = 3$ two-class partitions

$$(\{a, b\}, \{c\}), \quad (\{a, c\}, \{b\}), \quad (\{b, c\}, \{a\})$$

of N' by choosing one of these partitions, then choosing one of its two classes, and finally by adding d to the class chosen.   □

Example 3   Use Theorem 1 to find $S(5,3)$.

Solution: We have $S(4,2) = 7$ and $S(4,3) = 6$ from Example 1. Then we find by Theorem 1 that $S(5,3) = S(4,2) + 3\,S(4,3) = 7 + 3 \cdot 6 = 25$.   □

The Pascal recursion $C(n+1, k) = C(n, k-1) + C(n, k)$ used to compute the binomial coefficients has a similar form, but the coefficient in the second term of the sum is 1 for $C(n, k)$ and k for $S(n, k)$.

Using the recurrence relation in Theorem 1, we can obtain each of the Stirling numbers $S(n, k)$ from the two Stirling numbers $S(n-1, k-1)$, $S(n-1, k)$ previously found. These are given in Table 1 for $1 \le k \le n \le 6$.

n \ k	1	2	3	4	5	6
1	1					
2	1	1				
3	1	3	1			
4	1	7	6	1		
5	1	15	25	10	1	
6	1	31	90	65	15	1

Table 1.   Stirling numbers of the second kind, S(n,k).

Inverse Partitions of Functions

Recall that a function $f : N \rightarrow K$ is *onto* if every element $b \in K$ is an image of some element $a \in N$, so $b = f(a)$. If we denote the set of images by $f(N) = \{f(a) | a \in N\}$, then f is onto if and only if $f(N) = K$.

Example 4   Suppose $N = \{a, b, c, d\}$, $K = \{1, 2, 3\}$, and the function f is defined by $f(a) = f(b) = f(d) = 2$, $f(c) = 1$. Then $f(N) = \{1, 2\} \ne K$, so f is not onto.   □

Every function $f : N \rightarrow K$ determines an equivalence relation on N under which two elements of N are related if and only if they have the same image under f. Since the equivalence classes form a partition of N, we make the following definition.

Definition 2   The *inverse partition* defined by a function $f : N \rightarrow K$ is the partition $P(f)$ of N into equivalence classes with respect to the the equivalence relation R_f defined by $aR_f b$ if and only if $f(a) = f(b)$.   □

Given the function f, every element $b \in f(N)$ determines an equivalence class of R_f. Suppose we denote by $f^{-1}(b)$ the set of elements in N that have b as their image*. Then $f^{-1}(b)$ is an equivalence class, called the **inverse image** of b. It follows that

$$a \in f^{-1}(b) \quad \text{if and only if} \quad b = f(a).$$

Thus, the equivalence classes $f^{-1}(b)$ for $b \in f(N)$ form the inverse partition $P(f)$ of N, and the number of equivalence classes is the size of the set $f(N)$. Therefore $f : N \rightarrow K$ is onto if and only if $P(f)$ has k classes.

Example 5   Find the inverse partition of N defined by the function f of Example 4.

Solution: For the function f in Example 4, the set of elements of N with image 1 is $f^{-1}(1) = \{a, b, d\}$, while the set of elements with image 2 is $f^{-1}(2) = \{c\}$. Since no elements have 3 as an image, the set $f^{-1}(3)$ is empty, so it is not an equivalence class. Thus the inverse partition of N defined by f is the 2-class partition $P(f) = (\{a, b, d\}, \{c\})$.   □

An Identity for Stirling Numbers

We can classify the k^n distributions of n distinguishable balls into k distinguishable cells by the number j of nonempty cells. Such a distribution is determined by a j-class partition P of the set of balls together with an injective function φ from the j classes of P to the k cells. The classification obtained in this way leads to an identity involving the Stirling numbers of the second kind. Denote by $F(N, K)$ the set of functions $f : N \rightarrow K$. Recall that the size of $F(N, K)$ is k^n. Let us classify the functions $f \in F(N, K)$ according to the size of their image sets $f(N)$, or equivalently, according to the number of classes in their inverse partitions $P(f)$.

---

* What we have denoted by f^{-1} is actually a function from K to the power set $P(N)$ of N, and not the inverse function of f. The function $f : N \rightarrow K$ has an inverse function from K to N if and only if it is a one-to-one correspondence.

Given a j-class partition $P = \{A_1,, A_2, \ldots, A_j\}$ of N, consider the set of functions $f \in F(N, K)$ for which $P(f) = P$. Two elements in N can have the same image if and only if they belong to the same A_i. Hence a function f has $P(f) = P$ if and only if there is a one-to-one function $\varphi : \{A_1, A_2, \ldots, A_j\} \to K$ such that $f(a) = \varphi(A_i)$ for all i and all $a \in A_i$. The number of one-to-one functions from a j-set to a k-set is the **falling factorial**

$$(k)_j = P(k, j) = k(k - 1) \cdots (k - j + 1).$$

Hence, for any j-class partition P, the number of functions $f \in F(N, K)$ such that $P(f) = P$ is $(k)_j$. Since there are $S(n, j)$ j-class partitions of N, by the product rule there are $S(n, j)(k)_j$ functions $f \in F(N, K)$ such that $f(N)$ has size j. Summing over j gives us

$$k^n = \sum_{j=1}^{k} S(n, j)(k)_j. \tag{2}$$

The jth term in the sum is the number of functions f for which $|f(N)| = j$.

We noted earlier that the onto functions correspond to distributions in the occupancy problem where the balls and the cells are distinguishable and there must be at least one ball in each cell. If we remove the restriction that there must be at least one ball in each cell, then a distribution corresponds to a function $f : N \to K$. Classification of the k^n distributions according to the number of nonempty cells gives (2). If we consider the term where $j = k$ in (2), and note that $(k)_k = k!$, we have the following theorem.

Theorem 2   The number of functions from a set with n elements onto a set with k elements is $S(n, k)k!$.   ∎

The inclusion-exclusion principle can be used to show that the number of onto functions from a set with n elements to a set with k elements is

$$\sum_{i=0}^{k} (-1)^i C(k, i)(k - i)^n. \tag{3}$$

By Theorem 2, we may equate (3) to $S(n, k)k!$, and we obtain

$$S(n, k) = \frac{1}{k!} \sum_{i=0}^{k} (-1)^i C(k, i)(k - i)^n. \tag{4}$$

Example 6   Let $n = 5$, $k = 3$. Then if the 3^5 functions $f : N \to K$ are classified according to the number of classes in their inverse partitions, we obtain

$$3^5 = \sum_{j=1}^{3} S(5,j)(3)_j = 1 \cdot 3 + 15 \cdot 6 + 25 \cdot 6 = 243,$$

which is of course easily verified. Theorem 2 shows that the number of these functions that are onto is $S(5,3)3! = 25 \cdot 6 = 150$. Alternatively, by the inclusion-exclusion expression (3), we have

$$\sum_{i=0}^{3} (-1)^k C(3,i)(3-i)^5 = 3^5 - 3 \cdot 2^5 + 3 \cdot 1^5$$
$$= 243 - 96 + 3 = 150. \qquad \square$$

Before turning to polynomials in a real variable x, we need to write the summation in (2) in a different form. Since $S(n,j) = 0$ for $j > n$ and $(k)_j = 0$ for an integer $j > k$, the term $S(n,j)(k)_j$ in (2) can be nonzero only when $j \leq n$ and $j \leq k$. Thus we can replace the upper limit k in (2) by n, which gives

$$k^n = \sum_{j=1}^{n} S(n,j)(k)_j. \qquad (2')$$

Stirling Numbers and Polynomials

Recall that a *polynomial of degree n* in a real variable x is a function $p(x)$ of the form

$$p(x) = a_n x^n + a_{n-1} x^{n-1} + \cdots + a_0,$$

where $a_n, a_{n-1}, \ldots, a_0$ are constants with $a_n \neq 0$. Suppose we extend the definition of the falling factorial $(k)_n$ from the set $\mathcal{N} \times \mathcal{N}$ to the set $\mathcal{R} \times \mathcal{N}$ by defining the function $(x)_n$ for any *real number* x and any nonnegative integer n to be $(x)_n = 1$ when $n = 0$ and $(x)_n = x(x-1)\cdots(x-n+1)$ when $n \geq 1$. Equivalently, define $(x)_n$ recursively by $(x)_0 = 1$ and $(x)_n = (x-n+1)(x)_{n-1}$. As the product of n linear factors, $(x)_n$ is a polynomial of degree n. We can then replace k by x in $(2')$ to obtain

$$x^n = \sum_{j=1}^{n} S(n,j)(x)_j. \qquad (5)$$

Subtracting the right-hand side from each side gives

$$x^n - \sum_{j=1}^{n} S(n,j)(x)_j = 0. \qquad (6)$$

But $(x)_j = x(x-1)\cdots(x-j+1)$ is a polynomial of degree j, for $1 \leq j \leq n$. Hence the left-hand side of (6) is a polynomial $p(x)$ of degree at most n. But since $p(x) = 0$ for every positive integer x and since a polynomial of degree n has at most n real roots, $p(x)$ must be identically zero. Then we obtain for every real number x

$$x^n = \sum_{j=1}^{n} S(n,j)(x)_j. \tag{7}$$

Equation (7) represents (2′) extended from positive integers k to arbitrary real numbers x. Since k does not appear in (7), we may replace the index variable j by k, rewriting (7) as

$$x^n = \sum_{k=1}^{n} S(n,k)(x)_k. \tag{7′}$$

Equation (7′) represents (7) in a form convenient for comparison with (10) in the next section.

Example 7   Let $n = 3$. Then $(x)_1 = x$, $(x)_2 = x(x-1) = x^2 - x$, and $(x)_3 = x(x-1)(x-2) = x^3 - 3x^2 + 2x$. Substituting these into the right-hand side of (5) gives

$$\begin{aligned}
S(3,1)(x)_1 + &S(3,2)(x)_2 + S(3,3)(x)_3 \\
&= 1 \cdot x + 3 \cdot (x^2 - x) + 1 \cdot (x^3 - 3x^2 + 2x) \\
&= x^3.
\end{aligned}$$ □

Stirling Numbers of the First Kind

There is an interpretation of (7) that will be understood more readily by readers who are familiar with linear algebra. The set of polynomials $p(x)$ with real coefficients (or with coefficients in any field) forms a *vector space**. A *fundamental basis* of this vector space is a sequence of polynomials $\{p_k(x) | k = 0, 1, \ldots\}$ such that $p_k(x)$ has degree k. Every polynomial can be uniquely expressed as a linear combination of the polynomials in a fundamental basis. Two important fundamental bases are the *standard basis* $\{x^k | k = 0, 1, \ldots\}$ and the *falling factorial basis* $\{(x)_k | k = 0, 1, \ldots\}$. The standard basis is in fact the one used in the definition of a polynomial in x, since a polynomial is defined as a linear combination of the powers of x. Then Equation (7) expresses the basis $\{x^k\}$ in terms of the basis $\{(x)_k\}$.

---

* This vector space has infinite (but countable) dimension.

In fact, (7) was Stirling's original definition of the numbers $S(n, k)$ as the coefficients in changing from the falling factorial basis $\{(x)_k\}$ to the standard basis $\{x^k\}$. These numbers were said to be of the *second kind* since they change a basis *to* the standard basis. More commonly, we would be changing *from* the standard basis to another basis, and the coefficients would be of the *first kind*. When the other basis is the sequence $\{(x)_k\}$ of falling factorial polynomials, we encounter the Stirling numbers of the first kind.

To illustrate these ideas, let us first suppose we want to express the basis $\{(x - 1)^k\}$ in terms of the standard basis $\{x^k\}$. Using the Binomial Theorem, we can express the polynomial $(x - 1)^n$ as

$$(x - 1)^n = \sum_{k=0}^{n}(-1)^{n-k}C(n, k)x^k. \tag{8}$$

The coefficients $(-1)^{n-k}C(n, k)$ in (8), that change the standard basis to the other basis (and which are the coefficients when the product $(x - 1)^n$ of n identical factors is expanded), by analogy would be called binomial coefficients of the first kind. On the other hand, if we express x as $(x - 1) + 1$ and apply the Binomial Theorem, we obtain

$$x^n = ((x - 1) + 1)^n = \sum_{k=0}^{n}C(n, k)(x - 1)^k. \tag{9}$$

Thus, the binomial coefficients $C(n, k)$ are used in (9) to change from the other basis to the standard basis, and would therefore be referred to as the binomial coefficients of the second kind.

The coefficients needed to change the falling factorial basis $\{(x)_k\}$ to the standard basis $\{x^k\}$ can be obtained by simply expanding the product $(x)_n = x(x - 1)\ldots(x - n + 1)$.

Example 8   Write $(x)_3$ in terms of the standard basis $\{x^k\}$.

Solution: Let $n = 3$. Then expanding the product $(x)_3$ and reversing the order of the terms gives

$$\begin{aligned} (x)_3 &= x(x - 1)(x - 2) \\ &= x^3 - 3x^2 + 2x \\ &= 2x - 3x^2 + x^3. \end{aligned}$$

$\square$

Let us now define the Stirling numbers of the first kind.

Definition 3   The *Stirling numbers of the first kind* $s(n, k)$ are the numbers satisfying

$$(x)_n = \sum_{k=0}^{n} s(n, k) x^k. \tag{10}$$

That (10) uniquely determines the coefficients $s(n, k)$ follows either from the definition of multiplication of polynomials or from the fact that every polynomial can be uniquely expressed as a linear combination of the polynomials in a basis.

Example 9   Find the Stirling numbers which express $(x)_3$ in terms of the polynomials $1, x, x^2$.

Solution: Using the definition of $s(n, k)$ and Example 8, we have

$$(x)_3 = s(3,0) \cdot 1 + s(3,1)x + s(3,2)x^2 + s(3,3)x^3$$
$$= 2x - 3x^2 + x^3.$$

Hence, the Stirling numbers of the first kind which express $(x)_3$ in terms of the polynomials $1, x, x^2$ and x^3 in the standard basis are $s(3,0) = 0$, $s(3,1) = 2$, $s(3,2) = -3$, $s(3,3) = 1$.   □

Note that in Example 9 some of the Stirling numbers $s(n, k)$ of the first kind can be negative. Hence, unlike the Stirling numbers of the second kind, those of the first kind cannot represent the sizes of sets. (But their absolute values do. See Exercise 16.)

Consider for a fixed n the sequence of numbers $s(n, k)$. These are zero when $n > k$. We can determine their sum over $1 \le k \le n$ immediately from (10). The polynomial $(x)_n$ vanishes whenever x is a positive integer and $n > x$. Thus, on setting $x = 1$ in (10), we get

$$\sum_{k=1}^{n} s(n, k) = 0 \quad \text{for} \quad n \ge 2. \tag{11}$$

There is a recurrence relation for $s(n, k)$ analogous to the recurrence relation in Theorem 1 for $S(n, k)$, but we will obtain this one by a method different from the combinatorial argument given there. We start by finding the boundary values where $k = 0$. Using the convention that $(x)_0 = 1$ if $x = 0$ and 0 otherwise, we have $s(0,0) = 1$. And since x is a factor of $(x)_n$ for $n \ge 1$, the constant term is 0, so $s(n,0)$ for $n \ge 1$.

The analogue of Theorem 1 is then given by the following theorem.

Theorem 3   Let n and k be positive integers. Then

$$s(n+1, k) = s(n, k-1) - n\, s(n, k). \tag{12}$$

Proof: We make use of the fact that $(x)_{n+1} = x(x-1)\cdots(x-n+1)(x-n) = (x-n)(x)_n$. Then by (10),

$$(x)_{n+1} = \sum_{k=0}^{n+1} s(n+1, k)x^k. \tag{13}$$

But

$$(x)_{n+1} = (x-n)(x)_n$$
$$= \sum_{j=0}^{n} s(n, j)x^{j+1} - n \sum_{j=0}^{n} s(n, j)x^j. \tag{14}$$

When we equate the coefficients of x^k in (13) and (14), we find that $s(n+1, k) = s(n, k-1) - n\, s(n, k)$. ∎

Example 10   Use recurrence relation (12) to find $s(5, 3)$.

Solution: We see from Example 9 that $s(3, 1) = 2$, $s(3, 2) = -3$, and $s(3, 3) = 1$. Thus, by (12), we find $s(4, 2) = 2 - 3\cdot(-3) = 11$ and $s(4, 3) = -3 - 3\cdot 1 = -6$. We then obtain $s(5, 3) = 11 - 4\cdot(-6) = 35$. □

The values of $s(n, k)$ for $1 \le k \le n \le 6$ shown in Table 2 were computed using (12).

n \ k	1	2	3	4	5	6
1	1					
2	-1	1				
3	2	-3	1			
4	-6	11	-6	1		
5	24	-50	35	-10	1	
6	-120	274	-225	85	-15	1

Table 2.   Stirling numbers of the first kind, s(n,k).

Comments

When we observe the tables of values of the Stirling numbers for $1 \le k \le n \le 6$, we notice that the numbers in certain columns or diagonals come from well-known sequences. We will examine some of these. Proofs will be left for the exercises.

First consider the numbers $S(n, 2)$ in the second column of Table 1. For $2 \leq n \leq 6$ these are $1, 3, 7, 15, 31$. It appears that $S(n, 2)$ has the form $2^{n-1} - 1$ (Exercise 14). The numbers $S(n, n-1)$ just below the main diagonal in Table 1 are $1, 3, 6, 10, 15$ for $2 \leq n \leq 6$, suggesting (Exercise 13) that $S(n, n-1)$ is the **triangular number**

$$C(n, 2) = \frac{1}{2}n(n - 1).$$

Next consider Table 2, which gives the values $s(n, k)$ of the Stirling numbers of the first kind. We can easily verify that the row sums are zero for $2 \leq n \leq 6$, as given for all $n \geq 2$ by (9). Observe that the numbers $s(n, 1)$ in the first column of Table 2 satisfy $s(n, 1) = (-1)^{n-1}(n - 1)!$ for $1 \leq n \leq 6$. This in fact holds for all n (Exercise 14). The numbers $s(n, n-1)$ just below the main diagonal in Table 2 are the negatives of the Stirling numbers $S(n, n-1)$ of the second kind, which are apparently the triangular numbers $C(n, 2)$ (Exercise 13).

Note also that the numbers $s(n, k)$ alternate in sign in both rows and columns. It is not difficult to prove (Exercise 16) that the sign of $s(n, k)$ is $(-1)^{n-k}$, so that the absolute value of $s(n, k)$ is

$$t(n, k) = (-1)^{n-k}s(n, k).$$

These integers $t(n, k)$ are the **signless Stirling numbers of the first kind**. As nonnegative integers, these numbers have a combinatorial interpretation (Exercise 18).

Suggested Readings

A basic treatment of the Stirling numbers is in reference [2]. A great deal of information about the generating functions of the Stirling numbers and further properties of these numbers can be found in the more advanced books [1], [3], [4], and [5].

1. M. Aigner, *Combinatorial Theory*, Springer-Verlag, New York, 1979.

2. K. Bogart, *Introductory Combinatorics*, Harcourt Brace Jovanovich, New York, 1990.

3. L. Comptet, *Advanced Combinatorics*, D.Reidel, Boston, 1974.

4. R. Stanley, *Enumerative Combinatorics*, Wadsworth and Brooks/Cole, Belmont, Cal., 1986.

5. H. Wilf, *generatingfunctionology*, Academic Press, San Diego, Cal., 1990.

Exercises

1. For $n = 7$ and $1 \leq k \leq 7$, find the Stirling numbers $S(n, k)$ and $s(n, k)$.

2. Express $(x)_4$ as a polynomial by expanding the product $x(x-1)(x-2)(x-3)$.

3. Express the polynomial x^4 as a linear combination of the falling factorial polynomials $(x)_k$.

4. Find the number of onto functions from an eight-element set to a five-element set.

5. Let $n = 3$ and $x = 3$. Classify the $x^n = 27$ functions f from $N = \{1, 2, 3\}$ to $X = \{a, b, c\}$ according to the size of the image set $f(N)$ to verify that there are $S(3, j)(3)_j$ such functions f with $|f(N)| = j$, for $1 \leq j \leq 3$.

6. In how many ways can seven distinguishable balls be placed in four identical boxes so that
   a) there is at least one ball in each box?
   b) some box(es) may be empty?

7. Suppose each of a group of six people is assigned one of three tasks at random. Find the probability (to three decimal places) that
   a) task 3 is not assigned.
   b) all three tasks are assigned.
   c) exactly two of the tasks are assigned.

8. In how many ways can a set of 12 people be divided into three (nonempty) subsets.

9. Suppose a k-sided die is rolled until each of the numbers $1, 2, \ldots, k$ have appeared at least once, at which time the rolls are stopped. Give an expression for the number of possible sequences of n rolls that satisfy the condition.

10. A computer is programmed to produce a random sequence of n digits.
    a) How many possible sequences are there?
    b) How many of these sequences have each of the 10 digits appearing?

11. A pool table has four corner pockets and two center pockets. There is one white ball (the cue ball) and 15 colored balls numbered $1, 2, \ldots, 15$. In a game each of the numbered balls is sunk into a pocket (and remains there) after being struck by the cue ball, which the player has propelled with a cue stick. Thus a game produces a distribution of the numbered balls in the set of pockets.
    a) Assuming the pockets are distinguishable, how many distributions are there?

b) Suppose we assume the corner pockets are identical and the center pockets are identical, but that a corner pocket is distinguishable from a center pocket. Give an expression for the number of distributions in which all of the numbered balls are sunk in corner pockets or they are all sunk in center pockets.

12. Let n and k be positive integers with $n + 1 \geq k$. Prove that $S(n + 1, k) = \sum_{j=0}^{n} C(n, j)S(n - j, k - 1)$.

13. Prove that
    a) $S(n, n - 1) = C(n, 2)$.
    b) $s(n, n - 1) = -C(n, 2)$.

14. Prove that
    a) $S(n, 2) = 2^{n-1} - 1$.
    b) $s(n, 1) = (-1)^{n-1}(n - 1)!$.

15. Let m and n be nonnegative integers with $n \leq m$. The *Kronecker delta function* $\delta(m, n)$ is equal to 1 if $m = n$ and 0 otherwise. Prove that

$$\sum_{k=n}^{m} S(m, k)s(k, n) = \delta(m, n).$$

In Exercises 16–20, let n and k be positive integers with $k \leq n$.

16. Prove that the sign of the Stirling number of the first kind is $(-1)^{n-k}$. (Thus the signless Stirling number of the first kind $t(n, k) = |s(n, k)|$ is equal to $(-1)^{n-k}s(n, k)$.)

17. Find a recurrence relation for the signless Stirling numbers $t(n, k)$ of the first kind similar to the recurrence relation (12) satisfied by the Stirling numbers $s(n, k)$ of the first kind.

18. A **cyclic permutation** (or **cycle**) of a set A is a permutation that cyclically permutes the elements of A. For example, the permutation σ, with $\sigma(1) = 2$, $\sigma(2) = 4$, $\sigma(3) = 1$, $\sigma(4) = 5$, $\sigma(5) = 3$, is cyclic, and denoted by (12453) or any of its cyclic equivalents, such as (24531) or (31245). It can be shown that every permutation of a set N can be expressed as a product of cycles that cyclically permute disjoint subsets of N, unique except for the order of the cycles. Thus, for example, (153)(24) is the **cyclic decomposition** of the permutation σ given by $\sigma(1) = 5$, $\sigma(2) = 4$, $\sigma(3) = 1$, $\sigma(4) = 2$, $\sigma(5) = 3$. Prove that $t(n, k)$ is the number of permutations of an n-element set that have exactly k cycles in their cyclic decomposition. *Hint:* Use Exercise 17.

19. Suppose a computer is programmed to produce a random permutation of n different characters.

a) Give an expression for the probability that the permutation will have exactly k cycles.

b) Calculate the probabilities with $n = 8$ that the permutation will have two cycles and that it will have three cycles. Which is more likely?

$\star$**20.** Let $a(n, k)$ be the sum of the products $1^{c_1} 2^{c_2} \cdots k^{c_k}$, taken over all k-tuples $(c_1, c_2, \ldots, c_k)$ such that c_i is a nonnegative integer for $i = 1, 2, \ldots, k$ and the sum of the c_is is $n - k$. Prove that $a(n, k)$ satisfies the initial conditions and the recurrence relation (1) for the Stirling numbers $S(n, k)$ of the second kind. (This shows that $S(n, k) = a(n, k)$.)

21. (Requires calculus.) Let k be a fixed positive integer. It can be shown that the ratios $S(n, k - 1)/S(n, k)$ and $s(n, k - 1)/s(n, k)$ both approach 0 as a limit as n approaches ∞. Use these facts to find

a) $\displaystyle\lim_{n \to \infty} S(n + 1, k)/S(n, k)$.

b) $\displaystyle\lim_{n \to \infty} s(n + 1, k)/s(n, k)$.

$\star$**22.** (Requires calculus.) The *exponential generating function* of a sequence (a_n) is defined to be the power series

$$A^*(x) = \sum_{n=0}^{\infty} a_n \frac{x^n}{n!}.$$

Let k be a fixed positive integer and let $a_n = S(n, k)$. Prove that

$$A^*(x) = \frac{(e^x - 1)^k}{k!}.$$

$\star$**23.** Find the expansion of the polynomial $P_k(x) = (1 - x)(1 - 2x) \ldots (1 - kx)$.

Computer Projects

1. Write a computer program that uses the recurrence relation (1) to compute Stirling numbers of the second kind.

2. Write a computer program that uses the recurrence relation (12) to compute Stirling numbers of the first kind.

7

Catalan Numbers

Author: Thomas A. Dowling, Department of Mathematics, Ohio State University.

Prerequisites: The prerequisites for this chapter are recursive definitions, basic counting principles, recurrence relations, rooted trees, and generating functions. See, for example, Sections 3.1–3.3, 4.1–4.4, 5.1, 5.2, 8.1–8.3, and Appendix 3 of *Discrete Mathematics and Its Applications*, Second Edition, by Kenneth H. Rosen.

Introduction

Sequences and arrays whose terms enumerate combinatorial structures have many applications in computer science. Knowledge (or estimation) of such integer-valued functions is, for example, needed in analyzing the complexity of an algorithm. Familiar examples are the polynomials in n, exponential functions (with an integer base) with exponent a polynomial in n, factorials, and the binomial coefficients. Less familiar are the Stirling numbers considered elsewhere in this book. The sequence of positive integers to be met here, called the Catalan* numbers, enumerate combinatorial structures of many different

---

* Eugène Charles Catalan (1814–1894) was a prominent Belgian mathematician who had numerous publications on multiple integrals, general theory of surfaces, mathematical analysis, probability, geometry, and superior arithmetic.

types. Those include nonnegative paths in the plane, well-formed sequences of parentheses, full binary trees, well-parenthesized products of variables, stack permutations, and triangulations of a convex polygon.

After defining the Catalan numbers explicitly by formula, we will show by a *combinatorial argument* that they count nonnegative paths in the plane. The size of each set of structures subsequently considered is shown to be a Catalan number by establishing a one-to-one correspondence between that set and a set of structures shown earlier to be of that size.

Using *recurrence relations* and *generating functions*, we will show by a different approach that the size of one of these sets (well-parenthesized products of variables) is a Catalan number. All the sets considered are then enumerated by Catalan numbers in view of the existence of the one-to-one correspondences previously established. The asymptotic behavior of the sequence is investigated, and we obtain the order of magnitude of the nth Catalan number.

Paths and Catalan Numbers

Suppose $m = a + b$ votes were cast in an election, with candidate A receiving a votes and candidate B receiving b votes. The ballots are counted individually in some random order, giving rise to a sequence of a As and b Bs. The number of possible ballot sequences is the number $C(m, a)$ of a-element subsets of the set $\{1, 2, \ldots, m\}$, since each such subset indicates which of the m ballots were cast for candidate A. Assuming all such sequences are equally likely, what is the probability that candidate A led throughout the counting of the ballots?

Every sequence of m ballots can be represented by an ordered m-tuple $(x_1, x_2, \ldots, x_m)$ with $x_i = 1$ if the ith ballot was a vote for A and $x_i = -1$ if it was for B. Then after i ballots are counted, the ith *partial sum* $s_i = x_1 + x_2 + \ldots + x_i$ (with $s_0 = 0$) represents A's "lead" over B. If we denote by $P(a, b)$ the number of sequences $(x_1, x_2, \ldots, x_m)$ with the partial sums $s_i > 0$ for $i = 1, 2, \ldots, m$, then the probability that A led throughout is $P(a, b)/C(m, a)$.

The Catalan numbers arise in the case where $a = b$, which we shall now assume. Denote the common value of a and b by n, so that $m = 2n$. Suppose we seek the probability that A never trailed throughout the counting. There are $C(2n, n)$ possible sequences of n 1's and n -1s. We seek the number for which $s_i \geq 0$ for $i = 1, 2, \ldots, 2n - 1$.

We can represent the sequence $(x_1, \ldots, x_{2n})$ by a *path* in the plane from the origin to the point $(2n, 0)$ whose *steps* are the line segments between $(i - 1, s_{i-1})$ and (i, s_i), for $i = 1, 2, \ldots, 2n$. The ith step in this path then has slope $s_i - s_{i-1} = x_i \in \{1, -1\}$.

Example 1   Let $n = 5$, so the paths run from the origin to the point $(10, 0)$. We display three such sequences and their partial sum sequences. For clarity, the 1s in the sequence are represented by plus signs and the -1s by minus signs. Draw the corresponding paths.

	Sequence	**Partial sum sequence**
(i)	$(-, -, +, +, +, +, -, -, -, +)$	$(0, -1, -2, -1, 0, 1, 2, 1, 0, -1, 0)$
(ii)	$(+, +, -, +, -, -, +, +, -, -)$	$(0, 1, 2, 1, 2, 1, 0, 1, 2, 1, 0)$
(iii)	$(+, +, -, +, +, -, +, -, -, -)$	$(0, 1, 2, 1, 2, 3, 2, 3, 2, 1, 0)$

Solution: The corresponding paths are shown in Figure 1. $\square$

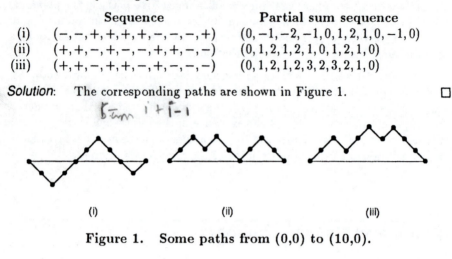

(i)   (ii)   (iii)

Figure 1.   Some paths from (0,0) to (10,0).

Note that in sequence (i) the partial sum sequence has both positive and negative entries, so the path lies both above and below the x-axis. In sequence (ii) all the partial sums are nonnegative, so the path does not go below the x-axis. But in sequence (iii), we have $s_i > 0$ for $i = 1, 2, \ldots, 2n - 1$. Hence, except for its two endpoints, the path lies entirely above the x-axis.

We call a path from $(0, 0)$ to $(2n, 0)$ **nonnegative** if all $s_i \geq 0$ and **positive** if $s_i > 0$ for $i = 1, 2, \ldots, 2n - 1$. Thus, a nonnegative path corresponds to a ballot sequence in which candidate A and candidate B both received n votes, but candidate A never trailed. Similarly, a positive path represents a ballot sequence in which candidate A was leading all the way until the final ballot brought them even.

We shall see that the number of nonnegative paths and positive paths from the origin to the point $(2n, 0)$ are both Catalan numbers. Before proceeding with this ballot problem, let us define the Catalan numbers.

Definition 1   The *Catalan number* c_n, for $n \geq 0$, is given by

$$c_n = \frac{1}{n+1} C(2n, n).$$ $\square$

The values of c_n for $n \leq 10$ are given in Table 1.

n	0	1	2	3	4	5	6	7	8	9	10
c_n	1	1	2	5	14	42	132	429	1,430	4,862	16,796

Table 1.   **The first eleven Catalan numbers.**

Example 2   Find all the nonnegative paths from the origin to $(6,0)$. Which of these are positive paths?

Solution: There are $C(4,2) = 6$ slope sequences of length 6 that start with 1 and end with -1. To check for nonnegativity, we compute their partial sums, and we find the nonnegative paths have slope sequences

$$(+,-,+,-,+,-), \quad (+,-,+,+,-,-), \quad (+,+,-,-,+,-),$$

$$(+,+,-,+,-,-), \quad (+,+,+,-,-,-),$$

with respective partial sum sequences

$$(0,1,0,1,0,1,0), \quad (0,1,0,1,2,1,0), \quad (0,1,2,1,0,1,0),$$

$$(0,1,2,1,2,1,0), \quad (0,1,2,3,2,1,0).$$

These paths are shown in Figure 2.   □

Figure 2.   **The nonnegative paths from the origin to $(6,0)$.**

Let us now show that the numbers of nonnegative and positive paths are Catalan numbers.

Theorem 1   The number of paths from the origin to $(2n, 0)$ that are
- (i)   positive is the Catalan number c_{n-1},
- (ii)   nonnegative is the Catalan number c_n.

Proof: We shall first establish a one-to-one correspondence between positive paths of length $2n$ and nonnegative paths of length $2n - 2$. Let $(s_0, s_1, \ldots, s_{2n})$ be the partial sum sequence of a positive path P. Then $s_0 = s_{2n} = 0$ and $s_i \geq 1$ for $i = 1, 2, \ldots, 2n - 1$. Let $\mathbf{x} = (x_1, x_2, \ldots, x_{2n})$ be the corresponding slope sequence of the steps, so $x_i = s_i - s_{i-1} \in \{1, -1\}$. Since $s_1 \geq 1$ and $s_0 = 0$, we must have $s_1 = 1$. Hence the path P passes through the point $(1,1)$. Similarly, since $s_{2n-1} \geq 1$ and $s_{2n} = 0$, we have $s_{2n-1} = 1$. Therefore P passes through the point $(2n-1, 1)$. If we omit the first and last terms from the slope sequence, we have a sequence $\mathbf{x}'$ that has $n-1$ 1s and $n-1$ -1s. Further, the partial sums for $\mathbf{x}'$ satisfy

$$
\begin{aligned}
s_i' &= x_1' + x_2' + \ldots + x_i' \\
&= x_2 + x_3 + \ldots + x_{i+1} \\
&= s_{i+1} - 1 \\
&\geq 0
\end{aligned}
$$

for $0 \leq i \leq 2n - 2$. Thus the positive path P from the origin to $(2n, 0)$ corresponds to a nonnegative path P' from the origin to $(2n - 2, 0)$. Geometrically, the path P' is produced from P by taking the segment of P from $(1, 1)$ to $(2n - 1, 1)$ relative to the new coordinate system obtained by translating the origin to the point $(1, 1)$.

Since the first and last terms of P must be 1 and -1, respectively, the operation of deleting those terms is reversed by adding 1 before and -1 after P'. Thus the function that takes P to P' is invertible. Hence, if a_n is the number of positive paths and b_n the number of nonnegative paths from the origin to $(2n, 0)$, then $a_n = b_{n-1}$. Part (ii) will then follow from (i) once we establish that $a_n = c_{n-1}$, since we would then have $b_n = a_{n+1} = c_n$.

A positive path P from the origin to $(2n, 0)$ is determined uniquely by its segment P' from $(1, 1)$ to $(2n - 1, 1)$, which lies entirely above the x-axis. But the number of such paths P' is the difference between $C(2n-2, n-1)$, the total number of paths from $(1, 1)$ to $(2n - 1, 1)$, and the number of paths Q from $(1, 1)$ to $(2n - 1, 1)$ that meet the x-axis.

Thus, we can determine the number of paths P' by counting the number of such paths Q. Suppose that Q first meets the x-axis at the point $(k, 0)$. Then $k \geq 2$ since Q begins at the point $(1, 1)$. If we reflect the segment Q_1 of Q from $(1, 1)$ to $(k, 0)$ about the x-axis, we obtain a path Q_1' from $(1, -1)$ to $(k, 0)$. Then if we adjoin to Q_1' the segment Q_2 of Q from $(k, 0)$ to $(2n - 1, 1)$, we obtain a path $Q^* = Q_1' Q_2$ from $(1, -1)$ to $(2n - 1, 1)$. But every such path Q^* must cross the x-axis, so we can obtain the path Q from Q^* by reflecting the segment of Q^* from $(1, -1)$ to its first point on the x-axis.

Hence we have a one-to-one correspondence between the paths Q and Q^*, so the number of paths Q from $(1, 1)$ to $(2n-1, 1)$ that meet the x-axis is equal to the number of paths Q^* from $(1, -1)$ to $(2n - 1, 1)$. Every such path Q^* must have two more increasing steps than decreasing steps, so it has n increasing steps and $n - 2$ decreasing steps. The number of such paths Q^* is therefore $C(2n - 2, n - 2)$, and this is equal to the number of such paths Q.

The number, a_n, of positive paths P from the origin to $(2n, 0)$ can now be calculated. Since it is equal to the number of positive paths P' from $(1, 1)$ to $(2n - 1, 1)$, and this is the difference between the total number $C(2n - 2, n - 1)$ of paths from $(1, 1)$ to $(2n - 1, 1)$ and the number $C(2n - 2, n - 2)$ of paths Q

from $(1,1)$ to $(2n-1,1)$ that meet the x-axis, we have

$$
\begin{aligned}
a_n &= C(2n-2, n-1) - C(2n-2, n-2) \\
&= \frac{(2n-2)!}{(n-1)!(n-1)!} - \frac{(2n-2)!}{(n-2)!n!} \\
&= \frac{(2n-2)!}{(n-2)!(n-1)!} \left(\frac{1}{n-1} - \frac{1}{n} \right) \\
&= \frac{(2n-2)!}{(n-2)!(n-1)!} \frac{1}{n(n-1)} \\
&= \frac{1}{n} \frac{(2n-2)!}{(n-1)!(n-1)!} \\
&= \frac{1}{n} C(2n-2, n-1) \\
&= c_{n-1}.
\end{aligned}
$$
■

Well-formed Sequences of Parentheses

The Catalan numbers count several structures important in computer science. Let us consider first the set of *well-formed sequences of parentheses*, which can be defined recursively (see Section 3.3 in *Discrete Mathematics and Its Applications*, Second Edition, by Rosen).

Definition 2   A sequence of parentheses is *well-formed* if and only if it can be derived by a finite sequence of the following rules:

The empty sequence is well-formed.

If A is well-formed, then (A) is well-formed.

If A and B are well-formed, then AB is well-formed.

We say that the right parenthesis following A in the second rule *closes* the left parenthesis preceding A.   □

Example 3   Find a sequence of $n = 4$ parentheses that is not well-formed and a sequence that is well-formed.

Solution: The sequence $(())( )$ is not well-formed since only one of the third and fourth left parentheses can be closed by the single right parenthesis that follows them. But the sequence $(())()( )$ is well-formed since each left parenthesis is closed by the first right parenthesis following it that does not close a left parenthesis between them.   □

Clearly each well-formed sequence of parentheses must have an equal number of left parentheses and right parentheses. Further, in any initial string consisting of the first i parentheses of a well-formed sequence of $2n$ parentheses, there must be at least as many left parentheses as right parentheses. Thus, if we replace left parentheses by 1s and right parentheses by -1s in a well-formed sequence of parentheses, we obtain a sequence $(x_1, x_2, \ldots, x_{2n}) \in \{1, -1\}^{2n}$ with all partial sums $s_i \geq 0$, and hence a nonnegative path from $(0,0)$ to $(2n,0)$. Conversely, any nonnegative path from $(0,0)$ to $(2n,0)$ produces a well-formed sequence of parentheses. By Theorem 1 and this one-to-one correspondence, we have established the following result.

Theorem 2   The number of well-formed sequences of parentheses of length $2n$ is the Catalan number c_n.   ■

Example 4   Find the well-formed sequences of parentheses of length $2n = 6$.

Solution: Since $n = 3$, by Theorem 2 there are exactly $c_3 = 5$ such sequences. They are found to be

$$( )( )( ), \quad ( )(( )), \quad (( ))( ), \quad (( ) ( )), \quad ((( ))).$$ □

Stack Permutations

In *Fundamental Algorithms*, Volume 1, of his classic series of books, *The Art of Computer Programming*, Donald Knuth posed the problem of counting the number of permutations of a particular type that arise in the computer. A **stack** is a list which can only be changed by insertions or deletions at one distinguished end, called the **top** of the list. When characters are individually inserted and deleted from the stack, the last one inserted must be the first one deleted from the stack (*lifo*). An insertion to the top of the stack is called a **push**; a deletion from the top is called a **pop**. We can interpret a stack as a stack of plates, with a push representing the placement of a plate on top, and a pop corresponding to the removal of a plate from the top.

A sequence of pushes and pops is **admissible** if the sequence has an equal number n of pushes and pops, and at each stage the sequence has at least as many pushes as pops. If we identify pushes with 1s and pops with -1s, then an admissible sequence corresponds to a nonnegative path from the origin to the point $(2n, 0)$. Thus, by Theorem 1, the number of admissible sequences of pushes and pops of length $2n$ is the Catalan number c_n.

When applied in a computer, an admissible sequence of pushes and pops of length $2n$ transforms an input string of length n to an output string with the same symbols, but in a possibly different order. Suppose we have as an initial input string the standard permutation $123\ldots n$ of the set $N = \{1, 2, \ldots, n\}$

and an admissible sequence of pushes and pops of length 2n. Each push in the sequence transfers the last element of the input string to the top of the stack, and each pop transfers the element on top of the stack to the beginning of the output string. After the n pushes and n pops have been performed, the output string is a permutation of N called a **stack permutation**.

Example 5   Let $n = 4$ and consider the admissible sequence

$$(+, +, +, -, -, +, -, -),$$

where a plus sign represents a push and a minus sign represents a pop. Find the stack permutation produced by this sequence of pushes and pops.

Solution: We will denote the result of each operation of the admissible sequence of pushes and pops by a string of the form $\alpha[\sigma]\beta$, where α is the current input string, β the current output string, and $[\sigma]$ the current stack, with the first element of σ being the top of the stack. Then the admissible sequence given proceeds as follows to produce the stack permutation 4132:

Sequence	$\alpha[\sigma]\beta$	Operation
	1234[ ]	
+	123[4]	Push 4
+	12[34]	Push 3
+	1[234]	Push 2
−	1[34]2	Pop 2
−	1[4]32	Pop 3
+	[14]32	Push 1
−	[4]132	Pop 1
−	[ ]4132	Pop 4.

□

A stack permutation of $123\ldots n$ is defined as one produced from $1, 2, \ldots, n$ by an admissible sequence of pushes and pops. But we have seen that there is a one-to-one correspondence between admissible sequences of pushes and pops of length $2n$ and nonnegative paths from the origin to the point $(2n, 0)$. The stack permutation can be found from its corresponding nonnegative path in the plane as follows.

Let i index the horizontal axis and s the vertical axis, and suppose the path passes through the points (i, s_i), $i = 0, 1, 2, \ldots, 2n$. Let k be the maximum ordinate s_i of the path.
(1)   Draw (segments of) the horizontal lines with equations $s = j$ for $j = 1, 2, \ldots, k$. The region bounded by the lines $i = 0$, $i = 2n$, $s = j - 1$, $s = j$ will be called box j.

(2)   Label the increasing steps of the path from left to right with $n, n-1, \ldots, 1$.

(3)   For $j = 1, 2, \ldots, k$, label each decreasing step in box j with the label of the last increasing step in box j that precedes it.

(4)   The stack permutation is the sequence *from right to left* of labels on the n decreasing steps.

Since the path starts at the origin, never crosses the i-axis (with equation $s = 0$), and ends on the i-axis at $(2n, 0)$, each box j must contain an equal number of increasing and decreasing steps. Further, they must alternate increasing-decreasing from left to right in box j, starting with an increasing step. Thus the labeling of the increasing steps in step (2) and the decreasing steps in step (3) establishes a one-to-one correspondence between the n increasing steps and the n decreasing steps of the path, where corresponding steps have the same label.

The label l on the increasing step in box j represents the element pushed onto the stack at that term of the admissible sequence of pushes and pops. Element l is not popped until the path first returns to box j by the decreasing step labeled l. The distinct labels on the steps between the two steps labeled l each occur twice, and represent the elements that were pushed, and hence must be popped, while l was on the stack.

Alternatively, in the well-formed sequence of parentheses corresponding to the nonnegative path, each increasing step is regarded as a left parenthesis, and the corresponding decreasing step is regarded as the right parenthesis that closes it.

Example 6   Draw the nonnegative path produced by the admissible sequence in Example 5, and find the corresponding stack permutation by labeling the steps.

Solution: The sequence of ordinates of the path is the partial sum sequence

$$s = (0, 1, 2, 3, 2, 1, 2, 1, 0)$$

computed from the admissible sequence (slope sequence)

$$(+, +, +, -, -, +, -, -)$$

given in Example 5. The nonnegative path, with maximum ordinate $k = 3$, is displayed in Figure 3, along with (segments of) the lines $s = 1, 2, 3$. The $n = 4$ increasing steps are labeled from left to right as $4, 3, 2, 1$. The decreasing steps are then labeled as shown in accordance with (3). When read from right to left, the labels on the decreasing steps produce the stack permutation 4132.   □

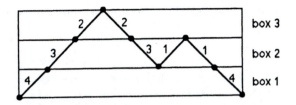

Figure 3.   Stack permutation 4132 from a nonnegative path with n = 4.

A stack permutation can only be produced by a unique admissible sequence, and therefore by a unique nonnegative path. We can recover the admissible sequence, and hence the path, from the stack permutation as follows. Starting with the stack permutation, precede it by the empty input string α and the empty stack $[\sigma]$ as in Example 5. Begin with an empty push-pop sequence. Then, given a current content $\alpha[\sigma]\beta$ of the input, stack, and output, respectively, with at least one of σ and β nonempty, proceed repeatedly as follows:

If the stack is empty or both of σ and β are nonempty, with the first element b of β less than the first element s of σ, transfer b to the left of σ (b was just popped) and add $-$ to the right of the push-pop sequence.

If the output is empty or both of σ and β are nonempty, with the first element b of β greater than the first element s of σ, transfer s to the right of α (s was just pushed) and add $+$ to the right of the push-pop sequence.

When the input string is $\alpha = 12\ldots n$, σ and β are empty and the admissible sequence that produced the stack permutation is the push-pop sequence constructed.

Example 7   Find the the admissible sequence of pushes and pops that produces the stack permutation 4213.

Solution:

$\alpha[\sigma]\beta$	Operation	Sequence
[ ]4213		
[4]213	4 Popped	$-$
[24]13	2 Popped	$-$
[124]3	1 Popped	$-$
1[24]3	1 Pushed	$+$
12[4]3	2 Pushed	$+$
12[34]	3 Popped	$-$
123[4]	3 Pushed	$+$
1234[ ]	4 Pushed	$+$

The admissible sequence, obtained by reading the sequence in the third column upward, is $(+, +, -, +, +, -, -, -)$. □

It follows from the foregoing that there is a one-to-one correspondence between the set of stack permutations of N and the set of nonnegative paths, or between the set of stack permutations of N and set of admissible sequences. By Theorem 1 we have the following theorem.

Theorem 3   The number of stack permutations of an n-element set is the Catalan number c_n.   ∎

Well-parenthesized Products

Consider an algebraic structure S with a binary operation, which we will refer to as multiplication. Then, as usual, we can denote the product of $x, y \in S$ by xy. Let us further assume that the operation is *not commutative*, so that $xy \neq yx$ in general. The product $x_1 x_2 \cdots x_{n+1}$ of $n + 1$ elements of S in that order is well-defined provided that multiplication is associative, i.e. that $(xy)z = x(yz)$ for all $x, y, z \in S$. But let us suppose that multiplication in S is *not associative*. Then a product $x_1 x_2 \cdots x_{n+1}$ is defined only after parentheses have been suitably inserted to determine recursively pairs of elements to be multiplied. However, we will refer to the sequence $x_1 x_2 \cdots x_{n+1}$ without parentheses simply as a product.

We shall determine the number of ways a product $x_1 x_2 \cdots x_{n+1}$ can be parenthesized. The assumption that the binary operation is noncommutative and nonassociative allows us to interpret this number as the maximum number of different elements of S that can be obtained by parenthesizing the product. However, we could instead consider the x_is to be real numbers and the binary operation to be ordinary multiplication. In this case we are seeking the number of ways that the product $x_1 x_2 \cdots x_{n+1}$ can be computed by successive multiplications of exactly two numbers each time. This was Catalan's original formulation of the problem.

Example 8   Find the distinct ways to parenthesize the product $x_1 x_2 x_3 x_4$.

Solution: Whenever a left parenthesis is closed by a right parenthesis, and we have carried out any products defined by closed pairs of parentheses nested between them, we must have a product of exactly two elements of S. The well-parenthesized sequences for the product $x_1x_2x_3x_4$ are found to be

$$((x_1(x_2x_3))x_4), \quad (x_1((x_2x_3)x_4)), \quad ((x_1x_2)(x_3x_4)),$$

$$(x_1(x_2(x_3x_4))), \quad (((x_1x_2)x_3)x_4). \qquad \square$$

Note that we used $n = 3$ pairs of parentheses in each parenthesized product in Example 8. Although not necessary, it is convenient to include outer parentheses, where the left parenthesis is first and the right parenthesis last.

We will now formally define what is meant by parenthesizing a product.

Definition 3   A product is *well-parenthesized* if it can be obtained recursively by a finite sequence of the following rules:

Each single term $x \in S$ is well-parenthesized.

If A and B are well-parenthesized, then (AB) is well-parenthesized. $\square$

Note that a well-parenthesized product, other than a single element of S, includes outer parentheses. Thus, (xy) is well-parenthesized, but xy is not. We can then use mathematical induction to prove that n pairs of parentheses must be added to $x_1x_2 \cdots x_{n+1}$ to form a well-parenthesized product.

If the $n+1$ variables $x_1, x_2, \ldots, x_{n+1}$ are deleted from a well-parenthesized product, the n pairs of parentheses that remain must be a well-formed sequence of parentheses. But not every well-formed sequence of n pairs of parentheses can arise in this way. For example,

$$(( )( )( ))$$

is a well-formed sequence of $n = 4$ pairs of parentheses, but since the operation is binary, the outer pair of parentheses would call for the undefined product of the three elements of S that are to be computed within the inner parentheses.

Example 9   Show by identifying A and B at each step that

$$((x_1(x_2x_3))(x_4x_5))$$

is obtained from the product $x_1x_2x_3x_4x_5$ by the recursive definition, and hence is a well-parenthesized product.

Solution:

$$x_1x_2x_3x_4x_5$$

$x_1(x_2x_3)x_4x_5$	$A = x_2, \quad B = x_3$
$(x_1(x_2x_3))x_4x_5$	$A = x_1, \quad B = (x_2x_3)$
$(x_1(x_2x_3))(x_4x_5)$	$A = x_4, \quad B = x_5$
$((x_1(x_2x_3))(x_4x_5))$	$A = (x_1(x_2x_3)), \quad B = (x_4x_5). \qquad \square$

We will now show that there is a one-to-one correspondence between well-parenthesized products of $x_1, x_2, \cdots, x_{n+1}$ and nonnegative paths from the origin to the point $(2n, 0)$. A well-parenthesized product forms a string **p** of length $3n + 1$ with three types of characters: n left parentheses, $n + 1$ variables, and n right parentheses. But the slope sequence of the nonnegative paths from the origin to the point $(2n, 0)$ has just two different numbers, 1 and -1, with n of each. To obtain a sequence from **p** with a structure similar to that of the slope sequence, we form a string $\mathbf{q} = S(\mathbf{p})$ of length $2n$ by deleting the last variable x_{n+1} and the n right parentheses.

Example 10   Find the string **q**, if $\mathbf{p} = ((x_1(x_2x_3))(x_4x_5))$ is the well-parenthesized product in Example 8.

Solution: Deleting x_5 and the right parentheses from **p** gives

$$\mathbf{q} = ((x_1(x_2x_3(x_4.$$ $\square$

Let us examine the properties of this string $\mathbf{q} = S(\mathbf{p})$ obtained from a well-parenthesized product **p**. We will then show that **p** can be obtained from a string **q** with these properties. By the way that **q** was defined, we first note the following.

Lemma 1   The string $\mathbf{q} = S(\mathbf{p})$ has n left parentheses and the n variables $x_1, x_2, \ldots, x_n$ in that order.   ∎

Since **p** cannot have a left parenthesis between x_n and x_{n+1}, the last character of the string **q** must be x_n. This is in fact implied by a more general property that **q** satisfies, analogous to the property satisfied by nonnegative paths, which we state in the following lemma.

Lemma 2   Let $\mathbf{q} = S(\mathbf{p})$, where **p** is a well-parenthesized product of the variables $x_1, x_2, \ldots, x_{n+1}$. For $i \leq 2n$, the number of left parentheses in the string $q_1q_2 \cdots q_i$ is at least as large as the number of variables.

Proof: We will prove the lemma by induction on n. If $n = 1$, then we must have $\mathbf{p} = (x_1x_2)$, so $\mathbf{q} = (x_1$ and the conclusion holds.

Suppose $n \geq 2$ and that the conclusion holds whenever **q** is obtained from a well-parenthesized product **p** of $k \leq n$ variables. Let **p** be a well-parenthesized product of $n + 1$ variables. From the recursive definition, $\mathbf{p} = (AB)$ is the product of two nonempty well-parenthesized products, A and B. The first left parenthesis in **p** is placed before AB, so the number of left parentheses up to each character of **p** preceding B is one more than in A. But if x_k is the last variable in A, then it does not appear in $S(A)$, but does appear following x_{k-1} in $\mathbf{q} = S(\mathbf{p})$. Thus the difference between the number of left parentheses and the number of variables in $\mathbf{q}$ exceeds the corresponding difference in $S(A)$ by one until x_k is reached, where it becomes zero. The differences at each character of B are then the same as they are at that character in $\mathbf{p}$. Since A is a well-parenthesized product of $k \leq n$ variables, it then follows by the inductive hypothesis that the number of left parentheses in $q_1 q_2 \cdots q_i$ for $i \leq 2n$ is at least as large as the number of variables. ∎

We say that a string $\mathbf{q}$ satisfying Lemmas 1 and 2 is **suitable**.

Theorem 4   There is a one-to-one correspondence between the set of suitable strings of length $2n$ and the set of well-parenthesized products of length $3n + 1$.

Proof: We will show that the function S is a one-to-one correspondence. Let $\mathbf{q}$ be a suitable string. We need to show that we can reconstruct the well-parenthesized product $\mathbf{p}$ such that $\mathbf{q} = S(\mathbf{p})$. First we adjoin x_{n+1} to the right of $\mathbf{q}$ and call the new string $\mathbf{q}' = \mathbf{q}x_{n+1}$. Then by Lemma 1 we have the following.

Lemma 1′   The string $\mathbf{q}'$ has n left parentheses and the $n + 1$ variables $x_1, x_2, \ldots, x_{n+1}$ in that order.

Since $\mathbf{q}$ and $\mathbf{q}'$ agree in the first $2n$ positions, we will denote the character of $\mathbf{q}'$ in position i by q_i for $i \leq 2n$. Then $\mathbf{q}'$ satisfies the conclusion of Lemma 2.

Let us prove the theorem by mathematical induction. If $n = 1$ then $\mathbf{q}' = (x_1 x_2$, so we must have $\mathbf{p} = (x_1 x_2)$.

Assume that $n \geq 2$ and the theorem is true with $n - 1$ replacing n. By Lemmas 1 and 2 the last two characters of $\mathbf{q}$ are either $x_{n-1} x_n$ or $(x_n$, so the last three characters of $\mathbf{q}'$ are either $x_{n-1} x_n x_{n+1}$ or $(x_n x_{n+1}$. By Lemma 1′, in either case $\mathbf{q}'$ will have three consecutive characters of the form $(x_j x_{j+1}$ for some $j \geq 1$. Let j_1 be the minimum such j. When right parentheses are inserted in $\mathbf{q}'$ to form a well-parenthesized product, a right parenthesis must immediately follow $(x_{j_1} x_{j_1+1}$, so $\mathbf{p}$ would contain $(x_{j_1} x_{j_1+1})$. Replace $(x_{j_1} x_{j_1+1})$ by a new variable y_1 in $\mathbf{q}'$ to form a string $\mathbf{q_1}$. Then $\mathbf{q_1}$ has $n - 1$ left parentheses and n variables. Further, $\mathbf{q_1}$ satisfies the conclusion of Lemma 1′ with $n-1$ replacing n. Then by our inductive hypothesis, the well-parenthesized product $\mathbf{p_1}$ can be recovered. Substituting $(x_{j_1} x_{j_1+1})$ for y_1 in $\mathbf{p_1}$ gives a well-parenthesized product $\mathbf{p}$ such that $\mathbf{q} = S(\mathbf{p})$. Since S is one-to-one and can be inverted, it is a one-to-one correspondence. ∎

Example 11   Recover the well-parenthesized product **p** from the suitable string

$$q = (x_1((x_2((x_3x_4x_5$$

so that $q = S(p)$.

Solution: We form $q' = (x_1((x_2((x_3x_4x_5x_6$ by adding x_6 to the right of q. Then locate at each stage j the first occurrence of a left parenthesis immediately followed by two variables, and replace this string of length three by the new variable y_j equal to this string with a right parenthesis added on the right as a fourth character.

$$
\begin{aligned}
q' &= (x_1((x_2((x_3x_4x_5x_6 \\
&= (x_1((x_2(y_1x_5x_6 & y_1 &= (x_3x_4) \\
&= (x_1((x_2y_2x_6 & y_2 &= (y_1x_5) \\
&= (x_1(y_3x_6 & y_3 &= (x_2y_2) \\
&= (x_1y_4 & y_4 &= (y_3x_6) \\
&= y_5 & y_5 &= (x_1y_4)
\end{aligned}
$$

Then, on setting $p = y_5$ and successively substituting for the new variables $y_5, y_4, \ldots, y_1$ their values on the right we obtain

$$
\begin{aligned}
p &= y_5 \\
&= (x_1y_4) \\
&= (x_1(y_3x_6)) \\
&= (x_1((x_2y_2)x_6)) \\
&= (x_1((x_2(y_1x_5))x_6)) \\
&= (x_1((x_2((x_3x_4)x_5))x_6)).
\end{aligned}
$$

□

Corollary 1   The number of well-parenthesized products of $n + 1$ variables is the Catalan number c_n.

Proof: By Theorem 4, each well-parenthesized sequence from $x_1x_2 \cdots x_{n+1}$ corresponds to a suitable string q of length $2n$ with n left parentheses and the n variables $x_1, x_2, \ldots, x_n$. Define a sequence $z = (z_1, z_2, \ldots, z_{2n})$ by

$$
z_i = \begin{cases} 1 & \text{if } q_i \text{ is a left parenthesis} \\ -1 & \text{if } q_i \text{ is a variable } x_j. \end{cases}
$$

Then it follows from Lemma 2 that the partial sums s_i of z are nonnegative. Thus, corresponding to q is a nonnegative path from $(0, 0)$ to $(2n, 0)$. Consequently, by Theorem 1, the number of well-parenthesized products is c_n. ∎

Full Binary Trees

Recall (see Section 8.1 of *Discrete Mathematics and Its Applications*, Second Edition, by Rosen) that a **full binary tree** is a rooted tree in which each internal vertex has exactly two children. Thus, a full binary tree with n internal vertices has $2n$ edges. Since a tree has one more vertex than it has edges, a full binary tree T with n internal vertices has $2n + 1$ vertices, and thus $n + 1$ leaves. Suppose we label the leaves of T as they are encountered along a transversal (preorder, postorder, or inorder; see Section 8.1 of *Discrete Mathematics and Its Applications*) with $x_1, x_2, \ldots, x_{n+1}$. Then T recursively defines a well-parenthesized product of $x_1, x_2, \cdots, x_{n+1}$ by the following rule.

Labeling rule: If v is an internal vertex with left child a and right child b, having labels A and B, respectively, then label v with (AB).

The label on the root of the tree will be the well-parenthesized product.

Conversely, given a well-parenthesized product of $n+1$ variables $x_1, x_2, \ldots, x_{n+1}$, a labeled full binary tree is determined by first labeling the root with the well-parenthesized product, then moving from the outer parentheses inward by adding two children labeled A and B to each vertex v with label (AB). The leaves of the tree will be labeled with the variables $x_1, x_2, \ldots, x_{n+1}$ in the order encountered by a traversal. Consequently, there is a one-to-one correspondence between the well-parenthesized products of $n + 1$ variables and the full binary trees with $n + 1$ leaves and n internal vertices. By Theorem 4 we therefore have the following result.

Theorem 5   The number of full binary trees with n internal vertices is the Catalan number c_n. ∎

Example 12   Draw and label the full binary tree defined by the well-parenthesized product $((1(23))(45))$.

Solution: The full binary tree is shown in Figure 4.   □

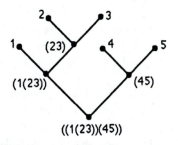

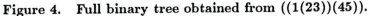

Figure 4.   Full binary tree obtained from $((1(23))(45))$.

Triangulations of a Convex Polygon

In this section we consider a geometric interpretation of the Catalan numbers. An *n*-gon ($n \geq 3$) in the plane is a polygon P with n vertices and n sides. Let $v_0, v_1, \ldots, v_{n-1}$ be the vertices (in counterclockwise order). Let us denote by $v_i v_j$ the **line segment** joining v_i and v_j. Then the n sides of P are $s_i = v_{i-1} v_i$ for $1 \leq i \leq n-1$ and $s_0 = v_n v_0$. A **diagonal** of P is a line segment $v_i v_j$ joining two nonadjacent vertices of P. An *n*-gon P is **convex** if every diagonal lies wholly in the interior of P.

Let D be a set of diagonals, no two of which meet in the interior of a convex *n*-gon P, that partitions the interior of P into triangles. The sides of the triangles are either diagonals in D or sides of P. The set T of triangles obtained in this way is called a **triangulation** of P. Three triangulations of a convex hexagon are shown in Figure 5.

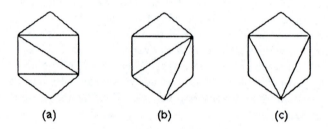

| (a) | (b) | (c) |

Figure 5.   Three triangulations of a convex hexagon.

We shall next determine the number of diagonals needed to form a triangulation.

Lemma 3   A triangulation of a convex *n*-gon has $n - 2$ triangles determined by $n - 3$ diagonals.

Proof: We shall argue by induction on n. If $n = 3$ there is one triangle and no diagonals, while if $n = 4$ there are two triangles and one diagonal.

Assume that $n \geq 5$ and that the conclusion holds for triangulations of a convex *m*-gon with $3 \leq m < n$. Let P be a convex *n*-gon and let T be a triangulation of P with diagonal set D. Since $n > 3$ there must be at least one diagonal in D, say $v_0 v_k$, where $2 \leq k \leq n - 2$. The diagonal $v_0 v_k$ of P then serves jointly as a side of the convex $(k + 1)$-gon P_1 with vertices $v_0, v_1, \ldots, v_k$ and the convex $(n - k + 1)$-gon P_2 with vertices $v_0, v_k, v_{k+1} \ldots, v_{n-1}$. Triangulations T_1 and T_2 of these two convex polygons are defined by subsets D_1 and D_2, respectively, of the set D of diagonals of P other than $v_0 v_k$. Since $k + 1 \leq n$ and $n - k + 1 \leq n$, we may apply the inductive hypothesis. Then T_1 and T_2

have $k-1$ and $n-k-1$ triangles defined by $k-2$ and $n-k-2$ diagonals, respectively. Adding the numbers of triangles gives $(k-1)+(n-k-1)=n-2$ triangles in T. We add 1 (for $v_0 v_k$) to the sum $(k-2)+(n-k-2)=n-4$ of the numbers of diagonals to get $n-3$ diagonals in D.   ∎

It is convenient now to assume that P is a convex $(n+2)$-gon for $n \geq 1$, with vertices $v_0, v_1, \ldots, v_{n+1}$ and sides $s_0, s_1, \ldots, s_{n+1}$. Then, by Lemma 3, every triangulation of P is defined by $n-1$ diagonals and has n triangles.

Let t_n be the number of triangulations of a convex $(n+2)$-gon P. Then clearly $t_1 = 1$ and $t_2 = 2$.

Example 13   Draw all the triangulations of a convex pentagon to show that $t_3 = 5$.

Solution: Since $n = 3$, each triangulation has three triangles defined by two diagonals. If $v_i v_j$ is one of the diagonals, the other diagonal must meet v_i or v_j. Thus each of the two diagonals must join the common endpoint to a nonadjacent vertex. We find the five triangulations shown in Figure 6.   □

Figure 6.   The triangulations of a convex pentagon.

Consider the string $s_1 s_2 \cdots s_{n+1}$ formed by taking the $n+1$ sides of P other than s_0 in order around P. We shall show that the product $s_1 s_2 \cdots s_{n+1}$ is well-parenthesized by a triangulation of P. One side, s_0, is excluded above in order that the remaining sides form an open path in the plane. The sides, taken in the order of the path, then form a sequence analogous to the product of $n+1$ variables considered earlier.

Let T be a triangulation of P defined by a set D of $n-1$ diagonals, where $n \geq 4$. Each side s_i of P is a side of exactly one of the n triangles of T. There are two types of triangles in T that contain sides of P:

(i) The three sides of an **outer triangle** are two adjacent sides s_i, s_{i+1} of P and the diagonal $v_{i-1} v_{i+1}$ of D.

(ii) The three sides of an **inner triangle** are a side $s_i = v_{i-1} v_i$ of P and the two diagonals $v_{i-1} v_j$, $v_i v_j$ of D for some vertex v_j, with $j \neq i-2, i+1$.

For example, hexagons (a) and (b) in Figure 5 each have two outer triangles, while (c) has three. In order to establish a one-to-one correspondence between triangulations and well-parenthesized products, we must show that any triangulation has an outer triangle not having s_0 as a side.

Lemma 4   If $n \geq 2$, every triangulation T of a convex $(n + 2)$-gon P has at least two outer triangles.

Proof: Suppose that at most one of the n triangles of T has two sides of P as sides. Let n_i be the number of sides of P that are sides of the ith triangle. Then $n_i = 1$ for at least $n - 1$ triangles and $n_i = 2$ for at most one. When we sum these n numbers n_i, we conclude that P has at most $n + 1$ sides. But P has $n + 2$ sides, so we have a contradiction. Thus P must have at least two outer triangles.   ∎

Theorem 6   The number of triangulations of a convex $(n + 2)$-gon is the Catalan number c_n.

Proof: By Corollary 1, it will suffice to establish a one-to-one correspondence between triangulations of a convex $(n + 2)$-gon P and well-parenthesized products of the $n + 1$ sides of P other than s_0.

Let $n \geq 2$ and assume such a one-to-one correspondence exists for $(n + 1)$-gons. Let T be a triangulation of the convex $(n + 2)$-gon P. Since every side of P is a side of exactly one triangle of T, and by Lemma 4 there are at least two outer triangles, there must be an outer triangle in T that does not have s_0 as a side. This triangle has vertices v_{i-1}, v_i, v_{i+1} for some i, $1 \leq i \leq n$, so has as sides the two sides s_i, s_{i+1} of P and the diagonal $v_{i-1}v_{i+1}$ in D. Label this diagonal with $(s_i s_{i+1})$. If we delete vertex v_i and replace sides s_i, s_{i+1} by the diagonal labeled $(s_i s_{i+1})$, we have a convex $(n + 1)$-gon P'. By the inductive hypothesis we can establish a one-to-one correspondence between triangulations T' of P' and well-parenthesized products of the sides of P' other than s_0. But one of the sides of P' is labeled with the well-parenthesized product $(s_i s_{i+1})$ of two sides of P. Thus the well-parenthesized product of the sides of P' represents a well-parenthesized product of the sides of P.

Conversely, each innermost pair of parentheses in a well-parenthesized product of the sides of P other than s_0 indicates that the two sides within that pair are in an outer triangle. Then the diagonal completing the outer triangle must be included in D. Each closing of parentheses acts in this way to add diagonals that complete outer triangles on the reduced polygon until a triangulation of P is obtained.   ∎

Summary of Objects Counted by the Catalan Numbers

The one-to-one correspondences we have established between the sets of triangulations of a convex $(n+2)$-gon, well-parenthesized products of $n+1$ variables, well-formed sequences of n pairs of parentheses, stack permutations of $12\cdots n$, and nonnegative paths from the origin to the point $(2n,0)$ are illustrated in Figure 7 for the case $n=4$.

The side s_0 in the hexagon that does not correspond to a variable in the corresponding well-parenthesized product of $n+1$ variables is shown as a dashed line segment. For clarity, each of the other sides, s_i, which corresponds to a variable in the corresponding well-parenthesized product, is labeled simply i.

The Generating Function of the Catalan Numbers

We started by defining the Catalan number c_n by means of a formula, and we then showed by a combinatorial argument that it enumerates nonnegative paths in the plane. We subsequently found one-to-one correspondences between several different types of combinatorial structures, starting with the nonnegative paths. It followed that the number of structures of each type must be equal to the number c_n of nonnegative paths. Having established the one-to-one correspondences, the same conclusion would follow if we showed (combinatorially or otherwise) that the number of structures of any particular type is given by

$$c_n = \frac{1}{n+1}\, C(2n, n). \tag{1}$$

In this section we will obtain (1) as the number of well-parenthesized products of $n+1$ variables using recurrence relations and generating functions (see Chapter 5 and Appendix 3 of *Discrete Mathematics and Its Applications*). In the next section we will investigate the behavior of the sequence $\{c_n\}$ for large values of n.

A sequence $\{a_n\} = a_0, a_1, \ldots$ satisfies a linear homogeneous recurrence relation of degree k with constant coefficients if each term a_n for $n \geq k$ can be computed recursively from the previous k terms by means of

$$a_n = C_1 a_{n-1} + C_2 a_{n-2} + \cdots + C_k a_{n-k} \tag{2}$$

for some constants C_i, $1 \leq i \leq k$, with $C_k \neq 0$. Any sequence satisfying (2) is completely determined by its k initial values.

The generating function of a sequence $\{a_n\}$ is the power series

$$A(x) = \sum_{n=0}^{\infty} a_n x^n.$$

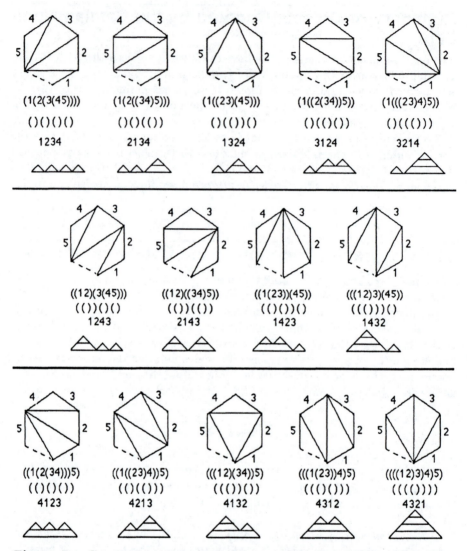

Figure 7. One-to-one correspondences with n = 4 between the sets of triangulations of a convex hexagon, well-parenthesized products, well-formed sequences of parentheses, stack permutations, and non-negative paths.

If the sequence satisfies a linear homogeneous recurrence relation with constant coefficients of some fixed degree k, the generating function is a rational function of x. The polynomial in the numerator depends only on the k initial values, while the polynomial in the denominator depends only on the recurrence relation. Once the roots of the polynomial in the denominator are found (or estimated by an algorithm), the value of any term of the sequence can be obtained by means of partial fractions and known power series.

Suppose we define a_n to be the number of well-parenthesized products of n variables. We showed earlier that a_{n+1} is the Catalan number c_n given by (1). But let us find a_n using recurrence relations and generating functions. To form a well-parenthesized product of $n \geq 2$ variables $x_1, x_2, \cdots, x_n$ by the recursive definition, the outer parentheses would be the last ones added to form (AB), where A and B are well-parenthesized products, each having at least one of the variables. The outer parentheses then would enclose AB, where A is one of the a_i well-parenthesized products of the first i variables and B is one of the a_{n-i} well-parenthesized products of the last $n - i$ variables, for some i satisfying $1 \leq i \leq n - 1$. Then, by the product rule and the sum rule, we obtain

$$a_n = a_1 a_{n-1} + a_2 a_{n-2} + \cdots + a_{n-1} a_1 = \sum_{i=1}^{n-1} a_i a_{n-i}. \tag{3}$$

Note that (3) is a homogeneous recurrence relation with constant coefficients. However, it is not linear, but *quadratic*. In addition, since the number of previous terms that determine a_n depends on n, and the degree of a recurrence relation is defined only when this number is some fixed integer k, the degree is not defined in (3).

If we define $a_0 = 0$, then the terms $a_0 a_n$ and $a_n a_0$ can be added to the right-hand side of (3) without changing its value, and we obtain

$$a_n = a_0 a_n + a_1 a_{n-1} + \cdots + a_n a_0 = \sum_{i=0}^{n} a_i a_{n-i}. \tag{4}$$

The right-hand side of (4) is zero for $n \leq 1$, but for $n \geq 2$ it is the coefficient of x^n in the square of the generating function $A(x) = \sum_{i=0}^{\infty} a_n x^n$. Since $a_1 = 1$, it follows that
$$A^2(x) = A(x) - x,$$
which is a quadratic equation in $A(x)$. By the quadratic formula, we obtain as solutions

$$A(x) = \frac{1}{2}(1 \pm \sqrt{1 - 4x}). \tag{5}$$

Since $A(0) = a_0 = 0$, and when we set $x = 0$ the right-hand side of (5) with the plus sign is 1, we must take the minus sign. Thus the generating function of the sequence a_n is

$$A(x) = \frac{1}{2}(1 - \sqrt{1 - 4x}). \tag{6}$$

Using a generalization of the binomial theorem, it can be shown that

$$\sqrt{1 - 4x} = (1 - 4x)^{1/2} = 1 + \sum_{n=1}^{\infty} (-1)^n \frac{(\frac{1}{2})_n}{n!} 4^n x^n, \tag{7}$$

where $(\frac{1}{2})_n$ is the *falling factorial* function $(x)_n = x(x-1)\cdots(x-n+1)$ evaluated at $x = 1/2$. The terms in the sum in (7) can be simplified after writing 4^n as $2^n 2^n$, carrying out the multiplication of $(\frac{1}{2})_n = (\frac{1}{2})(\frac{1}{2} - 1)\cdots(\frac{1}{2} - n + 1)$ by $(-1)^n 2^n$ termwise, writing the remaining factor 2^n as $2(2^{n-1})(n-1)!/(n-1)!$, and noting that $2^{n-1}(n-1)! = 2\cdot 4\cdots(2n-2)$. We then obtain

$$\sqrt{1-4x} = 1 - 2\sum_{n=1}^{\infty} \frac{1}{n} C(2n-2, n-1)\, x^n. \tag{8}$$

From (6) and (8) we obtain the generating function

$$A(x) = \sum_{n=1}^{\infty} \frac{1}{n} C(2n-2, n-1)\, x^n. \tag{9}$$

Thus the coefficient of x^{n+1} in (9) is $a_{n+1} = \frac{1}{n+1} C(2n, n)$, which by (1) is the Catalan number c_n. Similar methods could be used to show that the sizes of the other structures considered are Catalan numbers. It would suffice to show that the sequence satisfied the recurrence relation (4) and that the initial values agree, perhaps after a shift.

Asymptotic Behavior of the Catalan Numbers

Let us consider the behavior of the sequence $\{c_n\}$ of Catalan numbers for large values of n. In the previous section we let a_n be the number of well-parenthesized products of n variables and showed that the sequence $\{a_n\}$ satisfies the recurrence relation (3). Using the generating function $A(x)$ of the sequence $\{a_n\}$, we found that a_{n+1} is equal to the Catalan number c_n given by (1). If we substitute c_j for a_{j+1} in (3) and adjust the range of the index variable i, we see that the sequence $\{c_n\}$ satisfies the recurrence relation

$$c_n = c_0 c_{n-1} + c_1 c_{n-2} + \cdots + c_{n-1} c_0 = \sum_{i=0}^{n-1} c_i c_{n-i-1} \tag{10}$$

with $c_0 = 1$. This is a quadratic homogeneous recurrence relation with constant coefficients, but with the degree undefined. The asymptotic behavior of the sequence $\{c_n\}$ can be more easily found by showing that it satisfies a second homogeneous recurrence relation, one that is linear of degree one but with a *variable* coefficient. The linear recurrence relation could have been found earlier using Definition 1 of the Catalan numbers, but we will find it using the solution given by (1) to the quadratic recurrence relation (10).

A linear homogeneous recurrence relation of degree one with a constant coefficient has the form $a_n = C a_{n-1}$. On iterating this recurrence relation $n-1$

times, we obtain the formula $a_n = C^n a_0$. Suppose that instead of making our original definition of c_n, which is the same as (1), we had defined c_n as the number of well-parenthesized products of $n + 1$ variables. Then we would find, as in the last section, that the sequence $\{c_n\}$ satisfies the quadratic recurrence relation (10), and that the solution is given by (1). On using the formula for the binomial coefficient, it can be then be shown (see Exercise 6) that

$$c_n = \frac{4n - 2}{n + 1} c_{n-1},$$ (11)

so that the constant coefficient C is replaced by a variable coefficient

$$C(n) = \frac{4n - 2}{n + 1} = 4 - \frac{6}{n + 1}.$$

Clearly $C(n)$ increases to 4 as a limit as $n \to \infty$. However, this does not imply that c_n can be approximated by a constant multiple of 4^n. That would be the case if fact $C(n)$ was identically equal to the constant $C = 4$.

However, on using the familiar expression for a binomial coefficient involving three factorials, and replacing each of those factorials by an approximate value, we can approximate c_n, and use this approximation to find a function $f(n)$ with a relatively simple form such that $c_n = O(f(n))$. The simplest form of **Stirling's approximation** s_n of $n!$ is given by

$$s_n = \sqrt{2\pi n}\, e^{-n} n^n.$$ (12)

Using this approximation, it can be shown (see Exercise 7) that

$$c_n = O(n^{-3/2} 4^n).$$ (13)

Suggested Readings

1. K. Bogart, *Introductory Combinatorics*, Harcourt, Brace, Jovanovich, New York, 1990.

2. L. Comptet, *Advanced Combinatorics*, D. Reidel, Boston, 1974.

3. W. Feller, *An Introduction to Probability Theory and Its Applications*, Second Edition, Wiley, 1961.

4. F. Roberts, *Applied Combinatorics*, Prentice-Hall, Englewood Cliffs, N.J., 1984.

Exercises

In Exercises 1–4 find the structures that correspond to the given structures under the one-to-one correspondences established.

1. Given the sequence $(+ + - + - + - - + + --)$ of ± 1s with nonnegative partial sums, find or draw the corresponding
   a) well-formed sequence of six pairs of parentheses
   b) nonnegative path from the origin to $(12, 0)$
   c) stack permutation of 123456.

2. Given the sequence $(+ + - + - - + + --)$ of ± 1s with nonnegative partial sums, find or draw the corresponding
   a) well-parenthesized product of six variables
   b) full binary tree with six leaves whose vertices are labeled with well-parenthesized products
   c) triangulation of a convex septagon.

3. Given the following triangulation of a convex octagon, find or draw the corresponding
   a) well-parenthesized product of seven variables
   b) sequence of twelve ± 1s with nonnegative partial sums
   c) nonnegative path from the origin to $(12, 0)$
   d) stack permutation of 123456.

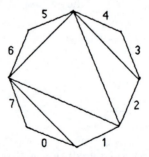

4. Given the well-parenthesized product $((1(23))((45)6))$ of six variables (with x_i denoted by i), find or draw the corresponding
   a) sequence of ten ± 1s with nonnegative partial sums
   b) stack permutation of 12345
   c) triangulation of a convex septagon.

5. Find the sequence of ten pushes $(+)$ and pops $(-)$ that produces the stack permutation 42135, and draw the corresponding nonnegative path.

6. Prove that the Catalan numbers c_n satisfy the recurrence relation (11).

7. Use the Stirling approximation (12) for $n!$ to prove that the Catalan number c_n satisfies (13).

In Exercises 8–10, suppose that T is a triangulation of a convex $(n + 2)$-gon P with diagonal set D. Let $v_0 v_1 \cdots v_{n+1}$ be the vertices of P in order, and let s_i be the side $v_{i-1} v_i$ for $1 \le i \le n+1$, $s_0 = v_0 v_{n+1}$. Denote by **p** the corresponding well-parenthesized product $s_1 s_2 \cdots s_{n+1}$ of its sides other than s_0.

8. Prove that the diagonal $v_i v_j$ is in the diagonal set D if and only if the product $s_{i+1} s_{i+2} \cdots s_j$ is well-parenthesized in **p**.

9. Let $1 \le k \le n - 1$. Prove that the nonnegative path corresponding to T meets the x-axis at the point $(2k, 0)$ if and only if D contains the diagonal $v_k v_{n+1}$.

10. Prove that the nonnegative path corresponding to T is positive if and only if D contains the diagonal $v_0 v_n$.

Computer Projects

1. Given a positive integer n as input, find the Catalan number c_n using
   a) the recurrence relation (10).
   b) the recurrence relation (11).

2. Given positive integers n and N, find N random sequences $x_j = \{x_{ij}\}$ of n 1s and n −1s, compute the corresponding sequences $s_j = \{s_{ij}\}$ of partial sums $s_{ij} = x_{1j} + x_{2j} + \cdots + x_{ij}$, and let a, b be the number of positive, nonnegative sequences s_j, respectively. Compute the ratios
   a) $a/C(2n, n)$.
   b) $b/C(2n, n)$.
   c) a/b.

3. Given a positive integer n, find a random sequence x of n 1s and n −1s that has a nonnegative sequence s of partial sums. Using s, produce the corresponding
   a) well-formed sequence of parentheses.
   b) stack permutation.
   c) well-parenthesized product.
   d) full binary tree (graphics).
   e) triangulation of a convex polygon (graphics).

8

Ramsey Numbers

Author: John G. Michaels, Department of Mathematics, State University of New York, College at Brockport.

Prerequisites: The prerequisites for this chapter are the pigeonhole principle and basic concepts of graphs. See, for example, Sections 4.2, 7.2 and 7.3 of *Discrete Mathematics and Its Applications*, Second Edition, by Kenneth H. Rosen.

Introduction

Suppose there are 6 people at a party, where each pair of people are either friends or strangers. We can show that there must be either 3 mutual friends or 3 mutual strangers at the party. To do this, we set up a graph G with 6 vertices (corresponding to the 6 people), where edges represent friendships. We need to show that there must be a triangle (i.e., a simple circuit of length 3) in G or else a triangle in $\overline{G}$, the complement of G.

This problem can be rephrased as the following edge-coloring problem: Show that if every edge of K_6 is colored red or green, then there must be either a red triangle or a green triangle. To see that these two problems are equivalent, take G to be the subgraph of K_6 consisting of the 6 vertices and the red edges; therefore $\overline{G}$ consists of the 6 vertices and the green edges. A red triangle in K_6 corresponds to a set of 3 mutual friends in G, whereas a green triangle corresponds to a set of 3 mutual strangers.

The proof that there is either a red or a green triangle in K_6 is a simple application of the pigeonhole principle. Begin by choosing a vertex v in K_6. We let the edges on v represent pigeons and the colors red and green be the names of two pigeonholes. Since $d(v) = 5$ and each edge on v is either red or green, we have 5 pigeons and 2 pigeonholes. Therefore some pigeonhole holds at least 3 pigeons; that is, there are at least 3 red edges or 3 green edges incident on v. Assuming that v has at least 3 red edges, say $\{v, a\}, \{v, b\}$, and $\{v, c\}$, we examine the edges joining a, b, c. If any of these 3 edges is red, we obtain a red triangle. If none of the 3 edges is red, then we have a green triangle joining a, b, c. (A similar argument works if v has at least 3 green edges.) Thus, we are guaranteed of obtaining a *monochromatic* triangle, that is, a triangle such that all its edges are of the same color.

In this chapter we extend these ideas further, examining questions such as the following. What is the minimum number of people needed at a party in order to guarantee that there are at least 4 mutual friends or 4 mutual strangers? What is the minimum number needed to guarantee that there are 3 mutual friends or 5 mutual strangers? What is the minimum number needed to guarantee that there are 4 mutual close friends, 7 mutual acquaintances who are not close friends, or 9 mutual strangers?

The minimum numbers in problems such as these are called Ramsey numbers, named after Frank Ramsey*, who in 1930 published a paper [8] on set theory that generalized the pigeonhole principle.

Ramsey Numbers

As we saw earlier, no matter how the edges of K_6 are colored red or green, K_6 contains a subgraph K_3 all edges of which are colored red or a subgraph K_3 all edges of which are colored green. That is, K_6 contains either a red K_3 or a green K_3. We say that the integer 6 has the $(3, 3)$-Ramsey property. More generally, we have the following definition.

Definition 1   Let i and j be integers such that $i \geq 2$ and $j \geq 2$. A positive integer m has the (i, j)-*Ramsey property* if K_m contains either a red K_i or a green K_j as a subgraph, no matter how the edges of K_m are colored red or green.   □

---

* See *Discrete Mathematics and Its Applications*, Second Edition, for biographical information on Ramsey.

From the above discussion, we know that 6 has the $(3,3)$-Ramsey property. But is 6 the smallest such number? Suppose we take K_5 and "color" its 10 edges using 1s and 2s, as in Figure 1a.

There are no monochromatic triangles in either Figure 1b or 1c. Therefore this coloring shows that 5 does not have the $(3,3)$-Ramsey property. It is easy to see that no positive integer smaller than 5 has the $(3,3)$-Ramsey property. (See Exercise 3.) Therefore, 6 is the smallest integer with this property, and is called a Ramsey number.

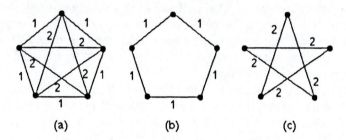

(a)   (b)   (c)

Figure 1. A coloring of K_5.

Definition 2   The *Ramsey number* $R(i,j)$ is the smallest positive integer that has the (i,j)-Ramsey property.   □

For example, $R(3,3) = 6$, since 6 has the $(3,3)$-Ramsey property but no smaller positive integer has this property.

Example 1   Find $R(2,7)$, the smallest positive integer that has the $(2,7)$-Ramsey property.

Solution: We begin by examining the positive integers n such that every coloring of the edges of K_n with red and green results in either a red K_2 (i.e., a red edge) or a green K_7. The number $R(2,7)$ is the smallest positive integer with this property. Consider any coloring of the edges of K_7. Either there is at least one red edge, or else every edge is colored green. If there is a red edge, then we have the desired red K_2. If every edge was colored green, then we have the desired green K_7. Thus 7 has the $(2,7)$-Ramsey property, which says that $R(2,7) \leq 7$.

But $R(2,7) \not< 7$. To see this, consider the coloring of K_6 where each edge is colored red. Then K_6 has neither a red K_2 nor a green K_7, and so 6 does not have the $(2,7)$-Ramsey property.

Therefore $R(2,7) = 7$.   □

The argument in the above example can be generalized by replacing 7 with any integer $k \geq 2$ to obtain:

$$R(2, k) = k.$$

(This is left as Exercise 4.) This example also leads us to make four other observations:

1. For all integers $i \geq 2$ and $j \geq 2$, $R(i, j) = R(j, i)$.

2. If m has the (i, j)-Ramsey property, then so does every integer $n > m$.

3. If m does not have the (i, j)-Ramsey property, then neither does any integer $n < m$.

4. If $i_i \geq i_2$, then $R(i_1, j) \geq R(i_2, j)$.

Proofs of these four facts are left to the reader as Exercises 5-8.

Note that when we try to find $R(i, j)$, we are looking for a red K_i or a green K_j; that is, "red" is associated with the variable i and "green" is associated with the variable j. Likewise, when we try to find $R(j, i)$, "red" is associated with j and "green" with i. Since $R(i, j) = R(j, i)$, we need only look for a monochromatic K_i subgraph or a monochromatic K_j subgraph.

The definition of the Ramsey number $R(i, j)$ requires us to find the *smallest* positive integer with the (i, j)-Ramsey property. But suppose that for some i and j there is *no* positive integer with the (i, j)-Ramsey property? In such a case there would be no Ramsey number $R(i, j)$. This leads us to the question: For every choice of positive integers $i \geq 2$ and $j \geq 2$, is there a Ramsey number $R(i, j)$? The following lemma and theorem provide an affirmative answer to this question.

Lemma 1   If $i \geq 3$ and $j \geq 3$, then

$$R(i, j) \leq R(i, j - 1) + R(i - 1, j). \tag{1}$$

Proof: Let $m = R(i, j - 1) + R(i - 1, j)$. We will show that m has the (i, j)-Ramsey property. Suppose the edges of K_m have been colored red or green and v is a vertex of K_m. Partition the vertex set V into 2 subsets:

$$A = \text{all vertices adjacent to } v \text{ along a red edge}$$
$$B = \text{all vertices adjacent to } v \text{ along a green edge}.$$

Since

$$|A| + |B| = |A \cup B| = m - 1 = R(i, j - 1) + R(i - 1, j) - 1,$$

either $|A| \geq R(i - 1, j)$ or $|B| \geq R(i, j - 1)$. If this were not the case, we would have $|A| < R(i - 1, j)$ and $|B| < R(i, j - 1)$, which would imply that

$$|A \cup B| < R(i - 1, j) + R(i, j - 1) = m - 1.$$

This would contradict the fact that $|A \cup B| = m - 1$.

Consider the case where $|A| \geq R(i - 1, j)$. Now consider the complete subgraph on the vertices in A. This is a subgraph of K_m, which we call $K_{|A|}$. We will show that $K_{|A|}$ contains either a red K_i or a green K_j. Since $|A| \geq R(i-1, j)$, $K_{|A|}$ has either a red K_{i-1} or a green K_j. If we have a red K_{i-1}, we add the red edges joining v to the vertices of K_{i-1} to obtain a red K_i. Thus, $K_{|A|}$, and hence K_m, has either a red K_i or a green K_j. This says that m has the (i, j)-Ramsey property. (The case where $|B| \geq R(i, j - 1)$ is left as Exercise 9.) Therefore, inequality (1) has been proved.   □

This lemma establishes a relationship that Ramsey numbers must satisfy. The following theorem uses mathematical induction together with this relationship to prove the existence of the Ramsey numbers.

Theorem 1   Ramsey's Theorem   If i and j are integers ($i \geq 2$ and $j \geq 2$), then there is a positive integer with the (i, j)-Ramsey property (and hence $R(i, j)$ exists).

Proof: We use (1) and the Principle of Mathematical Induction to prove that for all integers $i \geq 2$ and $j \geq 2$ there is a positive integer with the (i, j)-Ramsey property. Let $P(n)$ be the statement:

$$P(n):\ \text{If } i + j = n, \text{ then there is an integer with the}$$
$$(i, j)\text{-Ramsey property.}$$

The base case is $P(4)$, since the smallest values of i and j under consideration are $i = j = 2$. We know from the comments following Example 1 that there is an integer with the $(2, 2)$-Ramsey property. Therefore $P(4)$ is true.

Now we assume that $P(n)$ is true and show that $P(n + 1)$ is also true. Assume that $i + j = n + 1$. Therefore $i + (j - 1) = n$ and $(i - 1) + j = n$. $P(n)$ states that there are integers with the $(i, j - 1)$-Ramsey property and the $(i - 1, j)$-Ramsey property. Hence the Ramsey numbers $R(i, j - 1)$ and $R(i - 1, j)$ exist. Inequality (1) guarantees that $R(i, j)$ must also exist. Therefore $P(n + 1)$ is also true. The Principle of Mathematical Induction guarantees that $P(n)$ is true for all $i \geq 2$ and $j \geq 2$. This shows that $R(i, j)$ exists if $i \geq 2$ and $j \geq 2$.   ∎

So far we know the values of the following Ramsey numbers:

$$R(2, k) = R(k, 2) = k$$
$$R(3, 3) = 6.$$

If $i \geq 2$ and $j \geq 2$, it rapidly becomes very difficult to find $R(i, j)$ because of the large number of possible edge colorings of the graphs K_n. Hence, it is no surprise that the list of Ramsey numbers whose exact values are known is very short. We will now evaluate some of these.

Example 2   Find $R(3,4)$.

Solution: From Lemma 1 we know that

$$R(3,4) \leq R(3,3) + R(2,4)$$
$$= 6 + 4$$
$$= 10.$$

To determine if $R(3,4) < 10$, we might consider looking at all possible red/green colorings of the edges of K_9. If one of these colorings has no red K_3 or green K_4, we can conclude that $R(3,4) = 10$. However, if every red/green coloring of K_9 produces either a red K_3 or a green K_4, we must then look at colorings of K_8, etc. Examining all possible red/green colorings of the edges of K_9 is not an easy task—K_9 has 36 edges, so initially there would be $2^{36} \approx 69,000,000,000$ colorings to examine.

Fortunately, we can avoid examining the colorings of K_9, because of the following fact:

If $i \geq 3$, $j \geq 3$, and if $R(i, j-1)$ and $R(i-1, j)$ are even,
then $R(i,j) \leq R(i, j-1) + R(i-1, j) - 1.$ (2)

The proof of this fact follows the proof of Lemma 1, and is left as Exercise 10.

Using (2) with $i = 3$ and $j = 4$ yields

$$R(3,4) \leq R(3,3) + R(2,4) - 1$$
$$= 6 + 4 - 1$$
$$= 9$$

and we therefore know that $R(3,4) \leq 9$.

To see that 8 does not have the (3,4)-Ramsey property, consider the coloring of the graph K_8, where the red edges are drawn in Figure 2(a) and the green edges in Figure 2(b).

It is easy to see that there is no triangle in 2(a). In Exercise 11 the reader is asked to check that there is no K_4 in 2(b).

Thus, $R(3,4) = 9$. $\square$

Example 3   Find $R(3,5)$.

Solution: From (1) we know that

$$R(3,5) \leq R(3,4) + R(2,5)$$
$$= 9 + 5$$
$$= 14$$

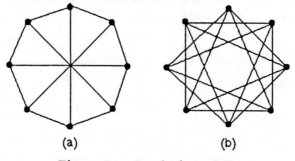

(a)   (b)

Figure 2.   A coloring of K_8.

In fact, $R(3,5) = 14$. To see this, we show that 13 does not have the $(3,5)$-Ramsey property. Draw K_{13} with vertices labeled $1, 2, \ldots, 13$. Color the edge $\{i, j\}$ red if $|i - j| = 1$, 5, 8 or 12, and color the edge green otherwise. We leave it to the reader to verify in Exercise 12 that this graph has no red K_3 or green K_5.   □

There are a few other Ramsey numbers whose values are known exactly. Table 1 lists these numbers and ranges for some of the smaller Ramsey numbers. For example, $R(5,4) = R(4,5)$ is known to be 25, 26, or 27.

i \ j	2	3	4	5	6
2	2				
3	3	6			
4	4	9	18		
5	5	14	25–27	43–52	
6	6	18	34–43	57–94	102-169
7	7	23	≥ 49	≥ 76	
8	8	28	≥ 53	≥ 94	
9	9	36	≥ 69		

Table 1.   Ramsey Numbers $R(i,j)$.

From the remark following Example 1, we know exact values of all Ramsey numbers $R(i,j)$ when $i = 2$ or $j = 2$. Aside from these, only eight other Ramsey numbers have known values. The Ramsey numbers $R(3,3)$, $R(4,3)$, $R(5,3)$, and $R(4,4)$ were found in 1955 by A. M. Gleason and R. E. Greenwood; $R(6,3)$ was found by J. G. Kalbfleisch in 1966; $R(7,3)$ was found by J. E. Graver and J. Yackel in 1968; $R(8,3)$ was found recently by B. McKay and Z. Ke Min; $R(9,3)$ was found by C. M. Grinstead and S. M. Roberts in 1982.

Many upper and lower bounds for Ramsey numbers are known. The following theorem gives one of these.

Theorem 2   If $i \geq 2$ and $j \geq 2$, then $R(i,j) \leq C(i+j-2, i-1)$.

Proof: A proof by induction can be given here, following closely the induction proof given for Theorem 1. This is left as Exercise 14. ∎

It is also known that if $k \geq 2$, then $2^{k/2} \leq R(k,k) \leq 2^{2k-3}$, and if $j \geq 13$, then $R(3,j) \leq C(j,2) - 5$. Proofs of these facts can be found in Tomescu [10].

Generalizations

The Ramsey numbers discussed in the last section represent only one family of Ramsey numbers. In this section we will briefly study some other families of these numbers.

For example, suppose we take K_n and color its edges red, yellow, or green. What is the smallest positive integer n that guarantees that K_n has a subgraph that is a red K_3, a yellow K_3, or a green K_3? We might also think of this problem in terms of friendships rather than colors. A group of n countries each send a diplomat to a meeting. Each pair of countries are friendly toward each other, neutral toward each other, or enemies of each other. What is the minimum number of countries that need to be represented at the meeting in order to guarantee that among the countries represented there will be 3 mutual friends, 3 mutually neutral ones, or 3 mutual enemies? The minimum such number is written $R(3,3,3;2)$. The "2" is written as part of $R(3,3,3;2)$ because edges (i.e., the objects being colored) are determined by 2 vertices. (As we shall see, the 2 can be replaced by a larger positive integer.)

The three 3s can be replaced by any number of positive integers to obtain other families of Ramsey numbers. For example, using the 3 colors red, yellow, and green, $R(5,4,7;2)$ is the smallest positive integer n with the property that if the edges of K_n are colored with the 3 colors, then K_n contains a red K_5, a yellow K_4, or a green K_7.

Definition 3   Suppose $i_1, i_2, \ldots, i_n$ are positive integers, where each $i_j \geq 2$. A positive integer m has the $(i_1, \ldots, i_n; 2)$-*Ramsey property* if, given n colors $1, 2, \ldots, n$, K_m has a subgraph K_{i_j} of color j, for some j, no matter how the edges of K_m are colored with the n colors.

The smallest positive integer with the $(i_i, \ldots, i_n; 2)$-Ramsey property is called the **Ramsey number** $R(i_i, \ldots, i_n; 2)$. □

Note that if $n = 2$, the Ramsey numbers $R(i_1, i_2; 2)$ are the Ramsey numbers $R(i_1, i_2)$ studied in the previous section.

Again we are faced with the question: Do these numbers always exist? That is, for a given list $i_i, \ldots, i_n$, are there positive integers with the $(i_i, \ldots, i_n; 2)$-Ramsey property so that there is a smallest one (i.e., the Ramsey number $R(i_i, \ldots, i_n; 2)$)? The answer is yes, and a proof using the Principle of Mathematical Induction can be found in Graham, Rothschild, and Spencer [6].

Very little is also known about the numbers $R(i_1, \ldots, i_n; 2)$ if $n \geq 3$. However, if $i_j = 2$ for all j, then

$$R(2, \ldots, 2; 2) = 2.$$

This is left as Exercise 15. If each $i_j \geq 3$, the only Ramsey number whose value is known is $R(3, 3, 3; 2)$.

Example 4   Show that $R(3, 3, 3; 2) = 17$.

Solution: Consider any coloring of the edges of K_{17}, using the colors red, yellow, and green. Choose any vertex v. Of the 16 edges incident on v, there is a single color that appears on at least 6 of them, by the Pigeonhole Principle. Suppose this color is red, and that there are 6 red edges joining v to vertices labeled $1, 2, 3, 4, 5, 6$. If one of the edges joining i and j ($1 \leq i \leq 6$, $1 \leq j \leq 6$) is also red, then we have a red K_3. Otherwise, every one of the edges joining i and j is yellow or green. These edges give a graph K_6 colored with 2 colors, and we know that such a graph has a monochromatic K_3 (yellow or green) since $R(3, 3) = 6$. This says that K_{17} must have a K_3 that is red, yellow, or green. Therefore $R(3, 3, 3; 2) \leq 17$.

To see that $R(3, 3, 3; 2) \geq 17$, consult Berge [1, opposite p.420] for a coloring of K_{16} with 3 colors that has no monochromatic triangle.   □

So far we have dealt with Ramsey numbers of the form $R(i_1, \ldots, i_n; 2)$ by looking at them from the standpoint of coloring the edges of the graph K_m with n colors and looking for monochromatic subgraphs K_{i_j}. But there is another way to develop these numbers and further generalize ideas.

Consider the problem in the Introduction—the problem of finding a red or green subgraph K_3 in K_6. Start with K_6 and its vertex set V. Take all 2-element subsets of V (i.e., the edges of K_6) and divide these subsets into 2 collections C_1 and C_2. The number 6 has the $(3, 3)$-Ramsey property if and only if:

(i) There is a 3-element subset of V with all its 2-element subsets in C_1, or

(ii) There is a 3-element subset of V with all its 2-element subsets in C_2.

Thinking of C_1 as the set of edges colored red and C_2 as the set of edges colored green, we see that we have a red triangle if and only if condition (i) is satisfied, and we have a green triangle if and only if condition (ii) is satisfied.

But note that this statement of the Ramsey property does not require us to use a graph. The property is phrased only in terms of a set and properties of a certain collection of its subsets. This notion can be extended to include dividing subsets of size r (rather than 2) into any number of collections (rather than only the two collections C_1 and C_2).

This leads us to the following general definition of the classical Ramsey numbers.

Definition 4   Suppose that $i_1, i_2, \ldots, i_n, r$ are positive integers where $n \geq 2$ and each $i_j \geq r$. A positive integer m has the $(i_1, \ldots, i_n; r)$-*Ramsey property* if the following statement is true:

> If S is a set of size m and the r-element subsets of S are partitioned into n collections $C_1, \ldots, C_n$, then for some j there is a subset of S of size i_j such that each of its r-element subsets belong to C_j.

The **Ramsey number** $R(i_1, \ldots, i_n; r)$ is the smallest positive integer that has the $(i_1, \ldots, i_n; r)$-Ramsey property.   □

In particular, when $r = 2$, we can think of this definition in terms of coloring the edges of K_m with n colors and taking C_j as the set of edges of color j. The numbers i_j give the number of vertices in the monochromatic K_{i_j} subgraphs.

We mention without proof Ramsey's Theorem regarding the existence of these Ramsey numbers. A proof can be found in Graham, Rothschild, and Spencer [6].

Theorem 3 Ramsey's Theorem   If $i_1, \ldots, i_n, r$ are positive integers where $n \geq 2$ and each $i_j \geq r$, the Ramsey number $R(i_1, \ldots, i_n; r)$ exists.   ∎

Earlier in this chapter we displayed the known Ramsey numbers of the form $R(i_1, i_2; 2)$. We also proved that $R(3, 3, 3; 2) = 17$. If $r \geq 3$, very little is known about exact values of the Ramsey numbers. See Exercise 17 for an example of one type of Ramsey number whose exact value is known.

If $r = 1$, the Ramsey numbers $R(i_1, \ldots, i_n; 1)$ are easy to find, since in this case we need only consider the 1-element subsets of S. The following theorem gives a formula for these numbers.

Theorem 4 $R(i_1, \ldots i_n; 1) = i_1 + \ldots i_n - (n-1)$.

Proof: Let $i_1 + \ldots + i_n - (n-1) = m$. We first show that the integer m has the $(i_1, \ldots, i_n; 1)$-Ramsey property.

Take a set S of size m and divide its 1-element subsets into n classes $C_1, \ldots, C_n$. Observe that there must be a subscript j_0 such that $|C_{j_0}| \geq i_{j_0}$. (If $|C_j| < i_j$ for all j, then $|C_j| \leq i_j - 1$. Therefore $m = |C_1| + \ldots + |C_n| \leq (i_1 - 1) + \ldots + (i_n - 1) = i_1 + \cdots + i_n - n = m - 1$, and hence $m \leq m - 1$, which is a contradiction.) If we take any i_{j_0} elements of C_{j_0}, we have a subset of S of size i_{j_0} that has all its 1-element subsets belonging to C_{j_0}. This shows that $R(i_1, \ldots, i_n; 1) \leq i_1 + \cdots + i_n - (n-1)$.

We now show that $m - 1 = i_1 + \cdots + i_n - n$ does not have the $(i_1, \ldots, i_n; 1)$-Ramsey property. Take a set S where $|S| = i_1 + \cdots + i_n - n$. Partition its 1 - element subsets into n classes $C_1, \ldots, C_n$ where $|C_j| = i_j - 1$. With this partition there is no subset of S of size i_j that has all its 1-element subsets belonging to C_j. ∎

Note the particular case of this theorem when $i_1 = \cdots = i_n = 2$:

$$R(2, \ldots, 2; 1) = n + 1.$$

This fact shows how Ramsey theory can be thought of as a generalization of the pigeonhole principle. In the terminology of Ramsey numbers, the fact that $R(2, \ldots, 2; 1) = n + 1$ means that $n + 1$ is the smallest positive integer with the property that if S has size $n + 1$ and the subsets of S are partitioned into n sets $C_1, \ldots, C_n$, then for some j there is a subset of S of size 2 such that each of its elements belong to C_j. Hence, some C_j has at least 2 elements. If we think of a set S of $n + 1$ pigeons and the subset C_j, $(j = 1, \ldots, n)$ as the set of pigeons roosting in pigeonhole j, then some pigeonhole must have at least 2 pigeons in it. Thus, the Ramsey numbers $R(2, \ldots, 2; 1)$ give the smallest number of pigeons that force at least 2 to roost in the same pigeonhole.

Schur's Theorem

Suppose the integers $1, 2, 3, 4, 5$ are each colored red or green. That is, suppose $S = \{1, 2, 3, 4, 5\}$ is partitioned into 2 subsets, R and G, where the integers in R are colored red and the integers in G are colored green. Then it is known that the equation

$$x + y = z$$

has a monochromatic solution. (See Exercise 18.) That is, the equation $x + y = z$ is satisfied for some $x, y, z \in R$ or some $x, y, z \in G$. For example, if $R = \{2, 4, 5\}$

and $G = \{1,3\}$, we have a red solution: $2 + 2 = 4$. Also, if $R = \{2,5\}$ and $G = \{1,3,4\}$, we have a green solution: $1 + 3 = 4$.

However, if $S = \{1,2,3,4\}$, we are not guaranteed a monochromatic solution. To see this, take $R = \{1,4\}$ and $G = \{2,3\}$. The equation $x + y = z$ is not satisfied for any choices of $x, y, z \in R$ or for any choices of $x, y, z \in G$.

The number 5 can be looked on as a "dividing point" here. If $n \geq 5$, then partitioning $\{1,\ldots,n\}$ into red and green sets will always result in a monochromatic solution to $x + y = z$, whereas if $n < 5$, we may fail to have a monochromatic solution. We write

$$S(2) = 5,$$

where the number 2 indicates the fact that we are using 2 colors. The letter "S" is used in honor of I. Schur*, who in 1916 developed this material while studying a problem related to Fermat's Last Theorem ($x^n + y^n = z^n$ has no integer solutions if $n > 2$).

Rather than work with only 2 colors, we can color $\{1,2,\ldots,n\}$ with k colors and look for the minimum value of n, written $S(k)$, that guarantees a monochromatic solution to $x + y = z$.

If $k = 1$, it is easy to see that

$$S(1) = 2.$$

(If $\{1,2\}$ is colored with 1 color, then we have the solution $1+1 = 2$; the smaller set $\{1\}$ yields no solution to $x + y = z$.) If $k = 3$, it is known that

$$S(3) = 14.$$

That is, no matter how the integers in the set $\{1,\ldots,14\}$ are colored with 3 colors, $x + y = z$ will have a monochromatic solution.

It is natural to ask the question: For each positive integer k, is there a number $S(k)$? For example if we wish to use 4 colors, is there a positive integer $S(4)$ such that any coloring of $\{1,\ldots,S(4)\}$ with 4 colors will give a monochromatic solution? The following theorem shows that the numbers $S(k)$ always exist and are bounded above by the family of Ramsey numbers $R(3,\ldots,3;2)$.

Theorem 5   If k is a positive integer, then

$$S(k) \leq R(3,\ldots,3;2)$$

(where there are k 3s in the notation for the Ramsey number).

---

* Issai Schur (1875–1941) was a Russian mathematician who attended schools in Latvia and Germany. Most of his teaching career was spent at the University of Berlin. Forced into retirement by the Nazis in 1935, he eventually emigrated to Palestine where he died two years later. He contributed to many areas of mathematics, and is best known for his work in the area of abstract algebra called the representation theory of groups.

Proof: We will show that if the integers $1, 2, \ldots, R(3, \ldots, 3; 2)$ are colored with k colors, then the equation $x + y = z$ will have a monochromatic solution. (This implies that $S(k) \leq R(3, \ldots, 3; 2)$ since $S(k)$ is the smallest integer with the monochromatic solution property.)

Let $n = R(3, \ldots, 3; 2)$ and color the integers $1, 2, \ldots, n$ with k colors. This gives a partition of $1, 2, \ldots, n$ into k sets, $S_1, S_2, \ldots, S_k$, where integers in the same set have the same color.

Now take the graph K_n, label its vertices $1, 2, \ldots, n$, and label its edges according to the following rule:

$$\text{edge } \{i, j\} \text{ has label } |i - j|$$

This labeling has a special feature: every triangle has two sides with labels whose sum is equal to the label on the third side. (To see this, suppose we have a triangle determined by i_1, i_2, i_3, and assume $i_1 > i_2 > i_3$. The 3 edge labels are $i_1 - i_2$, $i_2 - i_3$, and $i_1 - i_3$, and we have $(i_1 - i_2) + (i_2 - i_3) = (i_1 - i_3)$.)

We will use these labels to color the edges of K_n: use color m on edge $\{i, j\}$ if its label $|i - j| \in S_m$. This gives a coloring of K_n with the k colors used for the elements in the sets $S_1, \ldots, S_k$. Since $n = R(3, \ldots, 3; 2)$, n has the $(3, \ldots, 3; 2)$-Ramsey property, and so there must be a monochromatic triangle in K_n. If its 3 vertices are i_1, i_2, i_3, and if we let $x = i_1 - i_2$, $y = i_2 - i_3$, and $z = i_1 - i_3$, then we have $x + y = z$ where all 3 values have the same color. ∎

Note that the theorem shows only the existence of $S(k)$, by showing that these numbers are bounded above by certain Ramsey numbers. For example, if $k = 3$, the theorem states that

$$S(3) \leq R(3, 3, 3; 2) = 17.$$

Therefore, we know that $x + y = z$ has a monochromatic solution, no matter how the integers $1, \ldots, 17$ are colored with 3 colors. But the theorem does not give the value of the minimum number with this property, $S(3)$, which is known to be 14.

It is natural to ask what happens if we have more than 3 variables in the equation. For an extension to equations of the form $x_1 + \ldots + x_{n-1} = x_n$, see Beutelspacher and Brestovansky [2].

Convex Sets

In this section we will show how Ramsey numbers play a role in constructing convex polygons. A **convex polygon** is a polygon P such that if x and y are points in the interior of P, then the line segment joining x and y lies completely inside P. In Figure 3 the hexagon (6-gon) is convex, whereas the quadrilateral (4-gon) is *concave* (i.e., not convex) since the line segment joining x and y intersects the exterior of the 4-gon.

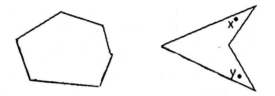

Figure 3.   Two polygons.

If we take $n(\geq 3)$ points in the plane, no 3 of which are collinear, we can always connect then to form an n-gon. But can we guarantee that the n-gon will be convex? (The answer is no, even for 4 points, as shown by the 4-gon in Figure 3.) But suppose we do not select all n points? For example, given 5 points, no 3 of which are collinear, can we always find 4 of the 5 points so that when they are connected we obtain a 4-gon that is convex? Then answer is yes, and is left to the reader as Exercise 19.

In general, suppose we want to guarantee that we can obtain a convex m-gon by connecting m of n given points, no 3 of which are collinear. Is there always an integer n that guarantees a convex m-gon, and, if so, how large must n be? For example, if we want a convex 5-gon, how many points, n, must we start with in order to guarantee that we can obtain a convex 5-gon? The following theorem, proved by Erdös and Szekeres [3] in 1935, shows that Ramsey numbers can be used to find a solution. In fact, it was this paper that provided the impetus for the study of Ramsey numbers and suggested the possibility of its wide applicability in mathematics.

Theorem 6   Suppose m is a positive integer and there are n given points, no 3 of which are collinear. If $n \geq R(m, 5; 4)$, then a convex m-gon can be obtained from m of the n points.

Proof: Suppose $n \geq R(m, 5; 4)$ and S is a set of n points in the plane, with no 3 points collinear. Since n has the $(m, 5; 4)$-Ramsey property, no matter how we divide the 4-element subsets of S into 2 collections C_1 and C_2, either
(i) There is a subset of S of size m with all its 4-element subsets in C_1, or
(ii) There is a subset of S of size 5 with all its 4-element subsets in C_2.

We will take C_1 to be the collection of all subsets of S of size 4 where the 4-gon determined by the points is convex and take C_2 to be the collection of all subsets of S of size 4 where the 4-gons are concave.

But note that alternative (ii) cannot happen. That is, it is impossible to have 5 points in the plane that give rise only to concave 4-gons. (This is Exercise 19.) Therefore, we are guaranteed of having a subset $A \subseteq S$ where $|A| = m$ and all 4-gons determined by A are convex.

We will now show that the m points of A determine a convex m-gon. Let k be the largest positive integer such that k of the m points form a convex k-gon. Suppose G is a convex m-gon determined by k of the points of A. If $k < m$, then at least one of the elements of A, say a_1, lies inside the convex k-gon G. Therefore there are 3 vertices of G, say a_2, a_3, a_4, such that a_1 lies inside the triangle determined by these vertices. Hence, the set $\{a_1, a_2, a_3, a_4\}$ determines a concave 4-gon, contradicting the property of A that all its 4-gons are convex. Therefore $k \not< m$, and we must have $k = m$. This says that the m points of A determine the desired convex m-gon. ∎

The Ramsey number $R(m, 5; 4)$ in Theorem 7 gives a set of values for n that guarantee the existence of a convex m-gon. But it remains an unsolved problem to find the smallest integer x (which depends on m) such that if $n \geq x$, then a convex m-gon can be obtained from m of the n points.

Graph Ramsey Numbers

So far, we have examined colorings of K_m and looked for monochromatic K_i subgraphs. But suppose we don't look for complete subgraphs K_i, but rather try to find other subgraphs, such as cycle graphs (C_i), wheels (W_i), complete bipartite graphs ($K_{i,j}$), or trees? Problems such as these give rise to other families of Ramsey numbers, called *graph Ramsey numbers*.

Definition 5   Suppose $G_1, \ldots, G_n$ are graphs, each with at least one edge. An integer m has the $(G_1, \ldots, G_n)$-*Ramsey property* if every coloring of the edges of K_m with the n colors $1, 2, \ldots n$ yields a subgraph G_j of color j, for some j.

The *graph Ramsey number* $R(G_1, \ldots, G_n)$ is the smallest positive integer with the $(G_1, \ldots, G_n)$-Ramsey property. □

We note that, just as in the case of the classical Ramsey numbers discussed earlier, the "order" of particular colors does not matter. That is, if every coloring of K_m has a red G_1 or a green G_2, then every coloring of K_m has a green G_1 or a red G_2, and vice versa. Therefore, $R(G_1, G_2) = R(G_2, G_1)$, and the problem can be phrased as one of finding a monochromatic G_1 or G_2 (rather than a G_1 or G_2 of a specified color).

Example 5   Some graph Ramsey numbers are easy to determine because they are the classical Ramsey numbers in disguise.

Suppose we want to find $R(W_3, C_3)$, where W_3 is the wheel with 3 spokes and C_3 is the cycle of length 3. Since W_3 is the graph K_4 and C_3 is K_3, we have

$$R(W_3, C_3) = R(K_4, K_3) = R(4, 3) = 9.$$

Similarly, to find $R(K_{1,1}, W_3)$, we must be able to guarantee either a red $K_{1,1}$ (i.e., a red edge) or a green W_3. Therefore,

$$R(K_{1,1}, W_3) = R(K_2, K_4) = 4.$$

The graph Ramsey numbers always exist, and are bounded above by related classical Ramsey numbers. To see this, suppose we wish to prove the existence of $R(G_1, \ldots, G_n)$ where each graph G_j has i_j vertices. If we let $m = R(i_1, \ldots, i_n; 2)$, then Theorem 4 guarantees that every coloring of K_m with the n colors $1, 2, \ldots, n$ yields a subgraph K_{i_j} of color j, for some j. But G_j is a subgraph of K_{i_j}, and hence we obtain a subgraph G_j of K_m that has color j. Therefore $R(G_1, \ldots, G_n)$ is bounded above by $R(i_1, \ldots, i_n; 2)$. We state this as the following theorem.

Theorem 7   For $j = 1, \ldots, n$, suppose that G_j is a graph with i_j vertices (where $i_j \geq 2$). Then the graph Ramsey number $R(G_1, \ldots, G_n)$ exists, and

$$R(G_1, \ldots, G_n) \leq R(i_1, \ldots, i_n; 2). \qquad \blacksquare$$

This area of Ramsey theory has been a focus of much activity by many mathematicians, including Erdös and Graham*, during the last twenty years. See, for example Gardner [5] and Graham, Rothschild, and Spencer [6].

The case where a monochromatic K_i subgraph is "almost" obtained has also been studied. That is, rather than looking for the monochromatic K_i subgraphs (which is done when we try to find the classical Ramsey numbers $R(i, j)$), we look for monochromatic subgraphs $K_i - e$, where $K_i - e$ is the graph K_i with any one edge removed. The following example gives one of these numbers.

---

* Ronald L. Graham (1935–) was born in Taft, California, and received his bachelor's degree from the University of Alaska while in the Air Force. He received his Ph.D. from Berkeley (at which time he was also a member of a trampoline group) and then went to work at Bell Laboratories. At Bell Labs he has headed the Mathematical Studies Center and is currently Adjunct Director of the Research Information Sciences Division. His research work has been in the area of combinatorial mathematics, with many contributions in the field of Ramsey Theory. For his work in this area, in 1972 he was named a corecipient of the Polya Prize, given by the Society for Industrial and Applied Mathematics. He has also earned acclaim for his skill as a juggler, and has been past president of the International Jugglers Association.

Example 6   Prove that $R(K_3 - e, K_3 - e) = 3$.

Solution: First note that $K_3 - e$ is the graph on 3 vertices consisting of 2 edges. No matter how the 3 edges of K_3 are colored red or green, there are at least 2 of the same color, thereby giving the monochromatic subgraph $K_3 - e$. Therefore $R(K_3 - e, K_3 - e) \leq 3$. It is easy to see that $R(K_3 - e, K_3 - e) > 2$, since we can take K_2 and color one edge red and the other green. Therefore

$$R(K_3 - e, K_3 - e) = 3. \qquad \square$$

It is also known that

$$R(K_4 - e, K_4 - e) = 10$$
$$R(K_5 - e, K_5 - e) = 22$$
$$42 \leq R(K_6 - e, K_6 - e) \leq 86$$
$$R(K_4 - e, K_5 - e) = 13$$
$$R(K_4 - e, K_6 - e) = 17$$
$$R(K_4 - e, K_7 - e) = 28.$$

For more information on these numbers, the reader is referred to Faudree, Rousseau, and Schelp [4] and Radziszowski [7]. The last two numbers in this list were found by J. McNamara (personal communication, August 14, 1990).

Suggested Readings

1. C. Berge, *Graphs and Hypergraphs*, American Elsevier, New York, 1973.

2. A. Beutelspacher and W. Brestovansky, "Combinatorial Theory," Proceedings, *Lecture Notes in Mathematics*, Vol. 969, 1982, Springer-Verlag, Berlin, pp. 30–38.

3. P. Erdös and G. Szekeres, "A Combinatorial Problem in Geometry," *Compositio Mathematica*, Vol. 2, 1935, pp. 463–470.

4. R. Faudree, C. Rousseau, and R. Schelp, "Studies Related to the Ramsey Number $R(K_5 - e)$," in *Graph Theory and Its Application to Algorithms and Computer Science*, ed. Y. Alavi, 1985.

5. M. Gardner, "Mathematical Games," *Scientific American*, Vol. 235, No. 5, 1977, pp. 18–28.

6. R. Graham, B. Rothschild, and J. Spencer, *Ramsey Theory*, Wiley, New York, 1980.

7. S. Radziszowski, "Small Ramsey Numbers", unpublished.

8. F. Ramsey, "On a Problem of Formal Logic," *Proceedings of the London Mathematical Society*, Vol. 30, 1930, pp. 264–286.

9. F. S. Roberts, *Applied Combinatorics*, Prentice-Hall, Englewood Cliffs, N. J., 1984.

10. I. Tomescu, *Problems in Combinatorics and Graph Theory*, translated by R. Melter, Wiley, New York, 1985.

Exercises

1. Prove that $R(2,3) = 3$, by showing that every coloring of the edges of K_3 with red and green gives either a red K_2 or a green K_3, and then showing that K_2 does not have this property.

2. Prove that $R(3,4) > 6$ by finding a coloring of the edges of K_6 that has no red K_3 or green K_4.

3. Prove that if $0 < n < 5$, then n does not have the $(3,3)$-Ramsey property.

4. Prove that $R(2,k) = k$ for all integers $k \geq 2$.

5. Prove that $R(i,j) = R(j,i)$ for all integers $i \geq 2$, $j \geq 2$.

6. Suppose that m has the (i,j)-Ramsey property and $n > m$. Prove that n has the (i,j)-Ramsey property.

7. Suppose that m does not have the (i,j)-Ramsey property and $n < m$. Prove that n does not have the (i,j)-Ramsey property.

8. Prove that $R(i_1,j) \geq R(i_2,j)$ if $i_1 \geq i_2$.

9. In the proof of Lemma 1, prove that if $|B| \geq R(i, j-1)$, then m has the (i,j)-Ramsey property.

⋆10. Suppose $i \geq 3$, $j \geq 3$, and $R(i, j-1)$ and $R(i-1, j)$ are even integers. Prove that $R(i,j) \leq R(i, j-1) + R(i-1, j) - 1$. (*Hint:* Follow the proof of Lemma 1, choosing the vertex v so that it has even degree.)

11. Prove that the graph in Figure 2(b) does not contain K_4 as a subgraph.

⋆12. Draw K_{13} and color its edges red and green according to the rule in Example 3. Then prove that the graph has no red K_3 or green K_5.

13. Use inequality (1) of Lemma 1 to prove that $R(4,4) \leq 18$. (*Note:* Roberts [9, p.330] contains a coloring of K_{17} that contains no monochromatic K_4. This proves that $R(4,4) = 18$.)

14. Prove that if G has nine vertices, then either G has a K_4 subgraph or $\overline{G}$ has a K_3 subgraph.

15. Prove Theorem 3.

⋆16. Suppose $i_1 = \cdots = i_n = 2$. Prove that $R(i_1, \ldots, i_n; 2) = 2$, for all $n \geq 2$.

⋆17. Prove that $R(7, 3, 3, 3, 3; 3) = 7$. (*Note:* This example can be generalized to $R(m, r, r, \ldots, r; r) = m$ if $m \geq r$).

18. Prove that $S(2) = 5$ by showing that $x + y = z$ has a monochromatic solution no matter how $1, 2, 3, 4, 5$ are colored with two colors.

⋆19. Prove that $S(3) > 13$ by showing that there is a coloring of $1, \ldots, 13$ with three colors such that the equation $x + y = z$ has no monochromatic solution.

⋆20. Prove that for every five points in the plane (where no three are collinear), four of the five points can be connected to form a convex 4-gon.

21. Consider the following game for two players, A and B. The game begins by drawing six dots in a circle. Player A connects two of the dots with a red line. Player B then connects two of the dots with a green line. The player who completes a triangle of one color wins.

    a) Prove that this game cannot end in a draw.

    b) Prove that this game can end in a draw if only five dots are used.

    c) Suppose the game is played with six dots, but the player who completes a triangle of one color loses. Prove that the game cannot end in a draw.

22. Suppose the game in Exercise 20 is modified for three players, where the third player uses the color blue.

    a) Prove that the game can end in a draw if 16 points are used.

    b) Prove that there must be a winner if 17 points are used.

23. Suppose the game of Exercise 20 is played by two players with 54 dots, and the winner is the first player to complete a K_5 of one color. If the game is played and happens to end in a tie, what conclusion about a Ramsey number can be drawn?

24. Verify that $R(K_{1,1}, K_{1,3}) = 4$.

Computer Projects

1. Write a computer program that proves that $R(3, 3) \leq 6$, by examining all colorings of the edges of K_6 and showing that a red K_3 or a green K_3 is always obtained.

2. Write a computer program that checks all edge-colorings of K_5 and determines the number of colorings that contain neither a red K_3 nor a green K_3.

3. Write a computer program that finds all colorings of $\{1, \ldots, 13\}$ with three colors such the the equation $x + y = z$ has no monochromatic solution.

9

Arrangements with Forbidden Positions

Author: John G. Michaels, Department of Mathematics, State University of New York, College at Brockport.

Prerequisites: The prerequisites for this chapter are basic counting techniques and the inclusion-exclusion principle. See, for example, Sections 4.1, 4.3, 5.4, and 5.5 of *Discrete Mathematics and Its Applications*, Second Edition, by Kenneth H. Rosen.

Introduction

In this chapter we will discuss the problem of counting arrangements of objects where there are restrictions in some of the positions in which they can be placed. For example, we may need to match applicants to jobs, where some of the applicants cannot hold certain jobs; or we may wish to pair up players to form two-person teams, but some of the players cannot be paired up with some of the other players.

Problems such as these, where we want to find the number of arrangements with "forbidden" positions, have a long history. They can be traced back to the

early eighteenth century when the French mathematician Pierre de Montmort*
studied the *problème des rencontres* (the matching problem). In this problem
an urn contains n balls, numbered $1, 2, \ldots, n$, which are drawn out one at a
time. de Montmort wanted to find the probability that there are no matches
in this process; that is, that ball i is not the ith ball drawn. This problem is
really one of counting *derangements* — permutations of a set where no element
is left in its own position. (The formula for D_n, the number of derangements
of n objects, can be found in Section 5.5 of *Discrete Mathematics and Its
Applications*, Second Edition, by Rosen.)

Another problem of arrangements, called the *problème des ménages* (the
problem of the households), asks for the number of ways to arrange n couples around a table so that the sexes alternate and no husband and wife are
seated together. This problem was solved in 1891 by E. Lucas**. We will solve
problems such as these by defining a polynomial called a *rook polynomial* and
showing how to use this to count arrangements.

Arrangements with Forbidden Positions

Example 1   Suppose an office manager places an ad for some part-time
help: a keyboard operator (K), a file clerk (F), a stenographer (S), a delivery
person (D), and someone to work in the warehouse (W). Five people answer
the newspaper ad and are interviewed for the jobs. Figure 1 shows which jobs
each of the five applicants (1, 2, 3, 4, and 5) is qualified to handle.

Each square in this figure is either shaded or unshaded. A shaded square
represents a "forbidden position"; that is, the person cannot perform that job.
An unshaded square represents an "allowable position". For example, Appli-
cant 1 cannot hold the job of stenographer, but can hold any of the other jobs.
In how many ways can the office manager place the five applicants in jobs for

---

* Pierre-Rémond de Montmort (1678–1719) was born into the French nobility,
received his father's large fortune at age 22, studied philosophy and mathematics
with Father Nicholas de Malebranche, and held the position of canon at Notre-Dame.
He married and began his study of probability, possibly because of his contacts with
the Bernoulli family. In 1708 he published his *Essai d'Analyse sur les Jeux de Hasard*.
One of the games studied in this work was the matching game treize. The significance
of his contributions in mathematics lies in his use of algebraic methods to study games
of chance.

** Edouard Lucas (1842–1891) was a French number theorist. In 1876 he proved
that the Mersenne number $M_{67} = 2^{67} - 1$ was not prime. In that year he also
proved that $M_{127} = 2^{127} - 1$ was prime; for 75 years this was the largest number
proven to be prime. Lucas attached the name "Fibonacci" to the Fibonacci sequence
$1, 1, 2, 3, 5, 8, \ldots$ and studied the closely-related Lucas sequence, $1, 3, 4, 7, 11, 18, \ldots$.

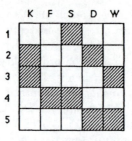

Figure 1.   Job applicants and possible jobs.

which they are qualified?

Solution: A matching of the applicants with the jobs is called an **arrangement with forbidden positions**. Two possible job assignments are:

1–keyboard, 2–stenographer, 3–delivery, 4–warehouse, 5–file clerk,

1–warehouse, 2–stenographer, 3–file clerk, 4–delivery, 5–keyboard.

We can think of Figure 1 as a 5×5 chessboard with nine squares removed. A **rook** is a chess piece that moves horizontally or vertically and can take (or capture) a piece if that piece rests on a square in the same row or column as the rook (assuming that there are no intervening pieces). For example, a rook on square $(2, F)$ can capture an opponent's piece on any of the squares in row 2 or column F, but cannot capture a piece on square $(1, K)$. A matching of applicants to jobs corresponds to a placing of five rooks on the unshaded squares so that no rook can capture any other rook. These are called "nontaking" rooks. Thus, the number of acceptable job assignments is equal to the number of ways of placing five nontaking rooks on this chessboard so that none of the rooks is in a forbidden position.

The key to determining this number of arrangements is the inclusion-exclusion principle. To set up the problem so that we can use the inclusion-exclusion principle, we let

$$A_i = \text{the set of all arrangements of 5 nontaking rooks}$$
$$\text{with the rook in row } i \text{ in a forbidden square,}$$

for $i = 1, 2, 3, 4, 5$.

If we let U be the set of all possible job assignments, then the solution to our problem is $|U - (A_1 \cup A_2 \cup A_3 \cup A_4 \cup A_5)|$. Applying the inclusion-exclusion principle to $|A_1 \cup \cdots \cup A_5|$ yields

$$|A_1 \cup \cdots \cup A_5| = \sum |A_i| - \sum |A_i \cap A_j| + \sum |A_i \cap A_j \cap A_k| \qquad (1)$$
$$- \sum |A_i \cap A_j \cap A_k \cap A_l| + |A_1 \cap A_2 \cap A_3 \cap A_4 \cap A_5|,$$

where we sum over the appropriate sets of subscripts.

The problem of placing nontaking rooks on allowable squares has now been reduced to a series of problems of counting the number of ways of placing nontaking rooks on forbidden squares. We need to determine the size of each of the 31 sets on the right side of (1). To simplify the solution, we introduce some notation. Let

$$r_i = \text{the number of ways of placing } i \text{ nontaking rooks}$$
$$\text{on forbidden squares of a board.}$$

If we need to emphasize the fact that we are working with a particular board B, we will write $r_i(B)$ instead or r_i.

Each of the five expressions on the right side can be written in terms of r_i, for $i = 1, 2, 3, 4, 5$. The number $|A_i|$ counts the number of ways of placing 5 nontaking rooks, with the rook in row i on a forbidden square. For example, $|A_3| = 2 \cdot 4!$ since there are two ways to place a rook on a forbidden square of row 3 and 4! ways to place four other nontaking rooks. Therefore $\sum |A_i| = r_1 \cdot 4!$. Similar reasoning applies to $\sum |A_i \cap A_j| = r_2 \cdot 3!$, $\sum |A_i \cap A_j \cap A_k| = r_3 \cdot 2!$, $\sum |A_i \cap A_j \cap A_k \cap A_l| = r_4 \cdot 1!$, and $|A_1 \cap \cdots \cap A_5| = r_5 \cdot 0!$. Making these substitutions allows us to rewrite (1) as

$$|A_1 \cup \cdots \cup A_5| = r_1 \cdot 4! - r_2 \cdot 3! + r_3 \cdot 2! - r_4 \cdot 1! + r_5 \cdot 0!.$$

Hence, the solution to our problem can be written as

$$5! - (r_1 \cdot 4! - r_2 \cdot 3! + r_3 \cdot 2! - r_4 \cdot 1! + r_5 \cdot 0!). \tag{2}$$

It is easy to see that $r_1 = 9$, since there are nine ways to place a rook on a forbidden square. It is also not difficult to see that $r_2 = 28$ by counting the 28 ways to place two nontaking rooks on forbidden squares. However the problems grow increasingly more difficult when we try to find the coefficients r_3, r_4, and r_5. This leads us to look for techniques to help simplify the counting process.

Our technique for simplification is one that is often used in problems of counting — relate the given problem to a series of smaller problems, each of which is easier to solve. We begin by taking the given chessboard and changing the order of the rows and the order of the columns to obtain the board B in Figure 2.

With this rearrangement, the original board B of forbidden squares can be broken into two disjoint subboards, B_1 and B_2, shown in Figure 2. (We say that two boards are *disjoint* if they have no rows or columns in common.) The problem of computing the right side of (1) by placing nontaking rooks on forbidden squares of B is reduced to two smaller problems: placing nontaking rooks on the forbidden squares of B_1 and placing nontaking rooks on the forbidden squares of B_2.

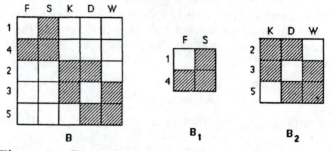

Figure 2.   Rearrangement of board of Figure 1, and two disjoint subboards.

For example, to find $r_1(B)$ either we place 0 rooks on B_1 and 1 on B_2, or else we place 1 rook on B_1 and 0 on B_2. That is,

$$r_1(B) = r_0(B_1) \cdot r_1(B_2) + r_1(B_1) \cdot r_0(B_2)$$
$$= 1 \cdot 6 + 3 \cdot 1 = 9.$$

To find $r_2(B)$, we observe that placing two nontaking rooks on the forbidden squares of B gives us three cases to consider: place 0 on B_1 and 2 on B_2, place 1 on B_1 and 1 on B_2, or place 2 on B_1 and 0 on B_2. That is,

$$r_2(B) = r_0(B_1) \cdot r_2(B_2) + r_1(B_1) \cdot r_1(B_2) + r_2(B_1) \cdot r_0(B_2)$$
$$= 1 \cdot 9 + 3 \cdot 6 + 1 \cdot 1 = 28.$$

Similar reasoning can be used to show that:

$$r_3(B) = \sum_{i=0}^{3} r_i(B_1) \cdot r_{3-i}(B_2)$$
$$= 1 \cdot 2 + 3 \cdot 9 + 1 \cdot 6 + 0 \cdot 1 = 35,$$

$$r_4(B) = \sum_{i=0}^{4} r_i(B_1) \cdot r_{4-i}(B_2)$$
$$= 1 \cdot 0 + 3 \cdot 2 + 1 \cdot 9 + 0 \cdot 6 + 0 \cdot 1 = 15,$$

$$r_5(B) = \sum_{i=0}^{5} r_i(B_1) \cdot r_{5-i}(B_2)$$
$$= 1 \cdot 0 + 3 \cdot 0 + 1 \cdot 2 + 0 \cdot 9 + 0 \cdot 6 + 0 \cdot 1 = 2.$$

Substituting the values of $r_i(B)$ into (2) yields the solution of the original problem:

$$5! - (r_1 \cdot 4! - r_2 \cdot 3! + r_3 \cdot 2! - r_4 \cdot 1! + r_5 \cdot 0!)$$
$$= 5! - (9 \cdot 4! - 28 \cdot 3! + 35 \cdot 2! - 15 \cdot 1! + 2 \cdot 0!)$$
$$= 15.$$

Hence the original job assignment problem can be done in 15 ways. $\qquad\square$

Rook Polynomials

The numbers $r_0(B) = 1, r_1(B) = 9, r_2(B) = 28, r_3(B) = 35, r_4(B) = 15$, and $r_5(B) = 2$ in Example 1 can be stored as coefficients of a polynomial:

$$1 + 9x + 28x^2 + 35x^3 + 15x^4 + 2x^5.$$

More generally, we have the following.

Definition 1   If B is any board, the *rook polynomial* for B, written $R(x, B)$, is the polynomial of the form

$$R(x, B) = r_0(B) + r_1(B)x + r_2(B)x^2 + \cdots + r_n(B)x^n$$

where $r_i(B) = $ the number of ways of placing i nontaking rooks on forbidden squares of the board. $\qquad\square$

The rook polynomial is not only a convenient bookkeeping device for storing the coefficients $r_i(B)$, but the algebraic properties of polynomials can also be used to help solve problems of counting arrangements.

In the previous example the coefficients were found by breaking board B into 2 disjoint subboards B_1 and B_2. Each of these subboards has its own rook polynomial:

$$R(x, B_1) = 1 + 3x + x^2, \qquad R(x, B_2) = 1 + 6x + 9x^2 + 2x^3.$$

(The reader is asked to verify this in Exercise 1.) If we multiply these polynomials, we obtain

$$
\begin{aligned}
R(x, B_1) \cdot R(x, B_2) &= (1 + 3x + x^2)(1 + 6x + 9x^2 + 2x^3) \\
&= (1 \cdot 1) + (1 \cdot 6 + 3 \cdot 1)x + (1 \cdot 9 + 3 \cdot 6 + 1 \cdot 1)x^2 \\
&\quad + (1 \cdot 2 + 3 \cdot 9 + 1 \cdot 6)x^3 + (3 \cdot 2 + 1 \cdot 9)x^4 + (1 \cdot 2)x^5 \\
&= 1 + 9x + 28x^2 + 35x^3 + 15x^4 + 2x^5 \\
&= R(x, B).
\end{aligned}
$$

Thus, the rook polynomial for B is the product of the rook polynomials for the subboards B_1 and B_2. The fact that a similar result is always true is stated in Theorem 1.

Theorem 1   If a board B is broken into 2 disjoint subboards B_1 and B_2, then $R(x, B) = R(x, B_1) \cdot R(x, B_2)$.

Proof: We will prove that the 2 polynomials, $R(x, B)$ and $R(x, B_1) \cdot R(x, B_2)$, are equal. To do this, we will show that, for each i, the x^i term of $R(x, B)$ is equal to the x^i term of the product $R(x, B_1) \cdot R(x, B_2)$. To see that this is always true, consider the product of the two rook polynomials

$$R(x, B_1) \cdot R(x, B_2) = (r_0(B_1) + r_1(B_1)x + \cdots + r_m(B_1)x^m)$$
$$\cdot (r_0(B_2) + r_1(B_2)x + \cdots + r_n(B_2)x^n).$$

Multiplying these two polynomials and combining like terms yields the x^i term

$$(r_0(B_1) \cdot r_i(B_2) + r_1(B_1) \cdot r_{i-1}(B_2) + \cdots + r_i(B_1) \cdot r_0(B_2))x^i.$$

This sum gives the number of ways of placing i nontaking rooks on B, broken down into $i + 1$ cases according to the number of rooks on B_1 and the number of rooks on B_2. Therefore this coefficient is equal to $r_i(B)$, which yields the term $r_i(B)x^i$ of $R(x, B)$. Since the corresponding terms of $R(x, B_1) \cdot R(x, B_2)$ and $R(x, B)$ are equal, we have $R(x, B) = R(x, B_1) \cdot R(x, B_2)$.   ∎

The following example illustrates the technique of this theorem.

Example 2   A woman on a sales trip brought four skirts (blue, brown, gray plaid, green stripe) and five blouses (yellow, pink, white, tan, and blue). Some of the skirts cannot be worn with some of the blouses, as shown by the shaded squares in Figure 3. In how many ways can she make four outfits by pairing the four skirts with four of the five blouses?

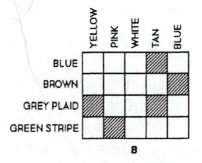

Figure 3.   **Possible skirt and blouse outfits.**

Solution: (Note that in this example we are matching a set of four objects into a set of five objects. We will find the rook polynomial for the board B and then use the inclusion-exclusion principle to finish the counting process. Since the board is not square, we will need to suitably adjust our counting when we use the inclusion-exclusion principle.)

We observe that this board B of forbidden positions can be broken into two disjoint subboards B_1 and B_2, as in Figure 4.

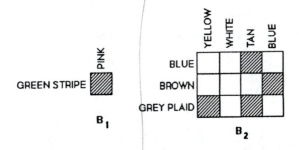

Figure 4.   Disjoint subboards for the board of Figure 3.

It is not difficult to compute the rook polynomials for each of these boards:

$$R(x, B_1) = 1 + x$$
$$R(x, B_2) = 1 + 4x + 4x^2 + x^3.$$

(This is left as Exercise 2.) By Theorem 1,

$$R(x, B) = R(x, B_1) \cdot R(x, B_2)$$
$$= (1 + x)(1 + 4x + 4x^2 + x^3)$$
$$= 1 + 5x + 8x^2 + 5x^3 + x^4.$$

Therefore $r_0 = 1$, $r_1 = 5$, $r_2 = 8$, $r_3 = 5$, $r_4 = 1$. Now that we know the number of ways to place nontaking rooks on forbidden squares, we use the inclusion-exclusion principle to obtain the final answer:

$$|U - (A_1 \cup \cdots \cup A_4)| = |U| - |A_1 \cup \cdots \cup A_4|$$
$$= |U| - \left(\sum |A_i| - \sum |A_i \cap A_j| \right.$$
$$\left. + \sum |A_i \cap A_j \cap A_k| - |A_1 \cap A_2 \cap A_3 \cap A_4| \right)$$
$$= 5 \cdot 4 \cdot 3 \cdot 2 - \left(5(4 \cdot 3 \cdot 2) - 8(3 \cdot 2) + 5(2) - 1(1)\right)$$
$$= 39.$$

(Note that $|U| = 5 \cdot 4 \cdot 3 \cdot 2$ since $|U|$ is equal to the number of ways to place four nontaking rooks on the 4×5 board. Also, $\sum |A_i| = 5(4 \cdot 3 \cdot 2)$ since $r_1 = 5$

and there are $4 \cdot 3 \cdot 2$ ways to place the three other nontaking rooks in three of the other four columns.)   □

The following theorem summarizes the technique of using a rook polynomial together with the inclusion-exclusion principle to count arrangements with forbidden positions.

Theorem 2   The number of ways to arrange n objects among m positions (where $m \geq n$) is equal to

$$P(m,n)\big[r_1(B) \cdot P(m-1, n-1) - r_2(B) \cdot P(m-2, n-2) + \cdots$$

$$+ (-1)^{n+1} r_n(B) \cdot P(m-n, 0)\big]$$

where the numbers $r_i(B)$ are the coefficients of the rook polynomial for the board of forbidden positions.

In particular, if $m = n$, the number of arrangements is

$$n! - \big[r_1(B) \cdot (n-1)! - r_2(B) \cdot (n-2)! + \cdots + (-1)^{n+1} r_n(B) \cdot 0!\big]. \quad ■$$

Example 3   Problème des rencontres   An urn contains n balls, numbered $1, 2, \ldots, n$. The balls are drawn out one at a time and placed in a tray that has positions marked $1, 2, \ldots, n$, with the ball drawn first placed in position 1, the ball drawn second placed in position 2, etc. A *rencontre*, or match, occurs when ball i happens to be placed in position i. In how many ways can the balls be drawn from the urn so that there are no matches?

Solution: We need to find D_n = the number of derangements of $1, 2, \ldots, n$. We will do this by using rook polynomials. Since a match occurs when ball i is in position i, we shade the square (i, i), for $i = 1, 2, \ldots, n$, of board B, as in Figure 5.

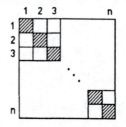

Figure 5.   An $n \times n$ board.

Board B can be broken into n disjoint subboards $B_1, B_2, \ldots, B_n$, each consisting of the single square (i, i).

Each subboard has the rook polynomial $R(x, B_i) = 1 + x$. Theorem 1 applies here (using n instead of 2), and we have

$$R(x, B) = R(x, B_1) \cdot R(x, B_2) \ldots R(x, B_n)$$
$$= (1 + x)(1 + x) \ldots (1 + x)$$
$$= (1 + x)^n$$
$$= C(n, 0) + C(n, 1)x + C(n, 2)x^2 + \cdots + C(n, n)x^n$$

using the Binomial Theorem at the last step to expand $(1 + x)^n$. Therefore, by Theorem 2, the number of arrangements with no matches is equal to

$$n! - \left[C(n, 1)(n - 1)! - C(n, 2)(n - 2)! + \cdots + (-1)^{n+1}C(n, n)0! \right]$$

$$= n! - n! + \frac{n!}{2!} - \frac{n!}{3!} + \cdots + (-1)^n \frac{n!}{n!}$$
$$= n!(\frac{1}{2!} - \frac{1}{3!} + \cdots + (-1)^n \frac{1}{n!}). \qquad \square$$

The method of simplifying the counting process by breaking a chessboard into two or more disjoint subboards works well when it can be done, as in Examples 2 and 3. But suppose it is impossible to break up a given board? The following example illustrates how to handle such a problem.

Example 4   Suppose a person has four gifts (1, 2, 3, 4) to give to four people — Kathy (K), Fred (F), Dave (D), and Wendy (W). The shaded squares in Figure 6 show which gifts cannot be given to the various people. Assuming that each person is to receive a gift, find the number of ways the four gifts can be given to the four people.

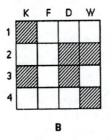

Figure 6.   Possible distributions of gifts.

Solution: In this case it is not possible to break the board into two distinct subboards. (To see why, consider row 1. If square $(1, K)$ is in a subboard B_1, this would force the forbidden square $(3, K)$ to also be in board B_1. This forces the forbidden square $(3, D)$ to be in B_1. This forces the forbidden squares in row 2 to be in B_1, which in turn forces square $(4, W)$ to be in B_1. Therefore B_1 is the entire board B and we have not simplified the problem.)

To solve a problem involving such a board, we simplify the problem by examining cases. We want to find the rook polynomial $R(x, B)$. To find $r_i(B)$ we begin by choosing a forbidden square, such as $(3, K)$. Either we place a rook on this square (and hence no other rook in row 3 or column K) or else we do not place a rook on this square. In either case we are left with smaller boards to consider.

If we place a rook on square $(3, K)$, then the remaining $i - 1$ rooks must be placed on forbidden squares of the board B' in Figure 7. This can be done in $r_{i-1}(B')$ ways. If we do not place a rook on square $(3, K)$, then the i rooks must all be placed on forbidden squares of the board B'' in Figure 7. This can be done in $r_i(B'')$ ways.

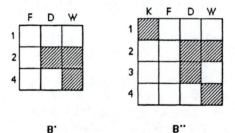

Figure 7.   Subboards of the board of Figure 6.

Since these two cases exhaust all possibilities, we have

$$r_i(B) = r_{i-1}(B') + r_i(B''). \tag{3}$$

This recurrence relation can be used to build the rook polynomial for B. Since $r_i(B)$ is to be the coefficient of x^i in the rook polynomial for B, multiply equation (3) by x^i to obtain

$$r_i(B)x^i = r_{i-1}(B')x^i + r_i(B'')x^i. \tag{4}$$

Summing equations (4) with $i = 1, 2, 3, 4$ gives

$$\sum_{i=1}^{4} r_i(B)x^i = \sum_{i=1}^{4} r_{i-1}(B')x^i + \sum_{i=1}^{4} r_i(B'')x^i$$

$$= x \sum_{i=1}^{4} r_{i-1}(B')x^{i-1} + \sum_{i=1}^{4} r_i(B'')x^i$$

$$= x \sum_{i=0}^{3} r_i(B')x^i + \sum_{i=1}^{4} r_i(B'')x^i.$$

Using the fact that $r_0(B)x^0 = 1$ for any board B, we add $r_0(B)x^0$ to the left side and $r_0(B'')x^0$ to the second sum on the right side, obtaining

$$\sum_{i=0}^{4} r_i(B)x^i = x\sum_{i=0}^{3} r_i(B')x^i + \sum_{i=0}^{4} r_i(B'')x^i,$$

or

$$R(x,B) = xR(x,B') + R(x,B''). \tag{5}$$

It is easy to see that

$$R(x,B') = 1 + 3x + x^2.$$

It is also not difficult to find the rook polynomial for B'', since its board already appears as disjoint subboards:

$$R(x,B'') = (1+x)(1+4x+3x^2)$$
$$= 1 + 5x + 7x^2 + 3x^3.$$

Substituting these in equation (5) gives

$$R(x,B) = xR(x,B') + R(x,B'')$$
$$= x(1+3x+x^2) + (1+5x+7x^2+3x^3)$$
$$= 1 + 6x + 10x^2 + 4x^3.$$

By Theorem 2, the number of ways to distribute the four gifts is

$$4! - (6\cdot3! - 10\cdot2! + 4\cdot1!) = 4. \qquad \square$$

The analog of equation (5) holds for all boards, which gives the following theorem.

Theorem 3   If (a,b) is a square on board B, if board B' is obtained from B by removing all squares in row a and column b, and if board B'' is obtained from B by removing the one square (a,b), then

$$R(x,B) = xR(x,B') + R(x,B''). \qquad \blacksquare$$

Example 5   A tennis coach wants to pair five men (1, 2, 3, 4, 5) and five women (6, 7, 8, 9, 10) for some practice sessions in preparation for a mixed doubles tournament. Based on the players' schedules and levels of ability, the

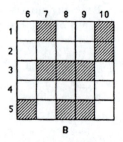

Figure 8.   Possible pairings of tennis players.

coach knows that certain pairs cannot be formed, as shown by the shaded squares in Figure 8. In how many ways can the five men and the five women be paired?

Solution: Since it is not possible to break board B into disjoint subboards (the reader should check this), we use Theorem 3 to find $R(x, B)$.

If we begin with square $(3, 8)$ in Theorem 3, we obtain the boards B' and B'' of Figure 9.

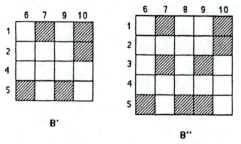

Figure 9.   Subboards of board of Figure 8.

Board B' can be broken into two disjoint subboards (using squares $(5, 6)$ and $(5, 9)$ as one board), and its rook polynomial is

$$R(x, B') = (1 + 2x)(1 + 3x + x^2)$$
$$= 1 + 5x + 7x^2 + 2x^3.$$

However, it is not possible to break board B'' into disjoint subboards.

To find the rook polynomial for board B'', we need to use Theorem 3 again. Using square $(5, 9)$ in the theorem, we obtain

$$R(x, B'') = x(1 + 4x + 3x^2) + (1 + 2x)(1 + 5x + 6x^2 + x^3)$$
$$= 1 + 8x + 20x^2 + 16x^3 + 2x^4.$$

(The details are left as Exercise 8.) Therefore,

$$R(x, B) = x R(x, B') + R(x, B'')$$
$$= x(1 + 5x + 7x^2 + 2x^3) + (1 + 8x + 20x^2 + 16x^3 + 2x^4)$$
$$= 1 + 9x + 25x^2 + 23x^3 + 4x^4.$$

From Theorem 3, it follows that the tennis coach can pair the five men and five women in 12 ways.   □

Suggested Readings

1. R. Grimaldi, *Discrete and Combinatorial Mathematics*, Addison-Wesley, Reading, Mass., 1985.

2. J. Riordan, *An Introduction to Combinatorial Analysis*, Wiley, New York, 1958.

3. F. Roberts, *Applied Combinatorics*, Prentice-Hall, Englewood Cliffs, N.J., 1984.

4. A. Tucker, *Applied Combinatorics*, Second Edition, Wiley, New York, 1985.

Exercises

1. Verify that $R(x, B_1) = 1 + 3x + x^2$ and $R(x, B_2) = 1 + 6x + 9x^2 + 2x^3$ for the boards of Figure 2.

2. Verify that $R(x, B_1) = 1 + x$ and $R(x, B_2) = 1 + 4x + 4x^2 + x^3$ for the boards of Figure 4.

3. Prove that it is impossible to break the board B of Figure 8 into disjoint subboards.

In Exercises 4–7 find the rook polynomial and the number of arrangements with no object in a forbidden position for the given board.

4.

5.

6.

7.

8. Carry out the details to find $R(x, B'')$ in Example 5.

9. Find the number of permutations of $1, 2, 3, 4$ where 1 is not in position 3, 2 is not in positions 3 or 4, and 4 is not in position 1.

10. A professor has divided a discrete mathematics class into four groups. Each of the groups is to write a biography on one of the following mathematicians: Boole, DeMorgan, Euclid, Euler, Hamilton, and Pascal. Group 1 does not want to write on Euler or Pascal, Group 2 does not want to write on DeMorgan or Hamilton, Group 3 does not want to write on Boole, DeMorgan, or Pascal, and Group 4 does not want to write on Boole or Euler. If the professor wants each group to write on a different mathematician, in how many ways can the professor assign a different mathematician to each group?

11. Suppose B is a 4×4 board with four forbidden positions, all in the last column. Use the method of rook polynomials to prove that there are no possible arrangements.

12. Suppose B is a 4×4 board with no forbidden positions. Use the method of rook polynomials to find the number of arrangements of the four objects.

13. Let $A = \{1, 2, 3, 4\}$. Find the number of 1-1 functions $f : A \to A$ such that $f(1) \neq 3$, $f(2) < 3$, and $f(4) > 1$.

14. The head of a mathematics department needs to make summer teaching assignments for five courses: numerical analysis, mathematical modeling, discrete mathematics, precalculus, and applied statistics. Professor Bloch does not want to be assigned to either mathematical modeling or precalculus, Professor Mahoney will not teach applied statistics, Professor Nakano does not want to teach numerical analysis or discrete mathematics, Professor Rockhill will teach any course except applied statistics, and Professor Sommer is willing to teach anything except numerical analysis. In how many ways can the department head match the five faculty to the five courses so that the wishes of the faculty are followed?

⋆15. (A *problème des ménages*) Four married couples are to be seated around a circular table so that no two men or two women are seated next to each other and no husband is to sit next to his wife. Assuming that arrangements such as $123 \cdots 78$ and $234 \cdots 81$ are different, how many arrangements are possible? (*Hint*: First determine the number of ways in which the four women can be seated. Then set up a board to determine the forbidden positions for the four men.)

Computer Projects

1. Write a computer program that takes a board of forbidden positions as input and determines whether the board can be written as two disjoint subboards.

2. Write a computer program that uses Theorem 3 to find the rook polynomial for a board of forbidden positions.

3. Write a computer program that takes a board of forbidden positions as input and gives as output the number of arrangements such that no object is in a forbidden position.

10

Block Designs and Latin Squares

Author: William C. Arlinghaus, Department of Mathematics and Computer Science, Lawrence Technological University.

Prerequisites: The prerequisites for this chapter are properties of integers and basic counting techniques. See, for example, Sections 2.3 and 4.1 of *Discrete Mathematics and Its Applications*, Second Edition, by Kenneth H. Rosen.

Introduction

Suppose that you were given $25,000 to conduct experiments in the following situation. Five different chemicals can be added during a manufacturing process. This process can take place at five different temperatures. Finally, the process can be performed on any of five different machines. Also, performing the process once costs $1000.

To obtain the most information possible, you would want to perform the process with each different chemical as an additive at each different temperature on each different machine. By the product rule of counting, this would require 125 experiments, and you would need five times as much money as you have been allotted.

Fortunately, statistical analysts have come up with a tool called *analysis of variance* which can draw conclusions from less information. If each chemical can be used at each different temperature and on each different machine, much information can be obtained. Consider the matrix

$$
\begin{array}{c c}
 & \begin{matrix} T_1 & T_2 & T_3 & T_4 & T_5 \end{matrix} \\
\begin{matrix} C_1 \\ C_2 \\ C_3 \\ C_4 \\ C_5 \end{matrix} &
\begin{pmatrix}
1 & 4 & 5 & 2 & 3 \\
3 & 1 & 2 & 4 & 5 \\
2 & 5 & 1 & 3 & 4 \\
5 & 3 & 4 & 1 & 2 \\
4 & 2 & 3 & 5 & 1
\end{pmatrix}
\end{array}
$$

Let the rows represent the five chemical additives C_1, C_2, C_3, C_4, C_5; the columns represent the temperatures T_1, T_2, T_3, T_4, T_5; and let the (i,j)th entry of the matrix be the machine number on which the process is performed. Since each of the numbers 1, 2, 3, 4, 5 appears exactly once in each row and exactly once in each column, every chemical appears with every machine, every temperature appears with every machine, and every (*chemical,temperature*) permutation appears exactly once. So the experiments above can be performed for the allotted $25,000, and statistics can be used to gain meaningful information about the relations among additive, temperature, and machine. A matrix of the type above is known as a *Latin square*.

Latin Squares

To generalize this idea to an arbitrary number n, we need an arrangement of rows and columns in which each of the numbers $1, 2, \ldots, n$ appears exactly once in each row and column, permitting n tests to create a mix of the n states represented by the rows and the n states represented by the columns. Hence we have the following definition.

Definition 1   A *Latin square of order n* is an $n \times n$ matrix whose entries are the integers $1, 2, \ldots, n$, arranged so that each integer appears exactly once in each row and exactly once in each column.   □

Example 1   One Latin square of order 5 is the matrix

$$
\begin{pmatrix}
1 & 2 & 3 & 4 & 5 \\
2 & 3 & 4 & 5 & 1 \\
3 & 4 & 5 & 1 & 2 \\
4 & 5 & 1 & 2 & 3 \\
5 & 1 & 2 & 3 & 4
\end{pmatrix}
$$

It is easy to generalize this example to any n by making the first row $1, 2, \ldots, n$; the second row $2, 3, \ldots, n, 1$; and so on.   ☐

In more complicated experiments, it may be necessary to have more than one Latin square of a given order. But we need some concept of what "different" means. Certainly

$$\begin{pmatrix} 1 & 2 & 3 \\ 2 & 3 & 1 \\ 3 & 1 & 2 \end{pmatrix} \quad \text{and} \quad \begin{pmatrix} 2 & 3 & 1 \\ 1 & 2 & 3 \\ 3 & 1 & 2 \end{pmatrix}$$

should not be different. To help clarify the situation, we introduce the idea of a *reduced* Latin square.

Definition 2   A Latin square is *reduced* if in the first row and in the first column the numbers $1, 2, \ldots, n$ appear in natural order.   ☐

Example 2   The Latin square

$$\begin{pmatrix} 2 & 3 & 1 \\ 1 & 2 & 3 \\ 3 & 1 & 2 \end{pmatrix}$$

can be transformed into reduced form by reversing the first two rows, obtaining

$$\begin{pmatrix} 1 & 2 & 3 \\ 2 & 3 & 1 \\ 3 & 1 & 2 \end{pmatrix}$$ ☐

Since interchanges of rows and columns only amount to changing the names of those rows and columns, it is always permissible to do this. Thus we can always transform a Latin square to reduced form. Of course, interchanging numbers inside the matrix only amounts to a renumbering of the "machines", which still is not essentially different.

Definition 3   Two Latin squares are *equivalent* if one can be transformed into the other by rearranging rows, rearranging columns, and renaming elements.   ☐

Even reduced Latin squares can be equivalent, as illustrated in the following example.

Example 3   Show that the Latin squares

$$A = \begin{pmatrix} 1 & 2 & 3 & 4 \\ 2 & 4 & 1 & 3 \\ 3 & 1 & 4 & 2 \\ 4 & 3 & 2 & 1 \end{pmatrix} \quad \text{and} \quad B = \begin{pmatrix} 1 & 2 & 3 & 4 \\ 2 & 3 & 4 & 1 \\ 3 & 4 & 1 & 2 \\ 4 & 1 & 2 & 3 \end{pmatrix}$$

are equivalent.

Solution: We first interchange rows 3 and 4 of A to obtain

$$\begin{pmatrix} 1 & 2 & 3 & 4 \\ 2 & 4 & 1 & 3 \\ 4 & 3 & 2 & 1 \\ 3 & 1 & 4 & 2 \end{pmatrix} .$$

We then interchange columns 3 and 4, obtaining

$$\begin{pmatrix} 1 & 2 & 4 & 3 \\ 2 & 4 & 3 & 1 \\ 4 & 3 & 1 & 2 \\ 3 & 1 & 2 & 4 \end{pmatrix}$$

Finally, by interchanging the "names" 3 and 4, we obtain B.   □

Evidently, it is not obvious whether or not two Latin squares are equivalent. But, since equivalence is an equivalence relation on Latin squares, there is some finite number of distinct classes of non-equivalent Latin squares of order n.

Orthogonal Latin Squares

Now reconsider the problem of the Introduction. Suppose in addition to chemical, temperature, and machine, the day of the week on which the process is performed is also significant. Still each chemical and temperature must go together — now not only on each machine exactly once, but also on each day of the week exactly once.

If we use two Latin squares, one for the machine number and the other for the day of the week, the machines and days of the week will still be properly mixed if the two Latin squares are related properly, referred to as *orthogonal*.

Definition 4   Two $n \times n$ Latin squares $L_1 = (a_{ij})$ and $L_2 = (b_{ij})$ are called *orthogonal* if every ordered pair of symbols (k_1, k_2), $1 \leq k_1 \leq n$, $1 \leq k_2 \leq n$, occurs among the n^2 ordered pairs (a_{ij}, b_{ij}).   □

Example 4   Show that the two Latin squares

$$L_1 = \begin{pmatrix} 1 & 4 & 5 & 2 & 3 \\ 3 & 1 & 2 & 4 & 5 \\ 2 & 5 & 1 & 3 & 4 \\ 5 & 3 & 4 & 1 & 2 \\ 4 & 2 & 3 & 5 & 1 \end{pmatrix} \quad \text{and} \quad L_2 = \begin{pmatrix} 1 & 2 & 4 & 3 & 5 \\ 3 & 4 & 1 & 5 & 2 \\ 2 & 3 & 5 & 4 & 1 \\ 5 & 1 & 3 & 2 & 4 \\ 4 & 5 & 2 & 1 & 3 \end{pmatrix}$$

are orthogonal.

Solution: Simply looking at the 25 pairs (a_{ij}, b_{ij}), where a_{ij} is the entry in row i and column j of L_1 and b_{ij} is the entry in row i and column j of L_2 establishes the fact. Note, for instance, that the pair $(1, 1)$ comes from row i, column 1; $(1, 2)$ from row 4, column 4; $(1, 3)$ from row 5, column 5; $(1, 4)$ from row 2, column 2; and $(1, 5)$ from row 3, column 3.   □

Suppose we use the two Latin squares in Example 4 to schedule our 25 experiments. Looking at row i, column j tells us when to use chemical C_i and temperature T_j. The entry from L_1 tells the machine, and the entry from L_2 tells the day of the week. Hence, since in row 2 and column 4, L_1 has entry 4 and L_2 has entry 5, chemical C_2 would be used with temperature T_4 on machine 4 on day 5 (Friday). Since L_1 and L_2 are orthogonal, each (*machine,day*) pair occurs exactly once, as of course does each (*chemical,temperature*) pair.

Of course, this is just an illustration when $n = 5$. But the same principles clearly apply for every n. Thus, we obtain the following theorem.

Theorem 1   If there are two orthogonal Latin squares of order n, it is possible to schedule a series of n^2 experiments with four different variable elements, each of which has n possible states, such that any ordered pair of two states appears exactly once with each ordered pair of the other two states.   ∎

The problem of determining for which n there are orthogonal Latin squares of order n has a long history. There are, in fact, no two orthogonal Latin squares of orders 2 or 6. For a long time it was conjectured that there were no orthogonal Latin squares of order $2n$ if n is odd. But in fact such squares have been found for $2n \geq 10$, where n is odd.

Finite Projective Planes

In fact, it is sometimes possible to find $n-1$ mutually orthogonal Latin squares of order n. The simplest such example consists of the orthogonal Latin squares

$$\begin{pmatrix} 1 & 2 & 3 \\ 2 & 3 & 1 \\ 3 & 1 & 2 \end{pmatrix} \quad \text{and} \quad \begin{pmatrix} 1 & 2 & 3 \\ 3 & 1 & 2 \\ 2 & 3 & 1 \end{pmatrix}$$

of order 3. With each set of $n-1$ mutually orthogonal Latin squares of order n, it is possible to associate a geometric object called a *finite projective plane*.

Definition 5   A *projective plane* consists of two sets of elements called points and lines (each line is a subset of points) such that each two points belong to exactly one line and each two lines intersect in exactly one point.   □

The $n-1$ mutually orthogonal Latin squares of order n, when they exist, can be used to generate a projective plane of order n. We state the following theorem without proof and then illustrate it with an example.

Theorem 2   A finite projective plane necessarily has the same number of points, $n+1$, on every line. (Such a plane is said to be of *order n*.) It also has $n+1$ lines through every point, and a total of n^2+n+1 points and n^2+n+1 lines.   ■

Example 5   Find the projective plane associated with $n-1$ mutually orthogonal Latin squares $L_1, \ldots, L_{n-1}$ of order n, and illustrate it when $n=3$.

Solution: Let the points be

$$\{a_{ij} \mid 1 \leq i, j \leq n\} \cup R \cup C \cup \{P_i \mid 1 \leq i \leq n-1\}.$$

The a_{ij} correspond to the entries in the matrix, R is for row, C is for column, and the P_i correspond to the $n-1$ Latin squares.

The lines are

1) $a_{11}, a_{12}, \ldots, a_{1n}, R$

$\vdots$

n) $a_{n1}, a_{n2}, \ldots, a_{nn}, R$

n+1) $a_{11}, a_{21}, \ldots, a_{n1}, C$

$\vdots$

2n) $a_{1n}, a_{2n}, \ldots, a_{nn}, C$

These correspond to the rows and columns of the matrices.

There are also lines joining the points whose entries in L_1 are 1 and P_1, whose entries in L_1 are 2 and P_1, ..., whose entries in L_1 are n and P_1. There is a similar set of n lines for each Latin square (lines found using the kth Latin square include the point P_k). Finally, there is the line containing R, C, P_1, ..., P_{n-1}.

In particular, when $n = 3$ there are 13 points:

$$a_{11}, a_{12}, a_{13}, a_{21}, a_{22}, a_{23}, a_{31}, a_{32}, a_{33}, R, C, P_1, \text{ and } P_2.$$

The thirteen lines are

   1) $a_{11}, a_{12}, a_{13}, R$
   2) $a_{21}, a_{22}, a_{23}, R$
   3) $a_{31}, a_{32}, a_{33}, R$
   4) $a_{11}, a_{21}, a_{31}, C$
   5) $a_{12}, a_{22}, a_{32}, C$
   6) $a_{13}, a_{23}, a_{33}, C$

from L_1:

   7) $a_{11}, a_{23}, a_{32}, P_1$
   8) $a_{12}, a_{21}, a_{33}, P_1$
   9) $a_{13}, a_{22}, a_{31}, P_1$

from L_2:

  10) $a_{11}, a_{22}, a_{33}, P_2$
  11) $a_{12}, a_{23}, a_{31}, P_2$
  12) $a_{13}, a_{21}, a_{32}, P_2$

from the extra points:

  13) R, C, P_1, P_2

Examination shows that every line contains four points, every point is on four lines, every two lines intersect in a point, every two points determine a line. □

The theory of finite projective planes is extremely rich. Both Ryser [5] and Hall [3] have entire chapters on the subject. Ryser shows that there is always a projective plane of order p^k is p is a prime and k is a positive integer. He also shows that if $n \equiv 1$ or 2 (mod 4) and some prime factor of n which is congruent to 3 (mod 4) occurs to an odd power in the prime factorization of n, then there is no projective plane of order n.

Block Designs

We now return to the situation of the Introduction, but we suppose that there are only four temperatures that are possible, instead of five. Still, deleting the last column of the Latin square gives a reasonable experimental design.

Example 6   The matrix

$$\begin{pmatrix} 1 & 4 & 5 & 2 \\ 3 & 1 & 2 & 4 \\ 2 & 5 & 1 & 3 \\ 5 & 3 & 4 & 1 \\ 4 & 2 & 3 & 5 \end{pmatrix}$$

is obtained from the Latin square of the Introduction by deleting the last column. This effectively removes one temperature. Still, each machine number occurs four times, once in each column, and it appears in exactly four of the five rows. So, while it is not complete, it is still balanced. $\square$

For the general situation, the machine numbers are called **varieties**, the rows **blocks**, and the number of columns k.

Definition 6   A *balanced incomplete block design* (BIBD), also called a (b, v, r, k, λ)-*design*, comprises a set of v varieties arranged in b blocks in such a way that

    i) each block has the same number $k < v$ of varieties, with no variety occurring twice in the same block;

    ii) each variety occurs in exactly r blocks;

    iii) each pair of varieties occurs together in exactly λ blocks. $\square$

For instance, the 5×4 matrix of Example 6 is a $(5, 5, 4, 4, 3)$-design.

Since each pair of varieties occurs together in the same number of blocks, the design is called *pairwise balanced*. In general, if each set of t varieties occurs together in the same number of blocks, the design is called a t-**design**. The design in Example 6 is both a 4-design (every ordered 4-tuple appears once) and a 3-design (every ordered triple appears twice). Note that the only thing that prevents a Latin square from being a BIBD is its completeness ($k = v$). Since the symmetry occurring in a Latin square is rarely present in actual experiments, the construction of BIBDs is an important ability in designing experiments.

Usually, BIBDs are specified by listing their blocks. For instance, the $(5, 5, 4, 4, 3)$–design in Example 6 is

$$\{\{1, 2, 4, 5\}, \{1, 2, 3, 4\}, \{1, 2, 3, 5\}, \{1, 3, 4, 5\}, \{2, 3, 4, 5\}\}.$$

There are several relationships among the parameters b, v, r, k, and λ, as stated in the following theorem.

Theorem 3   In a (b, v, r, k, λ)-design,

   i) $bk = vr$

   ii) $\lambda(v - 1) = r(k - 1)$

   iii) $r > \lambda$

   iv) $b \geq v$.

Proof: Only the first three parts will be proved; the fourth is beyond the scope of the book; see [5] for a proof.

   i) Since each of the b blocks has k varieties, bk counts the total number of varieties; but since each variety is in r blocks, vr also counts this. Hence $bk = vr$.

   ii) Since each pair of varieties occurs in exactly λ blocks, the total number of varieties (other than v_1) occurring in the blocks containing v_1 is $\lambda(v - 1)$. But since v_1 occurs in exactly r blocks, that number is also $r(k - 1)$.

   iii) Since $k < v$, we have $k - 1 < v - 1$. But, $r(k - 1) = \lambda(v - 1)$, so we must have $r > \lambda$.   ∎

As noted in the discussion preceding Theorem 3, if every set of t varieties occurs in the same number of blocks, λ_t, the design is called a t-design. So, of course, every BIBD is a 1-design (with $\lambda_1 = r$) and a 2-design (with $\lambda_2 = \lambda$), from Definition 6. Usually, a design is called a t-design for the largest t possible for that design. In fact, a t-design is often referred to as a t-(b, v, k, λ_t) design, and the r and k of Definition 6 are not given. The following theorem shows that they can be determined from t, b, v, k, and λ_t.

Theorem 4   If $0 < s < t$, and D is a t-(b, v, k, λ_t) design, then D is also an s-(b, v, k, λ_s) design, where λ_s can be determined from λ_t.

Proof: We need only show D is a $(t - 1)$-design. To do this, let S be a fixed set of $t - 1$ varieties, and suppose S is a subset of λ_{t-1} blocks of D. Each block containing S also contains $k - (t - 1)$ other varieties. Any one of these together with S forms a t-set containing S. Since S is in λ_{t-1} blocks, there are $\lambda_{t-1}(k - t + 1)$ such t-sets altogether.

   But we can count this number of t-sets in another way. The design D contains $v - (t - 1)$ varieties other than the ones in S. Each one of these together with S forms a t-set. By hypothesis, each such t-set is in λ_t blocks. Thus, the number of t-sets is also $\lambda_t(v - t + 1)$.

   Hence $\lambda_{t-1}(k - t + 1) = \lambda_t(v - t + 1)$, and so λ_{t-1} is independent of the choice of S.   ∎

Corollary 1   Every t-design is a BIBD with $r = \lambda_1$, $\lambda = \lambda_2$.   ∎

For instance, the BIBD obtained at the beginning of this section is a 4-design with $b = 5$, $v = 5$, $k = 4$, $\lambda_4 = 1$. From the formula of the proof,

$$\lambda_3(4 - 4 + 1) = \lambda_4(5 - 4 + 1), \text{ so } \lambda_3 = 2$$

$$\lambda_2(4 - 3 + 1) = \lambda_3(5 - 3 + 1), \text{ so } \lambda_2 = 3$$

$$\lambda_1(4 - 2 + 1) = \lambda_3(5 - 2 + 1), \text{ so } \lambda_1 = 4$$

Thus, this 4-design is indeed a $(5, 5, 4, 4, 3)$-design.

Of course, any Latin square of order n can be used to obtain an $(n - 1)$-design just by deleting one column.

Some other interesting designs that occur are the $(n^2 + n + 1, n^2 + n + 1, n + 1, n + 1, 1)$ designs obtained from the projective plane of order n by making the varieties the points and making the blocks the lines. Since every line contains $q + 1$ points, every point is on $q + 1$ lines, and two points determine a unique line, this is indeed a BIBD.

Steiner Triple Systems

Another often-studied class of BIBDs is the class with $k = 3$ and $\lambda = 1$.

Definition 7   A $(b, v, r, 3, 1)$-design is called a *Steiner triple system*.   □

While these are named for Jacob Steiner, they first arose in a problem called *Kirkman's Schoolgirl Problem* (1847).

Example 7   Suppose that 15 girls go for a walk in groups of three. They do this each of the seven days of the week. Can they choose their walking partners so that each girl walks with each other girl exactly once in a week?

Solution: This amounts to finding a Steiner triple system with $v = 15$ (girls), $b = 35$ (there are five groups of girls each day for seven days), and $r = 7$ (each girl walks on seven days). Further, the 35 blocks must be divided into seven groups of five so that each girl appears exactly once in each group.

Number the girls $0, 1, 2, \ldots, 14$. Let the first group be

$$\{14, 1, 2\}, \{3, 5, 9\}, \{11, 4, 0\}, \{7, 6, 12\}, \{13, 8, 10\}.$$

Then let group i $(1 \le i \le 6)$ be obtained as follows:

a) 14 remains in the same place,
b) if $0 \le k \le 13$, k is replaced by $(k + 2i) \bmod 14$.

It is left as an exercise to show that the seven groups obtained actually give 35 different blocks of the type desired.   □

Steiner conjectured in 1853 that Steiner triple systems exist exactly when $v \geq 3$ and $v \equiv 1$ or $3 \pmod 6$. This has proven to be the case. In the case where $v = 6n + 3$, we have $b = (2n + 1)(3n + 1)$. (See Exercise 9.)

If the b triples can be partitioned into $3n + 1$ components with each variety appearing exactly once in each component, the system is called a *Kirkman triple system*. Notice that the solution to the Kirkman schoolgirl problem has $n = 2$. For more results about Steiner triple systems, see [3] or [5].

Suggested Readings

1. P. Dembowski, *Finite Geometries*, Springer-Verlag, Berlin, 1968.

2. J. Denes and A. Keedwell, *Latin Squares and their Applications*, Academic Press, New York, 1974.

3. M. Hall, *Combinatorial Theory*, Blaisdell, Massachusetts, 1967.

4. J. Riordan, *An Introduction to Combinatorial Analysis*, Wiley, New York, 1958.

5. H. Ryser, *Combinatorial Mathematics*, Carus Monograph #14, Mathematical Association of America, 1963.

Exercises

1. Show that

$$\begin{pmatrix} 1 & 2 & 3 & 4 \\ 2 & 1 & 4 & 3 \\ 3 & 4 & 2 & 1 \\ 4 & 3 & 1 & 2 \end{pmatrix} \quad \text{and} \quad \begin{pmatrix} 1 & 2 & 3 & 4 \\ 2 & 3 & 4 & 1 \\ 3 & 4 & 1 & 2 \\ 4 & 1 & 2 & 3 \end{pmatrix}$$

are equivalent.

2. Find a reduced Latin square equivalent to

$$\begin{pmatrix} 1 & 4 & 5 & 2 & 3 \\ 3 & 1 & 2 & 4 & 5 \\ 2 & 5 & 1 & 3 & 4 \\ 5 & 3 & 4 & 1 & 2 \\ 4 & 2 & 3 & 5 & 1 \end{pmatrix}$$

⋆**3.** Show that "equivalent" is an equivalence relation on the set of $n \times n$ Latin squares.

4. Find a Latin square orthogonal to

$$\begin{pmatrix} 1 & 2 & 3 & 4 \\ 2 & 1 & 4 & 3 \\ 3 & 4 & 1 & 2 \\ 4 & 3 & 2 & 1 \end{pmatrix}$$

⋆**5.** a) Find a set of three mutually orthogonal Latin squares of order 4.
 b) How many points are there in a finite projective plane of order 4?
 c) How many points are on a typical line?
 d) List all the points and lines.

6. Suppose a BIBD has 69 blocks, 24 varieties, and 8 varieties in a block. What are all the parameters?

7. Delete a column from the Latin square of Exercise 4 to obtain a 3-design. What are its parameters?

8. Construct a BIBD from the finite projective plane in the text. What are its parameters?

9. Suppose a Steiner triple system has $6n + 3$ varieties. Show that $r = 3n + 1$ and $b = (2n + 1)(3n + 1)$.

10. a) Find the other six groups of the solution to the Kirkman schoolgirl problem.
 b) With whom does schoolgirl 5 walk on Thursday (assume Sunday is day 0).
 c) When does schoolgirl 14 walk with schoolgirl 0? Who is their companion?

⋆**11.** Alice, Betty, Carol, Donna, Evelyn, Fran, Georgia, Henrietta, and Isabel form a swimming group. They plan to swim once a week, with one group of three swimming each of Monday, Wednesday, and Friday. Over the course of four weeks, each woman wants to swim with each other woman. Construct a schedule for them.

⋆**12.** There is a unique Steiner triple system with $v = 7$.
   a) What are its parameters as a BIBD?
   b) Construct it.
   c) Use it to construct a finite projective plane. What order is it?

Computer Projects

1. Write a computer program to determine whether or not two Latin squares are orthogonal.

2. Write a computer program to determine r and λ in a BIBD if b, v, and k are given. The output should list all of b, v, k, r, λ and should say "this is an impossible configuration" if r or λ turns out not to be an integer.

11

Scheduling Problems and Bin Packing

Author: Robert A. McGuigan, Department of Mathematics, Westfield State College.

Prerequisites: The prerequisites for this chapter are basic concepts of graph theory. See, for example, Sections 7.1 and 7.2 of *Discrete Mathematics and Its Applications*, Second Edition, by Kenneth H. Rosen.

Introduction

Imagine a job which is composed of a number of different tasks. To complete the job all the tasks must be completed. The tasks are performed by a number of identical *processors* (machines, humans, etc.) Each task has an associated length of time required for its completion. A **scheduling problem**, then, is to decide in what order and at what times the tasks should be assigned to processors; that is, how the tasks should be scheduled. These problems are found in many places. They can be involved in such activities as budgeting and resource allocation, making work assignments, manufacturing, and planning. Scheduling problems also arise in the efficient use of highly parallel computers.

The goal in scheduling may be to achieve the shortest possible time for completion of the job, to use the smallest possible number of processors to complete the job within a specified time, or to optimize performance according to some other criterion.

Scheduling Problems

In order to make our problem more specific and for simplicity, we need to make some assumptions. First we will assume that any processor can work on any task. In addition we will always assume the following two rules:

(i) No processor can be idle if there is some task it can be doing.

(ii) Once a processor has begun a task, it alone must continue to process that task until it is finished.

We make these rules to simplify our discussion. Rule (i) seems reasonable if our goal is efficiency. Rule (ii) seems more restrictive. After all, a lot of jobs are done by teams, and a processor might well do part of a task, leave it or turn it over to another processor, and work on some other task. In theory, though, we could consider very small, "atomic" tasks that could not be shared. An example might be punching a key on a keyboard. For such tasks rule (ii) does not seem unreasonable. We can also make a case for rule (ii) on the grounds of efficiency. If the processors are people, time may be lost in the change of processors in mid-task.

Example 1   Suppose two people are planning a dinner party. Both people are skilled cooks and can do any of the tasks associated with this job, so rules (i) and (ii) are satisfied. Suppose the job of giving the dinner party is composed of the following tasks and completion times.

Task	Time (in minutes)
Decide guest list (GL)	15
Plan the menu (M)	30
Clean house (CH)	80
Purchase food (PF)	45
Cook food (CF)	124
Set table (ST)	15
Serve food (SF)	15

Some of these tasks must be done before others can be begun. For example, the food must be purchased before it is cooked or served. When this happens we say that purchasing the food is a **precedent** of cooking the food. Whenever task A must be completed before task B can be started we say A is a **predecessor** or a **precedent** of B. Dependence of tasks on the completion of other tasks is common in complex projects. We can state the precedence relations for our cooking project in the following list.

Task	Must be preceded by task(s)
Decide guest list (GL)	none
Plan the menu (M)	GL
Clean house (CH)	none
Purchase food (PF)	M
Cook food (CF)	CH, PF
Set table (ST)	CH, M
Serve food (SF)	ST, CF

□

Another way to describe the precedence relationship between tasks is by a directed graph. Each task is represented by a vertex and there is a directed edge from A to B if A must be completed before B can be begun. The graph can be simplified (if desired) by eliminating an edge from A to B if there is a different directed path from A to B. This simplification is not essential for the way we are going to use the graph, but it makes it easier to understand. We do not lose any precedence information this way since if we delete edge (A, B) there must be an alternative directed path from A to B. The fact that A must be completed before B is started is implied by the directed path.

The completion time for each task is written inside the circle for the vertex representing that task. A graph of this sort is called an **order requirements digraph**.

Example 2   Draw the order requirements digraph for the dinner party of Example 1.

Solution: The digraph is drawn in Figure 1.   □

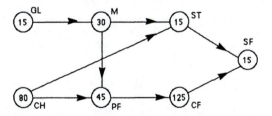

Figure 1.   An order requirements digraph.

An important feature of an order requirements digraph is the *critical path*.

Definition 1   A *critical path* in an order requirements digraph is a directed path such that the sum of the completion times for the vertices in the path is the largest possible.   □

It is possible that there may be more than one critical path in an order requirements digraph. In that case all critical paths must have the same sum of times for their vertices.

Since the tasks on a critical path must be done in the order they occur on the path, the sum of the times for a critical path gives us a lower bound for the completion time for the whole project. If the number of processors available is unlimited, then the total time for the critical path is the shortest possible completion time for the project.

To see this, note that the earliest starting time (where the start of the project is time 0) for any task T is the largest sum of times on a directed path to that task. Every precedent of T will be on a directed path to T. Since we look for the longest such directed path, all precedents of T will be finished before we start T.

If there are a limited number of processors, then this method of determining the starting time of a task does not apply since it might be necessary to wait until a processor is available.

Example 3   Find the critical path for the party digraph in Figure 1.

Solution: The critical path for the party digraph is:

$$GL \rightarrow M \rightarrow PF \rightarrow CF \rightarrow SF$$

with a total time of 230 minutes. A schedule which is completed within this time limit is shown in Figure 2. Time is measured horizontally from left to right. The shaded areas indicate times when the processor is idle.   □

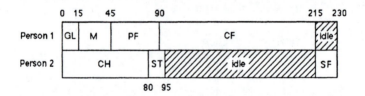
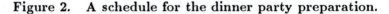

Figure 2.   A schedule for the dinner party preparation.

If there is a limited, perhaps small, number of processors, then we could easily build up a backlog of tasks which have their predecessors completed but can't be begun because there is no free processor. When a processor does become free, which of these ready tasks should be assigned to it?

We amend our definition of the critical path method to state that the ready task which heads the directed path with the greatest sum of processing times should be assigned to the next free processor. If there is more than one such task, then any of them may be chosen at random. This criterion only applies when the number of processors is limited. In the unlimited case, every task can be assigned to a processor immediately when its predecessors have been completed.

Example 4   Our critical path method can yield a very bad schedule in some cases. The example in Figure 3, due to Graham [3], using four processors, shows the tasks $(A-L)$, their times, and the order requirement digraph. Figure 4 shows the critical path schedule and an optimal schedule for this example.   □

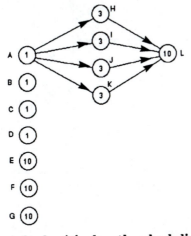

Figure 3.   A bad critical path scheduling problem.

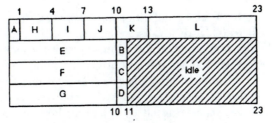

Critical Path Schedules

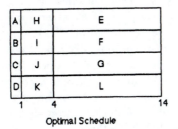

Optimal Schedule

Figure 4.   Critical path and optimal schedules.

If we carry out the critical path method for the order requirement digraph of Figure 3 assuming there are no limitations on the number of processors, then we would obtain the schedule shown in Figure 5.

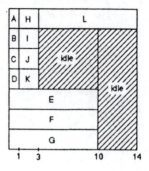

Figure 5.   An optimal schedule.

In this case we would use seven processors and still obtain an optimal completion time of 14 time units.

Optimal Algorithms

Since optimal schedules are by definition the best possible, it is natural to ask whether some efficient algorithm other than the critical path method would always yield the optimal schedule for a job. We ask for an efficient algorithm because it is always possible to find an optimal schedule by exhaustive search. That is, we simply examine all possible schedules and select one that takes the least time to complete. The problem with this approach is that if the number of tasks is very large, generating all possible schedules takes an unacceptable amount of time even using a computer.

Algorithm analysis is concerned with measuring how much time (or number of steps) is necessary for execution of an algorithm, as a function of the size of the problem. In the case of scheduling, the size might be measured by the number of tasks. An algorithm is generally considered efficient if the number of steps for its execution is bounded above by a polynomial function of the size of the problem. Then we would say that there is a *polynomial time* algorithm for the problem. For an exhaustive search to find an optimal schedule for n tasks we would expect the number of steps to grow at a rate similar to that of $n!$. Exhaustive search is thus highly inefficient.

Mathematicians have developed a term which describes algorithmic problems for which no polynomial time algorithm has been found, but which have a similar property. Specifically, a problem belongs to the **class NP** if having somehow (even by guessing) obtained the correct solution, it is possible to check it in polynomial time. Many difficult algorithmic problems have been shown to belong to class NP. In fact, many such problems are what is known as **NP complete**. This means that they belong to class NP and that if they have a polynomial time solution algorithm, then so do *all other problems in* NP. It is generally conjectured, but not yet proved, that NP-complete problems do not have polynomial time solution algorithms. It has been proved that the general problem of finding optimal schedules is NP-complete.

In view of this, we have little hope of finding efficient algorithms for the general optimal scheduling problem. Therefore, it becomes interesting and important to find efficient algorithms which, while not always yielding optimal schedules, do produce schedules which are close to optimal, or at least not too far from optimal.

It can be shown that the ratio of the completion time of a critical path schedule to that of an optimal schedule can never be greater than 2. That is, critical path schedules can never take more than twice the time of optimal schedules. In certain cases the critical path method does even better. If the tasks are independent (that is, there are no precedence relations among the tasks), then a critical path schedule never takes more than one third more time than an optimal schedule. (See reference [3].)

Critical path schedules could easily not be optimal, but as a practical matter we have seen that there is a limit to how bad they can be. Furthermore, it may be relatively easy to modify a critical path schedule to get an optimal one.

A special case in which good methods do exist for determining an optimal schedule occurs when there are just two processors and all the tasks have equal length. We describe two such methods here. Since all the tasks are assumed to take the same amount of time to process, we will not mention the time for each task explicitly.

Example 5   The Fujii-Kasami-Ninomiya method, developed in 1969, makes use of the idea that two tasks A and B can be executed during the same time interval only if they are incomparable, i.e. there is no directed path from one to the other. Start with an order-requirement digraph. Create a second, non-directed graph called the *incomparability graph* of the tasks by having a vertex for each task and connecting two vertices by an edge if and only if the corresponding tasks are incomparable. Figure 6 shows an order-requirement digraph and its incomparability graph.

Now find in the incomparability graph the largest set of edges having no two with a vertex in common. In Figure 6 the edges AB, CD, EF, GH, and IJ form such a set of edges. These pairs of vertices then show the tasks to execute simultaneously. The rest (if any) are executed one at a time.

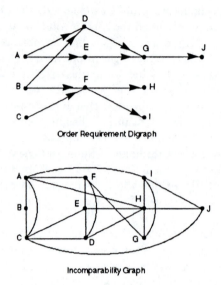

Order Requirement Digraph

Incomparability Graph

Figure 6.   An order requirement digraph and incomparability graph.

Sometimes this method does not yield pairs of tasks which can be executed simultaneously. For example, instead of the edges we chose above suppose we had picked AB, CG, EF, DH, and IJ. Then we cannot execute C and G simultaneously and D and H simultaneously. In this and similar cases it is necessary to exchange some vertices to obtain simultaneously executable pairs. Here we would exchange G and D to get our original set.   □

Good algorithms exist for finding the required maximal set of disjoint edges.

Example 6   The second method we present is the Coffman-Graham algorithm. This algorithm works only with the order-requirement digraph. To begin, remove all unnecessary directed edges from the order-requirement digraph. That is, if there is a directed edge from A to B and some other directed path also from A to B, then remove the directed edge. This must be done as much as possible.

Now choose a vertex with no outgoing directed edges, i.e. no successor vertices, and assign it label 1. Continue numbering tasks with no successors with 2, 3, etc., until all such tasks are numbered.

For each task which has all its successor vertices numbered, create a sequence of all its successors' numbers in decreasing order and assign that sequence as a temporary label to the vertex. Once all possible temporary sequence labels have been assigned, determine the vertex whose sequence label comes first in dictionary order and assign that vertex the next available number as a permanent label. Recall that in dictionary order $(5, 6, 1)$ is smaller than $(6, 2, 1)$, $(5, 6, 1, 7)$, and (7). Repeat this process until all vertices have been assigned permanent number labels. The optimal schedule is now obtained by assigning to any free processor the highest numbered task not yet processed. Figure 7 shows the digraph in Figure 6 with labels assigned.

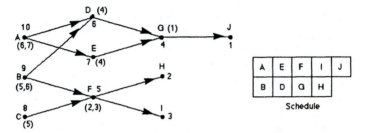

Figure 7. Labeled order requirement digraph.

The idea behind this algorithm is to place earlier in the schedule tasks which either head long directed paths or have many successors. This differs from the critical path method which only considers whether a task heads a long path.   ☐

To describe the Coffman-Graham algorithm (Algorithm 1) in pseudocode, let $T(v)$ be the temporary label of v, $L(v)$ be the permanent label of v, and let $S(v)$ be the set of all successors of the vertex v, i.e. the set of all vertices w such that there is a directed edge from v to w.

Bin Packing

Up to now we have been studying the problem of finding the shortest completion time for a job when the number of processors is fixed in advance. Now we ask, given a deadline time d, what is the minimum number of processors needed to complete the job within the deadline? This sort of problem is known as a **bin packing** problem. For bin packing we imagine a set of objects $O_1, \ldots, O_n$ with weights $w_1, \ldots, w_n$. The goal is to pack the objects into the minimum number of identical bins, each having the same capacity of holding at most a total weight of W. In the scheduling version the processors are the bins, the tasks are the objects, and the weights are the times of the tasks. We try to assign tasks to the fewest possible processors provided that no processor can be assigned tasks whose total time exceeds the deadline time.

Bin packing problems are very common. For example, consider the problem of determining the minimum number of standard length boards needed to

---

ALGORITHM 1   Coffman-Graham Algorithm.

procedure *Coffman-Graham*(G: order requirement digraph)
$\{G$ has vertices $v_1, \ldots, v_n\}$
for all pairs of vertices u, v of G
    if (u, v) is a directed edge and there is a different directed
        path from u to v **then** delete (u, v)
$U :=$ set of all vertices of G
$\{U$ is the set of unlabeled vertices$\}$
for all $v \in U$ $L(r) := \infty$
$c := 1$
$\{c$ is next available value for $L\}$
for $i := 1$ **to** n
    if $outdegree(v_i) = 0$ **then**
    begin
        $L(v_i) := c$
        $c := c + 1$
    end
    $\{$all vertices with no successors are labeled$\}$
while $U \neq \emptyset$
    for all vertices $v \in U$
    begin
        if $L(w) \neq \infty$ for all $w \in S(v)$ **then** $T(v) :=$ the decreasing
            sequence of $L(w)$ for all $w \in S(v)$
        among all v with $L(v) = \infty$ and $T(v)$ assigned, choose
            v with minimal $T(v)$ in dictionary order
        $L(v) := c$
        $\{v$ has a permanent label$\}$
        $c := c + 1$
        $U := U - \{v\}$
    end
    $\{$assign the vertices to processors in decreasing order of $L(v)\}$

---

produce a certain amount of boards of various non-standard lengths. In this case the objects are the shorter boards and the bins are the standard length boards. A more obvious example of bin packing is the problem of loading objects onto trucks for transportation. Each truck has a limit to the amount of weight it can carry and we wish to use as few trucks as possible. Consider also the problem of scheduling patients in an emergency room setting. Each doctor can only provide a limited amount of service, we want to have each patient taken care of as soon as possible with as few personnel as possible.

Analogous situations occur whenever some commodity is supplied in standard amounts and must be subdivided into given smaller amounts. In the context of scheduling theory we shall consider only the case where there are no precedence relations among the tasks, i.e., the tasks are independent. Even in this simplified situation no good algorithm is known which produces optimal solutions in every case. The only known algorithm which always produces optimal solutions is exhaustive search: examine all possible packings and choose the best one. This method is so inefficient that even moderate size problems would require more computing capacity than currently exists in the world.

Again we are forced to try for algorithms which will not produce packings that are too bad. One approach is known as **list processing**. The objects to be packed are arranged in a list according to one of many possible algorithms and then processed in the order of the list. For example, consider the **first-fit** algorithm. The weights are arranged arbitrarily in a list $(w_1, w_2, \ldots, w_n)$. We then pack the objects in the order of the list, putting an object in the first bin it will fit into and opening a new bin when the current weight will not fit in any previously opened bin. Let $FF(L)$ be the number of bins required for the list L according to the first-fit algorithm and let $OPT(L)$ be the smallest possible number of bins for L. In 1973, Jeffrey Ullman showed that

$$FF(L) \le \frac{17}{10} OPT(L) + 2$$

for any list of weights L.

Algorithm 2 gives the pseudocode description of the first-fit algorithm.

ALGORITHM 2   First-fit Algorithm.

procedure $FF(W$: an arbitrary list $w_1, \ldots, w_n)$
$\{b_1, \ldots$ is the list of bins; object O_i has weight w_i; $L(b_j) =$
   total weight placed in $b_j\}$
$k := 1$
$\{k$ is number of bins opened$\}$
for $i := 1$ **to** n
begin
$\{$find first available bin$\}$
   $j := 1$
   while O_i not packed and $j \le k$
   begin
      if $L(b_j) + w_i \le d$ **then** pack O_i in b_j
      $j := j + 1$
   end
   if j=k+1 **then** open b_j and pack O_i in b_{k+1}
end

One of the reasons FF(L) might be large is the arbitrary order of the weights in L. The large weights might come at the end of the list. Perhaps a more efficient packing could be accomplished if the weights were first sorted into decreasing order. This method is known as **first-fit-decreasing**, and the number of bins it requires is FFD(L). It has been shown that

$$FFD(L) \leq \frac{11}{9}OPT(L) + 4.$$

For lists requiring a large number of bins, the 4 is relatively insignificant and FFD is much more efficient than FF.

Example 7   Use the first-fit algorithm to pack the following weights in bins of capacity 100:

$$7 \quad 7 \quad 7 \quad 7 \quad 7 \quad 12 \quad 12 \quad 12 \quad 12 \quad 12 \quad 15 \quad 15 \quad 15$$
$$36 \quad 36 \quad 36 \quad 36 \quad 36 \quad 52 \quad \quad 52 \quad 52 \quad 52 \quad 52 \quad 52 \quad 52.$$

Solution: The first-fit algorithm yields the following bin packing:

bin 1:	7	7	7	7	7	12	12	12	12	12

bin 2:	15	15	15	36	bin 3:	36	36
bin 4:	36	36			bin 5:	36	52
bin 6:	52				bin 7:	52	
bin 8:	52				bin 9:	52	
bin 10:	52				bin 11:	52.	

However, an optimal packing uses only 7 bins:

bin 1:	52	36	12	
bin 2:	52	36	12	
bin 3:	52	36	12	
bin 4:	52	36	12	
bin 5:	52	36	12	
bin 6:	52	15	15	15
bin 7:	52	7	7	7	7	7.

This packing is optimal because the total weight to be packed is 684, so it cannot be packed in 6 bins of capacity 100.   □

Though FFD is more efficient, FF has at least one advantage. FF can be used when the list of weights is not completely available while the packing is being done. This could easily occur in a factory where trucks are loaded as objects are produced.

The scheduling and bin packing problems presented here are typical. Perhaps the reader can think of many more; indeed they are ubiquitous in modern life. Furthermore, as is the case with many difficult algorithmic problems, it is most likely impossible to find efficient optimal algorithms. Thus research is focussed on finding algorithms which yield good solutions or ones that are not too far from optimal. This topic is the subject of much current research. The reader interested in additional results, more technical details, and additional technical references is urged to consult the references below.

Suggested Readings

1. M. Garey and D. Johnson, *Computers and Intractability*, Freeman, San Francisco, 1978.

2. M. Garey, R. Graham, and D. Johnson, "Performance guarantees for scheduling algorithms", *Operations Research*, Vol. 26, 1978, pp. 3–21.

3. R. Graham, "Combinatorial Scheduling Theory", *Mathematics Today*, ed. L. Steen, Springer-Verlag, 1978.

Exercises

1. A researcher plans a survey consisting of the following tasks:

Task	Precedences	Time (days)
Design of questionnaire (A)	none	5
Sample design (B)	none	12
Testing of questionnaire (C)	A	5
Recruit interviewers (D)	B	3
Train interviewers (E)	D, A	2
Assign areas to interviewers (F)	B	5
Conduct interviews (G)	C, E, F	14
Evaluate results (H)	G	20

Construct the order requirement digraph for this project.

2. A construction company assembles prefabricated houses in its factory and transports them to the site where they are attached to the foundations. The job consists of the following tasks:

Task	Precedences	Time (days)
Inspect site and prepare plans (A)	none	3
Level site and build foundation (B)	A	4
Construct wall panels, floors roof, and assembly (C)	A	5
Transportation to site and positioning on foundation (D)	C	1
Attach to foundation and make final installation (E)	B, D	4

Construct the order requirement digraph for this project.

3. A publisher wishes to put out a new book. What is the earliest date that the book can be ready? The following tasks and times are involved. Assume unlimited processors. Find the optimal schedule.

Task	Precedences	Time (weeks)
Appraisal of book by reviewers (A)	none	8
Initial pricing (B)	none	2
Market assessment (C)	A, b	2
Revision by author (D)	A	6
Editing of final draft (E)	C, D	4
Typesetting (F)	E	3
Preparation of plates (G)	E	4
Design of jacket (H)	C, D	6
Printing and binding (I)	F, G	8
Inspection and final assembly (J)	I, H	1

4. Find the critical path schedule for the job with the following order requirement digraph.
   a) With unlimited processors.
   b) With only two processors.

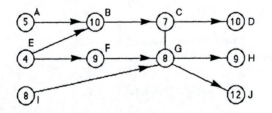

5. Consider the following order requirement digraph.
   a) Assuming only two processors, find the critical path schedule.
   b) What is the optimal schedule for two processors?
   c) What about unlimited processors?

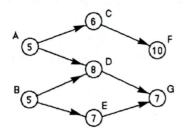

6. Apply the Fujii-Kasami-Ninomiya method to the following order requirement digraph.

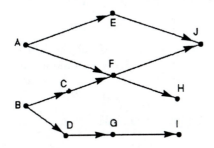

7. Apply the Coffman-Graham algorithm to the following order requirement digraph.

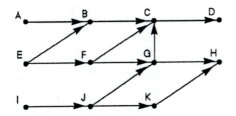

8. A certain type of carton can hold a maximum of 140 pounds. Objects weighing 85, 95, 135, 55, 65, 25, 95, 35, 35, and 40 pounds are to be packed in these cartons.

   a) Use first-fit on the list as given to determine how many cartons are required.

   b) Use first-fit decreasing to determine how many cartons are required.

   c) What is the optimal number of cartons for these weights?

9. A shelf system is to be constructed. It requires boards of lengths 7, 7, 6, 6, 6, 5, 5, 5, 5, 3, 3, 3, 3, 4, 4, 8, 8, 6, 6, 9, 9, 5, 5, and 6 feet. The lumber yard only sells boards with length 9 feet.

   a) Determine how many boards must be bought using FF.

    b) Determine how many boards must be bought using FFD.

    c) What happens if the boards at the lumber yard are 10 feet long?

10. Make up a list processing method different from FF and FFD. Are there cases where your method might be preferable to FF and FFD?

Computer Projects

1. Implement the FF algorithm for bin packing.

2. Implement the FFD algorithm for bin packing.

3. Carry out an empirical investigation of the relative efficiency of FF and FFD by generating lists of weights at random and bin sizes at random, running both algorithms on the same weights many times, and repeating this many times.

4. Implement the Coffman-Graham algorithm.

12

Burnside–Polya
Counting Methods

Author: Jonathan L. Gross, Department of Computer Science, Columbia University.

Prerequisites: The prerequisites for this chapter are combinations, equivalence relations, and bijections on sets. See, for example, Sections 4.3, 6.5, and 1.6, of *Discrete Mathematics and Its Applications*, Second Edition, by Kenneth H. Rosen.

Introduction

If a game of tic-tac-toe is played out until all spaces are filled, then the resulting grid will have five crosses and four naughts (also called "oh"s). From counting combinations, it follows that the number of 3×3 grids with five crosses and four naughts is $C(9,5)$, which equals 126.

In playing tic-tac-toe, it is natural to regard two configurations as equivalent if one can be obtained from the other by rotating or reflecting the board. For instance, in Figure 1, configuration (B) can be obtained by rotating configuration (A) counterclockwise 90°, and (C) can be obtained by reflecting (A) horizontally. If one considers such configurations to be the "same", then how many "really different" configurations are there?

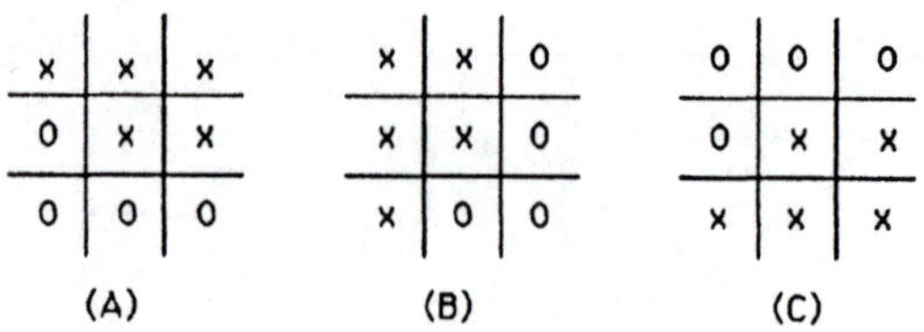

Figure 1.   Three equivalent tic-tac-toe configurations.

We can formalize this intuitive concept of "sameness" by calling two tic-tac-toe configurations **congruent** if one can be obtained from the other by a rotation or by a reflection.   Congruence is an equivalence relation, in the usual sense, and the equivalence classes into which it partitions the set of all configurations of the tic-tac-toe board are called **congruence classes**. Thus, we seek the solution to the following problem:

> **Congruence-Class Counting Problem** ($CCCP$): Count the number of different congruence classes among the configurations with five crosses and four naughts.

If all the congruence classes were the same size, then we could solve $CCCP$ by dividing the uniform class-size into $C(9,5)$, the total number of, individual configurations. Unfortunately, it is not quite this simple, as now illustrated.

Example 1   Count the numbers of configurations that are equivalent to each of the configurations (D), (E), and (F) in Figure 2.

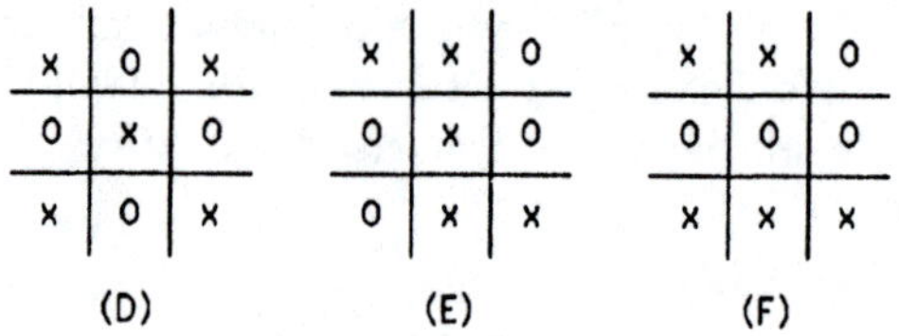

Figure 2.   Configurations with equivalence classes of different sizes.

Solution: Every rotation and reflection of configuration (D) always yields (D) itself, so its congruence class has cardinality equal to one. Every configuration congruent to (E) is a pattern with one of its two diagonals filled with crosses and either its middle row or its middle column filled with crosses. Conversely, every such pattern is congruent to (E). Since there are four such patterns, it follows that the congruence class of (E) has cardinality equal to four.

The total number of rotations and reflections of the tic-tac-toe board onto itself is eight, that is, there are four rotations and four reflections. The four different rotations correspond to zero, one, two, or three quarter-turns of the tic-tac-toe board. We can reflect the board horizontally through its middle row, vertically through its middle column, through the "major" diagonal row that runs from the upper left to the lower right, or through the "minor" diagonal row that runs from the upper right to the lower left. Applying each of these eight rotations and reflections to configuration (F) yields a different configuration. □

As illustrated by the method we have just applied to configuration (F), we can easily calculate the size of the congruence class of any given configuration. That is, we simply apply all eight rotations to the given configuration, and we see how many different ones we obtain.

Our method for counting the congruence classes, known as **Burnside–Polya enumeration theory**, also involves these rotations and reflections. This is an extremely important counting technique, since it can also be used to count graph isomorphism classes (see Section 7.3 of *Discrete Mathematics and Its Applications*, Second Edition, by Kenneth H. Rosen), equivalence classes of graph colorings (see Section 7.8 of Rosen's book), equivalence classes of finite-state automata (see Sections 10.2 and 10.3 of Rosen's book), and many other kinds of equivalence classes involving structural symmetries.

We shall ultimately solve *CCCP* by calculating that there are exactly 23 different congruence classes of configurations with five crosses and four naughts. A good exercise is to try to derive this number without using Burnside–Polya theory, by systematically applying ad hoc methods. It is easy to make mistakes in such an endeavor. Burnside–Polya theory offers two advantages: it reduces the chance of error inherent in ad hoc methods, and it is applicable in other calculations involving cardinalities so large that ad hoc counting is infeasible.

Permutation Groups

A rotation or a reflection on a tic-tac-toe board is a special case of a bijection (i.e., a one-to-one, onto function) from a finite set to itself, which is commonly called a **permutation**. This relationship becomes clear if we label the nine squares of the tic-tac-toe board with the integers from 1 to 9, as illustrated in Figure 3.

$$\begin{array}{c|c|c} 1 & 2 & 3 \\ \hline 4 & 5 & 6 \\ \hline 7 & 8 & 9 \end{array}$$

Figure 3. The labeling of tic-tac-toe squares with integers.

Then rotating a quarter-turn counterclockwise takes square 1 to square 7, square 2 to square 4, square 3 to square 1, and so on. The change on every position of the tic-tac-toe board can be recorded in a 2×9 matrix, as follows:

$$\begin{pmatrix} 1 & 2 & 3 & 4 & 5 & 6 & 7 & 8 & 9 \\ 7 & 4 & 1 & 8 & 5 & 2 & 9 & 6 & 3 \end{pmatrix}.$$

In each of the nine columns, the entry in the top row is mapped to the entry immediately below it. In general, any permutation on a finite set of cardinality n can be fully described by such a $2 \times n$ matrix.

All 9! permutations on the set $\{1, 2 \ldots, 9\}$ can be described by 2×9 matrices, but only four of them represent rotations on the tic-tac-toe board and only four others represent reflections. For the sake of simplification, we turn for the moment to 2×2 tic-tac-toe, whose squares are labeled as in Figure 4.

Figure 4.   A 2x2 tic-tac-toe board.

All 4! permutations on the set $\{1, 2, 3, 4\}$ can be described by 2×4 matrices. The eight of them that represent rotations and reflections are as follows:

rotations:

$$
\begin{array}{cccc}
90° & 180° & 270° & 360°
\end{array}
$$

$$
\begin{pmatrix} 1 & 2 & 3 & 4 \\ 3 & 1 & 4 & 2 \end{pmatrix}
\quad
\begin{pmatrix} 1 & 2 & 3 & 4 \\ 4 & 3 & 2 & 1 \end{pmatrix}
\quad
\begin{pmatrix} 1 & 2 & 3 & 4 \\ 2 & 4 & 1 & 3 \end{pmatrix}
\quad
\begin{pmatrix} 1 & 2 & 3 & 4 \\ 1 & 2 & 3 & 4 \end{pmatrix}
$$

reflections:

$$
\begin{array}{cccc}
\text{horizontal} & \text{vertical} & \text{main diagonal} & \text{minor diagonal}
\end{array}
$$

$$
\begin{pmatrix} 1 & 2 & 3 & 4 \\ 3 & 4 & 1 & 2 \end{pmatrix}
\quad
\begin{pmatrix} 1 & 2 & 3 & 4 \\ 2 & 1 & 4 & 3 \end{pmatrix}
\quad
\begin{pmatrix} 1 & 2 & 3 & 4 \\ 1 & 3 & 2 & 4 \end{pmatrix}
\quad
\begin{pmatrix} 1 & 2 & 3 & 4 \\ 4 & 2 & 3 & 1 \end{pmatrix}
$$

If the elements on the set being permuted are integers (or any other ordered set), then it is natural to arrange the columns of the matrix so that the elements of the first row are in ascending order. However, any ordering of the columns equally well expresses the action of the permutation on every element.

One instance in which it is convenient to consider other orderings is in calculating the composition $g \circ f$ of two permutations. To do this operation, write the $2 \times n$ matrix representation of g immediately below the $2 \times n$ matrix representation of f. The columns of f should be ordered as usual,

$$1, 2, \ldots, n.$$

The columns of g should be ordered so that the top row is in the order

$$f(1), f(2), \ldots, f(n)$$

which matches the bottom row of the matrix for f. Then the bottom row of the matrix for g will appear in the order

$$g(f(1)), g(f(2)), \ldots, g(f(n)).$$

It follows that the $2 \times n$ matrix representing composition $g \circ f$ is formed by writing the bottom row of the matrix for g in that order immediately below the top row of the matrix for f.

For instance, suppose that we take the quarter-turn counterclockwise as f and the horizontal reflection as g, for the 2×2 board. Then this process is as follows:

$$\begin{pmatrix} 1 & 2 & 3 & 4 \\ 3 & 1 & 4 & 2 \end{pmatrix} \qquad\qquad \text{1/4 turn counterclockwise}$$

$$\begin{pmatrix} 3 & 1 & 4 & 2 \\ 1 & 3 & 2 & 4 \end{pmatrix} = \begin{pmatrix} 1 & 2 & 3 & 4 \\ 3 & 4 & 1 & 2 \end{pmatrix} \qquad \text{horizontal reflection}$$

$$\begin{pmatrix} 1 & 2 & 3 & 4 \\ 1 & 3 & 2 & 4 \end{pmatrix} \qquad\qquad \text{reflection through main diagonal}$$

In addition to reviewing the mechanics of the process on the left by which the matrix representation of the composition is calculated, you should also apply your spatial perceptions to the corresponding description at the right of the composition, as viewed geometrically.

The following properties of 2×2 tic-tac-toe boards can be proved either by applying the composition rule for $2 \times n$ matrix representations or by geometric reasoning:

(1) The composition of two rotations is a rotation.

(2) The composition of two reflections is a rotation.

(3) The composition of a rotation with a reflection or of a reflection with a rotation is a reflection.

From the combination of these three assertions, we immediately infer the following theorem.

Theorem 1   The composition of a rotation or a reflection of a 2×2 tic-tac-toe board with another rotation or reflection is a rotation or a reflection. ∎

A collection of permutations on a finite set is said to be **closed under composition** if whenever any two of them are composed, the resulting permutation is also in the collection.

Example 2   Show that the collection of rotations and reflections on the 2×2 tic-tac-toe board is closed under composition.

Solution: We have established this with Theorem 1.   □

Example 3   Show that the collection of all four rotations on the 2 × 2 tic-tac-toe board is closed under composition.

Solution: This is obvious from geometry.   □

Example 4   Show that the collection of permutations on the 2 × 2 tic-tac-toe board consisting of the 360° rotation alone is closed under composition.

Solution: Its composition with itself is itself.   □

Example 5   Show that the collection of all four reflections on the 2 × 2 tic-tac-toe board is not closed under composition.

Solution: This follows from property (2) preceding Theorem 1.   □

Since a permutation π is a bijective function from a set to itself, it has an inverse, denoted $\text{inv}(\pi)$ or π^{-1}, which is also a bijective function from that set to itself. In other words, the inverse of a permutation on any set is a permutation on the same set. To calculate the inverse of a permutation in terms of its $2 \times n$ matrix representation, simply swap the two rows. If you want the top row of the result to be sorted, you can rearrange the columns accordingly.

For instance, it is clear from geometric reasoning that the inverse of a quarter-turn counterclockwise is a three-quarter turn counterclockwise. Here is how our calculation rule applies to this example.

$$\text{inv}\begin{pmatrix} 1 & 2 & 3 & 4 \\ 3 & 1 & 4 & 2 \end{pmatrix} = \begin{pmatrix} 3 & 1 & 4 & 2 \\ 1 & 2 & 3 & 4 \end{pmatrix}$$
$$= \begin{pmatrix} 1 & 2 & 3 & 4 \\ 2 & 4 & 1 & 3 \end{pmatrix}.$$

These two additional properties of 2 × 2 tic-tac-toe boards both follow immediately from geometric reasoning:

(4) The inverse of a rotation is a rotation.

(5) The inverse of a reflection is that same reflection.

From the combination of these two properties, we immediately infer the following theorem.

Theorem 2   The inverse of a rotation or a reflection of a 2 × 2 tic-tac-toe board is also a rotation or a reflection.   ■

A collection of permutations on a finite set is said to be **closed under inversion** if the inverse of every permutation in the collection is also in the collection.

There is a special name for a collection of permutations that is closed both under composition and under inversion. It is called a **permutation group.**

Example 6   Show that the collection of all rotations and reflections on the 2 × 2 tic-tac-toe board form a permutation group.

Solution: This follows from Theorems 1 and 2 together.   □

Example 7   Show that the collection of all rotations and reflections on the 3 × 3 tic-tac-toe board form a permutation group.

Solution: This follows from applying to the 3 × 3 board the same methods used for the 2 × 2 board.   □

Example 8   Show that the collection of all permutations on a finite set forms a permutation group.

Solution: Since the composition of any two permutations is a permutation and since the inverse of any permutation is a permutation, this follows immediately.
   □

Example 9   Show that the singleton collection containing only the identity permutation (which fixes every element, just like any other identity function on a set) is a permutation group.

Solution: The composition of the identity with itself is the identity, and the inverse of the identity is the identity, so the collection is closed both under composition and under inversion.   □

We conclude this section by placing the concept of congruence classes of tic-tac-toe boards into a context of greater generality, amenable to the Burnside–Polya theory of counting.

When a permutation group G acts on a set Y, we often call the elements of that set *objects*. In particular, the tic-tac-toe configurations with five crosses and four naughts are the objects, when the permutation group is the collection of rotations and reflections on the 3 × 3 tic-tac-toe board.

If y is any object in the set Y, then for every permutation $\pi \in G$, the object $\pi(y)$ is considered to be related to y. We write yRy' if y and y' are related this way, and we say that R is the **relation induced by the action** of G.

Theorem 3   The relation R induced by the action of a permutation group P on a set of objects Y is an equivalence relation.

Proof: Given any object y, let I denote the identity permutation. Then we have $y\,R\,I(y)$. In other words, every object y is related to itself, from which it follows that the relation R is reflexive.

Next, given any two objects, y and y', suppose that yRy', which means that there exists a permutation π in the group G such that $\pi(y) = y'$. Since a permutation group is closed under inversion, it follows that $\pi^{-1} \in G$. Evidently, we have $\pi^{-1}(y') = y$, from which it follows that $y'Ry$. Thus, we have established that the relation R is symmetric.

Finally, if yRy' and $y'Ry''$, then there exist permutations π and μ in G such that $\pi(y) = y'$ and $\mu(y') = y''$. Obviously, $\mu \circ \pi(y) = y''$. Since the permutation group G is closed under composition, it is clear that $\mu \circ \pi \in G$. Hence, we have yRy'', from which it follows that the relation R is transitive.

Having established reflexivity, symmetry, and transitivity for relation R, we conclude that it is an equivalence relation.   ∎

The equivalence classes induced by the action of a permutation group on a set of objects are often called **orbits**.

Example 10   What are the orbits induced by the action of the group of rotations and reflections on the configurations of a tic-tac-toe board?

Solution: They are simply the congruence classes.   □

Example 11   When the group of all possible permutations acts on a set of objects, how many orbits are formed?

Solution: There is only one orbit, which comprises all elements of the set. □

The introduction of these algebraic concepts enables us to formulate the objective of Burnside–Polya enumeration theory most clearly, as a method for counting the orbits of a permutation group acting on a finite set. Actually, Frobenius invented the method for counting orbits, but its appearance in a classic tract of Burnside [1] led to its being called "Burnside's Lemma".

Polya* [3] augmented this theory with a means to assign "weights" to orbits

---

* George Polya (1887–1985) was a Hungarian mathematician who received his Ph.D. in probability theory from the University of Budapest. He taught at the Swiss Federal Institute of Technology and Brown University before taking a position at Stanford University in 1942. He published over 250 articles in various areas of mathematics and wrote several books on problem-solving.

and to decompose the total number of orbits into a sum of numbers of orbits of each weight class. Actually Polya rediscovered methods already known to Redfield [4], whose paper had escaped most attention. F. Harary (see [2]) developed the use of Burnside–Polya enumeration theory for graphical enumeration, which has attracted many mathematicians to its further application.

We will show how to count the 23 congruence classes of configurations cited in the introduction, and thereby solve *CCCP*, by a detailed application of Burnside–Polya theory. Along the way, we shall strive for the intermediate goal of counting the congruence classes of the 2×2 tic-tac-toe configurations of naughts and crosses in which no square is left empty.

There are 16 such configurations, since the filling of each of four squares involves a binary choice. Burnside's methods alone enable us to establish that there are six orbits, and Polya's augmentation provide an "inventory" of these six orbits into subclasses, as follows:

> 1 orbit with four crosses and zero naughts
>
> 1 orbit with three crosses and one naught
>
> 2 orbits with two crosses and two naughts
>
> 1 orbit with one cross and three naughts
>
> 1 orbit with zero crosses and four naughts.

Figure 5 provides one example configuration for each of these six orbits. You can easily demonstrate that every one of the 16 configurations can be rotated or reflected into one of the six examples shown.

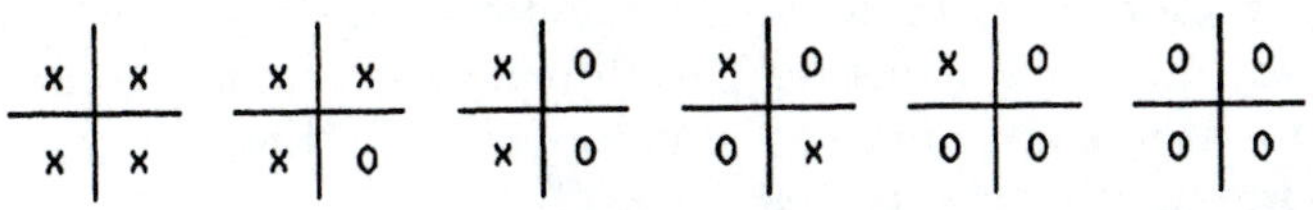

Figure 5. One configuration from each of the six orbits of 2×2 tic-tac-toe under the group of rotations and reflections.

The Cycle Structure of Permutations

We now return to the 2×9 representation of the counterclockwise quarter-turn on the 3×3 tic-tac-toe configurations.

$$\begin{pmatrix} 1 & 2 & 3 & 4 & 5 & 6 & 7 & 8 & 9 \\ 7 & 4 & 1 & 8 & 5 & 2 & 9 & 6 & 3 \end{pmatrix}$$

When we apply this permutation, the content (cross or naught) of location 1 will move to location 7, as we see from column 1. Column 7 indicates that the content of location 7 moves to location 9. Column 9 says that the content of location 9 moves to location 3. We also note that column 3 says the content of location 3 moves to location 1. In other words, the contents of the four locations 1, 7, 9, 3 move in a closed cycle.

Similarly we note that the contents of locations 2, 4, 8, and 6 moves in another closed cycle of length four. We also note that the permutation fixes the content of location 5, the center of the board. We may regard this as a cycle of length one. The two cycles of length four together with the cycle of length one account for the content of all nine of the locations of the board.

This analysis enables us to represent the permutation as a composition

$$(1 \ 7 \ 9 \ 3)(2 \ 4 \ 8 \ 6)(5)$$

of cycles, from which we could easily reconstruct the $2 \times n$ matrix representation. We can encode the fact that there are two 4-cycles and one 1-cycle as the multivariate monomial $t_1 t_4^2$. (By a *monomial*, we mean a polynomial with only one term. By *multivariate*, we mean it has more than one variable. In this case, its variables are t_1 and t_4.) In general, such a monomial is called the **cycle structure** of the permutation.

We observe that the objects in any one cycle are disjoint from the objects in any of the other cycles. In general, any permutation can be represented as a composition of disjoint cycles, and we call such a representation the **disjoint cycle form** of the permutation.

Table 1 indicates the disjoint cycle form and the cycle structure for all rotations and reflections on the 2×2 tic-tac-toe configurations.

We see from the table that there is one permutation with cycle structure t_1^4, two with structure $t_1^2 t_2$, three with structure t_2^2, and two with structure t_4. When we add the cycle structures for all permutations in a group G together and divide by the cardinality of the group, the resulting polynomial is called the **cycle index** of G, and is denoted $Z(G)$.

Example 12   What is the cycle index of the group of rotations and reflections on the 2×2 configurations?

Solution: $\frac{1}{8}(t_1^4 + 2t_1^2 t_2 + 3t_2^2 + 2t_4)$.   □

Example 13   Calculate the cycle index of the group of rotations and reflections on the 3×3 tic-tac-toe configurations.

Solution: The cycle index is

$$\frac{1}{8}(t_1^9 + 4t_1^3 t_2^3 + t_1 t_2^4 + 2t_1 t_4^2).$$

Its first term corresponds to the null (i.e., 360°) rotation; its second term corresponds to the four reflections, since each of them fixes three squares and swaps three pairs; its third term corresponds to the 180° rotation; and its fourth term accounts for the quarter-turn and the three-quarter turn.   □

rotations	cycle form	cycle structure
$\begin{pmatrix} 1 & 2 & 3 & 4 \\ 3 & 1 & 4 & 2 \end{pmatrix}$	(1 3 4 2)	t_4
$\begin{pmatrix} 1 & 2 & 3 & 4 \\ 4 & 3 & 2 & 1 \end{pmatrix}$	(1 4)(2 3)	t_2^2
$\begin{pmatrix} 1 & 2 & 3 & 4 \\ 2 & 4 & 1 & 3 \end{pmatrix}$	(1 2 4 3)	t_4
$\begin{pmatrix} 1 & 2 & 3 & 4 \\ 1 & 2 & 3 & 4 \end{pmatrix}$	(1)(2)(3)(4)	t_1^4
reflections		
$\begin{pmatrix} 1 & 2 & 3 & 4 \\ 3 & 4 & 1 & 2 \end{pmatrix}$	(1 3)(2 4)	t_2^2
$\begin{pmatrix} 1 & 2 & 3 & 4 \\ 2 & 1 & 4 & 3 \end{pmatrix}$	(1 2)(3 4)	t_2^2
$\begin{pmatrix} 1 & 2 & 3 & 4 \\ 1 & 3 & 2 & 4 \end{pmatrix}$	(1)(2 3)(4)	$t_1^2 t_2$
$\begin{pmatrix} 1 & 2 & 3 & 4 \\ 4 & 2 & 3 & 1 \end{pmatrix}$	(1 4)(2)(3)	$t_1^2 t_2.$

Table 1. Cycle forms and cycle structures for rotations and reflections on 2×2 tic-tac-toe configurations.

Burnside's Lemma

The Burnside–Polya counting method is based upon substitutions into the cycle index. A simple illustration of how this works is to substitute the number 2 for each variable in the cycle index

$$\tfrac{1}{8}(t_1^4 + 2t_1^2 t_2 + 3t_2^2 + 2t_4).$$

The result of the substitution is the arithmetic expression

$$\tfrac{1}{8}(2^4 + 2 \cdot 2^2 2 + 3 \cdot 2^2 + 2 \cdot 2).$$

This simplifies to

$$\tfrac{1}{8}(16 + 16 + 12 + 4) = 6,$$

exactly the number of configurations appearing in Figure 5.

The mathematical result that this process always yields the total number of orbits is called Burnside's Lemma. Its proof will be obtained here with the aid of three auxiliary lemmas.

Let G be a permutation group acting on a set Y of objects. By the **stabilizer** of an object y, denoted Stab(y), we mean the collection of permutations in G that map y to itself.

It is clear that the composition of two permutations that fix y is also a permutation that fixes y. It is also clear that the inverse of a permutation that fixes y is also a permutation that fixes y. Thus, Stab(y) is also a permutation group. Since it is wholly contained in the group G, we call Stab(y) a **subgroup** of G.

Example 14   What is the stabilizer of the 2×2 tic-tac-toe configuration with crosses in locations 1 and 4 and naughts in locations 2 and 3?

Solution: Its stabilizer is the subgroup comprising these four permutations

$$(1)(2)(3)(4) \qquad (1\ 4)(2\ 3) \qquad (1\ 4)(2)(3) \qquad (1)(2\ 3)(4). \qquad \square$$

The necessary and sufficient condition on a permutation for fixing that configuration is that all the locations occurring within each cycle be marked the same, that is, all with crosses or all with naughts.

Just as we associate with each object y the collection Stab(y) of permutations that fix y, we associate with each permutation π the set of objects that it fixes. This set is called the **fixed-point set** of π and it is denoted Fix(π), and it comprises the set of objects that occur in 1-cycles of the disjoint cycle form of π.

Example 15   What 2×2 tic-tac-toe configurations are fixed by the permutation $(1)(2)(3)(4)$?

Solution: It fixes all 16 completely filled 2×2 tic-tac-toe configurations. $\square$

Example 16   What 2×2 tic-tac-toe configurations are fixed by the permutation $(1\ 4)(2\ 3)$?

Solution: When the permutation $(1\ 4)(2\ 3)$ acts on the 2×2 tic-tac-toe configurations, it swaps the marks in locations 1 and 4, and it swaps the marks in locations 2 and 3. Therefore, it fixes a tic-tac-toe configuration if and only if the contents of locations 1 and 4 are the same and the contents of locations 2 and 3 are the same. Since each of the four locations is to be filled with either a cross or a naught, there are two choices for the kind of mark for locations 1 and 4 and two choices for the kind of mark for locations 2 and 3. Thus, $(1\ 4)(2\ 3)$ fixes four tic-tac-toe configurations. $\square$

Example 17   What 2×2 tic-tac-toe configurations are fixed by the permutation $(1\ 4)(2)(3)$?

Solution: By the same analysis we just performed for Example 16, we see that $(1\ 4)(2)(3)$ fixes a configuration if and only if locations 1 and 4 are filled with the same mark; the marks in locations 2 and 3 are both arbitrary. Thus, we have three binary choices for marks: the mark for locations 1 and 4, the mark for location 2, and the mark for location 3. It follows that the permutation $(1\ 4)(2)(3)$ fixes eight (i.e., 2^3) configurations.   □

The first of the three lemmas needed for the proof of Burnside's Lemma concerns the effect of interchanging the indices for a double summation. Its proof involves the use of the *Iverson truth function* $\text{true}(p)$, whose value is 1 if p is a true statement, and whose value is 0 otherwise.

Lemma 1   The sum of the cardinalities of the stabilizers, taken over all objects of a permuted set Y, equals the sum of the cardinalities of the fixed-point sets, taken over all permutations in the group G that acts on Y. That is,

$$\sum_{y \in Y} |\text{Stab}(y)| = \sum_{\pi \in G} |\text{Fix}(\pi)|.$$

Proof: Since $\text{Stab}(y) = \{\pi : \pi(y) = y\}$, it follows that

$$|\text{Stab}(y)| = \sum_{\pi \in G} \text{true}(\pi(y) = y).$$

Therefore,

$$\sum_{y \in Y} |\text{Stab}(y)| = \sum_{y \in Y} \sum_{\pi \in G} \text{true}(\pi(y) = y)$$

$$= \sum_{\pi \in G} \sum_{y \in Y} \text{true}(\pi(y) = y)$$
(by interchanging indices of summation)

$$= \sum_{\pi \in G} |\text{Fix}(\pi)|.$$
(because $\sum_{y \in Y} \text{true}(\pi(y) = y) = |\text{Fix}(\pi)|$)

∎

Lemma 2   For any object y in a set Y of permuted objects under the action of a permutation group G,

$$|\text{Stab}(y)| = \frac{|G|}{|\text{orbit}(y)|}.$$

Proof: Suppose that $\mathrm{orbit}(y) = \{y_1, y_2, \ldots, y_n\}$, where $y = y_1$. Then for $j = 1, 2, \ldots, n$, we define

$$G_j = \{\pi \in G : \pi(y) = y_j\}.$$

In other words, G_j is the subset of permutations in G that map y to y_j. Clearly, $\{G_1, G_2, \ldots, G_n\}$ is a partition of the permutations in the group, and $G_1 = \mathrm{Stab}(y)$.

For $j = 1, 2, \ldots, n$, let π_j be any permutation such that $\pi_j(y) = y_j$. Then composition with π_j maps every permutation in G_1 to a permutation in G_j, and composition with π_j^{-1} maps every permutation in G_j to a permutation in G_1. It follows that composition with π_j is a bijection from G_1 to G_j, which implies that $|G_j| = |G_1| = |\mathrm{Stab}(y)|$.

Since $\{G_1, G_2, \ldots, G_n\}$ is a partition of G into subsets of size $|\mathrm{Stab}(y)|$, it follows that the product of $|\mathrm{Stab}(y)|$ with the number $n = |\mathrm{orbit}(y)|$ of subsets equals $|G|$. Equivalently, $|\mathrm{Stab}(y)| = |G|/|\mathrm{orbit}(y)|$. ∎

Example 14, revisited.   We recall that the configuration with crosses on its main diagonal (i.e., in locations 1 and 4) and naughts on its minor diagonal (i.e., in locations 2 and 3) has four elements in its stabilizer. Since the only other configuration in its orbit is the configuration with crosses on its minor diagonal and naughts on its main diagonal, its orbit has cardinality two. Since there are eight rotations and reflections in the permutation group acting on the set of configurations, the equation

$$4 = 8/2$$

serves as empirical evidence of the correctness of Lemma 2. □

Lemma 3   Let G be a permutation group acting on a set of objects Y. Then

$$\sum_{y \in Y} \frac{1}{|\mathrm{orbit}(y)|} = \#\ \mathrm{orbits}.$$

Proof: Suppose that $\#\ \mathrm{orbits} = k$, and that $Y_1, Y_2, \ldots, Y_k$ are the orbits. Then

$$\sum_{y \in Y} \frac{1}{|\mathrm{orbit}(y)|} = \sum_{j=1}^{k} \sum_{y \in Y_j} \frac{1}{|\mathrm{orbit}(y)|}$$

$$= \sum_{j=1}^{k} \sum_{y \in Y_j} \frac{1}{|Y_j|}$$

$$= \sum_{j=1}^{k} \frac{1}{|Y_j|} \sum_{y \in Y_j} 1$$

$$= \sum_{j=1}^{k} \frac{1}{|Y_j|} |Y_j|$$

$$= \sum_{j=1}^{k} 1$$

$$= k$$

$$= \text{# orbits.}$$

(This lemma is really a fact about partitions of sets, and depends in no way upon the algebra of permutation groups.) ∎

Theorem 4   (Burnside's Lemma)   Let G be a permutation group acting on a set of objects Y. Then

$$\text{# orbits} = \frac{1}{|G|} \sum_{\pi \in G} |\text{Fix}(\pi)|.$$

Proof: Having already proved Lemmas 1, 2, and 3, we may prove Burnside's Lemma by a sequence of substitutions.

$$\frac{1}{|G|} \sum_{\pi \in G} |\text{Fix}(\pi)| = \frac{1}{|G|} \sum_{y \in Y} |\text{Stab}(y)| \qquad \text{by Lemma 1}$$

$$= \frac{1}{|G|} \sum_{y \in Y} \frac{|G|}{|\text{orbit}(y)|} \qquad \text{by Lemma 2}$$

$$= \frac{1}{|G|} |G| \sum_{y \in Y} \frac{1}{|\text{orbit}(y)|}$$

$$= \sum_{y \in Y} \frac{1}{|\text{orbit}(y)|}$$

$$= \text{# orbits.} \qquad \text{by Lemma 3} \ \square$$

For a direct application of Burnside's Lemma, we add the values of $|\text{Fix}(\pi)|$, the number of objects fixed, over all permutations π in the group G, and then divide their sum by $|G|$, the number of elements of the group. Theorem 5 generalizes the analysis of Examples 14, 15, and 16 into a method for calculating the values of $|\text{Fix}(\pi)|$, and Corollary 1 employs the result of Theorem 5 in establishing how to count the number of congruence classes of configurations.

Theorem 5   Let π be a permutation of the completely filled configurations of 2×2 tic-tac-toe boards, and let π have exactly r cycles in its disjoint cycle form. Then $|\text{Fix}(\pi)| = 2^r$.

Proof: The permutation π fixes a configuration if any only if, for each cycle in its disjoint cycle form, all the locations are marked the same.   ∎

Corollary 1   The number of congruence classes of completely filled 2×2 tic-tac-toe configurations equals the value of the arithmetic expression obtained by substituting the number 2 into the cycle index for the action of the group of rotations and reflections.

Proof: Theorem 5 indicates that this is exactly how to apply Burnside's Lemma to this counting problem.   ∎

Example 18   At the beginning of this section, we performed this calculation and confirmed that the result was 6, exactly the number of configurations appearing in Figure 5. A related question we might ask is this: if some of the locations of the 2×2 board remain unfilled, then how many congruence classes of configurations are there?

Solution: An analysis analogous to Examples 14, 15, and 16 and Corollary 1 indicates that the answer can be obtained by substituting the number 3 for each variable in the cycle index $\frac{1}{8}(t_1^4 + 2t_1^2t_2 + 3t_2^2 + 2t_4)$, an operation which we now perform.

$$\frac{1}{8}(3^4 + 2 \cdot 3^2 3 + 3 \cdot 3^2 + 2 \cdot 3) = \frac{1}{8}(81 + 54 + 27 + 6)$$
$$= \frac{1}{8}(168)$$
$$= 21.   \qquad \square$$

One way to confirm the validity of this result is to draw representative configurations from each of the 21 congruence classes, and then to confirm that the list of drawings is complete and non-repetitive. However, there is an easier approach that still uses Figure 5, if we regard "empty" as just another kind of mark on a tic-tac-toe board.

First of all, only one congruence class of configurations uses exactly one mark. Since there are three possible marks, we have three orbits with exactly one mark. Figure 5 shows four congruence classes with exactly two different marks. Since we have three choices of two kinds of marks from the set {cross, naught, empty}, there are 12 orbits (i.e., $3 \cdot 4$) with exactly two marks. That makes 15 orbits so far, and it remains to count the orbits with three different kinds of marks.

Suppose that we intend to use two crosses, one naught, and one empty location. There are two different possible orbits, one with the two crosses in horizontally or vertically adjacent locations, and the other with two crosses juxtaposed diagonally. Since the same analysis applies to counting orbits with two naughts, one cross, and one empty or orbits with two empties, one cross, and one naught, it follows that there are six (i.e., $3 \cdot 2$) orbits with three different marks. Since $15 + 6 = 21$, we have another empirical verification of the validity of Burnside's Lemma and of our method of applying it to configuration counting problems.

Polya's Inventory Method

Polya's augmentation of Burnside's Lemma involves the assignment of a monomial weight to each configuration so that any two configurations in the same orbit are assigned the same weight. When a weighting polynomial is substituted into the cycle index, the resulting polynomial provides an enumeration of the orbits according to weight.

As a first illustration of how Polya's method is used and the inventoried information it provides, we continue the analysis of 2×2 tic-tac-toe configurations. The weight assigned to a configuration with r crosses and $4 - r$ naughts is the monomial x^r. Observe carefully how we perform the substitution into the multivariate cycle index

$$\tfrac{1}{8}(t_1^4 + 2t_1^2 t_2 + 3t_2^2 + 2t_4).$$

For $r = 1, 2, 3, 4$, the binomial $1 + x^r$ is substituted for each instance of the variable t_r. The resulting expression is

$$\tfrac{1}{8}((1 + x)^4 + 2(1 + x)^2(1 + x^2) + 3(1 + x^2)^2 + 2(1 + x^4)),$$

which we expand into

$$
\begin{aligned}
\tfrac{1}{8}(\quad & 1 + 4x + 6x^2 + 4x^3 + \ x^4 \\
+\ & 2 + 4x + 4x^2 + 4x^3 + 2x^4 \\
+\ & 3 \qquad\quad + 6x^2 \qquad\quad + 3x^4 \\
+\ & 2 \qquad\qquad\qquad\qquad\quad + 2x^4 \ ).
\end{aligned}
$$

By collecting terms of like degree, we obtain the univariate polynomial

$$\tfrac{1}{8}(\quad 8 + 8x + 16x^2 + 8x^3 + 8x^4 \quad)$$

which simplifies to

$$1 + \ x + \ 2x^2 + \ x^3 + \ x^4.$$

Our interpretation of this simplified univariate polynomial is that there is one orbit with no crosses, one orbit with one cross, two orbits with two crosses, one orbit with three crosses, and one orbit with four crosses, exactly what we saw in Figure 5. That is, the coefficient of the term of degree r is the number of orbits of weight x^r, which we designed to equal the number of orbits with r crosses.

Theorem 6 formalizes this counting technique. Its proof involves the derivation of a "weighted" version of Burnside's Lemma.

Theorem 6   Let π be a permutation of the completely filled configurations of 2×2 tic-tac-toe boards, and let

$$t_1^{e_1} t_2^{e_2} t_3^{e_3} t_4^{e_4}$$

be the cycle structure of π. For $r = 1, 2, 3, 4$, substitute the binomial $1 + x^r$ for t_r (and collect terms of like degree). Then the coefficient of the term of degree r in the resulting polynomial equals the number of orbits of weight x^r. ∎

Solving CCCP   With the aid of Theorem 6, we are ready to solve *CCCP*. We begin by recalling from Example 13 that the cycle index for the action of the group of rotations and reflections on the 3×3 tic-tac-toe configurations is the multivariate polynomial

$$\tfrac{1}{8}(t_1^9 + 4t_1^3 t_2^3 + t_1 t_2^4 + 2t_1 t_4^2).$$

If we need to know the number of congruence classes for each possible number of crosses from zero to nine, with naughts in all other grid locations, then we substitute $(1 + x^r)$ for each instance of the variable t_r in the cycle index above and proceed as in our calculation for the 2×2 configurations.

Since *CCCP* restricts its concern to counting the configurations with five crosses, our task is somewhat reduced. That is, it is sufficient to calculate, for each of the four terms of the cycle index, the coefficient of x^5 that results when we substitute $(1 + x^r)$ for each instance of the variable t_r in that term, for $r = 1, 2, \ldots, 9$. Here are the details of this step.

term	substitution	coefficient of x^5	value
t_1^9	$(1+x)^9$	$C(9,5)$	126
$4t_1^3 t_2^3$	$4(1+x)^3(1+x^2)^3$	$4(C(3,1)C(3,2) + C(3,3)C(3,1))$	48
$t_1 t_2^4$	$(1+x)(1+x^2)^4$	$C(1,1)C(4,2)$	6
$2t_1 t_4^2$	$2(1+x)(1+x^4)^2$	$2C(1,1)C(2,1)$	4
		sum $=$	184

The sum of the values in the rightmost column is 184. Division by 8, the cardinality of the permutation group, yields 23, which is the number of congruence classes of configurations with five crosses and four naughts that we previously promised. Figure 6 provides a complete list of representatives of the 23 congruence classes.

Boldface crosses are used to organize these 23 congruence classes into subsets that can be easily checked by ad hoc methods for completeness and non-duplication. For instance, there are nine classes in which an entire side contains crosses.

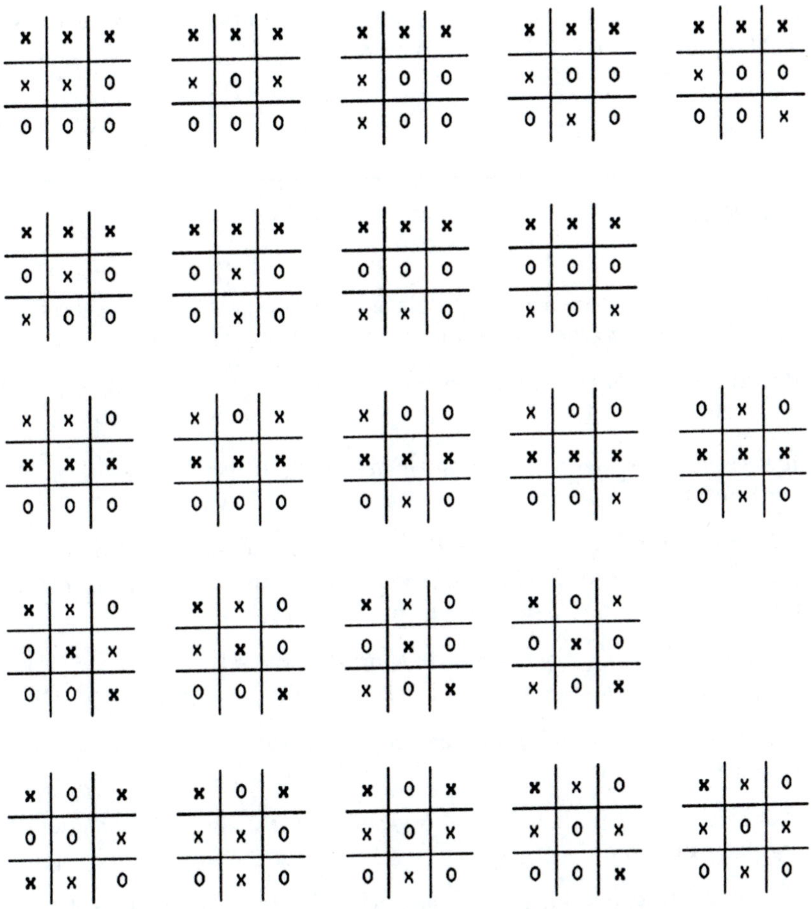

Figure 6. The **23 different** 3×3 **tic-tac-toe configurations with five crosses and four naughts.**

Suggested Readings

1. W. Burnside, *Theory of Groups of Finite Order*, Second Edition, Cambridge University Press, Cambridge, 1911.

2. F. Harary and E. Palmer, *Graphical Enumeration*, Academic Press, New York and London, 1973.

3. G. Polya, "Kombinatorische Anzahlbestimmungen für Gruppen, Graphen, und chemische Verbindungen", *Acta Mathematica*, Vol. 68, 1937, pp. 344–51.

4. J. Redfield, "The theory of group-reduced distributions", *American Journal of Mathematics*, Vol. 49, 1927, pp. 433–55.

Exercises

1. Draw a 3×3 tic-tac-toe configuration with two crosses and seven naughts such that the congruence class has cardinality equal to two.

2. Represent the four rotations on the 3×3 tic-tac-toe board of Figure 3 by 2×9 matrices.

3. Represent the four reflections on the 3×3 tic-tac-toe board of Figure 9 by 2×9 matrices.

4. Use the composition rule for $2 \times n$ matrix representations of permutations to show that the composition of the 90° rotation and the 180° rotation of the 2×2 tic-tac-toe board is the 270° rotation.

5. Use $2 \times n$ matrix representations to show that the inverse of the 90° rotation of the 2×2 tic-tac-toe board is the 270° rotation.

6. Calculate the cycle index for the group of rotations and reflections on an equilateral triangle.

7. Calculate the cycle index for the group of rotations and reflections on a regular pentagon.

8. Calculate the cycle index for the group of rotations and reflections on a regular hexagon.

9. How many congruence classes are there for a 3×3 tic-tac-toe board with crosses and naughts everywhere but the center, which is left unfilled?

10. In Exercise 9, suppose we further require that there are four crosses and four naughts. How many congruence classes meet this additional restriction?

Computer Projects

1. Write a computer program that takes as input a 3×3 array of 0s and 1s and prints all reflections and rotations of this array.

2. Write a computer program that accepts as input a completely filled-in 3×3 tic-tac-toe configuration and determines its orbit.

3. Write a computer program that takes a cycle index, substitutes $1 + x^r$, and evaluates and collects like terms to produce a polynomial in x.

PART III

GRAPH THEORY

13

Food Webs

Author: Robert A. McGuigan, Department of Mathematics, Westfield State College.

Prerequisites: The prerequisites for this chapter are basic concepts of graph theory. See, for example, Sections 7.1 and 7.2 of *Discrete Mathematics and Its Applications*, Second Edition, by Kenneth H. Rosen.

Introduction

A food web is a directed graph modeling the predator-prey relationship in an ecological community. We will use this directed graph to study the question of the minimum number of parameters needed to describe ecological competition. For this purpose we will consider how graphs can be represented as intersection graphs of families of sets.

We will also investigate the axiomatic description of measures of status in food webs.

Competition

In an ecological system, the various species of plants and animals occupy niches defined by the availability of resources. The resources might be defined in terms of factors such as temperature, moisture, degree of acidity, amounts of nutrients, and so on.

These factors are subject to constraints such as temperature lying in a certain range, pH lying within certain limits, etc. The combination of all these constraints for a species then defines a region in n-dimensional Euclidean space, where n is the number of factors. We can call this region the *ecological niche* of the species in question.

For example, suppose we restrict ourselves to three factors, such as temperature, nutrients, and pH. Assume that the temperature must be between t_1 and t_2 degrees, the amount of nutrients between n_1 and n_2 and the pH between a_1 and a_2. Then the ecological niche these define occupies the region of 3-dimensional Euclidean space shown in Figure 1.

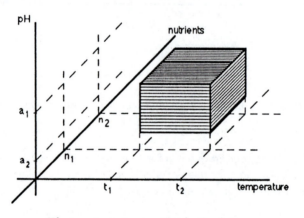

Figure 1.   An ecological niche.

Euclidean space which has as dimensions the various factors of temperature, pH, etc., is called an **ecological phase space**. Generally, no two distinct species will have the same ecological niche in phase space; however, two species **compete** if their ecological niches have non-empty intersection. A basic principle of ecology, known as the **principle of competitive exclusion**, dictates that species whose niches are too similar, or overlap too much, cannot coexist. If the factors defining the niche are independent, then the niche in phase space would be a box such as that in Figure 1. If the factors are not independent, i.e. the level of one depends on levels of others, then the niche would be some other type of set, e.g. convex, but not a box.

For example, consider the two factors temperature (t) and per cent humidity (h). We might have constraints such as: t must be between 0 and 100, and h must be between 0 and $100t - t^2$. In this case temperature and humidity are not independent; the possible values of h depend on the values of t. The region in two-dimensional space defined by these constraints is not a rectangle.

Our discussion of ecological communities and related concepts such as species, food webs, and competition will be somewhat oversimplified in order to make a brief presentation possible. Interested readers should consult reference [1] for an in-depth treatment of these topics. Our mathematical treatment follows that of reference [6].

Food Webs

It may be difficult to know all the factors which determine an ecological niche, and some factors may be relatively unimportant. Hence it is useful to start with the concept of competition and try to find the minimum number of dimensions necessary for a phase space in which competition can be represented by niche overlap.

One approach to this question is to consider the notion of the *food web* of an ecological community.

Definition 1   A *food web* of an ecological community is a directed graph with a vertex for each species in the community and a directed edge from the vertex representing species A to the vertex representing species B if and only if A preys on B.   □

Figure 2 shows a simple food web for a community of seven species: robin, fox, grasshopper, raccoon, salamander, milksnake, and toad.

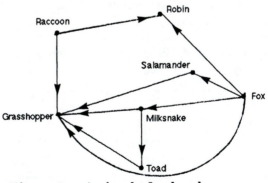

Figure 2.   A simple food web.

We can define *competition* using the food web. Two species *compete* if and only if they have a common prey. Thus, in the example of Figure 2, raccoon and fox compete (since robin is a common prey), milksnake and raccoon compete, while salamander and robin do not compete. We use this competition relation to define a graph called the competition graph.

Definition 2   The *competition graph* of a food web is a simple graph with a vertex for each species. Two vertices are joined by an (undirected) edge if and only if the species they represent have a common prey.   □

Example 1   Find the competition graph for the food web of Figure 2.

Solution: The competition graph for this food web is shown in Figure 3.   □

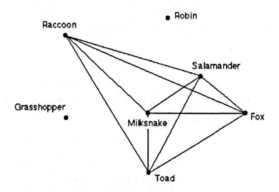

Figure 3.   A competition graph.

To represent the competition relation in phase space we want to assign to each vertex of the competition graph a subset of Euclidean space of some dimension in such a way that two vertices are joined by an edge in the competition graph if and only if the sets assigned to these vertices have non-empty intersection. Figure 4 shows a representation of the competition graph of Figure 3, using an interval for each vertex. We have thus represented the competition graph using only one dimension.

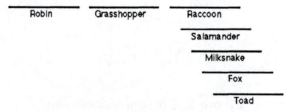

Figure 4.   Interval representation of a competition graph.

We can now state a general mathematical problem, but first we need to develop some terminology.

Definition 3   A graph is an *intersection graph* for a family of sets if each vertex is assigned a set in such a way that two vertices are joined by an edge if and only if the corresponding sets have non-empty intersection.   □

Definition 4   A graph is called an *interval graph* if it is the intersection graph for a family of closed intervals.   □

Our goal is the representation of competition graphs of families of sets in Euclidean n-space. Clearly the simplest case would be that of competition graphs that are interval graphs. This would mean that only one ecological factor is necessary to describe niche overlap.

Example 2   Find the interval graph for the family of closed intervals $A = [1, 3]$, $B = [2, 6]$, $C = [5, 8]$, $D = [4, 5]$.

Solution: We use the definition of intersection graph to obtain the graph of Figure 5.   □

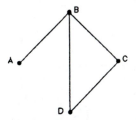

Figure 5.   An intersection graph.

Example 3   Prove that the 4-cycle graph C_4 of Figure 6 is not an interval graph.

Solution: The proof depends on the order properties of the real numbers. Let the interval corresponding to vertex n be $[n_l, n_r]$. Since the intervals for vertices 1 and 2 overlap, we must have either $1_l \leq 2_l \leq 1_r \leq 2_r$ or $2_l \leq 1_l \leq 2_r \leq 1_r$, Assume for specificity that $1_l \leq 2_l \leq 1_r \leq 2_r$. The argument for the other case is analogous.

Since the interval for vertex 3 must meet that for vertex 2 and must not meet that for vertex 1, we must have $1_l \leq 2_l \leq 1_r < 3_l \leq 2_r$. Now the interval for vertex 4 must meet those for both vertices 1 and 3, so we have to have $1_l \leq 4_l \leq 1_r$ and $3_l \leq 4_r \leq 3_r$ since interval 1 lies entirely to the left of interval 3. However, since $2_l \leq 1_r < 3_l \leq 2_r$, the intervals for vertices 2 and 4 overlap, which is forbidden.   □

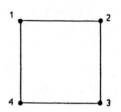

Figure 6.   A graph that is not an interval graph.

The 4-cycle can, however, be represented as the intersection graph of a family of boxes in Euclidean 2-space, as shown in Figure 7.

There are several methods known for determining whether a simple graph is an interval graph. A detailed discussion of this topic may be found in Roberts' book [6]. We simply state the characterization due to Gilmore and Hoffman [3] without proof. Before the characterization can be stated, we need some definitions.

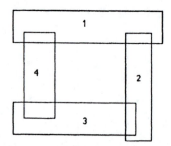

Figure 7.   A box representation.

Definition 5   A graph H is a *generated subgraph* of a graph G if the vertices of H are a subset of the vertices of G and vertices in H are adjacent in H if and only if they are adjacent in G.   □

Definition 6   The *complement* of a graph G is the graph $\overline{G}$ where the vertices of $\overline{G}$ are the vertices of G, and two vertices in $\overline{G}$ are adjacent if and only if they are not adjacent in G.   □

Definition 7   An *orientation* of a graph G is an assignment of a direction to each edge in G (which makes G into a directed graph).

An orientation is *transitive* if whenever (u, v) and (v, w) are directed edges, then (u, w) is a directed edge.   □

The characterization due to Gilmore and Hoffman is given by the following theorem.

Theorem 1   A graph G is an interval graph if and only if it satisfies the following two conditions:

(i) The four-cycle C_4 is not a generated subgraph of G,

(ii) The complement of G is transitively orientable.   ∎

Our goal in our study of ecological competition is the representation of niches in Euclidean space and competition by niche overlap. It seems desirable in an ideal representation that the factors determining the dimension of the ecological phase space would be independent and the niches would be represented as "boxes", or Cartesian products of intervals. This leads us to the next part of this discussion, namely, when can we represent a graph as the intersection graph of a family of boxes in n-space.

Boxicity

Definition 8   The *boxicity* of a graph G is the smallest n such that G is the intersection graph of a family of boxes in Euclidean n-space.   □

Note that an interval graph is simply a graph with boxicity equal to 1. It is not entirely clear that every simple graph has a boxicity. The following theorem resolves this difficulty.

Theorem 2   Every graph G with n vertices is the intersection graph of a family of boxes in Euclidean n-space.

Proof: Let $v_1, v_2, \ldots, v_n$ be the vertices of G. A box in Euclidean n-dimensional space is the set of all n-tuples of real numbers $(x_1, x_2, \ldots, x_n)$ such that each x_i is in some closed interval I_i. Now, for each $k = 1 \ldots, n$ and each vertex v_i, define closed intervals $I_k(v_i)$ as follows.

$$I_k(v_i) = \begin{cases} [0,1] & \text{if } i = k \\ [1,2] & \text{if } i \neq k \text{ and } \{v_i, v_k\} \text{ is an edge in } G \\ [2,3] & \text{if } i \neq k \text{ and } \{v_i, v_k\} \text{ is not an edge in } G. \end{cases}$$

For each vertex v_i define a box $B(v_i)$ in Euclidean n-space by

$$B(v_i) = \{(x_1, x_2, \ldots, x_n) \mid x_j \in I_j(v_i) \text{ for } j = 1, \ldots, n\}.$$

Thus, the box $B(v_i)$ corresponding to v_i is the Cartesian product of the intervals $I_j(v_i)$ for $j = 1, \ldots, n$.

Now we show that v_i and v_j are adjacent in G if and only if $B(v_i) \cap B(v_j) \neq \emptyset$. Thus the graph G is the intersection graph of the family of boxes $B(v_i)$. First, suppose that there is an edge joining v_l and v_m. If k is different from both l and m, then according to the definition, $I_k(v_l) \cap I_k(v_m)$ is $[1, 2] \cap [1, 2], [1, 2] \cap [2, 3]$, or $[2, 3] \cap [2, 3]$. In any case we have $I_k(v_l) \cap I_k(v_m) \neq \emptyset$. If k=l or k=m then $I_k(v_l) \cap I_k(v_m) = [1, 2] \cap [0, 1] \neq \emptyset$. So, if there is an edge joining v_e and v_m, then for all k, $I_k(v_l) \cap I_k(v_m) \neq \emptyset$. Hence $B(v_l) \cap B(v_m) \neq \emptyset$.

Now suppose that $B(v_l) \cap B(v_m) \neq \emptyset$. Then for each k from 1 to n, $I_k(v_l) \cap I_k(v_m) \neq \emptyset$. Set $k = l$ then $I_l(v_l) = [0, 1]$ and $I_l(v_m)$ must be $[1, 2]$ for the intersection to be nonempty. By definition of $I_l(v_m)$, v_l and v_m are adjacent. Thus G is the intersection graph of the family of boxes $B(v_i)$. ∎

This theorem shows that boxicity is well-defined. Unfortunately, there is no efficient algorithm known for determining the boxicity of a general graph. There is no characterization known for graphs of any specific boxicity other than 1.

In fact, there are not many general classes of graphs for which the boxicity is known. It is not hard to see that the boxicity of the n-cycle C_n is 2 for $n = 4$ or larger, and this is left as Exercise 6. Another general class of graphs for which the boxicity is known is the *complete p-partite* graphs. These are the graphs $K_{n_1, n_2, \ldots, n_p}$ defined as follows: there are $n_1 + \cdots + n_p$ vertices partitioned into p classes, where the ith class has n_i vertices. Within a class no vertices are adjacent, and every vertex in any class is adjacent to all vertices in the other classes. Roberts [6] showed that the boxicity of $K_{n_1, \ldots, n_p}$ is equal to the number of n_i that are larger than 1.

One result which helps somewhat in calculating the boxicity of a graph is due to Gabai [2]. This theorem depends on the concept of *independence* of a set of edges.

Definition 9   A set of edges in a graph is *independent* if they have no vertices in common. □

Gabai's theorem [2] is the following, stated without proof.

Theorem 3   Let G be a simple graph. If the maximum size of an independent set of edges of $\overline{G}$ is k, then G has boxicity less than or equal to k. Also, if $\overline{G}$ has a generated subgraph consisting of k independent edges then the boxicity of G is greater than or equal to k. ∎

Gabai's theorem is useful in determining the boxicity of relatively small graphs and for certain families. In any case it limits the amount of trial and error needed.

In our study of competition we search for the representation of the competition graph of a food web as the intersection graph of a family of sets in Euclidean n-space for some n. As a consequence of the theorem proved above, this representation is always possible. Furthermore, we can use the boxicity of the competition graph as an indicator of the minimum number of factors essential for describing competition in the community. Cohen [1] has studied more than 30 single-habitat food webs published in the ecological literature and has found that the competition graphs of all of them are interval graphs. That is, in all cases one dimension suffices to represent competition by niche overlap. It is not known whether this is a general law of ecology, but it does raise many interesting questions. In some single-habitat communities a single dimension for the niche space can be identified. It may be some obviously linear factor such as temperature, body length or depth in water. However, it may well be that more than one single dimension will work. And, of course, we can't expect the single-niche dimension to be the same from community to community.

Hypothetical food webs have been constructed such that their competition graphs are not interval graphs, but these combinations of species have never been observed in nature at the same time and place.

The representation of graphs as intersection graphs of boxes has important applications in ecology, as we have seen. Applications to such diverse fields as archaeology and automobile traffic control have also been investigated (see reference [6]). We conclude with an additional application of food webs.

Trophic Status

In the study of social systems it is often useful to measure the status of an individual in an organization. Harary [4] first introduced the idea of measuring the status of a species in a food web. In ecology this status is usually called the **trophic level** and is helpful in assessing the complexity and diversity of a web. The idea is that a web with many species at each trophic level has a high degree of complexity. In ecology it is generally thought that more complex ecosystems are more stable. In this section we study the question of how trophic status can be defined in a food web.

If the food web is simply a directed path (a food chain) then it is easy to define trophic status; just follow the order of the species in the chain. Some other structures also allow for an easy definition of trophic status. For example, we might think of species with no outgoing edges as being at the *bottom* of the web. Suppose that for every vertex, all directed paths to vertices at the bottom have the same length. Examples of such webs are given in Figure 8.

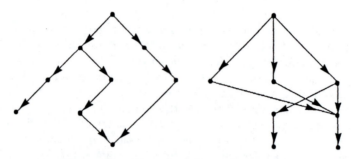

Figure 8.   Graphs of two food webs.

In this kind of web, the trophic status of a vertex can be defined as the length of a directed path from the vertex to the bottom.

In general it is difficult to define trophic status in complicated food webs. Because more than one approach may be possible, we will use the term *trophic status* in this context rather than the term trophic level which is well-known in the context of food chains. Our goal is to investigate how trophic status could be measured rather than to develop a unique possibility.

To start, we need some basic assumptions about food webs. In particular, we assume that our food web is *acyclic*, i.e. that the directed graph has no cycles. Thus, there are no species $s_1, \ldots, s_n$ such that for $i = 1, \ldots, n-1$, s_i preys on s_{i+1} and s_n preys on s_1. In particular there are no two species such that each preys on the other. Thus, the prey relationship is *asymmetric*.

We will take an axiomatic approach to defining measures of trophic status. That is, we will state conditions which any reasonable measure should satisfy in the form of axioms. A measure will then be acceptable if and only if it satisfies the axioms. The axioms will define an ideal model for the concept of measure of trophic status. Our approach will follow that of Harary [4] and Kemeny and Snell [5], who work with status in an organization, and the treatment in Roberts [6], which is more detailed.

Definition 10   In a food web a species v is a *direct prey* of a species u if there is a directed edge from u to v. A species v is an *indirect prey* of u if there is a directed path from u to v.   □

It could well happen that there are two species u and v neither of which is an indirect prey of the other.

Definition 11   If v is a direct or indirect prey of u, then the *level of v relative to u* is the length of the shortest directed path from u to v.   □

We can now state some reasonable axioms for measures of trophic status. Let $t_W(u)$ be the measure of status in the food web W. The axioms are:

Axiom 1: If a species u has no prey then $t_W(u) = 0$.

Axiom 2: If, without otherwise changing the food web, we add a new vertex which is a direct prey of u to get a new web W', then $t_{W'}(u) > t_W(u)$.

Axiom 3: Suppose the web W is changed by adding edges and/or vertices in such a way that the level of some direct or indirect prey of u is increased, and no direct or indirect prey of u has its level relative to u decreased. If W' is the new web, then $t_{W'}(u) > t_W(u)$.

These axioms make sense intuitively when we consider that we are saying that a species with no prey is at the bottom level (Axiom 1), that if the number of prey of a species increases its status increases (Axiom 2), and that the status of a species increases if its level relative to some indirect prey is increased (Axiom 3).

There is a measure of status which satisfies the axioms. Harary [4] suggested the following definition.

Definition 12   If a species u has n_k species at level k relative to u for each k, then

$$h_W(u) = \sum_k k n_k. \qquad \square$$

Theorem 4   The measure $h_W(u)$ satisfies Axioms 1-3.

Proof: If u has no prey, then $h_W(u) = 0$ because all the $n_k = 0$.

If we add a direct prey for u, then n_1 increases by 1, so the sum defining $h_W(u)$ also increases.

Likewise, if some direct or indirect prey of u at level k relative to u is moved to level $k + n$ below u and no other direct or indirect prey of u has its level decreased, the sum for h increases by at least kn, verifying Axiom 3. ∎

Kemeny and Snell [5] also show that if t_W is any other measure of trophic status satisfying Axioms 1–3 and having all its values nonnegative, then for all species u, $t_W(u) \geq h_W(u)$. Thus, h is in a sense a minimal measure of trophic status.

While h satisfies our axioms it fails to have other desirable properties. For example, it seems reasonable that if t_W is a measure of trophic status and v is a direct or indirect prey of u, then

$$t_W(u) \geq t_W(v).$$

The measure h does not have this property. Figure 9 shows an example of an acyclic food web W with two vertices u and v for which v is a direct prey of u but $h_W(v) > h_W(u)$.

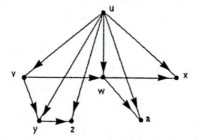

Figure 9.   An acyclic food web.

In this example, $h_W(u) = 6$ and $h_W(v) = 8$.

The problem we have found can be avoided if we modify our definition of level of one species relative to another: If v is a direct or indirect prey of u, then the *level of v relative to u* is the length of the *longest* directed path from u to v.

It is not hard to show that if h is defined by the same formula as before, but using the new definition of level, then h satisfies Axioms 1–3 as well as having the property that any species has higher status than any of its direct or indirect prey (see reference [5]). The problem we encountered here demonstrates one of the difficulties with the axiomatic approach. Our problem lay in the definition of level and this would not show up in any consideration of the reasonableness of the axioms. Ideally, all of the terms used in specifying the axioms should either be left undefined or else be checked for "reasonableness", just as the axioms themselves are. In this light we would also have to examine the new definition of level.

Without referring to the notion of relative level in a food web, perhaps the only requirement we can state for a measure of trophic status is that if there is a directed path from u to v, then $t_W(u) \geq t_W(v)$.

There are other ways to investigate complexity of food webs and relative importance of species in food webs. General methods of measuring complexity in graphs can be applied to competition graphs and food webs. For example, such ideas as the number of edges divided by the number of vertices, and the average out-degree and average in-degree might be useful. The importance, or criticality, of a species in a food web could be studied by investigating what happens to the web when the species is deleted from the web. For example, if the web is disconnected when a species is removed that would indicated a high level of importance. More information on these questions can be found in [6].

Suggested Readings

1. J. Cohen, *Food Webs and Niche Space*, Princeton University Press, 1978.

2. H. Gabai, "*N*-dimensional Interval Graphs", mimeographed, York College, C.U.N.Y., New York, 1974.

3. P. Gilmore and A. Hoffman, "A Characterization of Comparability Graphs and Interval Graphs", *Canadian J. Math.*, Vol. 16, 1964, pp. 539–548.

4. F. Harary, "Status and Contrastatus", *Sociometry*, Vol. 22, 1959, pp. 23–43.

5. J. Kemeny and J. Snell, *Mathematical Models in the Social Sciences*, MIT Press, Cambridge, MA, 1972.

6. F. Roberts, *Discrete Mathematical Models*, Prentice-Hall, 1976.

Exercises

1. Find the ecological niche in Euclidean space of the appropriate dimensions in each case.

   a) Temperature between $10°F$ and $90°F$; nitrate concentration in soil between 1% and 5%.

   b) Carbon monoxide in atmosphere between 0% and 1%; relative humidity between 20% and 100%; nitrogen gas content in atmosphere between 15% and 20%.

2. Find the competition graph for the given food webs in each case:

   a)   b)

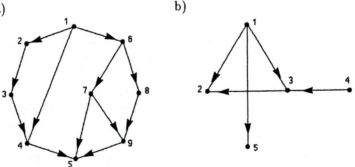

3. Find a representation for each graph as the intersection graph of a family of rectangles in the plane.

a)   b)

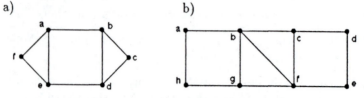

4. Find a representation for each graph as the intersection graph of a family of intervals on the line.

a)   b)

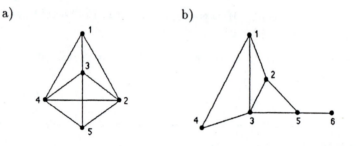

5. Show that if a graph G is an interval graph then it satisfies the conditions of the theorem of Gilmore and Hoffman characterizing interval graphs. *Hint:* For an interval representation let $I(v)$ be the interval assigned to the vertex v. If u and v are adjacent in $\overline{G}$, make the orientation (u, v) if and only if $I(u)$ lies entirely to the left of $I(v)$.

6. Show that if C_n is the cycle of length n, then the boxicity of C_n is 1 for $n = 3$ and 2 for $n \geq 4$.

7. According to Roberts' result quoted in the text, the boxicity of the complete bipartite graph $K(3,3)$ is 2. Find a representation of $K(3,3)$ as the intersection graph of a family of boxes in the plane.

8. Let Q_3 be the graph formed by the edges and corners of a cube in Euclidean three space. Is Q_3 an interval graph? Why? Determine the boxicity of Q_3.

9. A food web for some species in the Strait of Georgia, B.C. ([1], page 165) is given by the following table. The numbers atop columns indicate predator (consuming) species and those at the left of rows indicate prey (consumed) species. An entry 1 indicates that the predator in that column consumes the prey for that row, an entry 0 that it does not. The key identifies the various species.

	1	2	3	4	5	Key
2	1	0	0	0	0	1. Juvenile pink salmon
3	1	0	0	0	0	2. P. minutus
4	0	0	1	0	0	3. Calanus and Euphausiid furcilia
5	1	0	0	1	0	4. Euphausiid eggs
6	0	1	1	0	1	5. Euphausiids
7	0	0	1	0	1	6. Chaetoceros socialis and debilis
						7. mu-flagellates

a) Construct a directed graph for this food web.

b) Construct the competition graph for this food web.

c) Find a set of intervals on the real line such that the graph of part b) is the intersection graph of this family of intervals.

10. Repeat Exercise 9 for the following food web for a community of pine feeders [1], p.148.

	2	3	4	5	6	7	8	9	10	Key
1	1	1	0	0	0	0	0	0	0	1. Pine
2	0	0	1	1	0	0	0	0	0	2. Caterpillars, moths
3	0	0	1	0	1	1	1	1	1	3. Aphids, secretion
4	0	0	0	0	0	0	0	0	1	4. Digger wasps
5	0	0	0	0	0	0	0	0	1	5. Ichneumons
8	0	0	0	0	0	0	0	0	1	6. Bugs
9	0	0	0	0	0	0	0	0	1	7. Ants
10	0	0	1	0	0	0	0	0	0	8. Syrphids
										9. Ladybugs
										10. Spiders

11. Give an example of a food web which has two species, neither of which is a direct or indirect prey of the other.

12. In the section on trophic status two different definitions of relative level were given and two corresponding versions of the measure of trophic status h_W were also given. Calculate the trophic status of each vertex in each of the following food webs using both versions of h.

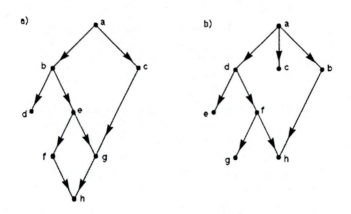

13. If the only requirement we make for a measure of trophic status t_W is that if there is a directed path from u to v then $t_W(u) > t_W(v)$, show that every acyclic food web has such a measure of trophic status.

14. (Roberts [6]) If relative level is measured using the length of the shortest directed path (our first definition), a plausible measure of trophic status is

$$t_W(u) = \sum_v h_W(v),$$

where the sum is taken over all vertices v for which there is a directed path from u to v. Show that this possible measure has the property that if there is a directed path from u to v, then $t_W(u) \geq t_W(v)$. Which of the Axioms 1–3 does this measure satisfy?

15. In our discussion of trophic status we assumed that the food web was acyclic. How restrictive is this assumption? Can you think of two species each of which could have the other as prey?

Computer Projects

1. Write a program to calculate trophic status in acyclic food webs.

2. Write a program to calculate the adjacency matrix for the intersection graph of a family of intervals given as pairs (a, b) of their endpoints.

14

Applications of
Subgraph Enumeration

Author: Fred J. Rispoli, Department of Mathematics, Dowling College.

Prerequisites: The prerequisites for this chapter are counting, probability, graphs, and trees. See, for example, Sections 4.1–4.4, 7.1–7.6, 8.1, and 8.5 of *Discrete Mathematics and Its Applications*, Second Edition, by Kenneth H. Rosen.

Introduction

Many applications of graph theory involve enumerating subgraphs to determine the number of subgraphs satisfying various properties, or to find a subgraph satisfying various properties. Some interesting examples are:

Example 1 How many distinct paths are there joining locations v_1 to v_3 in the transportation network represented by the graph in Figure 1? Given the length, l, and cost, c, of each edge, as displayed in Figure 1, does there exist a path joining v_1 to v_3 with total length 15 or less, and total cost \$40 or less? □

Example 2 How many different isomers are there of the saturated hydrocarbons C_5H_{12}? □

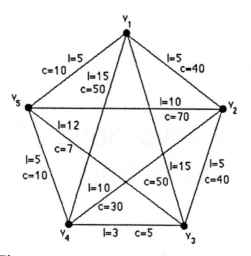

Figure 1.   A transportation network.

Example 3   How many ways are there to construct an electrical network which connects all of the nodes in the network and uses the smallest number of wires possible?   □

Example 4   A salesman wishes to visit a number of cities and return to the starting point in such a way that each city is visited exactly once. How many ways can this be done? If a route is selected at random, what is the probability that two given cities are visited in succession? Given the distances between cities, what route should be chosen so that the total distance covered is as short as possible?   □

In this chapter we will discuss how to solve these problems, and other similar problems. The approach is to define each problem in terms of subgraphs of K_n, the complete graph on n vertices, and then derive a method to generate and count the set of all subgraphs of K_n satisfying the required conditions. In particular, we will count the number of simple paths joining any pair of vertices in K_n, the number of spanning trees in K_n, the number of Hamilton circuits in K_n, and the number of perfect matches in K_n. These counts will then be used to determine the algorithmic complexity of exhaustive search procedures, to compute various probabilities, and to solve some counting problems.

Counting Paths

We begin by discussing paths and enumeration problems involving paths. Given any graph $G = (V, E)$ and a positive integer n, a *path of length n* from vertex u

to vertex v is a sequence of edges $e_1, e_2, \ldots, e_n$ of E such that $e_1 = \{x_0, x_1\}$, $e_2 = \{x_1, x_2\}, \ldots, e_n = \{x_{n-1}, x_n\}$ where $x_0 = u$ and $x_n = v$. A path is *simple* if it does not contain the same edge more than once.

Since any path of a graph $G = (V, E)$ consists of a subset of vertices of V and a subset of edges of E, a path is a subgraph of G. We will only consider simple paths in this chapter, and will omit the term "simple".

Theorem 1 and its proof allow us to solve Example 1 of the introduction. We use the notation

$$P(n, r) = n(n - 1)(n - 2) \ldots (n - r + 1) \qquad \text{if } r > 0,$$

and $P(n, 0) = 1$.

Theorem 1   Given any two vertices in K_n, the complete graph with n vertices, the number of paths joining them is

$$\sum_{k=1}^{n-1} P(n - 2, k - 1) = O(n^{n-2}).$$

Proof: Let K_n have vertex set $V = \{v_1, v_2, \ldots, v_n\}$ and let v_i and v_j be any pair of vertices in K_n. We count the number of paths joining v_i to v_j of length k, by establishing a one-to-one correspondence from the set of paths joining v_i to v_j of length k to the set of $(k+1)$-permutations of the set $\{1, 2, \ldots, n\}$ which begin with i and end with j.

Given any path P of length k joining v_i to v_j, to obtain a $(k + 1)$-permutation simply list the subscripts of the vertices that P visits as it is traversed from v_i to v_j. Conversely, let $i_1 i_2 \ldots i_{k+1}$ be a $(k + 1)$-permutation of $\{1, 2, \ldots, n\}$ such that $i_1 = i$ and $i_{k+1} = j$. The corresponding path P is made up of edges $\{v_{i_s}, v_{i_{s+1}}\}$, for $s = 1, 2, \ldots, k$. Since every path joining v_i to v_j of length k corresponds to a unique $(k+1)$-permutation of $\{1, 2, \ldots, n\}$ beginning with i and ending with j, and every $(k + 1)$-permutation of $\{1, 2, \ldots, n\}$ which begins with i and ends with j of length k corresponds to a unique path joining v_i to v_j, the correspondence between these two sets is one-to-one. The number of $(k + 1)$-permutations of $\{1, 2, \ldots, n\}$ which begin with i and end with j is $P(n - 2, k - 1)$. Thus the total number of paths joining v_i to v_j is obtained by summing $P(n - 2, k - 1)$ as k varies from 1 to $n - 1$.

To obtain the big-O estimate, note that

$$P(n - 2, k - 1) = (n - 2)(n - 3) \ldots (n - k) \le nn \ldots n = n^{k-1}.$$

Hence,

$$\sum_{k=1}^{n-1} P(n - 2, k - 1) \le n^0 + n^1 + \cdots + n^{n-2} = O(n^{n-2}). \qquad \blacksquare$$

The proof of Theorem 1 indicates how to enumerate all paths joining any pair of vertices in K_n by generating permutations. (A method for generating permutations is given in Section 4.7 of the text.) This allows us to solve Example 1 using an exhaustive search.

Solution to Example 1.   By Theorem 1, there are

$$\sum_{k=1}^{4} P(3, k-1) = 1 + 3 + 6 + 6 = 16$$

paths joining v_1 to v_3. To determine if there is a path from v_1 to v_3 with total length 15 or less and total cost \$40 or less, we list each $(k+1)$-permutation of $\{1, 2, 3, 4, 5\}$ beginning with 1 and ending with 3 corresponding to a path, along with its total length and total cost for $k = 1, 2, 3, 4$.

Paths with 1 or 2 edges

13	length: 15, cost: 50
123	length: 10, cost: 80
143	length: 18, cost: 55
153	length: 17, cost: 17

Paths with 3 edges

1243	length: 18, cost: 75
1423	length: 30, cost: 120
1253	length: 27, cost: 117
1523	length: 20, cost: 120
1453	length: 32, cost: 67
1543	length: 13, cost: 25

Paths with 4 edges

12453	length: 32, cost: 87
12543	length: 23, cost: 125
14253	length: 47, cost: 157
15243	length: 28, cost: 115
14523	length: 35, cost: 170
15423	length: 25, cost: 90

This shows that there is one path joining v_1 to v_3 which has total length 15 or less, and total cost \$40 or less, namely the path corresponding to 1543. □

Example 1 is an example of a *shortest weight-constrained path problem*, which we now define.

Shortest Weight-Constrained Path Problem: Given positive integers W and L, and a weighted graph $G = (V, E)$ with weights $w(e)$ and lengths $l(e)$, which are both positive integers, for all $e \in E$. Is there a path between two given vertices with weight $\leq W$ and length $\leq L$?

There is no known algorithm with polynomial complexity which solves the shortest weight-constrained problem. (See [2] in the suggested readings for an explanation why.) Thus, using an exhaustive search is a useful method for solving such a problem, as long as n is not too large. Theorem 1 tells us precisely just how large n can be. For example, suppose $n = 10$, and each path along with its weight and length can be computed in 10^{-4} seconds of computer time. Then, by Theorem 1, the are at most 10^8 paths to consider in K_{10}. So the problem can be solved in at most $10^8 \cdot 10^{-4} = 10^4$ seconds, or roughly 3 hours. Whereas if $n = 20$, the amount of computer time required is at most $20^{18} \cdot 10^{-4}$ seconds, or roughly $8 \cdot 10^{12}$ years.

A problem closely related to the above problem is the well-known shortest path problem, defined as follows.

> **Shortest Path Problem**: Given a weighted graph, find a path between two given vertices that has the smallest possible weight.

The shortest path problem may also be solved using an exhaustive search. However, Dijkstra's algorithm is a much better method. (See Section 7.6 of the text for a description of the algorithm). This is true because Dijkstra's algorithm requires $O(n^2)$ operations (additions and comparisons) to solve the problem. Whereas, if an exhaustive search is used, the number of additions used to compute the weight of each path is $O(n)$, and, by Theorem 1, there are $O(n^{n-2})$ such paths to examine. Thus, the number of additions required to compute the weight of all paths is $O(n^{n-1})$. This shows that Dijkstra's algorithm is much more efficient than an exhaustive search.

Counting Spanning Trees

In this section we shall study the enumeration of spanning trees. Recall that a *tree* is a connected graph with no circuits. If $G = (V, E)$ is a graph, a *spanning tree* of G is a subgraph of G that is a tree containing every vertex of V.

Spanning trees were first used by the German physicist Gustav Kirchoff who developed the theory of trees in 1847. Kirchoff used spanning trees to solve systems of simultaneous linear equations which give the current in each branch and around each circuit of an electrical network.

In 1857, the English mathematician Arthur Cayley independently discovered trees when he was trying to enumerate all isomers for certain hydrocarbons. Hydrocarbon molecules are composed of carbon and hydrogen atoms where each carbon atom can form up to four chemical bonds with other atoms, and each hydrogen atom can form one bond with another atom. A saturated hydrocarbon is one that contains the maximum number of hydrogen atoms for a given number of carbon atoms. Cayley showed that if a saturated hydrocarbon has n carbon atoms, then it must have $2n + 2$ hydrogen atoms, and hence has the chemical formula $C_n H_{2n+2}$. His approach was to represent the structure of a hydrocarbon molecule using a graph in which the vertices represent atoms of hydrogen (H) and carbon (C), and the edges represent the chemical bonds between the atoms (see Figure 2). He then showed that any graph representing a saturated hydrocarbon must be a tree. Thus, any graph representing the saturated hydrocarbon $C_n H_{2n+2}$ must be a tree with n vertices of degree 4 and $2n + 2$ vertices of degree 1.

When two molecules have the same chemical formula but different chemical bonds they are called isomers. One can enumerate the isomers of $C_n H_{2n+2}$ by enumerating the nonisomorphic trees with n vertices of degree 4 and $2n + 2$ vertices of degree 1. The problem may be simplified further by removing vertices representing hydrogen atoms, thereby obtaining a subgraph called the *carbon-graph*. The vertices of carbon-graphs all represent carbon atoms and the edges represent chemical bonds between the carbon atoms. Given any graph representing a saturated hydrocarbon $C_n H_{2n+2}$, removing all vertices of degree 1 leaves a tree, namely, the carbon-graph, containing n vertices which all have degree at most 4.

Conversely, given any tree T with n vertices such that every vertex has degree at most 4, edges may be added to T to obtain a tree, T', in which all of the original n vertices have degree 4. So T' represents a molecule with the chemical formula $C_n H_{2n+2}$. Since any tree with n vertices such that every vertex has degree at most 4 corresponds to a unique isomer with chemical formula $C_n H_{2n+2}$, and vice versa, there is a one-to-one correspondence between the isomers of $C_n H_{2n+2}$ and the nonisomorphic trees with n vertices such that every vertex has degree at most 4. We shall exploit this fact to solve the problem posed in Example 2.

Solution to Example 2:   Figure 2 gives all nonisomorphic trees with 5 vertices such that every vertex has degree 4 or less. The corresponding isomer is given below each tree along with its name.   □

Cayley did not immediately succeed at obtaining a formula, in terms of n, for the number of isomers of $C_n H_{2n+2}$. So he altered the problem until he was able to obtain such a formula for trees satisfying various conditions. In 1889 he discovered Theorem 2, known as Cayley's Theorem, which states: the number of spanning trees of K_n is n^{n-2}. The proof we will give was discovered by H. Prüfer in 1918. Several other completely different proofs are also known. (See [5] in the suggested readings.) The idea behind the proof is to establish a one-to-one correspondence from the set of all spanning trees of K_n to the set of ordered $(n-2)$-tuples $(a_1, a_2, \ldots, a_{n-2})$, where each a_i is an integer satisfying $1 \leq a_i \leq n$. Given any spanning tree T of K_n, we obtain an $(n-2)$-tuple

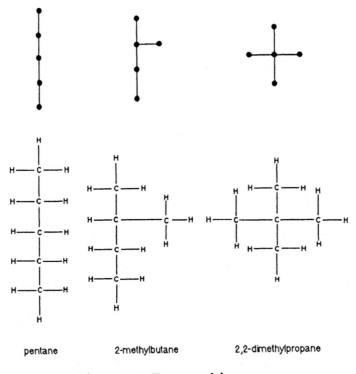

pentane   2-methylbutane   2,2-dimethylpropane

Figure 2.   Trees and isomers.

as follows. Choose a vertex of degree 1 . (The existence of such a vertex is proved in Exercise 5.) Assume the vertices are labeled $v_1, \ldots, v_n$ and remove the vertex of degree 1 with with the smallest subscript, along with its incident edge. Let a_1 be the subscript of the unique vertex which was adjacent to the removed vertex. Repeat this procedure on the remaining tree with $n-1$ vertices to determine a_2. Iterate this procedure until there are only two vertices left, thereby obtaining the $(n-2)$-tuple, $(a_1, a_2, \ldots, a_{n-2})$.

Example 5   Find the 5-tuple which corresponds to the spanning tree given in Figure 3.

Solution: Figure 3 corresponds to the 5-tuple $(2, 3, 4, 3, 6)$. To see this, notice that v_1 is the vertex with the smallest subscript which has degree 1 and v_2 is adjacent to v_1, thus $a_1 = 2$. Now remove edge $\{v_1, v_2\}$. In the reduced graph, v_2 is the vertex with the smallest subscript which has degree 1. Vertex v_3 is adjacent to v_2; thus $a_2 = 3$. Now remove edge $\{v_2, v_3\}$. Iterating this procedure gives the result. $\square$

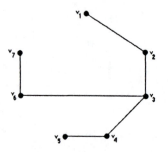

Figure 3.   A spanning tree.

To obtain a spanning tree of K_n, given any $(n-2)$-tuple, begin with the list $\{1, 2, \ldots, n\}$. Find the smallest number, i, in the list but not in the $(n-2)$-tuple and take the first number in the $(n-2)$-tuple, a_1. Then add the edge joining the vertices v_i and v_{a_1}. Remove i from the list and a_1 from the $(n-2)$-tuple and repeat the procedure. Iterate until there are only two numbers left in the list, then join the vertices with these subscripts. The graph G thus obtained does not contain any circuits. For if C is a circuit in G, let $\{u, v\}$ be the last edge in C adjoined to G. Then both u and v were included in an edge previously adjoined to G. If the first time u was included in an edge adjoined to G, u was from the list, then u was not in the tuple, and was crossed off the list. So it may not be an endpoint of any edge subsequently adjoined to G. Thus u must have been from the tuple the first time it was an endpoint of an edge adjoined to G. Similarly, v must have been from the tuple the first time it was an endpoint of an edge adjoined to G. Now let $v_1, v_2, \ldots, v_k$ be the vertices visited by C, where $u = v_1$ and $v = v_k$, as C is traversed from u to v without passing through edge $\{u, v\}$. Since v_1 was in the tuple when edge $\{v_1, v_2\}$ was adjoined to G, v_2 must have been from the list. This implies v_2 must have been from the tuple when $\{v_2, v_3\}$ is adjoined to G, hence, v_3 is from the list when $\{v_2, v_3\}$ is adjoined to G. Similarly, v_4 must have been from the list when $\{v_3, v_4\}$ was adjoined to G, and so on. But this implies that $v_k = v$ was from the list when $\{v_{k-1}, v_k\}$ was adjoined to G, a contradiction. Thus G can not have any circuits. Exercise 6 shows that any graph with n vertices, $n-1$ edges, and no circuits must be a tree. Thus G is a spanning tree of K_n. We have shown that every spanning tree of K_n corresponds to a unique $(n-2)$-tuple and every $(n-2)$-tuple corresponds to a unique spanning tree of K_n. Therefore, there is a one-to-one correspondence between these two sets.

Example 6   Find the spanning tree of K_7 which corresponds to the 5-tuple $(7, 2, 1, 2, 1)$.

Solution: The spanning tree is given in Figure 4. To see why, start with the list $\{1, 2, 3, 4, 5, 6, 7\}$. The number 3 is the smallest number in the list but not

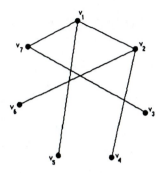

Figure 4.   The spanning tree corresponding to (7,2,1,2,1).

in $(7, 2, 1, 2, 1)$, and 7 is the first number in the 5-tuple. So we adjoin edge (v_3, v_7). Now remove 3 from the list to obtain the new list $\{1, 2, 4, 5, 6, 7\}$, and remove 7 from the 5-tuple to obtain the 4-tuple $(2, 1, 2, 1)$. The number 4 is the smallest number in the list but not in $(2, 1, 2, 1)$, and 2 is the first number in the 4-tuple. So we adjoin edge (v_4, v_2). Iterate this procedure until there are only two numbers left, namely 1 and 7. Now adjoin edge (v_1, v_7) to obtain the tree. $\qquad\square$

Theorem 2 Cayley's Theorem   The number of spanning trees of K_n is n^{n-2}.

Proof: Construct the one-to-one correspondence outlined above from the set of all spanning trees of K_n with vertices $\{v_1, v_2, \ldots, v_n\}$, to the set of all $(n-2)$-tuples $(a_1, a_2, \ldots, a_{n-2})$, where each a_i is an integer satisfying $1 \le a_i \le n$. The count is obtained by observing that there are n^{n-2} such $(n-2)$-tuples, since there are n ways to select each a_i. $\qquad\blacksquare$

Examples 7 and 8 involve a direct application of Cayley's Theorem.

Example 7   How many ways are there to construct an electrical network with 12 nodes which connects all of the nodes using the fewest possible number of wires?

Solution: Any electrical network consisting of 12 nodes and wires connecting the nodes can be represented by a subgraph of K_{12}, where each node is represented by a vertex, and each wire is represented by an edge. The graph representing any electrical network which connects all 12 nodes and uses the fewest number of wires, must be a connected graph with no circuits. Hence, it must be a spanning tree of K_{12}. By Cayley's Theorem, there are 12^{10} spanning trees of K_{12}. Thus, there are 12^{10} ways to construct the electrical network. $\qquad\square$

Example 8   Determine the probability that a spanning tree selected at random from K_n does not contain a given edge e.

Solution: Exercise 22 shows that the number of spanning trees of the graph obtained by deleting the edge e from K_n is $(n-2)n^{n-3}$. By Cayley's Theorem, the number of spanning trees of K_n is n^{n-2}. So the probability is

$$\frac{(n-2)n^{n-3}}{n^{n-2}} = \frac{n-2}{n} = 1 - \frac{2}{n}.$$ □

The proof of Theorem 2 describes how the set of all spanning trees of K_n may be generated by generating $(n-2)$-tuples. We now describe an algorithm which generates n-tuples $(a_1, a_2, \ldots, a_n)$, where each a_i is an integer satisfying $r \leq a_i \leq s$, where r and s are any integers satisfying $r < s$. The algorithm is based on the *lexicographic ordering* of n-tuples. In this ordering, the n-tuple $(a_1, a_2, \ldots, a_n)$ precedes the n-tuple $(b_1, b_2, \ldots, b_n)$ if, for some k with $1 \leq k \leq n$, $a_1 = b_1, a_2 = b_2, \ldots, a_{k-1} = b_{k-1}$, and $a_k < b_k$. In words, an n-tuple precedes a second n-tuple if the number in this n-tuple in the first position where the two n-tuples disagree is smaller than the number in that position in the second n-tuple. For example, the 5-tuple $a = (2,3,1,5,7)$ precedes the 5-tuple $b = (2,3,1,6,2)$, since $a_1 = b_1$, $a_2 = b_2$, $a_3 = b_3$, but $a_4 < b_4$.

Example 9   What is the next largest 5-tuple in lexicographic order after $(3,2,4,7,7)$ in the set of all 5-tuples $(a_1, a_2, a_3, a_4, a_5)$, with $1 \leq a_i \leq 7$?

Solution: To find the next largest 5-tuple, find the largest subscript i such that $a_i < 7$, which is $i = 3$. Then add one to a_3. This gives the 5-tuple $(3,2,5,7,7)$. Any other 5-tuple $(a_1, a_2, a_3, a_4, a_5)$ that is larger than $(3,2,5,7,7)$ satisfies either $a_1 > 3$, or $a_1 = 3$ and $a_2 > 2$, or $a_1 = 3$, $a_2 = 2$, and $a_3 > 5$. In every case $(a_1, a_2, a_3, a_4, a_5)$ is larger than $(3,2,4,7,7)$. Therefore, $(3,2,5,7,7)$ is the next largest 5-tuple.   □

Algorithm 1 displays the pseudocode description for finding the next largest n-tuple after an n-tuple that is not $(s, s, \ldots, s)$, which is the largest n-tuple.

Next we look at a problem for which there is no known algorithm. Given any weighted graph G and any spanning tree T of G, define the **range** of T to be the weight of the edge in T with the largest weight minus the weight of the edge in T with the smallest weight.

Example 10   Use an exhaustive search to find a spanning tree with the smallest possible range for the graph in Figure 5.

ALGORITHM 1.   **Generating the next largest n-tuple in lexicographic order.**

procedure *next n-tuple* $((a_1, a_2, \ldots, a_n)$: n-tuple of integers
  between r and s, $r < s$, not equal to $(s, s, \ldots, s))$
$j := 1$
for $i := 1$ **to** n
  if $a_i < s$ **then** $j := i$
$\{j$ is the largest subscript with $a_j < s\}$
$a_j := a_j + 1$
$\{(a_1, a_2, \ldots, a_n)$ is now the next largest n-tuple$\}$

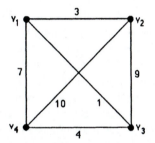

Figure 5.   A weighted graph.

Solution: By Cayley's Theorem there are $4^2 = 16$ spanning trees of K_4.
We list each 2-tuple corresponding to a spanning tree of K_4, along with the
corresponding range of each spanning tree:

(1,1) range: 6	(2,1) range: 6	(3,1) range: 8	(4,1) range: 9
(1,2) range: 9	(2,2) range: 7	(3,2) range: 9	(4,2) range: 3
(1,3) range: 3	(2,3) range: 6	(3,3) range: 8	(4,3) range: 5
(1,4) range: 4	(2,4) range: 7	(3,4) range: 9	(4,4) range: 6

This shows that the spanning trees corresponding to $(1,3)$ or $(4,2)$, having
range 3, are spanning trees with the smallest possible range.   □

Another important problem involving spanning trees is the well known
minimal spanning tree problem.

Minimal Spanning Tree Problem: Given a weighted graph, find
a spanning tree with the smallest possible weight.

This problem may also be solved using an exhaustive search. However this approach should be avoided in this case since there are several well known algorithms which are much more efficient. For example, Prim's algorithm is known to find a minimal spanning tree for a graph with n vertices using $O(n^2)$ comparisons and no additions. (See Section 8.6 of *Discrete Mathematics and Its Applications*, Second Edition, by Rosen for a description of Prim's algorithm.) Whereas if an exhaustive search were used, the number of additions required to compute the weights of each spanning tree is $n - 2 = O(n)$. By Cayley's Theorem, this must be performed at most $n^{n-2} = O(n^{n-2})$ times. Thus, the number of additions required to compute the weights of the spanning trees of K_n is $O(n^{n-1})$. This shows that Prim's algorithm is much more efficient than an exhaustive search.

Counting Hamilton Circuits

Next we discuss Hamilton circuits and some related problems. Given any graph $G = (V, E)$, a path is called a *circuit* if it begins and ends at the same vertex. A circuit $x_0, x_1, \ldots, x_n$, where $x_0 = x_n$, is called a *Hamilton circuit* if $V = \{x_0, x_1, \ldots, x_n\}$ and $x_i \neq x_j$, for $0 \leq i < j \leq n$.

The terminology is due to the Irish mathematician Sir William Rowan Hamilton, who was a child prodigy, and is famous for his contributions in algebra. Perhaps his most famous discovery was the existence of algebraic systems in which the commutative law for multiplication $(ab = ba)$ does not hold. His *algebra of quaternions* , as it is now known, can be expressed in terms of Hamilton circuits on the regular dodecahedron (a regular solid with 20 vertices and 12 regular pentagons as faces). Hamilton's discovery lead to a puzzle in which the vertices of the dodecahedron are labeled with different cities of the world. The player is challenged to start at any city, travel "around the world", and return to the starting point, visiting each of the other 19 cities exactly once. In the puzzle that was marketed in 1859, the player must find a Hamilton circuit starting with five given initial cities.

An important problem involving Hamilton circuits is the *traveling salesman problem*. In such problems, a salesman wishes to visit a number of cities and return to the starting point, in such a way that each city is visited exactly once, and the total distance covered is as small as possible. The problem may also be stated using graph terminology.

Traveling Salesman Problem: Given a weighted graph, find a Hamilton circuit that has the smallest possible weight.

The origin of the traveling salesman problem is somewhat obscure. George Dantzig, Ray Fulkerson, and Selmer Johnson were among the first mathematicians who studied the problem in 1954. They showed that a certain Hamilton circuit of a graph representing 49 cities, one in each of the 48 contiguous states and Washington D.C., has the shortest distance. (See [1] in the suggested readings.) Since then, many researchers have worked on the problem. However, there is no known algorithm having polynomial complexity which solves the traveling salesman problem. On the other hand, there has been a lot of progress towards finding good algorithms which either solve the problem, or find approximate solutions to the problem. (This problem is also studied in another chapter of this book. In addition, see [4] in the suggested readings for a comprehensive discussion.)

Theorem 3 and its proof allow us to solve the traveling salesman problem using an exhaustive search, as well as determine probabilities concerning Hamilton circuits selected at random. To enumerate the Hamilton circuits in K_n, we establish a one-to-one correspondence that characterizes the set of all Hamilton circuits of K_n in terms of permutations. The idea behind the correspondence is to label the vertices of K_n, using $v_1, v_2, \ldots, v_n$, and then associate a permutation of $1, 2, \ldots, n$ to every Hamilton circuit using the subscripts of the vertices v_i.

For example, consider the circuit C given in Figure 6. We can associate the permutation 13425 with C. However, the permutations 34251, 42513, 25134, 51342, and the permutations 15243, 52431, 24315, 43152, 31524 all give rise to the same circuit, C. To obtain a one-to-one correspondence, we will pick an arbitrary starting point v_1, and associate the permutation beginning with 1, in which the second number is smaller than the last. According to this rule, 13425 is the only permutation associated to C.

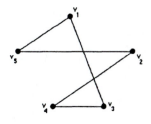

Figure 6.   A circuit C.

Theorem 3   The number of Hamilton circuits in K_n is $\frac{1}{2}(n-1)!$.

Proof: We show that the set of all Hamilton circuits in K_n is in one-to-one correspondence with the set of all permutations σ of $\{1, 2, \ldots, n\}$ beginning with 1, such that the second number of σ is smaller than the last. Let C be any Hamilton circuit in K_n. Take the vertex v_1 and let v_j and v_k be the two vertices which are joined to v_1 by edges in C. Clearly $j \neq k$, so assume $j < k$. To obtain the permutation σ corresponding to C let the ith element of σ be the subscript of the ith vertex visited by C as C is traversed by beginning at v_1 and proceeding in the direction such that v_1 is followed by v_j.

Conversely, given any permutation σ of $\{1, 2, \ldots, n\}$ beginning with 1, such that the second number of σ is smaller than the last, the Hamilton circuit corresponding to σ is obtained by starting at v_1, then visiting the vertices $\{v_2, v_3, \ldots, v_n\}$ in the order prescribed by σ.

The number of permutations of $\{1, 2, 3, \ldots, n\}$ beginning with 1, such that the second number is smaller than the last number, is equal to the number of ways to choose the second and last numbers times the number of ways to choose the remaining $n - 3$ numbers. Note that there is only one way to choose the first number since it must be 1. Moreover, when we choose two numbers, say a and b, one is larger than the other, so there is only one way to place them as second and last elements in the permutation. Therefore, the count is $C(n - 1, 2)(n - 3)! = \frac{1}{2}(n - 1)!$. ∎

We are now ready to answer the questions posed in Example 4 of the introduction.

Example 11   A salesman wishes to visit all the locations listed in Figure 7 and return to the starting point in such a way that each city is visited exactly once. If such a route is selected at random, what is the probability that the route visits v_1 and v_2 in succession?

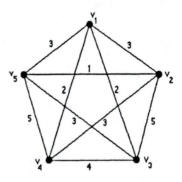

Figure 7.   Salesman's network.

Solution: The number of Hamilton circuits which visit v_1 and v_2 in succession is obtained by observing that if a Hamilton circuit passes through v_1 followed by v_2, then there are three ways to visit the next vertex, two ways to visit the next, and one way to visit the last. Thus, there are a total of $3 \cdot 2 \cdot 1 = 6$ Hamilton circuits. By Theorem 3, there are $\frac{1}{2}4! = 12$ Hamilton circuits in K_5. So the probability is $6/12 = 1/2$. □

Example 12   Use an exhaustive search to find a Hamilton circuit of smallest weight in the graph of Figure 7 by generating the permutations of $\{1, 2, 3, 4, 5\}$ which begin with 1, such that the second number is smaller than the last.

Solution: By Theorem 3, there are $\frac{1}{2}4! = 12$ Hamilton circuits in K_5. We give each permutation along with its corresponding weight.

12345	weight: 20	12354	weight: 18	12435	weight: 16
12453	weight: 16	12534	weight: 13	12543	weight: 15
13245	weight: 18	13254	weight: 15	13425	weight: 13
13524	weight: 11	14235	weight: 16	14325	weight: 15

This shows that the Hamilton circuit $v_1, v_3, v_5, v_2, v_4, v_1$, having weight 11, is a Hamilton circuit with the smallest possible weight.   □

Theorem 3 tells us that for a the graph K_{10} there would be $\frac{1}{2}9! = 181,440$ different Hamilton circuits. If each circuit could be found and its weight computed in 10^{-4} seconds, it would require approximately 3 minutes of computer time to solve a traveling salesman problem with 10 vertices. So an exhaustive search is a reasonable way to solve the problem. However, under the same assumption, a problem with 25 vertices would require $(3 \cdot 10^{23}) \cdot 10^{-4} = 3 \cdot 10^{19}$ seconds, or roughly $9.5 \cdot 10^{11}$ years.

Counting Perfect Matches

A class of ten students must be paired off to form five study groups. How many ways can the study groups be formed? After a preliminary examination the instructor assigns a rating from 1 to 10 to each pair such that the lower the rating, the more productive the pair, in the opinion of the instructor. How can the students be paired so that the sum of the ratings of the five pairs is minimal, thus maximizing the productivity of the class? These questions concern a certain type of matching, called a *perfect matching*, which we now define.

Definition 1   A *matching* in a graph $G = (V, E)$ is a subset of edges, M, contained in E such that no two edges in M have a common endpoint. A matching M is called *perfect* if every vertex of G is an endpoint of an edge of M.   □

For example, the set of all perfect matches of the graph given in Figure 8 are the matches

$$M_1 = \{\{1, 2\}, \{3, 4\}\} \qquad M_2 = \{\{1, 3\}, \{2, 4\}\} \qquad M_3 = \{\{1, 4\}, \{2, 3\}\}.$$

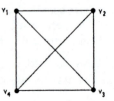

Figure 8.   Finding perfect matchings.

Theorems 1, 2, and 3 were all proved by establishing a one-to-one correspondence. The following theorem uses mathematical induction to count the perfect matches in K_n.

Theorem 4   The number of perfect matches in K_n is 0 if n is odd and $(n-1)(n-3)\ldots 5 \cdot 3 \cdot 1 = O(n^{n/2})$ if n is even.

Proof: We will prove this theorem using mathematical induction. If $n = 1$, there is no perfect matching and if $n = 2$, then there is only 1 perfect matching.

For the induction step, assume the theorem holds for all complete graphs with k vertices, where $k < n$. It is clear that K_n has no perfect matching if n is odd, so we assume n is even. We count the number of perfect matches in K_n by considering a vertex v_1, which can be matched to any of the other $n-1$ vertices. Suppose v_1 is matched to v_2. Then remove v_1, v_2, and all the edges incident to v_1 and v_2, to obtain the graph K_{n-2} with vertices $\{v_3, v_4, \ldots, v_n\}$. By the inductive assumption, since $n-2$ is even, the number of perfect matches in K_{n-2} is $(n-3)(n-5)\cdots 5 \cdot 3 \cdot 1$. Since there are $n-1$ ways to match v_1, and for each of these there are $(n-3)(n-5)\cdots 5 \cdot 3 \cdot 1$ ways to match the remaining $n-2$ vertices, the total number of perfect matches is

$$(n-1)(n-3)\ldots 5 \cdot 3 \cdot 1 \leq nn \ldots n = O(n^{n/2}). \blacksquare$$

Theorem 4 can be used to answer the question posed at the beginning of this section.

Example 13   How many ways can a class of 10 students be paired off to form 5 study groups?

Solution: The number of study groups is equal to the number of perfect matches in K_{10}. By Theorem 4, this number is $9 \cdot 7 \cdot 5 \cdot 3 \cdot 1 = 945$.   □

Example 14   Use an exhaustive search to find a perfect matching of minimal weight for the graph given in Figure 9 by listing all perfect matches along with their weights.

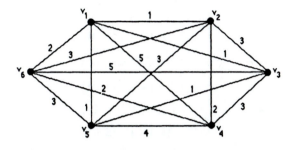

Figure 9.   A weighted graph.

Solution: By Theorem 4, there are $5 \cdot 3 \cdot 1 = 15$ perfect matches in K_6. We shall list the edges in each perfect matching of K_6 along with the weight of the matching.

$\{\{1,2\},\{3,4\},\{5,6\}\}$ weight: 7 $\{\{1,4\},\{3,5\},\{2,6\}\}$ weight: 9
$\{\{1,2\},\{3,5\},\{4,6\}\}$ weight: 4 $\{\{1,5\},\{2,3\},\{4,6\}\}$ weight: 6
$\{\{1,2\},\{4,5\},\{3,6\}\}$ weight: 10 $\{\{1,5\},\{2,4\},\{3,6\}\}$ weight: 8
$\{\{1,3\},\{4,5\},\{2,6\}\}$ weight: 8 $\{\{1,5\},\{3,4\},\{2,6\}\}$ weight: 7
$\{\{1,3\},\{2,4\},\{5,6\}\}$ weight: 6 $\{\{1,6\},\{3,4\},\{2,5\}\}$ weight: 8
$\{\{1,3\},\{2,5\},\{4,6\}\}$ weight: 6 $\{\{1,6\},\{2,3\},\{4,5\}\}$ weight: 9
$\{\{1,4\},\{2,3\},\{5,6\}\}$ weight: 11 $\{\{1,6\},\{2,4\},\{3,5\}\}$ weight: 5
$\{\{1,4\},\{2,5\},\{3,6\}\}$ weight: 13

This shows that the perfect matching $\{\{1,2\},\{3,5\},\{4,6\}\}$, with weight 4 is a perfect matching of the smallest possible weight.   ☐

Example 14 is an example of a *perfect matching problem*, defined as follows.

Perfect Matching Problem: Given a weighted graph, find a perfect matching that has the smallest possible weight.

The proof of Theorem 4 indicates how to recursively generate the set of perfect matches of K_n. Specifically, first generate all perfect matches of K_2, use these to generate all those of K_4, use the perfect matches of K_4 to generate those of K_6, and so on.

Example 15   Use the perfect matching $\{\{1,2\},\{3,4\}\}$ in K_4 to generate 5 perfect matches of K_6.

Solution: First, replace 1 by 5 and match 1 to 6 to obtain the perfect matching

$$\{\{5,2\},\{3,4\},\{1,6\}\}$$

in K_6. Next, replace 2 by 5 and match 2 to 6 to obtain the perfect matching

$$\{\{1,5\},\{3,4\},\{2,6\}\}$$

in K_6. Iterate this procedure two more times to get the perfect matches

$$\{\{1,2\},\{5,4\},\{3,6\}\}$$
$$\{\{1,2\},\{3,5\},\{4,6\}\}.$$

The fifth perfect matching is obtained by matching 5 to 6, giving

$$\{\{1,2\},\{3,4\},\{5,6\}\}. \qquad \square$$

The procedure used in the solution of Example 16 is generalized in Algorithm 2, which displays the pseudocode description for finding the $n-1$ perfect matches of K_n, given a perfect matching of K_{n-2}, where n is an even integer, $n \geq 4$.

ALGORITHM 2.　　**Generating $n-1$ perfect matches of K_n, given a perfect matching of K_{n-2}.**

procedure　　*perfect matches* $(\{\{a_1,a_2\},\{a_3,a_4\},\ldots,$
$\{a_{n-3},a_{n-2}\}\}$: a perfect matching of K_{n-2}, n an even integer, $n \geq 4$)
for $i := 1$ **to** $n-1$
begin
　　for $j := 1$ **to** $n-2$
　　　　if $j = i$ **then** $b_j := n-1$ **and** $b_{n-1} := a_i$
　　　　　　else $b_j := a_j$
　　if $i = n-1$ **then** $b_{n-1} := n-1$
　　$M_i := \{\{b_1,b_2\},\{b_3,b_4\},\ldots,\{b_{n-1},n\}\}$
end　$\{M_i$ is a perfect matching of $K_n\}$

Using Algorithm 2 one can solve a perfect matching problem using an exhaustive search. How efficient is this? The number of additions required to compute the weight of each perfect matching is $n/2 - 1 = O(n)$. By Theorem 4, the weights of $(n-1)(n-3)\cdots 5 \cdot 3 \cdot 1 = O(n^{n/2})$ perfect matches must be computed. So the number of additions required to compute the weights of all the perfect matches in K_n is $O(n^{\frac{n}{2}+1})$. There are more efficient ways to solve a perfect matching problem. For example, [3] in the suggested readings describes an algorithm that solves the perfect matching problem which requires $O(n^3)$ operations (additions and comparisons).

Suggested Readings

1. G. Dantzig, D. Fulkerson, and S. Johnson, "Solution of a Large-Scale Traveling Salesman Problem", *Operations Research*, volume 2 (1954), 393–410.

2. M. Garey and D. Johnson, *Computers and Intractability. A Guide to the Theory of NP-Completeness*, W. H. Freeman, San Francisco, 1979.

3. E. Lawler, *Combinatorial Optimization: Networks and Matroids*, Holt, Rinehart and Winston, New York, 1976.

4. E. Lawler, A. Lenstra, A. Rinnooy Kan, and D. Shmoys, editors, *The Traveling Salesman Problem*, John Wiley & Sons, New York, 1985.

5. J. Moon, "Various Proofs of Cayley's Formula for Counting Trees", *A Seminar on Graph Theory*, (ed. F. Harary), Holt, Rinehart and Winston, New York, 1967, 70–78.

Exercises

1. For the graph K_8, determine the number of
    a) paths joining any pair of vertices.   b) spanning trees.
    c) Hamilton circuits.   d) perfect matches.

2. For each of the following trees, determine the 5-tuple described in the proof of Cayley's Theorem.
    a)   b)

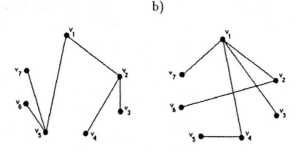

3. For each of the following 5-tuples, construct the corresponding spanning tree of K_7 as described in the proof of Cayley's Theorem.
   a) (7, 2, 4, 4, 1)
   b) (2, 2, 2, 4, 6).

4. List all the perfect matches of K_6 by first listing all the perfect matches of K_4 and then using these to obtain the perfect matches of K_6. (See Example 15.)

5. Show that any tree with at least two vertices has at least two vertices of degree 1.

6. Show that any graph with n vertices, n-1 edges, and no cycles is a tree.

7. How many different isomers do the saturated hydrocarbon C_6H_{14} have?

8. For the following graph determine if there is a path from A to C which has total length 40 or less and total cost $45 or less.

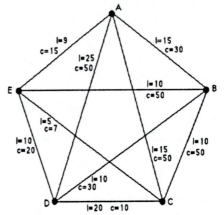

9. For the following graph
   a) find a spanning tree with the smallest possible range.
   b) find a Hamilton circuit with the smallest possible weight.
   c) find a perfect matching with the smallest possible weight.

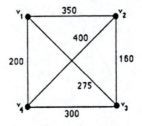

10. A doctor, who lives in village A, wishes to visit his patients who live in the four villages B, C, D, and E, as illustrated in the following graph. Find a route for him which involves the least possible total distance.

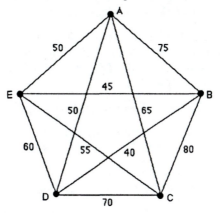

11. Let K_8 have the vertex set $V = \{v_1, v_2, \ldots, v_8\}$. Determine the probability that a path joining v_1 to v_5 selected at random from K_8 contains fewer than five edges.

12. Let K_n have vertex set $V = \{v_1, v_2, \ldots, v_n\}$. Determine the probability that a spanning tree selected at random from K_n contains a vertex having degree $n - 1$.

13. Let K_n have vertex set $V = \{v_1, v_2, \ldots, v_n\}$ where $n \geq 4$. Determine the probability that a Hamilton circuit selected at random from K_n visits v_1, v_2, and v_3 in succession.

14. Let K_n have vertex set $V = \{v_1, v_2, \ldots, v_n\}$ and assume n is even with $n \geq 6$. Determine the probability that a perfect matching selected at random from K_n contains the edges $\{v_1, v_2\}$ and $\{v_3, v_4\}$.

15. Determine the number of perfect matches in the complete bipartite graph $K_{n,n}$.

16. Explain how the perfect matches of the bipartite graph $K_{n,n}$ may be generated on a computer.

17. Given a perfect matching M of K_n, where n is even, determine how many spanning trees of K_n contain M.

18. a) Let $W = \{w_1, w_2, \ldots, w_n\}$ be a set of n real numbers and let r be an integer where $r < n$. Describe a procedure to find a subset of r numbers with the smallest possible sum, by checking all possible subsets of size r.

b) Give a formula in terms of n and r which indicates how many candidates must be checked to solve the problem.

19. a) Give an algorithm that is more efficient than the exhaustive approach for the problem described in Exercise 18.

    b) Provide a big-O estimate for your algorithm to prove that the algorithm is more efficient than the algorithm of Exercise 18.

20. Determine the largest value of n for which all of the Hamilton circuits of K_n may be generated in less than 10 minutes of computer time, assuming the computer requires 10^{-4} seconds of computer time to generate one Hamilton circuit and compute its weight.

21. How many spanning trees does the complete bipartite graph $K_{2,n}$ have?

22. Let $K_n - e$ be the graph obtained by deleting the edge e from K_n. Show that the number of spanning trees of $K_n - e$, for any edge e, is $(n-2)n^{n-3}$.

$\star$23. Let K_n have vertex set $V = \{v_1, v_2, \ldots, v_n\}$. Show that the number of spanning trees of K_n such that vertex v_i has degree d_i in the spanning tree is

$$\frac{(n-2)!}{(d_1 - 1)!(d_2 - 1)!\ldots(d_n - 1)!}.$$

$\star$24. Describe a method which generates the set of all spanning trees of K_n such that vertex v_i has degree d_i.

$\star\star$25. Let $K_{m,n}$ be the complete bipartite graph with vertices $V = V_1 \cup V_2$, where $V_1 = \{u_1, u_2, \ldots, u_m\}$ and $V_2 = \{v_1, v_2, \ldots, v_n\}$. Show that the number of spanning trees of $K_{m,n}$ such that vertex u_i has degree d_i and vertex v_j has degree f_j is

$$\frac{(m-1)!(n-1)!}{(d_1 - 1)!\ldots(d_m - 1)!(f_1 - 1)!\ldots(f_n - 1)!}.$$

Computer Projects

1. Let K_{10} have vertex set $V = \{v_1, v_2, \ldots, v_{10}\}$. Write a computer program that takes as input the weights of the edges of K_{10} and finds a path of length 3 of smallest possible weight that joins a given pair of vertices.

2. Write a program that generates all the Hamilton circuits of K_6.

3. Write a computer program that generates all the perfect matches of K_8.

15

Traveling Salesman Problem

Author: Arthur M. Hobbs, Department of Mathematics, Texas A&M University.

Prerequisites: The prerequisites for this chapter are graphs and trees. See, for example, Chapters 7 and 8 of *Discrete Mathematics and Its Applications*, Second Edition, by Kenneth H. Rosen.

Introduction

In the traveling salesman problem, we are given a list of cities including our own, and we are asked to find a route using existing roads that visits each city exactly once, returns to our home city, and is as short as possible. However, it is useful to formalize the problem, thus allowing other problems to be interpreted in terms of the traveling salesman problem. Thus we have the following definition.

Definition 1 Given a graph G in which the edges may be directed, undirected, or some of each, and in which a weight is assigned to each edge, the *traveling salesman problem*, denoted *TSP*, is the problem of finding a Hamilton circuit in G with minimum total weight, where the weight of a circuit is the sum of the weights of the edges in the circuit. Depending on the application, the weights on the edges will be called *lengths* or *costs*. □

Notice that the Hamilton circuit problem, to determine whether or not a given graph has a Hamilton circuit and to find one if it exists, is the special case of the TSP in which each of the edge weights is 1. Also, the feature that most distinguishes the TSP from the shortest path problem solved in Section 7.6 of *Discrete Mathematics and Its Applications*, Second Edition, by Rosen is the requirement in the TSP that *every* vertex of the graph must be included in the solution to the TSP.

We want to emphasize that the TSP calls for a Hamilton *circuit*, not a Hamilton path. Some applications would be more naturally stated in terms of Hamilton paths, but they can be translated into circuit problems (and this is done in the examples). For theoretical purposes, it is much better to have the symmetry that a Hamilton circuit allows, rather than having a pair of special vertices serving as the ends of a Hamilton path. Also, there is a forward-looking reason for favoring Hamilton circuits. The TSP is not solved, and any future complete or partial solutions of the TSP will be stated in terms of Hamilton circuits, rather than Hamilton paths. Thus it is better that our work now should be stated in terms of Hamilton circuits, so that future solutions can be immediately applied to it.

Example 1   Solve the TSP by finding all Hamilton circuits in the graph G_1 of Figure 1.

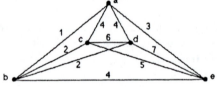

Figure 1.   Graph G_1.

Solution: Since G_1 is complete, any ordering of the vertices corresponds to a Hamilton circuit. By the nature of a circuit, we may suppose that all of the Hamilton circuits begin on the same vertex, e.g., vertex a. There are $(5-1)! = 24$ permutations of the vertices starting with a. But each Hamilton circuit is described by two of these permutations (see Exercise 5). Thus, there are $\frac{1}{2}(4!) = 12$ Hamilton circuits. These circuits and lengths are:

Permutation	Length	Permutation	Length
a, b, c, d, e, a	19	a, d, e, c, b, a	19
a, b, d, c, e, a	17	a, b, d, e, c, a	19
a, d, c, e, b, a	20	a, b, e, d, c, a	22
a, c, b, d, e, a	18	a, c, b, e, d, a	21
a, c, d, b, e, a	19	a, c, e, b, d, a	19
a, d, b, c, e, a	16	a, d, c, b, e, a	19

Thus the shortest Hamilton circuit, and hence the solution to the TSP in G_1, is given by the vertex sequence a, d, b, c, e, a with a total length of 16.   □

A variant of this procedure can be used when not all of the possible edges are present or when some edges are directed and circuits are constrained to pass through them in only the given direction. We may examine all the permutations, casting out those which do not correspond to Hamilton circuits. This is useful if the graph is nearly complete. If many edges are not present, however, we may do a depth-first search on paths starting at a, looking for those that extend to Hamilton circuits. The following example illustrates the first possibility.

Example 2   Solve the TSP for the graph of Figure 2.

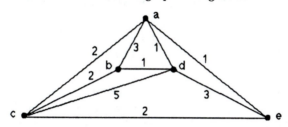

Figure 2.   Graph G_2.

Solution: This graph has five vertices, but one edge of the complete graph is omitted. We again list all of the permutations of the vertices starting with a, but for some of the permutations, we note that the corresponding circuit does not exist in the graph:

Permutation	Length	Permutation	Length
a, b, c, d, e, a	14	a, d, e, c, b, a	11
a, b, d, c, e, a	12	a, b, d, e, c, a	11
a, d, c, e, b, a	does not exist	a, b, e, d, c, a	does not exist
a, c, b, d, e, a	9	a, c, b, e, d, a	does not exist
a, c, d, b, e, a	does not exist	a, c, e, b, d, a	does not exist
a, d, b, c, e, a	7	a, d, c, b, e, a	does not exist

Examining the six cases of sequences which do correspond to Hamilton circuits in G, we find the shortest is a, d, b, c, e, a with total length 7.   □

These examples illustrate the most simple-minded algorithm for solving the traveling salesman problem: Just list all possible orderings of the vertices with one fixed beginning vertex, cast out orderings that fail to correspond to Hamilton circuits, and find the lengths of the rest, choosing the shortest. If there are n vertices, then there are $\frac{1}{2}(n-1)!$ orderings to examine. If no Hamilton circuit exists, the algorithm terminates, and the TSP has no solution in the graph. Otherwise, a shortest circuit is found, and its length is known. Because we must examine $\frac{1}{2}(n-1)!$ orderings of the vertices, this algorithm has complexity at least $O((n-1)!)$; such complexity is much worse than exponential complexity.

History

The roots of the traveling salesman problem problem are in the studies of knight's tours in chess and of Hamilton circuits. A *knight's tour* is a sequence of moves taken by a knight on a chessboard, that begins and ends on a fixed square a and visits all other squares, each exactly once. This can be seen as a Hamilton circuit in a graph in which each square of the board is a vertex and two vertices are joined by an edge if and only if a knight's move connects the corresponding squares. A solution of the knight's tour problem was given by Leonhard Euler [2].

The more general problem of Hamilton circuits apparently was first studied in 1856 by T. P. Kirkman; he was particularly interested in Hamilton circuits on the edges and vertices of certain kinds of geometric solids [5].

However, it was William Rowan Hamilton who exhibited "The Icosian Game" in 1857 (the game was marketed in 1859) and thus gained so much publicity for the problem that the problem was named for him. "The Icosian Game" provided a 20-vertex graph drawn on a board and 20 numbered pegs to place at the vertices; the object was to place the pegs in the order of a Hamilton circuit through the vertices of the graph. As a game "The Icosian Game" failed, but as publicity for a mathematical problem, however unintentionally, it was very effective. (One of the sources of mathematical interest in this game was that it serves as a model of a non-commutative algebra ("the Icosian calculus") and thus can be viewed as part of "the origin of group theory" [1], an important part of modern mathematics.)

The traveling salesman problem appears to have been first described some-time in the 1930s.* The problem became important during the late 1930s, just as the modern explosive growth of interest in combinatorics began. It was popularized by Merrill Flood of the RAND Corporation during the next two decades. The first important paper on the subject appeared in 1954 [1]; in it the authors George Dantzig, Ray Fulkerson, and Selmer Johnson of the RAND Corp. showed "that a certain tour of 49 cities, one in each of the [contiguous] 48 states and Washington, D. C., has the shortest road distance" [1]. The work was carried out using an ingenious combination of linear programming, graph theory, and map readings.

The study of the TSP has grown enormously since then; a monograph published in 1985 summarized the subject in 465 pages [6]. The literature on the problem is still growing rapidly.

---

* This was perhaps done in a seminar conducted by Hassler Whitney in 1934 [1,3], although he did not remember the event [1].

Applications

Even if there were no applications for a solution to the TSP, this problem would be important. It is an archetypical combinatorial problem: Other difficult combinatorial problems, such as the problem of finding the size of a smallest set S of vertices in a graph G such that every vertex in G is adjacent to a vertex in S, would be already solved if we could find a solution to the TSP [7]. There are literally hundreds of such problems [4], and their study has become a huge mathematical industry.

But there are important applications. We present three of them here. Others appear in Exercises 10–13, and still more appear in [6, Chapter 2].

Example 3   Schoolbus Routing   One of the earliest applications of the TSP was to the routing of school busses. In 1937, Merrill Flood studied this problem [1]: Suppose we have decided that a given school bus will pick up the children in a certain part of the city. What route will allow the bus to visit each child's home just once each morning and do so as cheaply as possible? This is just a restatement of the TSP in terms of a school bus, with children's homes for vertices and roads for edges. Its solution may save a school district thousands of dollars per year.   □

Example 4   Electronics   In electrical circuit design, it is common for several components to be connected electrically to the same terminal (for example, to the ground terminal). Further, it is common for the components (memory chips, cpu's, sockets, etc.) to be placed before the wiring diagram is completed. For example, memory chips on a computer's motherboard are generally neatly aligned in rows and columns on a certain area of the board. Once such components are placed on the board, we have a subset of the pins of these components that must be electrically connected. Now, electricity flows easily in both directions through a wire, so a tree of wires will serve for the connections, the pins acting as vertices and the wires as edges. Because the pins on the components are small and because of the limited space available for printed wires, at most two printed wires can be connected to each pin. But then the degree of each vertex is at most two; thus the tree will be a path. Circuit boards are crowded with wires, so minimizing the total length of wire is necessary both to allow all of the wires to fit and to keep down the signal transfer time. Thus, in the complete graph on the pins to be connected together, we wish to find a Hamilton path of shortest length.

This problem can easily be converted into the form of a TSP. Add one new vertex to the graph, and join it to every other vertex by an edge of length 0. Then the Hamilton circuits in this augmented graph correspond one-to-one with Hamilton paths in the complete graph, and a Hamilton circuit in the augmented graph is shortest if and only if the corresponding Hamilton path in the complete graph is shortest. (For further information, see Section 2.2 of [6].)   □

Array Clustering

Our third example involves a much more subtle use of the traveling salesman problem. But we must develop the problem quite far before we can get to the TSP. (See Section 2.5 of [6] for a more detailed treatment.)

Suppose that both Joe's Garage and Melissa's Shop rebuild both engines and carburetors but do no upholstery work, while Sam's Repairs and Anne's Annex reupholster auto seats and replace headliners but do no engine work. If we let the first capital letter of each of these companies stand for the company, and let a stand for engine rebuilding, b for carburetor rebuilding, c for reupholstering auto seats, and d for replacing headliners, we can represent the activities of these companies in the form of a matrix whose entries are 0s and 1s: Each row corresponds to a company, and each column to a possible activity of the company. A 1 is in a given row and column if the company carries out that activity; otherwise a 0 appears there. Then the activities of these companies are represented by both matrices X_1 and X_2, using different orderings of the rows and columns.

$$\mathbf{X_1} = \begin{array}{c} \\ J \\ M \\ S \\ A \end{array} \begin{pmatrix} \overset{a}{1} & \overset{b}{1} & \overset{c}{0} & \overset{d}{0} \\ 1 & 1 & 0 & 0 \\ 0 & 0 & 1 & 1 \\ 0 & 0 & 1 & 1 \end{pmatrix}$$

$$\mathbf{X_2} = \begin{array}{c} \\ J \\ S \\ M \\ A \end{array} \begin{pmatrix} \overset{a}{1} & \overset{c}{0} & \overset{b}{1} & \overset{d}{0} \\ 0 & 1 & 0 & 1 \\ 1 & 0 & 1 & 0 \\ 0 & 1 & 0 & 1 \end{pmatrix}.$$

Clearly the representation by matrix X_1 is better in that it groups the companies by their activities, or by industry. But matrix X_2 is obtained from X_1 by merely permuting the rows and columns of X_1. If we are to use a matrix representation such as that shown here, our problem is that of ordering the companies and the activities they might engage in so that we get a matrix like X_1 instead of one like X_2. This is not hard if there are only a few companies and activities involved, like we have here. But what if there are hundreds of each? That is the situation an economist studying the industries of the United States would face.

In general, let $\mathbf{A} = [a_{ij}]$ be an $m \times n$ matrix, where each row represents a company, each column represents a possible activity of a company, $a_{ij} = 1$ if company i has experience carrying out activity j, and $a_{ij} = 0$ if the company does not have such experience. The matrix $\mathbf{A}$ is called a **relationship matrix**.

In a complex economy, we may set up a relationship matrix and yet find that, like matrix X_2, it shows very little of the natural clusters, or industries, that are present. Could we introduce a function which would give a value to such matrices and which would show, for example, that X_1 is better than X_2? The answer is "yes." In matrices X_1 and X_2, notice that if we go along each of rows 1, 2, and 3, multiply each entry by the entry immediately below it, and add all the products, then in X_1 we get a sum of 4 while in X_2 we get a sum of 0. The reason we get a larger value from X_1 is that the 1s are bunched together there. The same thing happens if we go down columns 1, 2, and 3, multiply each entry by the entry to its immediate right, and add the products.

For a general $0, 1$-matrix $A = [a_{ij}]$ with m rows and n columns, the observations of the previous paragraph lead us to the function $f(A)$ given by

$$f(A) = \sum_{i=1}^{m-1} \sum_{j=1}^{n} a_{ij} a_{i+1,j} + \sum_{j=1}^{n-1} \sum_{i=1}^{m} a_{ij} a_{i,j+1}.$$

Notice that $f(X_1) = [1 \cdot 1 + 1 \cdot 1 + 0 \cdot 0 + 0 \cdot 0 + 1 \cdot 0 + 1 \cdot 0 + 0 \cdot 1 + 0 \cdot 1 + 0 \cdot 0 + 0 \cdot 0 + 1 \cdot 1 + 1 \cdot 1] + [1 \cdot 1 + 1 \cdot 1 + 0 \cdot 0 + 0 \cdot 0 + 1 \cdot 0 + 1 \cdot 0 + 0 \cdot 1 + 0 \cdot 1 + 0 \cdot 0 + 0 \cdot 0 + 1 \cdot 1 + 1 \cdot 1] = 8$ while similarly $f(X_2) = 0$. Further, if $\mathcal{M}$ is the set of all matrices obtainable from a given matrix M by a mixture of row and column permutations, then we want to find a matrix M^* in $\mathcal{M}$ such that $f(M^*) \geq f(M')$ for every $M' \in \mathcal{M}$. Note: There may be more than one M^* that will suffice here. For example, $f(X_3) = 8 = f(X_1)$ for the following matrix X_3.

$$X_3 = \begin{array}{c} \\ S \\ A \\ J \\ M \end{array} \begin{array}{cccc} a & b & c & d \\ \left(\begin{array}{cccc} 0 & 0 & 1 & 1 \\ 0 & 0 & 1 & 1 \\ 1 & 1 & 0 & 0 \\ 1 & 1 & 0 & 0 \end{array} \right) \end{array}.$$

It is possible to show that the result of any mixture of row and column permutations of a matrix can be produced by doing a single row permutation followed by a single column permutation. Further, permuting the rows does not affect which column a given entry is in. Thus, for example, if

$$X = \begin{pmatrix} a & b \\ c & d \end{pmatrix} \quad \text{and} \quad X' = \begin{pmatrix} c & d \\ a & b \end{pmatrix},$$

the interchange of rows 1 and 2 in going from X to X' leaves a and c in column 1 and b and d in column 2. Likewise, permuting the columns does not affect which row a given entry is in. Thus, if we can maximize each of

$$S_1(A) = \sum_{i=1}^{m-1} \sum_{j=1}^{n} a_{ij} a_{i+1,j}$$

and

$$S_2(\mathbf{A}) = \sum_{j=1}^{n-1} \sum_{i=1}^{m} a_{ij} a_{i,j+1},$$

separately, we will maximize $f(\mathbf{A})$.

Now we come to the traveling salesman problem; we will use it as a tool, and we will use it twice. First, to maximize S_1, it suffices to minimize

$$-S_1 = \sum_{i=1}^{m-1} \sum_{j=1}^{n} -a_{ij} a_{i+1,j}.$$

(This is needed because the TSP asks for a minimum.) Now, given matrix $\mathbf{A}$, for each row i we introduce a vertex i. For any two rows k and l, we join them by an undirected edge with weight

$$c_{kl} = \sum_{j=1}^{n} -a_{kj} a_{l,j}.$$

In the resulting undirected graph G_3', each Hamilton path h describes a permutation of the rows of $\mathbf{A}$. Further, if $\mathbf{A}' = [a_{ij}']$ is formed from $\mathbf{A}$ by carrying out this permutation of the rows for a minimum weight Hamilton path, then

$$\sum_{i=1}^{m-1} \sum_{j=1}^{n} -a_{ij}' a_{i+1,j}'$$

is precisely the sum of the weights along h. Since h is a minimum weight Hamilton path in G_3', this means that

$$\sum_{i=1}^{m-1} \sum_{j=1}^{n} a_{ij}' a_{i+1,j}'$$

is largest among all possible orderings of the rows of $\mathbf{A}$.

Thus the maximum value of this half of $f(\mathbf{A})$ is found by finding a minimum weight Hamilton path in G_3'. To convert this method to the TSP (for possible future solutions of the TSP as discussed before), add one more vertex 0 to G_3' and join 0 to each other vertex by an edge of weight 0, thus forming graph G_3. A solution of the TSP in G_3 corresponds to a permutation of the rows of $\mathbf{A}$ that maximizes S_1. A graph G_3 for the matrix $\mathbf{X_2}$ is shown in Figure 3, with a Hamilton circuit corresponding to the row ordering of matrix $\mathbf{X_1}$ shown by the bold edges. This circuit is read in the order J, M, S, A.

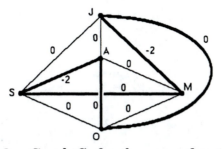

Figure 3.   Graph G_3 for the rows of matrix X_2.

We can do a similar thing with S_2, using a graph G_4 and starting with the columns of **A** for vertices (see Exercise 6). A graph G_4 for the matrix X_2 is shown in Figure 4, with a Hamilton circuit corresponding to the column ordering of matrix X_1 shown by the bold edges. This circuit is read in the order a, b, c, d to obtain X_1.

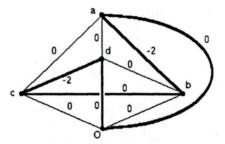

Figure 4.   Graph G_4 for the columns of matrix X_2.

Thus the data array rearrangement problem becomes a pair of TSPs.

Example 5   Suppose in polling companies, we obtained the 5×6 relationship matrix **Y** shown here.

$$\mathbf{Y} = \begin{array}{c} \\ A \\ B \\ C \\ D \\ E \end{array} \begin{array}{cccccc} a & b & c & d & e & f \\ \begin{pmatrix} 1 & 0 & 0 & 0 & 1 & 0 \\ 0 & 1 & 0 & 1 & 0 & 1 \\ 1 & 0 & 1 & 0 & 1 & 0 \\ 0 & 1 & 0 & 1 & 0 & 1 \\ 1 & 0 & 1 & 0 & 1 & 0 \end{pmatrix} \end{array}.$$

Find clusters for the five companies.

Solution: Following the procedure just described, we form the graph G_5 with vertices 0, A, B, C, D, and E, as shown in Figure 5. Solving the TSP there, we find the shortest Hamilton circuit shown by the bold edges in Figure 5. This corresponds to the ordering B, D, E, C, A of the rows of $\mathbf{Y}$. Reordering the rows of $\mathbf{Y}$ in this way produces $\mathbf{Y}'$.

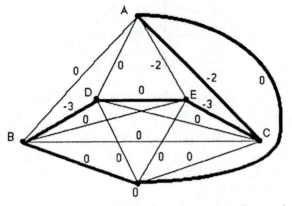

Figure 5.   Graph G_5 for the rows of matrix Y.

$$\mathbf{Y}' = \begin{array}{c} \\ B \\ D \\ E \\ C \\ A \end{array} \begin{array}{cccccc} a & b & c & d & e & f \\ \left(\begin{array}{cccccc} 0 & 1 & 0 & 1 & 0 & 1 \\ 0 & 1 & 0 & 1 & 0 & 1 \\ 1 & 0 & 1 & 0 & 1 & 0 \\ 1 & 0 & 1 & 0 & 1 & 0 \\ 1 & 0 & 0 & 0 & 1 & 0 \end{array}\right) \end{array}.$$

Next, we form the graph G_6 with vertices $0, a, b, c, d, e, f$, as shown in Figure 6. Solving the TSP here, we find the shortest Hamilton circuit shown by the bold edges, corresponding to the ordering f, b, d, e, a, c of the columns of $\mathbf{Y}'$ as well as of $\mathbf{Y}$. Carrying out this reordering, we get $\mathbf{Y}''$.

$$\mathbf{Y}'' = \begin{array}{c} \\ B \\ D \\ E \\ C \\ A \end{array} \begin{array}{cccccc} f & b & d & e & a & c \\ \left(\begin{array}{cccccc} 1 & 1 & 1 & 0 & 0 & 0 \\ 1 & 1 & 1 & 0 & 0 & 0 \\ 0 & 0 & 0 & 1 & 1 & 1 \\ 0 & 0 & 0 & 1 & 1 & 1 \\ 0 & 0 & 0 & 1 & 1 & 0 \end{array}\right) \end{array}.$$

Thus we see that companies B and D belong together in an industry carrying out activities b, d, and f, while companies A, C, and E belong in another industry which specializes in activities a, c, and e (although company A does not do activity c). Note that $f(\mathbf{Y}) = 0$ while $f(\mathbf{Y}'') = 17$. □

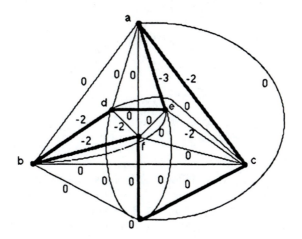

Figure 6.   Graph G_6 for the columns of matrix Y.

Reductions

No algorithm is known that has polynomial complexity and solves the TSP. Worse, it is strongly suspected that no TSP algorithm with polynomial complexity exists. Now, suppose we have selected an algorithm for solving the TSP and have programmed it for our computer. Since the algorithm does not have polynomial complexity, even a small reduction in the number of vertices in a graph we give it could result in a substantial reduction in the time our computer requires to solve the TSP.

One reduction which is easy to make, although it is not commonly possible, occurs when the graph G contains a subgraph H as shown in Figure 7, where vertices a and c may be incident with more edges than those shown, but the vertices b_i with $i \in \{1, 2, \ldots, k\}$ meet only the edges shown in the figure.

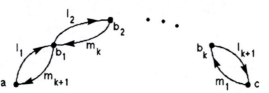

Figure 7.   A subgraph subject to a Type I reduction.

Then any Hamilton circuit in G contains exactly one of the two paths $a, b_1, b_2, \ldots, b_{k-1}, b_k, c$ or $c, b_k, b_{k-1}, \ldots, b_2, b_1, a$. Therefore, we can reduce the graph G to a graph G' by replacing the subgraph H with the subgraph H' shown in Figure 8, where the vertices a and c are as before, but the other vertices and the edges of H have been replaced by a single vertex b' and the four edges shown.

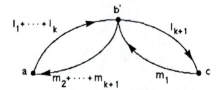

Figure 8.   Replacement subgraph produced by the Type I reduction from Figure 7.

The edge lengths in H' are as follows: edge (a, b') has length $l_1 + l_2 + \ldots + l_k$, edge (b', c) has length l_{k+1}, edge (c, b') has length m_1, and edge (b', a) has length $m_2 + m_3 + \ldots + m_{k+1}$. When a shortest Hamilton circuit has been found in G', exactly one of the two paths a, b', c or c, b', a must be in it, and we can replace that path by $a, b_1, b_2, \ldots, b_{k-1}, b_k, c$ or $c, b_k, b_{k-1}, \ldots, b_2, b_1, a$, respectively, to obtain a shortest Hamilton circuit in G. Hereafter we will call the reduction of replacing H with H' a **Type I reduction**.

Type I reductions are also available in the undirected case, as illustrated in the following example.

Example 6   Solve the TSP in the 8-vertex graph G_7 shown in Figure 9.

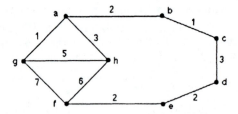

Figure 9.   Graph G_7 subject to a Type I reduction.

Solution: We can use a Type I reduction to replace the path a, b, c, d, e, f with the path a, b', f in which the edge $\{a, b'\}$ is given weight 2 and the edge $\{b', f\}$ is given weight $1 + 3 + 2 + 2 = 8$. The result G_8 is shown in Figure 10. In G_8, it is easy to see that there are only two Hamilton circuits, namely a, b', f, g, h, a and a, b', f, h, g, a. Since the first of these has length 25 while the second one has length 22, the second is clearly the solution to the TSP in G_8. Returning to Figure 9, b' is replaced by b, c, d, e to give the shortest Hamilton circuit $a, b, c, d, e, f, h, g, a$, having length 22 in G_7. $\square$

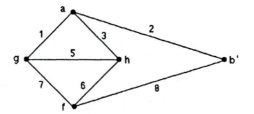

Figure 10.   Graph G_8 obtained from G_7 by a Type I reduction.

For a second reduction, as illustrated in Figure 11, suppose there is a subset A of $V(G)$ such that only one edge $e = (b, a)$ is directed from $b \in V(G) - A$ and toward $a \in A$; every other edge joining a vertex in A with a vertex in $V(G) - A$ is directed toward $V(G) - A$.

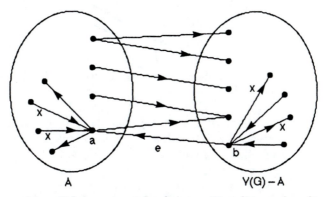

Figure 11.   Edge e must be in any Hamilton circuit of G.

Then any Hamilton circuit in G must include edge e since the Hamilton circuit must cross from $V(G) - A$ to A and only e is available. Hence no edge incident with b and directed away from b and no edge incident with a and directed toward a can be in any Hamilton circuit in G. These edges are marked with an "x" in Figure 11. Since these edges cannot be in a Hamilton circuit in G, there is no reason to leave them in G. Deleting them from the graph reduces it; indeed the reduced graph may have a new subset A' of the same type. We will call the deletion of unnecessary edges as described here a **Type II reduction**.

Example 7   Use reductions of Types I and II to find a Hamilton circuit in the graph of Figure 12.

Solution: In Figure 12, we find that we can replace vertices b_1, b_2, and b_3 with the single vertex b' by a Type I reduction, obtaining the graph shown in Figure 13. In Figure 13, we notice four occurrences of a set A suited to a Type II

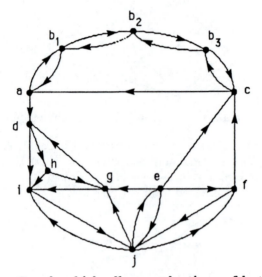

Figure 12.   **Graph which allows reductions of both Types I and II.**

reduction: $A_1 = \{e\}$, $A_2 = \{h\}$, $A_3 = \{i\}$, and $A_4 = \{a, b', c\}$. In Figures 13 and 14, for set A_i, circled by dashed lines, we label the edge uniquely directed toward or away from A_i by e_i, and we label all edges deletable by a Type II reduction as a result of e_i by x_i.

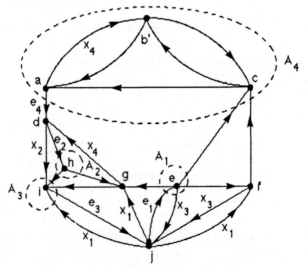

Figure 13.   **Graph obtained from Figure 12 by one Type I reduction.**

After applying Type II reductions to the graph of Figure 13, we get the graph shown in Figure 14.

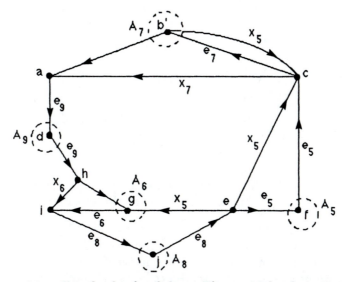

Figure 14.   Graph obtained from Figure 13 by four Type II reductions. Vertices d, f, and j yield two required edges, but A_8 and A_9 do not result in any edges removed.

There we see three new sets, $A_5 = \{f\}$, $A_6 = \{g\}$, and $A_7 = \{b'\}$. Each of these leads to the deletion of one or more further edges, resulting in the unique Hamilton circuit of Figure 15.

It follows that the graph of Figure 12 has the unique Hamilton circuit

$$a, d, h, g, i, j, e, f, c, b_3, b_2, b_1, a,$$

which is thus the solution of the TSP for this graph no matter what weights are placed on the edges.   □

Approximation Algorithms

Reductions do not always exist in a graph, and even when they do, they may not reduce the problem enough to make it solvable in a reasonable amount of time. When a solution must be found in spite of this problem, we may decide that a good approximation to the minimum solution will suffice.

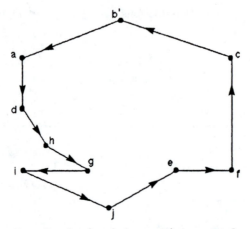

Figure 15.   Graph obtained from Figure 14 by 3 Type II reductions, and a Hamilton circuit in the graph of Figure 13.

Consider, for example, a package delivery company. Whenever the company has a truck load of packages to send out, the dispatcher has several choices of routing directions he could give. He could say simply, "Go out and deliver these packages," leaving it to the driver of the truck to find the best route to follow. But the driver might not know the city well, and so he might waste much time and money going out of the way to make deliveries that could have been made more efficiently. The dispatcher might instead give the driver a prepared route to follow. But who will prepare the route, and how? The dispatcher, at a time when he is directing the movements of 50 other trucks as well? No, the company provides the dispatcher with a computer programmed to solve the TSP for each truck that is sent out.

But even now there is a problem. One truck might well have packages to deliver to more than 100 different addresses. Thus we seem to be asking the computer to solve the TSP 50 or more times per day on graphs with 100 or more vertices each. As said before, in general we do not know how to solve this problem in less than many years per graph. An acceptable compromise would be to program the computer to spend just a few seconds to find a good, though not necessarily the best, route. But what does the term "good" mean in this context? One answer is that, if a shortest route has length k, a route is *good* if its length is at most $2k$, or some other small constant times k. Formally, we say we have a performance guarantee in this case.

Definition 2   A *performance guarantee* for an algorithm A is a theorem stating that there is a constant c such that, given a graph G with weighted edges and having a minimum Hamilton circuit of length k, the algorithm A will find a Hamilton circuit of length at most ck.   □

We have such an approximation algorithm in the case of graphs that satisfy the *triangle inequality*.

Definition 3   Let undirected graph G with vertices labeled $1, 2, \ldots, n$ have weight c_{ij} on edge $\{i, j\}$ for all adjacent i and j. We say that G satisfies the *triangle inequality* if $c_{ij} \leq c_{ik} + c_{kj}$ for every choice of i, j, and k.   □

We call this the "triangle inequality" because it is the inequality satisfied by the lengths of the three edges of a triangle in geometry. Its usefulness comes from the fact that, if we have a path a, b, c in a complete graph and if the vertex b is not needed in that path, there is a path of no greater length consisting of the edge $\{a, c\}$

One method of checking a graph to see if it satisfies the triangle inequality is to find all triangles in the graph, and then to check the sum of the lengths of each of the pairs of edges of each triangle against the length of the third side. Doing this in the four triangles a, b, c; a, b, d; a, c, d; and b, c, d of the graphs in Figures 16 and 17, we see that the graph G_9 of Figure 16 and graph G_{11} of Figure 17 do satisfy the triangle inequality, while graph G_{10} of Figure 17 does not $(1 + 2 < 6$ in triangle $a, b, c)$.

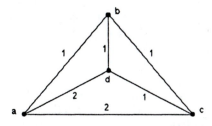

Figure 16.   **Graph G_9 satisfies the triangle inequality.**

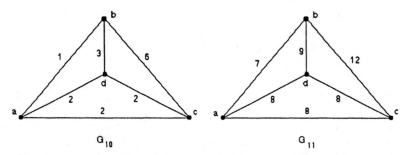

Figure 17.   Graph G_{10} does not satisfy the triangle inequality. Graph G_{11}, obtained from G_{10} by adding 6 to the weight of each edge, does satisfy the triangle inequality.

If G is a graph with finite nonnegative lengths c_{ij} on each edge $\{i, j\}$, then we can form a related graph G' which satisfies the triangle inequality. To do this, first let M be a constant such that $M \geq c_{ij}$ for all i and j. Then add M to every edge length in G to form G'. The triangle inequality is satisfied in G' since

$$c_{ij} + M \leq M + M \leq c_{ik} + M + c_{kj} + M$$

for every choice of i, j, and k. Further, not only does G' satisfy the triangle inequality, but we do not have to find many triangles and verify the inequality on each to know that G' satisfies it.

But the process described in the previous paragraph increases the length of every Hamilton circuit of G by exactly nM, where $n = |V(G)|$, so a shortest Hamilton circuit in G' has the same edges in the same order as a shortest Hamilton circuit in G. Hence solving the TSP in G' solves it in G.

Example 8   For the graph G_{10} of Figure 17 we can let $M = 6$. Adding 6 to the length of each edge of G_{10} yields the graph G_{11}, thus converting a graph which does not satisfy the triangle inequality into one that does. The three Hamilton circuits of G_{11} and their lengths are

Circuit	Length
a, b, c, d, a	35
a, b, d, c, a	32
a, c, b, d, a	37

The shortest of these is a, b, d, c, a with length 32. Returning to G_{10}, we see that Hamilton circuit a, b, d, c, a there has length $8 = 32 - 4(6)$ and it is easy to check that this is shortest.   □

Of course, we have no need for the triangle inequality if we are going to list all of the Hamilton circuits in the graph and find the shortest one. But in a complete weighted graph satisfying the triangle inequality, we can find a Hamilton circuit by a fast algorithm which has a performance guarantee that the circuit found will be no more than twice the length of a shortest Hamilton circuit.

Let us denote the weight c_{ij} of edge $\{i, j\}$ by $l(\{i, j\})$. Then for any subgraph H of weighted graph G, we let $l(H) = \sum_{e \in E(H)} l(e)$.

Let G be an undirected complete graph with a length c_{ij} on each edge. Suppose these lengths satisfy the triangle inequality. Let T be a minimal spanning tree of G (found by using Prim's algorithm, for example, as described in Section 8.6 of *Discrete Mathematics and Its Applications*, Second Edition, by Rosen). We will use T and the triangle inequality to find a Hamilton circuit C in G such that $l(C) \leq 2l(T)$.

In the algorithm *Short Circuit*, presented next, we begin with a circuit which includes all of the vertices and which has total length $2l(T)$ because it includes each edge of T exactly twice. Listing this circuit as a sequence of vertices, one at a time we delete second occurrences v of vertices, replacing each with the edge from the vertex immediately before v to the vertex immediately after v in the sequence. Each time, the circuit length stays the same or is reduced because the graph satisfies the triangle inequality. For example, for the graph G_{12} of Figure 18, we start with the vertex sequence a, b, c, b, a. Noting the presence of a second occurrence of b, we replace it with the edge $\{c, a\}$, thus obtaining the vertex sequence a, b, c, a which describes a Hamilton circuit.

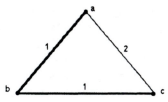

Figure 18.   Graph G_{12}. T is indicated by bold edges.

ALGORITHM 1   Short Circuit.

procedure *Short Circuit*(G: weighted complete undirected
   graph with $n \geq 3$ vertices; T: minimal spanning tree in G)
$T' :=$ graph formed from T by replacing each edge of T with
   two parallel edges
$v_1 :=$ vertex of degree 2 in T'
$C :=$ the vertex sequence of an Euler circuit in T' beginning
   at v_1
while a vertex other than v_1 is repeated in C
   begin
      $v :=$ the second occurrence of a vertex other that v_1 in C
      $C := C$ with v omitted
   end
end $\{C$ is a Hamilton circuit in G and $l(C) \leq 2l(T)\}$

Example 9   Use the Short Circuit algorithm to find a Hamilton circuit in the graph G_{13} of Figure 19.

Solution: Note that G_{13} satisfies the triangle inequality. The edges of a minimal spanning tree are drawn bold in Figure 19. The circuit C described

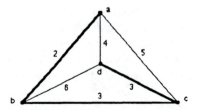

Figure 19.   Graph G_{13}. T is indicated by bold edges.

in the algorithm is a, b, c, d, c, b, a, and $l(C) = 2 + 3 + 3 + 3 + 3 + 2 = 16$. In this circuit, c is the first vertex that is repeated, so the circuit C becomes a, b, c, d, b, a, and then has length 16.   Next b is repeated, so the circuit C becomes a, b, c, d, a, having length 12.   Note that C is now a Hamilton circuit in G_{13}. This graph is small enough that we can list all of the Hamilton circuits in the graph (there are only three) and determine which is shortest. These three circuits have lengths $12, 16$, and 18; the one we found is shortest. $\square$

Example 10   Use the Short Circuit algorithm to find a Hamilton circuit in the graph G_1 of Figure 1.

Solution: Since $1 + 2 < 4$ in triangle a, b, c, this graph does not satisfy the triangle inequality. So we add $M = 7$, the largest edge length, to the length of each edge, obtaining the graph G_{14} of Figure 20. A minimal tree T is shown in Figure 20 with bold edges. Starting at d, we obtain $C = d, b, c, b, a, e, a, b, d$. Now b is the first repeated vertex, so we change C into d, b, c, a, e, a, b, d. Next a is the first repeated vertex, so C becomes d, b, c, a, e, b, d. Finally, b is repeated again, causing us to change C to d, b, c, a, e, d. This sequence corresponds to the same Hamilton circuit as the sequence a, c, b, d, e, a of Example 1, having length 18.   While this is not the shortest Hamilton circuit in G_1, it is not bad and it was quickly found. $\square$

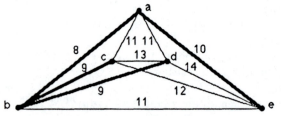

Figure 20.   Graph G_{14} obtained from graph G_1 of Figure 1 by adding 7 to the weight of each edge.

Notice in this last example that we did not use the new lengths shown in Figure 20; even T would use the same edges in G_1 as it does in G_{14}. In fact, for the purposes of algorithm *Short Circuit*, it is enough to know that the new lengths can be found, without bothering to actually find them. The real reason for the requirement that the lengths must satisfy the triangle inequality is to allow the proof of the next theorem, which is the performance guarantee for the algorithm *Short Circuit.*

Theorem 1   Let G be a weighted complete undirected graph in which the triangle inequality holds and in which all weights are nonnegative. Let C be a circuit obtained by the algorithm *Short Circuit*. If the minimum length Hamilton circuit in G has length k, then $l(C) \leq 2k$.

Proof: Let C' be a shortest Hamilton circuit in G, and let e be an edge of C'. Let $P = C' - e$. Then P is a spanning tree of G. Since T is a minimum spanning tree of G, we have $l(T) \leq l(P)$. Hence

$$l(C) \leq 2l(T) \leq 2l(P) \leq 2k. \qquad \blacksquare$$

Other approximation algorithms that have performance guarantees are described in Section 3 of Chapter 5 of [6]. The best of these (Christofides' algorithm) achieves a constant $c = 3/2$ as the multiplier of the minimum length k in the performance guarantee.

Suggested Readings

1. G. Dantzig, R. Fulkerson, and S. Johnson, "Solution of a large-scale traveling-salesman problem", *Operations Research*, Vol. 2, 1954, pp. 393–410.

2. L. Euler, "Solution d'une question curieuse qui ne paroit soumise à aucune analyse", *Mém. Acad. Sci. Berlin*, Vol 15, 1759, published 1766, pp. 310–337.

3. M. Flood, "The traveling-salesman problem", *Operations Research*, Vol. 4, 1956, pp. 61–75.

4. M. Garey and D. Johnson, *Computers and Intractability: A Guide to the Theory of NP-Completeness*, Freeman, San Francisco, 1979.

5. T. Kirkman "On the representation of polyhedra", *Phil. Trans. Royal Soc. London*, Vol. 146, 1856, pp. 413–418.

6. E. Lawler, J. Lenstra, A. Rinnooy Kan, and D. Shmoys, editors, *The Traveling Salesman Problem*, John Wiley & Sons, Chichester, 1985. (This is the primary reference for this chapter.)

7. L. Lovász and M. Plummer, *Matching Theory*, Elsevier Science Publ. Co., New York, 1986.

Exercises

1. Solve the traveling salesman problem by listing all of the possible Hamilton circuits and then choosing the shortest one. Notice sequences of vertices such as those forced by vertices of degree two; they can be used to reduce the number of possibilities. Also, use reductions when possible.

a)

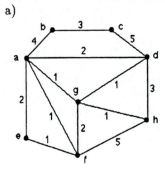

b)

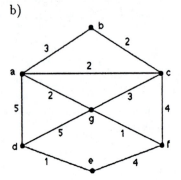

c)

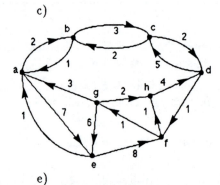

d)

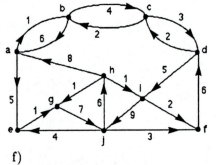

e)

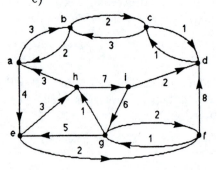

f)

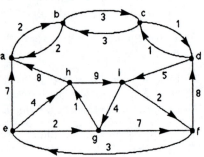

Hint for g) and h): Try working from the two different possible directions along a, b, c, d.

g)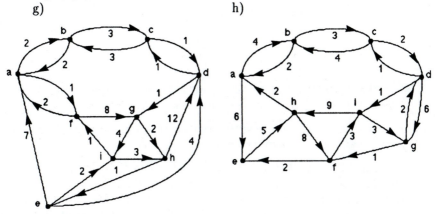

h)

2. Use the method shown in this chapter to permute the rows and columns of the given matrix and thus show the industrial groupings of the companies and their activities.

a)
$$
\begin{array}{c c}
 & \begin{array}{c c c c c} a & b & c & d & e \end{array} \\
\begin{array}{c} A \\ B \\ C \\ D \\ E \end{array} &
\left(\begin{array}{c c c c c}
1 & 1 & 0 & 0 & 0 \\
0 & 0 & 1 & 0 & 1 \\
0 & 1 & 0 & 1 & 0 \\
0 & 0 & 1 & 0 & 1 \\
0 & 1 & 0 & 1 & 0
\end{array}\right)
\end{array}
$$

b)
$$
\begin{array}{c c}
 & \begin{array}{c c c c c} a & b & c & d & e \end{array} \\
\begin{array}{c} A \\ B \\ C \\ D \end{array} &
\left(\begin{array}{c c c c c}
1 & 1 & 0 & 0 & 1 \\
1 & 0 & 0 & 1 & 1 \\
1 & 1 & 1 & 1 & 0 \\
0 & 1 & 1 & 0 & 0
\end{array}\right)
\end{array}
$$

3. Use procedure Short Circuit on the following graphs.

a)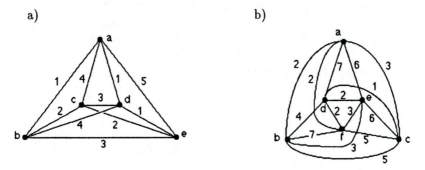

b)

⋆4. Find a minimum cost Hamilton circuit in the following graph. What strategy did you follow? Discuss the weaknesses of your strategy when applied to large examples.

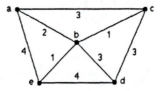

5. Show that each Hamilton circuit starting at a vertex a in a complete graph is described by two different permutations of the vertices.

6. In array clustering, show how the solution of a TSP in a graph G_4 can be used to find the maximum value of S_2.

7. How many different Hamilton circuits are there in K_7? One answer, $6!/2$, is given in Rosen's book *Discrete Mathematics and Its Applications*. Give at least two other answers, discussing how the meaning of the word "different" changes from one answer to another. Why is the text's choice of the meaning of "different" best, or is it?

8. Apply procedure Short Circuit to the following graph. Does anything go wrong? Why?

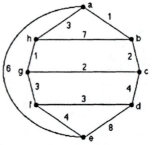

⋆9. The following figure shows a different sort of reducible graph, in which C and D are subgraphs of several vertices each, and a, b, c, d are four distinct vertices. Describe a reduction which will help solve the TSP in this graph and state how you can use the solution(s) in the reduced graph(s) to find a solution in the original graph.

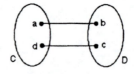

In Exercises 10–13, describe the vertices, edges, and edge weights that will convert the problem into a TSP.

10. An armored car must visit its list of banks as quickly as possible using routes thought to be safe.

11. A rail line from New York to San Francisco must pass through many specified cities at a minimum cost.

12. A package delivery company with many trucks clusters the deliveries and assigns a truck to each cluster. Each truck should make its deliveries in minimum time. *Note*: In this exercise, we see the TSP as a subproblem of a larger, even more difficult problem.

13. A commander needs to visit his front line units by the safest possible routes. *Hint*: Assign the degree of safety of a route a numerical value.

Computer Projects

1. Write a computer program to find all Type I reductions in a directed graph.

2. Write a computer program to find all Type II reductions in a directed graph.

3. Write a computer program calling on the procedures of Computer Projects 1 and 2 to exactly solve the TSP in a directed graph of at most 50 vertices.

16

The Tantalizing Four Cubes

Author: William C. Arlinghaus, Department of Mathematics and Computer Science, Lawrence Technological University.

Prerequisites: The prerequisites for this chapter are the basics of counting and graphs. See, for example, Sections 4.1, 7.1, and 7.2 of *Discrete Mathematics and Its Applications*, Second Edition, by Kenneth H. Rosen.

Introduction

The game of the four colored cubes consists of four cubes, each of whose sides is colored with one of four colors. The object of the game is to place the cubes next to each other in such a way that each of the long sides of the rectangular solid obtained has all four colors appearing on it. The game has been in existence since at least the 1940s, when it was sold commercially under the name "Tantalizer", and more recently as the popular puzzle "Instant Insanity". At the end of this chapter there is a template for a single cube. Readers may wish to copy it to make worksheets for themselves to follow the accompanying text — one sheet for each of the four cubes of the game.

The Game: Problem and Solution

For simplicity, we will exhibit each cube unfolded in the fashion of Figure 1. Thus, we want to arrange the cubes so that each of the four colors appears on each of the top, front, bottom, and back sides. The colors appearing on the left and right are not relevant to the solution.

Figure 1. 1. Cube top. 2. Cube front. 3. Cube bottom. 4. Cube back. 5. Left side of cube. 6. Right side of cube.

For example, if the four colors are red (R), white (W), blue (B), and green (G), four cubes arranged as in Figure 2 would provide a solution to the puzzle. Figure 3 shows the four cubes next to each other, viewed from the front, top, back, and bottom.

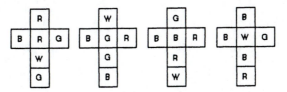

Figure 2.   A solution to the puzzle.

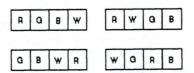

Figure 3. Upper left shows front view; upper right shows top view; lower left shows back view; lower right shows bottom view.

It should be fairly clear that the difficulty of finding a solution depends greatly on the color pattern on each cube. One extreme case would be to have each cube colored a single different solid color (one each of red, white, blue, green). In this case, it wouldn't matter how the cubes were rotated; every arrangement would be a solution. On the other hand, if all four cubes were colored solid red, no solution would be possible.

Our goal will be to use graph theory to simplify the search for a solution in some general situation and then to use our methods to find solutions in particular cases. But before we do this, it might help us to see how many different ways four cubes can be arranged. This may help us to realize why we need some method of simplifying the problem.

Example 1   Find the number of ways to arrange four cubes.

Solution: The first fact to note is that there are essentially only three ways to arrange the first cube; that is, choosing the pair of faces which are on the left and right specifies the cube. For once these faces are chosen, the remaining faces may be rotated (with left and right fixed) so that any of them becomes the front. Even reversing left and right makes no difference, since rotating the cube to reverse left and right just reverses front and back, so that the four faces of interest appear in reverse order.

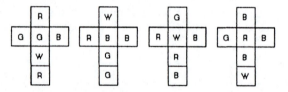

Figure 4.   Cubes of Figure 2 with left and right faces re-versed.

For example, Figure 4 exhibits the same cubes as Figure 2, but with left and right faces reversed. Once the first cube is positioned, however, the second cube may be positioned with respect to it in 24 ways. For the left-right pair may be chosen in 3 ways, either one of the pair may be the left face, and then the cube may be rotated to make any of the four remaining faces the front face. Similarly, each of the third and fourth cubes may be positioned in any of 24 different ways. Thus, the total number of positionings of the four cubes is $3 \cdot 24 \cdot 24 \cdot 24 = 41,472$. $\qquad \square$

So, picking an arrangement which is a solution could be quite difficult. But graph theory can be used to make finding a solution easier, by providing an analysis of what a solution looks like. Given a set of four cubes with faces colored red, white, blue, and green, define a graph with four vertices labeled R, W, B, G as follows. If cube i has a pair of opposite faces with colors x and y, draw an edge with label i between x and y.

Example 2   Use a graph to solve the puzzle for the cubes of Figure 5.

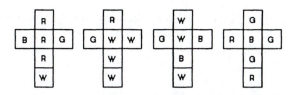

Figure 5.   From left to right: cubes 1, 2, 3, 4.

Solution: The graph of Figure 6 is the graph associated with the cubes of Figure 5. Note that both loops and multiple edges are allowed in this labeled graph.

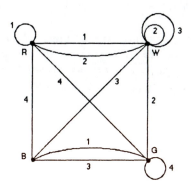

Figure 6.   Graph associated with cubes of Figure 5.

Now suppose that there is a solution of the puzzle with the cubes of Figure 5. Since the set of top and bottom faces must each have all four colors represented, the graph can be used to trace the colors on both faces simultaneously. Consider, for instance, the subgraph of Figure 6 shown in Figure 7.

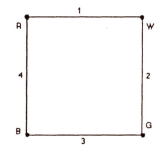

Figure 7.   Subgraph for top and bottom faces.

This subgraph can be used to place the top and bottom faces. Since cube 1 has a pair of opposite faces labeled R-W, place cube 1 with red as the top face and white as the bottom face. Now cube 2 has a W-G pair, so place cube 2 with white as the top face and green as the bottom face. Continue as the graph indicates, placing the top and bottom faces of cubes 3 and 4. At this point, the cubes appear as in Figure 8.

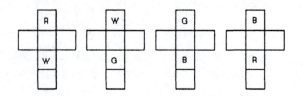

Figure 8.   Top and bottom faces.

The key facts about the subgraph of Figure 7 that made this work were that there were four edges, one with each of the labels 1,2,3,4, and that each vertex had degree 2, so that each color was represented exactly twice. Now the task is to rotate the remaining four faces of each cube to obtain a solution. This will be possible if there is another subgraph of the graph of Figure 6, like that of Figure 7 but with four different edges, since each edge represents a different pair of opposite faces, and the ones of Figure 7 have already been used. Such a subgraph is illustrated in Figure 9.

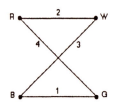

Figure 9.   Subgraph for front and back faces.

Using this subgraph to place the front and back faces of the cubes, the following solution to the problem of Figure 5 is obtained, in Figure 10.   □

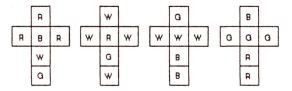

Figure 10.   Solution for cubes of Figure 5.

Note that, in this example, the positioning of the B-G pair in cube 1 was followed by the G-R pair in cube 4 since the label of the other edge incident with G was 4. Then the R-W pair of cube 2 was positioned, and finally the

W-B pair of cube 3 was placed. All of these positions were obtained by rotating the cubes with the top and bottom fixed. The colors on the left and right end up wherever this rotation takes them, although of course what colors are there doesn't affect the solution. The end result of this construction is the following theorem.

Theorem 1 A set of colored cubes has a solution if and only if its corresponding labeled graph has two disjoint subgraphs, each of which has every vertex of degree two and every label appearing exactly once. ∎

Several things should be noted about this theorem. First, if a loop is used in the subgraph, it contributes two to the degree of its vertex. For instance, subgraphs such as the ones of Figure 11 are acceptable subgraphs.

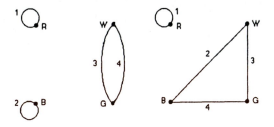

Figure 11. Acceptable subgraphs.

Second, there may be many such subgraphs available. What is necessary is to find two subgraphs of the proper type with no edges in common. There may be no such pair of subgraphs; there may be a unique pair of acceptable subgraphs, as in the problem of Figure 5; or there may be many possible subgraphs, as shown in the following example.

Example 3 Solve the problem of the cubes in Figure 12.

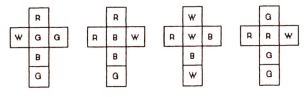

Figure 12. From left to right: cubes 1, 2, 3, 4.

Solution: The graph for these cubes is shown in Figure 13. There are six allowable subgraphs, shown in Figure 14.

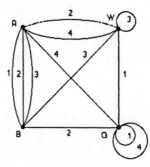

Figure 13.   The underlying graph for Figure 12.

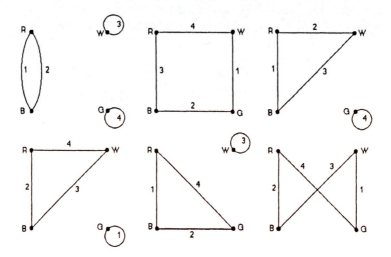

Figure 14.   Six acceptable subgraphs. Top row: left to right, A, B, C; bottom row: left to right, D, E, F.

Although Figure 14 exhibits six subgraphs of the type required by Theorem 1, there are only three pairs with distinct edges. They are AB, BC, and DE. Note that F cannot be paired with any other acceptable subgraph, so it is not of use in any solution. The three different solutions are exhibited in Figure 15 (the first subgraph of each pair is used for top and bottom).   □

Games are, of course, fun. How much fun they are depends on how successful the player is; knowledge is directly linked to success in games of skill. At a deeper level, games can help to train thought processes. Consider how this game might be like others. This is a combinatorial game; what is required is to position cubes in relation to each other according to some predetermined

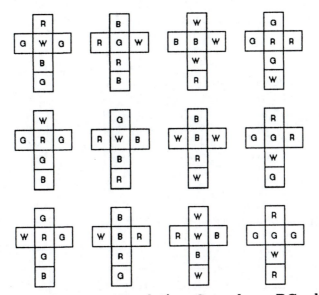

Figure 15.   First row: AB solution. Second row: BC solution. Third row: DE solution.

color scheme. Is any other game like this? Yes, "Rubik's Magic Cube" is, but this puzzle is much more complicated, as a combinatorial problem (see [3]). Then again, why confine the problem to cubical shapes. Might one construct puzzles with rules similar to those for the four colored cubes for prisms with a polygonal base and top other than a square? Learning to think creatively about puzzles, when translated to thinking creatively about mathematics (and other subjects), can reap rewards far beyond what might be expected!

Suggested Readings

1. R. Busacker and T. Saaty, *Finite Graphs and Networks*, McGraw-Hill, New York, 1965.

2. G. Chartrand, *Graphs as Mathematical Models*, PWS, Boston, 1977.

3. D. Singmaster, *Notes on Rubik's Magic Cube*, Enslow Publishers, Hillside, N. J., 1981.

4. J. Van Deventer, "Graph theory and 'Instant Insanity'", in *The Many Facets of Graph Theory*, G. Chartrand and S. Kapoor, eds., Springer-Verlag, Berlin, 1969.

Exercises

1. Solve the following puzzle.

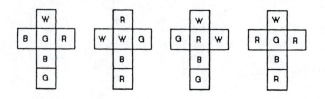

2. Solve the following puzzle.

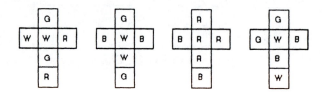

3. Find another solution to the puzzle for the previous exercise.

4. Solve the puzzle whose underlying graph is shown in the following figure.

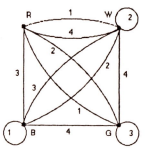

5. Construct a puzzle in which each color appears on at least four faces, but for which there is no solution.

★6. Construct a puzzle in which each color appears on each cube, but for which there is no solution.

★7. Construct a puzzle in which each color appears exactly six times and on each cube, but for which there is no solution.

★8. Construct a puzzle with exactly two solutions.

⋆9. How should the theorem be rephrased if
   a) there are 3 cubes and 3 colors;
   b) there are 3 cubes and 4 colors;
   c) there are 5 cubes and 5 colors.
   What kind of graphs would give solutions?

Computer Projects

1. Write a program that takes as input the pattern of colors on a set of four colored cubes and finds all solutions (if there are any).

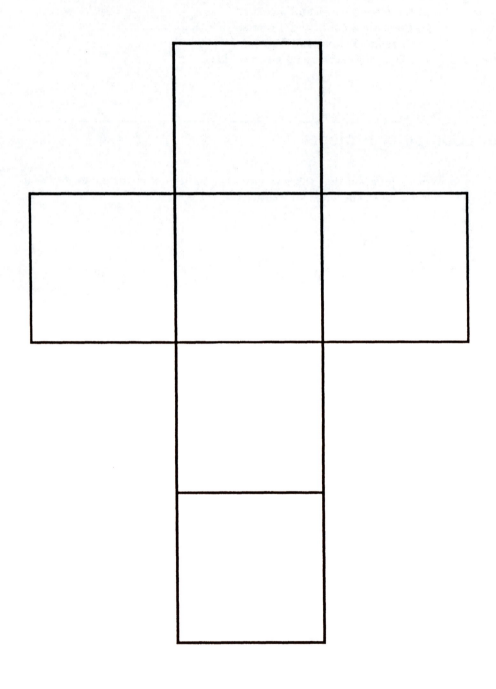

17

The Assignment Problem

Author: Fred J. Rispoli, Department of Mathematics, Dowling College.

Prerequisites: The prerequisites for this chapter are matrices, permutations, and basic concepts of graphs. See, for example, Sections 2.5, 4.3, 7.1, and 7.2 of *Discrete Mathematics and Its Applications*, Second Edition, by Kenneth H. Rosen.

Introduction

Consider the following problem: Given n workers $(i = 1, 2, \ldots, n)$ and n jobs $(j = 1, 2, \ldots, n)$, and the cost c_{ij} to train the ith worker for the jth job, find an assignment of one worker to each job which minimizes the total training cost. This problem is an example of an assignment problem, which we will define shortly. The assignment problem is particularly interesting because many seemingly different problems may be solved as assignment problems. Moreover, it is an important example of a combinatorial optimization problem; that is, a problem that seeks the best possible arrangement of objects among a specified set of many possible arrangements. Typically, the best possible arrangement means an arrangement with the smallest total cost possible.

Let us begin by looking at some examples.

Example 1   Job Assignment   Suppose three workers must be assigned to three jobs. The following matrix shows the cost of training each worker for each job.

$$\text{Worker Number} \begin{array}{c} \\ 1 \\ 2 \\ 3 \end{array} \begin{array}{ccc} & \textbf{Job Number} & \\ \textbf{1} & \textbf{2} & \textbf{3} \\ \left(\begin{array}{ccc} 5 & 7 & 9 \\ 14 & 10 & 12 \\ 15 & 13 & 16 \end{array} \right). \end{array}$$

One possible assignment is to assign worker 1 to job 2, worker 2 to job 1, and worker 3 to job 3. This assignment has a total cost of $7 + 14 + 16 = 37$. Is this an assignment with minimal total cost? We will discover the answer later in this chapter. □

Example 2   The Marriage Problem   A pioneering colony of 10 bachelors is joined by 10 prospective brides. After a short period of courting, it is decided to have an immediate ceremony. Each bride is given a list of 10 names on which she is to rank her preferences from 1 to 10; that is, she assigns 1 to her first choice, 2 to her second choice, and so on. Let c_{ij} be the rank bride i gives to bachelor j, and let $M = \{(1, j_1), (2, j_2), \ldots, (10, j_{10})\}$ be a set of 10 marriages where (i, j_i) pairs bride i with bachelor j_i. Then we assume that $\sum_{i=1}^{n} c_{ij_i}$ constitutes a valid measure of the anticipated "happiness" of the colony under the set of marriages M, in the sense that the smaller the sum, the happier the colony. What set of 10 marriages maximizes the happiness of the colony? □

Example 3   The Shortest Path Problem   Cargo must be delivered by train from New York to Los Angeles. The train routes available are shown in Figure 1, along with the time (in hours) required for each route. Notice that the time depends on the direction since some routes are express routes while others are not. What path from New York to Los Angeles gives the smallest total delivery time? □

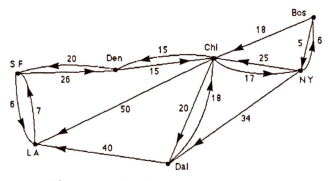

Figure 1.   Train routes and times.

These problems are all examples of problems which may be solved as assignment problems. In this chapter we will derive an efficient algorithm for solving assignment problems, and then discuss several problems which may be solved using this algorithm. The assignment problem will then be described in terms of graphs.

Solving Assignment Problems

Recall that a permutation of a set $N = \{1, 2, \ldots, n\}$ is a function $\sigma : N \to N$ which is one-to-one and onto. For example, the function from $\{1, 2, 3, 4, 5\}$ to itself where $\sigma(1) = 5$, $\sigma(2) = 4$, $\sigma(3) = 2$, $\sigma(4) = 1$, and $\sigma(5) = 3$, is a permutation which we denote 54213.

Definition 1   Given any $n \times n$ matrix $C = [c_{ij}]$, the *assignment problem* specified by C is the problem of finding a permutation σ of $\{1, 2, \ldots, n\}$ that minimizes

$$z = \sum_{i=1}^{n} c_{i\sigma(i)}.$$ □

One method for solving assignment problems is to generate all n! permutations of $\{1, 2, \ldots, n\}$ (a method for doing this is given in Section 4.7 of *Discrete Mathematics and Its Applications*, Second Edition, by Rosen), compute

$$z = \sum_{i=1}^{n} c_{i\sigma(i)}$$

for each permutation σ, and then find a permutation on which the minimum of z is attained.

Example 4   In the job assignment problem described in Example 1 of the Introduction, there are $3! = 6$ permutations:

$\sigma_1 = 123$ cost: 31 $\sigma_2 = 132$ cost: 30 $\sigma_3 = 213$ cost: 37

$\sigma_4 = 312$ cost: 36 $\sigma_5 = 231$ cost: 34 $\sigma_6 = 321$ cost: 34.

Thus, σ_2 solves the problem and indicates that the best assignment is to assign worker 1 to job 1, worker 2 to job 3, and worker 3 to job 2.   □

The above method is helpful only for n quite small, since one must check all n! possibilities. In practice assignment problems often have $n \geq 30$. If each permutation can be generated in just 10^{-9} seconds, an assignment problem with $n = 30$ would require at least $8 \cdot 10^{15}$ years of computer time to solve by generating all 30! permutations. Therefore a better method is needed.

Before developing a better algorithm, we need to set up a model for the assignment problem. Let $\mathbf{C} = [c_{ij}]$ be any $n \times n$ matrix in which c_{ij} is the cost of assigning worker i to job j. Let $\mathbf{X} = [x_{ij}]$ be the $n \times n$ matrix where

$$x_{ij} = \begin{cases} 1 & \text{if row } i \text{ is assigned to column } j \text{ (that is,} \\ & \text{worker } i \text{ is assigned to job } j) \\ 0 & \text{otherwise} \end{cases}$$

The assignment problem can then be expressed in terms of a function z as:

$$\text{minimize } z(\mathbf{X}) = \sum_{i=1}^{n} \sum_{j=1}^{n} c_{ij} x_{ij},$$

subject to the constraints

$$\sum_{j=1}^{n} x_{ij} = 1, \quad \text{for } i = 1, 2, \ldots, n \tag{1}$$

$$\sum_{i=1}^{n} x_{ij} = 1, \quad \text{for } j = 1, 2, \ldots, n \tag{2}$$

Notice that condition (1) guarantees that each row subscript i is assigned to exactly one column subscript. Condition (2) guarantees that each column subscript j is assigned to exactly one row subscript. Hence any matrix $\mathbf{X}$ satisfying conditions (1) and (2) is called a solution and corresponds to a permutation σ of N obtained by setting $\sigma(i) = j$ if and only if $x_{ij} = 1$. Furthermore, if $\mathbf{X}$ is a solution corresponding to σ, then

$$\sum_{j=1}^{n} c_{ij} x_{ij} = c_{i\sigma(i)}.$$

Summing over i from 1 to n, we obtain

$$\sum_{i=1}^{n} c_{i\sigma(i)} = \sum_{i=1}^{n} \sum_{j=1}^{n} c_{ij} x_{ij}.$$

Thus, any solution $\mathbf{X}$ on which $z(\mathbf{X})$ is minimum is called an **optimal solution**. For instance, in Example 1 it was noted that the permutation σ_2 given by 132 gives the best possible assignment of workers to jobs for that assignment problem. The permutation σ_2 corresponds to the matrix

$$\mathbf{X}^* = \begin{pmatrix} 1 & 0 & 0 \\ 0 & 0 & 1 \\ 0 & 1 & 0 \end{pmatrix}.$$

Since

$$C = \begin{pmatrix} 5 & 7 & 9 \\ 14 & 10 & 12 \\ 15 & 13 & 16 \end{pmatrix},$$

we have

$$z(\mathbf{X}^*) = \sum_{i=1}^{3} \sum_{j=1}^{3} c_{ij} x_{ij}^* = 5 + 12 + 13 = 30.$$

This model allows for the derivation of an efficient algorithm known as the **Hungarian method**. The idea behind the Hungarian method is to try to transform a given assignment problem specified by $\mathbf{C}$ into another one specified by a matrix $\widehat{\mathbf{C}} = [\widehat{c}_{ij}]$, such that $\widehat{c}_{ij} \geq 0$, for all pairs i, j, where both problems have the same set of optimal solutions. We then find a solution $\mathbf{X}^*$ for which

$$\widehat{z}(\mathbf{X}^*) = \sum_{i=1}^{n} \sum_{j=1}^{n} \widehat{c}_{ij} x_{ij}^* = 0.$$

Since $\widehat{c}_{ij} \geq 0$ (and hence $\widehat{z}(\mathbf{X}) \geq 0$ for all $\mathbf{X}$), $\mathbf{X}^*$ must be an optimal solution to the problem specified by $\widehat{\mathbf{C}}$, and hence must also be an optimal solution to the one specified by $\mathbf{C}$. Theorem 1 describes how we can transform a matrix into another one which has the same set of optimal solutions.

Theorem 1   A solution $\mathbf{X}$ is an optimal solution for

$$z(\mathbf{X}) = \sum_{i=1}^{n} \sum_{j=1}^{n} c_{ij} x_{ij}$$

if and only if it is an optimal solution for

$$\widehat{z}(\mathbf{X}) = \sum_{i=1}^{n} \sum_{j=1}^{n} \widehat{c}_{ij} x_{ij}$$

where $\widehat{c}_{ij} = c_{ij} - u_i - v_j$ for any choice of $(u_1, \ldots, u_n)$ and $(v_1, \ldots, v_n)$ where u_i and v_j are real numbers for all i and j.

Proof: We will show that the functions $z(\mathbf{X})$ and $\widehat{z}(\mathbf{X})$ differ only by the constant $\sum_{i=1}^{n} u_i + \sum_{j=1}^{n} v_j$.

$$\widehat{z}(\mathbf{x}) = \sum_{i=1}^{n} \sum_{j=1}^{n} \widehat{c}_{ij} x_{ij}$$

$$= \sum_{i=1}^{n} \sum_{j=1}^{n} (c_{ij} - u_i - v_j) x_{ij}$$

$$= \sum_{i=1}^{n} \sum_{j=1}^{n} c_{ij} x_{ij} - \sum_{i=1}^{n} \sum_{j=1}^{n} u_i x_{ij} - \sum_{i=1}^{n} \sum_{j=1}^{n} v_j x_{ij}$$

$$= \sum_{i=1}^{n} \sum_{j=1}^{n} c_{ij} x_{ij} - \sum_{i=1}^{n} \sum_{j=1}^{n} u_i x_{ij} - \sum_{j=1}^{n} \sum_{i=1}^{n} v_j x_{ij}$$

$$= z(\mathbf{x}) - \sum_{i=1}^{n} u_i \sum_{j=1}^{n} x_{ij} - \sum_{j=1}^{n} v_j \sum_{i=1}^{n} x_{ij}$$

$$= z(\mathbf{x}) - \sum_{i=1}^{n} u_i - \sum_{j=1}^{n} v_j.$$

The last equation follows from conditions (1) and (2). This shows that

$$z(\mathbf{X}) - \widehat{z}(\mathbf{X}) = \sum_{i=1}^{n} u_i + \sum_{j=1}^{n} v_j.$$

Thus, a solution $\mathbf{X}$ minimizes $z(\mathbf{X})$ if and only if it minimizes $\widehat{z}(\mathbf{X})$. ∎

To describe an optimal solution in terms of entries of a matrix the following notion of *independent* entries is needed. A set of entries of any matrix $\mathbf{A}$ is said to be **independent** if no two of them are in the same row or column.

Example 5　Apply Theorem 1 to the matrix given in Example 1 to obtain a new matrix with all nonnegative entries, which contains an independent set of three zeros and has the same set of optimal solutions as the original matrix.

Solution:　Let

$$\mathbf{C} = \begin{pmatrix} 5 & 7 & 9 \\ 14 & 10 & 12 \\ 15 & 13 & 16 \end{pmatrix}.$$

Subtract from each entry in each row the smallest entry in that row; that is, let $u_1 = 5$, $u_2 = 10$, $u_3 = 13$, and $v_1 = v_2 = v_3 = 0$. This gives the matrix

$$\begin{pmatrix} 0 & 2 & 4 \\ 4 & 0 & 2 \\ 2 & 0 & 3 \end{pmatrix}.$$

The new matrix has an independent set of two zeros, but we need three. Next, subtract from each entry in each column the smallest entry in that column, that is, let $u_1 = u_2 = u_3 = 0$, $v_1 = v_2 = 0$, and $v_3 = 2$. This gives

$$\widehat{C} = \begin{pmatrix} 0^* & 2 & 2 \\ 4 & 0 & 0^* \\ 2 & 0^* & 1 \end{pmatrix}.$$

The starred entries in $\widehat{C}$ form an independent set of three zeros. By Theorem 1 applied twice, $\widehat{C}$ and C have the same set of optimal solutions. $\square$

We are interested in obtaining a matrix with nonnegative entries with an independent set of three zeros because it is easy to obtain an optimal solution from such a matrix, as Example 6 illustrates.

Example 6   Solve the assignment problem specified by

$$C = \begin{pmatrix} 5 & 7 & 9 \\ 14 & 10 & 12 \\ 15 & 13 & 16 \end{pmatrix},$$

by obtaining an optimal solution to the problem specified by

$$\widehat{C} = \begin{pmatrix} 0^* & 2 & 2 \\ 4 & 0 & 0^* \\ 2 & 0^* & 1 \end{pmatrix}.$$

Solution: Define the solution

$$X^* = \begin{pmatrix} 1 & 0 & 0 \\ 0 & 0 & 1 \\ 0 & 1 & 0 \end{pmatrix}.$$

Then X^* solves the assignment problem specified by $\widehat{C}$ since $\widehat{z}(X^*) = 0$ and $\widehat{z}(X) \geq 0$ for any other solution X. By Example 5, X^* is also an optimal solution to the assignment problem specified by C. Note that X^* corresponds to the permutation 132. $\square$

The method used to obtain an optimal solution to the assignment problem specified by $\widehat{C}$ in Example 6 is generalized in Theorem 2.

Theorem 2   If $C = [c_{ij}]$ satisfies $c_{ij} \geq 0$ for all i and j ($1 \leq i \leq n$, $1 \leq j \leq n$), and $\{c_{1j_1}, c_{2j_2}, \ldots, c_{nj_n}\}$ is an independent set of n zeros in C, then $X^* = [x_{ij}^*]$ where $x_{1j_1}^* = 1, x_{2j_2}^* = 1, \ldots, x_{nj_n}^* = 1$, and $x_{ij}^* = 0$ for any other i and j, is an optimal solution to the assignment problem specified by C.

Proof: We must show that for any solution X, $z(X) \geq z(X^*)$. To see this, observe that

$$z(X^*) = \sum_{i=1}^{n} \sum_{j=1}^{n} c_{ij} x_{ij}^*$$

$$= \sum_{i=1}^{n} c_{ij_i} x_{ij_i}^*$$

$$= 0.$$

The second step follows from the definition of X^*, and the last step follows since $c_{ij_i} = 0$ for all i. Since $z(X) \geq 0$ for all solutions X, $z(X) \geq z(X^*)$, so X^* is an optimal solution.   ∎

The objective of the Hungarian method is to use Theorem 1 to transform a matrix C into another matrix $\hat{C}$, having the same set of optimal solutions as C, such that $\hat{C}$ contains an independent set of n zeros. Then, using Theorem 2, an optimal solution to both problems can be obtained.

Example 7   Use Theorem 1 to transform

$$C = \begin{pmatrix} 0 & 1 & 6 \\ 2 & -7 & 3 \\ -5 & 3 & 4 \end{pmatrix}$$

into a matrix with nonnegative entries containing an independent set of 3 zeros. Then use Theorem 2 to obtain an optimal solution to the assignment problem specified by C.

Solution: Let $u_1 = 0$, $u_2 = -7$, $u_3 = -5$, and $v_1 = v_2 = v_3 = 0$. Then apply Theorem 1 to obtain the matrix

$$\begin{pmatrix} 0 & 1 & 6 \\ 9 & 0 & 10 \\ 0 & 8 & 9 \end{pmatrix},$$

which has the same set of optimal solutions as C. This matrix does not have an independent set of 3 zeros. Letting $u_1 = u_2 = u_3 = v_1 = v_2 = 0$ and $v_3 = 6$ gives

$$\hat{C} = \begin{pmatrix} 0 & 1 & 0^* \\ 9 & 0^* & 4 \\ 0^* & 8 & 3 \end{pmatrix},$$

which also has the same set of optimal solutions as $\mathbf{C}$. By Theorem 2,

$$\mathbf{X}^* = \begin{pmatrix} 0 & 0 & 1 \\ 0 & 1 & 0 \\ 1 & 0 & 0 \end{pmatrix}$$

is an optimal solution to the problem $\widehat{\mathbf{C}}$, hence to the problem $\mathbf{C}$. Note that $\mathbf{X}^*$ corresponds to the permutation 321.   □

The matrix $\widehat{\mathbf{C}}$ in the solution of Example 7 is called a *reduced matrix* for $\mathbf{C}$, which we shall now define.

Definition 2   Given any $n \times n$ matrix $\mathbf{C} = [c_{ij}]$, let

$$u_i = \text{minimum } \{c_{i1}, c_{i2}, \ldots, c_{in}\}, \text{ for } i = 1, 2, \ldots, n,$$
$$v_j = \text{minimum } \{c_{1j} - u_1, c_{2j} - u_2, \ldots, c_{nj} - u_n\}, \text{ for } j = 1, 2, \ldots, n.$$

The $n \times n$ matrix $\widehat{\mathbf{C}} = [\widehat{c}_{ij}]$ given by $\widehat{c}_{ij} = c_{ij} - u_i - v_j$ for all pairs i and j is called the *reduced matrix* for $\mathbf{C}$.   □

In words, a reduced matrix is obtained by first subtracting from each row the smallest entry in each row and then subtracting from each column the smallest entry in each column. By Theorem 1, the assignment problems specified by a matrix $\mathbf{C}$ and by its reduced matrix $\widehat{\mathbf{C}}$ both have the same set of optimal solutions. Observe that all entries in the reduced matrix are nonnegative. However, the reduced matrix may not contain an independent set of n zeros.

Example 8   Determine the reduced matrix for

$$\mathbf{C} = \begin{pmatrix} 2 & 5 & 7 \\ 4 & 2 & 1 \\ 2 & 6 & 5 \end{pmatrix}.$$

Solution: The values of $u_1, u_2, u_3, v_1, v_2,$ and v_3, as defined in the definition of the reduced matrix are $u_1 = 2$, $u_2 = 1$, $u_3 = 2$, and $v_1 = 0$, $v_2 = 1$, and $v_3 = 0$. Therefore, the reduced matrix is

$$\widehat{\mathbf{C}} = \begin{pmatrix} 0 & 2 & 5 \\ 3 & 0 & 0 \\ 0 & 3 & 3 \end{pmatrix}.$$ □

The matrix $\hat{C}$ in the solution of Example 8 does not contain an independent set of three zeros. To obtain a new matrix having the same optimal solutions as $\hat{C}$, but containing more zeros, draw a set of lines through the rows and columns of $\hat{C}$ using as few lines as possible so that there is at least one line through every zero. This gives

$$\hat{C} = \begin{pmatrix} 0 & 2 & 5 \\ 3 & 0 & 0 \\ 0 & 3 & 3 \end{pmatrix}.$$

Observe that the minimum number of lines needed to cover all zeros is equal to the maximum number of independent zeros. Theorem 3, which we will need in order to show that the Hungarian method terminates after a finite number of steps, shows that this fact is true in general.

Theorem 3   The maximum number of independent zeros in a matrix is equal to the minimum number of lines needed to cover all zeros in the matrix.   ■

The proof is beyond the scope of the book. For a proof of Theorem 3, see [4] in the suggested readings.

Example 9   Use Theorem 1 to transform the reduced matrix

$$\hat{C} = \begin{pmatrix} 0 & 2 & 5 \\ 3 & 0 & 0 \\ 0 & 3 & 3 \end{pmatrix}$$

from Example 8 into a matrix with nonnegative entries containing an independent set of three zeros.

Solution: First, subtract from every entry in $\hat{C}$ the smallest entry not covered by any line (which is 2). This is the transformation with $u_1 = u_2 = u_3 = 2$ and $v_1 = v_2 = v_3 = 0$, and gives the matrix

$$\begin{pmatrix} -2 & 0 & 3 \\ 1 & -2 & -2 \\ -2 & 1 & 1 \end{pmatrix}.$$

Next, add 2 to every entry in every row and column covered by one line, and add 2 twice to any entry covered by two lines (note that the $(2,1)$ entry has 2 added to it twice, since it was covered twice). This is the transformation $u_1 = u_3 = v_2 = v_3 = 0$ and $u_2 = v_1 = 2$, and gives the matrix

$$\begin{pmatrix} 0 & 0^* & 3 \\ 5 & 0 & 0^* \\ 0^* & 1 & 1 \end{pmatrix}$$

which contains an independent set of three zeros.   □

The Hungarian Method

We will now display the algorithm called the Hungarian method. We shall assume that the costs c_{ij} are integers. To begin the algorithm, given an $n \times n$ matrix C, first obtain the reduced matrix $\hat{C}$ for C; that is, subtract from each entry of each row the smallest entry in that row. Then do the same for columns. Next perform the following two steps:

(i) Find a maximal independent set of zeros. If this set has n elements, an optimal solution is available. Otherwise go to step (ii).

(ii) Find a set of lines that cover all zeros using the smallest possible number of lines. Let k be the smallest entry not covered. Subtract k from each entry not covered by any line, and add k to each entry covered twice. Repeat step (i).

Algorithm 1 gives the pseudocode description of the Hungarian method.

Applying step (ii) of the algorithm produces a new matrix with the same set of optimal solutions as the original matrix, since step (ii) is equivalent to first subtracting k from every entry in the matrix, and then adding k to every entry covered by a line. Subtracting k from every entry is the transformation $u_i = k$, for all i, and $v_j = 0$, for all j. By Theorem 1, this does not change the set of optimal solutions. Adding k to every entry covered by a line is the transformation

$$u_i = \begin{cases} -k & \text{if there is a line through row } i \\ 0 & \text{otherwise} \end{cases}$$

$$v_j = \begin{cases} -k & \text{if there is a line through column } j \\ 0 & \text{otherwise.} \end{cases}$$

Again by Theorem 1, this does not change the set of optimal solutions.

We now show that the algorithm must terminate after a finite number of steps. (We leave it as Exercise 13 to show that, after performing the initial step, all entries in the reduced matrix are nonnegative.) We will show that the sum of all entries in the matrix decreases by at least 1 whenever step (ii) is performed. Clearly, if the sum of all entries is zero, then all entries in the matrix are zero and an independent set of n zeros exists. Thus, if the algorithm did not terminate, the sums of all matrix entries would give an infinite decreasing sequence of positive integers, which is impossible.

Step (ii) is performed only when no independent set of n zeros exists. Thus, if q is the minimum number of lines needed to cover all zeros, then Theorem 3 implies that $q < n$. Subtracting k from each entry subtracts kn^2 from the sum of entries, since there are n^2 entries in the matrix. Adding k to each covered entry adds qkn to the sum of entries, since there are q lines and n entries on each line. Therefore the net change in the sum of entries is $-kn^2 + qkn$. But $-kn^2 + qkn = kn(-n + q) < 0$, since $q < n$. Since k, q, and n are all integers, the sum of all entries must decrease by at least 1.

ALGORITHM 1.   Hungarian Method

procedure   *Hungarian* (C: $n \times n$ matrix of integers)
for $i := 1$ **to** n
begin
    $u_i :=$ smallest integer in row i of C
    for $j := 1$ **to** n
        $\hat{c}_{ij} := c_{ij} - u_i$
end
for $j := 1$ **to** n
begin
    $v_j :=$ smallest integer in column j of $\hat{C}$
    for $i := 1$ **to** n
        $\hat{c}_{ij} := \hat{c}_{ij} - v_j$
end
$\{\hat{C}$ is now the reduced matrix$\}$
$S :=$ an independent set of zeros of maximal size in $\hat{C}$
$q := |S|$
while $q < n$
begin
  $cover(\hat{C})$
  $k :=$ smallest entry in $\hat{C}$ not covered by a line
  for $i := 1$ **to** n
    for $j := 1$ **to** n
    begin
        if $\hat{c}_{ij}$ is not covered **then** $\hat{c}_{ij} := \hat{c}_{ij} - k$
        if $\hat{c}_{ij}$ is covered twice **then** $\hat{c}_{ij} := \hat{c}_{ij} + k$
    end
  $S :=$ an independent set of zeros of maximal size in $\hat{C}$
  $q := |S|$
end
for $i := 1$ **to** n
  for $j := 1$ **to** n
    if $\hat{c}_{ij} \in S$ **then** $x_{ij}^* := 1$ **else** $x_{ij}^* := 0$
$\{X^* = [x_{ij}^*]$ is an optimal solution$\}$

Exercise 17 shows that the number of iterations is $O(n^2)$. To compare the Hungarian method to the exhaustive search method mentioned above, suppose that each iteration can be performed in one second. Then an assignment problem with $n = 30$ can be solved in at most $30^2 = 900$ seconds, or 15 minutes of computer time.

The following example illustrates how the Hungarian method works.

Example 10   A foreman has five workers and five jobs to complete. The time in hours each worker needs to complete each job is shown in the following table.

	Job 1	Job 2	Job 3	Job 4	Job 5
Worker 1	3	4	8	7	8
Worker 2	2	5	3	2	6
Worker 3	7	9	1	8	3
Worker 4	5	3	4	6	6
Worker 5	8	9	7	5	8

How should the foreman make an assignment of one worker to each job so that the total time is minimized?

Solution: Let

$$C = \begin{pmatrix} 3 & 4 & 8 & 7 & 8 \\ 2 & 5 & 3 & 2 & 6 \\ 7 & 9 & 1 & 8 & 3 \\ 5 & 3 & 4 & 6 & 6 \\ 8 & 9 & 7 & 5 & 8 \end{pmatrix}.$$

The reduced matrix is

$$\begin{pmatrix} 0 & 1 & 5 & 4 & 3 \\ 0 & 3 & 1 & 0 & 2 \\ 6 & 8 & 0 & 7 & 0 \\ 2 & 0 & 1 & 3 & 1 \\ 3 & 4 & 2 & 0 & 1 \end{pmatrix}.$$

The minimum number of lines needed to cover all zeros of this matrix is four. For example, lines through row 3 and through columns 1, 2 and 4 will cover all zeros. Since we need an independent set of 5 zeros, step (ii) must be performed. This gives the matrix

$$\begin{pmatrix} 0^* & 1 & 4 & 4 & 2 \\ 0 & 3 & 0 & 0^* & 1 \\ 7 & 9 & 0^* & 8 & 0 \\ 2 & 0^* & 0 & 3 & 0 \\ 3 & 4 & 1 & 0 & 0^* \end{pmatrix}.$$

The starred entries indicate one possible independent set of five zeros. Thus an optimal solution is

$$\mathbf{X}^* = \begin{pmatrix} 1 & 0 & 0 & 0 & 0 \\ 0 & 0 & 0 & 1 & 0 \\ 0 & 0 & 1 & 0 & 0 \\ 0 & 1 & 0 & 0 & 0 \\ 0 & 0 & 0 & 0 & 1 \end{pmatrix},$$

which corresponds to the permutation 14325. An optimal job assignment is to assign Worker 1 to Job 1, Worker 2 to Job 4, Worker 3 to Job 3, Worker 4 to Job 2, and Worker 5 to Job 5. □

Example 11   Find a path which minimizes total delivery time from New York to Los Angeles in the shortest path problem given in Figure 1.

Solution: We solve the assignment problem specified by the following matrix. Exercise 16 shows that any optimal solution of this assignment problem will find a path which minimizes total delivery time. We assign a time of 100 hours to any route joining a pair of cities for which there is no train route. The choice of 100 prohibits such a route from occurring as part of an optimal solution. This is because the path

New York → Dallas → Los Angeles

is a path with total time 74 hours. Hence, any path which minimizes total delivery time can have a total time of at most 74 hours, so any route requiring more than 74 hours can not be part of an optimal solution.

	Bos	Chi	Dal	Den	SF	LA
N Y	6	25	34	100	100	100
Bos	0	18	100	100	100	100
Chi	100	0	20	15	100	50
Dal	100	18	0	100	100	40
Den	100	15	100	0	20	100
SF	100	100	100	26	0	6

By applying the Hungarian method, the optimal solution

$$\mathbf{X}^* = \begin{pmatrix} 1 & 0 & 0 & 0 & 0 & 0 \\ 0 & 1 & 0 & 0 & 0 & 0 \\ 0 & 0 & 0 & 1 & 0 & 0 \\ 0 & 0 & 1 & 0 & 0 & 0 \\ 0 & 0 & 0 & 0 & 1 & 0 \\ 0 & 0 & 0 & 0 & 0 & 1 \end{pmatrix}$$

is obtained (details are left as Exercise 5). This matrix shows that the shortest path is

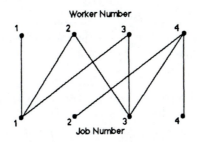

Figure 2.   Job assignments.

$$N\,Y \to Bos \to Chi \to Den \to S\,F \to L\,A.$$

(Note that the path does not pass through Dallas.)   □

The Hungarian method was discovered in 1955 by Harold Kuhn* of the Mathematics and Economics Departments of Princeton University (see [3] in the suggested readings for the original paper). The algorithm is called the "Hungarian" method in honor of Denes König**, who, in 1931, discovered Theorem 3. There are other efficient algorithms for solving the assignment problem. For example, [1] in the suggested readings describes an algorithm based on the degrees of vertices of certain spanning trees of $K_{n,n}$, the complete bipartite graph.

Perfect Matching Problems

Suppose four workers must be assigned to four jobs. The jobs that each worker can perform are indicated by an edge of the graph given in Figure 2. Is it possible to assign workers to jobs so that each worker is assigned one job and each job is assigned to one worker?

This problem may also be stated in terms of graphs. We need the following definition.

---

* Harold Kuhn (1925–) is an American mathematician who obtained his Ph.D. from Princeton University. Kuhn has made many fundamental contributions to the field of linear programming and is most famous for the Kuhn-Tucker conditions which characterize the set of optimal solutions of a linear program.

** Denes König (1884–1944) was a Hungarian mathematician. He is known as one of the pioneers of graph theory and is most famous for his work in matching theory.

Definition 3   Let $G = (V, E)$ be any bipartite graph with $V = V_1 \cup V_2$. A subset of edges M contained in E is called a *perfect matching* if every vertex in V is contained in exactly one edge of M.   □

For example, the bipartite graph given in Figure 3a contains the perfect matching given in Figure 3b.

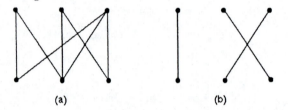

(a)   (b)

Figure 3.   A bipartite graph and a perfect matching.

The problem stated in the beginning of this section may now be stated as follows. Does there exist a perfect matching in the graph given in Figure 2? The problem of determining if a given bipartite graph contains a perfect matching was solved by Georg Frobenius* who proved the well known "Marriage Theorem". To state this theorem we will use the following notation: for any subset W contained in V_1 let $R(W)$ denote the set of vertices in V_2 adjacent to a vertex in W.

Theorem 4   Frobenius Marriage Theorem   A bipartite graph $G = (V, E)$ with $V = V_1 \cup V_2$ has a perfect matching if and only if $|V_1| = |V_2|$ and for every subset W contained in V_1, $|R(W)| \geq |W|$.   ■

The proof of Theorem 4 may be obtained by applying Theorem 3. The details are left for Exercises 18 and 19.

Example 12   Determine if the graph given in Figure 2 contains a perfect matching.

Solution: Let $W = \{\text{Worker 1, Worker 2, Worker 3}\}$. Then $R(W) = \{\text{Job 1, Job 3}\}$. Since $|R(W)| = 2$ and $|W| = 3$, Theorem 4 implies that the graph given in Figure 2 does not contain a perfect matching.   □

---

* Georg Frobenius (1848–1917) was a German mathematician who attended schools in Göttingen and Berlin. He was a professor of mathematics at both the University of Berlin and the Eidgenossische Polytechnikum in Zurich. Frobenius is best known for his contributions to algebra, particularly in group theory.

The **weight** of any perfect matching M is the sum of the weights of the edges in M. Many matching problems involve searching a weighted bipartite graph for a perfect matching which has the smallest possible weight.

Example 13   Suppose three workers must be assigned to three jobs. The graph given in Figure 4 indicates the cost of training each worker for each job. How should the workers be assigned to jobs so that each worker is assigned one job, each job is assigned one worker, and the total training cost is minimized?

Worker Number

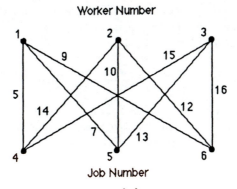

Job Number

Figure 4.   Training costs.

Solution: We solve the problem by listing the set of all perfect matches along with their weights:

$$M_1 = \{\{1,1\},\{2,2\},\{3,3\}\} \quad \text{weight: } 31$$
$$M_2 = \{\{1,1\},\{2,3\},\{3,2\}\} \quad \text{weight: } 30$$
$$M_3 = \{\{1,2\},\{2,1\},\{3,3\}\} \quad \text{weight: } 37$$
$$M_4 = \{\{1,3\},\{2,1\},\{3,2\}\} \quad \text{weight: } 36$$
$$M_5 = \{\{1,2\},\{2,3\},\{3,1\}\} \quad \text{weight: } 34$$
$$M_6 = \{\{1,3\},\{2,2\},\{3,1\}\} \quad \text{weight: } 34$$

This shows that M_2 is the perfect matching with the smallest possible weight. Thus Worker 1 should be assigned to Job 1, Worker 2 should be assigned to Job 3, and Worker 3 should be assigned to Job 2.   □

The reader should compare the perfect matches listed in the solution to Example 13 and the permutations $\sigma_1, \ldots, \sigma_6$ listed in Example 4. Note that the permutation σ_1 given by $\sigma_1(1) = 1$, $\sigma_1(2) = 2$, and $\sigma_1(3) = 3$, corresponds to the perfect matching M_1, which matches 1 to 1, 2 to 2, and 3 to 3. The permutation σ_2 given by $\sigma_2(1) = 1$, $\sigma_2(2) = 3$, and $\sigma_2(3) = 2$, corresponds to the perfect matching M_2 which matches 1 to 1, 2 to 3, and 3 to 2. Similarly the permutations σ_3, σ_4, σ_5, and σ_6 correspond to the perfect matches M_3, M_4, M_5, and M_6 respectively. Therefore, solving Example 13 is equivalent to solving the assignment problem specified by

$$C = \begin{pmatrix} 5 & 7 & 9 \\ 14 & 10 & 12 \\ 15 & 13 & 16 \end{pmatrix}$$

solved earlier. This is not a coincidence. Given any weighted complete bipartite graph $K_{n,n}$, any perfect matching M corresponds to a permutation σ of $\{1, 2, \ldots, n\}$ defined by $\sigma(i) = j$ if and only if edge $\{i, j\} \in M$. Moreover, if the weight of edge $\{i, j\}$ is c_{ij}, then

$$\text{weight of } M = \sum_{i=1}^{n} c_{i\sigma(i)}.$$

Thus, finding a perfect matching of minimum weight in a complete bipartite graph is equivalent to solving the assignment problem specified by $C = [c_{ij}]$. In fact, finding a perfect matching with the smallest possible weight is simply a search for the best possible assignment of the vertices in V_1 to those in V_2.

Example 14   Find a perfect matching with the smallest possible weight for the graph given in Figure 5.

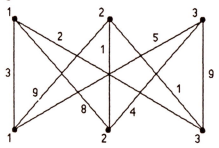

Figure 5.   A weighted graph.

Solution: The problem is solved by solving the assignment problem specified by

$$\begin{pmatrix} 3 & 8 & 2 \\ 9 & 1 & 1 \\ 5 & 4 & 9 \end{pmatrix}.$$

Applying the Hungarian method gives the reduced matrix

$$\begin{pmatrix} 0^* & 6 & 0 \\ 7 & 0 & 0^* \\ 0 & 0^* & 5 \end{pmatrix}$$

which contains an independent set of 3 zeros. An optimal solution is

$$\begin{pmatrix} 1 & 0 & 0 \\ 0 & 0 & 1 \\ 0 & 1 & 0 \end{pmatrix}$$

which corresponds to the perfect matching $M = \{\{1,1\},\{2,3\},\{3,2\}\}$.   □

Suggested Readings

1. M. Balinski, "Signature Methods for the Assignment Problem", *Operations Research*, Vol. 33, 1985, pp. 527–536.

2. D. Gale and L. Shapley, "College Admissions and the Stability of Marriage", *American Mathematical Monthly* 69, 1962, pp. 9–15.

3. H. Kuhn, "The Hungarian Method for the Assignment Problem" *Naval Res. Logist. Quart.*, Vol. 2, 1955, pp. 83–97.

4. M. Hall, *Combinatorial Theory*, Second Edition, Wiley, New York, 1986.

Exercises

In Exercises 1–4, solve the assignment problem specified by the given matrix.

1.

$$\begin{pmatrix} 5 & 8 & 3 & 9 \\ 2 & 6 & 1 & 9 \\ 3 & 9 & 4 & 8 \\ 4 & 7 & 2 & 9 \end{pmatrix}.$$

2.

$$\begin{pmatrix} 6 & 2 & 5 & 8 \\ 6 & 7 & 1 & 6 \\ 6 & 3 & 4 & 7 \\ 5 & 4 & 3 & 5 \end{pmatrix}.$$

3.

$$\begin{pmatrix} 7 & 5 & 9 & 7 & 8 & 6 \\ 1 & 2 & 4 & 1 & 3 & 1 \\ 9 & 9 & 8 & 8 & 9 & 3 \\ 4 & 7 & 5 & 6 & 3 & 4 \\ 5 & 3 & 7 & 4 & 3 & 5 \\ 3 & 2 & 2 & 1 & 2 & 1 \end{pmatrix}.$$

4.

$$\begin{pmatrix} -6 & 3 & 1 & 0 & 4 & 6 \\ 5 & -3 & 8 & 4 & 5 & 3 \\ -5 & 4 & 9 & 8 & 9 & 3 \\ 3 & 7 & 5 & -8 & 0 & 9 \\ 7 & 2 & 6 & 5 & 7 & 6 \\ -3 & 0 & 2 & -1 & 3 & 4 \end{pmatrix}.$$

5. Solve the assignment problem specified by the matrix in the solution to Example 11.

6. The coach of a certain swim team needs to assign swimmers to a 200-yard medley relay team . Most of his swimmers are quite fast in more than one stroke, so it is not clear which swimmer should be assigned to each of the four strokes. The four fastest swimmers and the best times they have achieved in each of the strokes, for 50 yards, are

Stroke	Ken	Rob	Mark	David
Backstroke	39.3	33.6	34.0	35.6
Breaststroke	34.2	41.8	38.7	33.7
Butterfly	29.5	30.6	33.1	31.8
Freestyle	28.7	27.6	30.3	29.3

How should the coach assign the four swimmers to the four different strokes to minimize the sum of the corresponding best times?

7. Find a set of marriages which maximizes the "happiness" of the following colony of 6 prospective brides and 6 bachelors, where the rating of the bachelors by the brides is given in the following table.

	John	Bill	Joe	Al	Bud	Hal
Jane	3	4	1	2	5	6
Mary	2	5	3	6	4	1
Carol	2	3	1	5	3	6
Jessica	1	2	5	6	3	4
Dawn	5	4	2	1	6	3
Lisa	4	3	6	2	1	5

8. The following figure indicates available train routes along with the time
   required to travel the route. Find a route from Boston to San Francisco
   which minimizes total time required.

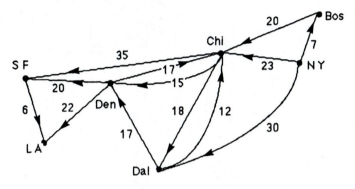

9. Determine which of the following bipartite graphs contain a perfect matching. List the edges in a perfect matching for those graphs that contain one,
   and show that Frobenius' Marriage Theorem does not hold for those graphs
   that do not contain a perfect matching.

   a)

   b)

   c)

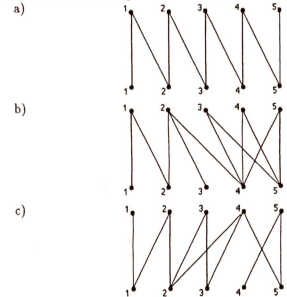

10. Find a perfect matching with the smallest possible weight in the following
    weighted graph. The weights of the edges are given in the following table.

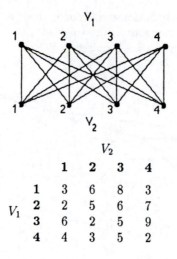

$$V_2$$

	1	2	3	4
1	3	6	8	3
V_1 2	2	5	6	7
3	6	2	5	9
4	4	3	5	2

11. a) Construct a 5×5 matrix C such that the assignment problem specified by C has more than one optimal solution.

   b) Construct a 5×5 matrix C such that the assignment problem specified by C has a unique optimal solution.

12. Show that any permutation of $\{1, 2, 3, 4\}$ solves the assignment problem specified by

$$\begin{pmatrix} 1 & 2 & 3 & 4 \\ 5 & 6 & 7 & 8 \\ 9 & 10 & 11 & 12 \\ 13 & 14 & 15 & 16 \end{pmatrix}.$$

13. Explain why the entries in the reduced matrix are nonnegative, even if the original costs are negative.

14. Given any $n \times n$ matrix C, describe how the Hungarian Method may be used to solve an assignment problem in which we seek a permutation σ of $\{1, 2, \ldots, n\}$ such that $\sum_{i=1}^{n} c_{i\sigma(i)}$ is *maximum*.

15. Use Exercise 14 to find a permutation which maximizes $\sum_{i=1}^{n} c_{i\sigma(i)}$, where C is the matrix given in Exercise 3.

16. Show that any optimal solution to the assignment problem specified by the matrix given in Example 11 finds a path from New York to Los Angeles which minimizes total delivery time. *Hint:* Suppose σ^* is an optimal solution and P is a path shorter than $\sum_{i=1}^{n} c_{i\sigma^*(i)}$.

17. Show that the Hungarian Method uses $O(n^2)$ iterations to find an optimal solution of an assignment problem.

A **vertex cover** Q of the edges of a graph G is a set of vertices such that each edge of G contains at least one vertex in Q.

18. Show that in a bipartite graph $G = (V, E)$ the maximum number of edges in a matching is equal to the minimum number of vertices in a vertex cover. *Hint*: Use Theorem 3.

19. Use Exercise 18 to prove Theorem 4.

Suppose that in a community of n bachelors together with n prospective brides each person ranks those of the opposite sex in accordance with his or her preferences for a marriage partner. A set of n marriages is called **unstable** if among the n marriages there are a man and a woman who are not married to each other, but prefer each other to the person they are married to; otherwise the set of marriages is called **stable**. (For a complete discussion of stable marriages see [2] in the suggested readings.)

20. If the first number of the following table gives the preferences of women by the men and the second number gives the preferences of men by the women, find a stable set of 4 marriages.

	Susan	Colleen	Nancy	Dawn
David	1,1	2,3	3,2	4,1
Richard	2,3	1,4	3,1	4,4
Paul	1,4	4,1	2,3	3,3
Kevin	3,2	1,2	4,4	2,2

⋆21. Prove that in any community of n men and n women there always exists a stable set of n marriages. *Hint*: Construct an iterative procedure for finding a stable set of n marriages.

Computer Projects

1. Write a program that inputs a 5×5 matrix C and solves the assignment problem specified by C by generating all the permutations of $\{1, 2, 3, 4, 5\}$.

2. Write a program that inputs a 5×5 matrix C and finds an independent set of zeros of maximum size in C.

18

Shortest Path Problems

Author: William C. Arlinghaus, Department of Mathematics and Computer Science, Lawrence Technological University.

Prerequisites: The prerequisites for this chapter are weighted graphs and Dijkstra's algorithm. See, for example, Section 7.6 of *Discrete Mathematics and Its Applications*, Second Edition, by Kenneth H. Rosen.

Introduction

One problem of continuing interest is that of finding the shortest path between points in a network. One traditional problem is that of finding the best route between two cities, given a complicated road network. A more modern one is that of transmitting a message between two computers along a network of hundreds of computers. The quantity to be minimized might be mileage, time, shipping cost, or any other measurable quantity.

Dijkstra's algorithm was designed to find the shortest path, in a weighted graph, between two points a and z. This is done by initially labeling each vertex other than a with ∞, labeling a with 0, and then modifying the labels as shortest paths within the graph were constructed. These labels are temporary; they become permanent when it becomes apparent that a label could never become smaller. (See the proof of Theorem 1 of Section 7.6 of *Discrete Mathematics and Its Applications*, Second Edition, by Rosen.)

If this process is continued until every vertex in a connected, weighted graph has a permanent label, then the lengths of the shortest paths from a to each other vertex of the graph are determined. As we will see, it is also relatively easy to construct the actual path of shortest length from a to any other point. Of course, this process can be repeated with any other point besides a as the initial point for Dijkstra's algorithm. So eventually all possible shortest paths between any two points of the graph can be determined. But, as a process to find all shortest paths, it is not very natural.

In the exercises of Section 7.6 of *Discrete Mathematics and Its Applications*, Floyd's algorithm was discussed. This algorithm computes the lengths of all the shortest distances simultaneously, using a triply-nested loop to do the calculations. Unfortunately, primarily since none of the calculations part of the way through the iterations have a natural graph-theoretic interpretation, the algorithm cannot be used to find the actual shortest paths, but rather only their lengths. This chapter will discuss a triple iteration, *Hedetniemi's algorithm*, in which intermediate calculations have a natural interpretation and from which the actual path can be constructed.

Further Reflections on Dijkstra's Algorithm

Dijkstra's algorithm traces shortest paths from an initial vertex a through a network to a vertex z. Each vertex other than a is originally labeled with ∞, while a is labeled 0. Then each vertex adjacent to a has its label changed to the weight of the edge linking it to a. The smallest such label becomes permanent, since the path from a to it is the shortest path from a to anywhere. The process continues, using the smallest non-permanent label as a new permanent label at each stage, until z gets a permanent label. In general, when Dijkstra's algorithm is used, a label attached to a vertex y is changed when the permanent label of a vertex x, added to the weight of the edge $\{x, y\}$, is less than the previous label of y. For instance, consider Figure 1. (Note that the vertices a, b, c here are the vertices b, c, g of Figure 4 of Section 7.6 of *Discrete Mathematics and Its Applications*.) In moving from a to b, the label on b was changed to 3, which is the sum of the permanent label, 2, of c and the weight, 1, of the edge between c and b.

Further, note that it is easy to keep track of the shortest path. Since an edge from c to b was added, the shortest path from a to b consists of the shortest path from a to c followed by the edge from c to b. Figure 1(c) keeps track of all the shortest paths as they are computed.

However, an efficient algorithm for finding the shortest path from a to z *need only keep track of the vertex from which the shortest path entered a given vertex*. For example, suppose that with the vector of vertices (a, b, c, d, e, z) we associate the vector of lengths $(0, 3, 2, 8, 10, 13)$ and the vector of vertices

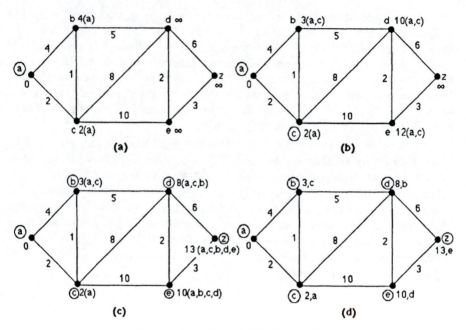

Figure 1.   **A weighted graph.**

$(-, c, a, b, d, e)$ from which the shortest path arrived at the vertex, as in Figure 1(d). Then the shortest path from a to z is of length 13, using the first vector. The path itself can be traced in reverse from the second vector as follows: z was reached from e, e from d, d from b, b from c, and c from a. Thus the shortest path is a, c, b, d, e, z.

Hedetniemi's Algorithm

One goal of shortest path algorithms is to find the lengths of all possible shortest paths in a weighted graph at the same time. For instance, given a road network with all lengths of roads listed, we would like to make a list of shortest distances between any two cities, not just the length from Detroit to Philadelphia or even from Detroit to all cities. In this section we discuss an algorithm to compute those lengths, developed recently by Arlinghaus, Arlinghaus, and Nystuen [1]. A program, never published previously, by which the computations were done for that research, is included.

The algorithm constructed here is based on a new way to compute powers of matrices, which we will call the *Hedetniemi matrix sum*. This sum was suggested to Nystuen at the University of Michigan by S. Hedetniemi, who was then a graduate student in mathematics. Hedetniemi later completed his doctorate under Frank Harary; and Nystuen, a professor of geography at Michigan remembered the method for later application.

Proceeding to the algorithm itself, suppose we begin with a connected, weighted graph with vertices $v_1, \ldots, v_n$. With this graph we associate the $n \times n$ "adjacency" matrix $\mathbf{A} = [a_{ij}]$ defined as follows:

$$a_{ij} = \begin{cases} 0 & \text{if } i = j \\ x & \text{if } i \neq j \text{ and there is an edge of weight } x \text{ between } i \text{ and } j \\ \infty & \text{otherwise.} \end{cases}$$

The symbol ∞ is used since ∞ can be printed in most computer programs; in computations within programs, some very large numbers should be used.

For example, the graph of Figure 2 has the following adjacency matrix $\mathbf{A}$.

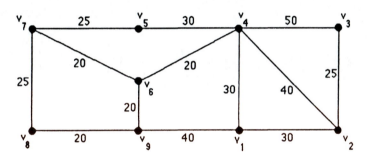

Figure 2.   A weighted graph with adjacency matrix A.

$$\mathbf{A} = \begin{pmatrix} 0 & 30 & \infty & 30 & \infty & \infty & \infty & \infty & 40 \\ 30 & 0 & 25 & 40 & \infty & \infty & \infty & \infty & \infty \\ \infty & 25 & 0 & 50 & \infty & \infty & \infty & \infty & \infty \\ 30 & 40 & 50 & 0 & 30 & 20 & \infty & \infty & \infty \\ \infty & \infty & \infty & 30 & 0 & \infty & 25 & \infty & \infty \\ \infty & \infty & \infty & 20 & \infty & 0 & 20 & \infty & 20 \\ \infty & \infty & \infty & \infty & 25 & 20 & 0 & 25 & \infty \\ \infty & \infty & \infty & \infty & \infty & \infty & 25 & 0 & 20 \\ 40 & \infty & \infty & \infty & \infty & 20 & \infty & 20 & 0 \end{pmatrix}.$$

We now introduce an operation on matrices called the Hedetniemi matrix sum, denoted by $\boxplus$.

Definition 1   Let $\mathbf{A}$ be an $m \times n$ matrix and $\mathbf{B}$ an $n \times p$ matrix. Then the *Hedetniemi matrix sum* is the $m \times p$ matrix $\mathbf{C} = \mathbf{A} \boxplus \mathbf{B}$, whose (i, j)th entry is

$$c_{ij} = \min\{a_{i1} + b_{1j}, a_{i2} + b_{2j}, \ldots, a_{in} + b_{nj}\}. \qquad \square$$

Example 1   Find the Hedetniemi matrix sum, $\mathbf{A} \mathbin{+\!\!+} \mathbf{B}$, of the matrices

$$\mathbf{A} = \begin{pmatrix} 0 & 1 & 2 \\ 2 & 0 & 3 \\ 5 & 6 & 0 \end{pmatrix} \text{ and } \mathbf{B} = \begin{pmatrix} 0 & 3 & 4 \\ 5 & 0 & 4 \\ 3 & 1 & 0 \end{pmatrix}.$$

Solution: We find that

$$\mathbf{A} \mathbin{+\!\!+} \mathbf{B} = \begin{pmatrix} 0 & 1 & 2 \\ 2 & 0 & 3 \\ 5 & 6 & 0 \end{pmatrix} + \begin{pmatrix} 0 & 3 & 4 \\ 5 & 0 & 4 \\ 3 & 1 & 0 \end{pmatrix} = \begin{pmatrix} 0 & 1 & 2 \\ 2 & 0 & 3 \\ 3 & 1 & 0 \end{pmatrix}.$$

For example, the entry c_{23} is computed as follows:

$$c_{23} = \min\{2 + 4, 0 + 4, 3 + 0\} = 3. \qquad \square$$

Example 2   Find $\mathbf{A} \mathbin{+\!\!+} \mathbf{B}$ if $\mathbf{A} = \begin{pmatrix} 0 & 1 & \infty \\ 1 & 0 & 4 \\ \infty & 4 & 0 \end{pmatrix}$ and $\mathbf{B} = \begin{pmatrix} 0 & 1 & \infty \\ 1 & 0 & 4 \\ \infty & 4 & 0 \end{pmatrix}.$

Solution: We see that

$$\mathbf{A} \mathbin{+\!\!+} \mathbf{B} = \begin{pmatrix} 0 & 1 & \infty \\ 1 & 0 & 4 \\ \infty & 4 & 0 \end{pmatrix} + \begin{pmatrix} 0 & 1 & \infty \\ 1 & 0 & 4 \\ \infty & 4 & 0 \end{pmatrix} = \begin{pmatrix} 0 & 1 & 5 \\ 1 & 0 & 4 \\ 5 & 4 & 0 \end{pmatrix}.$$

For example, c_{13} is computed using $c_{13} = \min\{0 + \infty, 1 + 4, \infty + 0\} = 5.$ $\quad\square$

But what has this to do with shortest paths? Consider our example of Figure 2. Let $\mathbf{A}^2 = \mathbf{A} \mathbin{+\!\!+} \mathbf{A}$, $\mathbf{A}^3 = \mathbf{A}^2 \mathbin{+\!\!+} \mathbf{A}$, ... Then,

$$\mathbf{A}^2 = \begin{pmatrix} 0 & 30 & 55 & 30 & 60 & 50 & \infty & 60 & 40 \\ 30 & 0 & 25 & 40 & 70 & 60 & \infty & \infty & 70 \\ 55 & 25 & 0 & 50 & 80 & 70 & \infty & \infty & \infty \\ 30 & 40 & 50 & 0 & 30 & 20 & 40 & \infty & 40 \\ 60 & 70 & 80 & 30 & 0 & 45 & 25 & 50 & \infty \\ 50 & 60 & 70 & 20 & 45 & 0 & 20 & 40 & 20 \\ \infty & \infty & \infty & 40 & 25 & 20 & 0 & 25 & 40 \\ 60 & \infty & \infty & \infty & 50 & 40 & 25 & 0 & 20 \\ 40 & 70 & \infty & 40 & \infty & 20 & 40 & 20 & 0 \end{pmatrix}.$$

Look at a typical computation involved in finding $\mathbf{A}^2 = [a_{ij}^{(2)}]$:

$$a_{13}^{(2)} = \min\{0 + \infty, 30 + 25, \infty + 0, 30 + 50,$$
$$\infty + \infty, \infty + \infty, \infty + \infty, \infty + \infty, 40 + \infty\}$$
$$= 55.$$

Notice that the value 55 is the sum of 30, the shortest (indeed, only) path of length 1 from v_1 to v_2, and 25, the length of the edge between v_2 and v_3. Thus $a_{13}^{(2)}$ represents the length of the shortest path of two or fewer edges from v_1 to v_3. So $\mathbf{A}^2$ represents the lengths of all shortest paths with two or fewer edges between any two vertices.

Similarly, $\mathbf{A}^3$ represents the lengths of all shortest paths of three or fewer edges, and so on. Since, in a connected, weighted graph with n vertices, there can be at most $n - 1$ edges in the shortest path between two vertices, the following theorem has been proved.

Theorem 1   In a connected, weighted graph with n vertices, the (i, j)th entry of the Hedetniemi matrix $\mathbf{A}^{n-1}$ is the length of the shortest path between v_i and v_j.   ∎

In the graph of Figure 2, with nine vertices, we have

$$\mathbf{A}^8 = \begin{pmatrix} 0 & 30 & 55 & 30 & 60 & 50 & 70 & 60 & 40 \\ 30 & 0 & 25 & 40 & 70 & 60 & 80 & 90 & 70 \\ 55 & 25 & 0 & 50 & 80 & 70 & 90 & 110 & 90 \\ 30 & 40 & 50 & 0 & 30 & 20 & 40 & 60 & 40 \\ 60 & 70 & 80 & 30 & 0 & 45 & 25 & 50 & 65 \\ 50 & 60 & 70 & 20 & 45 & 0 & 20 & 40 & 20 \\ 70 & 80 & 90 & 40 & 25 & 20 & 0 & 25 & 40 \\ 60 & 90 & 110 & 60 & 50 & 40 & 25 & 0 & 20 \\ 40 & 70 & 90 & 40 & 65 & 20 & 40 & 20 & 0 \end{pmatrix}.$$

Therefore, the shortest path from v_1 to v_7 is of length 70.

Perhaps the most interesting fact about this example is that $\mathbf{A}^4 = \mathbf{A}^8$. This happens because in the graph of Figure 2, no shortest path has more than 4 edges. So, no improvements in length can occur after 4 iterations. This situation is true in general, as the following theorem states.

Theorem 2   For a connected, weighted graph with n vertices, if the Hedetniemi matrix $\mathbf{A}^k \neq \mathbf{A}^{k-1}$, but $\mathbf{A}^k = \mathbf{A}^{k+1}$, then $\mathbf{A}^k$ represents the set of lengths of shortest paths, and no shortest path contains more than k edges.   ∎

Thus, this algorithm can sometimes be stopped short. Those familiar with sorting algorithms might compare this idea to that of a bubble sort and Floyd's algorithm to a selection sort (see Sections 8.4 and 7.6 of *Discrete Mathematics and Its Applications*).

Algorithm 1 gives the pseudocode for the Hedetniemi algorithm, which computes powers of the original weighted adjacency matrix $\mathbf{A}$, quitting when two successive powers are identical. We leave it as Exercise 3 to determine the efficiency of the algorithm.

ALGORITHM 1 Hedetniemi shortest path algorithm.

procedure Hedetniemi(G: weighted simple graph)
$\{G$ has vertices $v_1, \ldots, v_n$ and weights $w(v_i, v_j)$ with
$\quad w(v_i, v_i) = 0$ and $w(v_i, v_j) = \infty$ if (v_i, v_j) is not an edge$\}$
for $i := 1$ **to** n
$\quad$**for** $j := 1$ **to** n
$\quad\quad A(1, i, j) := w(v_i, v_j)$
$t := 1$
repeat
$\quad$*flag* := *true*
$\quad t := t + 1$
$\quad$**for** $i := 1$ **to** n
$\quad\quad$**for** $j := 1$ **to** n
$\quad\quad\quad A(t, i, j) := A(t - 1, i, j)$
$\quad\quad\quad$**for** $k := 1$ **to** n
$\quad\quad\quad\quad A(t, i, j) := \min\{A(t, i, j), A(t - 1, i, j) + A(1, k, j)$
$\quad\quad\quad$**if** $A(t, i, j) \neq A(t - 1, i, j)$ **then** *flag* := *false*
until $t = n - 1$ **or** *flag* = *true*
$\{A(t, i, j)$ is the length of the shortest path between v_i and $v_j\}$

All that remains is the calculation of the shortest paths themselves.

Shortest Path Calculations

To compute the actual shortest path from one point to another, it is necessary to have not only the final matrix, but also its predecessor and **A** itself. For example, in the graph of Figure 2, the predecessor of $\mathbf{A}^4(= \mathbf{A}^5 = \cdots)$ is

$$\mathbf{A}^3 = \begin{pmatrix} 0 & 30 & 55 & 30 & 60 & 50 & 70 & 60 & 40 \\ 30 & 0 & 25 & 40 & 70 & 60 & 80 & 90 & 70 \\ 55 & 25 & 0 & 50 & 80 & 70 & 90 & \infty & 90 \\ 30 & 40 & 50 & 0 & 30 & 20 & 40 & 60 & 40 \\ 60 & 70 & 80 & 30 & 0 & 45 & 25 & 50 & 65 \\ 50 & 60 & 70 & 20 & 45 & 0 & 20 & 40 & 20 \\ 70 & 80 & 90 & 40 & 25 & 20 & 0 & 25 & 40 \\ 60 & 90 & \infty & 60 & 50 & 40 & 25 & 0 & 20 \\ 40 & 70 & 90 & 40 & 65 & 20 & 40 & 20 & 0 \end{pmatrix}.$$

We now find the shortest path from v_1 to v_7 (a path of length 70). Now

$$a_{17}^{(4)} = a_{1k}^{(3)} + a_{k7}$$

for some k. But the entries $a_{1k}^{(3)}$ form the row vector

$$(0, 30, 55, 30, 60, 50, 70, 60, 40)$$

and the entries a_{k7} form the column vector

$$(\infty, \infty, \infty, \infty, 25, 20, 0, 25, \infty).$$

Since (other than for $k = 7$) the only way in which 70 arises is as the sum $50 + 20$ when $k = 6$, the shortest path ends with an edge of length 20 from v_6 to v_7, following a path with 3 or fewer edges from v_1 to v_6. (In fact, since 70 does arise as $70 + 0$ when $k = 7$, there is a path with *total* number of edges at most 3.)

Now we can look for the previous edge ending at v_6. Note that $a_{16}^{(4)} = 50$, as expected ($70 - 20 = 50$). The entries a_{k6} form the column vector

$$(\infty, \infty, \infty, 20, \infty, 0, 20, \infty, 20).$$

This time 50 arises, when $k = 4$, as $30 + 20$, so the shortest path of length 50 from v_1 to v_6 ends with an edge of length 20 from v_4 to v_6. Finally, the entries a_{k4} form the column vector

$$(30, 40, 50, 0, 30, 20, \infty, \infty, \infty),$$

and 30 arises only as $30 + 0$ or $0 + 30$, so there is an edge of length 30 from v_1 to v_4. So, the shortest path from v_1 to v_7 is v_1, v_4, v_6, v_7 (the edges of lengths 30, 20, 20).

Thus, the Hedetniemi method provides a graphical interpretation at each stage of the computation, and the matrices can be used to retrieve the paths themselves. Computationally, four copies of the matrix must be saved: the original "adjacency" matrix, the last matrix computed, and its two predecessors (the immediate predecessor is identical to the last matrix unless $n - 1$ iterations are required).

Suggested Readings

1. S. Arlinghaus, W. Arlinghaus, and J. Nystuen, "The Hedetniemi Matrix Sum: An Algorithm for Shortest Path and Shortest Distance", *Geographical Analysis*, Vol. 22, No. 4, October, 1990, pp. 351–360.

2. E. Dijkstra, "Two problems in Connexion with Graphs", *Numerische Mathematik*, Vol. 1, pp. 269–271.

Exercises

1. Use Dijkstra's algorithm to compute the length of the shortest path between v_2 and v_3 in the graph of Figure 2. What is the path?

2. Suppose Dijkstra's algorithm is used on a graph with vertices $v_1, \ldots, v_7$, length vector $(0, 6, 5, 8, 12, 13, 14)$, and vertex vector $(-, 1, 1, 3, 4, 4, 6)$, where vertex v_i is represented by i in the vertex vector.
   a) Find the shortest path from v_1 to v_7.
   b) Find the shortest path from v_1 to v_5.
   ⋆c) Draw the graph, if possible.

3.   a) Estimate the number of operations in Hedetniemi's algorithm.
   ⋆b) Are there any factors that could change the result?

4. Find the final Hedetniemi matrix for the following weighted graph.

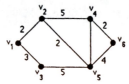

5. Find the final Hedetniemi matrix for the following weighted graph.

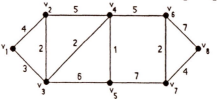

6. Use the Hedetniemi matrix to find the shortest path from v_3 to v_4 in the graph of Exercise 4.

7. Use the Hedetniemi matrix to find the shortest path from v_1 to v_6 in the graph of Exercise 4.

8. Use the Hedetniemi matrix to find the shortest path from v_1 to v_8 in the graph of Exercise 5.

⋆9. All the matrices in the Hedetniemi calculations are symmetric; that is, $a_{ij} = a_{ji}$ no matter what i and j are.
   a) How much time could be saved by taking this into account?
   b) Write an algorithm to exploit this fact.

⋆10. Is there any situation where nonsymmetric matrices might arise?

Computer Projects

1. a) Given a table of distances between some (but not necessarily all) pairs of cities in a road network, write a computer program that implements the Hedetniemi algorithm to find the shortest routes between all pairs of cities.

    b) Suppose there are roads from Detroit to Toledo of length 30 miles, from Toledo to Columbus of length 110 miles, from Columbus to Cincinnati of length 80 miles, from Detroit to Kalamazoo of length 100 miles, from Kalamazoo to Indianapolis of length 120 miles, from Indianapolis to Dayton of length 100 miles, from Dayton to Columbus of length 70 miles, from Dayton to Cincinnati of length 30 miles, from Indianapolis to Cincinnati of length 115 miles, and from Toledo to Dayton of length 120 miles. Use the program of part a) to find the shortest routes between all pairs of cities.

2. a) Given a table of distances between some (but not necessarily all) pairs of cities in a road network, write a computer program that implements Floyd's algorithm to find a mileage chart giving distances between all pairs of cities.

    b) Use the program of part a) to find a mileage chart giving distances between all pairs of cities in Computer Project 1b).

19

Network Survivability

Author: Arthur M. Hobbs, Department of Mathematics, Texas A&M University.

Prerequisites: The prerequisites for this chapter are graphs and trees. See, for example, Chapters 7 and 8 of *Discrete Mathematics and Its Applications*, Second Edition, by Kenneth H. Rosen.

Introduction

For the first two years after the end of World War II, there were essentially no atomic bombs available in the United States [10] and none anywhere else in the world. But by the mid 1950s, both the United States and the Soviet Union had not only fission bombs but fusion bombs ready for use. Since then, the number of countries having one or both kinds of bomb has grown alarmingly, and the arsenals have grown to frightening proportions.

At the moment, we may have no nuclear-equipped enemy, but that can change quite suddenly. Friends can become enemies overnight (witness Iraq and the United States in August, 1990). Worse, enemies can attain nuclear capabilities much faster than expected. (The Soviet Union was thought incapable of producing a nuclear bomb for several years at the time it exploded its first one.) Therefore, we should continue all possible peaceful preparations for protection against nuclear attack.

Among the essential requirements for an effective response to a nuclear attack are command, control and communications (C^3, in military parlence). Knowing this, the enemy is certain to attack them. He has several options: to attack the commanders, to attack the control systems used by the commanders, to attack the communications links between various commanders and between commanders and their forces, or to attack a mixture of these. In the United States, responsibility for the aspects of C^3 is divided among several agencies; the Defense Communications Agency (DCA) is responsible for the design and maintenance of the Defense Communications Systems [1].

There are several aspects of a nuclear strike that the communications system must take into account. The enemy is likely to allocate several weapons to high altitude (above 100 km) explosions at the very beginning of an attack, since one such explosion will black out radio communications (including transmissions between microwave towers) over several thousand square kilometers [1]. This will, of course, do little damage to properly protected equipment*, so that communications could be restored within a few hours, but it would seriously disrupt our early response. A surface detonation has a similar effect, but over a much smaller area [1], [3]. Burying communication cables a little less than a meter underground, will protect them from all but direct hits [1], but burying cables is expensive. Most communication links will remain microwave relays between towers and between satellites and ground stations.

Let us represent a communications network by a multigraph. We introduce a vertex for each command center and each switching center. Two vertices are joined by an edge whenever the corresponding centers are directly connected by a communications link (by a cable, or by a string of microwave antennae, or through a satellite, etc.). Because the term "multigraph" is a bit cumbersome, we will refer to multigraphs in this chapter as "graphs" except in definitions and theorems. When we need to discuss a graph without multiple edges, we will call it a "simple graph". We will reserve the word "network" for the communications network and we will call the multigraph a "graph representation of the network".

A good strategy is to build our network so that it satisfies the following two criteria:

(i) It should survive a limited attack, including attacks aimed at other nearby targets.

(ii) A careful study of our network by a knowledgeable enemy should reveal that the network is **bland**, in that it has no parts especially attractive to attack.

The thought behind "blandness" is that an attack is unlikely to be purposely

---

* However, there is an initial electromagnetic pulse of enormous size generated by a nuclear explosion; this pulse would destroy unprotected electrical equipment as effectively as a lightning bolt [1].

made against just part of a bland network, since no part of the network would appear more worth attacking than any other part.

We will address blandness shortly, but first we give a brief discussion of survivability of networks in limited attacks.

Cut Vertices and Blocks

One obvious failure of the first criterion for survivable networks occurs if every message traveling through the network must pass through one particular switch: One bomb on the switch would totally disable the network. In the graph representation, such a switch is a **cut vertex**, that is, a vertex such that removing the vertex and all edges incident with it leaves a subgraph with more connected components than in the original graph. We are interested in the subgraphs joined together by the cut vertices.

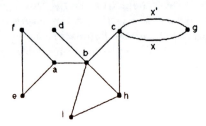

Figure 1.   Graph G_1 with cut vertices a, b, and c.

Example 1   Consider the graph G_1 of Figure 1. G_1 is connected, but the erasure of any one of vertices a, b or c produces a subgraph with two or more (connected) components; thus a, b and c are cut vertices of G_1. But look at the triangle aef. Although this subgraph includes the cut vertex a of G_1, a is not a cut vertex of the triangle by itself. On the other hand, if we try to expand triangle aef to a larger connected subgraph of G_1, as for example subgraph H in Figure 2, we find that a is a cut vertex of any such larger subgraph. Thus the triangle aef is a maximal connected subgraph of G_1 without cut vertices of its own.

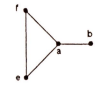

Figure 2.   Subgraph H of G_1.

The cut edge $\{a, b\}$ is another such subgraph. Indeed, there are five such maximal subgraphs of G_1, as shown in Figure 3. $\square$

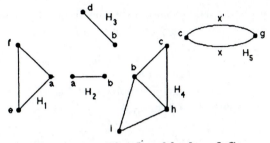

Figure 3. The five blocks of G_1.

This example suggests the following definition.

Definition 1   A *block* of a multigraph G is a maximal connected subgraph B of G such that B has no cut vertices of its own (although it may contain cut vertices of G). A multigraph is itself a *block* if it has only one block.   □

There are three types of blocks. One is an isolated vertex; we will not see these again. A second type is the graph having just one edge and two vertices. The third has more than one edge; in Theorem 1 we will show that any block of the third kind contains a circuit, just as do the subgraphs H_1, H_4, and H_5 shown in Figure 3. To distinguish the third sort of block from the first two, we say that a block with more than one edge is **2-connected**. We need a preliminary lemma first.

Lemma 1   Let G be a connected multigraph, and let a be a vertex of G. Then a is a cut vertex of G if and only if there are two vertices v and v' distinct from a in one component of G such that every path in G from v to v' includes vertex a.

Proof: The proof is left as Exercise 4.   ■

In Theorem 1, we prove even more than claimed previously. Notice that in subgraphs H_1, H_4, and H_5 of Figure 3 every edge is in some circuit of the subgraph. This is a general property of such blocks.

Theorem 1   Suppose G is a block with more than one edge. Then every edge of G is in a circuit of G.

Proof: The main idea of the proof of this theorem is that if G is a block, if G has more than one edge, and if an edge e of G is in no circuit of G, then G can be subdivided into two parts which are connected only by edge e. Then one of the ends of e must be a cut vertex of G, a contradiction. We leave the details of the proof to the reader.   □

Example 2   For each edge in the graph G_1 of Figure 1, either state that it is a cut edge or list a circuit containing it.

Solution:

Edge	Circuit or cut edge	Edge	Circuit or cut edge
$\{a, f\}$	a, e, f, a	$\{a, e\}$	a, e, f, a
$\{e, f\}$	a, e, f, a	$\{a, b\}$	cut edge
$\{b, d\}$	cut edge	$\{b, c\}$	b, c, h, i, b
$\{b, h\}$	b, c, h, b	$\{b, i\}$	b, c, h, i, b
$\{c, h\}$	b, c, h, i, b	$\{h, i\}$	b, c, h, i, b
x	c, g, c	x'	c, g, c

□

Suppose we have represented a communications system by a multigraph with at least two edges and have found that the graph is a block. By Theorem 1 every edge in the graph is in a circuit. If a single vertex of a circuit is deleted, any two of the remaining vertices are still connected by a path in the rest of the circuit. Thus the communications system can survive at least one destroyed switch, from any cause whatsoever. This gives at least a partial solution to the first criterion of a survivable network.

As seen here, the subject of survivability of networks to limited attack is closely bound to the concept of removing vertices from a graph and thus breaking the graph into pieces. This subject is treated at greater length under the heading "connectivity" in many books, as for example in [2]. We will examine further the first criterion that must be satisfied by a survivable communications network later in this chapter.

Density

When we say a network is "bland," we intend to mean that the network offers no especially attractive targets. One interpretation of this notion is that there are no parts that are crowded together, so the network is not "dense." Going over to graphs, we want the density of a graph to be a measure that increases as the number of edges of the graph is increased. Further, if we say the density is 1, for example, we do not want the meaning of that phrase to depend on the number of vertices in the graph. In addition, a scale for the density should be set so that every member of a recognizably uniform class of graphs has a constant density. Trees consitute such a class; let us make the density of any tree equal to 1. Further, we can make sure the density is not dependent on the number of vertices by having our formula for density include that number as a part of its denominator. These latter two ideas give us the following formula.

Definition 2   If G is a multigraph with vertex set $V(G)$ and edge set $E(G)$ and with $\omega(G)$ components*, then the *density* $g(G)$ of G is given by

$$g(G) = \frac{|E(G)|}{|V(G)| - \omega(G)}. \qquad \square$$

Notice that if T is a tree, then $\omega(T) = 1$ and $|E(T)| = |V(T)| - 1$, so $g(T) = 1$ in that case. Also, in a graph with a fixed number of components and a fixed number of vertices, it is clear that $g(G)$ will increase with increasing $|E(G)|$. Thus we can expect this measure of density to be useful in our analysis of communications networks.

Example 3   Compute $g(G)$ for C_3, C_n, K_4, K_n, $K_{2,3}$, $K_{2,n}$, and $K_{m,n}$.

Solution: Since a triangle C_3 has three edges and three vertices, $g(C_3) = 3/(3-1) = 3/2$. In general, if C_n is a circuit with $n > 1$ vertices, then $g(C_n) = n/(n-1)$.

Since K_4 has 6 edges and 4 vertices, we have $g(K_4) = 6/(4-1) = 6/3 = 2/1 = 4/2$. The general case here is that if K_n is a complete graph on $n \geq 2$ vertices, then $g(K_n) = n/2$, and this is an upper bound on $g(G)$ if G is a simple connected graph.

Because the complete bipartite graph $K_{2,3}$ has $2 \times 3 = 6$ edges and $2+3 = 5$ vertices, we get $g(K_{2,3}) = 6/(5-1) = 6/4 = 3/2$. In general, $g(K_{2,n}) = 2n/(n+2-1) = 2n/(n+1) = 2 - \frac{2}{n+1}$, and even more generally $g(K_{m,n}) = mn/(m+n-1)$. $\qquad \square$

But our comment about $g(G)$ increasing with $|E(G)|$ is not quite satisfactory. We did not intend to include a requirement that the number of components should not change. This problem is solvable, however. We first need an interesting arithmetic lemma.

Lemma 2   [6]   Let $p_1/q_1, p_2/q_2, \ldots, p_k/q_k$ be fractions in which p_i and q_i are positive integers for each $i \in \{1, 2, \ldots, k\}$. Then

$$\min_{1 \leq i \leq k} \frac{p_i}{q_i} \leq \frac{p_1 + p_2 + \cdots + p_k}{q_1 + q_2 + \cdots + q_k} \leq \max_{1 \leq i \leq k} \frac{p_i}{q_i}.$$

Proof: See Exercise 5.   ∎

---

* ω is the lower case Greek letter "omega".

For example, $\min(\frac{1}{2}, \frac{2}{3}, \frac{7}{7}, \frac{9}{5}) = \frac{1}{2} \leq \frac{1+2+7+9}{2+3+7+5} = \frac{19}{17} \leq \frac{9}{5} = \max(\frac{1}{2}, \frac{2}{3}, \frac{7}{7}, \frac{9}{5})$.

Since we are looking for the densest parts of the graph, we can restrict our attention to connected graphs G, as shown in the next theorem.

Theorem 2   Suppose multigraph G has components $H_1, H_2, \ldots, H_k$, and suppose l is an index such that $g(H_l) = \max_{1 \leq i \leq k} g(H_i)$. Then $g(H_l) \geq g(G)$.

Proof: We use Lemma 2, obtaining

$$
\begin{aligned}
g(G) &= \frac{|E(G)|}{|V(G)| - k} \\
&= \frac{|E(H_1)| + |E(H_2)| + \cdots + |E(H_k)|}{(|V(H_1)| - 1) + (|V(H_2)| - 1) + \cdots + (|V(H_k)| - 1)} \\
&\leq \max_{1 \leq i \leq k} \left(\frac{|E(H_1)|}{|V(H_1)| - 1}, \frac{|E(H_2)|}{|V(H_2)| - 1}, \ldots, \frac{|E(H_k)|}{|V(H_k)| - 1} \right) \\
&= \max_{1 \leq i \leq k} (g(H_i)) \\
&= g(H_l).
\end{aligned}
$$

∎

Example 4   Examine the function g for the graph G_2 of Figure 4.

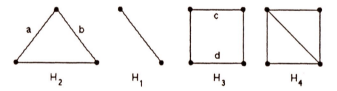

Figure 4.   Graph G_2 with four components.

Solution: In Figure 4, $G_2 = H_1 \cup H_2 \cup H_3 \cup H_4$. We see that $g(G_2) = 13/(13 - 4) = 13/9$. But $g(H_4) = 5/(4 - 1) = 5/3 > 13/9 = g(G_2)$.   □

Example 5   Find the densest part of G_3 of Figure 5.

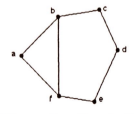

Figure 5.   Graph G_3.

Solution: The connected subgraphs of G_3 (other than trees and G_3 itself) are shown in Figure 6 (up to isomorphism). Calculating g for each of the subgraphs, we have $g(T) = 1$ for any tree in G_3, while $g(G) = 7/5$, $g(H_1) = 3/2$, $g(H_2) = 4/3$, $g(H_3) = 5/4$, $g(H_4) = 6/5$, $g(H_5) = 5/4$, $g(H_6) = 6/5$, and $g(H_7) = 6/5$. Since the largest of these is $3/2$, the triangle H_1 is the densest part of G_3. Thus, the part of the network whose graph representation is G_3 that is most likely to be heavily used is the triangle and that is the part that should be attacked.   □

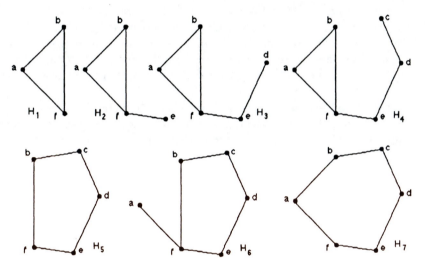

Figure 6.   Connected subgraphs of G_3.

The following definition formalizes the idea of this example*.

Definition 3   Given a multigraph G,

$$\gamma(G) = \max_{H \subseteq G} g(H) = \max_{H \subseteq G} \frac{|E(H)|}{|V(H)| - \omega(H)},$$

where the maximum is taken over all subgraphs H of G for which the denominator in $g(H)$ is not zero.   □

Clearly, a subgraph H of graph G which achieves the value of $\gamma(G)$ is a densest part of the graph and thus corresponds to a part of the communications network through which messages are most likely to pass.

---

* γ is the lower case Greek letter "gamma."

Notice that if H is a connected graph, then the number $g(H)$ is the number of edges of H divided by the number $|V(H)| - 1$ of edges in a spanning tree of H. Thus $g(H)$ is an upper bound on the number of edge-disjoint spanning trees that could appear in H. This bound is not always achieved. For example, it could not be achieved in a triangle T, where $g(T) = 3/2$. Because γ is more important than g, the bound is recognized in the name we give γ. The Latin term for a tree is *arbor*. Since, in addition, $\gamma(G)$ is a fraction, we call $\gamma(G)$ the **fractional arboricity** of G. It turns out (see [4], [8]) that $\gamma(G)$ is even more strongly associated with numbers of spanning trees in G than this simple upper bound would suggest, and so the name has a very strong justification.

By Theorem 2, it suffices to examine only connected subgraphs of G to determine $\gamma(G)$. For example, in Example 5 we listed all of the connected subgraphs of G_3, and there we found the densest connected subgraph was H_1 with density $3/2$. Then by Theorem 4 and the definition of γ, we have $\gamma(G_2) = 3/2$.

But even limiting ourselves to all connected subgraphs of G is not enough. It would be better to have to examine still fewer subgraphs H in the process of computing $\gamma(G)$. The following theorem gives a substantial reduction in the number of subgraphs to examine. For example, using it for finding $\gamma(G_3)$, it is necessary only to examine subgraphs H_1, H_5, H_7, and graph G_3 itself. The proof of this theorem is beyond the scope of this chapter.

Theorem 3   Let multigraph G consist of blocks $B_1, B_2, \ldots B_k$. Then

$$\gamma(G) = \max_{1 \le i \le k} (\gamma(B_i)). \qquad \blacksquare$$

There is one more aid available in computing γ. If H is a connected subgaph of graph G and if G contains an edge e which joins two vertices of H but is not in H, then adding e to H produces a subgraph H' with no more vertices than H has, but with another edge. Hence $g(H') > g(H)$. Thus it is not sensible for us to examine subgraphs like H when subgraphs like H' exist. For example, the subgraph H_4 in Figure 6 has all of the vertices of G_3, but it is missing the edge $\{b, c\}$. Thus it is not surprising that $g(G_3) = 7/5$, which is $1/5$ more than $g(H_4)$.

To make this idea formal, we say that a subgraph H of graph G is **induced** by its vertex set $V(H)$ if every edge of G joining two vertices in $V(H)$ is in H. Thus H_4 in Figure 6 is not an induced subgraph of G_3, nor are H_6 or H_7, but subgraphs H_1, H_2, H_3, and H_5 are induced subgraphs.

In computing $\gamma(G)$ for a connected graph G, we now must find only the 2-connected induced subgraphs of G, if any, compute the function g for each of them, and choose the largest among the number 1 ($= g(T)$ for any tree T of G) and the values of g computed.

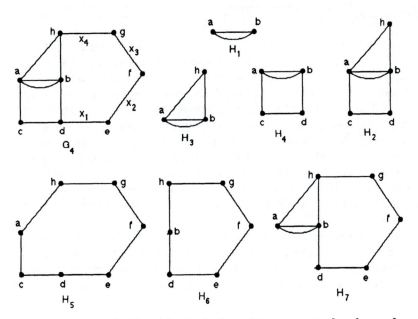

Figure 7.   Graph G_4 with its induced 2-connected subgraphs.

Example 6   Find $\gamma(G_4)$, where G_4 is shown in Figure 7.

Solution: Figure 7 also shows all of the induced 2-connected subgraphs of G_4. We find that $g(G_4) = 11/7$, $g(H_1) = 2$, $g(H_2) = 7/4$, $g(H_3) = 2$, $g(H_4) = 5/3$, $g(H_5) = 7/6$, $g(H_6) = 6/5$, and $g(H_7) = 3/2$. The largest of these is 2, so $\gamma(G_4) = 2$ and this value is attained by both H_1 and H_3. Since H_3 has H_1 as a subgraph, the most attackable part of the network is that corresponding to the subgraph H_3.   □

Even a slightly larger graph than G_4 would have too many induced 2-connected subgraphs for us to compute γ by hand. Worse, it turns out that the number of such subgraphs grows exponentially with increasing numbers of vertices of the graph. Thus even a computer would not be able to use this method to find $\gamma(G)$ for a graph representing a large communications system. However, several algorithms are given in [5], [7], and [9] for computing γ, and these have polynomial complexity. The descriptions of these algorithms are long, and the algorithms are hard to apply by hand, so we do not present them here.

Strength

We now return to our concern for protecting communications networks from limited attacks. In the first part of our study of this problem, we examined attacks on vertices of the graph, which represent command centers and switches in the network. But some command centers are buried, like the famous one in Cheyenne Mountain, Colorado, and others are mobile, as for example the United States' National Emergency Airborne Command Post [1]. The locations of the switching centers are far from other sorts of targets whenever possible, are concealed and kept secret, and some are hardened (buried). Thus the most vulnerable part of the communications system is that represented by the edges of the graph. If we had unlimited funds, we could simply use buried cables for all communications links except those going overseas and going to airborne posts. But we do not have unlimited funds.

So now we study attacks on the communication links by studying the effects of erasing edges in the graph representation. Our concern here is that the graph should not be too severely damaged by the erasure of edges. One reasonable measure of such damage is the number of additional components that are produced by the erasures. Specifically, given graph G, and given a set F of edges of G, denote by $G - F$ the graph obtained from G by erasing the edges in F from G. Then the number of additional components produced by the erasure of the edges in F is $\omega(G - F) - \omega(G)$.

Example 7   Remove $F = \{a, b, c, d\}$ from G_2.

Solution: Removing the edges of $F = \{a, b, c, d\}$ from the graph G_2 of Figure 4, we obtain the graph $G_2 - F$ of Figure 8, which has 6 components. Thus $\omega(G_2) - \omega(F) = 6 - 4 = 2$.   □

Figure 8.   Graph $G_2 - \{a, b, c, d\}$.

But $\omega(G - F) - \omega(G)$ is not a good measure of the resistance of graph G to edge erasure because it does not take into account the number of edges erased. The fact that erasing all of the edges of G assures $\omega(G - F) - \omega(G) = |V(G)| - \omega(G)$ does not say that G is necessarily weak. In order to take the size of F into account, we use a ratio, namely

$$\frac{|F|}{\omega(G - F) - \omega(G)}. \tag{1}$$

Notice that formula (1) is reduced if $|F|$ is reduced or if $\omega(G - F) - \omega(G)$

is increased. So, on a fixed graph, to find its weakest structure, we would search for the set F that minimized formula (1). This leads us to the following definition*.

Definition 4   The *strength* of a multigraph G is given by

$$\eta(G) = \min_{F \subseteq E(G)} \frac{|F|}{\omega(G - F) - \omega(G)},$$

where the minimum is taken over all subsets F of $E(G)$ for which $\omega(G - F) - \omega(G) > 0$.   □

The computation of η by using the definition is usually painfully tedious. We give one example here, but in the next section we present a method which uses γ and is much easier to apply.

When calculating η by the definition, we restrict ourselves to sets F of edges whose erasure increases the number of components of the graph. But in addition, since we are seeking a minimum value for the ratio (1), it is not useful to include an edge e in set F if e joins two vertices in the same component of $G - F$. In other words, the components of $G - F$ should be the subgraphs induced by the vertex sets of the components. We incorporate these two observations into the next example.

Example 8   Given the graph G_5 of Figure 9, use the definition of η to find $\eta(G_5)$.

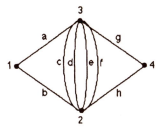

Figure 9.   Graph G_5.

Solution: In Table 1 we list values of ratio (1) for various subsets F of edges of G_5. This list is organized by the number of components in $G - F$. Since the components involved are induced by their sets of vertices, they are listed by their vertex sets.

---

* η is the lower case Greek letter "eta."

Number of components	Vertices of components			Edge set	Formula (1)
2	1	234		$\{a, b\}$	$2/1 = 2$
	2	134		$\{b, c, d, e, f, h\}$	$6/1 = 6$
	3	124		$\{a, c, d, e, f, g\}$	$6/1 = 6$
	4	123		$\{g, h\}$	$2/1 = 2$
	12	34		$\{a, c, d, e, f, h\}$	$6/1 = 6$
	13	24		$\{b, c, d, e, f, g\}$	$6/1 = 6$
3	1 2	34		$\{a, b, c, d, e, f, h\}$	$7/2$
	1 3	24		$\{a, b, c, d, e, f, g\}$	$7/2$
	1 4	23		$\{a, b, g, h\}$	$4/2 = 2$
	2 4	13		$\{b, c, d, e, f, g, h\}$	$7/2$
	3 4	12		$\{a, c, d, e, f, g, h\}$	$7/2$
4	1 2 3 4			$\{a, b, c, d, e, f, g, h\}$	$8/3$

Table 1.   Finding $\eta(G_5)$.

We notice that the minimum occurs three times, with edge sets $F_1 = \{a, b\}$, $F_2 = \{g, h\}$, and $F_3 = \{a, b, g, h\} = F_1 \cup F_2$. Thus $\eta(G_5) = 2$. The maximum damage at minimum cost comes in three sets, but the larger one does the damage of both of the smaller ones, so it would be sensible to carry out the attack indicated by the set F_3 of edges. If our job is to redesign the network to make an attack less attractive, then this is the place in the network we need to improve. ◻

Computing the Strength of a Graph

We begin with an apparent digression from the topic of this section, but it will be seen shortly that the subject of this digression is exactly what we need to compute η with some ease.

Example 9   Calculate $\gamma(G_5)$ in Figure 9.

Solution: In Figure 10, we see the induced 2-connected subgraphs of this graph. There, $g(H_1) = 4/1$, $g(H_2) = 6/2 = 3$, $g(H_3) = 6/2 = 3$, and $g(G_5) = 8/3$. Since the largest of these is 4, we see that $\gamma(G_5) = 4$. Recall that $\eta(G_5) = 2$, so $\gamma(G_5) > \eta(G_5)$. ◻

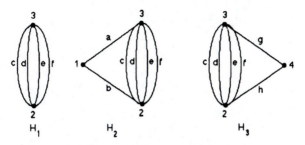

Figure 10.   The induced 2-connected subgraphs of G_5.

It is not a coincidence that $\gamma(G_5) > \eta(G_5)$. In fact, the next theorem shows that there is always a similar relationship between $\gamma(G)$ and $\eta(G)$. The proof of Theorem 4 exploits the fact that $\omega(G - E(G)) = |V(G)|$.

Theorem 4   For any multigraph G having at least one edge,

$$\gamma(G) \geq \frac{|E(G)|}{|V(G)| - \omega(G)} \geq \eta(G) \geq 1. \tag{2}$$

Proof: Since G has an edge, $\omega(G) < |V(G)|$, or $|V(G)| - \omega(G) > 0$. By their definitions,

$$\gamma(G) \geq \frac{|E(G)|}{|V(G)| - \omega(G)} \tag{3}$$

and

$$\eta(G) \leq \frac{|E(G)|}{\omega(G - E(G)) - \omega(G)} = \frac{|E(G)|}{|V(G)| - \omega(G)}. \tag{4}$$

Combining (3) and (4) we have $\gamma(G) \geq \frac{|E(G)|}{|V(G)|-\omega(G)} \geq \eta(G)$.

For $\eta(G) \geq 1$, see Exercise 8.   ∎

Actually, the connection between $\gamma(G)$ and $\eta(G)$ is even stronger than Theorem 4 suggests. The easiest way to see this is through the theory of contractions of subgraphs, and that theory will also give us a way to compute $\eta(G)$ by computing $\gamma(M)$ for several graphs M related to G.

Definition 5   Let G be a multigraph, and let e be an edge of G. We *contract e* by replacing e and its two ends by a single vertex v_e, letting each edge that met either end of e now be incident with v_e. For our purposes, we will allow multiple edges to be created by this process, but any loops generated will be erased. The resulting multigraph is denoted by G/e.   □

Example 10   Contract edge e of graph G_6 of Figure 11.

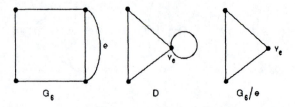

Figure 11.   Graph G_6 and its contraction to G_6/e.

Solution: When contracting edge e, the intermediate step is the pseudo-graph D shown in Figure 11. After erasing the loop of D, we obtain the graph G_6/e also shown in Figure 11.   ☐

To speed the process of contraction, we next define the contraction of a subgraph H of G.

Definition 6   Let G be a multigraph, and let H be a subgraph of G. We contract H by contracting every edge of H. The multigraph obtained by contracting subgraph H of multigraph G is denoted G/H and is called the *contraction of H in G.*   ☐

The graph G/H is independent of the order in which the edges of H are contracted, so our definition and notation does not need to mention that order. In our examples, we label each vertex formed by contraction with a concatenation of the labels of the vertices that became that vertex.

Example 11   Form G_5/H_1 using H_1 shown in Figure 10, and find the value of $\gamma(G_5/H_1)$.

Solution: The graph G_5 is shown in Figure 9 and the subgraph H_1 of G_5 shown in Figure 10. After contraction of H_1, we obtain the graph G_5/H_1 shown in Figure 12. Also in Figure 12 are the 2-connected induced subgraphs H_4 and H_5 of G_5/H_1. Notice that $g(H_4) = g(H_5) = g(G_5/H_1) = 2$. Thus $\gamma(G_5/H_1) = g(G_5/H_1) = 2$.   ☐

In the following definition, for brevity we let* $\Gamma(G)$ stand for a connected subgraph of G such that $\gamma(G) = g(\Gamma(G))$.

---

* Γ is the upper case Greek letter "gamma."

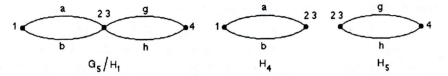

Figure 12.   Graph G_5/H_1 and its 2-connected subgraphs.

Definition 7   Given a multigraph G, we construct a sequence of multigraphs $H_1, H_2, \ldots, H_k$ by the following rules:

   (i) $H_1 = G$;

   (ii) For $i \geq 1$, if $\gamma(H_i) \neq g(H_i)$, we let $H_{i+1} = H_i/(\Gamma(H_i))$; and

   (iii) H_k is the first multigraph reached by this contraction process for which $\gamma(H_k) = g(H_k)$.

By Theorem 2, there is always a connected subgraph H of G for which $g(H) = \gamma(G)$. Thus H_k is defined for any multigraph G for which $\gamma(G)$ is defined. Because of its importance in calculating η, we call H_k an η–reduction of G, and we use G_0 to denote any η–reduction of G. When $G = G_0$, we say that G is η–reduced.   □

For example, we found in Example 12 that the η–reduced graph G_0 for G_5 is G_5/H_1. The following theorem justifies the operation described here. The proof of this theorem is beyond the scope of this chapter.

Theorem 5   There is only one η–reduction G_0 of a multigraph G. Further, G_0 satisfies $\eta(G) = \eta(G_0)$, and the edge set $E(G_0)$ is the largest edge set F of G such that

$$\eta(G) = \frac{|F|}{w(G - F) - w(G)}.$$ ■

This theorem gives us a way of computing $\eta(G)$ for any graph G — we simply find the η–reduction G_0 of G as described, and then compute $g(G_0)$.

Example 12   For the graph G_5 of Figure 9, compute $\eta(G_5)$.

Solution: In Example 9 we learned that $g(H_1) = \gamma(G_5)$ and in Example 11 we contracted that graph to obtain G_5/H_1 shown in Figure 12, determining that $\gamma(G_5/H_1) = 2$. Since $\gamma(G_5/H_1) = g(G_5/H_1)$, so that $G_0 = G_5/H_1$, it follows that $\eta(G_5) = 2$ and the largest subset of edges achieving this value in the definition of η is $\{a, b, g, h\}$. We learned this directly (the hard way) in Example 8.   □

Example 13   Compute $\eta(G_4)$ in Figure 7.

Solution: We learned in Example 6 that $\gamma(G_4) = 2$ and that $g(H_3)$ of Figure 7 is 2. Contracting H_3 yields the graph G_4/H_3 of Figure 13. The 2-connected induced subgraphs of G_4/H_3 are G_4/H_3 and the graphs H_8 and H_9 shown in Figure 13. Since $g(G_4/H_3) = 7/5$, $g(H_8) = 3/2$, and $g(H_9) = 5/4$, we have $\gamma(G_4/H_3) = g(H_8)$ and $\Gamma(G_4/H_3) = H_8$. Contracting H_8 results in the circuit C_4 having vertices $abcdh$, e, f, and g also shown in Figure 13. Since C_4 has only one 2-connected subgraph, we are done. We find that $\eta(G_4) = g(C_4) = 4/3$ and that the largest set of edges achieving this value in the definition of η is $\{x_1, x_2, x_3, x_4\}$ of Figure 7.   □

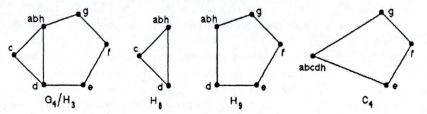

Figure 13. G_4/H_3, its 2-connected subgraphs, and $(G_4/H_3)/H_8 = C_4$.

Bland Networks

We have now seen three conditions in graphs that we would like to see considered in designing a communications network represented by the graph G:

(i)   The graph should be a block, so that the network will be protected against a limited attack or collateral damage,

(ii)   We should have $\gamma(G) = g(G)$ so that the network will not have any attractively dense parts, and

(iii)   We should have $\eta(G) = \frac{|E(G)|}{|V(G)| - \omega(G)}$ to assure that the network is adequately strong against direct attack on the communication links.

But $g(G) = \frac{|E(G)|}{|V(G)| - \omega(G)}$, so our second and third conditions are satisfied if $\gamma(G) = \eta(G)$.

Definition 8   A multigraph G is *uniformly dense* if $\gamma(G) = \eta(G)$. A communications network is *bland* if its graph representation is uniformly dense.   □

Example 14   Show that graph G_7 of Figure 14 is uniformly dense.

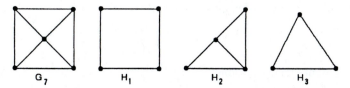

Figure 14.   Graph G_7 and its induced 2-connected subgraphs.

Solution: The graph G_7 is shown in Figure 14 together with its induced 2-connected subgraphs H_1, H_2, and H_3. Since $g(G_7) = 2$, $g(H_1) = 4/3$, $g(H_2) = 5/3$, and $g(H_3) = 3/2$, we see that $\gamma(G_7) = 2 = g(G_7)$. But it follows that the η-reduced graph $G_0 = G_7$. Hence $\eta(G_7) = \gamma(G_0) = \gamma(G_7) = 2$ and G_7 is uniformly dense. Note also that G_7 is a block, so it satisfies all three of our graph conditions. $\square$

The following theorem characterizes uniformly dense graphs.

Theorem 6   Let G be a multigraph with v vertices and e edges. The following are equivalent:

(a) $\gamma(G)(v - \omega(G)) = e$;

(b) $\eta(G)(v - \omega(G)) = e$;

(c) $\gamma(G) = \eta(G)$;

(d) G is η-reduced;

(e) There is a function $f : \{1, 2, \ldots, v - \omega(G)\} \to \mathcal{R}$ such that

   (i) $\dfrac{f(r)}{r} \le \dfrac{f(v - \omega(G))}{(v - \omega(G))}$ for $1 \le r \le v - \omega(G)$,

   (ii) $f(v - \omega(G)) = e$, and

   (iii) $|E(H)| \le f(|V(H)| - \omega(H))$ for each subgraph H of G that has $|V(H)| > \omega(H)$.

Proof: We leave the details of this proof to the reader. It is not difficult to prove that each of (a) and (d) is equivalent to (c), that (e) is equivalent to (a), and that (c) $\to$ (b). However, the proof that (b) $\to$ (c) is beyond the scope of this chapter; its proof can be found in [4]. $\blacksquare$

For our final example, we need the following corollary, in which we apply condition (e) with $f(r)/r$ nondecreasing. A **plane triangulation** is a connected simple graph drawn on the plane such that every face has exactly three edges on its boundary. It is known that if G is a connected planar simple graph with e edges and v vertices with $v \ge 3$, then $e \le 3v - 6$. It is easy to show that if G is a plane triangulation with e edges and v vertices, then $e = 3v - 6$ (see Exercise 9).

Corollary 1   The set of connected graphs G satisfying

$$\gamma(G) = \eta(G) = \frac{|E(G)|}{|V(G)| - 1}$$

includes all plane triangulations.

Proof: Let $f(r) = 3r - 3$ for $r \in \{1, 2, \ldots, v-1\}$. Then $f(v-1) = 3(v-1) - 3 = 3v - 6 = e$, so (ii) of part (e) of Theorem 6 is satisfied. Also, $f(r)/r = 3 - 3/r$, which increases in value as positive r increases in value. Since $r \leq v - 1$, we have

$$\frac{f(r)}{r} \leq \frac{f(v-1)}{v-1},$$

which is (i) of part (e) of Theorem 6. We leave the proof of (iii) of part (e) of Theorem 6 as Exercise 10.   ∎

Example 15   Is the graph G_8 shown in Figure 15 a good choice for a graph representation of a survivable network by the criteria described in this chapter?

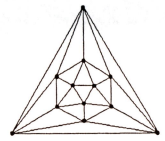

Figure 15.   Graph G_8, the icosahedron.

Solution: We notice first that G_8 is connected and has no cut vertices, so it is a block. Further, it is a plane triangulation, so $\gamma(G_8) = \eta(G_8)$. Thus it satisfies all conditions that we have placed on the graph representation of a network. It is a good choice.   □

We have arrived at one of the cutting edges of modern mathematical research. The following questions are not exercises; rather they are the questions being asked by some professional mathematicians in their research.

Given the graph G of an already existing communications network, and given that $\gamma(G) \neq \eta(G)$, what would be the best edge to add to G to reduce $\gamma(G) - \eta(G)$? What does "best" mean in the answer? Is it the cheapest edge whose addition will reduce $\gamma(G) - \eta(G)$, or does it reduce $\gamma(G) - \eta(G)$ by the largest amount? Would it be better to eliminate some edges already present and replace them by other edges? Which ones should be eliminated? Many other questions can be asked, and their answers could be critical to the survival of our communications system if we are ever subject to an attack on our homeland.

Suggested Readings

1. D. Ball, "Can Nuclear War be Controlled?", *Adelphi Papers*, No. 169, The International Institute for Strategic Studies, London, 1981.

2. J. Bondy and U. Murty, *Graph Theory with Applications*, American Elsevier, New York, 1976.

3. R. Cannell, *Live: A Handbook of Survival in Nuclear Attack*, Prentice-Hall, Inc., Englewood Cliffs, N.J., 1962.

4. P. Catlin, J. Grossman, A. Hobbs, and H.-J. Lai "Fractional arboricity, strength, and principal partitions in graphs and matroids" *Discrete Appl. Math*, (to appear).

5. W. Cunningham, "Optimal attack and reinforcement of a network", *J. Assoc. Comp. Mach.*, Vol. 32, 1985, pp. 549–561.

6. G. Hardy, J. Littlewood, and G. Polya, *Inequalities*, Cambridge University Press, Cambridge, 1952.

7. A. Hobbs, "Computing edge-toughness and fractional arboricity", *Contemporary Math.*, Vol. 89, 1989, pp. 89–106.

8. C. Nash-Williams, "Decompositions of finite graphs into forests", *J. London Math. Soc.*, Vol. 39, 1964, p. 12.

9. N. Tomizawa "Strongly irreducible matroids and principal partition of a matroid into strongly irreducible minors", *Elect. and Comm. in Japan*, Vol. 59A, No. 2, 1976, pp. 1–10.

10. A. Tucker "Communications black-out: Electromagnetic effects" *Nuclear Attack: Civil Defence*, ed. by the Royal United Services Institute for Defence Studies, Brassey's Publishers Ltd., Oxford, England, 1982, pp. 70–82.

Exercises

1. Draw the blocks of each graph. Then, for each edge, either state that it is a cut edge or list a circuit containing it.

a)

b)

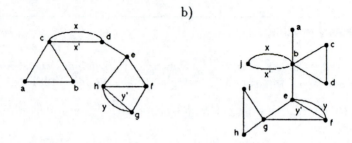

2. Find the values of γ and η for each of these graphs.

   a)   b)

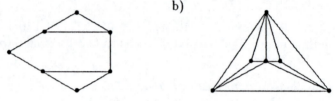

3. For each graph, find the value of γ. Then use contractions to find the η-reduction G_0 and the value of η.

   a)   b)

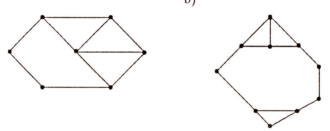

★4. Prove Lemma 1.

★5. Prove Lemma 2. *Hint:* Prove it first for $k = 2$ and then use induction.

6. Why are only eight subgraphs of G_4 (including G_4 itself) examined in determining $\gamma(G_4)$? For example, why not also look at the following subgraph? Give another 2-connected subgraph of G_4 that was omitted for the same reason.

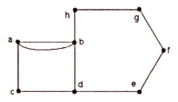

7. For any forest F with at least one edge, prove that $\gamma(F) = \eta(F) = 1$.

8. Prove that $\eta(G) \geq 1$ for any multigraph having at least one edge.

9. Prove that, if G is a plane triangulation with e edges and v vertices, then $e = 3v - 6$.

10. Prove that (iii) of part (e) of Theorem 6 is satisfied by the function f defined in the proof of Corollary 1.

Computer Projects

1. Write a computer program to calculate $\gamma(G)$ for a multigraph G.

2. Write a computer program which uses the program of Computer Project 1 to find the value of $\eta(G)$ for a multigraph G.

20

The Chinese Postman Problem

Author: John G. Michaels, Department of Mathematics, State University of New York, College at Brockport.

Prerequisites: The prerequisites for this chapter are Euler circuits in graphs and shortest path algorithms. See, for example, Sections 7.5 and 7.6 of *Discrete Mathematics and Its Applications*, Second Edition, by Kenneth H. Rosen.

Introduction

The solution of the problem of the seven bridges of Königsberg in 1736 by Leonhard Euler is regarded as the beginning of graph theory. In the city of Königsberg there was a park through which a river ran. In this park seven bridges crossed the river. The problem at the time was to plan a walk that crossed each of the bridges exactly once, starting and ending at the same point. Euler set up the problem in terms of a graph, shown in Figure 1, where the vertices represented the four pieces of land in the park and the edges represented the seven bridges. Euler proved that such a walk (called an **Euler circuit**, i.e., a circuit that traverses each edge exactly once) was impossible because of the existence of vertices of odd degree in the graph. In fact, what is known as Euler's Theorem gives the precise condition under which an Euler circuit exists in a connected graph: the graph has an Euler circuit if and only if the degree of every vertex is even.

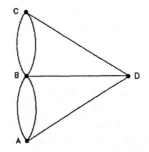

Figure 1. Königsberg bridge graph.

We now pose a related question about Figure 1. Starting and ending at point *A*, what is the minimum number of bridges that must be crossed in order to cross every bridge *at least* once? A problem of this type is referred to as a **Chinese Postman Problem**, named after the Chinese mathematician Mei-Ko Kwan, who posed such a problem in 1962 (see [3]). We will develop a method for solving problems of this type in this chapter.

Solution to the Problem

Before examining methods for solving Chinese Postman Problems, we first look at several applications of this type of problem. Suppose we have a road network which must be traversed by:

- a mail carrier delivering mail to buildings along the streets,
- a snowplow which must clear snow from each lane of the streets,
- a highway department crew which must paint a line down the center of each street,
- a police patrol car which makes its rounds through all streets several times a day.

In each case, the person (or vehicle) must traverse each street *at least once*. In the best situation, where every vertex (i.e., road intersection) has even degree, no retracing is needed. (Such retracing of edges is referred to as "deadheading".) In such a case, any Euler circuit solves the problem.

However, it is rarely the case that every vertex in a road network is even. (Examining a road map of any town or section of a city will confirm this.) According to Euler's Theorem, when there are odd vertices, it is impossible to plan a circuit that traces every edge exactly once. Since every road needs to be traced, some roads must be retraced. We pose a new problem — plan a route so that the total amount of retracing is as small as possible. More precisely, we have the following definition of the Chinese Postman Problem.

Definition 1   Given a connected weighted graph or digraph G, the *Chinese Postman Problem* is the problem of finding the shortest circuit that uses each edge in G at least once.   □

We will now study several examples, showing how to solve problems that can be phrased in terms of the Chinese Postman Problem.

The simplest case occurs when every vertex in the graph has even degree, for in this case an Euler circuit solves the problem. Any Euler circuit will have the minimum total weight since no edges are retraced in an Euler circuit.

However, the following example illustrates the case where there are vertices of odd degree. This example will provide us with the first step toward a solution to the more general type of Chinese Postman Problem.

Example 1   A mail carrier delivers mail along each street in the weighted graph of Figure 2, starting and ending at point A. The first number on an edge gives the length of time (in minutes) needed to deliver mail along that block; the second number gives the time for traveling along the block without delivering mail (i.e., the deadheading time). Assuming that mail is delivered to houses on both sides of the street by traveling once down that street, find the shortest route and minimum time required for the mail carrier to deliver the mail.

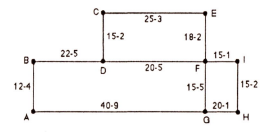

Figure 2.   Mail carrier's weighted graph.

Solution: The total time spent on the route is the sum of the mail delivery time plus any deadheading time. The mail delivery time is simply the sum of the mail delivery weights on the edges, which is 217 minutes. The problem is now one of determining the minimum deadheading time.

Observe that the graph has no Euler circuit since vertices D and G have odd degree. Therefore the mail carrier must retrace at least one street in order to cover the entire route. For example, the mail carrier might retrace edges $\{D, F\}$ and $\{F, G\}$. If we insert these two retraced edges in the graph of Figure 2, we obtain a multigraph where every vertex is even. The new multigraph therefore has an Euler circuit. This graph is drawn in Figure 3, where the edges are numbered in the order in which the mail carrier might follow them in an Euler circuit. (The deadheading edges appear as edges 7 and 12 in this multigraph.)

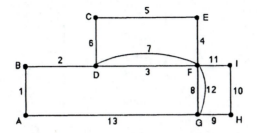

Figure 3. Mail carrier's route, including deadheading.

But is there a faster route? To answer this question, we examine the possible deadheading edges that could be added.

We claim that, no matter what route the mail carrier uses to deliver the mail, the edges used for deadheading will form a path joining D and G. To see this, consider the graph of Figure 3. Because D was odd in the original graph, a deadheading edge must be incident with D. (In our example, this is edge 7.) When this deadheading edge is added to the original graph, this causes its other endpoint, F, to become an odd vertex (its degree changed from 4 to 5). Since F is then odd, there must be another deadheading edge incident with F. (In our example, this is edge 12.) This will continue until a vertex that was originally odd is reached. (In our example, this stopped when G was reached.) Thus the deadheading edges will always form a path joining D and G.

Since the deadheading edges form a path joining D and G, to find the minimum weight of deadheading edges we need to find a path of minimum weight joining D and G in Figure 2.

The graph of Figure 2 is small enough that there are relatively few paths between D and G that we need to examine. (Note that we do not need to consider any path joining D and G that passes through a vertex more than once. Any such path could be replaced by a path of smaller weight that does not pass through any vertex more than once.) We list these paths along with their deadheading times:

Path	Time (minutes)
D, B, A, G	18
D, C, E, F, G	12
D, C, E, F, I, H, G	11
D, F, G	10
D, F, I, H, G	9

Therefore, the minimum deadheading time is nine minutes. This can be achieved by planning a route that uses the four edges $\{D, F\}$, $\{F, I\}$, $\{I, H\}$, and $\{H, G\}$. The multigraph with these deadheading edges added is shown in Figure 4.

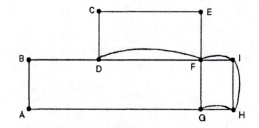

Figure 4.   Mail carrier's weighted graph, with deadheading edges for minimum route added.

Any Euler circuit in the graph of Figure 4 achieves the minimum time. Thus,

$$A, B, D, C, E, F, I, H, G, F, D, F, I, H, G, A$$

and

$$A, B, D, C, E, F, D, F, I, H, G, F, I, H, G, A$$

are both examples of fastest routes.

The minimum time is

delivery time $+$ deadheading time $= 217 + 9 = 226$ minutes.

(Note that the four deadheading edges do not have to be used in succession. Also note that the *number* of streets retraced does not matter. The route in Figure 3 only retraced two blocks, but was not as fast as either of the two routes in the graph of Figure 4.) $\square$

In this example we needed to traverse each edge at least once, forming a circuit that started and ended at A. No matter how we construct a circuit starting at A, we are forced to retrace edges. These retraced edges form a path between the two odd vertices. Therefore, to minimize the deadheading time, we need to find a path of minimum weight joining the two odd vertices.

In Example 1 there were sufficiently few paths joining the odd vertices that we could list them all and select one of minimum length. However, if there are many possibilities to consider, an algorithm for finding a shortest path should be used. (See the "Shortest Path Problems" chapter of this book or Dijkstra's shortest path algorithm in Section 7.6 of *Discrete Mathematics and Its Applications*, Second Edition, by Rosen.)

But now suppose that we are working with a weighted graph with *more than two* odd vertices. As in Example 1, we know that edges will need to be retraced and we need to minimize the total weight of the retraced edges. The following theorem, generalizing the idea developed in Example 1, shows an important property that the retraced edges have and helps us efficiently select the edges to be retraced.

Theorem 1   Suppose G is a graph with $2k$ odd vertices, where $k \geq 1$, and suppose C is a circuit that traces each edge of G at least once. Then the retraced edges in C can be partitioned into k paths joining pairs of the odd vertices, where each odd vertex in G is an endpoint of exactly one of the paths.

Proof: There are two parts to the proof. First we prove that the retraced edges of C can be partitioned into k paths joining pairs of odd vertices, and then we prove that each odd vertex is an endpoint of exactly one of these paths.

The proof of the first part follows the argument of Example 1. We choose an odd vertex v_1. Since v_1 has odd degree, the vertex must have at least one retraced edge incident with it. We begin a path from v_1 along this edge, and continue adding retraced edges to extend the path, never using a retraced edge more than once. Continue extending this path, removing each edge used in the path, until it is impossible to go farther. The argument of Example 1 shows that this path will only terminate at a second odd vertex v_2. The vertex v_2 must be distinct from v_1. (To see this, note that v_1 has odd degree in G. When the retraced edges are added to G, v_1 has even degree. Therefore there must be an odd number of retraced edges incident with v_1. One of these is used to begin the path from v_1; when it is removed, v_1 has an even number of retraced edges remaining. Therefore, if the path from v_1 ever reenters v_1, there will be a retraced edge on which it will leave v_1. Therefore, the path will not terminate at v_1.) We then begin a second path from another odd vertex v_3, which will end at another odd vertex v_4. (The parenthetical remarks earlier in this paragraph showing that v_2 must be distinct from v_1 can also be applied here to show that v_4 must be different from v_1, v_2, and v_3.) Proceeding in this fashion, every retraced edge will be part of one of these paths.

The second part of the theorem follows immediately, since each odd vertex appeared as an endpoint of some path, and once this happened, that vertex could never be an endpoint of a second path.   ∎

The following example illustrates the use of Theorem 1 in solving a problem of the Chinese Postman type.

Example 2   A truck is to paint the center strip on each street in the weighted graph of Figure 5. Each edge is labeled with the time (in minutes) for painting the line on that street. Find the minimum time to complete this job and a route that accomplishes this goal. Assume that the truck begins and ends at a highway department garage at A and that the time required for the truck to follow a street is the same regardless of whether or not the truck is painting or deadheading.

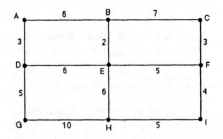

Figure 5.   Weighted graph for the line-painting truck.

Solution: Observe that there are four odd vertices — B, D, F, H. Therefore, traversing each edge on this graph at least once will require deadheading at each of these vertices. To minimize the total time for the job, we need to minimize the deadheading time. That is, we need to minimize the sum of the weights of all duplicated edges. Using Theorem 1 (with $k = 2$), we know that the deadheading edges form two paths joining pairs of the four odd vertices.

Therefore, to solve the problem we need to find the two paths with total weight as small as possible. We first need to list all ways to put the four odd vertices in two pairs. Then, for each set of two pairs we find a shortest path joining the two vertices in each of the two pairs, and finally we choose the set of pairs that has the smallest total weight of its two paths.

In this example, the pairings and shortest paths (with their weights) are

Pairing	Path	Weight	Path	Weight
$\{B,D\}, \{F,H\}$:	B,E,D	8	F,I,H	9
$\{B,F\}, \{D,H\}$:	B,E,F	7	D,E,H	12
$\{B,H\}, \{D,F\}$:	B,E,H	8	D,E,F	11

Of these three possible pairings, the pair $\{B,D\},\{F,H\}$ has smallest total weight, $8 + 9 = 17$ minutes. Therefore, the truck will spend 17 minutes deadheading, and the total time on the job spent by the truck will be

$$\text{painting time } + \text{ deadheading time} = 62 + 17 = 79 \text{ minutes.}$$

To find a specific route that achieves this time, take the given graph and add the retraced streets as multiple edges, as in Figure 6. This new graph has an Euler circuit, such as

$$A, B, C, F, E, B, E, D, E, H, I, F, I, H, G, D, A. \qquad \square$$

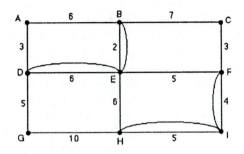

Figure 6. Weighted graph for a snow plow, with deadheading edges.

The key idea in the solution of the problem in Example 2 is finding a **perfect matching of minimum weight**, that is, a pairing of vertices such that the sum of the weights on the paths joining the vertices in each pair is as small as possible. To obtain such a matching, we examined all possible ways of matching the odd vertices in pairs, and then chose a minimum (i.e., shortest) matching. If there are n odd vertices, the number of perfect matchings to examine is $O(n^{n/2})$. (See the Chapter "Applications of Subgraph Enumeration" in this book for a method of enumerating these matchings.) Therefore, if n is large, we would need the assistance of a computer to accomplish the task. An algorithm of order $O(n^3)$ for finding a matching of minimum weight can be found in reference [4], for example.

Extensions

In each problem discussed in the last section, some simplifications were implicitly made. For example, in the mail carrier's problem of Example 1, we assumed that the person delivering the mail was restricted to traveling along only the streets in the given graph. Thus, when we minimized the deadheading time, we looked for the shortest path between D and G, *using only the given edges*. However, it is possible that there are additional paths or alleys (along which no mail is to be delivered) that will yield a shorter path between D and G. In this case we would need to expand the given graph to include all possible edges that could be used as parts of paths for deadheading, and then find a perfect matching of minimum weight in this new graph.

There are several other considerations that may need to be considered in a specific problem. For example, it may be difficult for a street sweeper to make a left turn at intersections. A snowplow may need to clear roads along a street network where some left turns are prohibited, some of the streets are one-way (and therefore may need to be followed twice in the same direction), or parked cars may prevent plowing during certain hours on one or both sides of a street. Also, it may be wise for the mail carrier to use a route where the deadheading periods occur as late as possible in the delivery route.

The Chinese Postman Problem can be even more complicated when handled on a large scale. For example, the postal service in city does not depend on one person to deliver mail to all homes and offices. The city must be divided into sections to be served by many mail carriers. That is, the graph or digraph for the city streets must be drawn as the union of many subgraphs, each of which poses its own Chinese Postman Problem. But how should the large graph be divided into subgraphs so that various factors (such as time and money) are minimized?

A model for solving problems such as this is explained in [7], where a model for street sweeping in New York City is discussed in detail. Two approaches to the problem are dealt with: one method that finds a single route for the entire graph and then divides this route into smaller pieces (the "route first–cluster second" approach), and a second method that first divides the graph into pieces and then works with each piece separately (the "cluster first–route second" approach). Methods such as these have been implemented and have resulted in considerable cost savings to the municipalities involved.

Suggested Readings

1. J. Edmonds, "The Chinese Postman Problem", *Operations Research*, Vol. 13, Supplement 1, 1965, B73.

2. S, Goodman and S. Hedetniemi, "Eulerian Walks in Graphs", *SIAM Journal of Computing*, Vol. 2, 1973, pp.16–27.

3. M. Kwan, "Graphics Programming Using Odd and Even Points", *Chinese Math.*, Vol. 1, 1962, pp. 237–77.

4. E. Lawler, *Combinatorial Optimization: Networks and Matroids*, Holt, Rinehart and Winston, New York, 1976.

5. E. Reingold and R. Tarjan, "On a Greedy Heuristic for Complete Matching", *SIAM Journal of Computing*, Vol. 10, 1981, pp. 676–81.

6. F. Roberts, *Applied Combinatorics*, Prentice-Hall, Englewood Cliffs, N.J., 1984.

7. A. Tucker and L. Bodin, "A Model for Municipal Street Sweeping Operations", Chapter 6 in *Discrete and System Models*, ed. W. Lucas, F. Roberts, and R. Thrall (Volume 3 of *Models in Applied Mathematics*), Springer-Verlag, New York, 1983, pp. 76–111.

Exercises

1. Solve Example 1 with the deadheading time on edge $\{F, I\}$ changed from 1 to 4.

2. A police car patrols the streets in the following graph. The weight on each edge is the length of time (in minutes) to traverse that street in either direction. If each street is a two-way street and the car starts and ends at A, what is the minimum time needed to patrol each street at least once?

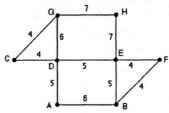

3. Solve Example 2 if the following times are changed: edge $\{G, H\}$ has weight 3 and edge $\{B, E\}$ has weight 5.

4. If each bridge in the Königsberg bridge graph (Figure 1) must be crossed at least once, what is the minimum number of bridges that must be crossed more than once, if the circuit begins and ends at A?

5. Find the minimum number of edges that must be retraced when drawing each graph as a circuit.
    a) K_6 b) K_n c) $K_{2,5}$ d) $K_{m,n}$.

6. A street washing truck needs to wash the streets of the following map. The labels on the edges give the time (in minutes) to wash that street. All streets are two-way, except that the street between D and C is one-way northbound. If the truck starts and ends its route at A, find a route that cleans all streets in the smallest amount of time. Assume that one pass down the center of a street washes the street and that the truck must observe the one-way restriction on the street joining D and C.

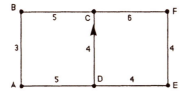

7. Find the minimum number of edges that must be retraced in the graph of the following figure, where each edge is traced at least once, starting and ending at vertex 1.

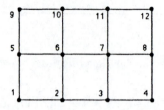

8. A computer plotter plots the following figure. It takes the plotter 0.05 seconds to plot each horizontal edge and 0.02 seconds to plot each vertical edge. Assuming that the time required to trace a line remains the same regardless of whether the plotter is plotting or deadheading and that the plotter must follow the positions of the lines, what is the minimum length of time required for the plotter to plot the figure? *Note:* See [5] for further details on this application.

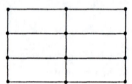

9. Suppose a mail carrier delivers mail to both sides of each street in the graph of Figure 2, and does this by delivering mail on only one side of the street at a time. The mail delivery time for each side of a street is half the weight on the edge. (For example, it takes 6 minutes to deliver mail on each side of street $\{A, B\}$). Find the minimum time needed to complete the route.

10. An 8×8 checkerboard is to be traced as a circuit. What is the smallest number of edges that must be retraced in order to trace the board?

Computer Projects

1. Write a program that inputs an unweighted graph and finds the minimum number of edges that must be retraced in a circuit that traces each edge at least once.

2. Write a program that inputs a weighted graph with two odd vertices and finds the minimum weight of a circuit that traverses each edge at least once.

3. Write a program that inputs a weighted graph with $2k$ odd vertices and finds the minimum weight of a circuit that traverses each edge at least once.

21

Graph Layouts

Author: Zevi Miller, Department of Mathematics and Statistics, Miami University.

Prerequisites: The prerequisites for this chapter are big-O notation and basic concepts of graphs and trees. See, for example, Section 1.8 and Chapters 7 and 8 of *Discrete Mathematics and Its Applications*, Second Edition, by Kenneth H. Rosen.

Introduction

In this chapter we will discuss a set of graph problems having a common theme. These problems deal with the question of how well a given graph G "fits" inside some other given graph H.

Why might we be interested in such problems? The answer is that solutions to such problems tell us much about the best design for interconnection networks of computers and for layouts of circuits on computer chips. The solution to a special case of one of these problems also sheds light on how to represent matrices in a compact way that makes it convenient to manipulate them when executing standard matrix operations.

Dilation

First consider a computer network based on a graph G. This network consists of a different computer located at each vertex of G, with two computers joined by a direct link when the corresponding vertices are joined by an edge in G. (We therefore continue to denote the network by G, its underlying graph.) We can imagine programming these computers to run in parallel, each computer receiving part or all of the original input data and then proceeding to perform its own private computations as specified by the master program controlling all the computers. At each time unit each computer is also allowed to pass the results of the computation just completed to one of its neighboring computers (i.e., the ones joined to it by an edge), and these neighbors will use these results as inputs into their own computations later. We call such a network G an **interconnection network** (or sometimes a **parallel computation network**). By dividing up the work between its different computers, we can expect that an interconnection network can solve at least some problems much faster than a single computer could.

We now take H to be an interconnection network different from G such that H has at least as many vertices as G; that is, $|V(G)| \leq |V(H)|$. Suppose that we have a program P for G to solve some problem as described in the last paragraph, but that G is not available while H is available. (In fact, even if G were available, we might still prefer to use H for standardization reasons.) The question then becomes how to "simulate" the program for G by a program for H which solves the same problem. Informally speaking, a simulation of G by H is a way of describing how, using the program P as a guide, H can accomplish the same task as G by assigning its computers the tasks assigned to those of G. One way of doing this is to make a *mapping* (or *correspondence*) between the vertices of G and the vertices of H so that corresponding vertices carry out the same tasks. The obvious question is how to define such a mapping, and the answer to this question in turn depends on how "effective" a given mapping is in doing the simulation.

Clearly, we need to be a bit more precise about how to evaluate the effectiveness of a mapping. We write

$$f : V(G) \rightarrow V(H)$$

to indicate that f is a one-to-one (though not necessarily onto) mapping from the vertices of G to the vertices of H. We will sometimes refer to such a mapping f as an **embedding** of G in H. In our simulation each computation of the program P at a vertex (i.e. computer) x in G will be replaced by the same computation at the corresponding vertex $f(x)$ in H. Also, each communication of P between adjacent vertices x_1 and x_2 of G will be replaced by the same communication between the corresponding vertices $f(x_1)$ and $f(x_2)$ in H.

Here is the place where we can measure the "effectiveness" of the map f. Notice that whereas x_1 and x_2 could communicate in some unit time t because they were adjacent, the vertices $f(x_1)$ and $f(x_2)$ require communication time $d \cdot t$ where d is the distance in H between $f(x_1)$ and $f(x_2)$. The simulation thus introduces a time delay factor d in the simulation of P, and the delay could even be worse if there is another adjacent pair z_1 and z_2 of G for which the distance in H between $f(z_1)$ and $f(z_2)$ is bigger than the distance between $f(x_1)$ and $f(x_2)$. We see therefore that one criterion for the effectiveness of f is that the worst possible delay factor (as measured over all possible adjacent pairs of vertices x_1 and x_2 in G) is minimized.

We now put these ideas into mathematical form. First we discuss distance. Throughout this chapter, if x and y are two vertices of G, then a **path** between x and y is a succession of vertices starting from x and ending at y in which every two successive vertices are joined by an edge, *and no vertex is repeated*. The **length** of a path is the number of edges on it (which is one less than the number of vertices on it). Now there may be many different paths of differing lengths between two given vertices in a graph. We define the **distance** between x and y in G, written $\text{dist}_G(x, y)$, to be the length of the shortest path in G from x to y.

Example 1   Find paths of lengths $2, 3, 4, 5$, and 6 between x and y in the graph of Figure 1.

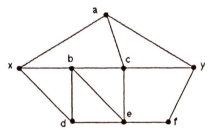

Figure 1.   Paths of various lengths between x and y.

Solution: Examples of these paths, in order of length, are

$$x, a, y \qquad x, b, c, y \qquad x, b, e, c, y \qquad x, b, e, c, a, y \qquad x, d, b, e, c, a, y.$$

There are other paths not listed here. Since the shortest path between x and y has length 2, we have $\text{dist}_G(x, y) = 2$.   □

We can now describe precisely the worst possible time delay of a map $f : V(G) \to V(H)$. For any two adjacent vertices x and y of G, the **delay** at the edge $\{x, y\}$ caused by f is the distance between $f(x)$ and $f(y)$ in H; that is, $\text{dist}_H(f(x), f(y))$. The worst possible delay, over all edges $\{x, y\}$ in G, caused by f is called the **dilation** of f and is denoted $\text{dil}(f)$. Put more precisely,

$$\text{dil}(f) = \max\{\text{dist}_H(f(x), f(y)) : \{x, y\} \in E(G)\}.$$

Example 2   Suppose that G is the graph obtained from K_4 by removing an edge (this graph is denoted $K_4 - e$) and H is the path on 4 vertices. In Figure 2 we illustrate two different maps from the vertices of G to the vertices of H, one having dilation 2 and the other having dilation 3. We have dil$(f) = 3$ because the edge $\{a, c\}$ of G is sent to the pair of vertices $f(a)$ and $f(c)$ in H which are distance 3 apart in H, and all other edges of G are sent to pairs that are at distance 2 or less apart. But we have dil$(g) = 2$, since any edge of G is sent by g to a pair of vertices in H that are distance 2 or less in H.   ☐

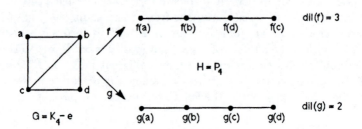

Figure 2.   Two different maps $f, g : V(G) \to V(H)$ where $G = K_4 - e$ and H is the path on four vertices. The second map is optimal, so $B(G, H) = 2$.

Finally, we want to find a map f having minimum worst possible time delay; that is, a map with **minimum possible dilation**. We call this minimum $B(G, H)$; or more precisely,

$$B(G, H) = \min\{\operatorname{dil}(f) : f \text{ a one–to–one map from } V(G) \text{ to } V(H)\}.$$

We see then that $B(G, H)$ measures the minimum possible worst case time delay when H simulates G, and so in some intuitive sense it measures how "compatible" G and H are. We call the map f **optimal** if dil$(f) = B(G, H)$, that is, if it has minimum possible dilation over all possible one-to-one maps from $V(G)$ to $V(H)$.

Example 3   What is $B(G, H)$ for the graphs G and H in Figure 2?

Solution: We could try all 4! maps from the vertices of G to the vertices of H, recording the dilation of each map as we go, and at the end we could scan our list to find the minimum dilation. This minimum is $B(G, H)$. We will not carry out this procedure here, but instead note the following. In Figure 2 we found a map $g : V(G) \to V(H)$ satisfying dil$(g) = 2$. This shows that $B(G, H) \leq 2$. In fact, we can also show that $B(G, H) \geq 2$ by proving that any map $M : V(G) \to V(H)$ must satisfy dil$(M) \geq 2$. We leave this to the reader as Exercise 2. Thus, $B(G, H) = 2$.   ☐

In the next two sections we will study the function $B(G, H)$ for certain types of graphs G and H that arise in various applications.

Bandwidth

The first of our minimum dilation problems arose originally in the context of sparse matrices. We call a matrix A **sparse** if the number of nonzero entries it has is small in comparison with its total number of entries. Such matrices arise frequently as coefficient matrices of systems of equations or systems of differential equations in numerical analysis and physics. When performing various operations on these matrices, such as matrix multiplication and matrix inversion, we notice that a large number of our computations involve multiplying 0s together. Even storing these matrices in a computer by recording every entry means storing a large number of 0s. In fact, such an $n \times n$ matrix would require storage of all its n^2 entries, most of them being 0. This suggests that we could perform our operations and our storage more efficiently if we concentrated on the nonzero entries, "filling in" the others in a predictably simple way depending on the operation at hand.

The focus on the nonzero entries of a matrix A is made easier if all these entries are concentrated in a "band" consisting of a small number of diagonals of A above and below the main diagonal. Such a concentration would speed up matrix multiplication and Gaussian elimination by making it possible to carry out only a small fraction of all the computations involved and still get the desired result, since the remaining computations (the ones involving entries outside the band) involve all 0 entries and thus have predictable results. A small band for A also allows us to use relatively little memory in storing A since we could keep track of each nonzero entry by simply recording the diagonal to which it belongs and where along that diagonal it can be found.

All this sounds promising, but what do we do if the nonzero entries of the matrix A do not all lie in a small band about the main diagonal of A? The key idea here is to permute the rows and columns of A, hoping to obtain a matrix that does have the required small band. That is, we perform a permutation (i.e. a renumbering) of the columns of A, and also the *same* permutation of the rows of A. Such an identical permutation of rows and columns is called a **symmetric permutation**. (In the case when A is the coefficient matrix of a system of equations, this permutation of the rows is the same as reordering the equations, and the permutation of the columns is the same as reindexing the variables in the system.) If the resulting matrix A' has a smaller band enclosing all its nonzero entries than does A, then we would prefer to work with A' rather than with A. The results of our work on A' can be easily translated back to results on A. (In the context of coefficient matrices, the translation just amounts to reindexing the variables again so that they have their original names.)

Example 4   In the 4×4 matrix at the top of Figure 3, only three super- and subdiagonals are needed to enclose the 1s. Now, by interchanging columns 3 and 4, and also interchanging rows 3 and 4, we obtain the bottom matrix in which only two super- and subdiagonals are needed to enclose all the 1s. This interchange of rows and columns amounts to interchanging the names (or subscripts) of variables 3 and 4 in the corresponding system of equations.   □

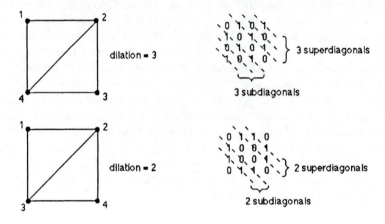

Figure 3.   Two numberings of a graph and the corresponding matrices.

What does all this have to do with dilation? The intriguing answer is that the smallest possible band achievable (over all row and column permutations) for a given matrix A is equal to $B(G, H)$ for certain graphs G and H which are defined in terms of A.

To understand this connection between bands of matrices and dilation, we start by defining the path graph on n vertices.

Definition 1   The *path graph* P_n is the graph whose vertices are the integers $1, 2, \ldots, n$ and whose edges are the successive pairs $\{i, i+1\}$, $1 \leq i \leq n-1$.   □

Figure 2 shows the path graph P_4.

Suppose G is a graph on n vertices. Then any one-to-one map $f : V(G) \to V(P_n)$ may be viewed as a numbering (or labeling) of the vertices of G by the integers $1, 2, \ldots, n$, and dil(f) is then the maximum distance between any two integers $f(x)$ and $f(y)$ for which $\{x, y\}$ is an edge of G. Then $B(G, P_n)$ is just the minimum possible dil(f) over all numberings of G with the integers $\{1, 2, \ldots, n\}$. The function $B(G, P_n)$ (of a graph G) has been extensively studied (see [5] or [3] for surveys), where it is called the *bandwidth* of G. We will abbreviate $B(G, P_n)$ by $B(G)$. We summarize the meaning of bandwidth in the following definition.

Definition 2   The *bandwidth* $B(G)$ of a graph G on n vertices is the minimum possible dilation of any numbering of G with the integers $1, 2, \ldots, n$. □

Example 5   Example 3 shows that $B(K_4 - e) = 2$. □

Now suppose we are given an $n \times n$ symmetric 0-1 matrix $A = [a_{ij}]$. Define a graph $G(A)$ by letting $V(G(A)) = \{1, 2, \ldots, n\}$ and saying that $\{i, j\}$ is an edge if and only if $a_{ij} = 1$. In Figure 3, referred to earlier, we see the 4×4 matrix A and the corresponding graph $G(A) = K_4 - e$. Notice that each possible numbering f of $G(A)$ for a matrix A corresponds to a symmetric permutation $P(f)$ of the rows and columns of A. Also, the dilation of any numbering f of $G(A)$ corresponds to the number of superdiagonals above and subdiagonals below the main diagonal containing all the 1s in the matrix resulting from the permutation $P(f)$. Hence $B(G(A))$ is the smallest possible band, over all symmetric permutations of rows and columns of A, of super- and subdiagonals of A which contain all the 1s of A. Finding this smallest band for A, or equivalently finding $B(G(A))$, is (as we said before) important in being able to efficiently store A, and in performing various operations on A such as Gaussian elimination and inversion.

Example 6   Figure 3 also shows the correspondence between the dilation of a numbering and the band of the corresponding matrix. □

Calculating and Bounding Bandwidth

Now that we have defined bandwidth of graphs and understand its relation to matrices, we will calculate the bandwidth of some familiar graphs and find upper and lower bounds for the bandwidth of arbitrary graphs.

We can easily calculate the bandwidths, $B(K_n)$ and $B(C_n)$, of K_n and C_n.

Example 7   What is $B(K_n)$ and $B(C_n)$?

Solution: Clearly $B(K_n) = n - 1$ since no matter what map $f : V(K_n) \rightarrow V(P_n)$ we consider, the two vertices mapped to 1 and n are joined by an edge, showing that $\text{dil}(f) = n - 1$. Since this is true for any map f, the smallest possible dilation is $n - 1$ and thus $B(K_n) = n - 1$.

To find $B(C_n)$, we can first show that $B(C_n) > 1$ (this is left to the reader). We can also show that $B(C_n) \leq 2$ by finding a map $f : V(C_n) \rightarrow V(P_n)$ with $\text{dil}(f) = 2$. This can be done by numbering the "left" half of C_n with the odd integers from 1 to n or $n-1$ (depending on whether n is odd or even respectively) in increasing order as we proceed counterclockwise around C_n, and numbering the "right" half with the even integers from 2 to n or $n-1$ (depending on whether n is even or odd respectively) in increasing order proceeding clockwise, starting from the vertex at clockwise distance one from the vertex numbered 1. This is illustrated in Figure 4. Since $1 < B(C_n) \le 2$, it follows that $B(C_n) = 2$. □

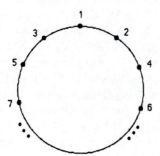

Figure 4.   An optimal numbering of C_n showing that $B(C_n) = 2$.

Example 8   What is is the bandwidth $B(K_{m,n})$ of $K_{m,n}$ where $m \le n$?

Solution: We will show that $B(K_{m,n}) = m - 1 + \lceil n/2 \rceil$, where $m \le n$.

We first show the upper bound $B(K_{m,n}) \le m - 1 + \lceil n/2 \rceil$ by constructing a map f for which $\text{dil}(f) = m - 1 + \lceil n/2 \rceil$. Let A and B be the disjoint sets of sizes m and n respectively defining the partition of the vertices of $K_{m,n}$ into two sets. We map $\lfloor n/2 \rfloor$ of the vertices in B to the integers $1, 2, \ldots, \lfloor n/2 \rfloor$, we then map all vertices in A to the integers $\lfloor n/2 \rfloor + 1, \ldots, \lfloor n/2 \rfloor + m$, and finally we map the remaining $\lceil n/2 \rceil$ vertices of B to the integers $\lfloor n/2 \rfloor + m + 1, \ldots, m + n$. With this map we see that the edge of $K_{m,n}$ that is stretched the longest is the one joining the vertex of A mapped to $\lfloor n/2 \rfloor + 1$ to the vertex of B mapped to $m + n$. This stretch is by definition the dilation of this map, and it has length $m - 1 + \lceil n/2 \rceil$.

We now prove the lower bound $B(K_{m,n}) \ge m - 1 + \lceil n/2 \rceil$. Let f be any numbering of $V(K_{m,n})$ by the integers $1, 2, \ldots, m + n$. Let m_1 and M_1 be the minimum and maximum of the set $f(A)$, and let m_2 and M_2 be the minimum and maximum of the set $f(B)$. Now at least one of the inequalities $m_2 \le M_1$ or $m_1 \le M_2$ holds, so that at least one of the intervals $[m_2, M_1]$ or $[m_1, M_2]$ is well defined. Then among either the one or the two intervals that are in this way defined, at least one must contain at least half the vertices in the set $f(B)$. This interval by its definition must also contain all the integers in the set $f(A)$. Since the first and last integers of this interval correspond to points on opposite sides of $K_{m,n}$, it follows that $\text{dil}(f)$ is at least the length of this interval. But this length is clearly at least $\lceil |f(B)|/2 \rceil + |f(A)| - 1 = \lceil n/2 \rceil + m - 1$. □

Example 9   Figure 5 shows the optimal numbering of $K_{4,4}$ given by the example.   □

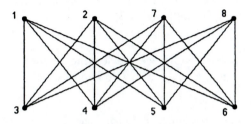

Figure 5.   An optimal numbering of $K_{4,4}$.

We will now derive some bounds on $B(G)$ in terms of other graph parameters. Before giving these bounds, we might well ask why we should be interested in such bounds. The reason is that up to now we have not stated a general procedure for computing $B(G)$ for an arbitrary graph G on n vertices. This is because there is no known procedure for doing this other than attempting all $n!$ possible maps $f : V(G) \rightarrow V(P_n)$, which is not a very appetizing prospect. In this light we can see that bounds for $B(G)$ which are easy to compute would be very welcome. For many graphs certain graph parameters can be easily computed, and in such cases the bounds on $B(G)$ which we will find are then also easy to compute.

The graph parameters we will use for our bounds are the number of vertices n, the number of edges q, the connectivity κ, the independence number β, and the diameter D.

Definition 3   We define the *connectivity* $\kappa(G)$, for a connected graph G, to be the smallest number of vertices whose removal from G (together with the removal of all edges incident on these vertices) leaves a disconnected graph. (By convention we take $\kappa(K_n) = n - 1$ and $\kappa(G) = 0$ for a disconnected graph G.)

The *independence number* $\beta(G)$ is the maximum number of vertices in any set S of vertices of G with the property that no two vertices in S are joined by an edge. (A set S with this property is called an *independent* set in G.)

The *diameter* $D(G)$ is the maximum distance between any two vertices of G.   □

Example 10   For the graph of Figure 1 we have $n = 8$, $q = 13$, $\kappa = 2$, $\beta = 3$, and $D = 3$. We have $\kappa = 2$ because the removal of the set $\{e, y\}$ of size 2 leaves a disconnected graph while the removal of any single vertex leaves the graph still connected.

We have $\beta = 3$ since there is an independent set $\{x, e, y\}$ of size 3 but no independent set of size 4 or greater.

Finally, we have $D = 3$ since the maximum distance between any two vertices is 3 (for example, $\text{dist}(x, y) = 3$). $\qquad \square$

The bounds on bandwidth we are looking for are based on two simple observations we will make in the next two lemmas.

Lemma 1   If G is a subgraph of H with the same number of vertices as H, i.e. $|V(G)| = |V(H)|$, then $q(G) \le q(H)$, $\kappa(G) \le \kappa(H)$, and $\beta(G) \ge \beta(H)$. $\qquad \blacksquare$

The reader should verify this. To see that the hypothesis $|V(G)| = |V(H)|$ is necessary, the reader is invited to find an example of a subgraph G of some graph H with $|V(G)| < |V(H)|$ for which $\kappa(G) > \kappa(H)$.

The second observation requires some notation. For any graph H let H^k be the graph having the same vertex set as H in which two vertices are joined by an edge if and only if they are at distance at most k in H.

Example 11   Draw the graph P_5^2.

Solution: The graph P_5^2 is illustrated in Figure 6. We obtain it by starting with P_5 and then joining by an edge every pair of vertices x and y separated by a distance of 2; in other words, joining "every other" vertex on P_5. $\qquad \square$

Figure 6.   The graph P_5^2.

Lemma 2   Let G be a graph on n vertices. Then $B(G) \le k$ if and only if G is a subgraph of P_n^k.

Proof: Recall that if the bandwidth of G satisfies $B(G) \le k$, then the vertices of G can be numbered with the integers 1 through n in such a way that for any edge $\{x, y\}$ the numbers given to x and y differ by at most k. Therefore this numbering is an embedding of G as a subgraph of P_n^k.

To establish the converse, we observe that an embedding f of G as a subgraph of P_n^k can also be viewed as a numbering satisfying $\text{dil}(f) \le k$. Hence $B(G) \le k$. $\qquad \blacksquare$

We are now ready to state our bounds on bandwidth.

Theorem 1   Let G be a graph having n vertices, q edges, connectivity κ, independence number β, and diameter D. Then

(i) $B(G) \geq n - \frac{1}{2}(1 + ((2n-1)^2 - 8q)^{1/2})$.

(ii) $B(G) \geq \kappa$.

(iii) $B(G) \geq \frac{n}{\beta} - 1$.

(iv) $B(G) \geq \frac{n-1}{D}$.

Proof: We first note that $\kappa(P_n^k) = k$, $\beta(P_n^k) = \lceil n/k \rceil$, and $|E(P_n^k)| = \frac{1}{2}k(2n - k - 1)$. We leave proofs of these facts as Exercise 4.

Now suppose $B(G) = k$.

To prove (i) we use Lemmas 1 and 2, obtaining

$$q \leq |E(P_n^k)| = \frac{1}{2}k(2n - k - 1).$$

Solving the quadratic inequality in k we obtain (i).

To prove (ii) we have similarly

$$\kappa(G) \leq \kappa(P_n^k) = k = B(G).$$

To prove (iii) we use Lemma 1 (as applied to β, with P_n^k playing the role of H) to get $\beta(G) \geq \beta(P_n^k)$. Exercise 4 asks the reader to prove that $\beta(P_n^k) = \lceil n/k \rceil$ and the right hand side is at least n/k. Hence (iii) follows.

To prove (iv), consider any numbering f of G with the integers $1, 2, \ldots, n$. Let $x = f^{-1}(1)$ and $y = f^{-1}(n)$. Clearly there is a path $x = x_0, x_1, x_2, \ldots, x_t = y$ in G from x to y of length $t \leq D$. The image of this path under f starts at 1 and ends at n. By the pigeonhole principle there must be an i such that

$$|f(x_i) - f(x_{i-1})| \geq \frac{n-1}{t} \geq \frac{n-1}{D}.$$

Thus dil$(f) \geq (n-1)/D$, and part (iv) follows.   ■

We remark that the simple lower bound in part (iv) of the previous theorem actually gives us the exact bandwidth in some important classes of graphs, as described in Theorem 2, which follows. Let T_k be the complete binary tree of k levels. Thus, T_k has a root at level 1, and 2^{i-1} vertices at level i for $i \leq k$.

Theorem 2   The bandwidth of T_k $(k \geq 1)$ is given by

$$B(T_k) = \left\lceil \frac{2^{k-1} - 1}{k - 1} \right\rceil.$$

Proof: Observe first that T_k has $2^k - 1$ vertices, and has diameter $2k - 2$. Hence $B(T_k) \geq \left\lceil \frac{2^{k-1}-1}{k-1} \right\rceil$ by part (iv) of Theorem 1. To prove that equality holds we can construct a numbering of T_k with dilation $\left\lceil \frac{2^{k-1}-1}{k-1} \right\rceil$. We leave this construction as a challenging problem for the reader.   ∎

Example 12   Figure 7 shows a numbering of T_4 with dilation 3. This numbering is optimal by Theorem 2.   □

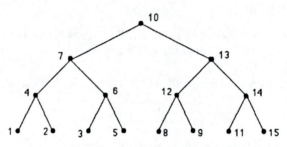

Figure 7.   An optimal numbering of T_4.

A little bit of thought gives a stronger lower bound than (iv) which is nonetheless based on the same idea. Define the **density** of a connected graph H to be

$$\text{den}(H) = \max \left\{ \left\lceil \frac{|V(G)| - 1}{D(G)} \right\rceil : G \text{ a connected subgraph of } H \right\}$$

where $D(G)$ denotes the diameter of a graph G.

Example 13   Calculate the density of the graph C shown in Figure 8.

Solution: Consider the subgraph G of C consisting of vertex 7 together with all its neighbors. For this G we have $\left\lceil \frac{|V(G)|-1}{D(G)} \right\rceil = 4$, and no other subgraph has a larger such ratio. Therefore $\text{den}(C) = 4$.   □

To get a feeling for $\text{den}(H)$, notice first that for any subgraph G of H the ratio $\left\lceil \frac{|V(G)|-1}{D(G)} \right\rceil$ measures how tightly packed or "dense" G is in the sense of packing in a number of vertices within a given diameter. Thus, although H may be dense in some parts and less dense in others, $\text{den}(H)$ measures the densest that H can be anywhere. Notice that when G is a subgraph of H we have $B(G) \leq B(H)$, while $B(G)$ is itself bounded below as in part (iv) of Theorem 1. We can in fact show the following.

Lemma 3   For any graph H, we have $B(H) \geq \text{den}(H)$.   ∎

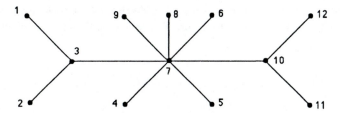

Figure 8.   A caterpillar C, and an optimal numbering of it.

It is now interesting to see that just as the trivial lower bound (d) is the actual value of the bandwidth for a natural class of graphs, the more general lower bound of Lemma 3 is the actual value of bandwidth for an additional (and also natural) class of graphs. Recall that a tree T is called a **caterpillar** if it contains a path such that every vertex not on the path is adjacent to some vertex on the path.

Theorem 3   For any caterpillar C we have $B(C) = \text{den}(C)$.   ■

We omit the proof here, though one can be found in [11] or [1] as a consequence of an algorithm for computing the bandwidth of any caterpillar.

Example 14   A caterpillar C, together with an optimal numbering of C, is shown in Figure 8. We saw in Example 13 that $\text{den}(C) = 4$. By Lemma 3 we have $B(C) \geq 4$, while the numbering given in the figure has dilation 4. It follows that $B(C) = 4 = \text{den}(C)$ (as claimed by Theorem 3).   □

Before leaving bandwidth, we mention a widely used algorithm for approximating $B(G)$ for arbitrary graphs G. It is called a "level algorithm" since it numbers the vertices of G by levels. Specifically, we begin by choosing a root v of G. Now let S_i be the set of vertices in G at distance i from v (we think of S_i as being "level i" of G). Now the algorithm lets $f(v) = 1$. Then it numbers the neighbors of v consecutively using the numbers 2 through $|S_1| + 1$, and the vertices at distance 2 from v consecutively using $|S_1| + 2$ through $|S_1| + |S_2| + 1$, etc. In general, the algorithm numbers the vertices in any given level with consecutive integers, with level i coming before level j if $i < j$. In other words, the algorithm maps S_i to the integers $|\cup_{t \leq i-1} S_t| + 2$ through $|\cup_{t \leq i} S_t| + 1$. Note that the resulting dilation is at most twice the size of the largest level S_i since edges of G can only run between successive levels.

Example 15   Figure 9 illustrates a numbering of a graph produced by the level algorithm. We see that there are five levels, and the vertices within each level are numbered consecutively.   □

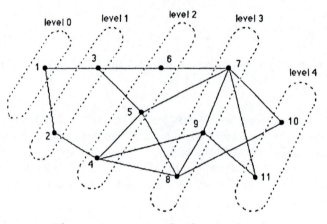

Figure 9.   A numbering by levels.

How good is this algorithm ? That is, how close to the actual bandwidth is the dilation of the numbering produced by the level algorithm ? The following example (taken from [10]) shows that this algorithm performs badly on at least some examples. First we need some notation (similar to the "big O") on growth of functions.

Definition 4   For two functions $f(n)$ and $g(n)$, we write

$$f(n) = \Omega(g(n))$$

if $f(n) \geq Kg(n)$ for some constant K when n is sufficiently large. We also write

$$f(n) = \theta(g(n))$$

to signify that $f(n) = \Omega(g(n))$ and $f(n) = O(g(n))$.   □

We see then that while $f = O(g(n))$ means that f is bounded above by a constant times g for n sufficiently large, the notation $f(n) = \Omega(g(n))$ means that f is bounded below by a constant times g for n sufficiently large and $f(n) = \theta(g(n))$ means that f is bounded both above and below by constants times g (the constant for the upper bound being usually different than the constant for the lower bound).

Example 16   For each integer $n \geq 1$ we construct a tree $L(n)$ as follows. Start with a path P_{2^n} on 2^n vertices. Now attach a path on 2^{n-1} vertices to the 2^{n-1}st vertex of P from the left. Then attach a path of 2^{n-2} vertices to the $2^{n-1} + 2^{n-2}$st vertex of P from the left, a path of 2^{n-3} vertices to the $2^{n-1} + 2^{n-2} + 2^{n-3}$st vertex of P from the left, etc. The tree $L(4)$ is illustrated in Figure 10. Now choose the leftmost vertex of P, call it v, as the root of $L(n)$ for the level algorithm. Observe that there are $n + 1$ vertices at distance $2^n - 1$ from v, and n vertices at distance $2^n - 2$ from v; that is, $|S_{2^n-1}| = n + 1$ and $|S_{2^n-2}| = n$. Also, every vertex of S_{2^n-1} is joined to some vertex of S_{2^n-2} by an edge. Hence any level algorithm with v as root will produce a numbering f of $L(n)$ such that

$$\text{dil}(f) \geq |S_{2^n-1}| = n + 1 = \Omega(\log|L(n)|).$$

On the other hand it can be shown that $B(L(n)) = 2$ for all n. Thus there is a gap between $B(L(n)) = 2$ and the estimate $\Omega(\log|L(n)|)$ for $B(L(n))$ proposed by the level algorithm that grows without bound as n approaches infinity. ☐

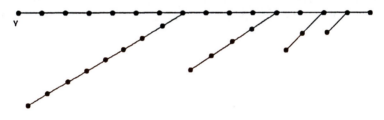

Figure 10. The tree $L(4)$. A level algorithm with v as root performs poorly.

Dilation Involving Other Pairs of Graphs

Let us now consider briefly the parameter $B(G, H)$ for graphs H other than just the path. Because cycles occur so frequently in graph theory we will first look at $B(C_n, H)$ where H is any connected graph on n vertices. Along the way we will find an interesting way of computing an upper bound on $B(C_n, T)$ where T is any tree on n vertices. Also because of its importance in circuit layout design on computer chips, we will study $B(G, G_2)$ where G is any graph and G_2 is the two-dimensional grid graph (to be defined later).

Our first result is perhaps surprising because of its constant upper bound applicable to a large class of graphs H.

Theorem 4   Let H be any connected graph on n vertices. Then $B(C_n, H) \leq 3$ where C_n denotes the cycle on n vertices. ∎

This result is found in [12]. We will sketch here the construction behind the proof because of its interesting algorithmic nature. First, however, we need to understand a connection between $B(Q, G_1)$ and $B(Q, G_2)$ when G_1 and G_2 are two graphs related in a special way, and Q is some third graph.

Lemma 4   Suppose that G_1 is a subgraph of a graph G_2 having the same number of vertices as G_2. If Q is a third graph with $|V(Q)| \leq |V(G_1)|$, then $B(Q, G_2) \leq B(Q, G_1)$.

Proof: Any map $f : Q \to G_1$ can also be viewed as a map $f' : Q \to G_2$, and we have $\text{dil}(f') \leq \text{dil}(f)$ since G_2 has all the edges which G_1 has, and possibly more. Now if we take $f : Q \to G_1$ to be a map with smallest possible dilation $B(Q, G_1)$, then since $B(Q, G_2)$ is the smallest possible dilation of any map from Q to G_2 (possibly even smaller than $\text{dil}(f')$) we get

$$B(Q, G_2) \leq \text{dil}(f') \leq \text{dil}(f) = B(Q, G_1). \qquad \blacksquare$$

Now we know that any connected graph H on n vertices has a spanning tree; that is, a subgraph T which is a tree on n vertices. If we apply Lemma 4 with C_n, H, and T playing the roles of Q, G_2, and G_1 respectively, then we get $B(C_n, H) \leq B(C_n, T)$. Therefore, if we could show that $B(C_n, T) \leq 3$ for any tree on n vertices, then Theorem 4 would be proved. This amounts to showing that there is a map $f : C_n \to T$ such that $\text{dil}(f) \leq 3$.

The following is an algorithm for constructing an embedding $f : C_n \to T$ into any tree T on n vertices satisfying $\text{dil}(f) \leq 3$. We denote the vertices of C_n by $1, 2, \ldots, n$ indexed in cyclic order. Given a root vertex $r \in T$ we let

$$\text{level}(x) = \text{dist}_T(r, x) \text{ for any } x \in T.$$

We will also refer to a depth first search of T as a DFS of T (See, for example, Section 8.5 of *Discrete Mathematics and Its Applications*, Second Edition, by Kenneth H. Rosen.)

We first describe this algorithm informally. We imagine walking through the vertices of T in the order of a DFS, and constructing our map f as we go. Suppose that we have so far mapped the first $i-1$ vertices $\{1, 2, \ldots, i-1\}$ of C_n to T, and we are now located at the vertex $f(i-1)$ of T. Our task is to decide how to map vertex i; that is, what vertex of T should be chosen as $f(i)$. We call a vertex of T "used" if it is $f(t)$ for some t where $1 \leq t \leq i-1$; that is, if it has been used as an image of the partially constructed map f. The algorithm moves to the first vertex of T following $f(i-1)$ (in the DFS) which is unused — call this vertex v. We must now decide whether to use v as $f(i)$. How do we make this decision? The answer depends on whether level(v) is even or odd. If level(v) is even then we use v; that is, we let $f(i) = v$. If level(v) is odd, skip v and continue walking on the DFS to an unused child of v, if such a child exists,

ALGORITHM 1.   Cycle-Tree.

procedure *cycle-tree* $(T$: a tree on n vertices)
choose a vertex $v_1 \in T$ as a root of T
$f(1) := v_1$
$S_1 := \{v_1\}$
order the vertices of T according to a DFS of T starting at
    the root v_1
for $i := 2$ **to** n
begin
{We assume that $f(1), f(2), \ldots, f(i-1)$ have been defined,
with values $v_1, v_2, \ldots, v_{i-1}$, respectively, and that $S_{i-1} = \{v_1, v_2, \ldots, v_{i-1}\}$.}
    $z :=$ the first vertex following v_{i-1} in the DFS such that
        $z \notin S_{i-1}$
    if level(z) is even **then** $v_i := z$
        else {level(z) is odd}
        if all children of z lie in S_{i-1} **then** $v_i := z$
        else $v_i :=$ the first child of z in the order of the DFS that
            is not in S_{i-1}
    $f(i) := v_i$
    $S_i := S_{i-1} \cup \{v_i\}$
end
{The output is $f(1) = v_1, f(2) = v_2, \ldots, f(n) = v_n$.}

and repeat the procedure. If all the children of v have been used, then use v by letting $f(i) = v$.

Algorithm 1 gives this algorithm in pseudocode. The input will be a tree T on n vertices and its output will be a one-to-one map $f : C_n \to T$ satisfying dil$(f) \leq 3$.

Example 17   Figure 11 shows an embedding $f : C_{15} \to T_4$ of C_{15} into the level 4 complete binary tree produced by Algorithm Cycle-Tree such that dil$(f) = 3$. It is instructive to go through the steps the algorithm follows to produce this embedding.   □

We omit the proof that the embedding $f : C_n \to T$ produced by Algorithm Cycle-Tree indeed satisfies dil$(f) \leq 3$. The details can be found in [12].

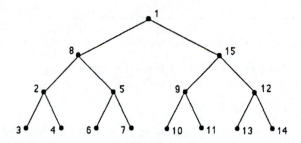

Figure 11. An embedding $F : C_{15} \to T_4$ produced by algorithm Cycle-Tree.

We now pass to a brief look at $B(T_r, G_2)$, where T_r is the level r complete binary tree, and G_2 is the infinite two-dimensional grid.

Definition 5   The *two dimensional grid* G_2 is the graph with vertices

$$V(G_2) = \{(x, y) : x \text{ and } y \text{ are integers}\}$$

and edges

$$E(G_2) = \{\{(x_1, y_1), (x_2, y_2)\} : |x_1 - x_2| + |y_1 - y_2| = 1\}. \qquad \Box$$

Thus, the vertices of G_2 are the lattice points in the plane (i.e., points with integer coefficients), and two lattice points are joined by an edge in G_2 when they are unit distance apart.

The grid graph G_2 is an especially important graph in applications. One of the commonly used interconnection networks, called the *mesh*, has the structure of a finite rectangle in G_2. (That is, the mesh is just an $m \times n$ subgrid of G_2 for some m and n.) Also, G_2 is useful in analyzing circuit layout on computer chips — but more on this later. For these reasons it is important to estimate $B(H, G_2)$ for various graphs H as a way of finding the communication delay when G_2 simulates H. Although this problem is difficult, we at least have a good lower bound for $B(T_r, G_2)$. We include the proof of this bound here because it is based on a very simple geometrical idea.

Theorem 5   The minimum possible dilation of any mapping of a complete binary tree on n vertices into the two-dimensional grid is bounded below by a constant times $\sqrt{n}/\log n$ when n is sufficiently large.

That is, we have

$$B(T_r, G_2) = \Omega(\sqrt{n}/\log n)$$

where $n = |T_r|$.

Proof: Let $f : T_r \rightarrow G_2$ be a one-to-one map, and let $d = \text{dil}(f)$. Also, let z be the root of T_r, that is, the vertex of degree 2 in T_r. Since every vertex of T_r is within distance $r - 1$ of z, it follows that every vertex in $f(T_r)$ can be found within distance (as measured in G_2) $d(r - 1)$ of $f(z)$, and hence within a circle or radius $d(r - 1)$ in the plane centered at $f(z)$. That is, we are saying that the entire image $f(T_r)$ must be contained in a circle C of radius $d(r - 1)$ in the plane centered at $f(z)$. Now this image consists of $|V(T_r)| = 2^r - 1$ lattice points, so C must contain at least $2^r - 1$ lattice points since it contains this image. But the number of lattice points contained within a circle in the plane is proportional to the area of that circle. Since the area of C is $\pi d^2(r - 1)^2$, it follows that $\pi d^2(r - 1)^2 \geq K(2^r - 1)$, for some constant K. Solving for d we get

$$d \geq \left(\frac{K(2^r - 1)}{\pi(r - 1)^2} \right)^{1/2} \geq L \frac{2^{r/2}}{r},$$

where L is some other constant (for example $L = K/(2\pi)$ will do). Now since $n = 2^r - 1$, we see that $2^{r/2}$ and r are proportional to $\sqrt{n}$ and $\log n$ (to the base 2) respectively. Therefore, we get

$$d = \Omega\left(\frac{2^{r/2}}{r} \right) = \Omega\left(\frac{\sqrt{n}}{\log n} \right),$$

and the theorem follows.   ■

It is remarkable that in fact this lower bound is, up to a constant factor, also an upper bound! That is, one can prove that $B(T_r, G_2) = O(\frac{\sqrt{n}}{\log n})$. Thus, the function $\sqrt{n}/\log n$ is, up to a constant factor, a correct estimate for $B(T_r, G_2)$. The proof of this, though requiring no special knowledge beyond the elements of graph theory, is still more complicated than the proof of Theorem 5. The interested reader may find it in [14], pp. 89–91.

Remembering that in applications we would only use a finite $m \times n$ subgrid of G_2 as an interconnection network, the reader may well wonder if one could get as good an upper bound for $B(T_r, H)$ as for $B(T_r, G_2)$ if H were a particularly small finite subgrid of G_2, say with just enough points to accommodate T_r. Intuitively, one would expect that being "hemmed in" by H would make it harder to find embeddings with small dilation than when we had as much of G_2 to work with as we wanted. We will return to this subject when we discuss the "area" of an embedding later. For now we try to be precise about relating the size of the target graph to the size of the domain graph in a graph embedding.

Definition 6   Consider a graph embedding $f : V(G) \rightarrow V(H)$. The *expansion* of f is $\exp(f) = |H|/|G|$.   □

Example 18   In Figure 12 the graph G on the left has 4 vertices while the graph H on the right has 7 vertices. Hence the map $f : V(G) \rightarrow V(H)$ satisfies $\exp(f) = 7/4$.   □

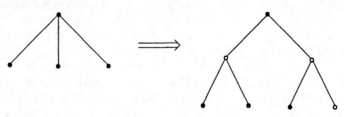

Figure 12.   Embedding complete ternary trees into complete binary trees.

Example 19   An example in which one extreme of this tradeoff can be easily seen is the embedding of complete ternary trees (i.e. 3-ary trees) into complete binary trees. Let $T(3)_r$ be the complete ternary tree with r levels, and thus $|T(3)_r| = (3^r - 1)/2$. The basic idea leading to an embedding $f : T(3)_r \rightarrow T_{2r}$ with $\text{dil}(f) = 2$ is indicated in Figure 12. The intended pattern is to embed level i of $T(3)_r$ into level $2i - 1$ of T_{2r} in the indicated manner for all $i \geq 1$. The fact that $\text{dil}(f) = 2$ is then easy to see. But what is $\exp(f)$?

Since T_{2r} has $2^{2r} - 1$ vertices, when we form the required ratio we get

$$\exp(f) = 2\left(\frac{2^{2r} - 1}{3^r - 1}\right) = \theta\left(\frac{2^{2r} - 1}{3^r - 1}\right) = \theta\left(\left(\frac{4}{3}\right)^r\right).$$

Now, letting $n = |T(3)_r|$, we should try to express the last quantity on the right as a function of n. One way to do this is to ask ourselves what power, call it α, we must raise n to in order to get this last quantity. We can answer this by working backwards. Writing $n^\alpha = \theta((\frac{4}{3})^r)$ and substituting $(3^r - 1)/2$ for n, we get $(3^r)^\alpha = \theta((\frac{4}{3})^r)$ (having absorbed the factor of 2 in our θ). Now taking the rth root of both sides, we can solve for α by taking logarithms and the result is $\alpha = \log_3(4/3)$. In conclusion, we have

$$\exp(f) = \theta(n^\alpha),$$

where $\alpha = \log^3(4/3)$.   □

Thus, in order to achieve a constant dilation of 2, we have paid the heavy price of expanding by a factor that grows as a fixed positive power of n. On the other hand, what price in dilation would we pay if we insisted on constant expansion? The fascinating answer is provided in [8] where it is shown that any embedding of a complete ternary tree into a complete binary tree with expansion less than 2 must have dilation $\Omega(\log \log \log n)$. The proof of this is beyond the scope of this chapter, but the interested reader is referred to [8] to see what is involved.

Min Sum and Cutwidth

In applications where a circuit (or graph) G is for automation purposes mapped on a path, the wires joining vertices of G must be placed on channels or tracks running parallel to the path. No two wires are allowed to overlap on the same track. Since the number of different tracks needed for the mapping essentially determines the area of the circuit layout (where the area is the product of the number of tracks and the length of the path), we would like to minimize the number of tracks. One way of doing this is to use each track "as much as possible". This amounts to constructing our map f in such a way that the edges of G, when drawn between points on the image path, overlap as little as possible.

We now express these ideas more precisely. Start with a one-to-one map $f : V(G) \to V(P_n)$ from G to the path on n vertices. For each interval $(i, i+1)$ of the "host" graph P_n we let cut(i) be the number of "guest" edges from G which pass over that interval; that is, we let

$$\text{cut}(i) = |\{\{f(x), f(y)\} : \{x, y\} \in E(G), f(x) \le i \text{ and } f(y) \ge i+1\}|.$$

Now we let value(f) be the maximum of cut(i) over all $1 \le i \le n - 1$. Thus, value(f) is the biggest overlap of edges that we have over any interval when we use the map f. Finally, we define the **cutwidth** of G, which is denoted $c(G)$, to be the smallest possible biggest overlap, taken over all possible maps f; that is,

$$c(G) = \min\{\text{value}(f) : f : V(G) \to V(P_n) \text{ a one-to-one map}\}.$$

Thus, $c(G)$ is proportional to the smallest area possible in a linear layout of G subject to the constraint that no two wires overlap in the same channel.

Example 20   In Figure 13 we illustrate a graph G with five vertices and two different maps from G to P_5. The second map has the smaller value; in fact it is easy to see that no map can have a smaller value; that is, $c(G) = 3$.   □

Another mapping problem which we will discuss follows immediately from the idea of dilation. When studying the dilation of a map $f : V(G) \to V(H)$ we are finding the worst possible time delay, over all edges in G, caused by f; that is, we are finding dil(f). It is also natural to consider the *average* time delay caused by f, since although dil(f) might be large it could happen that f might still be a "good" map if it has small time delay on a large fraction of all the edges of G. We would naturally calculate the average by adding up the individual delays and dividing by the total number of edges in G, and then we could ask for the smallest possible average over all possible maps f.

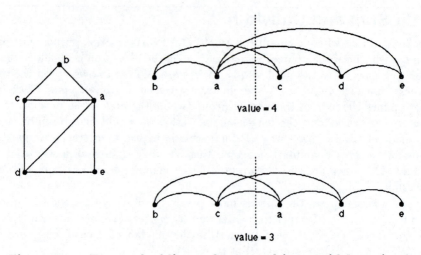

Figure 13. Two embeddings; the second is cutwidth optimal.

We now state all this precisely. Again we start with a one-to-one map $f : V(G) \to V(H)$. Define

$$\text{sum}(f) = \sum_{\{x,y\} \in E(G)} \text{dist}_H(f(x), f(y)),$$

which is the sum of the individual delays. We won't bother here to divide by the number of edges in G to get the average delay, since this number does not depend on the map f and we could do the division later if we care to. Now the minimum average we are looking for (apart from delaying the division until later) is

$$S(G, H) = \min\{\text{sum}(f) : f \colon V(G) \to V(H) \text{ a one-to-one map}\}.$$

Thus we may think of $S(G, H)$ as being the best average dilation (or time delay) obtainable over all embeddings $f : G \to H$.

Example 21   Find $\text{sum}(f)$ and $\text{sum}(g)$ where f and g are the dilation 3 and dilation 2 numberings respectively of $K_4 - e$ shown in Figure 3.

Solution: The number on a vertex of $K_4 - e$ indicates the vertex of P_4 to which it is mapped. Thus, for each edge $\{x, y\}$ of $K_4 - e$ the term $\text{dist}_H(f(x), f(y))$, with $H = P_4$, is just the difference between the numbers given to x and y. So, to calculate $\text{sum}(f)$ or $\text{sum}(g)$ we just need to add these differences over all edges in $K_4 - e$. Carrying out this addition we get $\text{sum}(f) = 8$ and $\text{sum}(g) = 7$.

□

Some elementary results on the min sum and cutwidth problems are summarized in the following examples. We abbreviate $S(G, P_n)$ by $S(G)$.

Example 22   What are $S(P_n)$, $S(C_n)$, $S(K_{1,n})$, and $S(K_n)$?

Solution: We have $S(P_n) = n - 1$, $S(C_n) = 2(n - 1)$, $S(K_{1,n}) = \lfloor n^2/4 \rfloor$, and $S(K_n) = n(n^2 - 1)$. (See Exercise 9.)   □

Example 23   What are $c(P_n)$, $c(C_n)$, $c(K_{1,n})$, and $c(K_n)$?

Solution: We have $c(P_n) = 1$, $c(C_n) = 2$, $c(K_{1,n}) = \lfloor n/2 \rfloor$, and $c(K_n) = \lfloor n^2/4 \rfloor$. (See Exercise 11.)   □

Some values for S and c are difficult to prove. Values of $S(T_k)$ and $c(T_{r,k})$ (where $T_{r,k}$ is the complete k-level r-ary tree) have been computed. See [4] and [9].

Although the computation of both $c(G)$ and $S(G)$ is in general difficult, polynomial time algorithms have been developed for computing $c(T)$ and $S(T)$ when T is a tree (see [15], [7], [6]). These results are well outside the scope of this chapter, but the reader is encouraged to study them in order to gain an appreciation for algorithms in graph theory.

The analogue of Theorem 4 for min sum is the following.

Theorem 6   [12] Let H be any connected graph on n vertices. Then

$$\frac{S(C_n, H)}{|E(H)|} \leq 2 - \frac{2}{n}.$$

The map $f : C_n \to H$ which provides the upper bound for $S(C_n, H)$ of Theorem 6 is the one produced in the algorithm Cycle-Tree (given earlier) applied to any spanning tree of H.

Area

In this section we discuss the area of a graph embedding into G_2, the 2-dimensional grid. Results in this subject have obvious applications to the layout of circuits on computer chips, these chips being wafers with vertical and horizontal tracks etched into them along which connections between circuit elements must run. Thus, we let H be an arbitrary graph, and we consider a one-to-one map $f : H \to G_2$. To make our analysis realistic, we apply generally accepted assumptions on how wires run along the tracks of the chip. These assumptions constitute the so called "Thompson grid model" [13]. Specifically, we view f not only as a map of vertices, but also as a map of the edges of H to paths in G_2, these paths of course running along the vertical and horizontal tracks of G_2. We also require that distinct edges e_1 and e_2 of H have images $f(e_1)$ and $f(e_2)$ which are not allowed to run along the same track (vertical or horizontal) of G_2 for any distance, although they may cross at a point when one image is running horizontally while the other is running vertically. A map satisfying these conditions is often called a *circuit layout* (with H being the electronic circuit).

Definition 7   The area $A(f)$ of an embedding $f : H \rightarrow G_2$ is the product of the number of rows and the number of columns of G_2 which contain any part of the layout $f(H)$.   □

Example 24   In Figure 14 we illustrate an embedding $f : K_4 - e \rightarrow G_2$ with area 6 (because we use 2 rows and 3 columns) and dilation 2, and an embedding $f : K_4 \rightarrow G_2$ with area 15 (because we use 3 rows and 5 columns) and dilation 8. Each unit segment in G_2 that is part of the layout has been labeled with the edge of the graph that runs along it. Notice that no two edges in the layout run along the same segment for any distance, though they may cross at the intersection points of the segments.

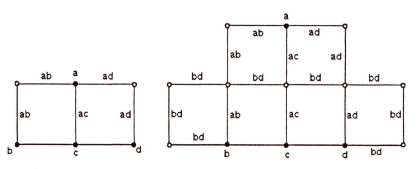

Figure 14.   Embeddings of $K_4 - e$ and K_4 in the grid G_2.

In chip manufacturing we are concerned with producing chips having as small an area as possible. Therefore, given a graph H, we are interested in finding a map $f : H \rightarrow G_2$ for which $A(f)$ is as small as possible.

In order to get a feeling for what is involved in minimizing area, we will consider here in some detail the relatively simple case when H is a complete binary tree T_{2k+1} on $2k + 1$ levels and height $2k$. We use an embedding called the *H-tree layout* because it follows a recursive pattern based on the letter H.

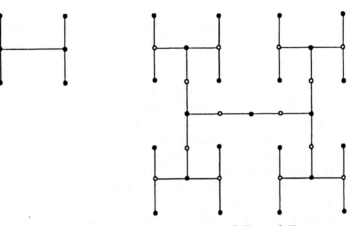

Figure 15.   *H*-tree layouts of T_3 and T_5.

We illustrate *H*-tree layouts of T_3 and T_5 in Figure 15. In general our goal is to embed T_{2k+1} into a square S in G_2 of dimensions $(2^{k+1} - 1) \times (2^{k+1} - 1)$.

An informal description of how this is done is as follows. We map the degree 2 node z of T_{2k+1} to the middle of S. We now use the horizontal and vertical tracks of G_2 which meet at z to separate S into four quadrants, each quadrant being a square of dimensions $(2^k - 1) \times (2^k - 1)$. Now recursively map the four subtrees isomorphic to T_{2k-1} and rooted at the grandchildren of z to these four quadrants. Finally use one of the two tracks separating the quadrants as part of the T_3 which interconnects z, its children, and its grandchildren.

From this recursive description of the *H*-tree layout, and with Figure 15 as an aid, we can establish the following which gives a good embedding of T_{2k+1} into G_2 from the standpoint of both area and dilation.

Theorem 7   There is an *H*-tree layout $f : T_{2k+1} \twoheadrightarrow G_2$ with the following properties. Let $n = |T_{2k+1}|$.

   (i) $f(T_{2k+1})$ is contained in a square of dimensions $(2^{k+1} - 1) \times (2^{k+1} - 1)$.

   (ii) $A(f) = O(n)$.

   (iii) $\mathrm{dil}(f) = O(\sqrt{n}\,)$.

Proof: For (i) we observe that a side of S must have length one more than twice a side of the square containing the *H*-tree layout of T_{2k-1}. Since the latter has side length $2^k - 1$ by induction, it follows that S has side length $2(2^k - 1) + 1 = 2^{k+1} - 1$, as claimed.

For (ii) we note that the area is $A(f) = O(2^{2k})$ while $n = 2^{2k+1} - 1$. Hence it is easy to see that $A(f) = O(n)$.

For (iii), we can check that the longest image of an edge is the one joining z to one of its children. The path in S to which this edge is mapped has length one more than half the side length of one of the quadrants. Since this side length is $2^{k+1} - 1$, we get $\text{dil}(f) = 1 + O(2^k) = O(\sqrt{n})$.   ∎

It is natural to ask how well the H-tree layout does, using area and dilation as yardsticks. Clearly the area of $O(n)$ achieved is optimal up to a constant factor since any n-vertex graph must use $\Omega(n)$ area. As for dilation, we already know from Theorem 5 that any embedding $f : T_{2k+1} \to G_2$ (even without the constraints of the Thompson model) satisfies $\text{dil}(f) = \Omega(\sqrt{n}/\log n)$. Hence the dilation $O(\sqrt{n})$ achieved by the H-tree layout is at most a factor of $\log n$ from the smallest possible that the dilation could be.

Finally, what about graphs other than complete binary trees? It can be shown that any n-vertex binary tree can be laid out in area $O(n)$, and any n-vertex planar graph can be laid out in area $O(n \log^2 n)$. These results, and more general ones applying to any class of graphs having "$f(n)$ separators" for some suitable function f, are outside the scope of this chapter. The reader is referred to [14] for a good exposition, and to [2] for some recent results.

Suggested Readings

1. S. Assman, G. Peck, M.Syslo, and M.Zak, "The bandwidth of caterpillars with hairs of length 1 and 2", *SIAM J. Alg.   Discrete Methods*, 1981, pp. 387–391.

2. S. Bhatt and F. Leighton, "A framework for solving VLSI graph layout problems", *J. of Computer and System Sciences*, Vol. 28, No. 2, 1984, pp. 300–343.

3. P. Chinn, J. Chvatalova, A. Dewdney, and N. Gibbs, "The bandwidth problem for graphs and matrices — a survey", *J. of Graph Theory*, Vol. 6, 1982, pp. 223–254.

4. F. Chung, "A conjectured minimum valuation tree", Problems and Solutions in *SIAM Review*, Vol. 20, 1978, pp. 601–604.

5. F. Chung, "Labelings of Graphs", in *Selected Topics in Graph Theory 3*, eds.   L. Beineke and R. Wilson, Academic Press Ltd., London, 1988, pp. 151–168.

6. F. Chung, "On optimal linear arrangements of trees", *Computers and Mathematics with Applications*, Vol. 10, 1984, pp. 43–60.

7. M. Goldberg and I. Klipker, "Minimal placing of a line" (in Russian), Technical Report, Phsico-Technical Institute of Low Temperatures, Academy of Sciences of Ukrainian SSR, USSR, 1976.

8. J. Hong, K. Melhorn, and A. Rosenberg, "Cost trade-offs in graph embeddings, with applications", *Journal of the ACM*, Vol. 30, No. 4, 1983, pp. 709–728.

9. T. Lengauer, "Upper and lower bounds on the complexity of the min-cut linear arrangement problem on trees", *SIAM J. Alg. Discrete Methods*, Vol. 3, 1982, pp. 99–113.

10. F. Makedon and I. Sudborough, "Graph layout problems", *Surveys in Computer Science*, ed. H. Maurer, Bibliographisches Institut, Zurich, 1984, pp. 145–192.

11. Z. Miller, "The bandwidth of caterpillar graphs", *Congressus Numerantium*, Vol. 33, 1981, pp. 235–252.

12. A. Rosenberg and L. Snyder, "Bounds on the cost of data encodings", *Mathematical Systems Theory*, Vol. 12, 1978, pp. 9–39.

13. C. Thompson, "Area-time complexity for VLSI", *Eleventh Annual ACM Symposium on Theory of Computing*, 1979.

14. J. Ullman, *Computational Aspects of VLSI*, Computer Science Press, Rockville, Md., 1984.

15. M. Yannakakis, "A polynomial algorithm for the min cut linear arrangement of trees", *Journal of the ACM*, Vol. 32, 1985, pp. 950–959.

Exercises

1. Show that if a graph G has a vertex of degree k, then $B(G) \geq \lceil k/2 \rceil$.

2. Show that $B(K_4 - e) \geq 2$.

3. Find the bandwidth of the following graph.

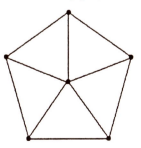

4. Show that
   a) $\kappa(P_n^k) = k$.   b) $\beta(P_n^k) = \lceil n/k \rceil$.
   c) $|E(P_n^k)| = \frac{1}{2}k(2n - k - 1)$.

5. Consider the following graph G. If f is a numbering of G obtained by a level algorithm with the indicated vertex v as the root, then what is the smallest that dil(f) can be? What is the largest that dil(f) can be for such an f?

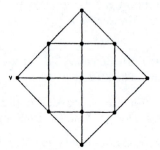

*6. Construct a sequence of graphs $\{H(n): n = 1, 2, 3, \ldots\}$ for which the estimate for $B(H(n))$ produced by the level algorithm differs from the true value of $B(H(n))$ by an amount that grows without bound as n approaches infinity no matter which vertex in $H(n)$ is chosen as a root. Hint: Use the graphs $L(n)$ described in the text by pasting them together somehow.

7. Use Algorithm Cycle-Tree to construct a dilation 3 map $f : C_{19} \rightarrow T$, where T is the tree in the following figure.

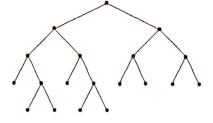

8. Construct layouts of K_5 and K_6 into G_2 (obeying the assumptions of the Thompson grid model) with the smallest area you can manage.

9. Show that
   a) $S(P_n) = n - 1$.   b) $S(C_n) = 2(n - 1)$.
   c) $S(K_{1,n}) = \lfloor n^2/4 \rfloor$.   d) $S(K_n) = n(n^2 - 1)$.

10. Show that if a graph G has a vertex of degree k, then $c(G) \geq \lceil k/2 \rceil$.

11. Show that
    a) $c(P_n) = 1$.   b) $c(C_n) = 2$.
    c) $c(K_{1,n}) = \lfloor n/2 \rfloor$.   d) $c(K_n) = \lfloor n^2/4 \rfloor$.

12. Consider the matrix

$$A = \begin{pmatrix} 0 & 0 & 0 & 1 & 1 & 1 \\ 0 & 0 & 0 & 1 & 1 & 1 \\ 0 & 0 & 0 & 1 & 1 & 1 \\ 1 & 1 & 1 & 0 & 0 & 0 \\ 1 & 1 & 1 & 0 & 0 & 0 \\ 1 & 1 & 1 & 0 & 0 & 0 \end{pmatrix},$$

which has a band of 5 diagonals above and below the main diagonal which enclose all the 1s.

a) Find a row and column permutation (the same permutation for both rows and columns) of A which results in a matrix A' requiring a band of only 4 such diagonals.

b) Find the graph $G(A)$, and show that $B(G(A)) = 4$.

13. Show that if a graph G on n vertices has a vertex of degree k with k even, then $S(G) \geq \frac{k}{2}(k + 2)$.

14. Show that if the level algorithm is applied to T_k (the complete binary tree on k levels with $2^k - 1$ vertices) with the degree 2 vertex as the root, then the biggest possible dilation that could result is $2^k - 2^{k-2} - 1$. What is the smallest value?

Computer Projects

1. Write a program which takes a tree T and produces a numbering of T with as small a dilation as you can manage. *Note*: Do not try to write a program which will calculate the exact smallest possible dilation numbering. There are theoretical reasons why such a program is likely to take much too long to run when the number of vertices in T is large. Instead of trying to write such a program, just develop some sensible heuristic idea and make it the foundation of your program.

2. Write a program which takes a tree T and produces a numbering f of T for which sum(f) is as small as you can manage.

3. Write a program which takes a tree T and produces a numbering f of T for which value(f) is as small as you can manage.

Note: In Projects 2 and 3, there are programs to calculate the smallest possible sum(f) and value(f) which are reasonably time efficient, but developing such a program is quite ambitious. Again, try to develop some sensible heuristic.

22

Graph Multicolorings

Author: Kenneth H. Rosen, AT&T Bell Laboratories.

Prerequisites: The prerequisites for this chapter are basic graph terminology and graph colorings. See, for example, Sections 7.1, 7.2 and 7.8 of *Discrete Mathematics and Its Applications*, Second Edition, by Kenneth H. Rosen.

Introduction

Graph coloring has been studied for many years and has been used in many different applications. In particular, graph colorings have been employed for over a hundred years to study map colorings. With each map we associate a graph — this graph has a vertex for each region of the map and an edge connecting two vertices if and only if the regions they represent share a common boundary. A coloring of the map so that no two regions with a common boundary have the same color corresponds to a coloring of the vertices of the associated graph so that no two adjacent vertices are assigned the same color. This traditional application of graph colorings has been one of the major factors in the development of graph theory.

However, there are many modern applications of graph colorings not involving maps. Some of these applications are task scheduling, meeting scheduling, maintenance scheduling, channel assignment for television stations, and frequency assignment for mobile telephones. To model variations of these applications we need various generalizations of graph colorings. In this chapter we will study these applications of graph colorings. We will make several different generalizations of graph colorings that are required to model variations of these problems.

Many of the generalizations of graph colorings that we will study in this chapter have been introduced and studied by Fred Roberts. More information about the topics covered, as well as the description of other applications, including traffic phasing and garbage collection, can be found in Roberts' survey article [5].

Applications of Graph Colorings

In this section we will describe a variety of applications of graph colorings. (Additional descriptions of these and other applications of graph colorings can be found in Section 7.8 of *Discrete Mathematics and Its Applications*, Second Edition, by Rosen, and in [4].)

Examination Scheduling   Consider the problem of scheduling 25 final examinations in the Computer Science Department of a college. The examinations need to be scheduled so that no student has two final exams at the same time and no professor has final exams for two different courses at the same time. To model this problem, we build a graph where a vertex is associated to each course and an edge connects two vertices if the courses they represent cannot have final examinations at the same time. In a coloring of the associated graph, colors represent time slots. In order to minimize the number of time slots needed to schedule all exams, we find the chromatic number of this graph (i.e., the minimum number of colors needed to color the vertices so no adjacent vertices have the same color).

Task Scheduling   Consider the problem of scheduling different tasks, some of which cannot be done at the same time. For example, a automobile repair shop may have 15 cars to repair, but only one machine used in a particular type of repair. To model this problem, we build a graph where a vertex is associated with each task and an edge connects two vertices if the tasks they represent are incompatible, that is, they cannot be done at the same time. For example, vertices representing car repairs that require the use of the same machine are joined by an edge. We use colors to represent time periods. Assuming that all tasks take the same time, to minimize the total time to complete the tasks we find the smallest number of colors needed to color the vertices of this graph. We find the chromatic number of this graph to minimize the time required to complete the tasks.

Meeting Scheduling Consider the problem of scheduling the meetings of different committees where some individuals serve on more than one committee. Clearly, no two committees can meet at the same time if they have a common member. Analogous to exam scheduling, to model this problem we build a graph where a vertex is associated to each committee and an edge connects two vertices if the committees they represent have a common member. In a coloring of this graph, colors represent time slots. We find the chromatic number of this graph to schedule all meetings in the least time.

Maintenance Scheduling A facility with repair bays is used to maintain a fleet of vehicles. Each vehicle is scheduled for regular maintenance during a time period and is assigned a repair bay. Two vehicles cannot be assigned the same space if they are scheduled for maintenance at overlapping times. To model this problem, we build a graph with vertices representing the vehicles where an edge connects two vertices if the vehicles they represent are assigned the same space for repair. We find the chromatic number of the associated graph to schedule maintenance for all vehicles using the smallest number of periods.

Channel or Frequency Assignment Two stations (radio, television, mobile telephone, etc.) that interfere, because of proximity, geography, power or some other factor, cannot be assigned the same channel. To model this problem we build a graph with vertices that represent the stations with an edge connecting two vertices if the stations they represent interfere. We find the chromatic number of the associated graph to assign frequencies to all stations using the smallest number of channels. (This mo del was first described by E. Gilbert in 1972 in unpublished work at Bell Laboratories.)

Many complications arise in these and other applications that make it necessary to apply generalizations of graph colorings. Using variations of some of these applications as motivation, we will now introduce several ways to generalize the notion of a graph coloring.

Graph Multicolorings

Suppose that there are two parts of each final examination at a college. Each part of an exam takes a morning or an afternoon. Therefore, we need to assign two time periods to each final. To model this problem, we need to assign *two* colors to each vertex of the associated graph, where each color represents a time period (such as Tuesday afternoon), so that no adjacent vertices are assigned a common color. This means that no student or faculty member is required to be at two final exams at the same time.

Consider the following variation of the channel assignment problem. Suppose we need to assign three channels to each station. For instance, backup channels may be needed when a channel is unusable; a station may need three channels to simultaneously broadcast three different programs; or a mobile radio station may need three different channels for teleconferencing. To model this problem, we need to assign *three* colors to each vertex of the associated graph, where each color represents a channel, so that no adjacent vertices are assigned a common color. This means that no stations that interfere will broadcast over the same channel.

These applications lead to the following definition.

Definition 1   An assignment of n colors to each vertex in a graph $G = (V, E)$ is called an *n-tuple coloring* or *multicoloring* if no two adjacent vertices are assigned a common color.   □

We often want to minimize the total number of colors used in an n-tuple coloring. For instance, we want to schedule two-part final examinations using the fewest periods. Similarly, we want to assign three channels to each station using the fewest channels.

Definition 2   The *n-tuple chromatic number* of a graph G, denoted by $\chi_n(G)$, is the minimum number of colors required for an n-tuple coloring of G.   □

For every graph G we have $\chi_n(G) \leq n\chi(G)$, where $\chi(G)$ is the chromatic number of G. To see this, note that we can construct an n-tuple coloring of G from a coloring of G by associating to each color n distinct new colors, with no new color associated to more than one of the original colors. As the next two examples illustrate, the equality $\chi_n(G) = n\chi(G)$ holds for some graphs, while for other graphs $\chi_n(G) < n\chi(G)$. Later we will see that equality holds for a large class of graphs.

Example 1   Find $\chi_2(K_4)$ and $\chi_3(K_4)$, where K_4 is the complete graph on four vertices.

Solution: Since every vertex of K_4 is adjacent to every other vertex, no color can be used more than once. Hence, a total of $4n$ colors are required for an n-tuple coloring of K_4. It therefore follows that $\chi_2(K_4) = 2 \cdot 4 = 8$ and $\chi_3(K_4) = 3 \cdot 4 = 12$.   □

Example 2   Find $\chi_2(C_4)$ and $\chi_2(C_5)$, where C_n is the n-cycle graph.

Solution: As Figure 1 shows, we can construct a 2-tuple coloring of C_4 using four colors. Since we must use at least four colors so that two colors are assigned to each of two adjacent vertices, no fewer than four colors can be used. Hence $\chi_2(C_4) = 4$.

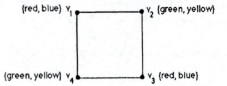

(red, blue) v_1 — v_2 (green, yellow)

(green, yellow) v_4 — v_3 (red, blue)

Figure 1.   A 2-tuple coloring of C_4 using four colors.

In Figure 2 we display a 2-tuple coloring of C_5 using just five colors (rather than six colors that would be used if we started with a coloring of C_5 and then assigned two new colors to each of the original colors in this coloring). Since it is impossible to construct a 2-tuple coloring of C_5 using four colors (as the reader can easily demonstrate), it follows that $\chi_2(C_5) = 5$.   □

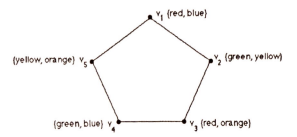

v_1 (red, blue)

(yellow, orange) v_5 v_2 (green, yellow)

(green, blue) v_4 v_3 (red, orange)

Figure 2.   A 2-tuple coloring of C_5 using five colors.

Although $\chi_n(G)$ may be less than $n\chi(G)$, there is an important class of graphs for which these quantities are equal. Before describing these graphs, we first give some definitions.

Definition 3   A *clique* in a graph G is a subgraph of G that is a complete graph.   □

Example 3   Find all cliques with four or more vertices in the graph G in Figure 3.

Solution: The subgraph containing the vertices a, b, d, and f, and the edges in G connecting these vertices, is a clique with four vertices. Inspection of the graph shows that there are no larger cliques and no other cliques with four vertices.   □

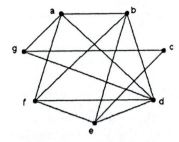

Figure 3.   The graph G.

Before describing a class of graphs for which the n-tuple chromatic number is n times the chromatic number, we need the following definition.

Definition 4   The *clique number* of a graph G, denoted by $\omega(G)$, is the largest integer k such that G contains a clique of k vertices.   □

Example 4   Find the clique number of the graph G in Figure 3.

Solution: By Example 3 we see that $\omega(G)$, the clique number of G, is 4 since G contains a clique of this size but no clique of a larger size.   □

The chromatic number of a graph must be at least as large as the clique number; that is, $\omega(G) \le \chi(G)$. This is true since any coloring of G will require $\omega(G)$ colors for the vertices in the largest clique. The other vertices in G may require additional colors. The special class of graphs we will be interested in have their clique numbers equal to their chromatic numbers, as described in the following definition.

Definition 5   A graph G is called *weakly γ-perfect* if its chromatic number equals its clique number, that is, if $\omega(G) = \chi(G)$.   □

Example 5   Is the graph G is Figure 3 weakly γ-perfect?

Solution: Coloring the vertices a and e red, b and c blue, d green, and f and g yellow produces a 4-coloring of G. Since any coloring of G uses at least four colors (since a, b, d, and f form a complete subgraph), we conclude that $\chi(G) = 4$. By Example 4 we know that $\omega(G) = 4$. Since $\chi(G) = \omega(G)$, it follows that G is weakly γ-perfect.   □

We can now state the following theorem, first proved by Roberts in [6].

Theorem 1   If a graph G is weakly γ-perfect, then $\chi_n(G) = n\chi(G)$.   ■

Example 6   Find $\chi_5(G)$ where G is the graph in Figure 3.

Solution: By Example 5 the graph in Figure 3 is weakly γ-perfect. As the solution to Example 5 shows, the chromatic number of G is four. Hence, by Theorem 1 it follows that $\chi_5(G) = 5 \cdot 4 = 20$.   □

Graph Set Colorings

In the last section we considered the problem of assigning the same number of colors to each vertex of a graph. This was useful in modeling several types of applications. However, there are situations for which this generalization of graph coloring is not adequate. For example, in the channel assignment problem, each station may be assigned one or more channels, where not all stations are assigned the same number of channels. In scheduling examinations, each examination may be taken by students at several different time periods, with possibly different numbers of periods assigned to different examinations. In scheduling tasks, each task may require one or more time periods, where it is not necessarily the case that all tasks are assigned the same number of time periods. In maintenance scheduling some vehicles may require two or more repair bays, where not all vehicles require the same number of bays. (A large plane may use five bays, while a two-seater may use only one bay). To model such applications we need to make the following definition.

Definition 6   Let $G = (V, E)$ be a graph. A function S that assigns a set of colors to each vertex in V is called a **set coloring** if the sets $S(u)$ and $S(v)$ are disjoint whenever u and v are adjacent in G.   □

Of course, an n-tuple coloring of a graph G is a special case of a set coloring in which every vertex is assigned the same number of colors. However, as the applications we have described show, it is often necessary to vary the number of colors assigned to different vertices.

Example 7   Construct a set coloring of C_5 where v_1, v_2, v_3, v_4, and v_5 are assigned 3 colors, 2 colors, 1 color, 3 colors, and 2 colors, respectively. (Here, the vertices of C_5 are as in Figure 2.)

Solution: We can construct such a coloring by assigning {red, green, blue} to v_1, {yellow, orange} to v_2, {red} to v_3, {green, blue, yellow} to v_4, and {orange, purple} to v_5.   □

For different applications we need to minimize different parameters associated to a set coloring. For example, when scheduling final examinations, with each examination using one or more possible time periods, we might want to minimize the number of time periods used. This corresponds to minimizing the total number of different colors used in the set coloring of the associated graph. This quantity, the number of different colors used in the set coloring, is called the **order** of the set coloring. On the other hand, if we want to limit the number of hours required for proctoring, we would need to limit the sum of the number of time periods available for each examination. This corresponds to minimizing the sum of the sizes of the sets of colors used in the set coloring of the associated graph. This quantity, the sum of the sizes of the sets of colors, is called the **score** of the associated set coloring

Example 8   What is the order and score of the set coloring in Example 7?

Solution: Six different colors are used in this set coloring in Example 7. Hence the order of this set coloring is 6. Its score is the sum of the number of colors it assigns to each vertices, namely $3 + 2 + 1 + 3 + 2 = 11$.   □

Graph T-Colorings

Consider the following channel assignment problem. Suppose that not only must interfering stations be assigned different channels, but also the separation between channels of interfering stations must not belong to a set of prohibited separations. For example, for the assignment of frequencies in ultra-high frequency (UHF) television, interfering stations cannot have the same frequency, nor can they have separations of 7, 14, or 15 channels. Suppose that in the maintenance of a fleet of planes, planes of a particular type cannot occupy repair bays that are adjacent because of interfering electrical signals. This leads us to the following definition.

Definition 7   Let $G = (V, E)$ be a graph and let T be a set of nonnegative integers containing 0. A function f from V to the set of positive integers is called a *T-coloring* if $|f(u) - f(v)| \notin T$ whenever u and v are adjacent vertices in G.   □

Example 9   Construct a T-coloring of K_3 when $T = \{0, 1, 4\}$.

Solution: Let the vertices of K_3 be v_1, v_2, and v_3. We assign color 1 to v_1. Since the difference of the colors of adjacent vertices cannot be in T, we cannot assign any of colors 1, 2, or 5 to v_2. Suppose we assign color 3 to v_2. Then we cannot assign any of colors 1, 2, 3, 4, 5, or 7 to v_3. We assign color 6 to v_3. This gives a T-coloring of K_3.

Similarly, we could have assigned color 4 to v_1, color 6 to v_2, and color 1 to v_3.   □

Example 10   Since ultra-high frequency (UHF) television stations that interfere cannot be assigned the same channel or channels differing by 7, 14, or 15 channels, to model the assignment of channels to UHF stations, we use a T-coloring where $T = \{0, 7, 14, 15\}$.   □

There are several different useful measures of the "efficiency" of a T-coloring of a graph. Sometimes we may be concerned with the total number of colors used, while at other times we may be concerned with the range of colors used. For example, in the channel assignment problem we may be interested in how many channels are used, or, instead, we may be interested in the range of channels used (that is, the required bandwidth). By the **order** of a T-coloring we mean the number of colors used. By the **T-span** of a T-coloring we mean the maximum difference between colors, that is,

$$\max\{|f(u) - f(v)| \, | u, v \text{ are vertices of G}\}.$$

When we want to minimize the number of colors used, such as when we want to use the fewest possible channels, we need to find the **T-chromatic number** of G. When we want to find the smallest possible T-span of a T-coloring, such as when we want to find the smallest range of channels required, we need to find the **T-span** of G.

Minimizing the order and minimizing the T-span of a graph often requires different colorings, as the following example, adapted from Roberts [5], shows.

Example 11   Let $T = \{0, 1, 4, 5\}$. Find the minimum order and minimum span of a T-coloring of C_5.

Solution: The minimum order of a T-coloring of C_5 with $T = \{0, 1, 4, 5\}$ is the same as the chromatic number of C_5, namely 3, since we can assign color 1 to v_1 and v_3, color 4 to v_2 and v_4, and color 7 to v_5 (where we are using the assignment of vertices in Figure 2). The reader should verify that this T-coloring of C_5 with three colors has minimum span.

On the other hand, using five colors we can construct a T-coloring of C_5 with span equal to 4 by assigning color 1 to v_1, color 4 to v_2, color 2 to v_3, color 5 to v_4, and color 3 to v_5. It is impossible to find a T-coloring with span smaller than 4, as the reader should verify. Therefore, the T-span of C_5 is 4. □

The solution of Example 11 shows that we cannot necessarily minimize both the order and span of a T-coloring of a graph simultaneously.

The following theorem is useful in the computation of T-spans. It shows that to compute the T-span of a graph G we need only find its chromatic number k and then find the T-span of the complete graph with k vertices. (Since the proof is complicated, we will not give it here. A proof can be found in Cozzens and Roberts [1].)

Theorem 2   If G is a weakly γ-perfect graph and $\chi(G) = m$, then the T-span of G equals the T-span of K_m.   ∎

Example 12   Let $T = \{0, 1, 3, 4\}$. What is the T-span of the graph G in Figure 3?

Solution: By Example 5 the graph G is weakly γ-perfect and its chromatic number is 4. Hence, the T-span of G is the T-span of K_4. When $T = \{0, 1, 3, 4\}$ the T-span of K_4 is 9, since the minimum span of a coloring of K_4 is achieved by the assignment of colors 1, 3, 8, and 10 to the four vertices of K_4. (The details of this demonstration are left as Exercise 9.)   □

Summary

We have seen how the study of applications of graph coloring to scheduling and assignment problems leads to the development of a variety of interesting generalizations of graph coloring. There are other generalization of graph coloring useful in constructing models which also have many interesting theoretical properties.

For example, in **list colorings** for vertices the colors that can be assigned to the vertices are restricted, in *I*-colorings an interval of real numbers is assigned to each vertex of a graph, and in *J*-colorings a union of intervals is assigned to each vertex of a graph. Also, to model some applications we need to combine two generalizations of graph colorings. For instance, we may need to assign two channels to broadcast stations so that interfering stations are not assigned the same channel or adjacent channels. This application requires the use of a combination of an n-tuple coloring and a T-coloring, which might be called an n-tuple T-coloring.

For more information and further references on these and other generalizations consult [5].

Suggested Readings

1. M. Cozzens and F. Roberts, "T-Colorings of Graphs and the Channel Assignment Problem," *Congressus Numerantium* , Vol. 35, 1982, pp. 191-208.

2. W. Hale, "Frequency Assignment: Theory and Applications," in *Proceedings of the IEEE*, Vol. 68, 1980, pp. 1497-1514.

3. R. Opsut and F. Roberts, "On the Fleet Maintenance, Mobile Radio Frequency, Task Assignment, and Traffic Phasing Problems," in *The Theory and Applications of Graphs*, Wiley, New York, 1981, pp. 479-492.

4. F. Roberts, *Applied Combinatorics*, Prentice-Hall, Englewood Cliffs, N.J., 1984.

5. F. Roberts, "From Garbage to Rainbows: Generalizations of Graph Coloring and their Applications", *Proceedings of the Sixth International Conference on the Theory and Applications of Graphs* , Wiley, New York (to appear).

6. F. Roberts, "On the Mobile Radio Frequency Assignment Problem and the Traffic Light Phasing Problem", Annals of the New York Academy of Science, Vol. 319, 1979, pp. 466-83.

Exercises

1. Find $\chi_2(G)$ for: a) K_4 b) C_6 c) C_7 d) W_6 e) W_7 f) Q_3.

2. Assign three channels to each of five mobile telephone stations, using the smallest number of different channels possible, if Station 1 interferes with Stations 2,4, and 5; Station 2 interferes with Stations 1,3, and 5; Station 3 interferes with Stations 2 and 4; Station 4 interferes with Stations 1,3, and 5; and Station 5 interferes with Stations 1,2, and 4.

3. At the end of the year, final examinations, each with two parts, are to be scheduled. Examinations are given either in the morning or afternoon each

day of a week. Schedule examinations using the smallest number of differ-
ent time periods for the following courses: Graph Algorithms, Operating
Systems, Number Theory, Combinatorics, Computer Security, Automata
Theory, and Compiler Theory, if no courses with the same instructor or
containing a common student can have a part scheduled at the same time.
Assume that Professor Rosen teaches Number Theory and Computer Secu-
rity, Professor Ralston teaches Graph Algorithms, Professor Carson teaches
Operating Systems and Automata Theory, and Professor Bastian teaches
Compiler Theory. Also assume that there are common students in Num-
ber Theory and Graph Algorithms, in Graph Algorithms and Operating
Systems, in Automata Theory and Compiler Theory, in Computer Security
and Automata Theory, Computer Theory and Graph Algorithms, and in
Computer Security and Compiler Theory.

4. Show that if G is a bipartite graph with at least one edge and n is positive
   integer, then $\chi_n(G) = 2n$.

5. Find the clique number of each of the following graphs.

   a)   b)

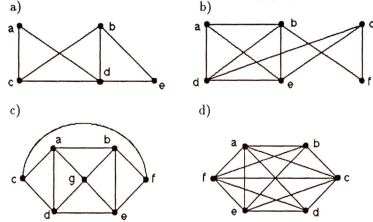

   c)   d)

6. Which of the graphs in Exercise 5 are weakly γ-perfect?

7. Show that every bipartite graph is weakly γ-perfect.

8. Find $\chi_2(G)$ for each graph G in Exercise 5.

9. Finish the argument in Example 12 to show that the T-span of K_4 is 9
   when $T = \{0, 1, 3, 4\}$.

★10. Find the T-chromatic number and T-span of C_5 if T is

   a) $\{0, 1\}$.   b) $\{0, 1, 3\}$.   c) $\{0, 1, 3, 4\}$.

★11. Find the T-chromatic number and T-span of K_4 for each of the sets T in
   Exercise 10.

★12. Find the T-span of each graph in Exercise 5, if $T = \{0, 1, 4\}$.

★13. We can use a greedy algorithm to construct an n-tuple coloring for a given graph G where n is a positive integer. First, we order the vertices of G as $v_1, v_2, ..., v_m$ and represent colors by positive integers. We assign colors $1, 2, ..., n$ to v_1. Then, once having assigned n colors to each of $v_1, v_2, ..., v_k$, we assign the smallest numbered colors to v_{k+1} not already assigned to a vertex adjacent to v_{k+1}.

   a) Use the greedy algorithm to construct a 2-tuple coloring of the following graph.

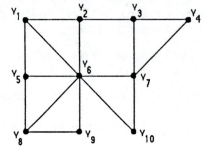

   b) Show that this algorithm does not always construct an n-tuple coloring of minimal order.

14. Describe a greedy algorithm that constructs a set coloring of a given graph G where each vertex v is to be assigned a set $S(v)$ of colors where the size of $S(v)$ is specified for each vertex.

★15. We can use a greedy algorithm to construct a T-coloring for a given graph G and set T. First, we order the vertices of G as $v_1, v_2, ..., v_n$ and represent colors by positive integers. We assign color 1 to v_1. Once we have assigned colors to $v_1, v_2, ..., v_k$, we assign the smallest numbered color to v_{k+1} so that the separation between the color of v_{k+1} and the colors of vertices adjacent to v_{k+1} that are already colored is not in T.

   a) Use this algorithm to construct a T-coloring of the graph G in Exercise 13 where $T = \{0, 1, 4, 5\}$.

   b) Show that this algorithm does not always construct a T-coloring of minimal span.

16. Describe two different problems that can be modeled using list colorings.

17. Describe two different problems that can be modeled using I-colorings.

18. Describe two different problems that can be modeled using J-colorings.

Computer Projects

1. Given the adjacency matrix of a graph G and a positive integer n, construct an n-tuple coloring of G.

2. Given the adjacency matrix of a graph G and a set of nonnegative integers T containing 0, construct a T-coloring of G.

23

Network Flows

Author: Arthur M. Hobbs, Department of Mathematics, Texas A&M University.

Prerequisites: The prerequisites for this chapter are graphs and trees. See, for example, Chapters 7 and 8 of *Discrete Mathematics and Its Applications*, Second Edition, by Kenneth H. Rosen.

Introduction

In this chapter we solve three very different problems.

Example 1   Joe the plumber has made an interesting offer. He says he has lots of short pieces of varying gauges of copper pipe; they are nearly worthless to him, but for only 1/5 of the usual cost of installing a plumbing connection under your house, he will use a bunch of T- and Y-joints he picked up at a distress sale and these small pipes to build the network shown in Figure 1. He claims that it will deliver three gallons per minute at maximum flow. He has a good reputation, so you are sure the network he builds will not leak and will cost what he promises, but he is no mathematician. Will the network really deliver as much water per minute as he claims?   □

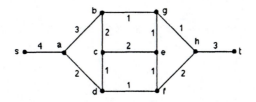

Figure 1.   A plumber's nightmare.

Example 2   We want to block access to the sea from inland town s on river R. We can do this by dropping mines in the river, but because the river spreads out in a wide delta with several outlets, the number of mines required depends on where we drop them. The number of mines required in a channel ranges from a high of 20 mines in R to a low of 1 in some channels, as shown in Figure 2. In that figure, each channel is shown with a number indicating how many mines will block it. What is the smallest number of mines needed to block off s's access to the sea, and where should the mines be placed?   □

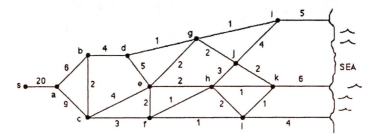

Figure 2.   Delta system of river R and numbers of mines needed to close channels.

Example 3   At Major University, Professor Johnson is asked to hire graders for 100 sections spread among 30 different courses. Each grader may work for one, two, or three sections, with the upper bound being the grader's choice, but the number actually assigned being Professor Johnson's choice. Professor Johnson contacts the potential graders, learns from each both his choice of number of sections and which courses he is competent to grade, and makes a table showing this information, together with the number of sections of each course being offered. Because the real problem is too large to use as an example here, Table 1 gives a smaller example. How should the assignment of graders be made?   □

In this chapter, we begin with Example 1, solve Example 2 on the way to solving Example 1, and then solve Example 3 by using the theory developed. Many more kinds of problems are solved using the methods of this chapter in the book *Flows in Networks* by Ford and Fulkerson [4].

	Course 1	Course 2	Course 3	Course 4	Max # Sec. Wanted
Student 1	yes	yes	no	no	3
Student 2	yes	no	yes	yes	2
Student 3	no	yes	yes	yes	3
# Sec. Needed	3	1	1	2	

Table 1.   Graders and courses.

Flow Graphs

In Example 1, we have a network of pipes that can be modeled by a graph with weights on the edges. Here, the T- and Y-joints and the inlet and outlet are represented by vertices, the pipes are represented by edges, and the weight on each edge is the capacity of the corresponding pipe in gallons per minute. Moreover, in this example we have water flowing from vertex s to vertex t as labeled in Figure 1. For a general solution to the problem, let us use the following terminology.

Definition 1   Let G be a graph in which there are two designated vertices, one the *source* of all flow, and the other the *sink*, or recipient of all flow. At every other vertex, the amount of flow into the vertex equals the amount of flow out of the vertex. The flows are limited by weights, or *capacities*, on the edges. The edges may be undirected or directed. We designate the capacity of an edge e by $c(e)$. We will call a graph with capacities on the edges, a source s, and a sink t, a *capacitated s,t-graph*.   □

Because we are searching for flows, we will show the flow through each edge of a capacitated s,t-graph as another number on the edge. To prevent confusion, we will designate the capacity of an edge and the amount of flow in it by a pair of numbers in parentheses on the edge, the capacity being the first number of the pair.

Example 4   Find a flow in the graph of Figure 3.

Solution: The path $p = s, b, a, t$ extends from s to t, and seen as a sequence of pipes, the largest amount of flow that could travel along it is the minimum of the capacities of the pipes comprising it. This minimum is 2, which is $c(s, b)$

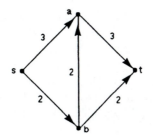

Figure 3.   A small capacitated s,t-graph.

and also $c(b, a)$. Thus we put number pairs on each of the edges, the second entry being 2 for each edge in the path and 0 for the other two edges. The result is shown in Figure 4.   □

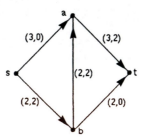

Figure 4.   Graph of Figure 3 with flow along path s,b,a,t.

There are two ways we can view a flow, and Example 4 illustrates them both. One view is to trace out the path from the source to the sink of one or more units of flow. In the example, path p is such a path. The other view is to measure the total flow in each edge of the graph. This view is shown in the example by our placing the amount of flow along each edge. Since there is actually only one flow, namely the orderly procession of fluid from the source to the sink through the network, these two views must be equivalent.

When solving the problem of finding maximum flows through the graph, the second view is preferable for two reasons. If we are searching a very large network by hand, it may well be impossible for us to find a best set of paths from the source to the sink, especially after several paths for flow have already been found. Searching for such paths is very like searching through a maze, since flow in an edge limits, perhaps to 0, the additional flow that may pass through that edge. For the second reason, we need only realize that problems of this sort are likely to be programmed on a computer, and computers are much better at examining local situations than global ones.

However, using the first view, we can detect rules that must be satisfied by a flow described as in the second view. To state these rules easily, we need to define several terms.

Let A be a subset of V in directed graph $G = (V, E)$, and let $B = V - A$. Let $c(A, B)$ be the sum of the capacities of the edges directed in G from vertices in A to vertices in B, and let $c(B, A)$ be the sum of the capacities of the edges directed in G from vertices in B to vertices in A. Similarly, let $f(A, B)$ be the amount of flow from A to B, i.e., the sum of the flows in the edges directed from vertices in A to vertices in B. Let $f(B, A)$ be the amount of flow from B to A. Then the **net flow** $F(A)$ from A is defined by

$$F(A) = f(A, B) - f(B, A).$$

For example, in Figure 4, if $A = \{s, b\}$, then $f(A, B) = 2$ and $f(B, A) = 0$. Hence $F(A) = 2$. Similarly, $F(\{b\}) = 2 - 2 = 0$ and $F(\{s, t\}) = 2 - 2 = 0$, while $F(\{b, t\}) = 2 - 2 - 2 = -2$.

Note that $F(\{s\})$ is the total number of units of flow moving from the source to the sink in the graph. Our objective is to find a flow for which $F(\{s\})$ is maximum.

Since every unit of flow that enters a vertex other than the source or sink must go out of that vertex, we have the following theorem.

Theorem 1   Suppose G is a directed capacitated s, t-flow graph, and suppose $A \subseteq V(G)$.
1. If $s \in A$ and $t \notin A$, then $F(A) = F(\{s\})$.
2. If $t \in A$ and $s \notin A$, then $F(A) = -F(\{s\})$.
3. If $A \cap \{s, t\} = \emptyset$ or if $\{s, t\} \subseteq A$, then $F(A) = 0$.

Proof: These facts are evident because all of the material flowing goes out of the source, the material all goes into the sink, and none is lost or gained at any other vertex. ∎

Although the definitions and theorem are given for directed graphs only, we can include undirected edges as follows. Although material can flow in either direction along an undirected edge, as a practical matter it will flow in only one direction (although we may not know in advance in which direction it will flow in a particular edge). Thus each undirected edge $e = \{a, b\}$ can be regarded as a pair of directed edges (a, b) and (b, a) joining the ends of e. Since the flow could go either way, we assign the capacity $c(e)$ of the edge e to both directed edges as $c(a, b)$ and $c(b, a)$. Further, using this device, we can designate the flow on the edge by $f(a, b)$ or $f(b, a)$ without ambiguity.

If, in the midst of an analysis, we discover we show flow going in both directions, it is clear that we can cancel the circulation in the two edges, leaving only that part of the flow which is actually passing through the pair of edges. For example, in Figure 5(a), we see a flow of 2 units from s to t, but $f(a, b) = 4$ while $f(b, a) = 2$. In Figure 5(b), the 2-unit circulation around the circuit a, b, a

has been eliminated (the 2 units along edge (b, a) have canceled 2 of the units along edge (a, b)) leaving the simpler, but equally accurate, picture of 2 units flowing from s to t through the path s, a, b, t. In general, if both (a, b) and (b, a) carry non-zero flow, we treat the combined flow by placing a flow of 0 on the smaller flow edge and replacing the flow on the other one by $|f(a, b) - f(b, a)|$.

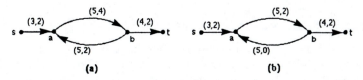

Figure 5.   Flow graph illustrating cancellation of flow in a pair of oppositely directed edges.

Increasing the Flow

Example 5   Increase the flow in the graph of Figure 4.

Solution: In Figure 4 it is easy to see that the flow shown is not the largest possible. In fact, consider the path s, a, t. Since $c(s, a) = 3$ while $f(s, a) = 0$, we could get three more units of flow to vertex a by using the edge (s, a). Then one of those units could go on to t through (a, t) since $c(a, t) = 3$ while $f(a, t) = 2$, or $c(a, t) - f(a, t) = 1$. Thus we can get $\min(3, 3 - 2) = 1$ unit of flow through s, a, t, producing the flow shown in Figure 6(a). $\square$

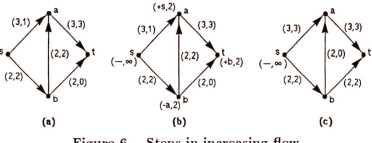

Figure 6.   Steps in increasing flow.

In general, if we can find a sequence $p = s, x_1, x_2, \ldots, x_n, t$ from the source s to the sink t in which every directed edge is directed in the same direction as the sequence (so that the sequence describes a path) and in which every edge has capacity exceeding the flow already in the edge, then we can increase the flow from s to t by simply adding flow to the path p. In such a case, the total amount of flow that can be added cannot exceed the additional amount that can be forced through any one of the edges in p, so the total flow increase by using such a path p is

$$\min_{e \in E(p)} (c(e) - f(e)).$$

But what if no such sequence of vertices exists?

Example 6   Increase the flow in the graph of Figure 6(a).

Solution: It is not obvious that the flow in this graph can be increased. However, we note that we could get $c(s,a) - f(s,a) = 2$ more units of flow from s to a, and if we had 2 more available at b, we could move them on through (b,t) to t. But let us rearrange the flow. If we erase the two units of flow in edge (b,a), then the two flowing through (s,b) become available at b to go out through (b,t). Further, the two additional units available at a can replace the two that used to go through (b,a) to a, thus allowing the flow of 2 units through (a,t) to continue. Thus we arrive at the flow shown in Figure 6(c).

An intermediate step can be interposed between Figures 6(a) and 6(c). This step is shown in Figure 6(b), where the flow is the same as that in Figure 6(a). What is different is a record at each vertex of a possibility of increasing flow. We may suppose that an infinite supply is always available at s, so we have labeled s with $(-, \infty)$, where the "$-$" indicates only that all flow begins at s. At vertex a, we see the label $(+s, 2)$, which signifies that two units of flow could come through edge (s,a) because $c(s,a) - f(s,a) = 2$. At vertex b is the label $(-a, 2)$, showing that 2 units of flow could come to b by canceling the flow on edge (b,a). The operation of cancellation is shown by the "$-$" attached to a in the label. Finally, t has the label $(+b, 2)$, showing that 2 units of flow are available at t, coming from b.   □

Let us look at the rearrangement of Example 6 another way. Consider the "path" s, a, b, t in Figure 6(b). We increased the flow on edges (s,a) and (b,t) by two units, and we decreased the flow on edge (b,a) by the same two units. These operations are signaled by the signs attached to the first label on each vertex as described in the example. The result was the increase of flow in the graph by two units.

Since s, a, b, t is not a path in Figure 6(a) (the edge (b,a) is directed against the order of the sequence), let us give such a sequence a name of its own.

Definition 2   A *chain* from x_0 to x_n in a directed graph G is a subgraph P of G whose vertices can be placed in a sequence $x_0, x_1, \ldots, x_n$ such that, for each $i \in \{0, 1, \ldots, n-1\}$, either $(x_i, x_{i+1}) \in E(P)$ or $(x_{i+1}, x_i) \in E(P)$ and no other edges are in $E(P)$.   □

Figure 7 shows an example of a chain from x_0 to x_5.

Figure 7.   **A chain from x_5 to x_5.**

Example 6 illustrates the following general principle.

Theorem 2   Suppose P with vertex sequence $x_0, x_1, \ldots, x_n$ is a chain from the source $s = x_0$ to the sink $t = x_n$ in a capacitated s, t-graph G, and suppose, for each i, either $(x_i, x_{i+1}) \in E(P)$ and $c(x_i, x_{i+1}) - f(x_i, x_{i+1}) > 0$, or $(x_{i+1}, x_i) \in E(P)$ and $f(x_{i+1}, x_i) > 0$. Let x be the smallest among the values $c(x_i, x_{i+1}) - f(x_i, x_{i+1})$ on edges $(x_i, x_{i+1}) \in E(P)$ and $f(x_{i+1}, x_i)$ on edges $(x_{i+1}, x_i) \in E(P)$. Then increasing the flow by x on the edges (x_i, x_{i+1}) and decreasing it by x on the edges (x_{i+1}, x_i) of P increases $F(\{s\})$ by x.   ∎

We call a chain like that described in Theorem 2 an **augmenting chain** in the capacitated s, t-flow graph.

The labels on the vertices are used to find augmenting chains. Let us visualize ourselves as exploring the graph, starting at vertex s with infinitely many units of flow available to us. As we move through the graph, searching for t, we keep a record of the amounts of new flow that can reach each vertex. This record is the set of vertex labels we show in Figure 6(b).

The labels are governed by two considerations.

1. If x units of flow can reach vertex m, and if edge (m, n) exists, and if $c(m, n) - f(m, n) > 0$, then $y = \min(x, c(m, n) - f(m, n))$ units can be gotten to n by following the chain from s to m already found and then pushing as much flow as possible through (m, n). (This amount of flow is the smaller of the amount available and the amount that can go through the edge.) This is signaled by placing the label $(+m, y)$ at vertex n.

2. If x units of flow can reach vertex m, if edge (n, m) exists, and if $f(n, m) > 0$, then $y' = \min(x, f(n, m))$ units become available at n by canceling y' units of flow from edge (n, m). The effect of the cancellation is to feed the $y' \leq x$ units of flow needed at m after the cancellation by using y' of the x units of new flow available at m, while using the y' units that were flowing through (n, m) as the source of the new y' units available at n.

When we label vertex n by using a label on vertex m and either edge (m, n) or edge (n, m), we say we **label n from m** and that we are **labeling across** edge (m, n) or (n, m).

We interpret the labels backwards to describe the augmenting chain. The first label on each vertex names the vertex preceding it on the chain from s found during the labeling process. For example, consider the labels on the flow graph shown in Figure 8(a). There (ignoring signs) the first label on t is a, so the augmenting chain vertex sequence ends with a, t. The first label on a is b, so the augmenting chain vertex sequence ends with b, a, t. Finally, the first label on b is s, so the augmenting chain vertex sequence is s, b, a, t.

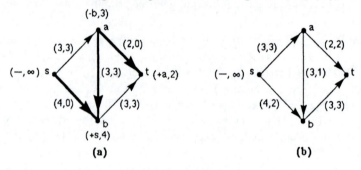

Figure 8. Showing an augmenting chain being found using labels and being used to increase flow.

When a vertex n is labeled from vertex m, the second label is always the minimum of the second label on m and the amount $c(m, n) - f(m, n)$ or $f(n, m)$ which can be gotten to n from m through the edge. Since the second label on s is ∞, the result is that the second label always gives the largest amount that can get to the vertex labeled. Thus when t is labeled, the second label of t states the increase of flow given by the augmenting chain specified by the labels. For example, in Figure 8(a) the augmenting chain has vertex sequence s, b, a, t, and the amounts of flow that can be forced through the edges of the chain are 4, 3, and 2, successively, with a minimum of 2. Because of the way second labels are chosen, the second label on t is this amount 2.

Example 7   Find an augmenting chain in the graph shown in Figure 8(a), in which there is a preexisting flow of 3 units.

Solution: We label s with $(-, \infty)$, and from there we label b with $(+s, 4)$. From b we can label a by canceling flow in (a, b), so a receives the label $(-b, 3)$. From a we can label t with label $(+a, 2)$. These labels are shown in Figure 8(a). Reading first labels backwards, we find the augmenting chain is s, b, a, t as discussed before, and the chain will increase the flow by 2 as the second label on t shows. The resulting flow is shown in Figure 8(b), where 3 units of flow go out of s to a and split there into 2 units that flow directly to t and one that goes to t through b. In addition, 2 units of flow go from s through b to t, making a total of 5 units of flow shown in Figure 8(b). □

While we are labeling we can keep track of what is possible, without concerning ourselves whether there is actually a chain available from s to t along which new flow can go. If we can label t, then the flow can be increased; we will show that if we cannot label t, then the flow cannot be increased.

We are also under no obligation to watch for a chain of labels. Since we always label an unlabeled vertex from a labeled vertex, s being always labeled with $(-,\infty)$, we automatically form a tree (disregarding the directions of edges). Thus for each labeled vertex x, our labels describe a unique chain from s to x. An example of such a tree is shown by boldface edges in Figure 8(a). As shown in that figure, if we mark on the graph the edges used in labeling vertices, we find the augmenting chain with vertices s, b, a, t shown in bold lines in Figure 8(a).

Example 8   Find a flow in the graph of Figure 1.

Solution: In Figure 9(a), the graph of Figure 1 is reproduced, except that each undirected edge has been replaced by two directed edges, one in each direction, each with the same capacity as the undirected edge. Also, the capacities have been written as the first entries of number pairs, with 0 for flow as the second number.* Starting with the label $(-,\infty)$ at s, we label across edges as described above. First a is labeled with $(+s, 4)$, and working from a we label b with $(+a, \min(4, 3)) = (+a, 3)$ and d with $(+a, \min(4, 2)) = (+a, 2)$, but we do not label s from a because s already has a label. Labeling from b, we do not need to label a, but we label c with $(+b, \min(3, 2)) = (+b, 2)$ and g with $(+b, \min(3, 1)) = (+b, 1)$. Then we label from c, placing $(+c, \min(2, 2)) = (+c, 2)$ on vertex e, but we place no label on d from c, since d already has a label. Next we label from d, placing label $(+d, \min(2, 1)) = (+d, 1)$ on vertex f. As before, we do not label a from d. Going on to vertex e, we label nothing from there, since all of its neighbors are already labeled. Next we label from f, placing label $(+f, \min(1, 2)) = (+f, 1)$ on vertex h. Since all neighbors of g are already labeled, we go on to h, from which we label t with $(+h, \min(1, 3)) = (+h, 1)$. Since t is labeled, we are done.

We use the labels to determine the chain from s to t that was found, along which a single unit of flow can flow (because the second label on t is 1). The first label on t is $+h$, showing that edge (h, t) is the last edge of the chain from s to t. The first label on h is $+f$, showing the next-to-the-last edge of the chain is (f, h). We continue reading backwards, using the first labels, obtaining the sequence "t, h, f, d, a, s" which reverses to give the chain s, a, d, f, h, t from s to t along which one unit of flow is added. The tree of edges used in our labeling is shown by bold lines in Figure 9(b), and Figure 10(a) shows the network with the flow we found. □

---

* In Figures 9(b) through 12, to simplify the figures we have shown only the directed edges that contain flow when flow is present and the undirected edges when it is not.

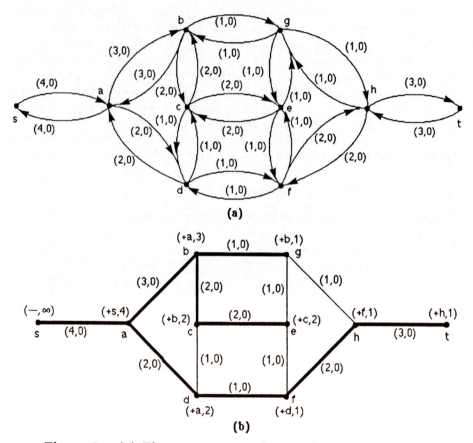

Figure 9.   (a) Figure 1 converted to a directed capacitated s,t-graph.   (b) The first labeling and the associated tree for Example 1.

To describe a procedure that can be programmed, we need a rule for deciding which edge to label across next. Many such rules are possible; the one we have adopted here and used in Example 8 is straightforward: Label from the alphabetically earliest vertex x which has a label and which meets an edge that has not yet been considered from vertex x, and label all possible vertices from x before going on to the next vertex. This rule is called the **lexicographic ordering rule**.

Once we have increased the flow, the labels we placed on the vertices other than s are wrong for the new combination of graph and flow, so we erase the vertex labels and start again from s. Again we explore the graph, searching for a chain from s to t along which we can increase the flow.

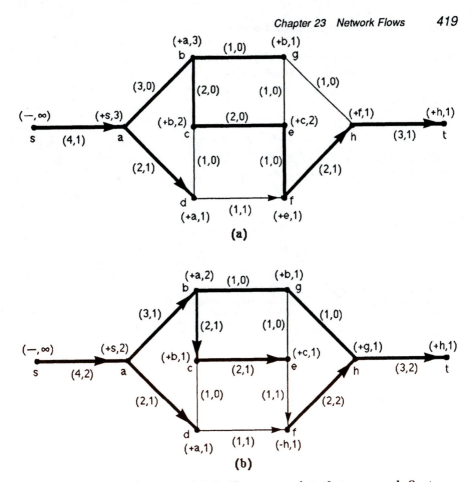

Figure 10.   (a) Second labeling, associated tree, and first flow for Example 1.   (b) Third labeling, associated tree, and second flow for Example 1.

Example 9   Increase the flow found in Example 8 as much as possible.

Solution: Labeling as before in the graph of Figure 10(a), we obtain the vertex labels shown in that figure. (Again the associated spanning tree is shown with bold lines.) Notice there that vertex f could not be labeled from d because $c(d, f) - f(d, f) = 1 - 1 = 0$. Hence f was labeled from e.

This time the augmenting chain is s, a, b, c, e, f, h, t, with one more unit of flow available. The resulting flow is shown in Figure 10(b). Again the labels are erased and new ones found. This time, since both $c(d, f) - f(d, f) = 0$ and $c(e, f) - f(e, f) = 1 - 1 = 0$, f has no label when labeling from e is completed. Hence we do not try then to label from f, but rather label from g. Later f does receive a label; indeed, its label shows that flow should be canceled to reach f. In a more complex graph, it would then be reasonable to label from f. In this graph, however, we reach t without using f again. The tree of edges used is shown in Figure 10(b) with bold edges, and the augmenting chain is s, a, b, g, h, t.

The resulting flow is shown in Figure 11. We label again, as shown in Figure 11, and we obtain the tree of edges used, again shown there. However, the tree does not contain t, so we have not found an augmenting chain. Does this mean there is no augmenting chain? □

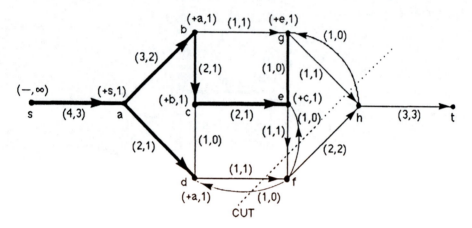

Figure 11.   Fourth labeling, associated tree, and a minimum cut.

For the answer to that question, we must bring up machinery appropriate to Example 2.

Definition 3   Given a directed graph G with capacities on the edges, and given a nonempty subset A of its vertices such that $V(G) - A$ is also nonempty, the set of all edges of G directed from vertices in A toward vertices in $V(G) - A$ is called the *cut* $(A, V(G) - A)$. The *capacity* $c(A, V(G) - A)$ of this cut is the sum of the capacities of the edges in it. If $s \in A$ and $t \in V(G) - A$, then we call the cut an *s, t-cut*. □

Our objective in Example 2 is to find a cut $(A, V(G) - A)$ such that $c(A, V(G) - A)$ is minimum. In Theorem 3, we begin to tie the maximum flow and the minimum cut together, and in Theorem 4 we will complete the connection.

Example 10   Discuss the cuts in the graph of Figure 11.

Solution: In Figure 11, the set of vertices in the tree is $A = \{s, a, b, c, d, e, g\}$. The set of edges directed from A to $V(G) - A = \{f, h, t\}$ is the cut $\{(d, f), (e, f), (g, h)\}$. Notice that on each of these edges the flow equals the capacity and that on the return edges (f, d), (f, e), (h, g) in $(V(G) - A, A)$ the flow is zero. The capacity of the cut is $c(d, f) + c(e, f) + c(g, h) = 1 + 1 + 1 = 3$. Notice also that this cut is an s, t-cut, and that the capacity of the cut is exactly the same as the total flow $F(A) = F(\{s\}) = 3$. $\square$

Theorem 3   The maximum flow from vertex s to vertex $t \neq s$ in a directed graph G with capacities on its edges is less than or equal to the capacity of any cut $(A, V(G) - A)$ having $s \in A$ and $t \notin A$.

Proof: Consider any s, t-cut $(A, V(G) - A)$ of graph G. Since any units of flow from s to t must pass through an edge of this cut, it follows immediately that $F(\{s\}) \leq c(A, V(G) - A)$.   ∎

In Example 10, several facts are evident. First, since s has a label and t does not, any flow from s to t must pass through one or another of the three edges in the cut $(A, V(G) - A)$. Second, since the return edges in $(V(G) - A, A)$ are empty, any flow passing through the three edges directed away from A must continue on toward t. Third, with the edges directed away from A full and the edge directed toward A empty, there is no conceivable way that the flow we have found could be increased. In other words, we have found a maximum flow in this graph from s to t, and its amount is equal to the sum of the capacities of the edges in this cut separating s from t.

Returning to the graph shown in Figure 6(c), we see another example of this situation. Vertex s is labeled $(-, \infty)$ as usual. Since $f(s, a) = c(s, a)$ and $f(s, b) = c(s, b)$, the tree of labeled vertices includes only vertex s, so $F(\{s\}) = c(\{s\}, \{a, b, t\}) = 5$.

Notice that there are no edges directed toward $\{s\}$, and both of the edges directed out of $\{s\}$ in Figure 6(c) are full. Thus, it is clear that the flow to vertex t cannot be increased from its value of 5 units shown in Figure 6(c), and the maximum flow is equal to the sum of the capacities of the edges in the set $\{(s, a), (s, b)\}$. (We will generalize these observations in Theorem 4, following Algorithm 1.)

The observations made in considering Examples 9 and 10 motivate Algorithm 1.

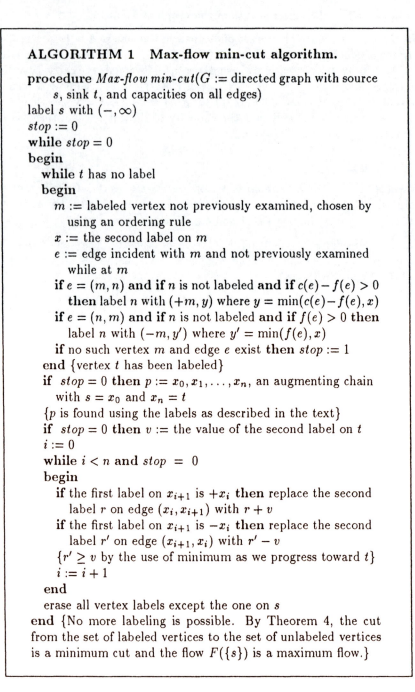

ALGORITHM 1   Max-flow min-cut algorithm.

procedure *Max-flow min-cut*($G :=$ directed graph with source
    s, sink t, and capacities on all edges)
label s with $(-, \infty)$
stop $:= 0$
while *stop* $= 0$
begin
  while t has no label
  begin
    $m :=$ labeled vertex not previously examined, chosen by
      using an ordering rule
    $x :=$ the second label on m
    $e :=$ edge incident with m and not previously examined
      while at m
    if $e = (m, n)$ and **if** n is not labeled and **if** $c(e) - f(e) > 0$
      then label n with $(+m, y)$ where $y = \min(c(e) - f(e), x)$
    if $e = (n, m)$ and **if** n is not labeled and **if** $f(e) > 0$ **then**
      label n with $(-m, y')$ where $y' = \min(f(e), x)$
    if no such vertex m and edge e exist **then** *stop* $:= 1$
  end {vertex t has been labeled}
  if *stop* $= 0$ **then** $p := x_0, x_1, \ldots, x_n$, an augmenting chain
    with $s = x_0$ and $x_n = t$
  {p is found using the labels as described in the text}
  if *stop* $= 0$ **then** $v :=$ the value of the second label on t
  $i := 0$
  while $i < n$ and *stop* $= 0$
  begin
    if the first label on x_{i+1} is $+x_i$ **then** replace the second
      label r on edge (x_i, x_{i+1}) with $r + v$
    if the first label on x_{i+1} is $-x_i$ **then** replace the second
      label r' on edge (x_{i+1}, x_i) with $r' - v$
    {$r' \geq v$ by the use of minimum as we progress toward t}
    $i := i + 1$
  end
  erase all vertex labels except the one on s
end {No more labeling is possible. By Theorem 4, the cut
from the set of labeled vertices to the set of unlabeled vertices
is a minimum cut and the flow $F(\{s\})$ is a maximum flow.}

Example 11   Solve the problem of Example 2.

Solution: Represent the river system as a graph by assigning a vertex to the town s, to the ocean t, and to each of the intersections of the channels. Join two vertices with an undirected edge if a river channel joins the corresponding points in the river system, and give the edge a capacity equal to the number of mines it takes to block the corresponding channel. The resulting graph is shown in Figure 12. Applying Algorithm 1 with the lexicographic ordering (see Exercise 7), we obtain a maximum flow of 7 with a minimum cut consisting of edges (d, g), (e, g), (e, h), (f, h), and (f, l). Thus the solution to the problem of Example 2 is to mine the channels corresponding to these five edges with a total of 7 mines.   □

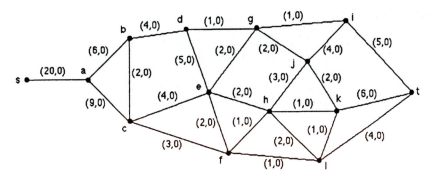

Figure 12.   The river delta of Example 2 converted to a capacitated s,t-graph.

Examples 9 and 11 point the way to the following theorem, which shows that Algorithm 1 solves our problem.

Theorem 4   The Max-flow Min-cut Theorem   The maximum s, t-flow in a capacitated s, t-graph is equal to the capacity of a minimum s, t-cut. Further, Algorithm 1 finds such a maximum flow and minimum cut.

Proof: We already know from Theorem 3 that the maximum flow amount

$$F(\{s\}) \leq c(A', V(G) - A')$$

for any minimum capacity s, t-cut $(A', V(G) - A')$. It will therefore suffice to find a flow f and an s, t-cut $(A, V(G) - A)$ such that $F(A) = c(A, V(G) - A)$ for the flow f.

Let Algorithm 1 run to completion, producing a flow f. Let A be the set of vertices labeled in the last pass through the algorithm. Since s always has a label, and since t could not be labeled on the last pass, $(A, V(G) - A)$ is an s, t-cut, and $F(A)$ is the amount of flow going from s to t as described by f.

Consider an edge (a, b) with $a \in A$ and $b \in V(G) - A$. Since a is labeled and b is not, we must have $f(a, b) = c(a, b)$ by the algorithm. Next, consider an edge (b', a') with $a' \in A$ and $b' \in V(G) - A$. Again, we note that a' has a label and b' does not; hence by the algorithm, $f(b', a') = 0$. Thus

$$F(A) = c(A, V(G) - A). \tag{1}$$

Since the maximum flow cannot be larger than $c(A, V(G) - A)$, $F(A)$ must be a maximum flow. The equality in (1) completes the proof of this theorem. ∎

Complexity

Given a capacitated s, t-graph G, let a be the largest edge capacity, let e be the number of edges of G, and let v be the number of vertices of G. In each search for an augmenting chain in the first half of Algorithm 1, we may have to examine nearly all of the edges, each from both ends, so each pass through that half of the algorithm takes $O(e)$ steps. Since each augmenting chain increases the flow by at least one unit, there can be no more than $a + 1$ searches for an augmenting chain. The second half of Algorithm 1 requires only $O(p)$ steps, where p is the number of edges in the augmenting chain. Thus the complexity of Algorithm is governed by the first half of the algorithm and is $O(ae)$.

Sometimes the capacity a is many orders of magnitude larger than the number e of edges or the number v of vertices. In such a case, we would like a measure of the complexity of the algorithm that does not depend on a. Edmonds and Karp [2] have shown that, if vertices are scanned in the same order in which they receive labels, instead of using the lexicographic ordering, then the complexity is $O(v^5)$.

Assignment of Graders

Example 12   Set up Example 3 as a flow graph problem.

Solution: Referring to the table given in Example 3, represent Students $1, 2$, and 3 by vertices S_1, S_2, and S_3, and represent Courses $1, 2, 3$, and 4 by vertices C_1, C_2, C_3, and C_4, respectively. Let s and t be two additional vertices. Join vertex s to S_1, S_2, and S_3 by directed edges, and assign capacity $c(s, S_i)$ equal to the number of sections Student i is willing to grade. Join each of vertices C_1, C_2, C_3, and C_4 to vertex t by directed edges, and assign capacity $c(C_i, t)$ equal to the number of sections of Course i being offered. For each i and j, add edge (S_i, C_j) if Student i is qualified to grade for Course j (i.e., if a "yes" appears in the row for Student i and the column for Course j of Table 1). For each such edge, let $c(S_i, C_j) = \infty$. The problem then becomes one of finding a maximum flow in the graph of Figure 13. □

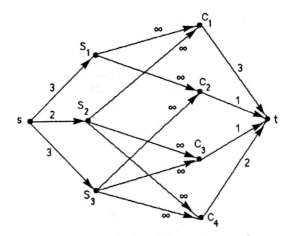

Figure 13. The flow graph for the grader assignment problem (Example 3).

By Theorem 4, the maximum flow in Figure 13 equals the capacity of the minimum cut. Let us look at a maximum flow as perceived under View 1 discussed early in this chapter. Each unit of flow passes from s to a vertex S_i, thence to a vertex C_j, and finally to vertex t. We may regard the unit as specifying an assignment of Student i to a section of Course j. For a fixed value of i, the number of units of flow passing through S_i cannot exceed $c(s, S_i)$, which is the maximum number of sections for which Student i wants to grade, so the assignment view of the units of flow cannot assign a student to more sections than he desires. Similarly, for a fixed value of j, the number of units passing through C_j cannot exceed $c(C_j, t)$, which is the number of sections needing graders. Thus no course will be assigned too many graders. Ideally, $(V(G) - \{t\}, \{t\})$ will turn out to be a minimum cut. Then by Theorem 4, the maximum flow will equal to capacity of that cut, and every section of every course will be assigned a grader.

Example 13   Solve Example 3.

Solution: Applying Algorithm 1 with lexicographic ordering to the graph of Figure 13, we find the flow shown in Figure 14, where the last labels and the associated tree (in bold edges) are also shown. From Figure 14, we see that $F(\{s\}) = c(V(G) - \{t\}, \{t\})$ as we hoped, so every section will get a grader. Further, interpreting the flow, we are told to assign Student 1 to all three sections of Course 1, Student 2 to the one section of Course 3 and one of the sections of Course 4, and Student 3 to the one section of Course 2 and to the other section of Course 4.   □

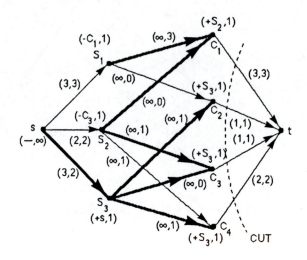

Figure 14.   Maximum flow, associated tree, and cut for the grader assignment problem (Example 3).

The generalization of Examples 3, 12, and 13 to other assignments is straightforward. The possibilities in such assignments are that the students become fully assigned without finding graders for every section, or that, as in the case of Example 3, the sections receive enough graders but some students do not work as much as they want, or that every student gets enough work and every section receives a grader, or that some students do not get enough work while some sections are not graded. The last case is illustrated in one of the examples of Exercise 8. In every case, a maximum flow obtained by using Algorithm 1 will determine an assignment of as many graders to as many sections as possible.

Historical Note

The 1950s were exciting years at the RAND Corporation, which had been set up after World War II to provide the government with well-founded scientific advice. Among the workers there were Lester Ford, Jr. and Ray Fulkerson, developers of the theory presented in this chapter, George Dantzig [1], one of the most important developers of linear programming, and Merrill Flood and Selmer Johnson, who worked with Fulkerson and Dantzig on the traveling salesman problem (see the "Traveling Salesman Problem" chapter in this book).

The problems which led to the theory that has been presented in this chapter were posed by the Air Force to Ford and Fulkerson in 1955 [4] as a problem in railway traffic flow. Their first work on it involved linear programming, but as they refined their understanding of the problem and available methods, they hit on the flow algorithm and labeling scheme we have presented here. Their development of the work was so fast that the entire theory of this chapter was published by 1957 [3].

Suggested Readings

1. G. Dantzig, *Linear Programming and Extensions*, Princeton University Press, Princeton, N. J., 1963.

2. J. Edmonds and R. Karp, "Theoretical improvements in algorithmic efficiency for network flow problems", *J. ACM*, Vol. 19, 1972, pp. 248–264.

3. L. Ford, Jr. and D. Fulkerson, "A simple algorithm for finding maximal network flows and an application to the Hitchcock problem", *Canadian J. Math.*, Vol. 9, 1957, pp. 210–218.

4. L. Ford, Jr., and D. Fulkerson, *Flows in Networks*, Princeton University Press, Princeton, N. J., 1962.

Exercises

In Exercises 1 and 2, one unit of flow is shown in the graph. Starting with that flow, use Algorithm 1 with the lexicographic ordering to find a maximum flow and a minimum cut in the graph.

1.

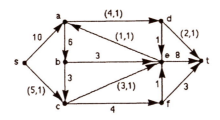

2.

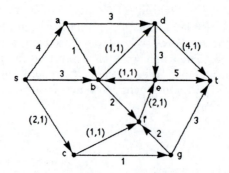

3. Using the graph and capacities of Exercise 1, find a maximum flow and minimum cut using Algorithm 1, but this time use the Edmonds and Karp ordering in which vertices are scanned in the same order in which they receive labels, instead of using the lexicographic ordering.

4. Using the graph and capacities of Exercise 2, find a maximum flow and minimum cut using Algorithm 1, but this time use the Edmonds and Karp ordering in which vertices are scanned in the same order in which they receive labels, instead of using the lexicographic ordering.

In Exercises 5 and 6, find a maximum flow and a minimum cut in the undirected graph by using Algorithm 1 with the lexicographic ordering.

5.

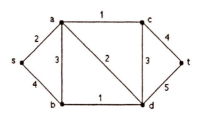

6.

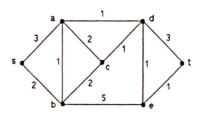

7. Apply Algorithm 1 with the lexicographic ordering to the graph shown in Figure 12.

8. For each of the following tables, find a maximal assignment of graders to sections of courses, as in Example 3.

(a)

	Course 1	Course 2	Course 3	Max. # Sec. Wanted
Student 1	yes	no	no	1
Student 2	yes	yes	no	1
Student 3	no	yes	yes	3
Student 4	yes	no	yes	1
# Sec. Needed	4	1	1	

(b)

	Course 1	Course 2	Course 3	Course 4	Max. # Sec. Wanted
Student 1	yes	yes	yes	yes	1
Student 2	yes	yes	no	no	2
Student 3	no	yes	yes	no	1
Student 4	no	yes	yes	yes	3
# Sec. Needed	2	2	2	1	

$\star\star$9. An undirected graph G is **bipartite** if $V(G)$ is the disjoint union of two nonempty sets V_1 and V_2 such that every edge of G joins a vertex of V_1 with a vertex of V_2. A **matching** in graph G is a set M of edges of G such that no two of the edges in M meet the same vertex of G. A **covering** of graph G is a set C of vertices of G such that every edge of G has at least one end in C. Prove König's Theorem: If G is an undirected bipartite graph, then the maximum number of edges possible in a matching in G equals the minimum number of vertices possible in a covering of G. *Hint*: use a source and sink connected to different subsets of $V(G)$ by edges of capacity 1.

$\star\star$10. (This problem requires information from the beginning of the chapter "Network Survivability".) Recall from that chapter that a block is a graph without cut vertices and that a graph is 2-connected if it is a block with at least two edges. Show that an undirected graph G with at least three vertices is 2-connected if and only if, for any two distinct vertices v and w of G, there are two simple paths joining v and w which have only the vertices v and w in common. Note: This is the 2- connected case of Menger's theorem. *Hint*: Replace each vertex x of G other than v and w by two new vertices x_1 and x_2 and a directed edge (x_1, x_2). For each edge $\{x, y\}$ of G, add edges (x_2, y_1) and (y_2, x_1), treating v and w suitably. Assign appropriate capacities and use Algorithm 1 and Theorem 4.

11. In the new factory of the Sampson Manufacturing Company, the workers are to be assigned to machines. One worker will use just one machine on the job. Each worker has stated in his job application which types of machines he is competent to operate, and the company knows how many of each type of machine they have to be manned. Describe how the problem of making the assignments can be solved by using a flow graph.

12. The Computer Information Company (CIC) sells information to computer owners who call in by modem. Due to the quality of their service, their telephone lines are very busy. But it turns out that their customers are not always able to get through to them, even when the company has idle lines coming in. It is obvious that the problem lies with the telephone network, but where is the bottleneck? Investigating the problem, the company finds that any call coming out of a switching center owned by the telephone company can reach the next switching center; the problem seems to be that some switching centers do not have enough capacity to handle all of the calls for CIC that come to them. Data from the telephone company tells CIC how many calls are coming into each switching center from local users of CIC and what the pass-through capacity of each switching center is. Many calls pass through several switching centers on their way to the CIC office. How can CIC determine which switching centers are blocking their calls (thus helping CIC management decide where they might build a subsidiary CIC station to reduce the pass-through load on the inadequate switches)? *Hint:* Try a flow from CIC to the users, connect a single sink to the switches with edges whose capacities are the number of local users attached to the switches, and replace switches in the telephone network by weighted directed edges.

Computer Projects

1. Write a computer program to find a maximum flow and a minimum cut in a directed capacitated s, t-graph.

2. Write a computer program to find a maximum matching in a bipartite graph. (See Exercise 9 and its solution for the necessary ideas and definitions.)

24

Petri Nets

Author: Robert A. McGuigan, Department of Mathematics, Westfield State College.

Prerequisites: The prerequisites for this chapter are graphs and digraphs. See, for example, Sections 7.1 and 7.2 of *Discrete Mathematics and Its Applications*, Second Edition, by Kenneth H. Rosen.

Introduction

Petri nets are mathematical structures which are useful in studying systems such as computer hardware and software systems. A system is modeled by a Petri net, the analysis of which may then reveal information about the structure and behavior of the system as it changes over time. Petri nets have been used to model computer hardware, software, operating systems, communications protocols, networks, concurrency, and parallelism, for example. Petri net models have been constructed for the CDC6400 computer and the SCOPE 3.2 operating system for the purpose of evaluating system performance (see references in [2]).

More generally, industrial production systems and even general social, ecological, or environmental systems can be modeled by Petri nets. In this chapter we will introduce the basic definitions of Petri net theory, study several examples in detail, and investigate some of the deeper concepts of the theory.

Petri Nets

A **Petri net** has four components: a set P of *places*, a set T of *transitions*, an *input function* I, and an *output function* O. The input function assigns to each transition a set of places known as the *input places* of the transition. The output function assigns to each transition a set of places known as the *output places* of the transition. Conceptually, places are passive components of the system. They may store things, represent states of the system, or make things observable, for example. Transitions are the active components of the system. They may produce things, transport things, or represent changes of state of the system. The following is the formal definition.

Definition 1   A *Petri net structure* is a four-tuple (P, T, I, O) such that P is a finite set (of *places*); T is a finite set (of *transitions*), with $P \cap T = \emptyset$; I (the input function) is a function from T to the set of all finite subsets of P; O (the output function) is a function from T to the set of all finite subsets of P.

A place p is an *input place* for a transition t if and only if p belongs to $I(t)$ and p is an *output place* for t if and only if p belongs to $O(t)$. □

Example 1   Consider a simple batch processing computer system. We suppose it has four states, or conditions:

1) a job is waiting for processing,
2) the processor is idle,
3) a job is being processed,
4) a job is waiting to be output.

There are four actions of the system:

1) a job is entered in the input queue,
2) a job is started on the processor,
3) a job is completed,
4) a job is output.

If a job is entered in the input queue, then a job is waiting; if a job is waiting and the processor is idle, then a job can be started. After a job is processed it can be completed and a job will be waiting for output and the processor will be idle. If a job is waiting for output then a job can be output. Using the rule of thumb about active and passive components of a system we should have places corresponding to the four states of the system and transitions corresponding to the four actions.

This simple system can be modeled by a Petri net having four places, p_1, p_2, p_3, p_4, corresponding to the four states, and four transitions, t_1, t_2, t_3, t_4, corresponding to the four actions.

The input and output functions I and O are defined by listing their values explicitly:

$$I(t_1) = \emptyset, \quad I(t_2) = \{p_1, p_2\}, \quad I(t_3) = \{p_3\}, \quad I(t_4) = \{p_4\}$$

$$O(t_1) = \{p_1\}, \quad O(t_2) = \{p_3\}, \quad O(t_3) = \{p_2, p_4\}, \quad O(t_4) = \emptyset.$$

Note that I assigns t_1 the subset $\emptyset$ of P and O assigns $\emptyset$ to t_4. This is the formal way of saying that a transition has no input or output places. □

There is a representation of Petri net structures using directed graphs, which makes it easier to see the structure. In drawing the directed graph representation of a Petri net, we make the following convention: *places will be represented by circular vertices and transitions by rectangular vertices.* If a place p is an input place for the transition t, then there is a directed edge from the vertex for p to that for t. If p is an output place for t, then a directed edge goes from t to p. It is easy to go back and forth between the two specifications.

Example 2   Construct a directed graph representation of the Petri net structure of Example 1.

Solution: Figure 1 shows such a directed graph and is labeled to show it as a model for the simple batch processing computer system. □

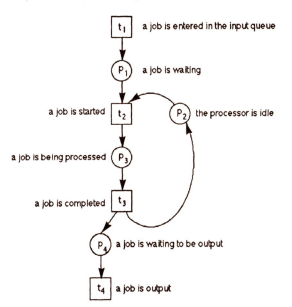

Figure 1.   A Petri net graph for a computer system.

Example 3   As another example (adapted from [2]), consider a library system. Users have access to three desks: the request desk, the collection desk, and the return desk. All books are kept in the stacks and every book has an index card. A user goes to the request desk to ask for a book. If the book is in the stacks it is removed and the borrowed book index is updated. The user gets the book at the collection desk. Books are returned to the return desk. Books returned are replaced in the stacks and the index is updated. A Petri net model of this system is given in graphical form in Figure 2.   □

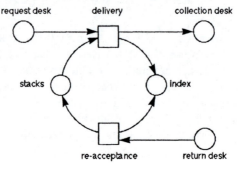

Figure 2.   A library system.

For the purpose of modeling more complex systems it is necessary to use a more complicated graph structure in which more than one directed edge may go from one vertex to another.

Example 4   Figure 3 shows an example of a graphical Petri net with multiple edges between some vertices.

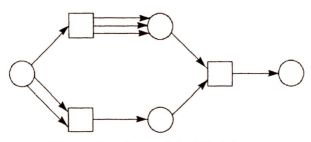

Figure 3.   A graphical Petri net.

This sort of structure requires a modification of the definition of Petri net structure given previously since a place cannot appear more than once as a member of a *set* of input or output places. To overcome this difficulty we need only change the ranges of the input function I and the output function O to be the set of all finite subsets of the Cartesian product of P and N, the set of positive integers. Thus an input or output place would be represented as an ordered pair (p, n) where the place is p and n is the number of edges between p and the transition in question. In what follows we will generally be using only the graphical representation of the net.

Modeling System Dynamics

In addition to having a static structure which is modeled by Petri net structures as discussed above, many systems change over time and it is of great interest to study this dynamic behavior. In Petri net theory this is accomplished through the use of *markings*.

Definition 2   A *marking* of a Petri net (P, T, I, O) is a function m from P to the nonnegative integers.   □

We think of the marking as assigning *tokens* to the places in the net. The number assigned to a place by the marking is the number of tokens at that place. In models of systems the tokens could have many interpretations. For example in modeling computer operating systems the tokens might represent the processes which compete for resources and which must be controlled by the operating system.

As we shall see, the tokens can move from place to place in the net simulating the dynamic behavior of the system. In the graphical representation of Petri nets the tokens are represented by solid dots in the circular vertices for the places. This is practical when the number of tokens at any place is small. If there are too many tokens then we write the number of tokens assigned to a place inside the circle.

Example 5   Figure 4 shows some examples of marked Petri nets.   □

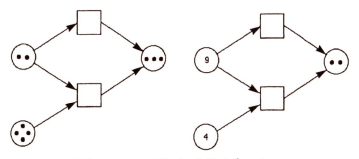

Figure 4.   Marked Petri nets.

The dynamic change of the Petri net model is controlled by the marking, i.e. the number of tokens assigned to each place, and by the *firing rules* for transitions.

Definition 3   A transition is *enabled for firing* if each of its input places has at least as many tokens in it as edges from the input place to the transition. A transition may fire only if it is enabled.   ☐

Example 6   Which of the transitions in Figure 5 are enabled for firing?

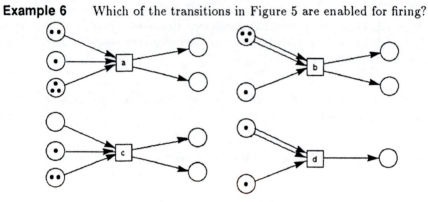

Figure 5.   Transitions.

Solution: Transitions a and b are enabled while c and d are not.   ☐

A transition is *fired* by removing one token from each input place for every edge from the input place to the transition and adding one token to each output place for every edge from the transition to that place.

Example 7   Show the result of firing each of the transitions in Figure 6.

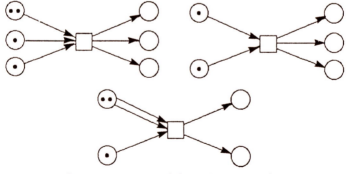

Figure 6.   Transitions before firing.

Solution: Figure 7 shows these transitions after firing.   ☐

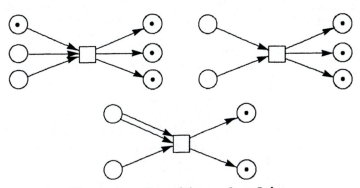

Figure 7. Transitions after firing.

Firing a transition generally changes the marking of the Petri net to a different one. Thus the dynamics of the system are acted out on the markings. Note that since only enabled transitions may be fired, the number of tokens at each place is always non-negative. Note also that firing transitions does not necessarily conserve the total number of tokens in the net.

We may continue firing transitions until there are no more enabled for firing. Since many transitions might at any time be enabled for firing, the sequence in which the transitions are fired might not be unique. The only restriction is that transitions do not fire simultaneously. Consequently, the marking which results after firing a certain number of transitions could vary depending on the particular transitions fired and their order.

Thus, there is possibly some nondeterminism in the execution of Petri net firing. Figure 8 shows an example of two transitions, each of which is enabled for firing, but once one of them is fired, the other is no longer enabled.

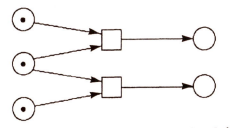

Figure 8.   Transitions enabled for firing.

The goal is to have the Petri net model the system, so each possible firing sequence would correspond to a possible behavior of the system, even though they would not all necessarily result in the same final marking.

Applications

We now look at some examples of Petri net models. The models we consider in detail all concern problems related to computer hardware and operating systems.

Example 8   Construct a Petri net model for calculating the logical conjunction of two variables x and y, each of which takes the values "true" or "false". Each is assigned a value independently of the other.

Solution: Figure 9 shows the required net. To see how this net works, we walk through the firing sequence corresponding to $x =$ "true" and $y =$ "false". We start with one token in the places corresponding to $x =$ "true" and $y =$ "false", the leftmost and rightmost places on the top line of Figure 9. Now only one transition is enabled for firing, the second one from the left. Firing that transition puts one token into the place labeled $x \wedge y =$ "false". No further transition firings are possible and the desired result is obtained. The reader may check that other choices for values of x and y also yield the correct results.

□

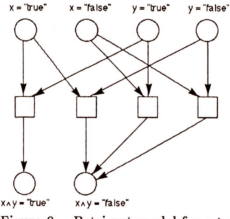

Figure 9.   Petri net model for $x \wedge y$.

Example 9   Construct a Petri net that computes the negation of x, which again takes only the values "true" and "false".

Solution: Figure 10 shows a net that computes the negation of the variable x. This net works similarly to that in Figure 9. If we want to know the value of $\neg x$ when x has a certain value, we put one token in the place for that value, carry out the firing, and observe which place has a token in it.   □

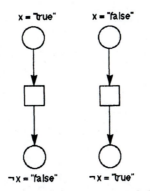

Figure 10.   Petri net model for $\neg x$.

Petri nets can be combined to form new nets. One way is simply to take the disjoint union of the two nets. This is accomplished for the graphical representation by simply drawing the graphs next to each other. Another method combines the nets in a way similar to the composition of functions. In many nets certain of the places could naturally be considered as input places, for example those labeled $x =$ "true" and $x =$ "false" in Figure 10. Others could be considered as output places, for example those labeled $\neg x =$ "false" and $\neg x =$ "true" in Figure 10. To compose two nets N_1 and N_2, the number of output places of N_1 must equal number of input places of N_2. The composition is obtained by identifying the output places of N_1 with the input places of N_2 in an appropriate manner.

Example 10   Construct a Petri net for computing $\neg(x \wedge y)$ by composing the nets in Figures 9 and 10.

Solution: Figure 11 shows the composition net. The input places for Figure 9 are the places labeled $x =$ "true", $x =$ "false", $y =$ "true", and $y =$ "false". The output places in Figure 9 are the places labeled $x \wedge y =$ "true", $x \wedge y =$ "false". The input places for Figure 10 are those labeled $x =$ "true" and $x =$ "false". To combine two nets we match up the input and output places as shown. It is also necessary to relabel some of the places to indicate their meaning in the composed net.   □

Now that we have seen how to use Petri nets to model conjunction and negation of propositional formulas we should note that we can represent all propositional functions using Petri nets since conjunction and negation are functionally complete, i.e. every possible truth table can be obtained as that of a propositional function using only conjunction and negation. (See Section 1.3

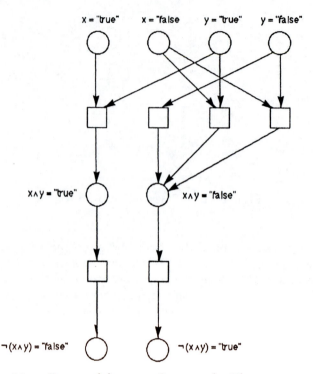

Figure 11.   Composition net for nets in Figures 9 and 10.

of *Discrete Mathematics and Its Applications*, Second Edition, by Kenneth Rosen.)

Using the correspondence between propositional functions and switching circuits we can observe that computer hardware can also be modeled using Petri nets. Figure 11 can thus be seen as modeling a NAND gate.

Our next examples of Petri nets show how they can be useful in studying parallelism in computer systems or problems of control in operating systems.

First we will examine the *readers/writers problem*. There are two types of processes: reader processes and writer processes. All processes share a common file or data object. Reader processes never modify the object but writer processes do modify it. Therefore, writer processes must exclude all other processes, but multiple reader processes can access the shared object simultaneously. This sort of thing happens frequently in database applications, for example, in airline reservation systems. Depending on the actual system, there may be limits on how many processes may access the memory area simultaneously. How can this situation be controlled?

Example 11   Construct a Petri net model for the readers/writers problem when there are six processes, two of which have write access and four have read access. Furthermore, suppose at most three reader processes can overlap in access to memory.

Solution: Figure 12 shows a Petri net model for this control problem. This example was adapted from one in reference [2]. In this example the processes are represented by the tokens, the places in the net represent the different things the processes might be doing, or states they might be in.

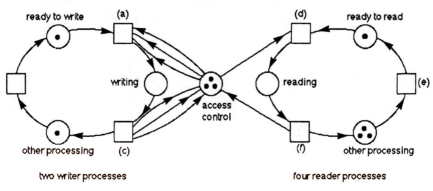

Figure 12.   Petri net model for readers/writers problem.

The assignment of tokens to places in Figure 12 is just one possibility, for illustrative purposes. Let us follow this system through some transition firings to see how it works. As the system is in Figure 12, no processes are reading or writing. Transition (a) is enabled for firing, as are (d), (e), and (b). If we fire (a) then one token is put into the writing place, the place labeled "ready to write" has one token removed from it, and the "access control" place has three tokens removed from it. After this firing, transition (d) is no longer enabled, so no process can enter the "reading" place. Even if there were another token in the "ready to write" place, we could not fire (a) again because there are no tokens in the access control place so (a) is not enabled. In fact, a little thought shows that if (a) has been fired to put a process in the write place then (a) and (d) become unable to fire, thus preventing any other process from either reading or writing. Now transition (c) is enabled. If it is fired we will have two tokens in the "other processing" place and three tokens will be put back in the access control place.

We now see how the net controls read access. Transition (e) is enabled for firing, and in fact we can fire it three times in succession so that the reader "other processing" place becomes empty and the "ready to read" place has four tokens in it. Transition (d) is now enabled for firing. Each time we fire transition (d), one token is removed from the "ready to read" place, one token is put in the reading place, and one token is taken out of the access control place. Once three firings of (d) have taken place, then the access control place is empty, transition (d) is no longer enabled, and no additional tokens can be put in the reading place.

What happens when processes stop reading? Every time transition (f) is fired, one token is put in the access control place and one token is put in the "other processing" place. Three firings of (f) will put three tokens into access control and if there are any tokens in the "ready to write" place, transition (a) will be enabled. We can see how the three tokens in the access control place implement the requirement that no more than three reader processes may have access simultaneously, and the three edges between transitions (a) and (e) and the access control place prevent access when a process is writing.   □

Next we examine the *producer/consumer problem*. Again we have a shared data object, but this time it is specified to be a buffer. A producer process creates objects which are put in the buffer. The consumer waits until there is an object in the buffer, removes it, and consumes it.

Example 12   Construct a Petri net model for the Producer/Consumer problem.

Solution: The net in Figure 13 is the required model.

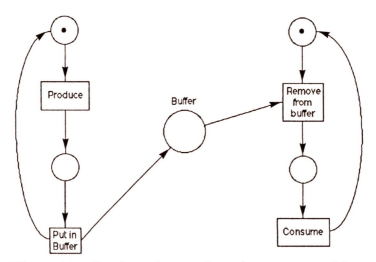

Figure 13.   Petri net for producer/consumer problem.

In this model each token in the buffer represents an object which has been

produced but not yet consumed. We can modify this example to work for the multiple producer/multiple consumer problem. In this case multiple producers produce objects which are stored in a common buffer for the use of multiple consumers. If there are n producers and k consumers, we need only start the system with n tokens in the initial place of the producer process and k tokens in the initial place of the consumer process, instead of one in each as shown in Figure 13. □

The *dining philosophers problem* was suggested in 1968 by Edsger Dijkstra, a great pioneer in computer science. Five philosophers alternatively think and eat. They are seated around a large round table on which are a variety of Chinese foods. Between each pair of philosophers is one chop stick. To eat Chinese food, two chopsticks are necessary; hence each philosopher must pick up both the chopstick on the left and that on the right. Of course, if all the philosophers pick up the chopstick on their right and then wait for the chopstick on their left to become free, they will wait forever — a *deadlock* condition. Dijkstra formulated this problem to illustrate control problems that confront operating systems in which processes share resources and may compete for them with deadlock a conceivable result. To solve the problem some philosophers must eat while others are meditating. How can this be accomplished?

Example 13   Construct a Petri net to solve the problem of the dining philosophers.

Solution: The Petri net in Figure 14 solves this problem.

Each philosopher is represented by two places, meditating (M_i) and eating (E_i). There are also two transitions for each philosopher for going from meditating to eating and vice-versa. Each chopstick is represented by a place (C_i). A token in an eating or meditating place indicates which condition that philosopher is in. A token in a chopstick place indicates that that chopstick is free. A philosopher can change from meditating to eating only if the chopsticks on the left and right are both free. □

Numerous other applications of Petri net models have been developed, not all in computer science. Petri nets have been used to study the PERT technique of project planning and in studying legal processes. More information on these topics can be found in reference [1]. The bibliography of reference [2] lists 221 items including 47 papers and books on applications of Petri nets.

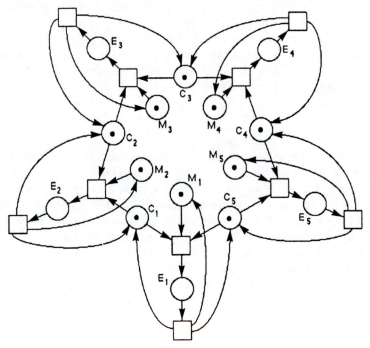

Figure 14. Petri net for dining philosophers problem.

Analysis of Petri Nets

We have seen how useful Petri nets can be in constructing models, but perhaps the most important purpose of modeling is to be able to analyze the model to answer questions about the system being modeled. In this section we consider some problems related to the analysis of Petri nets. The most important analysis problem is that of *reachability*.

Definition 4   Given a Petri net and a marking m, a marking m' is *immediately reachable* from m if there is some transition which, when fired, yields the marking m'.

A marking m' is *reachable* from the marking m if there is a sequence $m_1, \ldots, m_k$ of markings such that $m_1 = m$ and $m_k = m'$ and for all i, m_{i+1} is immediately reachable from m_i. If N is a Petri net and m is a marking of N, then the set of all markings reachable from m is called the *reachability set* of m and is denoted $R(N, m)$.   □

Example 14   Show that the marking of the net in Figure 15b is reachable from the marking in Figure 15a.

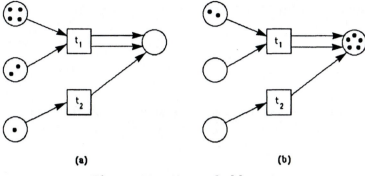

(a)   (b)

Figure 15. A reachable net.

Solution: Firing t_1 twice and then t_2 yields the marking in Figure 15b.   □

Many interesting analysis problems for Petri nets can be phrased as questions about what kinds of markings are reachable from others. For example we introduced the concept of *deadlock* in the discussion of the dining philosophers problem. A net is in **deadlock** if no transitions can fire. In any net we might be interested in knowing whether a deadlock marking is reachable from some initial marking.

If a Petri net is to be a model of a real hardware device, one of the important properties it should have is *safeness*.

Definition 5   A place p in a Petri net N with marking m is *safe* if and only if for all $m' \in R(N, m)$, $m'(p) \leq 1$. That is, p never has more than one token. A net is *safe* if every place in it is safe.   □

The reason safeness is important in modeling hardware devices is that if a place has either no tokens or one token in it, then that place can be implemented by a flip-flop. The nets in Figures 9, 10, and 11 are safe if the initial marking puts at most one token in each of the initial places. The producer/consumer net of Figure 13 is also safe with the marking shown.

Safeness is a special case of the property called *boundedness*. A place is k-**bounded** if the number of tokens in that place can never exceed k. A net is k-**bounded** if all of its places are k-bounded. Safeness is thus the same as 1-boundedness. A Petri net is **bounded** if it is k-bounded for some k. A Petri net which is bounded could be realized in hardware using counters for places while one with an unbounded place could not.

Petri nets can be used to model resource allocation systems. In this context the tokens might represent the resources to be allocated among the places. For these nets *conservation* is an important property.

Definition 6   A Petri net N with marking m is *conservative* if for all $m' \in R(N, m)$,

$$\sum_{p \in P} m'(p) = \sum_{p \in P} m(p). \qquad \qquad \square$$

Conservation thus means that the total number of tokens is the same for all markings reachable from m. This is an extremely strong requirement, as the following theorem shows.

Theorem 1   If N is a conservative net then for each transition the number of input places must equal the number of output places.

Proof: If t is a transition with differing numbers of input and output places then firing t will change the number of tokens in the net. (See, for example, the second transition in Figure 6.)   ∎

The concepts presented so far all involve reachability in some sense. How can they be analyzed? Numerous techniques have been developed and are discussed in detail in references [1] and [2]. We will limit ourselves here to a discussion of the *reachability tree*. The reachability tree of a Petri net is a graphical method of listing the reachable markings. Our treatment follows that of reference [1], Chapter 4, Section 2. To begin, we fix an ordered listing of the places so that a marking can be written as an ordered n-tuple of nonnegative integers. An entry in an n-tuple gives the number of tokens assigned to the place in that position in the list. The initial marking of the net corresponds to the root vertex of the tree. For each marking immediately reachable from the initial one, we create a new vertex and draw a directed edge to it from the initial marking. The edge is labeled with the transition fired to yield the new marking.

Now we repeat this process for all the new markings. If this process is repeated over and over, potentially endlessly, all markings reachable from the initial one will eventually be produced. Of course, the resulting tree may well be infinite. Indeed, if the reachability set of a net is infinite, then the tree must also be infinite.

Example 15   Carry out the first three steps in construction of the reachability tree for the net shown in Figure 16, with the initial marking given there.

Solution: Figure 17 shows the result. The tree is obtained as follows: the triple (x_1, x_2, x_3) gives the number of tokens assigned to the places p_1, p_2, p_3, in that order. From marking $(1, 0, 0)$, firing t_1 yields marking $(1, 1, 0)$. From

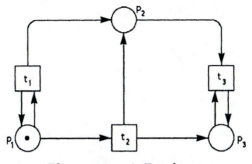

Figure 16. A Petri net.

marking $(1,0,0)$ firing t_2 gives marking $(0,1,1)$. From marking $(1,1,0)$, firing t_1 yields $(1,2,0)$ while firing t_2 yields $(0,2,1)$. From $(0,1,1)$, firing t_3 yields $(0,0,1)$. This completes the second level down from the top. The third level is constructed similarly. □

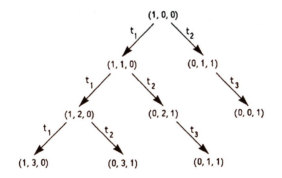

Figure 17. First three steps of reachability tree for Petri net of Figure 16.

If a net has an infinite reachability set, then of course its reachability tree will be infinite. However, it could happen that a net has a finite reachability set and still has an infinite reachability tree. This would be the case if a sequence of markings is repeated infinitely as in the net in Figure 18. For this net the tree is an infinite chain since the net alternates between the markings $(1,0)$ and $(0,1)$. As we have constructed it, the reachability tree contains the results of every possible sequence of transition firings, each sequence corresponding to some path from the root. Any reachability problem can, then, be solved by examining the reachability tree, though the search may be impractical.

While the reachability tree contains every reachable marking, its potential infiniteness poses a problem for analysis. Consequently, it is useful to have a finite representation of the reachability tree. We now describe a method for obtaining a finite representation of a reachability tree. For this purpose we

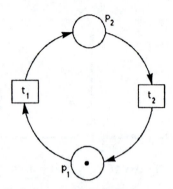

Figure 18.   Petri net with infinite reachability tree.

introduce a classification of vertices in the tree. The new markings produced at each step will be called *frontier* vertices. Markings in which no transition is enabled will be called *terminal* vertices. Markings which have previously appeared in the tree will be called *duplicate* vertices.

Terminal vertices are important because they yield no additional frontier vertices. Duplicate vertices yield no *new* frontier vertices, so no successors of duplicate vertices need be considered. We can thus stop generating frontier vertices from duplicate ones, thereby reducing the size of the tree. For the example in Figure 18 this will make the tree finite. In the example of Figures 16 and 17, the vertex $(0, 1, 1)$ in the third level from the root is a duplicate vertex and hence will produce no new markings.

One more case needs to be considered. If we examine the example of Figures 16 and 17 we can see that transition t_1 can be fired over and over endlessly, each time increasing the number of tokens at place 2 by one. This will create an infinite number of different markings. In this situation and in others like it there is a pattern to the infinite string of markings obtained. To aid in describing this pattern, it is useful to regard the n-tuples for markings as vectors and perform operations on them component-wise.

Suppose we have an initial marking m and some sequence of transition firings s yields a marking m' with $m' \geq m$ componentwise. We can think of m' as having been obtained from m by adding some extra tokens to some places so

$$m' = m + (m' - m)$$

componentwise, and $m' - m \geq 0$. Thus, firing the sequence s had the result of adding $m' - m$ to m. If we start from m' and fire s to get m'', then the result will be to add $m' - m$ to m', so

$$m'' = m + 2(m' - m).$$

In general we could fire the sequence n times to get a marking $m + n(m' - m)$.

We use a special symbol, ω, to represent the infinite number of markings which result from this type of loop. It stands for a number of tokens which can be made arbitrarily large. For the sake of simplifying our description it is useful to define some arithmetic "operations" using ω. For any constant a we define

$$\omega + a = \omega \qquad \omega - a = \omega \qquad a < \omega \qquad \omega \leq \omega.$$

These are all we will need in dealing with the reachability tree. We need one more notational device to simplify the description of the method for constructing the reduced reachability tree.

Definition 7   If m is a marking of a Petri net and t is a transition enabled for firing, then $\delta(m, t)$ is the marking produced from m by firing t.   □

In the reduced reachability tree each vertex x is an *extended marking*; that is, the number of tokens at a place is allowed to be either a nonnegative integer or the symbol ω. Each vertex is classified as either a frontier vertex, a duplicate vertex, a terminal vertex, or an interior vertex. Frontier vertices are vertices which have not been processed by the reduction algorithm; they are converted to terminal, duplicate, or interior vertices.

The algorithm begins by defining the initial marking to be the root of the tree and initially a frontier vertex. The algorithm continues until no more frontier vertices remain to be processed. If x is a marking written as an n-tuple, let x_i be the ith component of x.

Let x be a frontier vertex to be processed.

1. If there exists another vertex in the tree which is not a frontier vertex and is the same marking as x, then vertex x is a duplicate vertex.

2. If no transitions are enabled for the marking x, then x is a terminal vertex.

3. For all transitions t_j which are enabled for firing for the marking x, create a new vertex z in the tree. The components of z are defined as follows:

(a) If $x_i = \omega$ then $z_i = \omega$.

(b) If there exists a vertex y on the path from the root to x with $y \leq \delta(x, t_j)$ and $y_i < \delta(x, t_j)_i$ then $z_i = \omega$.

(c) Otherwise, $z_i = \delta(x, t_j)_i$. An edge labeled t_j is directed from vertex x to vertex z. Vertex x is classified as an interior vertex and z becomes a frontier vertex.

When there are no more frontier vertices, the algorithm stops.

Example 16   Construct the reduced reachability tree for the Petri net shown in Figure 16.

Solution: Figure 19 shows the required tree.   □

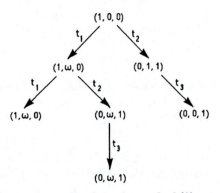

Figure 19.   Reduced reachability tree.

It has been proved that the algorithm for constructing the reduced reachability tree always terminates in a finite tree. The interested reader is referred to Chapter 4 of [1] for details.

Many questions about reachability can be answered using the reduced reachability tree. However, because the use of the symbol ω condenses infinitely many vertices into one, some information may be lost by this process. Often the ω indicates a pattern which can be recognized, thus reducing the loss of information. The special reachability questions we presented can be answered using the tree. A net will be safe if the vertices in the tree all have only 0s and 1s as components. A net will be bounded provided the symbol ω never appears. A net will be conservative if the sums of the components of all the vertices are equal.

Petri nets are perhaps the most widely used modeling tool in computer science. The references each contain large bibliographies; [1] has a bibliography extending over 38 pages.

Suggested Readings

1. J. Peterson, *Petri Net Theory and the Modeling of Systems*, Prentice-Hall, Inc., 1981.

2. W. Reisig, *Petri Nets, An Introduction*, Springer-Verlag, 1985.

Exercises

1. Construct a graph representation for the Petri net with places $\{p_1, p_2, p_3, p_4, p_5\}$, transitions $\{t_1, t_2, t_3\}$, and input function I and output function O defined by: $I(t_1) = \{p_1\}$, $I(t_2) = \{p_1\}$, $I(t_3) = \{p_2, p_3\}$, $O(t_1) = \{p_2\}$, $O(t_2) = \{p_3\}$, $O(t_3) = \{p_4, p_5\}$.

2. A small machine shop can make three different items, though it can work on only one item at a time. The shop can be in six different "states" corresponding to: an order is waiting, one of the three items is being made, an order is finished, and the shop is idle. There are six actions: order arriving, start work on item 1, start work on item 2, start work on item 3, finish processing, and order sent for delivery. Construct a Petri net model for this machine shop analogous to that in Figure 1.

3. Determine whether each transition is enabled for firing.

   a)   b)

   c)

4. Find the results of firing each transition.

   a)   b)

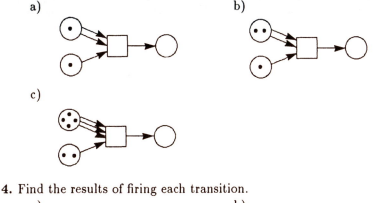

   c)

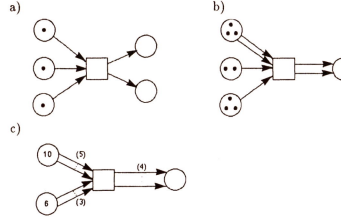

5. Construct a Petri net to calculate the propositional function $x \lor y$.

6. Construct a Petri net to calculate the propositional function $\neg x \land \neg y$.

7. Construct a Petri net for the propositional function $x \rightarrow y$.

8. Modify the example of Figure 12 to allow for three writer processes, five reader processes, and an access limit of only two reader processes at a time.

9. Construct a Petri net for the producer/consumer problem in which there are two producers and three consumers.

10. In our solution of the producer/consumer problem there is no limit on the number of tokens that could be in the buffer. Show how to modify the net so that at most three tokens can be in the buffer.

11. Consider the following marked Petri net.
   a) Is the net safe?
   b) Is the net bounded?
   c) Is the net conservative?

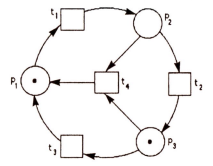

12. Analyze the following Petri net for safeness, boundedness, and conservativeness.

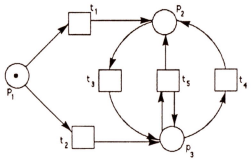

13. Construct the reachability tree for the following Petri net.

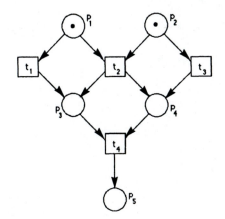

a) Is the net safe?
b) Is the net conservative?
c) Is the marking $(0, 0, 1, 0, 1)$ reachable from the initial marking?

14. Construct the first four levels of the reachability tree of the following Petri net. Is this net bounded?

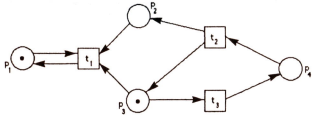

15. Construct the reduced reachability tree for the Petri net in Exercise 14.

Computer Projects

1. Implement computer models of Petri nets. That is, write a program which would simulate the behavior of a marked Petri net under transition firing.

2. Write a computer program to calculate the reachability tree up to ten levels (if necessary) for a Petri net.

3. Write a computer program to calculate the reduced reachability tree of a Petri net with a given marking.

Solutions to Exercises

Chapter 1   The Apportionment Problem

1. The apportionment for methods LF, GD, MF, and EP is (1, 1, 2, 4); for SD the apportionment is (1, 2, 2, 3).   **2.** This problem illustrates that ties can occur, thus violating the house size (this is not likely to occur if state populations are not essentially small integers). GD produces the apportionment (1, 1, 3, 4); EP and SD provide the apportionment (1, 2, 2, 4); but the allocation process under LF or MF encounters a tie rendering the apportionment $(1, 2, 3, 4)$ if an extra seat is assigned because of the tie.

3.

State	LF	GD	MF	EP	SD
NH	4	4	4	4	4
MA	11	12	11	11	11
RI	2	2	2	2	2
CT	7	7	7	7	7
NY	10	10	10	10	10
NJ	5	5	5	5	6
PA	13	13	13	13	13
DE	2	1	2	2	2
MD	8	8	8	8	8
VA	19	19	19	19	18
NC	10	11	10	10	10
SC	6	6	6	6	6
GA	3	3	3	3	3
VT	3	2	3	3	3
KY	2	2	2	2	2

4. Only EP and SD, because the denominators for the Huntington sequential method are zero, hence the ratios are infinite, until a seat has been assigned. **5. (a)** Since GD does not inherently assign even one seat per state, the natural method is to start the Huntington sequential method with $a_i = 3$ for each state. This is equivalent to employing $\sum max(3, \lfloor q_i/\lambda \rfloor) = H$ with the λ method.   **(b)** The proof of equivalence is the same inductive proof given for the regular case in the text.   **6.** The apportionment is $(3,3,4,5)$, which can be contrasted to $(1,3,5,6)$ if the three seat constraint does not exist.   **7.** The proof is the same as the proof of Theorem 1 with the "+1" following the a's omitted.   **8.** By Exercise 7, it suffices to consider the sequential algorithm; use induction on the number of seats assigned. Because this method assigns one seat per district before assigning subsequent seats (which is necessary in order that no p_i/a_i be infinite), assume that each state has one seat. The next seat is assigned to the state for which $p_i/1$ (the district size) is greatest; hence that state's district size must be reduced to minimize the maximum district size. After k of the seats have been assigned, the next state to receive a seat will be the one with the largest district size. This assignment is also necessary to reduce the maximum district size. If the maximum district size was as small as possible before the $(k+1)$st seat was assigned, any reallocation of seats will increase the maximum district size to at least the value with k seats assigned. **9. (a)** Let states $p_1 = 1000$, $p_2 = 10$, $p_3 = 10$, and $H = 3$.   **(b)** No, because the choice $\lambda = 1$ in the λ method provides each state with its upper quota, but too large a House. Increasing λ to decrease the total House size cannot increase the size of any state's delegation.   **10. (a)** For example, $\mathbf{p} = (24, 73, 83)$ with H changing from 18 to 19.   **(b)** No, because with only two states, a fractional part greater than 0.5 is necessary and sufficient for a state to receive its upper quota. Increasing the House size will increase its quota, which will still have a fractional part greater than 0.5 unless it has increased its integer part. **11.** $104!/(90!14!) \approx 8 \times 10^{16}$.   **12.** $434!/(385!49!)$.   **13.** Based on the census figures released in December, 1990 (which are subject to revision until July, 1991), 21 states receive the same number of representatives under all of the apportionment methods discussed in this chapter. These states (with their numbers of representatives) are: AL(7), AK(1), AR(4), CO(6), CT(6), GA(11), HI(2), IN(10), IA(5), MD(8), MN(8), MO(9), NV(2), NH(2), OR(5), SC(6), UT(3), VT(1), VA(11), WV(3), WY(1). The numbers of seats for states whose assignment depends on the apportionment method are given for greatest divisors, equal proportions (which is the method currently employed), and smallest divisors: AZ(6,6,7), CA(54,52,50), DE(1,1,2), FL(23,23,22), ID(1,2,2), IL(21,20,19), KS(4,4,5), KY(6,6,7), LA(7,7,8), ME(2,2,3), MA(11,10,10), MI(17,16,16), MS(4,5,5), MT(1,1,2), NE(2,3,3), NJ(14,13,13), NM(2,3,3), NY(33,31,30), NC(12,12,11), ND(1,1,2), OH(19,19,18), OK(5,6,6), PA(21,21,20), RI(1,2,2), SD(1,1,2), TN(8,9,9), TX(31,30,29), WA(8,9,9), WI(8,9,9). The major fractions method provides the same apportionment as equal proportions, except that MA would get 11 seats and OK would only get five. Largest fractions provides the same apportionment as equal proportions except for MA(11), NJ(14), MS(4), and OK(5). The classification of states with ten or more representatives as large states and those with fewer than ten as small states bears out the characterization of the various apportionment methods as favoring large or small states.   **14.(a)** We show $\log(\lim_{t\to 0}(0.5(a_i^t + (a_i + 1)^t))^{1/t}) = \log\sqrt{a_i(a_i + 1)}$, which is equivalent.

$$\lim_{t\to 0}\frac{1}{t}\log(0.5(a_i^t + (a_i + 1)^t)) =$$

$$\lim_{t\to 0}\frac{1}{t}\log(0.5((1 + t\log a_i) + (1 + t\log(a_i + 1)))) =$$

$$\lim_{t\to 0}\frac{1}{t}(0.5(t\log a_i + t\log(a_i + 1))) =$$

$$\lim_{t\to 0}0.5(\log a_i + \log(a_i + 1)) = \log\sqrt{a_i(a_i + 1)}.$$

(For each of the first two equalities, l'Hôpital's rule can be used to show that the ratio of the left side to the right side is 1.)   **(b)** The limit is manifestly less than or equal to $a_i + 1$ because $a_i < a_i + 1$, and replacing the former with the latter would provide equality. Because $(a_i + 1)^t < a_i^t + (a_i + 1)^t$, the limit is greater than $\lim_{t\to\infty}(0.5(a_i + 1)^t)^{1/t} = \lim_{t\to\infty}0.5^{1/t}((a_i + 1)^t)^{1/t} = a_i + 1$, since $0.5^{1/t}$ has 1 as limit.   **(c)** Letting $b_i = 1/a_i$ and $b_i' = 1/(a_i + 1)$, this limit is the reciprocal of the limit in part (b) for the bs. Since $b_i > b_i'$, the limit is the reciprocal of b_i (i.e., a_i).

Chapter 2   Finite Markov Chains

1. a) Looking at $\mathbf{T}^2$ (in Example 13), we find $p_{13}^{(2)} = 0.16$.   **b)** By Theorem 1, this is $q_2 p_{23} p_{31} p_{11} = 0.4 \times 0.2 \times 0.5 \times 0.3 = 0.012$.   **c)** The possible outcomes comprising this event are: $s_1 s_1 s_2$, $s_1 s_3 s_2$, $s_3 s_3 s_2$, $s_3 s_1 s_2$. We compute the probability of each of these, as in b), and add them, to get 0.144.   **2. T =**

$$\begin{bmatrix} 1 & 0 & 0 & 0 & 0 \\ 1-p & 0 & p & 0 & 0 \\ 0 & 1-p & 0 & p & 0 \\ 0 & 0 & 1-p & 0 & p \\ 0 & 0 & 0 & 0 & 1 \end{bmatrix}.$$

3. a) The state space here is $S = \{s_1 = 0, s_2 = 1, s_3 = 2\}$. The random process is a Markov chain since each day the marbles to be exchanged are chosen at random, meaning that previous choices are not taken into account. Thus, the probability of observing a particular number X_{k+1} of red marbles on day $k + 1$ depends only on how many red marbles were in the jar on day k.   **b) T =**
$$\begin{bmatrix} 0.8 & 0.2 & 0 \\ 0.09 & 0.82 & 0.09 \\ 0 & 0.2 & 0.8 \end{bmatrix}.$$ For example,

$p_{22} = 0.82$ is the probability that if each jar has one red marble in it, there will be one red marble in each after the exchange has been made. This event can occur if one *white* marble is chosen from each of the jars (each of which contains 9 white marbles); by the multiplication rule, there are a total of 100 possible pairs of choices and 81 ways to choose a white marble from each jar. This event would also occur if the one red marble in each jar is chosen; there is clearly only one way to do that. Thus, there are a total of 82 ways out of 100 possibilities of starting with a red in each jar, and ending with a red in each jar after the exchange is made (and 82/100=0.82). A similar use of the multiplication rule will yield the other probabilities found in the matrix.   **c)**
We begin by computing $\mathbf{T}^3 = \begin{bmatrix} 0.56 & 0.40 & 0.04 \\ 0.18 & 0.64 & 0.18 \\ 0.04 & 0.40 & 0.56 \end{bmatrix}$. We then see that $p_{32}^{(3)}$, the

probability that after 3 days there is one red marble in the jar, given that we start out with 2 red marbles, is 0.4.   **4.** p_{ij} is the probability that, starting in state s_i, the Markov chain moves to state s_j. Now the random process *must* move to one of the states s_j, $1 \le j \le N$, by definition of the state space. That is, it moves to exactly one of these states with probability 1, which (for the ith row) is $p_{i1} + p_{i2} + \cdots + p_{iN} = 1$, which is what is to be shown.   **5.**
The result is obtained by mathematical induction. The result is correct for $k = 1$ by the definition of p_{ij}. Assume it is true for $k = m$, i.e., for any i, l,
$p(X_m = s_l | X_0 = s_i) = p_{il}^{(m)}$. We must then deduce the result for $k = m + 1$.
We have

$$p_{ij}^{(m+1)} = P(X_{m+1} = s_j | X_0 = s_i) \qquad \text{by definition of } p_{ij}^{(m+1)}$$

$$= \frac{p(X_{m+1} = s_j, X_0 = s_i}{p(x_0 = s_i)} \qquad \text{by definition of conditional probability}$$

$$= \sum_{l=1}^{N} \frac{p(X_{m+1} = s_j, X_m = s_l, X_0 = s_i)}{p(X_0 = s_i)} \qquad \text{addition rule of probabilities}$$

$$= \sum_{l=1}^{N} \frac{p(X_m = s_l, X_0 = s_i)}{p(X_0 = s_i)} p(X_{m+1} = s_j | X_m = s_l, X_0 = s_i) \qquad \text{cond. prob.}$$

$$= \sum_{l=1}^{N} \frac{p(X_m = s_l, X_0 = s_i)}{p(X_0 = s_i)} p(X_{m+1} = s_j | X_m = s_l) \qquad \text{by (i)}$$

$$= \sum_{l=1}^{N} P(X_m = s_l | X_0 = s_i) p_{lj} \qquad \text{by (ii)}$$

$$= \sum_{l=1}^{N} p_{il}^{(m)} p_{lj} \qquad \text{by the induction assumption}$$

The last expression is the (i, j)th entry of $\mathbf{T}^{m+1}$.   **6. a)** $\mathbf{A}$ is not, since the first row is always (1 0 0) (see Exercise 8). $\mathbf{B}$ is, since $\mathbf{B}^3$ has all positive entries.

b) By the definition of a regular Markov chain, for some k, $\mathbf{T}^k$ has all positive entries. We will show that if $m > 0$ then $\mathbf{T}^{m+k}$ has all positive entries, which amounts to what was to be shown. Now $\mathbf{T}^{m+k} = \mathbf{T}^m \mathbf{T}^k$ which has as its (i,j)th entry $\sum_{n=1}^{N} p_{in}^{(m)} p_{nj}^{(k)} \geq p_{in}^{(m)} p_{nj}^{(k)}$, for any choice of n, since all of the terms of the sum are nonnegative. By assumption, $p_{nj}^{(k)} > 0$; furthermore, at least one of the $p_{in}^{(m)}$ must be greater than 0 since (see Exercise 4) the rows have entries adding up to 1. Thus for some n, $p_{in}^{(m)} p_{nj}^{(k)} > 0$, which yields the desired conclusion.

7. a) The state space $S = \{s_1, s_2\}$, where s_1 is the state that a women is a voter and s_2 that she is a nonvoter. Let X_k be the voting status of a woman in the kth generation of her family. This will be a Markov chain with matrix of transition probabilities $\mathbf{T} = \begin{bmatrix} 0.5 & 0.5 \\ 0.1 & 0.9 \end{bmatrix}$. **b)** $(p \ q) \begin{bmatrix} 0.5 & 0.5 \\ 0.1 & 0.9 \end{bmatrix} = (p \ q)$ is the system of equations $0.5p + 0.1q = p$, $0.5p + 0.9q = q$. We also have $p + q = 1$. Solving the system of three equations for the unknowns p and q yields $p = 0.167$ and $q = 0.833$. This may be interpreted to mean that in the long run (if these voting patterns remain unchanged) about 17% of women will be voters and the remaining 83% will be nonvoters.   **8. a)** 0 and 4 are absorbing states in Example 1.   **b)** Example 3 has none, since with positive probability, the process can leave any of the given states. This is of course true for any regular Markov chain.   **c)** No, it is not. If the Markov chain has an absorbing state, say s_i, then the ith row of the matrix of transition probabilities will have a 1 as the (i,i)th entry and all other entries in that row will be 0. When we perform the matrix multiplication, this row never changes. The underlying phenomenon is this: in a regular Markov chain, it must eventually be possible to reach any state from a particular state, since all the entries of some power of the matrix of transition probabilities are all positive. This clearly cannot happen if there is an absorbing state, since by the definition of such a state, no state can be reached from it no matter how long we wait.   **9. a)** Using the definition of conditional probability, the right hand side becomes $P(A)\frac{P(E \cap A)}{P(A)} + P(B)\frac{P(E \cap A)}{P(B)} = P(E \cap A) + P(E \cap B)$. Now, $E = (E \cap A) \cup (E \cap B)$ (since $A \cup B$ contains all possible outcomes) and $(E \cap A) \cap (E \cap B) = E \cap (A \cap B) = E \cap \emptyset = \emptyset$, so $P(E) = P(E \cap A) + P(E \cap B)$ ("addition rule" for probabilities), and we are done.   **b)** Using the hint, we compute $P(E) = P(A)P(E|A) + P(B)P(E|B)$. Now, $P(A) = P(B) = 1/2$. Also, $P(E|A) = r_{k+1}$, since the only way to win (starting with k dollars), given that we win the first round, is to win, given that we start with $k + 1$ dollars. (This is a consequence of property (i) in Definition 1; in this context, we might say that the Markov chain "forgets" that we have just won and thinks that we are starting with $k + 1$ dollars.) Similarly, $P(E|B) = r_{k-1}$, thus, $r_k = P(E) = \frac{1}{2}r_{k-1} + \frac{1}{2}r_{k+1}$, $0 < k < 4$, with $r_0 = 0$, $r_4 = 1$.   **c)** The identical argument yields $r_k = \frac{1}{2}r_{k-1} + \frac{1}{2}r_{k+1}$, $0 < k < N$, $r_0 = 0$, $r_N = 1$.   **d)** This is a straightforward verification by substitution.   **10. a)** Label the vertices of a pentagon $1,2,3,4,5$; thus, the state space is $S = \{1,2,3,4,5\}$. We then

have $\mathbf{T} = \begin{bmatrix} 0 & 1/2 & 0 & 0 & 1/2 \\ 1/2 & 0 & 1/2 & 0 & 0 \\ 0 & 1/2 & 0 & 1/2 & 0 \\ 0 & 0 & 1/2 & 0 & 1/2 \\ 1/2 & 0 & 0 & 1/2 & 0 \end{bmatrix}$.   b) Let $Q = [0.2\ 0.2\ 0.2\ 0.2\ 0.2]$.

Then $\mathbf{QT} = [0.2\ 0.2\ 0.2\ 0.2\ 0.2] = \mathbf{Q}$. In the long run, the probability of finding the drunkard at any particular corner of the building is $0.2=1/5$; that is, there is an equal chance of finding him at any particular corner.   c) Let the state space here be $S = \{1,2,3,4\}$. The matrix of transition prob-

abilities is $\mathbf{T} = \begin{bmatrix} 0 & 1/2 & 0 & 1/2 \\ 1/2 & 0 & 1/2 & 0 \\ 0 & 1/2 & 0 & 1/2 \\ 1/2 & 0 & 1/2 & 0 \end{bmatrix}$ and the equilibrium distribution is

$(0.25\ 0.25\ 0.25\ 0.25)$.   **11. a)** $S = \{\text{win, lose}, 3, 4, 5, 6, 7, 8, 9, 10, 11\}$ where $3, 4, \ldots, 11$ are the possible sums from which we can win (rolling a 2 or 12 immediately puts us in the "lose" state, since we must have rolled doubles). Note that once we are in one of the states $3, 4, \ldots, 11$, we stay there until we either win or lose.   **b)** The initial distribution (where the order is that given in the above description of S) is $[0\ 6/36\ 2/36\ 2/36\ 4/36\ 4/36\ 6/36\ 4/36\ 4/36\ 2/36\ 2/36]$. For example, there are 6 ways to roll doubles initially out of 36 possible outcomes so (since we lose when we roll doubles) the probability of losing right away is $6/36$. Of the 3 possible ways to roll a 4, $((1,3);(2,2);(3,1))$, only two, $(1,3)$ and $(3,1)$, correspond to the state "4"; $(2,2)$ corresponds to the

state "lose".   **c)** $T = \begin{bmatrix} 1 & 0 & 0 & 0 & 0 & 0 & 0 & 0 & 0 & 0 & 0 \\ 0 & 1 & 0 & 0 & 0 & 0 & 0 & 0 & 0 & 0 & 0 \\ \frac{2}{36} & \frac{6}{36} & \frac{28}{36} & 0 & 0 & 0 & 0 & 0 & 0 & 0 & 0 \\ \frac{2}{36} & \frac{6}{36} & 0 & \frac{28}{36} & 0 & 0 & 0 & 0 & 0 & 0 & 0 \\ \frac{2}{36} & \frac{6}{36} & 0 & 0 & \frac{26}{36} & 0 & 0 & 0 & 0 & 0 & 0 \\ \frac{4}{36} & \frac{6}{36} & 0 & 0 & 0 & \frac{26}{36} & 0 & 0 & 0 & 0 & 0 \\ \frac{6}{36} & \frac{6}{36} & 0 & 0 & 0 & 0 & \frac{24}{36} & 0 & 0 & 0 & 0 \\ \frac{4}{36} & \frac{6}{36} & 0 & 0 & 0 & 0 & 0 & \frac{26}{36} & 0 & 0 & 0 \\ \frac{4}{36} & \frac{6}{36} & 0 & 0 & 0 & 0 & 0 & 0 & \frac{26}{36} & 0 & 0 \\ \frac{2}{36} & \frac{6}{36} & 0 & 0 & 0 & 0 & 0 & 0 & 0 & \frac{28}{36} & 0 \\ \frac{2}{36} & \frac{6}{36} & 0 & 0 & 0 & 0 & 0 & 0 & 0 & 0 & \frac{28}{36} \end{bmatrix}$.

The idea is that once we roll a certain sum initially, we stay in that state until we either win or lose.   **12. a)** Reflexivity and symmetry are easy consequences of the definition of the relation. To show that the relation is transitive, we must prove that $s_i \leftrightarrow s_k$ and $s_k \leftrightarrow s_j$ implies $s_i \leftrightarrow s_j$. Since s_k is accessible from s_i, there is a number n such that $p_{ik}^{(n)} > 0$ and since s_j is accessible from s_k, $p_{kj}^{(m)} > 0$ for some number m. Now $\mathbf{T}^{n+m} = \mathbf{T}^n \mathbf{T}^m$, so the (i,j)th entry of $\mathbf{T}^{n+m}$ (which is, by Theorem 2, $p_{ij}^{(n+m)}$) can be computed as $p_{ij}^{(n+m)} = \sum_{l=1}^{N} p_{il}^{(n)} p_{lj}^{(m)} \geq p_{ik}^{(n)} p_{kj}^{(m)} > 0$. For $l = k$, we have $p_{ik}^{(n)} p_{kj}^{(m)} > 0$, so that the sum above (none of whose terms are negative) must in fact be larger than 0, which means that s_j is accessible from s_i. The identical argument demonstrates that s_i is accessible from s_j, so that these two states communicate. This establishes transitivity and hence that the relation $\leftrightarrow$ is an equivalence relation.   b) If s_k is absorbing, $p_{kk} = 1$ and $p_{kj} = 0$ for $j \neq k$, i.e., it is impossible for the process to leave state s_k and enter another state s_j. This means that for $j \neq k$, s_j is *not* accessible from s_k, so they cannot be communicating states.   c) No. A transient state like s_i is one that the process eventually leaves forever, whereas it returns over and over again to recurrent states (like s_j).   d) In Example 1, the equivalence classes are $\{0\}$, $\{4\}$, $\{1, 2, 3\}$. In Example 2, there is only one equivalence class $\{s_1, s_2, s_3\}$.   e) There is only one equivalence class. The fact that *all* entries of $\mathbf{T}^k$ are positive for some k means that for this k and for any i and j, we have $p_{ij}^{(k)} > 0$, which means that every pair of states communicate.   **13.** Let $p, q \geq 0$ with $p + q = 1$. Then $\mathbf{Q} = (p \ 0 \ 0 \ 0 \ q)$ is an initial probability distribution and it is easy to check that for such $\mathbf{Q}$ $\mathbf{Q} = \mathbf{Q}\mathbf{T}$. The idea is that there is a rather uninteresting equilibrium attained if we start out with probability p of having no money to start with and probability q of already at the beginning having the amount of money we want to end up with.   **14.** a) Choose a number e to be the error tolerance. We must show that for any choice of an initial probability distribution $\mathbf{Q}$, we have $|\sum_{i=1}^{N} q_i p_{ij}^{(k)} - r_j| < e$, $1 \leq j \leq N$, since $\sum_{i=1}^{N} q_i p_{ij}^{(k)}$ is the jth entry of $\mathbf{Q}_k$, which is supposed to be close to $\mathbf{Q}_e$. Now the entries of the jth column of $\mathbf{T}^{(k)}$ are by assumption all within e units of r_j. Also, $\sum_{i=1}^{N} q_i = 1$. We thus have $|\sum_{i=1}^{N} q_i p_{ij}^{(k)} - r_j| = |\sum_{i=1}^{N} q_i p_{ij}^{(k)} - \sum_{i=1}^{N} q_i r_j| = |\sum_{i=1}^{N} [q_i p_{ij}^{(k)} - q_i r_j]| \leq \sum_{i=1}^{N} |q_i (p_{ij}^{(k)} - r_j)| = \sum_{i=1}^{N} q_i |(p_{ij}^{(k)} - r_j)| \leq \sum_{i=1}^{N} q_i e = e$.   b) The $N \times N$ matrix $\mathbf{T}^2$ has N^2 entries. Each of these requires N additions and N multiplications, namely $p_{ij}^2 = \sum_{k=1}^{N} p_{ik} p_{kj}$. Thus, there are a total of N^3 additions and N^3 multiplications required to multiply two $N \times N$ matrices together. If this operation were to be repeated $k - 1$ times, which is the number of matrix multiplications required to compute $\mathbf{T}^k$, there would be a total of $(k - 1)N^3$ additions and $(k - 1)N^3$ multiplications required. Finally, to compute $\mathbf{Q}_k$, we must perform N additions and N multiplications for each of the N entries of the $1 \times N$ matrix $\mathbf{Q}_k = \mathbf{Q}\mathbf{T}^k$ for a grand total of $(k - 1)N^3 + N^2 \approx kN^3$ multiplications and additions to compute $\mathbf{Q}_k$.   c) $\mathbf{Q}_k = \mathbf{Q}\mathbf{T}^k = \mathbf{Q}\mathbf{T}^{k-1}\mathbf{T} = \mathbf{Q}_{k-1}\mathbf{T}$, which is what is to be shown. To compute $\mathbf{Q}_k$ using this idea, we must perform k operations of multiplying a $1 \times N$ matrix by an $N \times N$ matrix. Each one of these matrix multiplications requires N^2 multiplications and additions, for a total of kN^2 multiplications and additions for the computation of $\mathbf{Q}_k$, a very significant improvement over the method of part b).

Chapter 3   Rational Election Procedures

1. One example is the ranking of students by letter grades. If two students have the same grade, they are related to each other (XRY and YRX), hence it is not a total order.   **2.** The standard example of the power set of $\{a, b, c\}$ with a partial order defined by "is a subset of". It is not a weak order because $\{a\}$ and $\{b, c\}$ are not comparable.   **3.** Specializing XRY or YRX to the case $X = Y$ provides XRX.   **4.** Indifference is defined as $XIY \Leftrightarrow XRY \wedge YRX$. It is therefore symmetric. Since R is a weak order (which is transitive and reflexive), it is the intersection of two relations which are transitive and reflexive, hence is also transitive and reflexive.   **5.** It is connected since if there is a tie, the candidates are related to each other; else the winner is related to the loser. It is transitive since it is reflexive and any reflexive relation on two elements is transitive.   **6.** Majority rule with just two candidates satisfies PR since a stronger preference for candidate A entails giving him a vote previously assigned to B, which raises A's relative position, so he fares at least as well as before. IA is vacuously true since there are no candidates to withdraw from the contest if one wishes to compare the relative rankings of two.   **7.** If a relation is a total order, it is connected. If it is an equivalence relation it is symmetric. Combining $XRY \vee YRX$ with $XRY \Rightarrow YRX$ implies that XRY for all X and Y, i.e., everything is related to everything. This violates antisymmetry if the relation is on a set with more than one element.   **8.** Assume $X\widehat{P}_1 Y$ and $Y\widehat{R}X$. $Y\widehat{P}_2 X$ contradicts the hypothesis, hence $X\widehat{R}_2 Y$. But $X\widetilde{P}_1 Y$, $X\widehat{P}_2 Y$ and $Y\widehat{R}X$ contradicts Lemma 1, hence $X\widetilde{I}_2 Y$. By IA and PR, $X\widehat{P}_1 Y$ and $Y\widetilde{P}_2 X$ provide $Y\widetilde{R}X$, which violates the hypothesis of Lemma 2. Therefore the assumption $X\widehat{P}_1 Y$ and $Y\widehat{R}X$ cannot be true and Lemma 2 is proven.   **9.** If $XP_1 Y$, $YP_2 X$, and XPY; by symmetry with respect to candidates $YP_1 X$ and $XP_2 Y$ implies YPX and by symmetry with respect to voters $XP_2 Y$ and $YP_1 X$ implies XPY; which two implications provide a contradiction. Assuming initially YPX leads to the same contradiction, hence indifference must hold.   **10.** A has 4, B has 3, C has 2; hence none of the candidates has a majority of first place votes. A has a plurality.   **11.** If C is eliminated, B receives 5 first place votes while A still receives only 4. Hence B wins.   **12.** If only the favorite candidates are acceptable, approval voting is plurality voting for the favorite candidate, and A wins. If every voter approved his first two choices, A would still only get 4 votes, B would get six votes, and C would get 8 votes; hence C would win.   **13.** B would defeat A. C would then defeat B.   **14.** Yes, C would defeat either A or B in a two-way race.   **15.** The scoring is $2 - 1 - 0$. A gets 8, B gets 9, and C gets 10; hence C wins.   **16.** B receives 8, H receives 8, Y receives 2, and D receives 3; hence there is a tie between B and H.   **17.** C must beat D by transitivity; either outcome of the B-D competition will be consistent.   **18.** Three. No matter how many teams are in the tournament, if A defeats B, B defeats C, and C defeats A, transitivity will be violated.   **19.** If the number of voters is divisible by three, assign one-third to each preference schedule; for four voters, giving two voters to one preference schedule will result in contradicting transitivity with indiference instead of preference; for more than four voters assign the one or two voters in excess of a multiple of three to different (if the excess is two) candidates and the argument presented remains valid.   **20.** For the individual preferences BP_1C, CP_1A and CP_2A, AP_2B Lemma 1 provides CPA. BPC because it is true for P_1 (from above in the lemma). Hence BPA by transitivity. Lemma 2 (with IA and PR) provides this for all preferences compatible with BP_1A. Hence $BP_1A \Rightarrow BPA$. For CPA consider the preferences $C \succ B \succ A$ and $A \succ C \succ B$.   **21.** If YRX when more voters prefer X, then, by PR, YRX when more voters prefer Y, but XRY by symmetry. This is a contradiction if there is no indifference, hence XRY (which is consistent with indifference).   **22.** With three alternatives, there are a total of three two way contests; either each candidate wins one (no Copeland winner), or one candidate wins both contests in which he is involved (a Condorcet winner). If there are four candidates there are six two-way contests with each candidate involved in three of them. If no candidate wins three contests (hence there is no Condorcet winner), at least two candidates must win two contests (pigeonhole principle).   **23.** 315. (There are 3 ways to order teams B, C, and D; 3 ways to order teams F, G, and H; and 35 ways to interleaf the orderings of BCD with $EFGH$.   **24.** A *vs.* B and C *vs.* D or A *vs.* C and B *vs.* D. A *vs.* D initially if A is to lose.

Chapter 4   Gödel's Undecidability Theorem

1. $14 = 3 + 11$, $16 = 3 + 13$, $18 = 5 + 13$, $20 = 3 + 17$, $22 = 3 + 19$, $24 = 5 + 19$, $26 = 3 + 23$, $28 = 5 + 23$, $30 = 7 + 23$, $32 = 3 + 29$, $34 = 3 + 31$, $36 = 5 + 31$, $38 = 7 + 31$, $40 = 3 + 37$, $42 = 5 + 37$, $44 = 3 + 41$, $46 = 3 + 43$, $48 = 5 + 43$, $50 = 3 + 47$.   **2.** Starting with $n = 22$, repeated application of f gives the following sequence of integers: 22, 11, 34, 17, 52, 26, 13, 40, 20, 10, 5, 16, 8, 4, 2, 1. Hence $i = 15$. Starting with $n = 23$, repeated application of f gives: 23, 70, 35, 106, 53, 160, 80, 40, 20, 10, 5, 16, 8, 4, 2, 1. Hence $i = 15$.
3.   **4.**

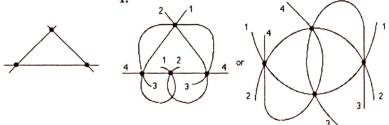

5. Same as solution to Exercise 3.

6.   **7.** Yes, as illustrated below.

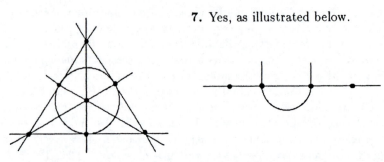

8. Suppose points a, b, c lie on line l_1, and d lies on l_2. Since l_2 contains three points and there are only four points in the system, at least two of the points a, b, c must also lie on l_2. This contradicts axiom (ii).   **9.** Suppose points a, b, c lie on line l_1. Since a lies on two lines, there is a line l_2 containing a. By axiom (ii), neither b nor c can lie on l_2, so l_2 must contain points d and e. Points b and d must also lie on another line, say l_3. The third point on l_3 cannot be a, c, or e; let f be this third point on l_3. Then a and f must lie on a line other than l_1 and l_2, which forces a to be on three lines, contradicting axiom (iii).   **10.** If the statement is true, then it is false. If the statement is false, then it is true. **11. a)** If a liar makes the statement, then "I am lying" is false, and hence the speaker is telling the truth (which contradicts the fact that the speaker never tells the truth). If a truth-teller makes the statement, then "I am lying" is true, and the speaker is lying (which contradicts the fact that the speaker always tells the truth). **b)** This is a paradox. If the person is a liar, then the statement is false. So I will know that he is telling the truth and so therefore he is a truth teller. But this truth teller says that I cannot know that he is truthful, which is an untrue statement since I do know. So, he is not a truth teller either. **12. a)** $2^{21}3^{19}5^{3}7^{3}11^{1}$ **b)** $2^{5}3^{11}5^{11}7^{21}11^{19}13^{1}17^{13}19^{7}23^{11}29^{23}31^{19}37^{1}41^{13}43^{13}$ **c)** $2^{9}3^{21}5^{17}7^{23}11^{11}13^{5}17^{11}19^{3}23^{21}29^{19}31^{23}37^{13}41^{13}$

d) $2^{9}3^{21}5^{11}7^{11}11^{21}13^{19}17^{3}19^{1}23^{13}29^{7}31^{5}37^{11}41^{21}43^{19}47^{3}53^{1}59^{13}61^{13}$

13. a) $2^{k_1}3^{k_2}5^{k_3}$, where $k_1 = 2^{21}3^{19}5^{3}7^{1}$, $k_2 = 2^{23}3^{19}5^{3}7^{21}$, and

$k_3 = 2^{23}3^{19}5^{3}7^{3}11^{1}$.   **b)** $2^{k_1}3^{k_2}5^{k_3}$, where $k_1 = 2^{17}3^{23}5^{11}7^{21}11^{19}13^{3}17^{23}19^{13}$, $k_2 = 2^{9}3^{23}5^{11}7^{5}11^{11}13^{1}17^{19}19^{3}23^{23}29^{13}31^{13}$, and $k_3 = 2^{5}3^{11}5^{21}7^{19}11^{1}13^{13}$.

14. a) $\neg(x = y)$.   **b)** $\forall x \exists y(x = fy)$.   **c)** $(x = 0) \lor \neg(y = 0)$.

15. a) $\left\{ \begin{array}{c} x = ff0 \\ \neg(y = x) \\ \neg(y = ff0) \end{array} \right\}$.   **b)** $\left\{ \begin{array}{c} \forall y \exists x \neg(x = y) \\ y = f0 \\ \exists x \neg(x = f0) \end{array} \right\}$.   **16.** Gödel's Undecidability Theorem predicts that there is some new statement G' in the larger system which is true but which cannot be proven within that system.

Chapter 5   Coding Theory

1. a) no   **b)** yes   **c)** yes   **d)** yes.   **2. a)** 5   **b)** 3   **c)** 4   **d)** 6.   **3.**
a) 0.9509900499   **b)** 0.096059601   **c)** 0.0000970299   **d)** 0.0000009801   **e)**
0.9990198504   **4. a)** detect 6, correct 3   **b)** detect 1, correct 0   **c)** detect
4, correct 2.   **5.** 0.999999944209664279880021   **6.** Let C be a binary
code with $d(C) = 4$. We can correct one error and detect two errors as follows. Let **y** be a bit string we receive. If **y** is a codeword **x** or has distance
1 from a codeword **x** we decode it as **x** since, as can be shown using the triangle inequality, every other codeword would have distance at least three from
y. If **y** has distance at least two from every codeword, we detect at least two
errors, and we ask for retransmission.   **7.** 11   **8.** The minimum distance of this code in n. We find that $2^n/(\sum_{j=0}^{(n-1)/2} C(n,j)) = 2^n/2^{n-1} = 2$,
since $\sum_{j=0}^{(n-1)/2} C(n,j) = (\sum_{j=0}^{n} C(n,j))/2 = 2^n/2 = 2^{n-1}$. Since there are two
codewords in this code and this is the maximum number of codewords possible
by the sphere packing bound, this code is perfect.   **9.** There is a 1 in a
specified position in **x** + **y** if there is a 1 in this position in exactly one of **x**
and **y**. Note that $w(\mathbf{x}) + w(\mathbf{y})$ is the sum of the number of positions where **x**
is 1 and the number of positions where **y** is 1. It follows that the number of
positions where exactly one of **x** and **y** equals 1 is this sum minus the number of positions where both **x** and **y** are 1. The result now follows.   **10.**

$$\mathbf{H} = (1\ 1\ 1\ 1\ 1).   \textbf{11. } \mathbf{H} = \begin{pmatrix} 1 & 0 & 0 & 1 & 0 & 0 & 0 & 0 & 0 \\ 0 & 1 & 0 & 0 & 1 & 0 & 0 & 0 & 0 \\ 0 & 0 & 1 & 0 & 0 & 1 & 0 & 0 & 0 \\ 1 & 0 & 0 & 0 & 0 & 0 & 1 & 0 & 0 \\ 0 & 1 & 0 & 0 & 0 & 0 & 0 & 1 & 0 \\ 0 & 0 & 1 & 0 & 0 & 0 & 0 & 0 & 1 \end{pmatrix}.   \textbf{12.}$$

$$\mathbf{H} = \begin{pmatrix} 1 & 1 & 0 & 1 & 1 & 0 & 0 \\ 1 & 0 & 1 & 1 & 0 & 1 & 0 \\ 1 & 1 & 1 & 0 & 0 & 0 & 1 \end{pmatrix}.   \textbf{13. } \mathbf{G} = \begin{pmatrix} 1 & 0 & 1 & 1 & 0 \\ 0 & 1 & 0 & 1 & 1 \end{pmatrix}.   \textbf{14.}$$

0000000, 0001111, 0010110, 0011001, 0110011, 0100101, 0101010, 0111100,
1000011, 1001100, 1010101, 1011010, 1100110, 1101001, 1110000, 1111111.
15. a) Suppose that when the codeword **x** is sent, **y** is received, where **y**
contains l erasures, where $l \le d - 1$. Since the minimum distance between
codewords is d there can be at most one codeword that agrees with **y** is the
$n - l$ positions that were not erased. This codeword is **x**. Consequently, we correct **y** to be **x**.   **b)** Suppose that when the codeword **x** is sent, **y** is received and
y contains at m errors and l erasures, such that $m \le t$ and $l \le r$. Suppose that
S is the set of bit strings that agree with **y** in the $n - l$ positions that were not
erased. Then there is a bit string $s_1 \in S$ with $d(\mathbf{x}, s_1) \le t$. We will show that
x is the only such codeword. Suppose that there was another codeword $z \in S$.
Then $d(\mathbf{z}, s_2) \le t$ for some string $s_2 \in S$. By the triangle inequality, we then
would have $d(\mathbf{x}, \mathbf{z}) \le d(\mathbf{x}, s_1) + d(s_1, s_2) + d(s_2, \mathbf{z})$. But since the first and third

terms in the sum of the right hand side of this inequality equal m and the middle term is no larger than l, it follows that $d(\mathbf{x}, \mathbf{z}) \leq m + l + m = 2m + l \leq 2t + r$, which is a contradiction since both $\mathbf{x}$ and $\mathbf{z}$ are codewords and the minimum distance between codewords is $d = 2t + r + 1$.

Chapter 6   Stirling Numbers

1. Using $S(7, k) = S(6, k - 1) + k\, S(6, k)$ and the values of $S(6, k)$ in Table 1, we get 1, 63, 301, 350, 140, 21, 1 as the values of $S(7, k)$. For the $s(7, k)$, use $s(7, k) = s(6, k - 1) - 6\, s(6, k)$ and Table 2 to get the values 720, -1764, 1624, -735, 115, -21, 1.   **2.** $(x)_4 = x(x - 1)(x - 2)(x - 3) = x^4 - 6x^3 + 11x^2 - 6x$.
3. Write $x^4 = (x)_4 + a_3(x)_3 + a_2(x)_2 + a_1(x)_1 = (x^4 - 6x^3 + 11x^2 - 6x) + (x^3 - 3x^2 + 2x)a_3 + (x^2 - x)a_2 + xa_1$ for unknown coefficients a_i. Equating the coefficients of x^j above, we get the equations $-6 + a_3 = 0$, $11 - 3a_3 + a_2 = 0$, $-6 + 2a_3 - a_2 + a_1 = 0$, and find the solution $a_3 = 6 = S(4, 3)$, $a_2 = 7 = S(4, 2)$, $a_3 = 1 = S(4, 1)$.   **4.** The number of onto functions from an 8-element set to a 5-element set is, by (3), $\frac{1}{5!} \sum_{i=0}^{5} (-1)^i C(5, i)(5 - i)^8 = 1050$.   **5.** Writing each function f as an ordered triple $f(1)f(2)f(3)$, the functions f with $|f(N)| = 1$ are the $S(3, 1)(3)_1 = 1 \cdot 3 = 3$ functions aaa, bbb, ccc. Those with $|f(N)| = 2$ are the $S(3, 2)(3)_2 = 3 \cdot 6 = 18$ functions aab, aba, baa, aac, aca, caa, bba, bab, abb, bbc, bcb, cbb, cca, cac, acc, ccb, cbc, and bcc. The $S(3, 3)(3)_3 = 1 \cdot 6 = 6$ functions f with $|f(N)| = 3$ are abc, acb, bac, bca, cab, and cba.   **6.** Since the balls are distinguishable and the boxes are identical, we can interpret the balls in a nonempty box as a class of a partition of the set of balls. Then the numbers are given by: a) $S(7, 4) = 350$;
b) $S(7, 1) + S(7, 2) + S(7, 3) + S(7, 4) = 1 + 63 + 301 + 350 = 715$.   **7.**
a) $2^6/3^6 = 64/729 = 0.088$.   b) $S(6, 3)\, 3!/3^6 = 90 \cdot 6/729 = 0.741$.   c)
$S(6, 2)(3)_2 = 31 \cdot 6/729 = 0.255$.   **8.** Using Theorem 1 with $k = 3$, recursively compute $S(n, 3)$ for $n = 3, 4, \ldots, 12$. Then the number of partitions of the set of 12 people into three subsets is $S(12, 3) = 86,526$.   **9.** After $n - 1$ rolls, all but one of the k numbers have appeared, and it, say x, appears on roll n. The first $n - 1$ rolls then define a function from the set $\{1, 2, \ldots, n - 1\}$ onto the set of $k - 1$ numbers other than x. Since x can be chosen in k ways, by Theorem 2 and the product rule the number of possible sequences is $S(n - 1, k - 1)k!$.
10. The sequence corresponds to a function from the set of n positions to the set of 10 digits. The function is arbitrary in a) and onto in b), so the numbers are: a) 10^n;   b) $S(n, 10) \cdot 10!$.   **11.** Here the pockets are the cells of the distribution.   a) The distribution corresponds to a function from the set of 15 numbered balls to the set of six pockets, so the number is 6^{15}.   b) The distributions in the four identical corner pockets correspond to partitions of the set of 15 distinguishable balls into at most four classes, while the distributions in the two identical center pockets correspond to partitions into at most two classes.

By the sum rule, the number of distributions is $\sum_{k=1}^{4} S(15, k) + \sum_{k=1}^{2} S(15, k)$.
12. The $S(n + 1, k)$ partitions into k classes of an $(n + 1)$-set $S = \{0, 1, \ldots, n\}$ can be classified according to the number of elements other than 0 in the class containing 0. The number of these partitions in which the class containing 0 has size $j + 1$ is obtained by choosing a j-element subset J of the n-set $\{1, 2, \ldots, n\}$ to put in a class with 0 and then choosing a $(k - 1)$-class partitions of the set of $n - j$ remaining elements. Apply the product rule and sum over j.   **13.**
a) A partition of an n-set N into $n - 1$ classes must have one class of size two, and the remaining classes of size one. Since it is determined uniquely by the class of size two, the number of these partitions equals $C(n, 2)$, the number of 2-subsets of N.   **b)** Since $s(n, n - 1)$ is the coefficient of x^{n-1} in the expansion of $(x)_n = x(x - 1) \ldots (x - n + 1)$, it is equal to -1 times the sum of the positive integers $1, 2, \ldots, n - 1$, which is $-n(n - 1)/2 = -C(n, 2)$.   **14. a)**
The number of ordered partitions (A, B) of an n-element set into two nonempty subsets is $2!$ times the number $S(n, 2)$ of such unordered partitions, since the two classes can be ordered in $2!$ ways. But there are $2^n - 2$ nonempty proper subsets A of the n-set, and then B is uniquely determined as the complement of A. Thus $S(n, 2) = (2^n - 2)/2! = 2^{n-1} - 1$.   **b)** The coefficient $s(n, 1)$ of x in the expansion of $(x)_n = x(x - 1) \cdots (x - n + 1)$ is the product of the terms $-1, -2, \ldots, -(n - 1)$ in the last $n - 1$ factors, which is $(-1)^{n-1}(n - 1)!$ **15.**
This follows immediately from the fact that the $S(n, k)$, $s(n, k)$ are the entries for exchanging between the two bases $\{x\}$, $\{(x)_n\}$ of the vector space. From the definitions $x^m = \sum_{k=0}^{m} S(m, k)(x)_k = \sum_{k=0}^{m} S(m, k) \sum_{n=0}^{k} s(k, n)x^n = \sum_{n=0}^{m} (\sum_{k=n}^{m} S(m, k)s(k, n))x^n$, where we have used the fact that $0 \le n \le k \le m$ and $S(m, k) = 0$ for $k > m$, $s(k, n) = 0$ for $k > n$. Equating the coefficients of x^n on both sides gives the result.   **16.** Replace x by $-x$ in (8), and note that $(-x)_n = (-1)^n x(x + 1) \cdots (x + n - 1) = (-1)^n (x)^n$, where $(x)^n = x(x + 1) \cdots (x + n - 1)$ is the **rising factorial**. This gives $(x)^n = \sum_{k=0}^{n} (-1)^{n-k} s(n, k)x^k = \sum_{k=0}^{n} t(n, k)x^k$ and the coefficients of x^k in the expansion of $(x)^n$ are clearly positive.   **17.** From Exercise 16 we have $t(n, k) = (-1)^{n-k} s(n, k)$, which is equivalent to $s(n, k) = (-1)^{n-k} t(n, k)$. Substituting for $s(n, k)$ in (12) gives $t(n, k) = t(n - 1, k - 1) + (n - 1)t(n - 1, k)$.
18. Let $p(n, k)$ be the number of permutations of an n-element set with k cycles in their cycle decomposition. For a fixed k, assume that $p(n-1, k) = t(n-1, k)$. Then a k-cycle permutation σ of the n-set $\{1, 2, \ldots, n\}$ can be obtained from either: (i) a $(k - 1)$-cycle permutation of the $(n - 1)$-set $\{1, 2, \ldots, n - 1\}$ by adding (n) as a cycle of length one (fixed point), or (ii) a k-cycle permutation of $\{1, 2, \ldots, n - 1\}$ by choosing one of the $n - 1$ elements a and inserting n as the new image of a, with the image of n being the previous image of a. The two cases are exclusive. There are $p(n - 1, k - 1)$ of type (i) and $(n - 1)p(n - 1, k)$ of type (ii). Thus $p(n, k)$ satisfies the recurrence relation satisfied by $t(n, k)$ (Exercise 17). Since $p(n, k) = t(n, k)$ for the initial values with $n = k, k + 1$, the two sequences are equal.   **19.** Since the permutations are given as random, we

assume each of the $n!$ permutations has equal probability $1/n!$. Let X be the number of cycles. **a)** By Exercise 18 the number of permutations with k cycles is $t(n, k)$, so the probability is $p(X = k) = t(n, k)/n!$. **b)** The total number of permutations is $8! = 40{,}320$. Using results from Exercises 1, 16, and 17, $t(8, 2) = t(7, 1) + 7t(7, 2) = 720 + 7 \cdot 1764 = 13{,}068$, $t(8, 3) = t(7, 2) + 7t(7, 3) = 1764 + 7 \cdot 1624 = 13{,}132$, so the probabilities are $p(X = 2) = 13{,}068/40{,}320 = 0.3241$, $p(X = 3) = 13{,}132/40{,}320 = 0.3257$. It is slightly more likely that the number of cycles is 3 than it is 2.   **20.** Let $C(n, k)$ be the set over which the sum is taken, so $a(n, k) = \sum\limits_{(c_1, c_2, \ldots, c_k) \in C(n,k)} 1^{c_1} 2^{c_2} \cdots k^{c_k}$. Partition $C(n, k)$ into two classes $A(n, k) = \{(c_1, c_2, \ldots, c_k) | c_k = 0\}$, $B(n, k) = \{(c_1, c_2, \ldots, c_k) | c_k \geq 1\}$. Then $a(n, k) = \sum\limits_{A(n,k)} 1^{c_1} 2^{c_2} \cdots k^{c_k} + \sum\limits_{B(n,k)} 1^{c_1} 2^{c_2} \cdots k^{c_k}$. But the first sum is unchanged if we omit the k^{c_k} factor in each term, since $k^{c_k} = 1$ when $c_k = 0$. But then it is equal to $\sum\limits_{C(n,k-1)} 1^{c_1} 2^{c_2} \cdots (k - 1)^{c_{k-1}} = a(n - 1, k - 1)$ since $c_1 + c_2 + \cdots + c_{k-1} = (n - 1) - (k - 1)$. In the second sum where $c_k \geq 1$, factor out k to reduce k^{c_k} to k^{c_k-1} inside the summation. Then $c_1 + c_2 + \cdots + (c_k - 1) = n - k - 1 = (n - 1) - k$, and all the new c_i's are non-negative, so $\sum\limits_{B(n,k)} 1^{c_1} 2^{c_2} \cdots k^{c_k} = k \sum\limits_{C(n-1,k)} 1^{c_1} 2^{c_2} \cdots k^{c_k} = k\, a(n - 1, k)$. Thus $a(n, k) = a(n - 1, k - 1) + k\, a(n - 1, k)$ which is equivalent to (1). For the initial conditions, the sum is vacuous if $k > n$, so $a(n, k) = 0$ when $k > n$. When $k = 1$, the only term in the sum is $1^{n-1} = 1$, so $a(n, 1) = 1$. Since $a(n, k)$ and $S(n, k)$ satisfy the same recurrence relation and have the same initial values, it follows that $S(n, k) = a(n, k) = \sum\limits_{C(n,k)} 1^{c_1} 2^{c_2} \cdots k^{c_k}$.   **21. a)** Dividing both sides by $S(n, k)$ of the recurrence relation in (1) gives $\frac{S(n+1,k)}{S(n,k)} = \frac{S(n,k-1)}{S(n,k)} + k$, so $\lim\limits_{n \to \infty} \frac{S(n+1,k)}{S(n,k)} = \lim\limits_{n \to \infty} \frac{S(n,k-1)}{S(n,k)} + k = k$. **b)** Here we divide the recurrence relation in (12) by $s(n, k)$ to get $\frac{s(n+1,k)}{s(n,k)} = \frac{s(n,k-1)}{s(n,k)} - n$, and on taking limits we get $\lim\limits_{n \to \infty} \frac{s(n+1,k)}{s(n,k)} = \lim\limits_{n \to \infty} \frac{s(n,k-1)}{s(n,k)} - n = -n$.   **22.** By the Binomial Theorem,

$$\frac{1}{k!}(e^x - 1)^k = \frac{1}{k!} \sum_{j=0}^{k} (-1)^j C(k, j) e^{(k-j)x}. \text{ Now use the fact that } e^{ax} = \sum_{n=0}^{\infty} a^n \frac{x^n}{n!}$$

to get $\frac{1}{k!}(e^x - 1)^k = \frac{1}{k!} \sum\limits_{j=0}^{k} (-1)^j C(k, j) \sum\limits_{n=0}^{\infty} (k - j)^n \frac{x^n}{n!} =$

$$\sum_{n=0}^{\infty} \left(\sum_{j=0}^{k} \frac{(-1)^j}{k!} C(k, j)(k - j)^n \right) \frac{x^n}{n!} = \sum_{n=0}^{\infty} S(n, k) \frac{x^n}{n!} \text{ by (4).}$$

    23. The polynomial $p_k(x) = \prod\limits_{i=1}^{k} (1 - ix)$ can be written as $p_k(x) = \prod\limits_{i=0}^{k} (1 - ix)$ since the added term for $i = 0$ doesn't change the product. Then divide each of the $k + 1$ factors by x and multiply $p_k(x)$ by x^{k+1}, to get $p_k(x) = x^{k+1} \prod\limits_{i=0}^{k} \left(\frac{1}{x} - i \right) =$

$$x^{k+1}(x^{-1})_{k+1} = x^{k+1} \sum_{j=0}^{k+1} s(k+1,j)x^{-j} = \sum_{j=0}^{k+1} s(k+1,j)x^{k+1-j} =$$

$$\sum_{j=0}^{k+1} s(k+1, k+1-j)x^j.$$

Chapter 7   Catalan Numbers

1. a) Substituting left parentheses for 1 and right parentheses for -1 gives the well-formed sequence (( )( )( ))(( )).

b)

c) Starting with 123456[ ], and interpreting each $+$ as a push and each $-$ as a pop, the sequence successively produces: 12345[6],1234[56], 1234[6]5, 123[46]5, 123[6]45, 12[36]45,12[6]345, 12[ ]6345, 1[2]6345, [12]6345, [2]16345, [ ]216345. The stack permutation is therefore 216345.   **2. a)** The string q of left parentheses and the first five variables is ((1(23((45. Adding the last variable on the right and closing parentheses from the left gives the well-parenthesized product $\mathbf{p} = ((1(23))((45)6))$.

b)   **c)**

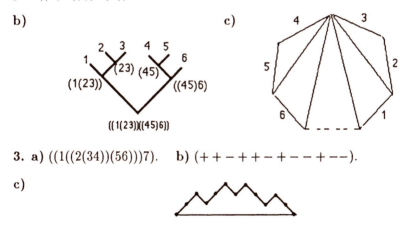

3. a) ((1((2(34))(56)))7).   **b)** $(++-++-+--+--)$.

c)

d) 12345[6], 1234[56], 1234[6]5, 123[46]5, 12[346]5, 12[46]35, 1[246]35, 1[46]235, 1[6]4235, [16]4235, [6]14235, [ ]614235.   **4. a)** $(+++---++--+-)$.   **b)** 12345[6], 1234[56], 123[456], 123[56]4, 123[6]54, 123[ ]654, 12[3]654, 1[23]654, 1[3]2654, 1[ ]32654, [1]132654, [ ]132654.

c)

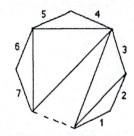

5.

[ ]42135		
[4]2135	4 Popped	−
[24]135	2 Popped	−
[124]35	1 Popped	−
1[24]35	1 Pushed	+
12[4]35	2 Pushed	+
12[34]5	3 Popped	−
123[4]5	3 Pushed	+
1234[ ]5	4 Pushed	+
1234[5]	5 Popped	−
12345[ ]	5 Pushed	+

The admissible sequence is therefore $(+ - + + - + + - - -)$. The path is the following.

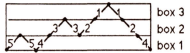

box 3
box 2
box 1

6. $c_n = \dfrac{1}{n+1} \dfrac{(2n)!}{(n!)^2} = \dfrac{2n(2n-1)}{(n+1)n^2} \dfrac{(2n-2)!}{((n-1)!)^2} = \dfrac{(4n-2)\cdot(2n-2)!}{(n+1)n\cdot((n-1)!)^2} = \dfrac{4n-2}{n+1} c_{n-1}.$

7. Substituting Stirling's approximation for the factorials in c_n gives $c_n = \dfrac{1}{n+1} \dfrac{(2n)!}{n!n!} \approx \dfrac{1}{n+1} \dfrac{\sqrt{4\pi n} \,(2n)^{2n}}{2\pi n \, n^{2n}} = \dfrac{2^{2n}}{(n+1)\sqrt{\pi n}} \approx \dfrac{4^n}{\sqrt{\pi}\, n^{3/2}} = O(n^{-3/2}\, 4^n).$ **8.** If $v_i v_j \in D$, then the polygon P' with vertices $v_i, v_{i+1}, \ldots, v_j$ is triangulated by the set D' of diagonals of D that are also diagonals of P'. With $v_i v_j$ serving as the excluded side of P', the product of sides $s_{i+1} s_{i+2} \cdots s_j$ is well-parenthesized into $\mathbf{p}'$ by recursively parenthesizing the two polygon sides that are sides of outer triangles, and then reducing the polygon. The order of reducing the polygons does not affect the well-parenthesized product finally obtained, so $\mathbf{p}'$ will be a subsequence of consecutive terms of $\mathbf{p}$. Conversely, if $s_{i+1} s_{i+2} \cdots s_j$ is well-parenthesized in p as $\mathbf{p}'$, then $\mathbf{p}'$ will appear on the diagonal joining the end vertices of the path formed by the sides in $\mathbf{p}'$. But that diagonal is $v_i v_j$.   **9.** Suppose that D contains the diagonal $v_k v_{n+1}$. Then after putting $i = k, j = n + 1$ in Exercise 8, the product $s_{k+1} s_{k+2} \cdots s_{n+1}$ is well-parenthesized as a sequence $\mathbf{p}'$. Corresponding to $\mathbf{p}'$ is a nonnegative path from the origin to $(2(n - k), 0)$. Translating this path to the right $2k$ units identifies it with the segment of the path corresponding to T from $(2k, 0)$ to

$(2n, 0)$. Conversely, suppose the nonnegative path corresponding to T meets the x-axis at the point $(2k, 0)$. On removing s_{n+1} and the n right parentheses from the corresponding well-parenthesized sequence $\mathbf{p}$ of the product $s_1 s_2 \cdots s_{n+1}$, we obtain a sequence $\mathbf{q}$ with n left parentheses interlaced with the product $s_1 s_2 \cdots s_n$. Since the path passes through the point $(2k, 0)$, the first $2k$ terms of $\mathbf{q}$ has k left parentheses interlaced with $s_1 s_2 \cdots s_k$. Hence the subsequence $\mathbf{q}'$ consisting of the last $2(n - k)$ terms of $\mathbf{q}$ interlaces $n - k$ left parentheses with $s_{k+1} s_{k+2} \cdots s_n$. Since the path is nonnegative, the segment corresponding to $\mathbf{q}'$ is nonnegative, and so corresponds to a triangulation of the $(n - k + 2)$-gon with sides $s_{k+1} s_{k+2} \cdots s_{n+1}$ and the diagonal (of P) joining the end vertices of the path. But that diagonal is $v_k v_{n+1}$.   **10.** If D contains the diagonal $v_0 v_n$, then $v_n v_{n+1} v_0$ is an outer triangle, so no diagonals on v_{n+1} can be in D. By Exercise 9 the corresponding path cannot meet the x-axis at any point $(2k, 0)$ for $1 \le k \le n - 1$. Since the path starts on the x-axis, it can only return to the x-axis after an even number $2k$ of steps. Thus the path is positive. Conversely, if the path is positive, then D contains no diagonals $v_k v_{n+1}$ for $1 \le k \le n - 1$. Since every side of P is in exactly one triangle of T, s_n, s_0 must be in the same triangle. But the outer triangle $v_n v_{n+1} v_0$ is the only triangle that can contain both. Thus T contains the diagonal $v_0 v_n$.

Chapter 8   Ramsey Numbers

1. There are 4 colorings of K_3 to consider: all 3 edges red, 2 red and 1 green, 1 red and 2 green, all 3 edges green. The first 3 colorings yield a red K_2, while the last yields a green K_3. The coloring of K_2 where both edges are green fails to have a red K_2 or a green K_3.   **2.** Draw K_6 as a hexagon with all its diagonals. Color the edges of the outer hexagon red and all diagonals green. Clearly, there is no red K_3. To see that there is no green K_4, number the vertices clockwise with $1, \ldots, 6$. If vertex 1 were a vertex of a green K_4, then vertices 3,4,5 must also be in K_4 (since K_4 has 4 vertices). But vertices 3 and 4, for example, are not joined by a green edge, and hence no K_4 subgraph using vertex 1 is possible. Similar reasoning shows that none of the vertices $2, \ldots, 6$ can be in a green K_4.   **3.** The coloring of Figure 1(a) shows that 5 does not have the $(3, 3)$-Ramsey property. Suppose $m < 5$, and choose any m vertices from this figure and consider the subgraph K_m of K_5 constructed on these m vertices. This gives a coloring of the edges of K_m that has no red K_3 or green K_3, since the original coloring of the edges of K_5 has no red K_3 or green K_3. **4.** Since every coloring of the edges of K_k either has a red K_2 (i.e., a red edge) or else every edge is colored green (which gives a green K_k). Therefore $R(2, k) \le k$. If we color every edge of K_{k-1} green, then K_{k-1} does not have either a red K_2 or a green K_k. Therefore $R(2, k) > k - 1$, and hence $R(2, k) = k$.   **5.** Let $R(i, j) = n$. We show that $R(j, i) \le R(i, j)$ and $R(i, j) \le R(j, i)$. To show that

$R(j, i) \leq R(i, j)$, we show that every coloring of the edges of K_n also contains either a red K_j or a green K_i. Choose any coloring, C, of K_n and then reverse the colors to get a second coloring, D. Since $R(i, j) = n$, the coloring D contains either a red K_i or a green K_j. Therefore, coloring C contains either a red K_j or a green K_i. This shows that $R(j, i) \leq n = R(i, j)$. A similar argument shows that $R(i, j) \leq R(j, i)$.   **6.** Suppose m has the (i, j)-Ramsey property and $n > m$. Consider any coloring of the edges of K_n with red and green. Choose any m vertices of K_n and consider the subgraph K_m determined by these m vertices. Then K_m, with the coloring that is inherited from the coloring of K_n, must have a subgraph that is a red K_i or a green K_j. Hence K_n also has a red K_i or a green K_j. Therefore n has the (i, j)-Ramsey property.   **7.** Suppose n did have the (i, j)-Ramsey property. By Exercise 6, every larger integer also has the (i, j)-Ramsey property. In particular, m must have the (i, j)-Ramsey property, which is a contradiction of the assumption.   **8.** We will show that if m has the (i_1, j)-Ramsey property, then m also has the (i_2, j)-Ramsey property. If m has the (i_1, j)-Ramsey property, then every coloring of the edges of K_m with red and green contains a red K_{i_1} or a green K_j. If K_m has a red K_{i_1}, then it also has a red K_{i_2} (since $i_1 \geq i_2$). Therefore K_m has either a red K_{i_2} or a green K_j. Hence K_m has the (i_2, j)-Ramsey property and therefore $m \geq R(i_2, j)$. This shows that every integer m with the (i_1, j)-Ramsey property also satisfies $m \geq R(i_2, j)$. Therefore, the smallest integer m with this property, namely $R(i_1, j)$, must also satisfy $R(i_1, j) \geq R(i_2, j)$.   **9.** We assume that $|B| \geq R(i - 1, j)$ and must show that m has the (i, j)- Ramsey property. Then $K_{|B|}$ contains either a red K_{i-1} or a green K_j. If we have a red K_{i-1}, we add the red edges joining v to the vertices of K_{i-1} to obtain a red K_i. Thus, $K_{|B|}$, and hence K_m, has either a red K_i or a green K_j. Therefore m has the (i, j)-Ramsey property.   **10.** The proof follows the proof of Lemma 1. We know that either $|A| \geq R(i, j-1)$ or $|B| \geq R(i-1, j)$. But m is even, so $\deg(v)$ is odd. Therefore, either $|A|$ or $|B|$ is odd. Let $m = R(i, j-1) + R(i-1, j) - 1$, which is an odd number. Suppose the edges of K_m are colored red or green. Choose any vertex v and define the sets A and B as in the proof of the Lemma. It follows that either $|A| \geq R(i, j - 1)$ or $|B| \geq R(i - 1, j) - 1$. But $\deg(v)$ is even since v is joined to the $m - 1$ other vertices of K_m. Since $|A \cup B| = |A| + |B| = m - 1$ (which is even), either $|A|$ or $|B|$ are both even or both odd. If $|A|$ and $|B|$ are both even, then $|B| > R(i - 1, j) - 1$, since $R(i - 1, j) - 1$ is odd. If $|A|$ and $|B|$ are both odd, then $|A| > R(i, j - 1)$, since $R(i, j - 1)$ is even. Therefore $m - 1 = |A| + |B| > R(i - 1, j) + R(i, j - 1) - 1$.   **11.** Suppose that the vertices of the graph in Figure 2(b) are numbered $1, \ldots, 8$ clockwise. By the symmetry of the figure, it is enough to show that vertex 1 cannot be a vertex of a K_4 subgraph. Suppose 1 were a vertex of a K_4 subgraph. Since vertex 1 is adjacent to only 3,4,6,7, we would need to have 3 of these 4 vertices are all adjacent to each other (as well as to 1). But this is impossible, since no 3 of the vertices 3,4,6,7 are all adjacent to each other.   **12.** Suppose that the graph

had a red K_3 and vertex 1 were a vertex of a red triangle. Vertex 1 is adjacent to vertices 2,6,9,13, but none of these 4 vertices are adjacent. Therefore, 1 is not a vertex of a red triangle. Similar reasoning applies to each of the other 12 vertices. Thus, K_{13} has no red K_3. We next show that K_{13} has no green K_5. Suppose it did, and vertex 1 were a vertex of the K_5. Then the other 4 vertices must come from the list 3,4,5,7,8,10,11,12. If vertex 3 were also in K_5, then the other 2 vertices must come from 5,7,10,12 (since there are the only vertices adjacent to 1 and 3). But we cannot choose both 5 and 10 or 7 and 12 since they are not adjacent. Thus, we can only pick 4 vertices: 1,3, and two from 5,7,10,12. Hence there is no K_5 if we use both 1 and 3. Similar reasoning shows that we cannot build a K_5 by using 1 and 4, 1 and 5, 1 and 7, etc. Thus vertex 1 cannot be a vertex in a K_5 subgraph. By the symmetry of the graph, the same reasoning shows that none of the vertices $2, 3, \ldots, 13$ can be part of K_5. Therefore, the graph contains no green K_5.   **13.** $R(4,4) \leq R(4,3) + R(3,4) = 9 + 9 = 18$.
14. Consider G as a subgraph of K_9. Color the edges of G red and color the edges of $\overline{G}$ (also a subgraph of K_9) green. Since $R(3,4) = 9$, K_9 has either a red K_4 or a green K_3. But a red K_4 must be a subgraph of G and a green K_3 must be a subgraph of $\overline{G}$.   **15.** Basis step: $R(2,2) = 2 \leq C(2,1)$. Induction step: We must prove that if $i + j = n + 1$, then $R(i,j) \leq C(i + j - 2, i - 1)$. Using (1), $R(i,j) \leq R(i, j-1) + R(i-1, j) \leq C(i+j-3, i-1) + C(i+j-3, i-2) = C(i + j - 2, i - 1)$.   **16.** We first show that 2 has the $(2, \ldots, 2; 2)$-Ramsey property. K_2 has only 1 edge, so 1 of the colors $1, \ldots, n$ must have been used to color this edge. If this edge has color j, then K_2 has a subgraph K_2 of color j. Thus $R(2, \ldots, 2; 2) \leq 2$. But $R(2, \ldots, 2; 2) > 1$ since K_1 has 0 edges and thus cannot have a subgraph K_2 of any color.   **17.** We first show that 7 has the $(7, 3, 3, 3, 3; 3)$-Ramsey property. Let $|S| = 7$ and suppose that its 3-element subsets are partitioned into 5 collections $C_1, C_2, \ldots, C_5$. If all the 3-element subsets are in C_1, we can take S itself as the subset that satisfies the definition of the $(7, 3, 3, 3, 3; 3)$-Ramsey property. If some C_j (for some $j > 1$) has at least one 3-element subset in it, then this 3-element subset of S satisfies the definition. Therefore 7 has the $(7, 3, 3, 3, 3; 3)$-Ramsey property. We now show that 6 fails to have the $(7, 3, 3, 3, 3; 3)$-Ramsey property. Suppose $|S| = 6$ and all 3-element subsets are placed in C_1. The value $j = 1$ does not work in the definition since S has no subset of size $i_1 = 7$. The values $j = 2, 3, 4, 5$ do not work since these C_j contain no sets. Therefore $R(7, 3, 3, 3, 3; 3) = 7$.
18. Suppose we have a partition with no monochromatic solution. We must have either $1 \in R$ or $1 \in G$. Assume $1 \in R$. Then $2 \in G$ (otherwise we have a red solution $1 + 1 = 2$). Since $2 \in G$, we must have $4 \in R$ (otherwise we have a green solution $2 + 2 = 4$). Then we must have $3 \in G$ to avoid the red solution $1 + 3 = 4$. If $5 \in R$, we have the red solution $1 + 4 = 5$, and if $5 \in G$, we have the green solution $2 + 3 = 5$. This contradicts the assumption that we have no monochromatic solution. A similar argument holds if $1 \in G$.   **19.** Use one color for each of the following sets: $\{1, 4, 10, 13\}, \{2, 3, 7, 11, 12\}, \{5, 6, 8, 9\}$.

20. Suppose the 5 points are a, b, c, d, e. Form the smallest convex polygon P that contains these 5 points either inside P or on P itself. If at least 4 of the 5 points lie on P, then we obtain a convex polygon by joining these 4 points. If P contains only 3 of the 5 points, say a, b, and c, the points d and e lie inside P. Draw the straight line through d and e. Two of the points a, b, c lie on one side of the line. Then these two points, together with d and e determine a convex 4-gon   **21. (a)** If the game ended in a draw, we would have K_6 colored with red and green with no monochromatic K_3, contradicting the fact that $R(3,3) = 6$.   **(b)** The coloring of the graph of Figure 1 shows how the game could end in a draw.   **(c)** There must be a monochromatic K_3 since $R(3,3 = 6$. Therefore someone must lose.   **22. (a)** Example 4 shows that $R(3,3,3;2) = 17$. Therefore there is a coloring of K_4 with 3 colors that contains no monochromatic K_3. Thus, the game can end in a draw.   **(b)** Since $R(3,3,3;2) = 17$, there must be a monochromatic triangle, and therefore a winner.   **23.** We could conclude that $R(5,5) > 54$. (If this does happen, please inform your instructor.)   **24.** To show that $R(K_{1,1}, K_{1,3}) \leq 4$, take K_4 and color its edges red and green. If any edge is red, K_4 has a red $K_{1,1}$. If no edges are red, then K_4 has a green $K_{1,3}$. But $R(K_{1,1}, K_{1,3}) > 3$ since we can take K_3 and color its edges green, showing that K_3 has no red $K_{1,1}$ or green $K_{1,3}$.

Chapter 9   Arrangements with Forbidden Positions

1. For B_1, there are 3 ways to place 1 rook and 1 way to place 2 rooks ($(1, S)$ and $(4, F)$), so $R(x, B_1) = 1 + 3x + x^2$. For B_2, one rook can be placed in 6 ways, so $r_1 = 6$. Two rooks can be placed on $(2, K)$ and any of the squares $(3, W)$, $(5, D)$, $(5, W)$, on $(D, 2)$ and any of the squares $(3, K)$, $(3, W)$, $(5, W)$, on $(3, K)$ and either $(5, D)$ or $(5, W)$, or $(3, W)$ and $(5, D)$; thus $r_2 = 9$. Three rooks can be placed on $(2, K)$, $(3, W)$, $(5, D)$ or on $(2, D)$, $(3, K)$, $(5, W)$; thus $r_3 = 2$. Therefore, $R(x, B_2) = 1 + 6x + 9x^2 + 2x^3$.   **2.** Since there is only 1 way to place one rook on B_1, $R(x, B_1) = 1 + x$. For board B_2, there are 4 ways to place 1 rook on a forbidden square, so $r_1 = 4$. There are 4 ways to place 2 rooks—on (blue, tan) and (brown, blue), or on (blue, tan) and (plaid, yellow), or on (brown, blue) and (plaid, yellow), or on (brown, blue) and (plaid, tan)—so $r_2 = 4$. There is only 1 way to place 3 rooks—on (blue, tan), (brown, blue), (plaid, yellow)—so $r_3 = 1$. Therefore, $R(x, B_2) = 1 + 4x + 4x^2 + x^3$. **3.** Suppose B' is a subboard of B and $(5,6)$ is in B'. This forces row 5, and hence columns 8 and 9 to be in B'. This forces row 3 to be in B'. This in turn forces column 7 to be in B', which forces column 10 to be in B'. Thus, all five columns must be in B', and hence $B' = B$.   **4.** We can take B' to be the board with rows 1 and 3, and columns 1 and 2. Then $R(x, B') = 1 + 3x + x^2$. For B'' (rows 2 and 4, and columns 3 and 4), we have $R(x, B'') = 1 + 2x$. Hence $R(x, B) = R(x, B') \cdot R(x, B'') = (1 + 3x + x^2)(1 + 2x) = 1 + 5x + 7x^2 + 2x^3$. The number of arrangements is $4! - (5 \cdot 3! - 7 \cdot 2! + 2 \cdot 1!) = 6$.   **5.** This board cannot be split into disjoint subboards. Assume that the rows (and columns) are numbered $1, 2, 3, 4$. Choose the square $(4, 1)$. The rook polynomial for the board with row 4 and column 1 removed is $R(x, B') = 1 + 4x + 3x^2$. Also, $R(x, B'') = 1 + 5x + 11x^2 + 6x^3 + x^4$. Therefore, $R(x, B) = x(1 + 4x + 3x^2) + (1 + 5x + 11x^2 + 6x^3 + x^4) = 1 + 6x + 15x^2 + 9x^3 + x^4$, and the number of arrangements is $4! - (6 \cdot 3! - 15 \cdot 2! + 9 \cdot 1! - 1 \cdot 0!) = 10$.   **6.** The board cannot be split. Using square $(1, 1)$, the rook polynomial for the board with row 1 and column 1 removed is $R(x, B') = 1 + 5x + 7x^2 + 2x^3$. Also, $R(x, B'') = 1 + 7x + 16x^2 + 13x^3 + 3x^4$. Therefore $R(x, B) = R(x, B') + R(x, B'') = 1 + 8x + 21x^2 + 20x^3 + 5x^4$. Thus, the number of arrangements is $5 \cdot 4 \cdot 3 \cdot 2 - [8 \cdot 4 \cdot 3 \cdot 2 - 21 \cdot 3 \cdot 2 + 20 \cdot 2 - 5 \cdot 1] = 19$.   **7.** Split the board, using rows 1 and 2 and columns 1 and 2 for board B'. Therefore, $R(x, B) = R(x, B') \cdot R(x, B'') = (1 + 3x + x^2)(1 + 3x + 3x^2 + x^3) = 1 + 6x + 13x^2 + 13x^3 + 6x^4 + x^5$. Therefore, the number of allowable arrangements is $5! - 6 \cdot 4! + 13 \cdot 3! - 13 \cdot 2! + 6 \cdot 1! - 1 \cdot 0! = 33$.   **8.** Deleting row 5 and column 9 from B'' yields a board with rook polynomial $1 + 4x + 3x^2$. When only square $(5, 9)$ is deleted, we obtain a board B'''. This board can be broken up, using row 5 and columns 6 and 8 for the first board. Its rook polynomial is $1 + 2x$. The rook polynomial for the other part is $1 + 5x + 6x^2 + x^3$. Therefore, the rook polynomial for B''' is $(1 + 2x)(1 + 5x + 6x^2 + x^3)$. Theorem 3 then gives the rook polynomial for B''.   **9.** The rook polynomial is $1 + 4x + 4x^2 + x^3$. Therefore, the number of permutations is $4! - 4 \cdot 3! + 4 \cdot 2! - 1 \cdot 1! = 7$.   **10.** Using Theorem 3 with the square (3,DeMorgan), we obtain $x(1 + 5x + 7x^2 + 3x^3) + (1 + 2x)(1 + 6x + 9x^2 + 2x^3)$. (The second product is obtained by deleting the square (3,DeMorgan) and breaking the remaining board into 2 disjoint subboards, using row 2 and the De Morgan and Hamilton columns.) Therefore, the rook polynomial is $1 + 9x + 26x^2 + 27x^3 + 7x^4$ and the number of arrangements is $6 \cdot 5 \cdot 4 \cdot 3 - [9 \cdot 5 \cdot 4 \cdot 3 - 26 \cdot 4 \cdot 3 + 27 \cdot 3 - 7 \cdot 1] = 52$.   **11.** The rook polynomial is $1 + 4x$. Therefore, the number of arrangements is $4! - [4 \cdot 3!] = 0$.   **12.** The rook polynomial is 1. Therefore, the number of arrangements is $4! - [0 \cdot 3! - 0 \cdot 2! + 0 \cdot 1! - 0 \cdot 0!] = 4!$.   **13.** This is Exercise 9 in another form. The answer is 7.   **14.** Break the board into 2 disjoint subboards, using rows Nakano and Sommer, and columns numerical analysis and discrete math for the first subboard. This yields $(1 + 3x + x^2)(1 + 4x + 4x^2) = 1 + 7x + 17x^2 + 16x^3 + 4x^4$. Therefore, the number of arrangements is $5! - 7 \cdot 4! + 17 \cdot 3! - 16 \cdot 2! + 4 \cdot 1! = 26$.   **15.** Choose any seating arrangement for the 4 women $(1, 2, 3, 4)$ at the 4 points of the compass (N, E, S, W). Suppose that the 4 women are seated in the order $1, 2, 3, 4$, clockwise from north. Also suppose that the men are named $1, 2, 3, 4$ and the empty chairs for the men are labeled A, B, C, D (clockwise), where chair A is between woman 1 and woman 2., etc. Using Theorem 3 with the square

(1,A), the rook polynomial is $x(1+5x+6x^2+x^3)+(1+7x+15x^2+10x^\varepsilon + x^4) = 1 + 8x + 20x^2 + 16x^3 + 2x^4$. Therefore, Theorem 2 shows that the number of arrangements is $4! - 8 \cdot 3! + 20 \cdot 2! - 16 \cdot 1! + 2 \cdot 0! = 2$. Since there are 4! ways in which the 4 women could have been seated, the answer is $4! \cdot 2 = 48$.

Chapter 10   Block Designs and Latin Squares

1. Interchange rows 2 and 3, then interchange columns 2 and 3, and finally reverse the names 2 and 3 to obtain $\begin{pmatrix} 1 & 2 & 3 & 4 \\ 2 & 3 & 4 & 1 \\ 3 & 4 & 1 & 2 \\ 4 & 1 & 2 & 3 \end{pmatrix}$.   **2.** Move columns 4 and 5 to columns 2 and 3, then rearrange rows to obtain $\begin{pmatrix} 1 & 2 & 3 & 4 & 5 \\ 2 & 3 & 4 & 5 & 1 \\ 3 & 4 & 5 & 1 & 2 \\ 4 & 5 & 1 & 2 & 3 \\ 5 & 1 & 2 & 3 & 4 \end{pmatrix}$.

3. a) Reflexivity is clear.   **b)** Symmetry is shown by reversing the steps that show L_1 equivalent to L_2.   **c)** Execute the steps that show L_1 equivalent to L_2, followed by the steps that show L_2 equivalent to L_3; this shows L_1 equivalent to L_3.   **4.** $\begin{pmatrix} 1 & 3 & 4 & 2 \\ 4 & 2 & 1 & 3 \\ 2 & 4 & 3 & 1 \\ 3 & 1 & 2 & 4 \end{pmatrix}$.   **5. a)** $\begin{pmatrix} 1 & 2 & 3 & 4 \\ 2 & 1 & 4 & 3 \\ 3 & 4 & 1 & 2 \\ 4 & 3 & 2 & 1 \end{pmatrix}$, $\begin{pmatrix} 1 & 3 & 4 & 2 \\ 4 & 2 & 1 & 3 \\ 2 & 4 & 3 & 1 \\ 3 & 1 & 2 & 4 \end{pmatrix}$,

$\begin{pmatrix} 1 & 4 & 2 & 3 \\ 3 & 2 & 4 & 1 \\ 4 & 1 & 3 & 2 \\ 2 & 3 & 1 & 4 \end{pmatrix}$.   **b)** $4^2 + 4 + 1 = 17$ points.   **c)** $4 + 1 = 5$ points on a line.   **d)** points $\{a_{ij} | 1 \le i, j \le 4\}, R, C, P_1, P_2, P_3$; lines: $a_{11}, a_{12}, a_{13}, a_{14}, R$; $a_{21}, a_{22}, a_{23}, a_{24}, R$; $a_{31}, a_{32}, a_{33}, a_{34}, R$; $a_{41}, a_{42}, a_{43}, a_{44}, R$; $a_{11}, a_{21}, a_{31}, a_{41}, C$; $a_{12}, a_{22}, a_{32}, a_{42}, C$; $a_{13}, a_{23}, a_{33}, a_{43}, C$; $a_{14}, a_{24}, a_{34}, a_{44}, C$; from L_1: $a_{11}, a_{22}, a_{33}, a_{44}, P_1$; $a_{12}, a_{21}, a_{34}, a_{43}, P_1$; $a_{13}, a_{24}, a_{31}, a_{42}, P_1$; $a_{14}, a_{23}, a_{32}, a_{41}, P_1$; from L_2: $a_{11}, a_{23}, a_{34}, a_{42}, P_2$; $a_{14}, a_{22}, a_{31}, a_{43}, P_2$; $a_{12}, a_{24}, a_{33}, a_{41}, P_2$; $a_{13}, a_{21}, a_{32}, a_{44}, P_2$; from L_3: $a_{11}, a_{24}, a_{31}, a_{44}, P_3$; $a_{13}, a_{22}, a_{34}, a_{41}, P_3$; $a_{14}, a_{21}, a_{33}, a_{42}, P_3$; $a_{12}, a_{23}, a_{31}, a_{44}, P_3$; extra R, C, P_1, P_2, P_3.   **6.** Since $b = 69$, $v = 24$, and $k = 8$, $bk = vr$ gives $69(8) = 24r$, so $r = 23$. Then $\lambda(23) = 23(7)$, so $\lambda = 7$. Thus, this is a $(69, 24, 23, 8, 7)$-design.   **7.** Deleting column 4 yields the 3-design $\{\{1, 2, 3\}, \{2, 1, 4\}, \{3, 4, 1\}, \{4, 3, 2\}\}$. Clearly $b = 4$, $v = 4$, $k = 3$. Hence $r = 3$ $(bk = vr)$, so $3\lambda = 3(2)$. Thus $\lambda = 2$. This is a $(4, 4, 3, 3, 2)$-design.   **8.** Let a_{11} be 1, a_{12} be 2,..., a_{33} be 9, R be 10, C be 11, P_1 be 12, P_2 be 13. Then the

varieties are $1, 2, \ldots, 13$. The blocks are $\{1, 2, 3, 10\}$, $\{4, 5, 6, 10\}$, $\{7, 8, 9, 10\}$, $\{1, 4, 7, 11\}$, $\{2, 5, 8, 11\}$, $\{3, 6, 9, 11\}$, $\{1, 6, 8, 12\}$, $\{2, 4, 9, 12\}$, $\{3, 5, 7, 12\}$, $\{1, 5, 9, 13\}$, $\{2, 6, 7, 13\}$, $\{3, 4, 8, 13\}$, $\{10, 11, 12, 13\}$. This is a $(13, 13, 4, 4, 1)$-design.   **9.** Since $\lambda(v - 1) = r(k - 1)$, $\lambda = 1$, $k = 3$, and $v = 6n + 3$, we have $6n + 2 = 2r$, so $r = 3n + 1$. Also $bk = vr$, so $b = vr/k = (6n + 3)(3n + 1)/3 = (2n + 1)(3n + 1)$.   **10. a)** Taking group 0: $\{14, 1, 2\}$, $\{3, 5, 9\}$, $\{11, 4, 0\}$, $\{7, 6, 12\}$, $\{13, 8, 10\}$, and adding $2i$ to each number not equal to 14, then taking the result mod 14 to obtain group i gives:
group 1: $\{14, 3, 4\}$, $\{5, 7, 11\}$, $\{13, 6, 2\}$, $\{9, 8, 0\}$, $\{1, 10, 12\}$;
group 2: $\{14, 5, 6\}$, $\{7, 9, 13\}$, $\{1, 8, 4\}$, $\{11, 10, 2\}$, $\{3, 12, 0\}$;
group 3: $\{14, 7, 8\}$, $\{9, 11, 1\}$, $\{3, 10, 6\}$, $\{13, 12, 4\}$, $\{5, 0, 2\}$;
group 4: $\{14, 9, 10\}$, $\{11, 13, 3\}$, $\{5, 12, 8\}$, $\{1, 0, 6\}$, $\{7, 2, 4\}$;
group 5: $\{14, 11, 12\}$, $\{13, 1, 5\}$, $\{7, 0, 10\}$, $\{3, 2, 8\}$, $\{9, 4, 6\}$;
group 6: $\{14, 13, 0\}$, $\{1, 3, 7\}$, $\{9, 2, 12\}$, $\{5, 4, 10\}$, $\{11, 6, 8\}$.   **b)** Thursday is group 4, when 5 walks with 12 and 8.   **c)** 14 and 0 walk with 13 in group 6 (Saturday).   **11.** This amounts to finding a Kirkman triple system of order 9 with 12 blocks partitioned into four groups (weeks). Here is one solution (devised from letting $A, \ldots, I$ correspond to $0, \ldots, 8$; finding an original group; and adding $2i$ mod 8 to obtain other groups).

	Mon	Wed	Fri
Week 1	I, A, B	C, E, H	D, F, G
Week 2	I, C, D	E, G, B	F, H, A
Week 3	I, E, F	G, A, D	H, B, C
Week 4	I, G, H	A, C, F	B, D, E.

12. a) Since $k = 3$, $\lambda = 1$, $v = 7$, from $\lambda(v - 1) = r(k - 1)$ we obtain $6 = 2r$, so $r = 3$. Hence $b = 7$ $(bk = vr)$, so this is a $(7, 7, 3, 3, 1)$-design.   **b)** The blocks are $\{1, 6, 7\}$, $\{2, 5, 7\}$, $\{3, 5, 6\}$, $\{1, 2, 3\}$, $\{1, 4, 5\}$, $\{2, 4, 6\}$, $\{3, 4, 7\}$.   **c)** The blocks are the lines in this projective plane of order 2.

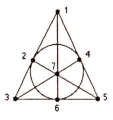

Chapter 11   Scheduling Problems and Bin Packing

1.

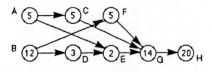

2.

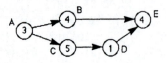

3. Order requirement digraph:

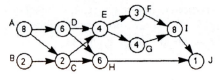

Critical path $A \to D \to E \to E \to G \to G \to I \to J$; length 31 weeks. Schedule (giving task and starting time for task in weeks after start of project): A, 0; B, 0; C, 8; D, 8; E, 14; F, 18; G, 18; H, 14; I, 22; J, 30.   **4. a)** Critical path: $A \to B \to C \to G \to J$; length 42. Schedule (giving task and starting time for task after start of project): A, 0; B, 5; C, 15; D 22; E, 0; F, 4; G, 22; H, 30; I, 0; J, 30.

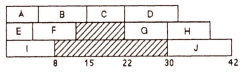

b)

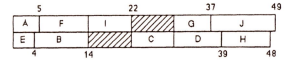

5. a)

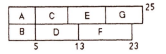

b) This schedule is optimal for two processors.   **c)** If there are unlimited processors, then the optimal schedule is the following:

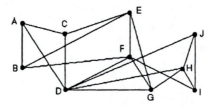

6. The incomparability graph is:

A maximal set of disjoint edges is AB, CD, EF, GH, IJ. The optimal schedule for this set is:

A	C	E	G	I
B	D	F	H	J

7. First delete FC as redundant. Next D and H receive permanent labels 1 and 2. Next C receives temporary label (1), G gets temporary label (2) and K gets temporary label (2). Next C gets permanent label 3, G gets 4, and K gets 5. Now B gets temporary label (3), F gets (4), and J gets (4,5). By dictionary order, B is labeled 6, F is labeled 7, and J is labeled 8. Now A gets temporary label (6), E gets (6,7), and I gets (8). These vertices then get permanent labels 9, 10, and 11, respectively. The schedule is then:

I	A	B	K	C	D
E	J	F	G	H	

8. a) Using FF, the bins contain: bin 1 – 85, 55; bin 2 – 95, 25; bin 3 – 135; bin 4 – 65, 35, 40; bin 5 – 95, 35.   **b)** Using FFD: bin 1 – 135; bin 2 – 95, 40; bin 3 – 95, 35; bin 4 – 85, 55; bin 5 – 65, 35, 25.   **c)** Both of these are optimal packings since the total weight to be packed is 665 pounds and four cartons can hold a maximum of 560 pounds.   **9. a)** 15 9-foot boards are needed for FF. **b)** 15 9-foot boards are needed for FFD.   **c)** 13 10-foot boards are needed for FF and FFD.   **10.** Next fit (NF) works like FF except that once a new bin is opened, the previous bin(s) is closed. This method might be preferable in the case of loading trucks from a single loading dock since only one bin at a time is used. Other list orders could be FFI (first-fit increasing) or (largest, smallest, next largest, next smallest,...) with FF.

Chapter 12   Burnside-Polya Counting Methods

1.

×	c	o
o	o	o
o	c	x

2. 90°: $\begin{pmatrix} 1 & 2 & 3 & 4 & 5 & 6 & 7 & 8 & 9 \\ 7 & 4 & 1 & 8 & 5 & 2 & 9 & 6 & 3 \end{pmatrix}$;

180°: $\begin{pmatrix} 1 & 2 & 3 & 4 & 5 & 6 & 7 & 8 & 9 \\ 9 & 8 & 7 & 6 & 5 & 4 & 3 & 2 & 1 \end{pmatrix}$;

270°: $\begin{pmatrix} 1 & 2 & 3 & 4 & 5 & 6 & 7 & 8 & 9 \\ 3 & 6 & 9 & 2 & 5 & 8 & 1 & 4 & 7 \end{pmatrix}$;

360°: $\begin{pmatrix} 1 & 2 & 3 & 4 & 5 & 6 & 7 & 8 & 9 \\ 1 & 2 & 3 & 4 & 5 & 6 & 7 & 8 & 9 \end{pmatrix}$.

3. Horizontal: $\begin{pmatrix} 1 & 2 & 3 & 4 & 5 & 6 & 7 & 8 & 9 \\ 7 & 8 & 9 & 4 & 5 & 6 & 1 & 2 & 3 \end{pmatrix}$;

Vertical: $\begin{pmatrix} 1 & 2 & 3 & 4 & 5 & 6 & 7 & 8 & 9 \\ 3 & 2 & 1 & 6 & 5 & 4 & 9 & 8 & 7 \end{pmatrix}$;

Main diagonal: $\begin{pmatrix} 1 & 2 & 3 & 4 & 5 & 6 & 7 & 8 & 9 \\ 1 & 4 & 7 & 2 & 5 & 8 & 3 & 6 & 9 \end{pmatrix}$;

Minor diagonal: $\begin{pmatrix} 1 & 2 & 3 & 4 & 5 & 6 & 7 & 8 & 9 \\ 9 & 6 & 3 & 8 & 5 & 2 & 7 & 4 & 1 \end{pmatrix}$.

4.

$\begin{pmatrix} 1 & 2 & 3 & 4 \\ 3 & 1 & 4 & 2 \end{pmatrix}$

180° $\begin{pmatrix} 3 & 1 & 4 & 2 \\ 2 & 4 & 1 & 3 \end{pmatrix} = \begin{pmatrix} 1 & 2 & 3 & 4 \\ 4 & 3 & 2 & 1 \end{pmatrix}$

270° $\begin{pmatrix} 1 & 2 & 3 & 4 \\ 2 & 4 & 1 & 3 \end{pmatrix}$

5.   90°   270°

inv $\begin{pmatrix} 1 & 2 & 3 & 4 \\ 3 & 1 & 4 & 2 \end{pmatrix} = \begin{pmatrix} 3 & 1 & 4 & 2 \\ 1 & 2 & 3 & 4 \end{pmatrix} = \begin{pmatrix} 1 & 2 & 3 & 4 \\ 2 & 4 & 1 & 3 \end{pmatrix}$.

6. $(1/6)(t_1^3 + 3t_1 t_2 + 2t_3)$.   **7.** $(1/10)(t_1^5 + 5t_1 t_2^2 + 4t_5)$.   **8.** $(1/12)(t_1^6 + 3t_1^2 t_2^2 + 4t_2^3 + 2t_3^2 + 2t_6)$.   **9.** The appropriate cycle index is $(1/8)(t_1^8 + 4t_1^2 t_2^3 + t_2^4 + 2t_2^2)$. Substitute 2 for every t_i to obtain 51.   **10.** You can draw the 13 configurations, or you may calculate the coefficient of x^4 in the polynomial $(1/8)((1 + x)^8 + 4(1 + x)^2(1 + x^2)^3 + (1 + x^2)^4 + 2(1 + x^4)^2)$.

Chapter 13   Food Webs

1. a)

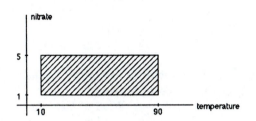

b)

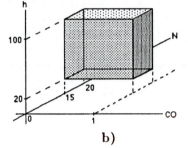

2. a)   **b)**

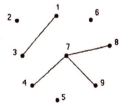

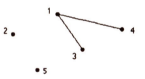

3. a)   **b)**

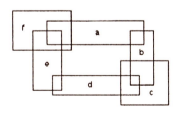

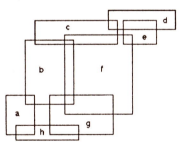

4. a)

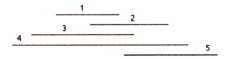

b)

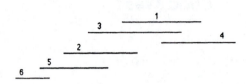

5. If G is an interval graph then it cannot have C_4 as a generated subgraph since otherwise the intervals corresponding to the vertices of that subgraph would constitute an interval representation of C_4, which is impossible. Using the orientation suggested by the hint establishes a transitive orientation of $\overline{G}$ since the ordering of the intervals on the line defined by the hint is transitive.

6. It is easy to find an interval representation of C_3; any set of three intervals, each intersecting the other two, will do. Thus C_3 has boxicity 1. If $n > 3$, let $v_1, \ldots, v_n$ be the vertices of G. The following diagram shows that the boxicity of G is no more than 2. C_n cannot have boxicity 1 by the same sort of argument used in the text to show that C_4 is not an interval graph.

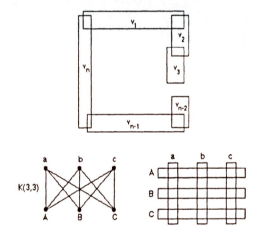

7.

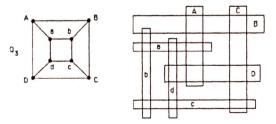

8. Q_3 is not an interval graph because the edges and corners of one face of the cube form a generated subgraph isomorphic to C_4. The following diagram shows a representation of Q_3 as the intersection graph of a family of boxes in two-space.

9. a)   **b)**

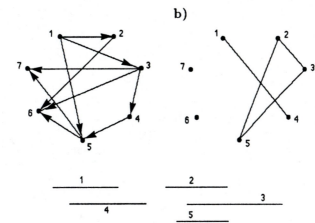

c)

$$\underline{\quad 1 \quad}$$ $$\underline{\quad 2 \quad}$$ $$\underline{\quad 3 \quad}$$

$$\underline{\quad 4 \quad}$$ $$\underline{\quad 5 \quad}$$

10. a)

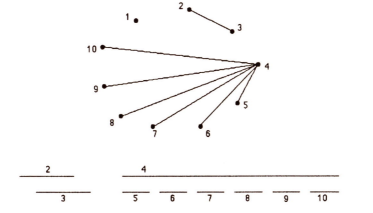

b)

c)

$$\underline{\quad 2 \quad}$$ $$\underline{\quad 4 \quad}$$

$$\underline{\quad 3 \quad}$$ $$\underline{5 \quad 6 \quad 7 \quad 8 \quad 9 \quad 10}$$

11.

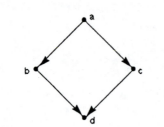

12. h_W via shortest path

   a)   b)

h_W via longest path

   a)   b)

vertex	h_W	vertex	h_W	vertex	h_W	vertex	h_W
a	14	a	12	a	16	a	15
b	9	b	1	b	9	b	1
c	3	c	0	c	3	c	0
d	0	d	6	d	0	d	6
e	4	e	0	e	4	e	0
f	1	f	2	f	1	f	2
g	1	g	0	g	1	g	0
h	0	h	0	h	0	h	0

13. The second version of h_W given in the text satisfies this condition and is defined for any acyclic food web. **14.** Suppose there is a directed path from u to v. Since every direct or indirect prey of v is also an indirect prey of u, every term in the sum for $t_W(v)$ is also a term in the defining sum for $t_W(u)$. Since all the values of h are non-negative, it follows that $t_W(u) \geq t_W(v)$. Axiom 1 is satisfied trivially. Axiom 2 is not satisfied. Suppose u is a vertex and we add a new species v which is a direct prey of u, but which itself has no prey. Then $h_W(v) = 0$, so the value of the sum for $t_W(u)$ is not increased. Axiom 3 is satisfied since increasing the level of v relative to u increases $h_W(v)$ and hence increases the sum defining $t_W(u)$. **15.** This assumption *is* restrictive. An example of two species which are mutual prey would be man and grizzly bear.

Chapter 14   Applications of Subgraph Enumeration

1. (a) 1957   **(b)** $8^6 = 262,144$ **(c)** 2520   **(d)** 105.   **2. (a)** $(2,2,1,5,5)$
(b) $(1,4,1,2,1)$.

3. a)   **b)**

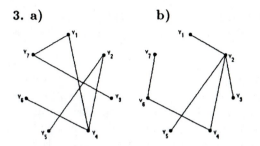

4. By Theorem 4, there are 15 perfect matches of K_6. Example 15 shows how to generate 5 perfect matches of K_6 using the matching $\{\{1,2\},\{3,4\}\}$ of K_4. The five perfect matches of K_6 generated from $\{\{1,3\},\{2,4\}\}$ are $\{\{5,3\},\{2,4\},\{1,6\}\}$, $\{\{1,5\},\{2,4\},\{3,6\}\}$, $\{\{1,3\},\{5,4\},\{2,6\}\}$, $\{\{1,3\},\{2,5\},\{4,6\}\}$, and $\{\{1,3\},\{2,4\},\{5,6\}\}$. The five perfect matches of K_6 generated from $\{\{1,4\},\{2,3\}\}$ are $\{\{5,4\},\{2,3\},\{1,6\}\}$, $\{\{1,5\},\{2,3\},\{4,6\}\}$, $\{\{1,4\},\{5,3\},\{2,6\}\}$, $\{\{1,4\},\{2,5\},\{3,6\}\}$, and $\{\{1,4\}, \{2,3\},\{5,6\}\}$.   **5.** Consider the longest path in the tree. Its two endpoints have degree 1.   **6.** Suppose G is a graph with n vertices, $n-1$ edges, and no circuits. The proof is complete if we show that G is connected. Suppose G is not connected. Then G is a forest with k components, where $k > 1$. Let $C_1, C_2, \ldots, C_k$ be the k components and let $n_1, n_2, \ldots, n_k$ be the number of vertices in each component. Then $\sum_{i=1}^{k} n_i = n$. Since each C_i is a tree, the number of edges in each C_i is $n_i - 1$. This implies that the number of edges in G is $\sum_{i=1}^{k}(n_i - 1) = (\sum_{i=1}^{k} n_i) - k = n - k < n - 1$, a contradiction.   **7.** 5
8. The path A, E, D, C has total length 39 and total cost \$45.

9. a)   **b)**   **c)**

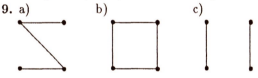

range 75   weight 1010   weight 360

10. Visit the villages in the order $ACEBD$.   **11.** 157/1957.   **12.** $1/n^{n-3}$.
13. $2/((n-1)(n-2))$.   **14.** $1/((n-1)(n-2))$.   **15.** The number of perfect matchings in $K_{n,n}$ is $n!$, which may be generated by observing that there is a one-to-one correspondence between the perfect matches in $K_{n,n}$ and the permutations on $\{1, 2, \ldots, n\}$.   **16.** Any perfect matching of $K_{n,n}$ may be described as a permutation of $\{1, 2, \ldots, n\}$. Hence, the perfect matches of $K_{n,n}$ can be generated by generating the permutations of $\{1, 2, \ldots, n\}$. A method for doing this is given in Section 4.7 of the textbook.   **17.** Let $m = |M| = n/2$. Then the number of spanning trees of K_n containing M is $2^{m-1}m^{m-2}$. To see this, consider the m edges of M as vertices of K_m which must be spanned by a tree. By Cayley's Theorem there are m^{m-2} such trees. Since every pair of edges of M may be connected by two different edges of K_n, every spanning tree of K_m gives rise to 2^{m-1} spanning trees of K_n containing

M.   **18. (a)** Generate all of the subsets of $\{1, 2, \ldots, n\}$ by generating the set of all r-combinations using the algorithm described in Section 4.7 of the textbook. For each subset $\{i_1, i_2, \ldots, i_r\}$ compute $z = w_{i_1} + w_{i_2} + \cdots + w_{i_r}$, then select a subset on which the minimum of z is attained.   **(b)** $C(n, r)$ candidates must be checked to solve the problem.   **19. (a)** Use the linear search algorithm to find the smallest element of W, say x_1. Remove x_1 from W and repeat the algorithm to find the smallest element of the remaining set, say x_2. Continue repeating the linear search algorithm n times, removing the smallest element after each repetition. This gives $\{x_1, x_2, \ldots, x_n\} = W$ such that $x_1 \leq x_2 \leq \cdots \leq x_n$. A subset of W of size r with the smallest possible sum is $\{x_1, x_2, \ldots, x_r\}$.   **(b)** This algorithm requires at most $O(n^2)$ comparisons. **20.** $n = 10$.   **21.** $n2^{n-1}$.   **22.** Let e be the edge $\{n-1, n\}$. Show there is a one-to-one correspondence between the spanning trees of $K_n - e$ and the $(n-2)$-tuples $(a_1, a_2, \ldots, a_{n-2})$ such that each a_i is an integer, $1 \leq a_i \leq n$, for $i = 1, 2, \ldots, n-3$, and $1 \leq a_{n-2} \leq n-2$. The result follows from the fact that there are $(n-2)n^{n-3}$ such $(n-2)$-tuples.   **23.** Show that the spanning trees of K_n such that vertex v_i has degree d_i are in one-to-one correspondence with the $(n-2)$-tuples $(a_1, a_2, \ldots, a_{n-2})$ such that the integer i appears $d_i - 1$ times. The result follows from counting all such $(n-2)$-tuples.   **24.** Use the method suggested by the solution to Exercise 23.   **25.** We use induction on $k = m + n$. The result can be checked directly for $m = 1$, $n = 3$, or $m = n = 2$. So, assume the result holds for all complete bipartite graphs with $m + n < k$, and let $K_{m,n}$ be one with $m + n = k$. Since every tree must have at least two vertices of degree 1, at least two of the d_i or f_j must be 1, say $d_1 = 1$. The number of spanning trees of $K_{m,n}$ such that vertex u_i has degree d_i, for all i, and vertex v_j has degree f_j, for all j, is equal to the number of spanning trees of $K_{m,n}$ such that vertex u_i has degree d_i and vertex v_j has degree f_j which contain edge $(1, 1)$, plus the number of such spanning trees which contain edge $(1, 2)$, plus the number of such spanning trees which contain $(1, 3)$, etc. The number of spanning trees such that vertex u_i has degree d_i, for all i, and vertex v_j has degree f_j, for all j, which contain edge $(1, k)$ is equal to 0 if $f_k = 1$, otherwise is equal to the number of spanning trees of $K_{m-1,n}$ such that vertex u_i has degree d_i (for $i = 2, 3, \ldots, m$), vertex v_k has degree f_{k-1}, and vertex v_j has degree f_j (for $j = 1, \ldots, k-1, k+1, \ldots, n$). By induction, the number of such trees is

$$\frac{(m-2)!(n-1)!}{(d_2 - 1)! \cdots (d_m - 1)!(f_1 - 1)! \cdots (f_{k-1} - 1)!(f_k - 2)!(f_{k+1} - 1)! \cdots (f_n - 1)!}.$$

The total number of spanning trees such that vertex u_i has degree d_i and vertex v_j has degree f_j is obtained by summing the above terms over all $k = 1, 2, \ldots, n$ such that $f_k \geq 2$. This sum is simplified by multiplying each term by $(f_k - 1)/(f_k - 1)$. Summing gives

$$\frac{(m-2)!(n-1)![(f_1 - 1) + (f_2 - 1) + \cdots + (f_n - 1)]}{(d_2 - 1)! \cdots (d_m - 1)!(f_1 - 1)! \cdots (f_n - 1)!}.$$

Since $(f_1-1)+(f_2-1)+\cdots+(f_n-1) = f_1+f_2+\cdots+f_n-n = m+n-1-n = m-1$. The solution is complete.

Chapter 15   Traveling Salesman Problem

1. a) f,e,a,b,c,d is forced, so the only Hamilton circuits are f,e,a,b,c,d,g,h,f of length 22 and f,e,a,b,c,d,h,g,f of length 21. The latter is the shorter, so the solution is f,e,a,b,c,d,h,g,f. **b)** a,b,c and d,e,f are forced, so the only Hamilton circuits are a,b,c,g,f,e,d,a of length 19 and a,b,c,f,e,d,g,a of length 21. The former is the shorter, so the solution is a,b,c,f,e,d,g,a. **c)** h,d,c,b,a,e,f,g,h is the only Hamilton circuit. Its length is 30. **d)** f,d,c,b,a,e,g,j,h,i,f is the only Hamilton circuit. Its length is 38. **e)** d,c,b,a,e,h,i,g,f,d with length 36 and d,c,b,a,e,f,g,h,i,d with length 23 are the only Hamilton circuits. The latter is shorter, so the solution is d,c,b,a,e,f,g,h,i,d. **f)** a,b,c,d,i,f,e,g,h,a with length 27 and a,b,c,d,i,g,f,e,h,a with length 37 are the only Hamilton circuits. The former is shorter, so the solution is a,b,c,d,i,f,e,g,h,a. **g)** a,b,c,d,g,h,e,i,f,a with length 15 and d,c,b,a,f,g,i,h,e,d with length 27 are the only Hamilton circuits. The former is shorter, so the solution is a,b,c,d,g,h,e,i,f,a. **h)** a,b,c,d,i,g,f,e,h,a with length 23 and d,c,b,a,e,h,f,i,g,d with length 34 are the only Hamilton circuits. The former is shorter, so the solution is a,b,c,d,i,g,f,e,h,a. **2.**

a) $M = $
$$\begin{array}{c} \\ C \\ E \\ A \\ D \\ B \end{array}\begin{array}{c} c\ \ e\ \ a\ \ b\ \ d \\ \left(\begin{array}{ccccc} 0 & 0 & 0 & 1 & 1 \\ 0 & 0 & 0 & 1 & 1 \\ 0 & 0 & 1 & 1 & 0 \\ 1 & 1 & 0 & 0 & 0 \\ 1 & 1 & 0 & 0 & 0 \end{array}\right) \end{array}$$
. Thus C and E are in an industry performing tasks b and d, A shares task b with them and does task a alone, and B and D

are in an industry doing tasks c and e. **b)** $M = $
$$\begin{array}{c} \\ B \\ A \\ C \\ D \end{array}\begin{array}{c} d\ \ e\ \ a\ \ b\ \ c \\ \left(\begin{array}{ccccc} 1 & 1 & 1 & 0 & 0 \\ 0 & 1 & 1 & 1 & 0 \\ 1 & 0 & 1 & 1 & 1 \\ 0 & 0 & 0 & 1 & 1 \end{array}\right) \end{array}.$$

Thus A, B, and C are in a single industry performing tasks a, d, and e (although A does not do d and C does not do e), C and D are in an industry performing tasks b and c, and A shares task b with C and D. **3. a)** The tree with edges $\{a,b\}$, $\{a,d\}$, $\{b,c\}$, and $\{d,e\}$ yields circuit c,b,a,d,e,c with length 7. **b)** The tree with edges $\{a,b\}$, $\{a,f\}$, $\{c,d\}$, $\{d,e\}$, and $\{d,f\}$ yields circuit b,a,f,d,e,c,b with length 19. **4.** $l(a,c,b,d,e,a) = 15$, $l(a,c,d,b,e,a) = 14$, $l(a,c,d,e,b,a) = 13$, $l(b,c,d,e,a,b) = 14$. The shortest of these is a,c,d,e,b,a with length 13. The strategy used here was just to find all Hamilton circuits in the graph. The weakness is that the number of Hamilton circuits rises extremely fast, so that there is not time enough to do it on larger graphs.   **5.** There are two directions around a Hamilton circuit. Starting at vertex a, the next vertex in one direction must be different from the next vertex in the other direction because there are at least three vertices in the graph. Hence the two permutations of the vertices are different.   **6.** To maximize S_2, it suffices to minimize $-S_2 = \sum_{j=1}^{n-1} \sum_{i=1}^{m} (-a_{ij} a_{i,j+1})$. Given matrix $\mathbf{A}$, for each column j we introduce a vertex j. For any two columns k and ℓ, we join them by an undirected edge with weight $c_{k\ell} = \sum_{i=1}^{m} (-a_{ik} a_{i,\ell})$. In the resulting undirected graph G_4', each Hamilton path h describes a permutation of the columns of $\mathbf{A}$. Further, if $\mathbf{A}' = [a_{ij}']$ is formed from A by carrying out this permutation of the columns for a minimum weight Hamilton path, then $\sum_{j=1}^{n-1} \sum_{i=1}^{m} (-a_{ij}' a_{i,j+1}')$ is precisely the sum of the weights along h. Since h is a minimum weight Hamilton path in G_4', this means that $\sum_{j=1}^{n-1} \sum_{i=1}^{m} (a_{ij}' a_{i,j+1}')$ is largest among all possible orderings of the columns of $\mathbf{A}$. Thus the maximum value of this half of $f(\mathbf{A})$ is found by finding a minimum weight Hamilton path in G_4'. To convert this method to the TSP, add one more vertex 0 to G_4' and join 0 to each other vertex by an edge of weight 0, thus forming graph G_4. A solution of the TSP in G_4 corresponds to a permutation of the columns of $\mathbf{A}$ that maximizes S_2. **7.** Let us represent the Hamilton circuits by sequences of vertex labels. We consider two circuits to be 'different' if the corresponding sequences are 'different.' Let s_1 and s_2 be two of these sequences of vertex labels. In terms of these sequences, the meaning of the word 'different' that was used in the text was that the sequences are 'different' unless they are identical or satisfy one or the other of the following two conditions: (a) s_1 begins with a label a, and if by starting at the occurrence of a in s_2, proceeding from left to right, jumping to the beginning of s_2 when its end is reached (without repeating the end label), and stopping when a is reached again, we can produce s_1, or (b) s_1 begins with a label a, and if by starting at the occurrence of a in s_2, proceeding from right to left, jumping to the end of s_2 when its beginning is reached (without repeating the end label), and stopping when a is reached again, we can produce s_1. An alternative meaning is that two are 'different' unless they are identical or satisfy (a), but not (b). In this case, the number of 'different' sequences, and thus 'different' Hamilton circuits, is 6!. A third meaning is that two sequences are 'different' unless they are identical. In this case, the number of 'different' sequences, and thus 'different' Hamilton circuits, is 7!. The text's choice of the meaning of "different" is best because it accurately represents the geometric structure of the graph.   **8.** Procedure Short Circuit fails because edges that it assumes are present are not in fact present. The procedure generates circuits in complete graphs, and the graph given is not complete.   **9.** In the figure, any Hamilton circuit must pass through both edges $\{a, b\}$ and $\{c, d\}$, and it must contain a Hamilton path from d to a in C and another Hamilton path from b to c in D. the TSP here can be reduced to two smaller TSPs, one in which C has been reduced to a single vertex ad and one in which D has been reduced to a single vertex bc, as shown in the figure below. Once Hamilton circuits solving the TSP have been found in each of the reduced graphs, the vertex ad can be removed from the one through D, and the resulting path can replace bc in the one through C, thus producing a Hamilton circuit through the graph given.

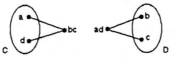

10. The banks are represented by vertices, and each safe route between two banks, or between the home base of the car and a bank, is represented by an edge joining the corresponding vertices, with the time it takes to travel the route as the weight on the edge.   **11.** The cities are represented by vertices, and each possible route for the railroad between two cities is represented by an edge. The weight on an edge is the cost of the rail line on that route. To make this a TSP problem, another vertex is added, with an edge of zero weight to each of the vertices representing New York and San Francisco.   **12.** There are several TSP problems, one for each truck. For a single truck, the destinations of the packages are represented by the vertices, and two vertices are joined by an edge if there is a route between the corresponding destinations. The weight on the edge is the time it takes a truck to travel the corresponding route.   **13.** Each front line unit is assigned a vertex. Edges join two vertices whenever there is any route that connects the corresponding units. A scale for safety is assigned with 0 representing a perfectly safe route and higher numbers indicating greater risk on the route. These numbers are the weights assigned to the edges of the graph.

Chapter 16   The Tantalizing Four Cubes

1. The underlying graph is

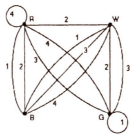

Two disjoint acceptable subgraphs are

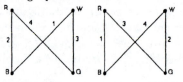

Hence a solution is

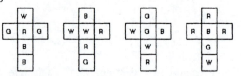

2. The underlying graph is

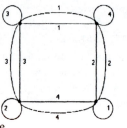

The acceptable subgraphs are

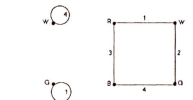

Thus one solution is

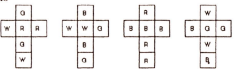

3. There are 2 disjoint versions of the second subgraph. Thus, another solution is

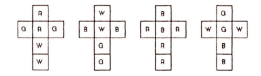

4. Two acceptable subgraphs are
Thus a solution is
The last left-right pair is R-W, but since the graph was given, not the cubes,

it is unknown which is left and which is right.

5. For example, there are no acceptable subgraphs in the following graph

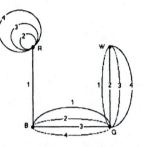

6. For example, there are no acceptable subgraphs in the following graph

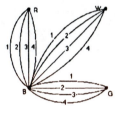

7. In the following graph,

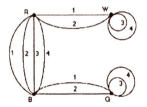

the only acceptable subgraphs are

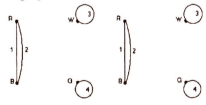

and they are not disjoint.

8. Again, the easiest way to find a puzzle with exactly two solutions is to construct the underlying graph. Here are two pairs of subgraphs

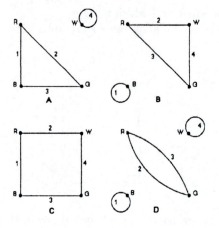

Of these four subgraphs, only the pairs AB and CD are disjoint. So they give two distinct solutions. If the additional four edges contribute no new acceptable subgraphs, these will be the only two solutions. So let all the other faces be red. The two solutions are

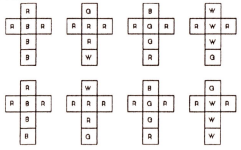

Note: To obtain the second solution from the first, leave cubes 1 and 3 the same, rotate the second cube 180° to the right and then 90° up, and rotate the fourth cube 90° down. **9. a)** If there are three cubes and three colors, the statement of the theorem remains the same. However, there are only three vertices and three labels. A typical acceptable subgraph is a triangle with three different labels, although a 2-cycle and a loop or three loops are possible. **b)** If there are three cubes and four colors, it is impossible for all colors to appear on the same side of a stack. **c)** If there are three cubes and five colors, the theorem remains the same. Now the graph has five vertices and five labels. A typical acceptable subgraph is a pentagon with five different labels, although numerous other configurations are possible.

Chapter 17   The Assignment Problem

1. 2143 is an optimal solution with $z = 20$.   **2.** 2341 is an optimal solution with $z = 13$.   **3.** 216354 is an optimal solution with $z = 18$.   **4.** 321465 is an optimal solution with $z = -6$.   **5.** 124356 is an optimal solution with $z = 65$.   **6.** Assign Ken to the Butterfly, Rob to the Freestyle, Mark to the Backstroke, and David to the Breaststroke, the minimum time is 124.8.   **7.** The following couples should marry: Jane and Joe, Mary and Hal, Carol and John, Jessica and Bill, Dawn and Al, and Lisa and Bud, giving a measure of anticipated "happiness" of 8.   **8.** The route New York, Chicago, Denver, Los Angeles is optimal with total time of 62 hours.   **9. a)** Edges $\{1,1\}$, $\{2,2\}$, $\{3,3\}$, $\{4,4\}$, and $\{5,5\}$ are a perfect matching.   **b)** No perfect matching exists. If $W = \{3,4,5\}$, then $R(W) = \{4,5\}$ and $|R(W)| < |W|$.   **c)** Edges $\{1,1\}$, $\{2,2\}$, $\{3,3\}$, $\{4,5\}$, and $\{5,4\}$ are a perfect matching.   **10.** The perfect matching $\{1,4\}$, $\{2,1\}$, $\{3,2\}$, $\{4,3\}$ has the smallest possible weight, which is 12.   **11. a)** Let $C = [c_{ij}]$ where $c_{ij} = 0$ for all i and j.   **b)** Let $C = [c_{ij}]$ where $c_{ii} = 0$ for $i = 1,2,3,4,5$, and $c_{ij} = 1$ for $i \neq j$.   **12.** Let $u_1 = 0$, $u_2 = 4$, $u_3 = 8$, $u_4 = 12$, and $v_1 = v_2 = v_3 = v_4 = 0$. Then apply

$$\text{Theorem 1 to obtain } \widehat{C} = \begin{pmatrix} 1 & 2 & 3 & 4 \\ 1 & 2 & 3 & 4 \\ 1 & 2 & 3 & 4 \\ 1 & 2 & 3 & 4 \end{pmatrix}. \text{ Then } C \text{ and } \widehat{C} \text{ have the same set}$$

of optimal solutions. But for any permutation σ of $\{1,2,3,4\}$, $\sum_{i=1}^{n} \widehat{c}_{i\sigma(i)} = 1 + 2 + 3 + 4 = 10$. So, any permutation is an optimal solution to the problem specified by $\widehat{C}$, and hence is an optimal solution to the problem specified by C.
13. If $c_{ij} \geq 0$ for all i and j, then subtracting the smallest entry from each row can not result in a negative entry. If some row, say $(c_{11}c_{12}\cdots c_{1n})$ has negative entries and, say, c_{11} is the smallest entry, then $\widehat{c}_{1j} = c_{1j} - c_{11} = c_{1j} + |c_{11}| \geq 0$, for $j = 1,2,\ldots,n$ since either $c_{1j} \geq 0$ or if $c_{1j} < 0$, then $|c_{1j}| \geq |c_{11}|$. Thus, after subtracting the smallest entry in each row, the resulting matrix has all nonnegative entries. Now subtracting the smallest entry from each column cannot result in a negative entry.   **14.** The problem may be solved by multiplying all entries in c by -1 since finding a permutation σ which maximizes $z = \sum_{i=1}^{n} c_{i\sigma(i)}$ is equivalent to finding a permutation σ which minimizes $-z = -\sum_{i=1}^{n} c_{i\sigma(i)}$.   **15.** 352461 is an optimal solution with $z = 35$.   **16.** Suppose σ^* is a permutation which solves the assignment problem specified by the matrix in Example 11. Suppose also that P is a path which has total delivery time less than $\sum_{i=1}^{n} c_{i\sigma^*(i)}$. Number the cities using $1,2,3,4,5,6,7$ representing New York, Boston, Chicago, Dallas, Denver, San Francisco, and Los Angeles respectively. Define the permutation σ as follows: if P visits city j immediately after P visits city i, then $\sigma(i) = j - 1$; if P does not visit city i, then $\sigma(i) = i - 1$. Then the total delivery time of P is $\sum_{i=1}^{n} c_{i\sigma(i)}$ since $c_{ii-1} = 0$, for $i = 2,3,4,5,6$. But this implies that $\sum_{i=1}^{n} c_{i\sigma(i)} < \sum_{i=1}^{n} c_{i\sigma^*(i)}$, a contradiction.
17. The number of iterations is at most the sum of all of the entries of the

reduced matrix. Let k be the largest entry in the reduced matrix, then the sum of all entries in the reduced matrix is at most kn^2. Thus the number of iterations is $O(n^2)$.   **18.** Given a bipartite graph $G = (V,E)$ define the matrix $\mathbf{A} = [a_{ij}]$ as follows. Let $a_{ij} = \begin{cases} 0 & \text{if edge } \{i,j\} \in E \\ 1 & \text{otherwise} \end{cases}$. Then matches correspond to independent sets of zeros in $\mathbf{A}$ and vertex covers correspond to line covers of $\mathbf{A}$. The result now follows from Theorem 3.   **19.** Let $G = (V, E)$ be a bipartite graph, with $V = V_1 \cup V_2$. If G has a perfect matching M, then $|V_1| = |M| = |V_2|$. For any W contained in V_1, let $W = \{w_1, w_2, \ldots, w_k\}$, and for any $w_i \in W$, let r_i be the vertex in V_2 such that $\{w_i, r_i\} \in M$. Then $r_1, r_2, \ldots, r_k$ are all distinct, and $\{r_1, r_2, \ldots, r_k\}$ is contained in $R(W)$, so $|R(W)| \geq |W|$. Conversely, assume $|V_1| = |V_2|$ and $|R(W)| \geq |W|$, for all W contained in V_1. Since every edge in E joins a vertex in V_1 to one in V_2, V_1 is a vertex cover. The proof is complete if we show that V_1 is a cover of minimal size. For then, Exercise 18 implies there is a matching of size $|V_1|$, which must be a perfect matching. Suppose Q is a vertex cover of the edges of minimum size, and $Q \neq V_1$. Let $U_1 = Q \cap V_1$ and let $U_2 = V_2 - U_1$. By assumption, $|R(U_2)| \geq |U_2|$. However, $R(U_2)$ is contained in $Q \cap V_2$ because edges not covered by vertices in V_1 must be covered by vertices in V_2. Thus, $|U_2| \leq |R(U_2)| \leq |Q \cap V_2|$. This implies that $|V_1| = |U_1| + |U_2| \leq |U_1| + |Q \cap V_2| = |Q \cap V_1| + |Q \cap V_2| = |Q|$. Since $|V_1| \leq |Q|$ and Q is a cover of minimum size, V_1 must be a cover of minimum size.   **20.** A stable set of four marriages is: David and Susan, Kevin and Colleen, Richard and Nancy, and Paul and Dawn.   **21.** We prove the existence of a stable set of n marriages by giving an iterative procedure which finds a stable set of marriages.

Initially, let each man propose to his favorite woman. Each woman who receives more than one proposal replies "no" to all but the man she likes the most from among those who have proposed to her. However, she does not give him a definite "yes" yet, but rather a conditional "yes" to allow for the possibility that a man whom she likes better may propose to her in the future.

Next, all those men who have not received a conditional "yes" now propose to the women they like second best. Each woman receiving proposals must now choose the man she likes best from among the men consisting of the new proposals and the man who has her conditional "yes", if any.

Continue to iterate this procedure. Each man who has not yet received a conditional "yes" proposes to his next choice. The woman again says "no" to all but the proposal she prefers thus far.

The procedure must terminate after a finite number of iterations since every woman will eventually receive a proposal. To see this, notice that as long as there is a woman who has not been proposed to, there will be rejections and new proposals. Since no man can propose to the same woman more than once, every woman will eventually receive a proposal. Once the last woman receives a proposal, each woman now marries the man who currently has her conditional "yes", and the procedure terminates.

The set of marriages produced is stable, for suppose David and Susan are not married to each other, but David prefers Susan to his own wife. Then David must have proposed to Susan at some iteration and Susan rejected his proposal in favor of some man she preferred to David. Thus Susan must prefer her husband to David. So there can be no instability.

Chapter 18   Shortest Path Problems

1. The length is 90. The path is v_2, v_1, v_9, v_8.   **2. a)** v_7 comes from v_6, v_6 from v_4, v_4 from v_3, v_3 from v_1. Thus the path is v_1, v_3, v_4, v_6, v_7.   **b)** v_5 comes from v_4, v_4 from v_3, v_3 from v_1. Thus the path is v_1, v_3, v_4, v_5.

c)

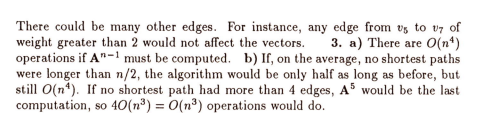

There could be many other edges. For instance, any edge from v_5 to v_7 of weight greater than 2 would not affect the vectors.   **3. a)** There are $O(n^4)$ operations if $\mathbf{A}^{n-1}$ must be computed.   **b)** If, on the average, no shortest paths were longer than $n/2$, the algorithm would be only half as long as before, but still $O(n^4)$. If no shortest path had more than 4 edges, $\mathbf{A}^5$ would be the last computation, so $4O(n^3) = O(n^3)$ operations would do.

4. $\mathbf{A} = \begin{pmatrix} 0 & 2 & 3 & * & * & * \\ 2 & 0 & * & 5 & 2 & * \\ 3 & * & 0 & * & 5 & * \\ * & 5 & * & 0 & 1 & 2 \\ * & 2 & 5 & 1 & 0 & 4 \\ * & * & * & 2 & 4 & 0 \end{pmatrix}$, $\mathbf{A}^5 = \mathbf{A}^4 = \begin{pmatrix} 0 & 2 & 3 & 5 & 4 & 7 \\ 2 & 0 & 5 & 3 & 2 & 5 \\ 3 & 5 & 0 & 6 & 5 & 8 \\ 5 & 3 & 6 & 0 & 1 & 2 \\ 4 & 2 & 5 & 1 & 0 & 3 \\ 7 & 5 & 8 & 2 & 3 & 0 \end{pmatrix}$.

5. $\mathbf{A} = \begin{pmatrix} 0 & 4 & 3 & * & * & * & * & * \\ 4 & 0 & 2 & 5 & * & * & * & * \\ 3 & 2 & 0 & 2 & 6 & * & * & * \\ * & 5 & 2 & 0 & 1 & 5 & * & * \\ * & * & 6 & 1 & 0 & * & 7 & * \\ * & * & * & 5 & * & 0 & 2 & 7 \\ * & * & * & * & 7 & 2 & 0 & 4 \\ * & * & * & * & * & 7 & 4 & 0 \end{pmatrix}$, $\mathbf{A}^6 = \mathbf{A}^5 =$

$$\begin{pmatrix} 0 & 4 & 3 & 5 & 6 & 10 & 12 & 16 \\ 4 & 0 & 2 & 4 & 5 & 9 & 11 & 15 \\ 3 & 2 & 0 & 2 & 3 & 7 & 9 & 13 \\ 5 & 4 & 2 & 0 & 1 & 5 & 7 & 11 \\ 6 & 5 & 3 & 1 & 0 & 6 & 7 & 11 \\ 10 & 9 & 7 & 5 & 6 & 0 & 2 & 6 \\ 12 & 11 & 9 & 7 & 7 & 2 & 0 & 4 \\ 16 & 15 & 13 & 11 & 11 & 6 & 4 & 0 \end{pmatrix}.$$

$$6.\ \mathbf{A}^3 = \begin{pmatrix} 0 & 2 & 3 & 5 & 4 & 8 \\ 2 & 0 & 5 & 3 & 2 & 5 \\ 3 & 5 & 0 & 6 & 5 & 8 \\ 5 & 3 & 6 & 0 & 1 & 2 \\ 4 & 2 & 5 & 1 & 0 & 3 \\ 8 & 5 & 8 & 2 & 3 & 0 \end{pmatrix}$$

$a_{3k}^3 = (3,5,0,6,5,8)$; $a_{k4} = (*,5,*,0,1,2)$; $5+1 = 6$, so there is an edge of weight 1 at the end from v_5 to v_4. $a_{k5} = (*,2,5,1,0,4)$. Only $5+0$ and $0+5$ arise, so there is an edge of weight 5 from v_3 to v_4. The path is v_3, v_5, v_4.
7. $a_{1k}^3 = (0,2,3,5,4,8)$; $a_{k6} = (*,*,*,2,4,6)$; $5+2 = 7$, so there is an edge of weight 2 from v_4 to v_6. $a_{k4} = (*,5,*,0,1,2)$; $4+1 = 5$, so there is an edge of weight 1 from v_5 to v_4. $a_{k5} = (*,2,5,1,0,4)$; $2+2 = 4$, so there is an edge of weight 2 from v_2 to v_5. $a_{k2} = (2,0,*,5,2,*)$. Only $2+0$ and $0+2$ arise, so there is an edge of weight 2 from v_1 to v_2. The path is v_1, v_2, v_5, v_4, v_6.

$$8.\ \mathbf{A}^6 = \mathbf{A}^5 = \begin{pmatrix} 0 & 4 & 3 & 5 & 6 & 10 & 12 & 16 \\ 4 & 0 & 2 & 4 & 5 & 9 & 11 & 15 \\ 3 & 2 & 0 & 2 & 3 & 7 & 9 & 13 \\ 5 & 4 & 2 & 0 & 1 & 5 & 7 & 11 \\ 6 & 5 & 3 & 1 & 0 & 6 & 7 & 11 \\ 10 & 9 & 7 & 5 & 6 & 0 & 2 & 6 \\ 12 & 11 & 9 & 7 & 7 & 2 & 0 & 4 \\ 16 & 15 & 13 & 11 & 11 & 6 & 4 & 0 \end{pmatrix},$$

$a_{1k}^4 = (0,4,3,5,6,10,12,16)$; $a_{k8} = (*,*,*,*,*,7,4,0)$ $16 = 12+4$, a vertex of weight 4 from v_7 to v_8; $a_{k7} = (*,*,*,*,7,2,0,4)$ $12 = 10+2$, a vertex of weight 2 from v_6 to v_7; $a_{k6} = (*,*,*,5,*,0,2,7)10 = 5+5$, a vertex of weight 5 from v_4 to v_6; $a_{k4} = (*,5,2,0,1,5,*,*)5 = 3+2$, a vertex of weight 2 from v_3 to v_4; $a_{k3} = (3,2,0,2,6,*,*,*)3 = 0+3$, a vertex of weight 3 from v_1 to v_3. The path is $v_1, v_3, v_4, v_6, v_7, v_8$.   9. a) Only half the calculations would be necessary at each stage. So, half the time could be saved.

b)
for $i := 1$ **to** n
   for $j := 1$ **to** i $\{j \le i$ always$\}$
     $A(1,i,j) = w(v_i, v_j)$
$i := 1$
repeat
   flag:=true
   $t := t + 1$
   for $i := 1$ **to** n
     for $j := 1$ **to** i
     $A(t,i,j) := A(t-1,i,j)$
     for $k := 1$ **to** $j - 1$
     $A(t,i,j) := \min\{A(t,i,j), A(t-1,i,k) + A(1,j,k)\}$
     for $k := j$ **to** $i - 1$
     $A(t,i,j) := \min\{A(t,i,j), A(t-1,i,k) + A(1,k,j)\}$
     for $k := i$ **to** n
     $A(t,i,j) := \min\{A(t,i,j), A(t-1,k,i) + A(1,k,j)\}$
if $A(t,i,j) \ne A(t-1,i,j)$ **then** *flag:=false*
until $t = n - 1$ **or** *flag=true*.

10. If the underlying graph is a directed graph, then edges are one-way, and the distance from i to j may not be the same as the distance from j to i. So, nonsymmetric are necessary.

Chapter 19 Network Survivability

1. a)

edge	circuit or cut edge	edge	circuit or cut edge
$\{a,b\}$	a,b,c,a	$\{a,c\}$	a,b,c,a
$\{b,c\}$	a,b,c,a	x	c,d,c
x'	c,d,c	$\{d,e\}$	cut edge
$\{e,f\}$	e,f,h,e	$\{e,h\}$	e,f,h,e
$\{f,g\}$	f,g,h,f	$\{f,h\}$	f,g,h,f
y	g,h,g	y'	g,h,g

b)

edge	circuit or cut edge	edge	circuit or cut edge
$\{a,b\}$	cut edge	x	b,j,b
x'	b,j,b	$\{b,c\}$	b,c,d,b
$\{b,d\}$	b,c,d,b	$\{c,d\}$	b,c,d,b
$\{b,e\}$	cut edge	$\{e,g\}$	e,f,g,e
y	e,f,e	y'	e,f,e
$\{f,g\}$	e,f,g,e	$\{g,h\}$	g,h,i,g
$\{g,i\}$	g,h,i,g	$\{h,i\}$	g,h,i,g

2. **a)** $\gamma(G) = \eta(G) = 9/6 = 3/2$. **b)** $\gamma(G) = \eta(G) = 12/5$. **3.** **a)** $\gamma(G) = 7/4$, $\eta(G) = 3/2$, and G_0 is the triangle K_3. (One contraction is needed to find G_0.) **b)** $\gamma(G) = 5/3$, $\eta(G) = 5/4$, and G_0 is the circuit C_5. (Two contractions are needed to find G_0.) **4.** Let G' be formed by erasing a and all edges of G incident with a. Suppose there are vertices v and v' of G which are distinct from a, are in the same component of G, and such that every path joining v with v' includes a. Then there can be no paths joining v and v' in G'. Thus v and v' are in different components of G'. But any component of G that does not contain a is a component of G'. Since v and v' are in the same component of G, they must be in the same component as a, and that component must have split into at least two components. Thus G' has more components than G, and a is a cut vertex of G. Now suppose a is a cut vertex of G. Then G' has a component H not in G. By the construction of G', the vertex a must be incident in G with an edge whose other end v is in H. But a cannot be adjacent only to vertices in H, for otherwise G and G' would have the same number of components. Hence there is a component H' of G' different from H that has a vertex v' adjacent to a in G. Now we have a path (v, a, v') in G joining v with v', whereas there are no such paths in G', since the two vertices are in different components of G'. Thus v and v' are in the same component of G, and a must be on every path joining v with v'. Lemma 1 follows. **5.** For $k = 2$, suppose $p_1/q_1 \le p_2/q_2$. Then $p_1 q_2 \le p_2 q_1$, so $p_1 q_1 + p_1 q_2 \le p_1 q_1 + p_2 q_1$. Dividing by $q_1(q_1 + q_2)$, we get $p_1/q_1 \le (p_1 + p_2)/(q_1 + q_2)$. But from $p_1 q_2 \le p_2 q_1$ we also get $p_1 q_2 + p_2 q_2 \le p_2 q_1 + p_2 q_2$. Dividing through this by $q_2(q_1 + q_2)$, we get $(p_1 + p_2)/(q_1 + q_2) \le p_2/q_2$. These two results show Lemma 2 for $k = 2$. Suppose the lemma is true for $k = n$, so that $\min_{1 \le i \le n} p_i/q_i \le (p_1 + p_2 + \cdots + p_n)/(q_1 + q_2 + \cdots + q_n) \le \max_{1 \le i \le n} p_i/q_i$. We will use the fraction in the middle of this last inequality as a single fraction to complete the proof. By the induction hypothesis and the first part of this proof, $\min_{1 \le i \le n+1} p_i/q_i = \min(\min_{1 \le i \le n}(p_i/q_i), p_{n+1}/q_{n+1}) \le \min\left(\frac{p_1 + p_2 + \cdots + p_n}{q_1 + q_2 + \cdots + q_n}, \frac{p_{n+1}}{q_{n+1}}\right) \le \frac{p_1 + p_2 + \cdots + p_{n+1}}{q_1 + q_2 + \cdots + q_{n+1}} \le \max\left(\frac{p_1 + p_2 + \cdots + p_n}{q_1 + q_2 + \cdots + q_n}, \frac{p_{n+1}}{q_{n+1}}\right) \le \max\left(\max_{1 \le i \le n}\left(\frac{p_i}{q_i}\right), \frac{p_{n+1}}{q_{n+1}}\right) = \max_{1 \le i \le n+1}(p_i/q_i)$. **6.** The graph shown is not induced, and adding the missing edge (edge $\{a, h\}$) gives a larger value of g. Other examples can be obtained from any subgraph shown in Figure 7 that includes the two edges joining a and b by leaving one of them out of the subgraph. **7.** By definition, each component of a forest is a tree and so has one fewer edges than vertices. Thus if forest F has k components, then $|E(F)| = |V(F)| - k = |V(F)| - \omega(F)$. But every subgraph of a forest is a forest. Thus, if H is any subgraph of forest F, and if H has an edge (so that $|V(H)| - \omega(H) > 0$), then $g(H) = |E(H)|/(|V(H)| - \omega(H)) = (|V(H)| - \omega(H))/(|V(H)| - \omega(H)) = 1$. Thus $\gamma(F) = \max_{H \subseteq G} g(H) = \max_{H \subseteq G} 1 = 1$. Now $\gamma(F) = 1 = g(F)$, so F is its η-reduced graph G_0. Thus $\eta(F) = \gamma(G_0) = \gamma(F) = 1$, and the claim is proved. **8.** Consider an arbitrary set F of edges of G. Let us erase the edges of F one at a time from G. We start with $\omega(G)$ components. Each time we erase an edge of F, the number of components either is unchanged or is increased by one because the edge has only two ends. Hence $w(G - F) \le w(G) - |F|$. This gives us $|F| \ge w(G) - w(G - F)$. Thus we have $F/(w(G) - w(G - F)) \ge 1$, for any set F for which $w(G) - w(G - F) > 0$. But $\eta(G)$ is the minimum of all such ratios, so $\eta(G) \ge 1$ also.   **9.** Let G be a plane triangulation with e edges, v vertices, and f faces. Since each edge is on exactly two faces (one face counted twice if the both sides of the edge are on the same face), and since each face has exactly three edges on its boundary, we have $2e = 3f$, or $f = (2/3)e$. By Euler's formula, $v - e + f = 2$. Hence $v - e + (2/3)e = 2$. simplifying and solving for e, we get $e = 3v - 6$, which is the claim.   **10.** Since any subgraph of a plane triangulation is a planar graph, we have $|E(H)| \le 3|V(H)| - 6$ for every connected subgraph of G. Let H be a subgraph of G, and let the components of H be $H_1, H_2, \cdots, H_k$. Then $|V(H)| = \sum_{i=1}^{k} |V(H_i)|$ and $|E(H)| = \sum_{i=1}^{k} |E(H_i)|$. Hence, since $w(H) = k$ and $k \ge 1$, $|E(H)| = \sum_{i=1}^{k} |E(H_i)| \le \sum_{i=1}^{k}(3|V(H_i)| - 6) = 3\sum_{i=1}^{k}(|V(H_i)| - 2) = 3(|V(H)| - 2k) = 3(|V(H)| - k) - 3k \le 3(|V(H)| - w(H)) - 3 = f(|V(H)| - w(H))$.

Chapter 20   The Chinese Postman Problem

1. 227 minutes. The minimum weight deadheading edges are $\{D, F\}$ and $\{F, G\}$, resulting in a ten-minute deadheading time. Any Euler circuit in the graph of Figure 3 gives a minimal route.   **2.** 73 minutes. Path G, D, E, B is the path of minimum weight joining G and B.   **3.** 76 minutes. There are two perfect matchings of minimum weight: $\{\{B, D\}, \{F, H\}\}$ and $\{\{B, F\}, \{D, H\}\}$, reach resulting in a deadheading time of 18 minutes. Add either pair of edges to the graph and use any Euler circuit to obtain an optimal route.
4. 2. Since we are counting the *number* of edges retraced, we can treat the graph as a weighted graph where every edge has weight 1. There are two perfect matchings: $\{\{A, B\}, \{C, D\}\}$ and $\{\{A, D\}, \{B, C\}\}$.   **5. a)** 3   **b)** 0 if n is odd, $n/2$ if n is even   **c)** 2   **d)** 0 if m and n are even, n if m is odd and n is even, m if m is even and n is odd, the larger of m and n if m and n are both odd.
6. $A, D, C, F, E, D, C, B, A$.   **7.** 3. There are 15 matchings to consider. The matchings $\{\{2, 5\}, \{3, 8\}, \{10, 11\}\}$ and $\{\{2, 3\}, \{5, 10\}, \{8, 11\}\}$ have minimum total weight.   **8.** 0.74 seconds. This is Exercise 7 again. The actual printing time is 0.58 seconds and the deadheading time is 0.16 seconds. There are six odd vertices. If we label them a, b, c, d, e, f clockwise from the top of the figure, the perfect matchings of minimum weight are: $\{\{a, b\}, \{c, d\}, \{e, f\}\}$ and $\{\{b, c\}, \{d, e\}, \{f, a\}\}$. Each of these matchings requires three vertical and two horizontal deadheading edges.   **9.** 217 minutes. Each block is traversed twice (once for each side of the street). Therefore the graph to consider is one where each street in the original map is replaced by a pair of multiple edges. The

degree of each vertex is even, so the graph has an Euler circuit. Following any Euler circuit will yield the minimal time.   **10. 16.** Of the 28 odd vertices, 24 are adjacent in pairs. The remaining four can be at best joined by pairs of length two.

Chapter 21   Graph Layouts

1. Let v be a vertex of degree k, and let $N(v)$ be the set of its neighbors in G. Then in any numbering f of G at least half the points of $N(v)$ must be mapped either to the left or to the right of v. This shows that dil(f) ≥ 2. Since this is true for any numbering, it follows that $B(G) \geq \lceil k/2 \rceil$.   **2.** This follows from Exercise 1 since $K_4 - e$ has a point of degree 3.   **3.** By part (iv) of Theorem 1 we have $B(G) \geq 5/2$, so $B(G) \geq 3$ since $B(G)$ is an integer. The opposite inequality $B(G) \leq 3$ follows by constructing a dilation 3 numbering of G.   **4. a)** If we remove any k consecutive vertices of P_n^k other than the first k or the last k, then the resulting graph is disconnected. This shows that $\kappa(P_n^k) \leq k$. You can see that $\kappa(P_n^k) > k - 1$ by noting that the removal of any set S of $k-1$ consecutive vertices from P_n^k still leaves a connected graph. This is true because the "long" edges $\{x, y\}$ of P_n^k joining x and y at distance k in P_n manage to tie together the two pieces of P_n that are left when S is removed. When the set S consists of nonconsecutive vertices, then even shorter edges of P_n^k tie the various pieces together.   **b)** An independent set S of P_n^k of size $\lceil n/k \rceil$ consists of vertices $1, k + 1, 2k + 2$, etc., showing that $\beta(P_n^k) \geq \lceil n/k \rceil$. On the other hand, if T is any set of vertices containing two vertices x and y with $\mathrm{dist}_{P_n}(x, y) \leq k$, then S is not independent in P_n^k. Thus, any independent set has size at most $|S|$, showing that $\beta(P_n^k) \leq \lceil n/k \rceil$.   **c)** The degrees of the vertices of P_n^k ($n \geq 2k + 1$), going from left to right, are $k, k + 1, k + 2, \ldots, 2k - 1, 2k, \ldots, 2k, 2k - 1, \ldots, k + 2, k + 1, k$. Now, to find the number of edges, add these degrees and divide by 2.   **5.** The smallest is 5, and the largest is 7. You get the smallest by using a numbering in which the highest number in a level is adjacent to the highest numbers (allowed by the edges) in the next level. You get the largest by using a numbering in which the lowest number in a level is adjacent to the highest numbers (allowed by the edges) in the next level.   **6.** The reader may well have wondered whether the poor performance of the level algorithm on the trees $L(n)$ is really due to the level algorithm itself, or rather to the bad choice of a root in $L(n)$. Indeed, if we took the rightmost vertex of the path P in $L(n)$ as our root then the level algorithm would produce a numbering of $L(n)$ with correct dilation 2. But, in fact, the bad performance is inherent in the level algorithm, as can be seen in the following modified example. We form a tree $H(n)$ by gluing two copies of $L(n)$ along the path P in reverse order. That is, we glue the leftmost vertex of P in the first copy to the rightmost vertex of P in the second copy, and in general the kth vertex from the left in the first copy to the $2^n - k + 1$st vertex from the right in the second copy. The tree $H(4)$ is illustrated in the following graph.

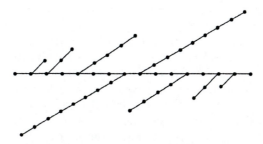

It can then be shown that $B(H(n)) = 3$ but that the level algorithm applied to $H(n)$ gives dilation $\Omega(\log|H(n)|)$ regardless of which vertex of $H(n)$ is chosen as root. We leave the proof that $B(H(n)) = 3$ to the reader (just find a dilation 3 numbering). The proof that $\text{dil}(f) \geq \Omega(\log|H(n)|)$ for any level numbering regardless of the root is based on the same idea as the corresponding proof for $L(n)$, except that the gluing of the two copies of $L(n)$ now makes every vertex on the path P behave in essentially the same way. That is, you can show that now matter what vertex v along P is chosen as a root, there are integers i for which the size of S_i is at least logarithmic in i.   **7.** The required embedding is illustrated in the following figure.

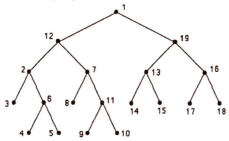

8. Just experiment and see how small you can make the area. You might notice that by allowing bigger area you can get smaller dilation.   **9. a) – d)** To see that $S(P_n) = n - 1$, map P_n to itself by the identity map. This gives the upper bound for $S(P_n)$. The upper bounds for $S(C_n)$ and for $S(K_{1,n})$ follow from the same maps described in the text that we used to calculate $B(C_n)$ and $B(K_{1,n})$. For $S(K_n)$, observe that since every pair of vertices in K_n is joined by an edge, all maps $f : K_n \to P_n$ have the same sum(f). To calculate sum(f), we let $x \in V(K_n)$ and calculate $S(x) = \sum_{y \neq x} \text{dist}(f(x), f(y))$. The desired sum$(f)$ is $\sum_{x \in V(K_n)} S(x)$. To calculate $S(x)$, suppose that $f(x) = i$. Then $S(x) = \sum_{f(y)<i} \text{dist}(f(x), f(y)) + \sum_{f(y)>i} \text{dist}(f(x), f(y)) = \sum_{t=1}^{i-1} t + \sum_{t=1}^{n-i} t = \frac{1}{2}((i-1)i + (n-i)(n-i+1))$. Now just sum this over all i to get the desired result. We leave the proofs of the lower bounds to the reader.   **10.** As in Exercise

1, in any numbering f of G at least half the points of $N(v)$ must be mapped either to the left or to the right of v. This forces an overlap of size at least half of k at the interval $(f(v), f(v) + 1)$ or at the interval $(f(v) - 1, f(v))$. Thus value$(f) \geq \lceil k/2 \rceil$, and since f was arbitrary this shows that $c(G) \geq \lceil k/2 \rceil$.
11. For $c(P_n) = 1$, map P_n by the identity map. If we denote the vertices of C_n by $1, 2, \ldots, n$ as we traverse C_n cyclically, then to get $c(C_n) \leq 2$ map vertex i of C_n to vertex i of P_n. The map which shows that $c(K_{1,n}) \leq \lfloor n/2 \rfloor$ puts the vertex in $K_{1,n}$ of degree n in the middle and the remaining vertices (of degree 1) anywhere arbitrarily. As in the calculation of $S(K_n)$, all maps f of K_n have the same value(f). The fact that $c(K_n) = \lfloor n^2/4 \rfloor$ follows since cut$(\lfloor n/2 \rfloor) = \lfloor n^2/4 \rfloor$ because every vertex x with $f(x) \leq \lfloor n/2 \rfloor$ is joined to every vertex x with $f(x) > \lfloor n/2 \rfloor$ causing an overlap of size $\lfloor n^2/4 \rfloor$ over the interval $(\lfloor n/2 \rfloor, \lfloor n/2 \rfloor + 1)$. We leave the lower bounds to the reader; Exercise 10 can be used here.   **12. a)** The matrix $\begin{pmatrix} 0 & 0 & 1 & 1 & 1 & 0 \\ 0 & 0 & 1 & 1 & 1 & 0 \\ 1 & 1 & 0 & 0 & 0 & 1 \\ 1 & 1 & 0 & 0 & 0 & 1 \\ 1 & 1 & 0 & 0 & 0 & 1 \\ 0 & 0 & 1 & 1 & 1 & 0 \end{pmatrix}$ has a band of 4 enclosing all the 1s, and is obtained by a permutation of the rows and columns of A.   **b)** The graph $G(A)$ is $K_{4,4}$, and it has bandwidth 4.   **13.** Let x be the vertex of degree k in G, and let $f : G \to P_n$ be any one-to-one map. Let $S(x) = \sum_{y \in N(x)} \text{dist}(f(x), f(y))$, where again $N(x)$ is the set of neighbors of x in G. Clearly $S(x)$ is minimized when half the vertices of $N(x)$ are mapped immediately to the left of $f(x)$ and the other half immediately to the right. Thus we get sum$(f) \geq S(x) \geq 2(\sum_{t=1}^{k/2} t) = \frac{k}{2}(k + 2)$.   **14.** The biggest dilation occurs when the vertex with smallest number in level $k - 1$ is joined to the vertex with biggest number in level k. The smallest number is $1 + 2^{k-2} - 1 = 2^{k-2}$ (i.e. one more than the number of vertices in T_{k-2}), and the biggest number is the number of vertices in T_k which is $2^k - 1$. The dilation that we get in that case is the difference between these two numbers, which is $2^k - 2^{k-2} - 1$. The smallest dilation occurs when the vertex with biggest number in level $k - 1$ is joined to the vertex with biggest number in level k, and smaller numbered vertices in level $k - 1$ are joined to smaller numbered vertices in level k. The biggest in level $k - 1$ is $2^{k-1} - 1$, and the biggest in level k is $2^k - 1$. Hence the dilation in this case is $2^k - 2^{k-1}$.

Chapter 22   Graph Multicolorings

1. a) 8   **b)** 4   **c)** 5   **d)** 6   **e)** 7   **f)** 4.   **2.** Station 1: channels 1,2,3; station 2: channels 4,5,6; station 3: channels 7,8,9; Station 4: channels 4,5,6; station 5: channels 7,8,9.   **3.** Graph Algorithms: Monday AM, Monday PM;

Operating Systems: Tuesday AM, Tuesday PM; Automata Theory: Monday AM, Wednesday AM; Number Theory: Tuesday PM, Wednesday AM; Computer Security: Monday PM, Tuesday AM; Compiler Theory: Tuesday PM, Wednesday PM; Combinatorics: Monday AM, Monday PM.   **4.** Let the edges in G be partitioned into disjoint nonempty subsets V_1 and V_2 such that every edge connects a vertex in V_1 and an edge in V_2. Assign colors $1, 2, ..., n$ to each vertex in V_1 and colors $n + 1, n + 2, ..., 2n$ to each vertex in V_2. This produces an n-tuple coloring using $2n$ colors. Therefore $\chi_n(G) \leq 2n$. But any edge in G will have $2n$ colors used for its endpoints, so $\chi_n(G) \geq 2n$. Hence $\chi_n(G) = 2n$.   **5. a)** 3 **b)** 4 **c)** 3 **d)** 5.   **6.** Graphs in parts a, b, and d are weakly γ-perfect.   **7.** It is easy to see that the clique number of a bipartite graph with at least one edge is 2. Since a bipartite graph has chromatic number equal to 2, such a graph is weakly γ-perfect. If no edge is present, both the clique number and chromatic number of the graph equal 1, so that graph is weakly γ-perfect.   **8. a)** 6 **b)** 8 **c)** 8 **d)** 10.   **9.** Suppose the vertices of K_4 are a, b, c, and d. By assigning color 1 to a, color 3 to b, color 8 to c, and color 10 to d, we get a T-coloring with span 9. To see that no T-coloring has smaller span, note that without loss of generality we can assume that a is assigned color 1. If the span is smaller than 9, since $T = \{0, 1, 3, 4\}$, the only available colors for b, c, and d are 3,6,7,8, and 9. But no three of these numbers have the property that all pairs of differences of the numbers are not in T.   **10. a)** T-chromatic number: 3, T-span: 4. **b)** T-chromatic number: 3, T-span: 4. **c)** T-chromatic number: 3, T-span: 6.   **11. a)** T-chromatic number: 4, T-span: 6. **b)** T-chromatic number: 4, T-span 6. **c)** T-chromatic number: 4, T-span: 9 (see Exercise 9).   **12. a)** 5 **b)** 7 **c)** 7 **d)** 10.   **13. a)** v_1: colors 1 and 2; v_2: colors 3 and 4; v_3: colors 1 and 2; v_4: colors 3 and 4; v_5: colors 3 and 4; v_6: colors 5 and 6; v_7: colors 7 and 8; v_8 colors 1 and 2; v_9: colors 3 and 4; v_{10}: colors 1 and 2.   **b)** It uses 6 colors for a 2-tuple coloring of C_5.   **14.** First, order the vertices as $v_1, v_2, ..., v_n$ and represent colors by positive integers. Assign as many colors as specified to v_1. Once having assigned as many colors as specified to each of $v_1, v_2, ..., v_k$, assign the smallest numbered colors of the quantity specified to v_{k+1} such that no color assigned is the same as a color assigned to a vertex adjacent to v_{k+1} that already was assigned a set of colors.   **15. a)** v_1: color 1; v_2: color 3; v_3: color 1; v_4: color 3; v_5: color 3; v_6: color 9; v_7: color 11; v_8: color 1; v_9: color 3; v_{10}: color 1.   **b)** It produces a span of 8 for C_5, but the T-span of C_5 is 4.   **16.** A list coloring is needed to model examination scheduling when particular examinations can only be given during restricted periods, to model maintenance scheduling when certain vehicles can only be maintained during particular times, or to model task scheduling when certain tasks can only be performed during specified times.   **17.** An I-coloring is needed to model assignments of frequency bands for mobile radios, to model space assignment in a maintenance facility laid out along a linear repair dock,

or to model task scheduling when tasks take an interval of time to complete.
18. A J-coloring is needed to model assignments of several frequency bands
for each station or to model task scheduling when tasks are completed during
more than one interval of time.

Chapter 23   Network Flows

1. The maximum flow is 13 with cut $\{(d,t),(d,e),(b,e),(c,e),(c,f)\}$.   2.
The maximum flow is 7 with cut $\{(a,d),(b,d),(f,e),(c,g)\}$.   3. The maximum flow is 13 with cut $\{(d,t),(d,e),(b,e),(c,e),(c,f)\}$.   4. The maximum flow is 7 with cut $\{(a,d),(b,d),(f,e),(c,g)\}$.   5. The maximum flow
is 4 with cut $\{\{a,c\},\{a,d\},\{b,d\}\}$.   6. The maximum flow is 4 with cut
$\{\{a,d\},\{c,d\},\{d,e\},\{e,t\}\}$.   7. The maximum flow is 7 with a minimum
cut consisting of edges (d,g), (e,g), (e,h), (f,h), and (f,l).   8. a) The maximum flow is 5 with minimum cut containing the edges (s,S_1), (s,S_2), (s,S_4),
(C_2,t), and (C_3,t). Interpreting a maximum flow, we find that an optimum
assignment has each of Students 1, 2, and 4 grading a section of Course 1,
and Student 3 grading one section of each of Courses 2 and 3. There are not
enough graders competent to grade all of the sections of Course 1, and there
are not enough sections in courses other than Course 1 to satisfy the desires
of all of the graders. (Notice that the edges of the minimum cut are directed
from $A = \{s,S_3,C_2,C_3\}$ to $V(G) - A$. Other edges between these two sets
of vertices are directed toward A.)   b) The maximum flow is 7 with minimum cut containing the edges (s,S_1), (s,S_2), (s,S_3), and (s,S_4). Examining a
maximum flow shows that an optimum assignment has Student 1 grading one
section of Course 1, Student 2 grading one section of each of Courses 1 and 2,
Student 3 grading the other section of Course 2, and Student 4 grading two
sections of Course 3 and the one section of Course 4. Both the students' desires and the needs of the courses are met with this assignment.   9. Let G
be an undirected bipartite graph, and suppose $V(G)$ is the disjoint union of
nonempty sets V_1 and V_2 such that every edge joins a vertex in V_1 with a vertex
in V_2. Form a directed capacitated s,t-graph H as follows: Direct every edge
of G from its end in V_1 to its end in V_2 and place a capacity of ∞ on each
such edge. Add a source vertex s and connect it to every vertex in V_1 with
an edge directed away from s of capacity 1. Add a sink vertex t and connect
each vertex in V_2 to t with an edge directed toward t of capacity 1. Now find
a maximum flow f in H and the corresponding minimum cut $(A, V(H) - A)$.
Since each unit of flow must travel from s to a vertex x in V_1 through an edge
of capacity 1, from x to a vertex y in V_2 through an edge originally in G, and,
because of the directions of the edges originally in G, must then go on directly
to t through another edge of capacity 1, the edges originally in G which are
used for flow must form a matching in G whose number of edges is the same

as the number of units of flow in H. Further, if M is a matching in G, then using the corresponding edges of H as the middle edges of a flow, there must be a flow in H whose number of units is equal to the size of M. Since f is a maximum flow, the edges originally in G used by the flow form a maximum matching of G. But the cut $(\{s\}, V(H) - \{s\})$ has capacity equal to the number of vertices in V_1, so the minimum cut $(A, V(H) - A)$ is finite. Hence it consists solely of edges of H incident with the vertices s and t, and so there is a one-to-one correspondence between the edges in $(A, V(H) - A)$ and vertices of G. Further, for each path s, m, n, t carrying a unit of flow, one of (s, m) or (n, t) must be in $(A, V(H) - A)$. Let the set of vertices of G met by edges in $(A, V(H) - A)$ be C, so that the size of C is the same as the size of $(A, V(H) - A)$. Suppose there is an edge e of G which does not meet a vertex in C, and let the edge of H corresponding to e be (m, n). Suppose $f(s, m) = 1$. Since m and n are not in C, neither (s, m) nor (n, t) is in $(A, V(H) - A)$, so the unit of flow from s to m must continue on to a vertex n' in V_2 with $n' \neq n$, and $(n', t) \in (A, V(H) - A)$. Hence n' received a label in the final labeling of the algorithm. Since $f(m, n') > 0$, m has a label, and since $c(m, n) = \infty$, n has a label. But t does not have a label, so $(n, t) \in (A, V(H) - A)$, contrary to our supposition. Thus $f(s, m) = 0$. Now in the final labeling of the algorithm, m and n receive labels, so $(n, t) \in (A, V(H) - A)$, again contrary to our assumption that neither m nor r is in C. Since we have a contradiction in either case, it follows that e cannot exist. Thus C is a cover of G. But by Theorem 4, the number of elements in $(A, V(H) - A)$ is the same as the number of units of flow in f, and those numbers are the same as the numbers of elements in C and M, respectively. The theorem follows.   **10.** Suppose G is 2-connected. Let $v, w \in V(G)$ with $v \neq w$. As suggested in the hint, replace each vertex x other than v and w with two new vertices x_1 and x_2 and a directed edge (x_1, x_2) with capacity 1. We will call this edge a "vertex-generated edge" generated by x. For every edge (x, y) not meeting v or w, replace it with the directed edges (x_2, y_1) and (y_2, x_1), both with capacity infinity. If edge $\{v, w\}$ is in $E(G)$, replace it with edge (v, w) having capacity 1. For each edge $\{v, x\}$ with $x \neq w$, replace it with an edge (v, x_1) having capacity infinity. Similarly, for each edge $\{w, x\}$ with $x \neq v$, replace it with an edge (x_2, w) having capacity infinity. The resulting directed graph H is a capacitated v, w-graph. Let f be a maximum flow in H from v to w. Since every unit of flow from v to w must pass through either edge (v, w) of capacity 1 or some vertex-generated edge (x_1, x_2) of capacity 1, f must have a finite value. Further, no two units of flow can have paths sharing a vertex other than v or w since (v, w) if it exists and all vertex-generated edges have capacities 1. By Theorem 4, the value of a maximum flow equals the capacity of a minimum cut in H between v and w. Since minimum cuts must be made of vertex-generated edges and (v, w), and since the removal of $\{v, w\}$ alone or of one vertex alone cannot disconnect G, there must be at least two edges in a minimum cut of H. Hence there must be at least two units of flow in f and thus at least two paths from v to w in H which share no vertices other than v and w. But these paths are easily translated back into paths in G with the same property, proving the theorem in one direction. Suppose that, for any distinct vertices v and w of G, there are two simple paths joining v with w which have only the vertices v and w in common. Suppose, for the sake of contradiction, that G has a cut vertex x. Form $G - x$ by erasing x and all edges incident with x in G. By the definition of a cut vertex, there must be vertices v and w in different components of $G - x$ which are in the same component of G. Let p_1 and p_2 be paths in G which join v and w and which share only those two vertices. Then x can be on at most one of p_1 or p_2; suppose x is not on the path p_2. Then p_2 is a path in $G - x$ joining v with w, so v and w are not in different components of $G - x$, contrary to the choice of v and w. It follows that G has no cut vertices. But G has at least three vertices, so it must have at least two edges. Thus G is 2-connected.   **11.** This is solved exactly as the problem of assigning graders to sections of classes is solved. The workers play the part of graders and the machines are the sections of the classes. Thus, we have a vertex for each worker and one for each type of machine, and we join a vertex for a worker to one for a type machine by an edge if the worker is competent to run the machine. We add a source s and a sink t. We join s to the vertex for each worker by an edge of capacity 1 (since each worker works on just one machine). We join the vertex for each type of machine to t by an edge of capacity equal to the number of machines of that type. Then a maximum flow in the graph will give the necessary assignment.   **12.** Let the CIC office be a vertex, introduce two vertices and a directed edge from one (the tail) to the other (the head) for each switch in the telephone network, and add one more sink vertex t. Give the capacity of a switch to the edge corresponding to that switch. Let the source vertex s be the CIC office. As suggested, join the head vertex for each switch to t by an edge directed toward t whose capacity is the number of local users tied to that switch. If there is a direct telephone link from one switch a to another b, introduce an edge from the head of the edge corresponding to a to the tail of the edge corresponding to b; since any call passing out of a switch reaches the next one, give a capacity of infinity to such edges. Join s to the tails of edges corresponding to switches to which the CIC office is directly connected by edges directed toward the switches, with capacity equal to the number of calls from that switch the company can accept. Then, given the reported trouble with calls coming to CIC, a minimum cut in the resulting graph will include edges corresponding to switches that are bottlenecks for the system. The max-flow min-cut algorithm will find such a minimum cut.

Chapter 24   Petri Nets

1.

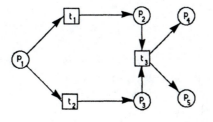

2.

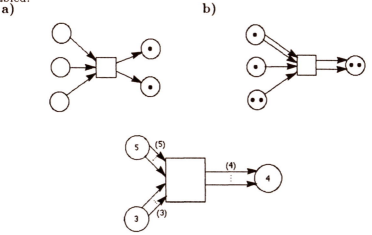

3. *a* is not enabled. The upper left place needs at least two tokens. *b* and *c* are enabled.

4. a)   **b)**

c)

5.

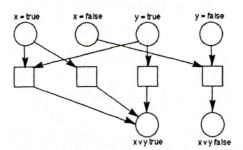

6. $\neg x \wedge \neg y$ is equivalent to $\neg(x \vee y)$, so the required net can be constructed from those for negation and disjunction, similarly to the way the net for $\neg(x \wedge y)$ was constructed in the text.   **7.** $x \rightarrow y$ is equivalent to $\neg x \vee y$. Thus, the required net can be constructed using those for negation and disjunction. **8.** The access control place should have only two tokens. There should be five "reader" tokens and three "writer" tokens. Instead of three multiple edges at the access control place, there should be two.

9.

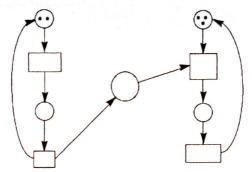

10. Add another place in the buffer which starts out with three tokens. Each time an object is put in the buffer, one token is removed from the new place. Each time an object is consumed, one token is added to the new place. See the following diagram, where B' is the new place.

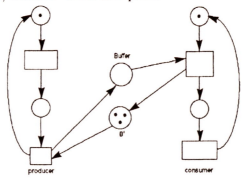

11. a) The net is not safe. Firing t_3 produces two tokens at p_1.   **b)** The

net is bounded. No place ever has more than two tokens.   **c)** The net
is not conservative. Firing t_1 puts one token in p_2 and removes one from p_1.
Then, firing t_4 puts one token in p_1 and removes one from each of p_2 and p_3,
reducing the number of tokens in the net.   **12.** Firing t_2 first and then t_5
puts one token in p_3 and p_2. From here repeat firings of t_5 increase the number
of tokens in p_2 each time by one. Thus, the net is not safe, not bounded, and
not conservative.

13.

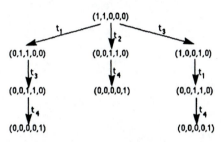

a) The net is safe, by inspection.   **b)** The net is not conservative since t_4
decreases the number of tokens.   **c)** $(0,0,1,0,1)$ is not reachable from
$(1,1,0,0,0)$, by inspection.

14.

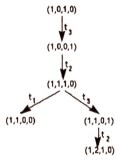

The net is not bounded. The number of tokens in place p_2 can be increased
without bound.

15.

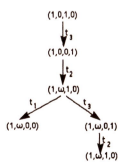

Index